BOLLINGEN SERIES LXX

THE KARIYE DJAMI

VOLUME 1 *of the publication*

of an archaeological project of

THE BYZANTINE INSTITUTE, INC.

Theodore Metochites, founder of the Monastery of the Chora. Detail

[3]

PAUL A. UNDERWOOD

THE KARIYE DJAMI

Volume 1   Historical Introduction
and Description of
the Mosaics and Frescoes

BOLLINGEN SERIES LXX / PANTHEON BOOKS

THIS IS THE FIRST VOLUME OF A PUBLICATION
CONSTITUTING THE SEVENTIETH WORK IN BOLLINGEN SERIES
PUBLISHED BY BOLLINGEN FOUNDATION

Library of Congress Catalogue Card No. 65–10404

Manufactured in the United States of America
DESIGNED BY ANDOR BRAUN

THIS VOLUME and the two volumes of plates which it accompanies constitute the systematic descriptive and illustrative record of all the mosaics and frescoes that still exist in the Kariye Djami, at Istanbul, which was known before the days of its conversion into a mosque as the church of the monastery of the Chora. My foremost purpose in the present volume is to assemble those types of historical, descriptive, and explanatory matter concerning the Kariye Djami and its representational arts that may be required by students and scholars of varied interests or approaches. In introductory sections the history of the monastery, the structural history of the church itself, and the architectural setting and layout of the iconographic program are discussed; separate chapters are devoted to the techniques that were employed by the mosaicists and painters. The major part of the text, however, consists of the descriptive record of the individual subjects of mosaic and fresco presented in catalogue form. No attempt is made to discuss, in the context of art history, the place of these works in either the stylistic or the iconographic development of Byzantine art. References are made to other monuments only if they provide strong evidence for the identification of fragmentary scenes or for determining the manner in which some partially preserved mosaics or paintings should be reconstructed.

A fourth volume, now being prepared by a number of authors and entitled *Studies in the Art of the Kariye Djami*, will be added to the present series in the near future; in it our works of early-fourteenth-century Palaeologan art will be placed in a broader context, in chapters dealing with the cultural and religious environment in which they were created and their relation to the iconographic traditions and stylistic development of Byzantine art in general. That volume will be illustrated with relevant works from other monuments, but for the representations in the Kariye Djami itself the reader will be referred to the plates in Volumes 2 and 3.

Since the representations, both narrative and figural, are distributed throughout the various parts of the building in accordance with a carefully conceived iconographic plan, iconography — or should we say iconology — does play a role in the arrangement of the sequence of the illustrations in the plate volumes and in the cataloguing of the scenes and figures; iconography will also come into play in this volume in my explanations of the narratives that are depicted, and when I point out the historical, allegorical, or dogmatic significance of scenes or figures. A tour through the narthexes, nave, and parecclesion soon reveals the sequence in which the Byzantine iconographer who devised the plan wished the subjects to be viewed. In accordance with this sequence, as I have determined it, I have assigned numbers — we might call them the key numbers — to all the subjects, or items, and have arranged the material pertaining to them in numerical order in both text and plate volumes. In most cases a single item, whether it be a scene within a narrative series or a figure within a category of figures, appears within an individual structural unit of wall or vault. The mosaics in the narthexes and the nave are numbered consecutively from [1] to [187]. The frescoes of the parecclesion, which comprise a coherent iconographic program independent of the mosaic program, are numbered from [201] to [269]. The user of these volumes will be assisted when he observes that the items numbered below two hundred are mosaics and are illustrated in Volume 2, while those in the two-hundred series are frescoes in the parecclesion and are illustrated in Volume 3. The key number for each item, in square brackets, appears in the descriptive section near the subject heading, and in the plate volumes it is centered beneath the caption for each illustration of that item. It is also placed in its proper position on the plans and sections of the church, which are included in each of the first three volumes, so that the location of any item in the building can easily be ascertained. Thus, whether he starts with the description of a subject, its illustrations, or a position in the building, the reader will quickly find the related information that is of interest to him In the text, cross references are usually to key numbers rather than pages, but since a given subject may have several illustrations, plate numbers are sometimes used to call attention to particular details.

In attempting to make of these volumes the basic source of information concerning the works of art themselves I have tried to anticipate the needs of a variety of readers. The catalogue entry for a subject commonly begins with a short English title of the subject followed by a reference to its primary literary sources (if it be an illustration of a scriptural or apocryphal text), a transcription of its Greek inscriptions, and a translation of the inscriptions. In transcribing the inscriptions I have supplied the missing letters of abbreviated words within parentheses and those portions of the lettering that are destroyed, but can be definitely reconstituted, within square brackets. Pointed brackets are used to enclose words that were omitted from inscriptions quoting established texts but that are essential to their meaning. In conjunction with the formal description that follows I have made comments clarifying the narrative when one is depicted and, where it seems pertinent, pointing out the didactic purpose of a given scene or figure. On the other hand, technical data on such matters as dimensions, condition, colors, and materials, which are likely to be of interest only to a relatively small number of specialists, are appended to the descriptions of all the mosaics and the frescoes in the parecclesion in concise, abbreviated form in two columns of small type and can thus be easily skipped by the reader to whom they may be of little or no concern.

In a sense, these volumes are the consummation of the cleaning and conservation work that was carried out over a period of years at the Kariye Djami under the auspices of the Byzantine Institute, Inc., and the museum and antiquities services of the Turkish government — work that was necessitated by the poor condition of the mosaics and frescoes and of the building itself. The mosaics were partially obscured by grime, yellow paint, and much residue of whitewash, and in places they were covered by patchings of plaster; the frescoes were all but invisible beneath coatings of partially disintegrated limewash and paint; and the paintings and mosaics in most of the sepulchral monuments of the church were buried behind rubble masonry fills. As a result of eleven seasons of work from 1948 to 1958, averaging seven months each, the mosaics now present themselves in an entirely new light and the frescoes and the sepulchral monuments, or wall tombs, are revealed to the fullest possible extent; most of the frescoes and the decorations in most of the tombs may be said to constitute newly discovered works of Byzantine art. In many respects, therefore, the excellent works in Russian of Feodor Shmit, of 1903 and 1906, published by the Russian Archaeological Institute of Constantinople (see Selected Bibliography) are now superseded. His is the only previous work that deals systematically with the Kariye Djami, its history, its architecture, and the mosaics as they were to be seen at the time. His plates, which reproduce the mosaics, are now obsolete because the newly cleaned mosaics, paintings, and tombs are illustrated completely in the present volumes. His text, however, although it contains numerous errors of fact and interpretation resulting in part from the conditions that then prevailed, still retains great value, especially in historical matters; the scholar is referred to it for its assembly of literary sources and its publication of a number of texts relating to the history of the monastery and its founder. The only other monograph on the subject of any importance today is Alexander Rüdell's architectural study of the Kariye Djami, published in 1908; in addition to plans, sections, elevations, and details it reproduces wash drawings of some of the mosaics and many of the ornamental motifs in both mosaic and fresco, and, for the first time, a few of the fresco scenes, although these were not clearly visible to Rüdell and some are wrongly identified.

The initial honors for the restorations at the Kariye Djami must go to the Byzantine Institute and its officers, supporters, and technical staff, as well as to the Dumbarton Oaks Center for Byzantine Studies, which, since 1950, has shared with the Institute the responsibilities for the conduct of the technical and scholarly work that has gone into the unveiling and study of these works of art. Under permits issued to the Byzantine Institute by the Ministry of National Education of the Turkish Republic, the work at the Kariye Djami was begun in 1948 by Thomas Whittemore, founder of the Institute, two years before his death on June 8, 1950. It was Mr. Whittemore's unique contribution to Byzantine studies that he conceived the plan of seeking out and revealing those mosaics that might exist in the former churches of Constantinople, the fountainhead of medieval Byzantine art, and that he acted upon the plan, beginning in 1932; his memory will long be honored especially for his work at the great church of Hagia Sophia. After 1950, when the association with Dumbarton Oaks began, it was my great privilege to direct the various projects of the Institute in Istanbul and to play a part in the striking transformation that has come about at the Kariye Djami. It should be mentioned that although the conservation work at the Kariye Djami was carried to completion in 1958 under the joint auspices of the sponsoring institutions, since 1962 the Byzantine Institute has relinquished the conduct of its field work to Dumbarton Oaks.

The restorations were accomplished with the cooperation, the generous support, or the active participation of governments, institutions, and many private individuals. Especial credit is due to the Moslem religious establishment and the government of Turkey for having secularized the mosque. By designating it as a public monument under the jurisdiction of the Department of Ancient Monuments and Museums, and placing it in the custody of the administration of Ayasofya Museum, along with several other former churches, they prepared the way for the restoration of the building and the works of art it contains. The officers, members, and staffs of the Byzantine Institute and Dumbarton Oaks are indeed most grateful to the Turkish administrative agencies and their personnel for entrusting us with the restoration of one of their truly important monuments. Particular thanks are due to those Turkish officials who shared most closely in this work and especially to the two directors of Ayasofya Museum to whom we were directly responsible during the period of our labors: the late Mr. Muzaffer Ramazanoglu and our colleague, the present director, Mr. Feridun Dirimtekin. Their many courtesies and sympathetic understanding of the problems involved are gratefully remembered.

It is a cause of deep regret that I cannot express my thanks by name to the very numerous individuals who so generously supported the Institute's conservation work. But when the roles of the two sponsoring institutions are acknowledged it should be understood that credit is imparted thereby to their officers and heads, for institutions do not function without men to guide and sustain their missions. It is my pleasure, especially, to extend my utmost thanks to Mr. John Nicholas Brown, who, as President, has guided the affairs of the Byzantine Institute since 1950. Sharing many of the burdens and responsibilities of this venture has been Mr. John S. Thacher, Director of Dumbarton Oaks and for a time Treasurer of the Institute; he has stood ever ready to render his personal assistance and his sound advice in the solution of problems both at home and in the conduct of the work in Istanbul.

Foremost among the sustaining American institutions whose assistance was of such vital importance in our work is the Bollingen Foundation. That it has, in addition, decided to undertake the publication of these volumes, as part of its distinguished Bollingen Series, adds immeasurably to our debt of gratitude. I wish to thank the officers of the Foundation and the staff of Bollingen Series for the patience and skills which they have exerted in the production of these volumes. I am also most grateful to Mrs. Pauline Manning Batchelder for her great care in editing my manuscript. To the Samuel H. Kress Foundation and to the Avalon and Old Dominion Foundations my warmest thanks are also extended for their generous help in sustaining the field work.

My sense of indebtedness cannot be adequately expressed to the staff of the Institute in Istanbul, who so skillfully and conscientiously carried out the actual work of restoration. Charged with the technical supervision and serving also in recent years as Assistant Field Director was Mr. Ernest J. W. Hawkins, who has seen this task through from beginning to end; his devotion, experience, and boundless energy are in great part responsible for the splendid results that have been achieved. For shorter periods others of the staff also assumed major responsibilities. Mr. Lawrence Majewski served most ably as Deputy Field Director during four seasons, bearing many administrative as well as supervisory duties with great skill and efficiency. During seven seasons Mr. Carroll Wales was in direct charge of the very delicate task of cleaning and repairing the frescoes, a task in which Mr. Constantine Tsaousis was closely associated. In this connection, my warmest thanks must be expressed to three of America's foremost specialists in the field of conservation for their expert advice and active participation in the treatment of the frescoes. The late Mr. Murray Pease, of the Metropolitan Museum of Art, New York, acted as consultant at the beginning of operations in the parecclesion; Mr. George Stout, Director of the Isabella Stewart Gardner Museum, Boston, generously gave of his time and energies in directing the removal and subsequent replacement of several of the frescoes; and Mr. R. J. Gettens, of the Freer Gallery of Art, Washington, made analyses of the materials and structure of the paintings. I wish also to express my gratitude to my friend Professor Ercüment Atabay for personal assistance and advice on innumerable occasions.

To several of my colleagues at Dumbarton Oaks I am greatly indebted for their assistance in the preparation of Volume 1. Many valuable suggestions were made by Professor Ernst Kitzinger, who was also kind enough to read parts of my manuscript. Professors Sirarpie Der Nersessian and Cyril Mango were ever willing to share their knowledge during the course of my studies. I should like to thank Dr. Herbert Kessler for his assistance in making the prints which have been used for many of the black and white illustrations in Volume 3. Finally, I wish to thank Mr. Charles W. Henstenburg, of New York, who, although in retirement, most graciously consented to assist the Bollingen Series by overseeing the preparation of the plates.

P. A. U.

Dumbarton Oaks
Washington, D. C.

Contents

PART ONE. The Mosaics

CONTENTS

x

PART TWO. The Frescoes

CONTENTS

List of Illustrations

Theodore Metochites, founder of the Monastery of the Chora. Detail

FIGURES IN THE TEXT

PLANS AND SECTIONS AT END OF BOOK

THE KARIYE DJAMI

Historical Introduction

Description of the Mosaics and Frescoes

Historical Introduction

PRIOR to the Turkish conquest of Constantinople in 1453 and the subsequent conversion of many of the city's Byzantine churches to Moslem use, the Kariye mosque was the church of the celebrated monastery of the Chora, a pious foundation whose origins, though they are obscure, are rooted in the early history of the city. The existing superstructure of the church, it should be said at the outset, is not of great antiquity but incorporates three major phases of Byzantine construction, of the eleventh, twelfth, and fourteenth centuries. In part they rest upon the substructures of a sixth-century building which has none of the features of a church.[1]

First a monastic church, then a mosque, the Kariye is now one of the museums of Istanbul. It is situated in the quarter of Edirne Kapou, scarcely more than a hundred meters from the massive ruins of the fifth-century city walls, which extend in a great arc from the Sea of Marmara to the Golden Horn, and at a point about midway between the Adrianople Gate and the Tekfur Saray, the so-called Palace of Constantine Porphyrogennitos. The main approach to the church is from the west (PL. 1); one descends a fairly steep hill, which becomes steeper beyond the façade (PL. 2 and 3) and continues to fall away toward the southeast in a series of terraces beyond the eastern side of the building.

Summary of the Early History of the Chora Monastery

THERE IS NO NEED here to repeat in detail what others have assembled concerning the early history of the monastery (which only indirectly relates to the existing building and its art), but it would be useful, perhaps, to summarize it briefly for the convenience of the reader.[2] Evidence concerning the existence of the Chora as a monastery prior to the seventh century is highly confusing and even contradictory. The traditions that would place its founding before the erection of the land walls of Theodosius II (A.D. 413) seem to have derived from a topographical interpretation of the meaning of its name and cannot be accepted as historically reliable evidence. One source, which purports to describe the circumstances of its founding in the sixth

---

1 See the plan executed by David Oates, reproduced below as text Fig. A, p. 5; and for a discussion of the successive phases of construction see his "Summary Report on the Excavations of the Byzantine Institute in the Kariye Camii: 1957 and 1958," *Dumbarton Oaks Papers*, 14 (Washington, 1960), 223–31.

2 The principal historical studies are contained in Feo-dor Shmit, *Kakhrie-dzhami* (Izvestiia Russkago Arkheologi-cheskago Instituta v Konstantinopole, XI; text, Sofia, album of plates, Munich, 1906), text, pp. 1–115; Alexander Van Millingen, *Byzantine Churches in Constantinople: Their History and Architecture* (London, 1912), pp. 288–316; R. Janin, *La Géographie ecclésiastique de l'Empire Byzantin*, Part I, Vol. 3, *Les Églises et les monastères* (Paris, 1953), pp. 545–53.

century, is of dubious historical value and in parts, at least, fictitious. Despite these words of caution, however, we should not categorically reject the possibility that various chapels, or even a monastery, had existed in the vicinity of the extant building before the more reliably documented establishment of the seventh century.

It has long been held, even by Byzantine writers, that the name *Chora*, by which the monastery has always been known, is in some sense a toponym, for the term and its cognates, *choros* and *chorion*, refer to such things as land, a landed estate, country, a country town, or even a suburban area outside the walls of a city. The name, therefore, has given rise to the view that at the time of its founding the monastery lay in a still-suburban area or that it was established in a small community, estate, or country town that had continued to be referred to as *chora* after the limits of the city had been expanded beyond it. The first of these suppositions implies that the monastery, or at least a hallowed site (a burial ground of Christian martyrs or a shrine commemorating them) which may later have prompted the founding of the monastery, had existed in the vicinity of the present church before the construction of the land walls of the early fifth century. As confirmation that the site of the Chora was a holy place at a very early date it would be tempting to accept the tradition that the bodies of St. Babylas and his eighty-four disciples were brought to Byzantium by ship shortly after their martyrdom in Nicomedia in A.D. 298 and buried in three tombs to the north of the city, at a place, as one text says, where the monastery of the Chora was later constructed.[3] The tradition associating this Babylas and his disciples with the Chora is reflected in other sources. For example, in the Life of Michael Syncellos, abbot of the Chora in the ninth century, it is said that the church of St. Anthimus, one of three churches or chapels of the ninth-century monastery, contained the relics of St. Babylas and his eighty-four disciples.[4] There is the possibility, however, that two saints of that name were confused, for the early Synaxaria of Constantinople record that the feast of St. Babylas of Antioch was celebrated at the Chora [5] but do not mention any connection between the Nicomedian Babylas and the monastery. The early and long-continued relationship between the Chora and Syrian monasticism would suggest that it was the Antiochene martyr-bishop who was especially revered at the Chora.

The view has been expressed, however, that the term *Chora*, as the name of the monastery, was employed from the beginning not in a topographical but in a mystical sense, as it assuredly was in the fourteenth century, to denote an attribute of Christ, if not also of the Virgin. It is true that many churches and monasteries of Constantinople were dedicated to Christ or to the Theotokos in one or another of the many qualities or attributes by which they were known: Christ as the Akataleptos (Incomprehensible), Dynamis (All-powerful), Evergetes (Benefactor), Pantocrator (Omnipotent); the Theotokos as the Eleousa (Merciful), Pammakaristos (All-blessed), Panachrantos (All-pure), etc. In the fourteenth century the name *Chora* was clearly thought to be an epithet that defined certain mystical qualities of Christ and the Theotokos, to whom the monastery was by then consecrated. This is made evident in the inscriptions that accompany several of their mosaic images in the church: numbers [1], [2], [3], [186], and [187] and the medallion of Tomb H (PL. 552 b). In four of these Christ is called the Chora (i.e., the land, sphere, or dwelling-place) of the Living, and in the other two the same epithet, in

---

3 Van Millingen, p. 288; Janin, p. 547.

4 Shmit, p. 257. The *Vita S. Michaelis Syncelli* is printed in Shmit, pp. 227–59.

5 *Propylaeum ad Acta Sanctorum Novembris: Synaxarium Ecclesiae Constantinopolitanae* (Brussels, 1902), col. 11.

4

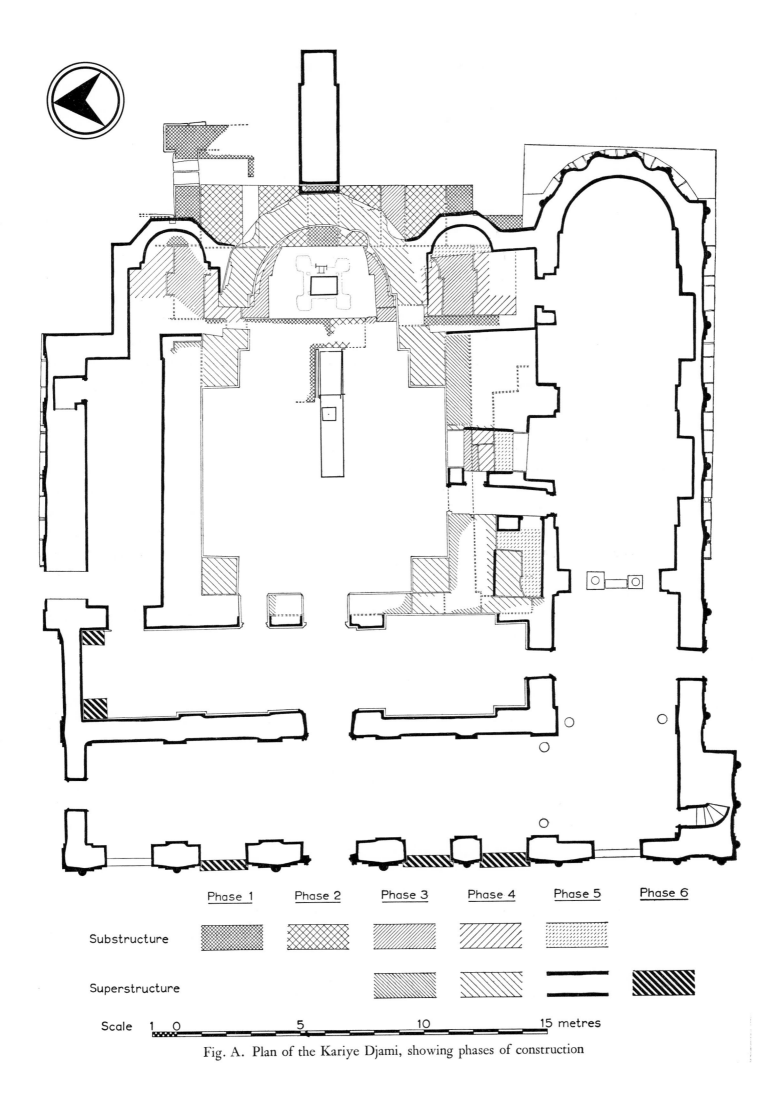

Phase 1   Phase 2   Phase 3   Phase 4   Phase 5   Phase 6

Substructure

Superstructure

Scale   1   0   5   10   15 metres

Fig. A. Plan of the Kariye Djami, showing phases of construction

a slightly different sense, is applied to the Mother of God: the Chora (i.e., the dwelling-place) of the Uncontainable (God).

There are two documentary sources that claim full knowledge of the circumstances surrounding the actual founding of the monastery called Chora. One places the event in the sixth century and associates it with the reign of Justinian; the other, which is more reliable as a historical document, places it in the early seventh century in the reigns of Phocas and Heraclius. The first is an anonymous biography of an otherwise unknown St. Theodore, who is alleged to have been an uncle of the Empress Theodora.[6] It has been suggested, with reason, that this account may well be an embroidery upon the second version, that of the *Patria* [history of origins] *of Constantinople*,[7] which ascribes the foundation to the son-in-law of the Emperor Phocas, a well-known personage named Crispus. The putative Theodore is described as a man of military accomplishments and a relative of the imperial family, like Crispus; both are said to have become monks at the monastery, the founder Theodore as its abbot, the founder Crispus as a monk-prisoner confined there by decree of the Emperor Heraclius. The first of the two accounts, in itself, does not constitute satisfactory evidence for a sixth-century foundation. On the other hand, as we shall see, the assertions of Nicephorus Gregoras that Justinian was the first builder of the Chora monastery, although not supported by Procopius (who wrote at great length on the subject of Justinian's building operations), and the fact that sixth-century substructures do underlie part of the existing building (see text Fig. A, phase 1) should make one hesitant in denying a sixth-century founding of the Chora.

According to the anonymous biography, St. Theodore had retired to a monastic life near Antioch after serving a distinguished military career. He was called to Constantinople by his imperial relatives to advise on theological matters, and there, it is said, he began construction of a monastery, shortly after 536, on part of the estate belonging to the Charisius family, close by the Charisius (Adrianople) Gate, which lay on the slope of the hill at the highest point of the Theodosian walls—a passage that describes quite accurately the present location of the church. A modest habitation of monks and a small chapel were already in existence when the saint began his new buildings. It is further stated that Theodore's monastery had been completed only three years when it was destroyed in an earthquake, presumably the severe tremors of the year 557; the Emperor Justinian then rebuilt it on a more magnificent scale and provided it with four churches, or chapels, dedicated to St. Anthimus of Nicomedia, the Forty Martyrs of Sebaste, St. Michael, and the Theotokos. A hostel for the use of Syrian monks visiting Constantinople and a hospital for the blind were also attached to the monastery.

The *Patria*, however, asserts that the Chora was founded by the general Crispus, count of the Excubiti and eparch of the city, who was the son-in-law of the tyrant Phocas. After having played a leading role in the overthrow of his father-in-law on behalf of Heraclius, Crispus was interned, by order of the new emperor, in his monastery, where he spent his last years as a monk.[8]

Of these two sources greater credence should be given to the *Patria* in view of the absence of any knowledge concerning a sainted uncle of the Empress Theodora. Conflicting claims to the founding or construction of a church or monastery sometimes arise, however, from the fact that

6 Janin, p. 546; Shmit, pp. 11–18, 27–29; M. I. Gédéon, Βυζαντινὸν ἑορτολόγιον (Constantinople, 1899), pp. 227–31.
7 Book III, Sec. 184 (in Theodore Preger, ed., *Scriptores*

Originum Constantinopolitanarum, II (Leipzig, 1907), 273.
8 Janin, p. 547 and n. 7.

after having fallen into disrepair or disuse such an establishment may be restored and refounded by a new patron, who is then called *ktetor*, or founder, without regard to its previous existence; it may even be given an entirely new dedication. It has been suggested, for example, that since the Chora was built upon land that belonged to the Charisius family, the Monastery of the Archangel Michael of Charisius, which existed in the early sixth century but was never referred to again after the reign of Justinian, may have been a predecessor of the Chora monastery; the Chora is said to have possessed for a time a church dedicated to the Archangel.[9]

Little is known of events or structural changes at the Chora during the period from the early seventh century to the middle of the ninth. The names of one or two of its abbots are recorded; otherwise, for this period, we know only of the confinement of certain personages to the monastery and the burial there of certain ecclesiastics of note. In 712 the Patriarch Kyros was confined to the monastery by the Emperor Philippicus,[10] and in 740, early in the period of the iconoclastic controversies, the deposed Patriarch Germanos, who had so firmly opposed the imperial decrees condemning the veneration of icons, was buried at the Chora.[11] Soon thereafter the patrician Bactagius, also an opponent of the iconoclastic emperors, was buried there, and his associate, Artavasdos, was imprisoned there by Constantine V after the latter had expelled the monks from the by then ruined monastery.[12] By 787, it would seem, the monastery was again in use, for its abbot, Simeon, took part in the second council of Nicaea.[13]

It seems almost certain that like many of the monasteries the Chora fell to a very low estate during the period of iconoclasm, but after the triumph of the orthodox iconodules in 843 it underwent a revival and entered upon a period of prosperity and influence under the rule of its famous abbot, Michael Syncellos.[14] Michael had come to Constantinople from Palestine in 813 to join in the opposition to the religious policies of Leo V, and for a time he received hospitality at the Chora. With him came his two disciples, the brothers Theodore and Theophanes.[15] In 836 the brothers were branded with hot irons by the iconoclasts (they were thenceforth known as the *graptoi*); Michael himself was banished to a monastery in Bithynia. On the triumph of Orthodoxy, in 843, Michael was made the syncellos of the new patriarch, Methodius, and was also named abbot of the monastery of the Chora. Theophanes was appointed Metropolitan of Nicaea, and upon his death, two years later, he was buried at the Chora. During Michael's brief rule (he died in 846) the monastery was restored, but the extent of the restoration is not detailed in the *Vita*. Mention is made, however, of the church of St. Anthimus, which is said to have contained the relics of St. Babylas of Nicomedia and his disciples; a chapel of St. Ignatius; and a church of the Forty Martyrs.[16]

For the period from the mid-ninth century to the last quarter of the eleventh there is a complete lack of information concerning the monastery and its buildings. What we learn at the end of this period of silence would indicate, however, that the monastery had come upon hard times and that its church, or churches, had fallen into a state of such extreme ruin as to require the

9 Van Millingen, p. 291 and n. 3; Janin, pp. 363 and 547.
10 Van Millingen, p. 293. Georgius Cedrenus, *Compendium Historiarum*, Vol. I; Bonn ed. (1838), I, 784. *Synaxarium Ecclesiae Constantinopolitanae*, col. 376, line 29.
11 *Synaxarium*, col. 677, line 55; Janin, p. 548; Van Millingen, p. 293.
12 Van Millingen, p. 293; Theophanes, *Chronographia*; Bonn ed. (1839), I, 648.

13 Janin, p. 548; Joannes Dominicus Mansi, *Sacrorum Conciliorum Nova, et Amplissima Collectio*, Vol. XII (Florence, 1766), col. 1111 D.
14 Van Millingen, p. 294; Janin, p. 548.
15 S. Vailhé, "Saint Michel le synkelle et les deux frères Grapti, Saint Théodore et Saint Théophane," *Revue de l'orient chrétien*, VI (1901), 313–32, 610–42.
16 *Vita S. Michaelis Syncelli*, in Shmit, pp. 257, 258.

construction of a new building; parts of this are incorporated in the existing structure of the Kariye Djami.

Structural History of the Church of the Chora

THE PRECEDING SUMMARY of the early history of the Chora monastery, much of it based on vague and often conflicting statements contained in the literary sources, has little or no bearing on the history of the structure that is now known as the Kariye Djami. For the history of the present building we have not only considerable historical documentation but also reliable archaeological evidence, which has been brought to light during the restorations and excavations of the Byzantine Institute in recent years (see text Fig. A).[17] In brief, the investigations have shown that a new church (text Fig. A, phase 3) was erected during the Comnene period, in the late eleventh century, on a site within the grounds of the ancient monastery which had not been occupied by any of the earlier churches. They have shown that this church was partly destroyed and was re-erected, also in the Comnene period, although this rebuilding (phase 4) is not recorded in any of the extant documents. Finally, in the second decade of the fourteenth century, as is very well attested, extensive restorations were carried out and new additions (phase 5) were made by Theodore Metochites, who, as its *ktetor*, took over responsibility for the well-being of the monastery.

THE FIRST COMNENE CHURCH, *Late Eleventh Century*

The historian Nicephorus Gregoras provides the only textual documentation regarding the construction of a church at the Chora in the late eleventh century. Although he wrote in the fourteenth century, the testimony of Gregoras on this point can be relied upon, for he was a protégé of Theodore Metochites, spent many years in residence at the Chora, and certainly had access to the traditions and records of the house. The excavations, moreover, bear him out with regard to the Comnene origin of the existing building. First, Gregoras tells us that the church of the Chora "had been built in ancient times by the emperor Justinian in an oblong shape," that is, in the form of a basilica. In this he seems to confirm the tradition elsewhere recorded only in the anonymous life of St. Theodore, which, as we have seen, is of doubtful historical value in many of its details. In the same passage Gregoras goes on to say that "time having destroyed . . . [Justinian's church] to its very foundations, the mother-in-law of the emperor Alexius Comnenus erected another church, from its foundations, in the form in which it is now seen, but inasmuch as time was again threatening to destroy it, . . . [Theodore Metochites], with a lavish hand, beautifully restored everything except the innermost naos." [18]

Aside from his reference to Justinian's church at the Chora, Gregoras speaks of only two phases of construction: the new church of the mother-in-law of Alexius Comnenus, and its restoration by Metochites. The excavations, however, show that not one, but two phases of Comnene construction preceded the fourteenth-century restorations. Beneath the existing apse the excavations exposed the foundations of a central apse, smaller than the existing one, flanked

17 Oates, "Summary Report."
18 Nicephorus Gregoras, *Byzantina Historia*, Bk. IX, Ch. 13; Bonn ed. (1829), I, 458 f.

by two narrow apsidioles; all three opened directly into the main body of the church (text Fig. A, phase 3). Doubtless this earliest church on the site had four free-standing columns or piers supporting a central dome with barrel vaults abutting against it on the four sides to provide a cruciform superstructure. The width of the nave, including the side apses, coincided with the width of the present nave.

The foundations of the apses of the first church were built upon an artificial terrace, which was formed by filling the space between two pre-existing, parallel walls with rather loose rubble. The two walls, which run north and south, are the ruins of a sixth-century structure that was not a church. The eastern wall consists of two great arches of what was originally a longer arcade, but at an early date, perhaps in the seventh century, the two existing arches were blocked with solid masonry (phase 2). When the first church was built this wall became, in effect, the re-taining wall for the fill on which the apsidal complex was founded. However, owing to subsid-ence of the terrain to the east, perhaps brought about by earthquakes, the eastern retaining wall and the rubble fill behind it moved eastward and caused the collapse of the apses of the church and perhaps other parts as well. In the subsequent restoration of the church the ruins of the original apses were dismantled to the top of their foundations to clear the area for the construc-tion of the entirely different apsidal arrangements of the second church (phase 4). However, to the west of the rubble fill the lower parts of the north, south, and west walls of the nave were preserved, and upon them were built the upper parts of the nave walls of the second church.

The evidence that enables us to date the first two churches in the Comnene period is of an archaeological nature. The brick masonry in all extant parts of both churches (phases 3 and 4) is of a type found only in eleventh- and twelfth-century structures in Constantinople and a number of other places in the Byzantine East.[19] It is characterized by exceedingly wide, but false, horizontal mortar joints, approximately three times the thickness of the bricks. In reality, alternate brick courses are slightly recessed and covered by the pointing mortar, which is struck flush with the projecting brick courses and scored with horizontal lines above and below the exposed courses.

Gregoras is so explicit in saying that the mother-in-law of Alexius built a new church from its very foundations that if we are to credit his knowledge of the history of the monastery, with which he was so intimately connected, we should assign the first of the two churches to her. The second of the two has proved so clearly to have been a restoration, though it involved alterations of plan, that his words are inapplicable to it. Van Millingen (p. 295), without citing his sources, identifies the mother-in-law of Alexius as Maria, the beautiful granddaughter of the Bulgarian king, Samuel, and niece of Aecatherina, the consort of Isaac I Comnenus. Maria married an Andronicus Ducas, whom Van Millingen identifies as a son of Michael VII Ducas. However, one of the principal historical sources for the events and personages of that time, the historian Nicephorus Bryennius,[20] states that Alexius' mother-in-law was the wife of Androni-cus, the eldest son of the Caesar John Ducas, uncle of Michael VII. The marriage of Maria's daughter, Irene Ducaena, to Alexius Comnenus, which occurred late in the year 1077 or early in

19 For a list of monuments erected in the "recessed brick" technique and for the chronological limits of its use in the vicinity of Constantinople and in Kievan Russia, see Cyril Mango, "The Date of the Narthex Mosaics of the Church of the Dormition at Nicaea," *D. O. Papers*, 13 (Washington, 1959), 249 ff. An illustration showing the use of this kind of masonry in the walls of the nave of the Kariye Djami can be found in Paul A. Underwood, "Notes on the Work of the Byzantine Institute in Istanbul: 1955–1956," *D. O. Papers*, 12 (Cambridge, Mass., 1958), Fig. 2, opp. p. 276.

20 *Commentarii*, Bk. III, Ch. 6; Bonn ed. (1836), p. 106 f.; Migne, *Patrologiae Graecae*, 127, col. 150. See also the French translation of Henri Grégoire in *Byzantion*, 25–27 (1955–57) fasc. 2, 885 ff.

1078,[21] was designed by Maria, against the powerful opposition of Alexius' mother, Anna Dalassena, to unite the rival houses of the Comnenes and the Ducases. (Bryennius does not record Maria's Christian name, but we learn it from the *Alexiad* of Anna Comnena, who says that she was of the first family of Bulgaria and who remarks, as does Bryennius, on her exceptional beauty and talents.) [22] In the interval between 1077 and 1081 — between the marriage and coronation of Alexius — efforts were made to have Alexius divorce Irene, but the consent of the patriarch Cosmas, who was a partisan of the Ducas faction, could not be obtained, and the patriarch refused to resign until he himself had crowned Irene. Seven days after Alexius' own coronation Cosmas crowned Irene, and soon afterward he abdicated. On his death Cosmas was buried at the Chora, a fact which suggests that the Chora was, by then, a foundation of the Ducas family, for it was a fitting honor to an ardent supporter of the Ducas cause that Cosmas should be buried in the church of the monastery that was erected and endowed by Maria Ducaena. The first church was most likely constructed between 1077 and 1081, the years in which Maria, who was *protovestiaria* at the imperial court, assumed a prominent role in the affairs of the Ducas and Comnenus families.

THE SECOND COMNENE CHURCH, *Early Twelfth Century*

After the partial destruction of Maria's church a nave of a type quite different from that of its predecessor was erected. The character of its masonry indicates that this rebuilding certainly took place in the Comnene period, and probably in the early twelfth century, as will be explained below. In its essential features the nave exists today (text Fig. A, phase 4; PL. 4–8). A single, large apse (PL. 4) was substituted for the triple-apsed sanctuary, and the small dome supported on four columns was replaced by a large dome, resting on relatively narrow arches carried on four corner piers (PL. 8), which provided a single-aisled nave of a type that is sometimes called a "domed basilica." This second nave was at once more spacious and of a more monumental character than its eleventh-century predecessor. Its pastophoria (prothesis and diaconicon), enclosed chambers that replaced the small side apses of the first church, were of necessity placed further to the north and south, respectively, and thus extended beyond the lateral walls of the nave. These no longer exist, but they were doubtless similar in form to the extant pastophoria, which are entirely of fourteenth-century construction, and stood in much the same positions. As others have observed, a wide, arched opening was constructed in the center of the south wall of the nave (text Fig. A); the northern face of the arch is now concealed by the marble revetments of the nave, but the upper part of the southern face can be seen in the narrow gallery constructed in the fourteenth century between the nave and the parecclesion.[23] The arch originally opened not into a southern side aisle, as has been conjectured,[24] but into an annex, which was possibly a parecclesion; the northwestern foundations of this annex were found beneath the floor of the small chamber that is situated between the nave and the western end of the existing, fourteenth-century parecclesion. The presence of the large arch in the south wall has

21 Ferdinand Chalandon, *Essai sur le règne d'Alexis Ier Comnène* (Paris, 1900), pp. 33 f.

22 *Alexias*, Bk. II, Ch. 6. See the edition, with French translation, of Bernard Leib, *Anne Comnène, Alexiade* (Collection Byzantine), Vol. I (Paris, 1937), p. 80, line 27, and

comments on p. 173 for p. 80, line 24.

23 See the plan at gallery level in Van Millingen, p. 320, Fig. 112 (lower left).

24 As shown by Van Millingen, p. 314, Fig. 102.

led to the further conjecture that an equivalent arch was provided in the north wall and that it too led to a side aisle, comparable to the existing, fourteenth-century northern annex.[25] Investigations have shown that no such arch existed in the north wall of the second nave.

The excavations have shown that the resemblance, remarked upon by Shmit,[26] between the nave and northern annex of the Kariye Djami, on one hand, and those of the fifth- to seventh-century churches of the Dormition at Nicaea, St. Clement at Ancyra, and St. Sophia at Salonika, on the other hand, is fortuitous and does not signify, as Shmit inferred, that Maria Ducaena's church of the late eleventh century was essentially a rebuilding of the seventh-century church of Crispus or a repetition of its plan. On the contrary, as we have seen, Maria's church was built *de novo* and was a typical four-column church. The single-aisled form given to the nave of its successor, which does resemble those of the early churches mentioned above, would seem to have grown out of a desire to enlarge the apse and dome and give the nave a more monumental aspect. In plan the church was not symmetrical, however, and except for its nave and the relation of its pastophoria to the sanctuary it did not resemble those early churches, which Shmit cited in support of his thesis that a seventh-century predecessor dictated the forms that still exist at the Kariye Djami.

It may be that one of the mosaic panels of the Kariye Djami offers a clue to the identification of the person who was responsible for the construction of this second Comnene church and thus enables us to date it. In the lower corners of the huge mosaic of the Deesis in the inner narthex ([6], PL. 36 and 37) are the portraits of two personages of royal lineage. That at the left depicts Isaac Comnenus, third son of the Emperor Alexius I Comnenus and Irene Ducaena and grandson of Maria Ducaena, the builder of the first Comnene church. The portrait at the right represents the Lady of the Mongols, a relative (probably a half sister) of the Emperor Andronicus II Palaeologos; she is depicted as a nun and inscribed as Melane, her name in religion.[27] These two figures, without a doubt, are integral parts of the mosaic as a whole, and this, in turn, is an integral part of the mosaic decorations installed in the church in the early fourteenth century by Theodore Metochites. Aside from his own portrait (frontispiece to this volume and PL. 26, 28), which he placed above the entrance to the nave in accordance with his rights as *ktetor*, or founder, of the monastery, the only portraits of historical personages which Metochites included in his program of decoration were those of Isaac and Melane the nun. The question thus arises as to his reasons for portraying them in one of the mosaics for which he was responsible. Although the two portraits in the Deesis panel look like donor figures, it is impossible that either person was a donor of the mosaic itself; Isaac had died more than a century and a half before the mosaic was made, and to judge from what is recorded in the historical sources, which include the testimony of Gregoras and of Metochites himself, it is hardly possible that the Lady of the Mongols, though she may have been a contemporary of Metochites, played any part in his restorations or the decoration of his church. In seeking a reason for their portrayal in the largest mosaic, and one of the most important ones, of the church—a panel that contains the colossal figures of Christ and the Virgin, to whom the church was dedicated—we should consider the possibility that both Isaac and the female relative of Andronicus were predecessors of Metochites as "founders" of

25 Van Millingen, loc. cit.; Shmit, text, PL. III, opp. p. 112.

26 Text, pp. 111 f. and PL. III, Figs. 1–4, opp. p. 112.

27 See item [6] in Part One for her identification and further references.

the monastery. Do we have here commemorative portraits of an earlier *ktetor* and an earlier *ktetorissa*, who had been of service to the Chora within the historical span of the existing building — that is, between the time of its extensive rebuilding, in the twelfth century, and about 1315, when Metochites assumed the ktetorship of the monastery and carried out his restorations?

When a monastery was newly founded or an old one was in need of new endowments and rebuilding, a patron who would assume the necessary responsibility was appointed by the emperor or by the patriarch, or both, and given the title of *ktetor*. Such a person, in a special and limited sense, assumed proprietary rights to the monastery, sometimes claiming it to be his privilege to bequeath it to his descendants or to others.[28] Thus, in Byzantium, many families acquired what were called family monasteries or family churches. Maria Ducaena doubtless was a *ktetorissa* of Chora and gave it a new church; and it is most likely that, in accordance with prevailing custom, the Chora continued for some time to enjoy the patronage of her descendants.

Although no historical source states that Isaac Comnenus was named as founder of the Chora, there is documentary evidence that for a time, at least, he had a personal interest, and perhaps certain proprietary rights, in the monastery and its church; with respect to Melane, on the other hand, we have no specific evidence to show the nature of her connection with the monastery, but that she had an interest in it is attested by her portrayal in the mosaic. Isaac Comnenus was the fifth child of Alexius I and Irene Ducaena. In the *Alexiad*, her account of the reign of her father, Anna Comnena says that she was the first-born child of Alexius; her birth, on December 1, 1083, was followed by that of a second daughter, then of the first son, John (the future Emperor John II), about 1088, then of Andronicus, and finally of Isaac, whose birth can be placed at about the year 1091–92.[29] In 1118, on the death of their father, Isaac helped his brother John, against the intrigues of their mother and eldest sister, to gain the throne, and soon thereafter Isaac was rewarded by being raised to the rank of Sebastocrator.[30] In about 1130, quarrels with the emperor and accusations of plotting against him led Isaac to flee to the East, but the brothers were reconciled in 1136.[31]

In that year the Emperor John II founded the monastery of the Pantocrator, in Constantinople; he had only recently constructed at the Pantocrator an imperial mausoleum to contain his own tomb and those of certain members of his immediate family.[32] But Isaac had already provided a tomb for himself in the church of the Chora, a fact which again suggests the possibility that he had become a patron, if not the founder, of the Chora monastery. This is known from the typicon, dated 1152, which Isaac granted to the monastery of the Theotokos Kosmosotira at Viros (modern Ferrai, Turkish Ferejik) in Thrace, which he founded at the age of about sixty.[33]

28 On the ownership of monasteries, see Emilio Herman, " 'Chiese private' e diritto di fondazione negli ultimi secoli dell'impero bizantino," *Orientalia christiana periodica*, XII (1946), 302–21, and his "Ricerche sulle istituzioni monastiche bizantine: Typika ktetorika, caristicari e monasteri 'liberi,' " ibid., VI (1940), 293–375.

29 *Alexias*, Bk. VI, Ch. 8. English translation by Elizabeth A. S. Dawes, *The Alexiad of the Princess Anna Comnena* (London, 1928), pp. 150 ff. See also Georgina Buckler, *Anna Comnena: A Study* (Oxford, 1929), p. 14 and genealogical chart; and for the date of John's birth, Chalandon, *Jean II Comnène et Manuel I Comnène* (Paris, 1912), p. 4.

30 Chalandon, *Jean II Comnène*, p. 17.

31 E. Kurtz, "Unedierte Texte aus der Zeit des Kaisers

Johannes Komnenos," *Byzantinische Zeitschrift*, 16 (1907), 102.

32 For a report on recently discovered evidence that establishes the sequence of construction of the three juxtaposed churches of the Pantocrator monastery, and comments on their dating, see Arthur H. S. Megaw, "Notes on Recent Work of the Byzantine Institute in Istanbul," *D. O. Papers*, 17 (Washington, 1963), 340–44.

33 L. Petit, "Typikon du monastère de la Kosmosotira près d'Aenos (1152)" (Izvestiia Russkago Arkheologicheskago Instituta v Konstantinopole, XIII, 1908), 17–77. See especially pp. 63 ff., where Isaac says that his portrait, if not his tomb, was set up in the Chora in his youth.

In that document he ordered that his tomb at the Chora, and certain other appurtenances—specifically the marbles of his tomb, its bronze railing, a portable mosaic icon of the Theotokos, with its stand, and the portraits of his father and mother—should be removed and brought to his newly built church at Viros. "As for my own portrait, which I made in my youth out of childish vanity," he says, "I do not wish it to be removed from Chora." The text does not indicate whether his portrait bore a physical relation to his tomb or whether it was prominently displayed as a ktetoric image. The latter possibility would account for his order that the portrait remain at the Chora. Since, as we know, at least the nave of the second Comnene church was decorated with mosaics, such a "founder portrait" might well have been a mosaic, affixed to the wall, so that it could not have been removed without being destroyed. In addition to the objects listed above, the typicon commanded that the monks of the Chora should relinquish certain other marbles; it is impossible to say whether these were structural materials, such as revetment slabs, or sculptured architectural members.

The impression we gain is that Isaac, even in his old age, retained a degree of authority at the Chora such as can best be explained on the grounds that it was he who rebuilt the church of his grandmother, became her successor as founder, and thereby merited the commemoration he received in the fourteenth-century Deesis mosaic we see today. It should be supposed that his tomb and his original portrait were placed in the church on completion of the restoration. The portrait, he says, was installed in his youth; perhaps this was soon after the death of his father and his elevation to the rank of Sebastocrator. These considerations would lead us to suggest a date of about 1120 for the construction of the second Comnene church.

Nothing is known of the fortunes of the monastery from the time of the construction and restorations under the Comnenes until the late thirteenth and early fourteenth centuries, during the rule of the Palaeologan dynasty. In the interval there occurred the disastrous conquest of Constantinople by the Latins of the Fourth Crusade and the establishment there of the Latin Empire, which endured throughout the greater part of the thirteenth century. It is not known whether the monastery was abandoned during this period (1204–61), but the testimony of Gregoras, quoted above, and the nature and extent of the restorations of the early fourteenth century, which we have been able to observe, indicate that the church had fallen into such disrepair as to render its continued use a serious danger. And yet, in 1275, shortly after the restoration of Byzantine rule, the monastery was occupied by the Patriarch John XI Bekkos,[34] probably because of its proximity to the Palace of Blachernae, which had become, beginning with the Comnenes, the principal residence of the emperors. In a similar way the Patriarch Athanasius I, at times during his two terms of office (1289–93, 1303–09), found it useful to reside at the monastery, because of its convenience to the imperial court.[35] There he conducted services and even convened his bishops before a visit to Blachernae Palace. The Chora was even nearer to another important residence, the palace of Theodore Metochites,[36] the high court functionary whose name was to be inseparably linked with that of the monastery—for it was he who was appointed by the emperor to assume the ktetorship of the Chora, re-endow it, and rebuild the church in the form and with the decorations that we see today.

---

34 Janin, p. 549 and n. 4.
35 Ibid. and n. 5 and 6.

36 See R. Guilland, "Le Palais de Théodore Métochite," *Revue des études grecques*, XXXV (1922), 82–95.

THE FOURTEENTH-CENTURY FOUNDER AND THE DATE OF HIS RESTORATIONS

Theodore Metochites (ca. 1269–1332), the final restorer of the Kariye Djami, was one of the great personalities of the Palaeologan era and a man of many accomplishments.[37] As the leading statesman of his day he served his emperor, Andronicus II, in many capacities. At about the age of thirty-six he rose to the position of *mesazon*, or prime minister, and he was given successively higher dignities at court, including the titles Logothete (or Controller) of the private purse (in 1295–96), Logothete of the general treasury (1305–06), and finally Grand Logothete (1321). His contemporaries, with a few dissents on the part of envious competitors, admired him for his great learning. A prolific author, whose works are still largely unedited and unpublished, he wrote commentaries on Aristotle and prided himself on his knowledge of ancient Greek literature. His greatest achievement as a savant, however, was in the field of astronomy, which he loved above all other studies; he presented himself as a renovator of the ancient scientists in the field. And he was a lover of books: perhaps his most cherished possession was the library that he collected and finally housed in his monastery of the Chora.

So eminent was Metochites' position at court and in the affairs of his day that his prestige to some degree was imparted to his descendants, who remained in the fore as one of the leading families during the last century of the empire.[38] Of his five sons, Nicephorus, a pupil of Gregoras, shared his father's love of learning and as a man of affairs became Grand Logothete in his turn under the Emperor John V Palaeologos; another son, Demetrius, was much more interested in horsemanship and racing than in his studies; and the youngest son, Alexius, rose to prominence at court as Grand Domestic. Some of the sons contracted marriages with women of the Palaeologan house; and for his daughter, Irene, Metochites arranged a most advantageous marriage to the nephew of Andronicus II, John Palaeologos, who became a favorite of the emperor and was elevated to the rank of Caesar.[39] Through these marriages Metochites himself became closely identified with the ruling family and especially with the fortunes of Andronicus II. However, his great wealth and power, and the fact that he was so firmly identified with the rule of the elder Andronicus, led to great tragedy at the end of his life. With the downfall of his emperor at the conclusion of the civil war of 1321–28 and the triumph of Andronicus III, Metochites became the prime victim of popular reaction against the rule of his master. He was imprisoned, his palace was destroyed, and his properties and wealth were confiscated. After a brief time he was exiled to Didymoteikhon in Thrace, but in 1330, after two years, he was permitted to return, dispirited and without hopes, to Constantinople. He was installed in his beloved monastery of the Chora, with all its reminders of his past fame and fortunes, and here, shortly before his death, he took the monastic vows and became Theoleptos the monk. His death occurred on

37 For an excellent sketch of the character and scholarly activities of Theodore Metochites, the reader is referred to the chapter by Ihor Ševčenko in Vol. 4, to be published in the near future. See also his *Études sur la polémique entre Théodore Métochite et Nicéphore Choumnos* (Corpus Bruxellense Historiae Byzantinae, Subsidia III, Brussels, 1962), which contains an excellent index; and Hans-Georg Beck, *Theodoros Metochites, die Krise des byzantinischen Weltbildes im 14. Jahrhundert* (Munich, 1952).

38 V. Laurent, "Le Dernier Gouverneur byzantin de Constantinople, Démétrius Paléologue Métochite, Grand Stratopédarque," *Revue des études byzantines*, XV (1957), 196; see also pp. 200–206, where the author sketches the career of the last prominent member of the family, Demetrius Palaeologos Metochites (ca. 1400–1453), Protovestiarius ca. 1433; Grand Primikirius ca. 1435; Grand Stratopedarch before 1444; and Governor of Constantinople from 1449 to May 29, 1453, when he died heroically in defense of the city.

39 For the sons of Metochites, see Laurent, pp. 201–02, and Beck, p. 10 and n. 7.

the 13th of March, 1332,[40] one month to the day after the death of his emperor, who ended his days as the monk Antonios.

The exact date when Metochites became *ktetor* of the Chora and began to restore its church is not known, but we are fortunate in having quite precise information from Gregoras concerning the completion of the decorations and the resumption of services in the newly finished church. In describing the deteriorating relations between the old emperor and his grandson, the co-Emperor Andronicus III, Gregoras says that during the festive week before Lent of the year 1321 the elder Andronicus determined to have his unruly grandson examined by the patriarch and the Senate and thereby to establish judicial grounds for his imprisonment. Metochites counseled a delay until the end of the festivities of that week because of the danger of a popular uprising in support of the younger Andronicus, for, it was argued, the people would be inflamed with much eating and drinking. To prove the wisdom of delay, Gregoras then tells of a bad omen that occurred in the palace in the middle of the night on the first Saturday of Lent (i.e., Mar. 7, 1321): a horse was heard neighing in the palace, where there were no horses. Messengers were sent to inform Metochites, but, Gregoras says, "the Logothete of the Genikon [Metochites' title at that time], having just completed the renovation of the monastery of Chora as regards its interior decorations, for that reason from time to time attended the night services with the monks."[41] Presumably he had to be called away from his devotions and the enjoyment of his newly finished church. The completion of the decoration of the Kariye Djami can therefore be dated as of the end of 1320 or the first months of 1321.

No documentary evidence exists concerning the beginning of the work or the length of time it took to carry out the building operations and the more imposing task of decorating the interiors — the floors and walls with marbles, the vaults of the two narthexes and the nave with mosaics, and the parecclesion, pastophoria, and passageways with frescoes. But to judge from his career, Metochites was hardly in a position to assume the heavy expenses of his ktetorship until after about 1308.[42] We can only hazard a guess as to the time required to accomplish it all. Metochites says in one of his poems that the structural work progressed rapidly, and from our present knowledge of the extent of fourteenth-century masonry in the various parts of the building, it can be estimated that one or two years should have sufficed for construction. The structural work in the nave, as we know from Gregoras[43] and from our own observations, was not extensive, and it would probably have been completed first, so that the decoration of the nave's interior could begin even before the masons' work was finished in the other parts of the church, all of which were constructed from their foundations. The making of mosaics is a relatively slow process, and in view of the great extent of the mosaic decoration in the narthexes and the nave it may have taken as much as three years to complete it. Medieval fresco painters, on the other hand, worked with great rapidity,[44] so that not much more than a year may have been required to execute the frescoes. On the basis of such estimates we may suppose that the entire program of restoration was carried out between the years 1315 and 1320–21.

It has been said repeatedly, but erroneously, that the mosaics of the Kariye Djami are pre-

---

40 For dates of events at the end of Metochites' life and references to sources, see Ševčenko, *Études sur la polémique*, p. 8, n. 2.

41 Gregoras, pp. 302 ff.

42 This opinion was given me verbally by Professor Ševčenko.

43 Pp. 458 f.

44 For a description of the fresco technique employed at the Kariye, see below, pp. 300–309.

cisely dated by an inscription at the year A.D. 1303.[45] What has been regarded as a set of numerals giving this date appears in the mosaic depicting The Miracle at Cana ([117], PL. 235, 237), in the northeastern pendentive of the axial bay of the outer narthex. Above the arched doorway of the house in the background is a device in tesserae of black glass, which has been interpreted as the Arabic numerals 6811. In terms of the customary Byzantine reckoning from the creation of the world such a date would indeed correspond to the year 1302–03 of the Christian era. Because of the importance this presumed date has assumed in the literature on the Kariye Djami mosaics it is necessary here to show in some detail that the device in question is not, in fact, a date but rather an ornament that quite by chance bears some resemblance to the Arabic numerals.

It is highly improbable that a Byzantine artist of the early fourteenth century would have recorded a date in such a place, or used mere numerals unaccompanied by a formal inscription, or employed Arabic numerals for the purpose. No parallel instances of such a method of dating can be cited in Byzantine art. Furthermore, the solely ornamental purpose of the device becomes evident once it is noted that throughout the mosaics and the paintings of the Kariye Djami, as in other contemporary Byzantine monuments, small embellishments of this type appear in representations of architecture and furniture, especially above doors and windows, on lintels, and on the narrow edges of footstools, daises, etc. These motifs usually consist of small hooks, curves, and vertical strokes symmetrically grouped either in single compositional units (e.g., PL. 93, 99, 112, 132, 160, 253) or in a number of repeats that form a continuous decoration (e.g., on the podia in PL. 132, 177, 460, and on the edge of the ladder in PL. 438). Symmetry is sometimes established by the use of a circle in the center and various little hooks and curves responding to one another at each side (PL. 112). At other times the central element resembles an inverted U (PL. 99). More important in the present context, however, is the frequent use of two short vertical strokes at the center and hooks and curved strokes at each side (PL. 160, 185, 253, 341, 363, etc.). It is this type of ornament that was used above the door in the Cana scene, but owing to the fact that the right wall of the building, drawn in pseudo-perspective (PL. 235), projects in front of part of the arch, only a little more than the left half of the arch is visible, and the ornament above it was necessarily rendered unsymmetrically as though the curves and hooks that belonged to the right of the two vertical bars forming the center of the whole motif were also obscured by the projecting wall. Once the intended, but incompleted symmetry is observed one can see that this is the same motif represented, with only minor variations, at the Kariye Djami in at least two instances, illustrated in Plates 253 and 460, on the side of the building in one case, and on the architecture immediately above the Ark of the Covenant in the other. A close examination of the first two strokes at the left in the alleged numerals will reveal that they cannot be thought to represent an Arabic number six, for they are separated quite widely from one another; to represent a six they should be closely joined. It is by chance that their positions in relation to one another produce a resemblance to that number. Finally, it should be pointed out that the same types of ornament that occur in the Kariye Djami are also to be found in other monuments. Almost the complete repertory was used at the church of the Holy Apostles, Salonika, and in at least one instance, on the architecture in the scene of The Entry into Jerusalem, there appears there the same motif that was used in the Cana scene, but completely drawn.[46]

45 It seems that Van Millingen was the first to regard a decorative motif in one of the mosaics as a date (in *Byzantine Churches*, p. 300).

46 A. Xyngopoulos, Ἡ ψηφιδωτὴ διακόσμησις τοῦ ναοῦ τῶν Ἁγίων Ἀποστόλων Θεσσαλονίκης (Ἑταιρεία Μακεδονικῶν Σπουδῶν, Μακεδονικὴ Βιβλιοθήκη 16, Salonika, 1953), PL. 25, 2.

DESCRIPTION OF THE FOURTEENTH-CENTURY STRUCTURE

Among the literary works of Metochites are two poems, one dedicated to Christ, the other to the Virgin, which are of special interest to us.[47] In them the restorer of the Chora monastery makes a number of statements concerning the nature and extent of the reconstruction of the building, its dedication, and the splendid gifts and furnishings he bestowed upon his monastery. His remarks on the dedication will be discussed below,[48] where they can be compared with the evidence to be derived from the iconographic program of the narthex mosaics. Here it will be useful to set down what he has to say about the structural aspects of his restoration [49] and compare them with the physical evidence that has emerged in the course of recent investigations in the building.

The work of structural demolition and construction, he says, was quickly done.[50] In two passages [51] he seems to imply what Gregoras [52] clearly states, namely, that little if any structural restoration was required in the nave [53] but that the annexes along the sides of the nave (see plan, Fig. 1) and the two narthexes (*pronaoi*) across the front were newly built by him; he does not characterize the two side annexes or state their function. In addition, he says, he provided marble floors and covered the walls to an appropriate height with matched slabs of marble. The context in which he comments on the marbles suggests that the floor and wall revetments in the nave were his work as well as those in the newly built narthexes.[54] He refers to the mosaics with which he decorated his church,[55] but surprisingly he does not dwell at any length on this most splendid aspect of his building. Among his other contributions to the enrichment of the Chora he mentions the holy vessels and silken vestments,[56] the icons,[57] and his famous library.[58]

The Nave

The conservation work of the Byzantine Institute offered an ideal opportunity to determine with new precision the various phases of construction. In the main, the rather vague testimony of Metochites and Gregoras is borne out by physical evidence. On removal of all modern plaster throughout the building it was found that, contrary to their statements, considerable reconstruction was carried out in the nave. The twelfth-century dome either had collapsed or was in such shattered condition that it had to be demolished and replaced by another. Indeed, the cornice of the earlier dome was also removed, and demolition of masonry extended into the up-

---

47 See *Dichtungen des Gross-Logotheten Theodoros Metochites*, ed. M. Treu (Programm des Victoria-Gymnasiums zu Potsdam, Ostern 1895, Potsdam, 1895), from which pertinent passages were excerpted by Shmit, pp. 41–42 and passim.

48 See pp. 27–28.

49 I wish to thank Professor Ševčenko for acquainting me with the content of the verses that relate to the structure of the Chora.

50 Poem A, lines 1019, 1020, 1025 (Treu, p. 28, and Shmit, pp. 41, 42).

51 Poem A, lines 1053 ff. (Treu, p. 29); and Poem B, lines 310 ff. (Treu, p. 46, and Shmit, p. 42).

52 See above, p. 8 and n. 18.

53 See below, however, for evidence that this is not literally true.

54 In Poem A, line 1032 (Treu, p. 28), where he refers to floors and revetments, he seems to mean those in the nave, since in lines 1047–48 he says that "such also" were provided for the *pronaoi*. There is reason to think, however, that the wall revetments of the nave may have been those of the twelfth century, reset and repaired by Metochites.

55 Poem A, lines 1039 ff. (Treu, p. 29).

56 Poem A, lines 1055 ff. (Treu, p. 29).

57 Poem A, lines 1087 f. (Treu, p. 30).

58 "In addition, I made it [i.e., the monastery] a treasury of various and numerous books," Poem A, lines 1145 ff. (Treu, p. 31).

per parts of the pendentives and even into the crown of the western arch, an extensive section of which was removed and rebuilt. In all these areas the masonry of the fourteenth century appears in clear contrast with that of the Comnene phases, which is described above.

Only the drum of Metochites' dome in the nave still exists; above the drum the dome is Turkish, made of timber and covered with plaster (PL. 8). Metochites' dome, perhaps duplicating the Comnene, was constructed with sixteen concave flutes, extending from summit to cornice, and was thus a larger version of the two domes of the inner narthex (PL. 42, 43; 66, 67). In the drum, each flute is pierced by a window. The masonry here consists of brick alternating every seven or eight courses with a single rather wide course of cut stone; only in this respect does it differ from the masonry normally used in Metochites' work, which will be described below. At the four axial points on the new dome cornice are bosses carved with monograms, which read (east, west, south, north): "Theodoros," "Metochites," "Logothetes," "kai Ktetor." In Plates 6, 7, and 8 the extent of reconstruction in the upper parts of the pendentives is clearly distinguishable, and in Plate 8 the rebuilt portion in the crown of the western arch (at the right) can be recognized. Because Metochites' annexes, built against the north and south sides of the nave (PL. 6, 7), and his inner narthex, built against the west side (PL. 5), were to rise in varying degrees above the sills of the great triple-arched windows in the three tympana, the masons found it necessary to fill the lower parts of the windows with new masonry to raise the sills above the surrounding roofs; thus they concealed at least portions of the twelfth-century mullions. The northern annex is a two-story structure, considerably higher than the others, and the windows of the northern tympanum (PL. 6) were filled to a height well above the mullions, which are thus completely incorporated within the fill, so that only the uppermost parts of the three arches remained open for glazing; in Turkish times even these were sealed, with slightly recessed masonry fills. The masonry of these window fills is quite rough and consists primarily of single courses of rough-hewn stone alternating with single courses of brick, the whole left without finished pointing.

The matched marble panels with which Metochites faced the lower parts of the walls of the nave extend from his marble floor (PL. 9) to the continuous cornice that marks the springing line of the great arches (PL. 4–8). It is not clear whether these slabs were newly supplied by Metochites or were in part survivors of the twelfth-century revetments, but it is evident that they were at least reset in the fourteenth century, for while the masonry walls incline slightly outward because of deformations induced by outward thrusts, the marbles are laid nearly vertically, with the result that there is a greater space behind them at the level of the lower edge of the narrow, ornamental intarsia frieze, immediately below the cornice, than at the floor; to compensate, the frieze was slanted back sharply to fit beneath the overhang of the cornice. All masonry surfaces above the cornice were covered with mosaics. Except for the three mosaic panels let into the zone of marble incrustation (PL. 4 and 8), and some remnants of ornamental mosaic in the arch soffits of the southern and western windows (PL. 6, far left, and 8), all nave mosaics have perished. A small piece of twelfth-century ornamental mosaic was found *in situ* on the right-hand reveal of the southern window, just above the original sill, concealed by the fourteenth-century fill—proof that the nave of the earlier church also had been decorated with mosaics.

The only other structural alterations of any importance carried out in the nave were the blocking of the door in the south wall of the bema which led to the earlier diaconicon and the partial filling of the large arch in the center of the south wall of the nave proper (text Fig. A), which had opened directly into a structure, possibly a parecclesion or burial chapel, that Metochites destroyed to make way for his new parecclesion. Within this latter fill a door and a small window were constructed (PL. 5, lower left), the door to provide access to a narrow passage leading to the new parecclesion and the window to illuminate a small interior chamber, which seems to have been an oratory.

Nothing survives of the furnishings of the bema, that is, of the altar, ciborium, and templon or iconostasis, and it is not known whether Metochites found it necessary to replace any or all of the furnishings of the earlier church. However, excavations in the apse revealed the emplacement for the altar and the foundations for the columns of a ciborium (text Fig. A). The excavations also disclosed, sunk beneath the altar, a large marble box filled with debris of many kinds from the destruction consequent upon the conversion of the church for Moslem use. In this debris were found quantities of painted window glass (blue, amber-yellow, green, purple-red, pink, and nearly colorless), and some of the H-section lead cames in which the pieces had been set were found under the apse floor in the parecclesion, proof that at least some of the windows, most probably those of the main apse, had been filled with painted colored glass, both figural and ornamental, of the sort that heretofore has been regarded as peculiar to medieval western Europe. These specimens make it evident that Byzantium possessed a highly developed art of painted windows. The glass from the Kariye Djami is very similar in style and technique to the painted glass subsequently found in the Constantinopolitan church of the Pantocrator (Zeyrek Djami), which dates from about 1126.[59] It is probable, therefore, that the glass from the Kariye is of similar date and that it belonged to windows (probably those in the apse) of the second Comnene church, which Metochites must have left *in situ* at the time of his restorations.

The Narthexes

The two narthexes of the Kariye Djami were entirely new constructions of Metochites.[60] In the vertical walls and lunettes his masonry, like that generally used in construction of the Palaeologan epoch, consists of bands of four courses of brickwork alternating with four courses of roughly dressed stone (PL. 1, 2, 10). The pointing, a deep pink owing to the use of pulverized brick as inert material, is beveled so that it underlaps slightly the course above it, while that of the stone masonry is almost flush. The differences between this masonry and that of the Comnene period, described above, are so pronounced that wherever they were exposed the two phases were easily distinguished.

The masonry in the arches and vaults is entirely of brick. The walls of both narthexes were faced with decorative slabs of marble, mainly Proconnesian (nearly white with gray veins) and verd antique, which extended from the floor to the cornice. Above the cornice all surfaces, including the arches, vaults, and lunettes, were covered with mosaics. Most of the revetments of the inner narthex (PL. 14–16) are intact, but the walls of the outer narthex (PL. 10–12) have

---

59 For the publication of information on the glass from the church of the Pantocrator and the Kariye Djami, see Megaw, "Notes on Recent Work of the Byzantine Institute in Istanbul," *D. O. Papers*, 17, 349–67; contains many illus-

trations.

60 Van Millingen (Fig. 105, p. 317) was mistaken as to the various phases of construction. See, instead, the plan of D. Oates, reproduced above—text Fig. A, p. 5.

been robbed of nearly all their marble sheathings. The marble floor of the inner narthex, like that of the nave, is nearly intact. The floor slabs of the outer narthex, however, had been removed, for over the years many burials were made beneath the floor, and ultimately the narthex was paved with large hexagonal bricks. These formed such an uneven surface and were so badly broken that in 1958 they were replaced by small slabs of precast concrete faced with terrazzo.

A glance at the plan (Fig. 1) will show that the decidedly unequal widths of the two lateral annexes resulted in a pronounced dissymmetry in the layout of the narthexes and conspicuous inequalities among the bays into which they were divided. Architectural tradition dictated that entrance to the narthexes and the nave beyond should be along an extension of the axis of the nave, which in these circumstances did not coincide with the center of the church as a whole. It is obvious also that direct access to the side annexes from one or both of the narthexes was to be provided. The plan that was adopted provided that the inner narthex should extend only across the front of the northern annex and the nave, giving direct access to both. But it made the outer narthex parallel the inner narthex to its full length, extend beyond it to the south the total width of the parecclesion, or southern annex, and turn around the southern end of the inner narthex to lead directly to the parecclesion.

The positions of the entrance bays in both narthexes being fixed by the axis of the nave, dissymmetry was bound to result. In the inner narthex, one large bay and a rather wide transverse arch were placed at the south end, to the right of the axial bay, while two smaller bays were placed to the left of the axial bay, to make up for the greater length on that side, so that the narthex was composed of four bays in all; each bay was separated from the next by a transverse arch. Since the inner narthex had only one exterior wall, the northern, through which light could be obtained, it was necessary to cover one or more of the bays with a dome raised on a drum, in which windows could be placed (PL. 1, 43, 67). For the southern bay, farthest removed from the exterior wall, such a dome was essential. The need for still more light, a feeling for symmetry, and, as will be seen, the requirements of the iconographic program of the mosaics were compelling reasons for placing another, smaller dome at the northern end. To accommodate the larger dome, at the south, it was necessary for the southern bay to be wider than the rest of the narthex. New masonry, about .57 m. thick, was applied to the face of the pre-existing Comnene wall, at the eastern side of the narthex, everywhere but in the southern bay, which was thus in effect recessed to a considerable depth (PL. 16); correspondingly, the newly constructed western wall was also recessed, though less deeply. The northern bay, which was to be covered by a smaller dome, was laid out as an approximate square. Space remained between the domes for two distinctly oblong bays (PL. 15, 108, 119). Since these were to be covered by domical vaults it was necessary to construct narrow arches against the eastern and western walls, joining one transverse arch to the next, to reduce the oblongs to squares. In the four bays of the inner narthex we therefore have units of three different sizes covered by vaults of two different types—domes and domical vaults.

The same factors that affected the layout of the inner narthex, except the problem of lighting, also affected that of the outer narthex. First, the position of the axial bay was fixed, and secondly, it being necessary to enter the parecclesion from the outer narthex, the latter was carried around the southwest corner of the inner narthex to join the west end of the parecclesion. As a result, the entrance bay is very much off the center of the narthex, and of the façade, and the bays had to be laid out in four different sizes and sets of proportions. The largest are the two bays at the south end (PL. 250, 258), which lead eastward to the parecclesion; the last bay was laid out as an approximate square, the corner bay as nearly so as possible; their dimensions were governed by the breadth of the parecclesion, which is somewhat greater than that of the narthex. So that its vault would be of maximum size and its importance would thus be accentuated, the entrance bay (PL. 228) was also made square. These three bays, being more or less square, could be covered with domical vaults the full width of the narthex. The remaining spaces, to left and right of the entrance bay, were of such dimensions as to require subdivision into two bays each, but their lengths were so unequal that the bays to the left of the entrance had to be considerably wider than those to the right; all four were distinctly oblong in shape. To cover these oblong bays (PL. 211, 216, 246, 249) with domical vaults it was necessary, as in the two central bays of the inner narthex, to reduce them to approximate squares by constructing arches against the eastern and western walls.

Because the outer narthex was exposed to the exterior throughout its length no domes were needed for its illumination. Its façade (PL. 1) was pierced by six tall arches, which reached from a point slightly above the floor into the lunettes above the interior cornice (see PL. 540, 546, 548). The arch in the entrance bay was of course filled with a great door and, above it, a glazed semicircular window; the arches in the other bays were originally filled with low marble balustrades at the bottom and glazed windows above.[61] At later dates three of these arches were formed into sepulchral niches by the insertion of thin masonry walls at the exterior plane of the building wall (see plan, Fig. 1, and text Fig. A). The seventh bay, at the entrance to the parecclesion, was given a triple-arched window, above the cornice in the southern lunette (PL. 182). The original aspect of the outer narthex, to its great detriment, has been altered by the later insertion of massive, slightly pointed reinforcing arches of roughly dressed stone within the original transverse arches of the sixth bay; these reinforcements rest at their imposts on Byzantine capitals carried on squat granite shafts without bases (plan; Figs. 1, 5, 6; and PL. 11).

The Parecclesion

Like the narthexes, the parecclesion (PL. 336, 337) was an entirely new construction of Metochites. It lies parallel to and attached to the south side of the nave and the diaconicon, to both of which it has access through doors in its north wall (see plan, Fig. 1). Its principal entrance, however, is at the western end: it is separated from the last bay of the outer narthex by two columns bearing a tympanum pierced by arches (PL. 335). Originally, the two side intercolumniations were blocked by screens about two and a half meters high and entry was confined to the central intercolumniation. Structurally, the parecclesion consists of two square bays (PL. 368, 408) and, at the east, a bema with a single apse, which is nearly the full width of the chapel (PL. 340). The western bay is covered by a ribbed dome on pendentives, which is raised on a drum containing twelve windows (PL. 408–10). On its east and west sides the dome is carried on two transverse arches. The eastern bay, between the dome and the bema, is covered by a domical vault (PL. 368) that in form and dimensions is very much like the vaults that cover

---

61 Underwood, "Notes on the Work of the Byzantine Institute in Istanbul: 1957,"
D. O. Papers, 13, p. 215 f. and Fig. 11.

the two bays of the outer narthex to the west of the parecclesion. The bema consists of an arch and an apse covered by a semidome.

Around the walls of the parecclesion, at the springing level of the arches, runs a cornice (PL. 336). The north and south walls below the cornice are articulated into bays by pilasters, which receive the three transverse arches. Four rectangularly recessed niches (arcosolia) were built within the thickness of the walls, one in each side of each of the two bays (see plan, Fig. 1, and PL. 533 *a* and *b*, 534, 537). Other penetrations occur in the north wall below the cornice — two doors, placed close beside the two arcosolia, enter respectively into a passage leading to the nave and into the southern pastophorium. In the pier at the northwest corner is a small window (PL. 508) providing indirect light to a small interior chamber. On the axis of the apse is a small triple-arched window. Above the cornice there are three openings in the side walls: in the center of each of the two southern tympana is a triple-arched window (PL. 453, 458), and in the northern tympanum of the western bay is a small arch (PL. 437) opening into a narrow vaulted gallery between the parecclesion and the nave.

The parecclesion, as will be seen below (pp. 188–89), was the mortuary chapel of the monastery, and the arcosolia in its walls were to serve as sepulchral monuments for the founder and other important personages. While it has sometimes been identified as the *trapeza*, or refectory, of the monastery, which is mentioned in one of Metochites' poems, evidence discovered during the course of the investigations of the Byzantine Institute, a reexamination of the text which led to this identification, and the iconography of its painted decoration show that the parecclesion should not be confused with the refectory, which must have been a detached building that has long since been destroyed.

The Pastophoria

In Byzantine churches the two apsidal chambers, or pastophoria, commonly flanking the great apse of the nave were set aside for special priestly functions associated with the service of the sanctuary, and they normally communicated directly with it. The recently completed restorations of these chambers at the Kariye Djami, undertaken because of the extensive structural damage they had suffered, have conclusively shown that they were built, from their foundations, as part of Metochites' campaign of reconstruction and are not contemporary with the main apse, as had been assumed formerly. They undoubtedly replaced earlier pastophoria, whose forms are now unknown.

The prothesis, the chamber to the north, has direct access to the main apse through the original, twelfth-century doorway. There is also a door in its west wall leading to the northern annex and the inner narthex beyond. The rectangular room (PL. 524) is covered by a low, windowless, fluted dome (PL. 521) resting on a cornice and four pendentives, and on its eastern side it has an apse lighted by a small triple-arched window. In the northern tympanum are two narrow windows above two small niches. All the walls and vaults were originally decorated with paintings, of which only fragments remain.

The original diaconicon, the chamber to the south of the main apse, had direct access to the sanctuary before the reconstructions of the fourteenth century. When it was rebuilt by Metochites, however, the doorway was blocked with masonry and covered, on the side that faced the main apse, with marble revetments; the new means of entrance was from the south, from the eastern bay of the parecclesion. So it is doubtful that the room, after its rebuilding, served as the diaconicon. Instead, it may have been used as a prothesis for the parecclesion — or perhaps as a baptistery, in view of the fact that in the center of the floor of its apse a small round sinking, lined with stone masonry, was discovered. This room, like the prothesis, is rectangular in plan, has an apse on its eastern side, and is covered by a dome. The apse is almost identical with that of the prothesis, but the dome (PL. 525), in contrast with the fluted prothesis dome, is divided by ribs into eight segments, and it is raised on a drum penetrated in its eastern side by three windows. Let into the western wall of the room are two small niches, and the northern and southern walls have one each. The dome still retains fragments of its paintings. The only other painted decorations are those that came to light in the soffit of the arch (PL. 529) that originally led into the sanctuary. These are undoubtedly of the twelfth century.

The Northern Annex

Another structure built by Metochites, according to his own words, is the two-storied annex adjoining the north side of the nave and parallel to it. The lower story (PL. 530) serves to connect the inner narthex, at the west, with the prothesis, at the east. Throughout its length the room is covered by a simple barrel vault springing at both sides from a cornice. To support the southern side of this vault and secure it firmly to the pre-existing nave, Metochites' masons thickened the old wall (text Fig. A) with a new facing of brick and dressed stone in a technique exactly like that used in the narthexes and the parecclesion. The exterior wall, at the north side, was made unusually thick so that there was room within it for a straight flight of stairs, starting near the eastern end of the passageway and leading to the upper room. The latter, though it has a much lower ceiling than the room below, is of equal area, and it too is roofed with a barrel vault. The barrel vault in the room at ground level was later reinforced at more or less regular intervals by three massive, slightly pointed arches of brick and stone masonry, which spring from a very low level and carry supporting walls of considerable height. The frescoed surface of the barrel vault is exposed only in the darkened intervals between the arches and even there is largely obscured from view.

The functions of the two rooms can now only be conjectured. It seems likely that the ground floor served as the diaconicon of Metochites' church — the room in which vestments, special icons, reliquaries, liturgical objects and service books could be kept available for the conduct of the liturgy. This function is suggested by the fact that Metochites blocked the door in the south side of the bema of the nave which in the Comnene church had led to a diaconicon situated to the south of the main apse. In the fourteenth-century church, therefore, what would normally have been the diaconicon became an adjunct of the parecclesion and could not well be used to serve the main sanctuary. The upper room of the northern annex, I would venture to suggest, was intended to serve as the *skevophylakion*, or treasury, or possibly to house Metochites's famous collection of manuscripts; in the two poems mentioned above, as well as in a letter written to the monks of the Chora while he was in exile, the founder speaks with great pride and concern of his library, housed at the Chora.

This survey of the structural history of the church of the Chora, in which the various phases of construction have been sorted out and described, shows, in brief, that beginning about the year 1315 Metochites demolished all the subsidiary structures of the Comnene church—its narthex or narthexes, pastophoria, and parecclesion—and left standing only its nave and apse; that even here it was necessary to build a new dome, replace the floor and all the mosaics, and even, perhaps, re-erect the marble sheathing of the walls; and that Metochites surrounded this nucleus with new pastophoria at the east, new annexes at the sides, including the imposing parecclesion, and entirely new narthexes at the west. The reader has thus become familiar with the structural framework for the extensive series of representations the church contains, and he will be prepared to consider, in their proper settings, the splendid mosaics and fresco paintings which are the principal subject of this publication.

PART ONE

The Mosaics

The Program and Layout

The mosaic depicting Theodore Metochites in the act of presenting a model of his church to Christ, "the chora of the living" (PL. 26), would make it appear that the church of the Chora was dedicated to Christ alone.[1] However, the testimony of the founder himself and that of the iconographic program of the mosaics in the narthexes make it clear that in endowing and rebuilding the monastery it was Metochites' intention to honor both Christ and the Theotokos, in nearly equal measure, and perhaps even to dedicate the monastery to them jointly. No doubt he was motivated in this by the fact that the term "chora," the name of the monastery, had come to denote certain mystical qualities attributed to Christ, as the Incarnate God, and to the Theotokos, as the instrument of the Incarnation. In addition to the panel of the donor before Christ, above the door to the nave ([3]), there are two images of Christ and two of the Virgin, arranged as pairs ([1]–[2], and [186]–[187]), which also convey dedicatory implications. As does the donor panel, the two images of Christ bear the epithet "the chora (dwelling-place) of the living," while those of the Virgin are inscribed with the words "the chora of the uncontainable."

The mid-fourteenth-century patriarch of Constantinople, Philotheos Kokkinos, surely had these mosaics and their epithets in mind when he stated that the monastery was named Chora in allusion to Christ, who was the chora of the living, and to the Theotokos, who was the chora of the uncontainable Christ.[2] And Metochites himself must have been mindful of the dedicatory nature of the images he had placed in his church when he said, in a poem written near the end of his life, "But thou, Oh Lady, hast become the instrument of this great miracle [the Incarnation] which gave life to mortals; and it is to bring a shrine [as a gift] to thee that I erected this monastery, calling it Chora after thee, the one who contained the uncontainable, to thee the shrine of the immortal God." [3] Elsewhere in his poems Metochites again implies that he dedicated the monastery to the Virgin: "To thee [the Theotokos] I have dedicated this noble monastery which is called by thy precious name of Chora;" [4] and in another passage he says, "I have made thee, Oh most pure Lady, my hope and the chora for the refuge of my life." [5] Referring to his return from exile, he writes, "I repaired to thy Chora, thou pure Chora of the uncontainable God." [6] It is curious, however, that although the images of Christ-chora are more numerous and more

---

1 As would the usual designation of the church as the church of the monastery of Christ in Chora, or St. Savior in Chora.

2 Migne, *Pat. Gr.*, 151, col. 652 C and D.

3 *Dichtungen des Gross-Logotheten Theodoros Metochites*, ed. M. Treu (Programm des Victoria-Gymnasiums zu Potsdam, Ostern 1895, Potsdam, 1895), Poem B, lines 14 ff., p. 38.

4 Poem A, lines 1340 ff. (Treu, p. 37).

5 Poem B, lines 104 ff. (Treu, p. 41).

6 Poem B, lines 154 ff. (Treu, p. 42).

prominent in his church than those of the Virgin-chora, only once, to my knowledge, does Metochites say in his verses that the monastery was dedicated to Christ: "And having conveyed these [gifts from the Emperor], together with my own gifts which I set apart from my many possessions, I dedicated these, Oh Lord Christ, to thee." [7] Whether the actual dedication of the church was to Christ, to the Virgin, or to both as sharers in the mystical connotations of the term chora, the fact is that the principal purpose of the iconographic program of the mosaics in the two narthexes, as of the paintings in the parecclesion, was to pay equal homage to both, and in the narrative cycles of their lives to recount the story of the Incarnation and the life-giving mission of the Son of God.

In addition to the mosaics with the inscribed epithets, placed in pendant relationship to one another, the visitor at the Chora will observe, at every turn throughout these parts of the building, a confrontation of other images of Christ and the Virgin, a host of portraits of their common ancestors, and a balancing and interweaving of the narrative cycles of their lives. Indeed, an examination of the iconographic program will show that with the exception of an array of saints and martyrs, such as is *de rigueur* in the decoration of churches, all representations in these parts of the church relate directly to them. None of the other cycles that so frequently find a place in church decoration of the time are included in the program at the Chora. For example, there are no cycles or scenes illustrating the lives of any of the saints or of any of the apostles; nor are there cycles of the Akathistos or of Old Testament subjects as such, although in the paintings of the parecclesion it will be seen that some of the latter were used as prefigurations of the Virgin. The mosaics that once adorned the vaults and tympana of the nave no longer exist, but it is highly improbable that they illustrated any of these subsidiary subjects. Some speculations on the content of the nave mosaics will be presented below; but it is important first to enumerate the constituent parts of the iconographic program in the narthexes and observe the order and manner of their distribution in the structural forms that were provided for them.

In arranging the iconographic program of the mosaics within the structural framework of the narthexes the iconographer intended to lead the beholder across the outer narthex at the entrance bay and into the inner narthex, for on this path he is confronted by the "dedicatory" images, above the doors through which he passes, of Christ-chora, the Virgin-chora, and the founder kneeling before the enthroned Christ-chora ([1]–[3]). Instead of entering into the nave, however, the beholder is drawn to the right, to the large bay at the south end of the inner narthex. There, on the east wall beneath the larger of the two narthex domes, is a huge devotional mosaic of the Deesis [6], depicting Christ Chalkites and the Virgin; this is a rather unusual version of the Deesis since it omits John the Baptist, showing again the intention to concentrate upon the persons of Christ and the Virgin.

At this point the visitor is impelled to look up into the dome above. Here is the starting point of the iconographic program that is to unfold in the two narthexes—that is, the cycles of the lives of the Virgin and Christ, which depict the story of the Incarnation and Christ's mission among men. In fact, not only does the program begin in the upper reaches of this dome but, after a complete circuit of both narthexes, it ends in the pendentives and vaults surrounding the dome's base. At the summits of the two domes of the inner narthex are medallion busts of Christ Pantocrator [7] and the Virgin [51], and in the flutes beneath them is an unusually extensive series of portraits of their ancestors, arranged in four zones (two zones in each dome) corresponding

7 Poem A, lines 1300 ff. (Treu, p. 35).

to four subdivisions within the genealogy: the early patriarchs from Adam to Jacob ([8]–[31]); the sons and immediate descendants of Jacob ([32]–[46]); the kings of the house of David, from David to Salathiel ([52]–[67]); and a group of "other ancestors outside the genealogy"[8] ([68]–[78]), whom Byzantine artists sometimes included in the ancestry because they were thought to have prefigured, or foretold, the Incarnation.

The genealogy in the domes serves as prelude to the narrative cycles of the lives of Mary and Christ, which comprise the major elements in the program; the life of Mary fills most of the remaining areas of the inner narthex, that of Christ all the major areas of the outer narthex and those beneath the southern dome of the inner. The narratives begin at the north ends of their respective narthexes, but although they form distinct cycles and are separated from one another by the wall between the narthexes, they are closely linked—one might say they form one continuous story, for the cycle of the outer narthex takes up the account at the precise point in Mary's life, as it is narrated in the apocryphal Protevangelium of James, where the Gospel accounts begin. In other words, the apocryphal story of Mary's life, depicted in the inner narthex, is discontinued at the very point where the Gospel texts overlap the apocryphal account and supersede it as the authority; the remainder of the story is illustrated in the mosaics of the outer narthex. It will be seen, however, that while the mosaics depicting the Infancy of Christ are based upon the Gospels and quote their texts in the inscriptions, at many points they illustrate details that are derived from the version of the Protevangelium.

The cycle of the Life of the Virgin ([82]–[99] and plan, Fig. 2) begins in the two northern pendentives of the northern dome and the lunette beneath them, continues from north to south in the lunettes and arches along the eastern side of the first three bays of the inner narthex and the vaults above them, and returns in the lunettes and arches along the west side, from south to north, to the point of origin at the north end of the narthex. The last episode in the cycle of the inner narthex, Joseph Reproaching the Virgin, is followed in the outer narthex by the cycle of the Infancy of Christ, as recounted in the Gospels, which begins with Mary's vindication when the angel appears to Joseph in a dream—the earliest incident concerning the birth of Christ to be recorded in the Gospel narrative (Matt. 1:20) and one of four illustrated episodes immediately preceding Christ's birth.

The cycle of the Infancy of Christ ([100]–[112]) was made to fit exactly within the fourteen available lunettes in the walls that encompass the outer narthex. There were sixteen lunettes altogether; two were devoted to "dedicatory" mosaics, and one of the remaining fourteen now retains no traces of its mosaics. The cycle ends with the episode that can be considered to mark the end of the infancy, in which Christ, at the age of twelve, is being taken by his parents to Jerusalem for Passover.

Beginning in the northern side of the domical vault of the northern bay (Bay 1, outer narthex), immediately above the first episodes of the Infancy Cycle, and continuing in the successive domical vaults of the outer narthex and the remaining areas beneath the southern dome of the inner narthex, is a series of subjects constituting a distinct narrative cycle, which may be termed the cycle of Christ's Ministry ([113]–[141]). The first subject, Christ among the Doctors, marks the start of his adult life, the occasion on which he began his mission among men —set out upon his Father's business, as he himself said (Luke 2:49). The greater part of this cycle consists of mosaics depicting Christ's miracles. There is no evidence among these fragmen-

8 See below, p. 36, and pp. 52–54 and n. 7 and 8, for an explanation of the sources of this term.

tary scenes that parables were interspersed among the miracles. The first few scenes ([113]–
[117]) depict early events of Christ's public life and are arranged in strict chronological
order: his appearance before the Doctors in the temple is followed by scenes of John the
Baptist preaching and bearing witness to Christ; then come the Temptation and the first of
Christ's miracles, The Marriage Feast at Cana. Thereafter chronology is abandoned. After running its course through the seven bays of the outer narthex the cycle ends in the fourth bay of
the inner narthex with eight miracles of healing. The mosaic cycle of Christ's Ministry originally consisted of at least thirty-two or at most thirty-six subjects, if we assume that scenes
were placed in the pendentives of the vault of the seventh bay; some of the subjects were
depicted in more than one episode. Although many of the scenes exist in fragmentary state, only
four, or eight, are completely destroyed, with no clue to their identification remaining. It is evident that the cycle did not encompass the entire life of Christ, stopping short of the great events
associated with the Passion. Scenes dealing with this subject, including such essential ones as The
Last Supper, The Washing of Feet, The Betrayal, and at least some of those concerning the
Crucifixion, Entombment, and Resurrection, would have found their place among the mosaics
which decorated the vaults of the nave.

It is to be noticed also that a number of the most important events within the chronological
limits of the three narrative cycles—events that were usually included among the Great Feasts
of the liturgical calendar—are not illustrated in the mosaics of the narthexes. Indeed, only three
of these essential events are depicted, namely, The Birth of the Virgin [87], The Presentation of the Virgin in the Temple [91], and The Nativity of Christ [102]. Conspicuous by
their absence are The Annunciation to the Virgin in her house (as distinguished from The Annunciation at the Well [98]), Christ's Presentation in the Temple, his Baptism, The Transfigu-
ration, The Raising of Lazarus, and The Entry into Jerusalem, all of which are events that often
figured in nave illustrations of the Great Feasts. The absence of these subjects signifies that
most, if not all, of them appeared among the mosaics of the nave and are now lost.

As was customary in Byzantine churches whose pictorial decoration was in mosaic, the nave
walls of the Kariye Djami, below the cornice marking the springing line of the vaults, were
covered with marble revetments. Only a limited number of mosaics, treated as framed panels,
could be introduced within the zone of marble. The three panels so set in the Kariye Djami still
exist. On the western faces of the two corner piers at the east, flanking the approach to the apse
(PL. 4), are standing figures of Christ [186] and the Virgin [187], which were intended to be
the monumental terminal icons of the templon, although they occur some distance in front of the
arch and step of the bema, where the iconostasis once stood. The third panel, which depicts The
Dormition of the Virgin [185], was set into the marble revetments above the western portal
(PL. 5). It is the sole surviving mosaic from what must have been an extensive series illustrating
the events commemorated on the Great Feasts of the church; all others in the series are among
the lost mosaics of the nave vaults.

One cannot now draw any conclusions concerning the number of scenes in the nave that
comprised the illustrations of the important feasts and the story of Christ's Passion, or the
manner in which they would have been disposed within the areas available to them. It can be
assumed, however, that they occupied all the arch soffits and the three tympana, that is to say,
the areas in the vaults exclusive of the dome and the conch of the apse. However, these architectural forms in the Kariye Djami are most ill suited to an orderly and monumental array of

narrative scenes, because all the arches except the bema arch are unusually narrow and the wall surfaces surrounding the triple windows of the tympana are irregular in shape and vary greatly from one tympanum to another. Especially in the soffits of the four arches that rest on the corner piers the scenes must have been greatly compressed in width and depicted at a small scale comparable to that of the Dormition.

The number of subjects employed in late-Byzantine church decoration in the domes of naves was rather restricted, and the choice of subjects was remarkably consistent. Although some other subjects are introduced in rare instances,[9] five themes appear with great frequency in the iconographic repertory of dome decoration in this period: *1*) the Christos Pantocrator, a bust figure enclosed in a rainbow-bordered medallion; *2*) the Celestial Powers, that is, seraphim, cherubim, and winged wheels disposed in zones around the medallion; *3*) the Divine Liturgy, consisting of angels serving as deacons in procession toward an altar placed on the eastern axis; *4*) the Prophets, holding inscribed scrolls; and *5*) the Four Evangelists, portrayed as seated figures in the act of writing their gospels. It was seldom that all five themes were, or could be, accommodated in a dome and its pendentives, as in the Catholicon of the Monastery of Chilandari on Mount Athos. However, three of the five seem to have been almost obligatory: the Pantocrator, at the summit of the dome; the Prophets, in the lower reaches; and the Evangelists, in the pendentives.[10] The other two themes, the Divine Liturgy and the Celestial Powers — sometimes one, sometimes the other, but seldom both — were sometimes introduced in the upper areas of the dome between the Prophets and the Pantocrator.[11] Whether these were included depended, at least in some measure, upon the relative size of the dome, the scale adopted for the figures, and whether figures could be placed between the windows in the drum. When there was room, a set of Prophets was usually inserted between the windows, and more frequently than not it was the Divine Liturgy that received preference as a fourth subject to occupy the zone above the windows and around the medallion of the Pantocrator.

In any conjectures regarding the iconographic program employed at the Chora in the dome of the nave, the precedents described above should be taken into account. But it should also be observed that the fourteenth-century dome, of which only the drum now exists (PL. 8), was composed of sixteen flutes, which would tend to divide the composition into sixteen segments, and that each flute was pierced by a window at the base of the dome. It is impossible to say whether the salient arrises between the concave flutes were decorated with ornamental borders, as they are in the two domes of the inner narthex (PL. 42 and 66), or whether, on the contrary, the segmental nature of the surface was minimized by the omission of borders so that the gold of the background could flow continuously over the arrises. It is evident, in any case, that figures would have been confined within the concavities of the sixteen flutes. The question is whether more than one zone of sixteen figures could have been accommodated below the medallion, in view of the fact that the drum was not available for figures because windows occupied all its flutes.

If the ratio between the diameter of the nave dome (7.20 m.) and its central medallion had

9 As at Sopoćani and Peć (both in the church of the Apostles and in St. Demetrius), where the Pantocrator became the central element of an Ascension.

10 Examples of churches in which only these three appear: Salonika, Holy Apostles (mosaic); Constantinople, the side chapel at the Fethiye Djami (Pammakaristos), where, however, the pendentives have lost their mosaics; Arilje, where

the Pantocrator is destroyed; Prizren, Bogorodica Ljeviška.

11 In addition to the three essential themes the Divine Liturgy appears, for example, at Studenica; Staro Nagoričino; Gračanica; Peć, church of the Virgin. On the other hand, the Celestial Powers were introduced into the domes at Arta, Panaghia Parigoritissa (mosaic), and the Catholicon of the Lavra on Mount Athos, among other places.

been similar to the ratios between the diameters of the two narthex domes (3.74 m. and 3.40 m.) and their respective medallions (1.24 m. and 1.14 m.), the diameter of the Pantocrator medallion in the nave would have been about 2.40 m.; but because its altitude was far greater than that of the medallions in the narthex domes, it is likely that it was made even larger. Now, if the size of the figures in the zone, or zones, between the medallion and the tops of the windows approximated the size of those in the two templon mosaics on the piers of the nave (ca. 2.20 m. in height, without halos, a minimal dimension for figures placed at such a lofty altitude in a dome), only one zone of figures could have been placed in the flutes of the nave dome, for above the level of a single zone of figures of such a dimension the flutes would have decreased in width to the point that figures of comparable size could not have been accommodated there. It seems evident, therefore, that the iconographic program of the dome, including its pendentives, would have consisted of three themes, and it is a logical conclusion that these comprised a Pantocrator, in the summit, a series of Prophets, one in each of the sixteen flutes above the windows, and the Four Evangelists, in the four pendentives. Under such a program the arrises of the flutes could well have been ornamented with borders, as they are in the two domes of the inner narthex.

In Byzantine church decoration the conch of the main apse had long been devoted to a monumental representation of the Virgin, and beginning in the twelfth century her attendant archangels, who had usually occupied the arch of the bema in front of the apse itself, were almost without exception placed within the conch, where they stood at each side of her.[12] While there is considerable variation in type, the Virgin most often is seated on a throne and holds the Christ Child in her lap, in a semireclining position [13] or seated upright.[14] Sometimes the enthroned Virgin holds an oval mandorla, as though it were a shield, within which is the seated figure of Christ Emmanuel.[15] At other times, the Virgin is depicted as a standing orant,[16] the Christ Child in an arc of heaven above her, or in the type of the standing Blachernitissa in orant pose with the half-figure of the Christ Emmanuel in an aureole on her breast;[17] a half-figure of the Virgin of the same type also appears in apse decoration.[18] We can be quite certain, therefore, that the lost mosaic in the conch of the main apse at the Kariye Djami depicted the Virgin flanked by two standing archangels. In view of the great emphasis on the Incarnation in the iconographic program of the Chora mosaics, a figure of the Virgin based upon the type of the Blachernitissa, which so clearly epitomizes that theme,[19] would have been most appropriate.

To conclude this brief outline of the iconographic program of the mosaics of the Chora and its layout in the structure only the series of portraits of martyrs and saints, all to be found in the outer narthex, remains to be considered. There are two categories of portraits: figures of martyrs ([142]–[178]), in the soffits of the arches that support the domical vaults of the bays, and figures of other sainted persons ([179]–[184]), on the pilasters that carry the transverse arches, in framed panels set into the marble revetments below the cornice.

The martyr portraits are of two kinds: small busts contained within roundels, and full-length frontal figures at a considerably larger scale. The busts in roundels occur in the relatively narrow relieving arches that support the east and west sides of the domical vaults of Bays 1, 2, 4,

---

12 This had sometimes occurred in pre-iconoclastic times, as in the apse mosaics of the Cypriote churches of the Panaghia Kanakaria, at Lythrangomi, and the Angeloktistos, at Kition.
13 As at Kurbinovo, or Staro Nagoričino.
14 As at Peć, church of the Virgin, or Studenica, church of Sts. Joachim and Anne.
15 See St. Sophia, at Ohrid.
16 As at Gračanica.
17 See Nerezi, St. Panteleimon.
18 As at Prizren, Bogorodica Ljeviška.
19 See the discussion of the Blachernitissa in [2], below.

and 5, and originally there were others in the summits of the six transverse arches that span the narthex; of the busts in the transverse arches only a small fragment of one now remains. (Further details concerning the arrangement, identification, and grouping of these martyr portraits will be found below, pp. 152–59.) The full-length standing figures, on the other hand, were disposed in confronted pairs in the six transverse arches, one pair in each arch; the mosaics in the last two arches, at the southwest corner of the narthex, were largely destroyed by the later insertion of reinforcing arches.

The mosaic panels of saints on the pilasters of the lower zone originally numbered twelve; half of these have been totally destroyed, and the remainder are in fragmentary state. Although it is possible that among the twelve one or more were martyr saints, five of the six partially preserved figures can be identified and no one of these represents a martyr. Indeed, it seems likely that the first six panels of the original twelve, which occur on the pilasters beneath the first three arches, in the northern part of the narthex, recall the general theme of the Incarnation, which we have seen to be central to the iconographic program of the narthex mosaics; for in all probability these six represented, as it were, the three holy families: Anne, with the infant Mary, opposite Joachim; Mary, with the infant Christ, opposite Joseph (now missing); and John the Baptist, opposite either Elizabeth or Zacharias (also missing).

The description of the layout of the mosaics in the two narthexes has made it evident that the iconographic program possesses a coherent plan and that a studied relationship exists between it and the architectural framework in which it is disposed. The question arises, therefore, whether the program and its disposition were entirely determined after the narthexes had been constructed or whether the requirements of the decorative program were anticipated, to some degree, in the architectural setting that was provided for it. In other words, is there evidence to indicate that the architecture was at all affected by the needs of an iconographer who, prior to the construction of the narthexes, had formulated the general outlines and nature of his program and was able to exert some influence in the determination of the architectural forms to be employed by the master builder? Though not all the happy coincidences that have been observed between the layout and the architecture can be attributed to the collaboration of builder and iconographer, a few phenomena do occur which strongly suggest that certain needs of the decorative program were consciously taken into account in the construction of the narthexes. The most important of these concerns the program's demand for a very large number of narrative scenes (as distinguished from individual portrait figures or busts in medallions) and the almost exclusive adoption of a most abnormal type of vaulting—abnormal, that is, in the construction of narthexes—which alone could meet this aspect of the program's requirements.

The narthex vaults provided space and suitable surfaces for approximately seventy narrative scenes, an extraordinarily large number of scenes for the narthexes of a church and one far exceeding that in any narthexes of comparable size in which representations, because they were executed in mosaic, were restricted to the zone of the vaults. This restriction, since it eliminated the use of the walls, makes the large number all the more remarkable. Such lavish use of scenes was made possible by the construction of domical vaults in nine of the eleven bays (the need for adequate light in the inner narthex and suitable spaces for the portrayal of Christ's ancestry led to the construction of lantern domes in the other two bays). Each of the nine domical vaults was capable of taking a number of scenes (as many as nine or ten were fitted into two of the vaults), arranged in a circular frieze around the perimeter, and in two instances the pendentives provided room as well. Moreover, the process of construction produced lunettes on the walls at two, or sometimes three, sides of each vault, adding a total of twenty lunettes, also admirably suited to the representation of scenes. When the transverse arches that separate the vaults were wide enough, as was the case in the inner narthex, there were surfaces suitable for still more scenes. It may be said, indeed, that no other method of vaulting could have provided for such an array of narrative scenes.

Now, it is a striking fact that the domical vault seldom appears in the narthexes of Constantinopolitan churches, or in those which clearly reflect the Constantinopolitan style of architecture, and never, to my knowledge, to an extent so nearly exclusive as in the Kariye Djami. We should eliminate from consideration the series of ten domical vaults covering the three narthexes that form a kind of perambulatory around the main church of the Pammakaristos (Fethiye Djami), which might be thought to provide a close parallel to those of the Chora, for they have been found by recent investigations to be Turkish additions or alterations.[20] At the Kilisse Djami three small, oblong domical vaults cover the inner narthex, and two larger square ones which alternate with three lantern domes cover the later outer narthex. In Constantinople the domical-vault form was frequently used, but in structures other than narthexes, and it had a long tradition; a number of the city's cisterns employed it exclusively and it was the principal form used in roofing the side galleries at Hagia Sophia.

The normal, and by far the most favored, vault form for narthexes was the groin or cross vault. It was used exclusively, for example, in the narthexes of Hagia Sophia, Saint Irene, and the two juxtaposed churches of the monastery of Constantine Lips (Fenari Isa Djami), in the original narthex of the Pammakaristos and that of its side chapel, the Pantepoptes (Eski Imaret), and in all the narthexes and galleries of the triple church of the Pantocrator. Why, then, did the builders not use the cross vault anywhere within the church of the Chora, and why, on the other hand, did they so abnormally, and so nearly exclusively, make use of the domical vault?

The answer might well be that the domical vault was admirably suited to the representation of narrative scenes, while the cross vault was among the most intractable of all vault forms as a setting for such scenes. In contrast to the domical vault with its single unbroken surface, the cross vault lacks continuity of flow, since its surface is broken up by the groins into irregular, angular forms radiating in four directions, and in such a setting it would be difficult to compose the individual scenes or to arrange them in sequences that could easily be followed by the be-

---

20 Observations made at the Fethiye Djami over a period of years by members of the staff of the Byzantine Institute while the interior masonry in the nave and narthexes was still bare of its covering plaster, and the exposure of some fragmentary frescoes in the south arm of the perambulatory, which required probings into the structure itself, have greatly clarified the structural history of this monument. A detailed account of these findings has been published by Cyril Mango and Ernest J. W. Hawkins, "Report on Field Work in Istanbul and Cyprus, 1962–1963," *D. O. Papers*, 18 (Washington, 1964), 319–33. The evidence shows that the walls, but not the domical vaults, of the perambulatory narthex on the north, west, and south sides of the nave were of late-Byzantine construction, dating perhaps even as late as the period when the church served as the Patriarchate of Constantinople (1455–1586), but in any case considerably later than the construction of the mortuary chapel (parecclesion) of Michael Glabas (ca. 1315); they are therefore much later than the narthexes of the Kariye Djami. The transverse arches and the domical vaults were found to be of Turkish masonry (dating after 1586, when the church was transformed into a mosque). For this see Mango and Hawkins, passim, and especially pp. 319, 328, and text Figs. A, C, and D. It is regrettable that H. Hallensleben's completely independent observations, published under the title, "Untersuchungen zur Baugeschichte der ehemaligen Pammakaristoskirche, der heutigen Fethiye camii in Istanbul," *Istanbuler Mitteilungen* (Deutsches Archäologisches Institut, Abteilung Istanbul), 13/14 (Tübingen, 1963–64), 128–193, were made after the church, save for the south arm of the perambulatory and the parecclesion (which now constitute a museum), had been restored as a mosque and the interior surfaces of its masonry had been covered with new plaster. His conclusions regarding the identification of the various phases of construction and some of the dates assigned to them are erroneous.

holder. These difficulties may be observed in the relatively few instances where the attempt was made to depict narrative subjects in a series of groin vaults: for example, in the narthexes of the Holy Apostles at Salonika or the Bogorodica Ljeviška at Prizren. At Dečani, where the vaulting system is similar to that of a Gothic church, the scenes are greatly distorted to fit the sharply triangular forms of the webbing between the ribbed groins. Normally, groin vaults were treated either decoratively, through the use of various ornamental motifs, or with a combination of ornament and medallion portraits, one in the center of each of the four segments. The latter approach was used, for example, in all the groin vaults at Hosios Loukas and the ones in the nave of the side chapel at the Pammakaristos; the groin vault in the bema of the Pammakaristos chapel still retains four medallions of archangels.

The barrel vault, of course, did lend itself to division into friezes, in which numerous scenes could readily be disposed. But the long, continuous barrel vault was seldom employed in middle and late Byzantine churches as a means of covering a narthex, although short units were sometimes used in combination with other vault forms. Its heaviness, its monotony, and the difficulties it imposed with regard to fenestration were probably factors which prevented its extensive use in the narthexes of churches of these periods.

The highly exceptional use of the domical vault at the Chora may therefore be explained on the grounds that the decision to include a very large number of narrative subjects in the decorative program had already been taken before the narthexes were constructed.

The fact that the cycles of the Life of the Virgin, the Infancy of Christ, and Christ's Public Ministry are so systematically arranged with regard to the structural parts of the narthexes (respectively they occur in the first three bays of the inner narthex, in the lunettes around the perimeter of the outer narthex, and in the successive domical vaults of the latter) does not necessarily mean that the program was completely outlined prior to construction. To the contrary, there is evidence that in the case of the cycles of the Life of the Virgin and the Infancy of Christ a degree of padding was required to fill out all the areas that were available. In the first of these cycles one subject—The Virgin Fed by an Angel—was twice depicted ([91] and [92]) and one scene—The Instruction of the Virgin in the Temple ([93]) — seems to have been made up *ad hoc* as a space filler; the subject of The Massacre of the Innocents ([107]–[110]) in the cycle of the Infancy was expanded inordinately over four lunettes in order to force all available lunettes into the cycle.

But when we examine the relationship between the layout of the Genealogy of Christ ([7]–[46], [51]–[78]) and the structural features of the two domes of the inner narthex, in which the ancestors are portrayed (PL. 42 and 66) — and especially those parts of the Genealogy allotted to the upper zones, which were not interrupted by windows—we again find clear evidence that the builders took into account some specific requirements of the iconographic program. Let us first consider the southern dome, where the Genealogy begins, and then proceed to its northern counterpart.

If we compare the four major domes in the Kariye Djami (PL. 8, 42, 66, and 409) with respect to the numbers and widths of their flutes or ribbed segments we are struck by the great number of excessively narrow flutes in the southern dome (PL. 42), which give it a very crowded appearance; the reasons for constructing the dome in this way can hardly be believed to have been architectural or aesthetic. The contrast can best be observed through a comparison of the number and width of the segments in each of the domes with the diameter of the dome. The southern dome of the inner narthex, which is here in question, has 24 flutes, a diameter of 3.74 m., and an average maximum flute width of about .49 m., measured from center to center of the bull's-nose borders between flutes. The corresponding numbers and dimensions for the other domes are: northern dome, 16 flutes, 3.40 m. diameter, and .667 m. flute width; nave dome, 16 flutes, 7.20 m. diameter, and 1.41 m. flute width; parecclesion dome, 12 ribbed segments, 4.70 m. diameter, and 1.23 m. between centers of ribs. We should inquire whether there were iconographic reasons for constructing the southern dome with as many as twenty-four flutes at the cost of such conspicuous overcrowding and in so great contrast to the other domes. We may then see whether there were comparable reasons for constructing its counterpart, the northern dome, with sixteen flutes.

Medieval iconographers who wished to portray the Genealogy of Christ were faced by the divergences that exist between the Gospels of Matthew and Luke in their recording of the Genealogy. The former begins with Abraham and traces the line through fourteen generations to David; then, by way of Solomon, through fourteen generations of kings of the House of David to Jechonias and the period of the Babylonian captivity; and finally, through Salathiel, born of Jechonias in captivity, through thirteen generations to Jesus, son of Joseph. Luke, on the other hand, begins with Adam and lists twenty-three generations through Jacob, then eleven generations more up through David. From here he traces the ancestry through forty-two generations to Jesus, son of Joseph, but through Nathan, another son of David, and not through the kings of the line of David and Solomon.

In late-Byzantine iconographic tradition, which is closely paralleled by the list in the painters' manual of Mount Athos, the *Hermeneia* of Dionysius of Fourna,[21] and reflected in the mosaic portraits of the Kariye Djami, considerable freedom was taken with the genealogies of the Gospels: portions were selected from both. Included also are the sons of Jacob, of whom only Judah was actually in the lineage, and a category was added, consisting of great Old Testament personages, mostly of the priestly class, who in one way or another were thought to have prophesied or to have prefigured the Incarnation. In addition to this last category, which was called "the other ancestors outside the genealogy," this "iconographer's genealogy," as it is more fully recorded in the *Hermeneia*, is composed of five groups: the early ancestors, called "the Just," in twenty-five generations from Adam to and including Jacob; the twelve sons of Jacob, who are called "patriarchs;" the line of Judah, who are also called "the Just," in ten generations from Zarah to Jesse; the fifteen kings of the House of David from David to Jechonias; and twelve generations, again called "the Just," extending from Salathiel, son of Jechonias, to Joseph, the "betrothed of the Theotokos."[22]

An examination of the layout of the Genealogy in the two domes of the inner narthex shows that the iconographer wished to devote the southern dome to the portrayal of as many generations as possible of the portion of the Genealogy from Adam to, but not including, David (he was forced by lack of space to omit the last eight generations preceding David), and to arrange the figures in two zones so that the early ancestors, from Adam to Jacob, would be in the upper zone while the sons of Jacob, and as many of Judah's immediate descendants as space permitted, would be in the lower zone, the available segments of which were greatly reduced in number because of the presence of windows. The northern dome was to contain two other categories

---

21 Ἑρμηνεία τῆς ζωγραφικῆς τέχνης, ed. A. Papadopoulos-Kerameus (St. Petersburg, 1909), pp. 73 ff.

22 For further discussion of the Genealogy, see below, pp. 52–54.

of the ancestry: the Kings of the House of David, in the upper zone, and "the other ancestors outside the genealogy," in the lower.

Now, according to the genealogy of St. Luke (3:34–38), the first category of ancestors, that is, the group from Adam through Jacob, comprised twenty-three generations. On the other hand, in the late-Byzantine iconographic tradition, as can be seen in the set at the Kariye Djami and in the list of the *Hermeneia*, this portion of the Genealogy was expanded to include two sons of Adam (Abel in addition to Seth) and two sons of Noah (Japheth in addition to Sem) and thus numbered twenty-five generations. It seems clear, therefore, that in providing the southern dome with the inordinately large number of twenty-four flutes the builders came as close as the laws of architectural composition would permit to supplying spaces in the upper zone to accommodate the number of generations required by the genealogies. Architectural practice dictated that the number of segments in a dome, whether it were fluted or ribbed, must always be a multiple of four and never an odd number such as twenty-three or twenty-five. It would be difficult to find an exception to this rule. As will be pointed out below, in connection with the description of the mosaics of the Genealogy, the iconographer got around the disparity among the strict genealogy of St. Luke, which calls for twenty-three generations, the iconographic tradition that calls for twenty-five generations, and the number of flutes—twenty-four—which the builder could provide, by adding two ancestors (Abel and Japheth) who were not in the lineage but who are listed in the *Hermeneia* and omitting one of the two Cainans who appear in Luke and in the *Hermeneia*. The implications of this procedure are that before the narthex was built it had been decided to provide for a Genealogy in its two domes, and to construct one of the domes with a quantity of flutes that would approximate as closely as possible the number of generations from Adam to Jacob.

Similar conclusions cannot be drawn so clearly in the case of the northern dome, for its flutes, unlike those of the southern dome, are not exceptional in number or proportions; it could have been constructed as it was, with sixteen flutes, without regard to the specific requirements of a predetermined iconographic program. However, when the layout of the Genealogy as a whole is recalled it becomes evident that in the upper zone of the northern dome the iconographer wished to emphasize the royal lineage of Christ (in contrast to his priestly "spiritual lineage," in the lower zone) and his line of descent from David and Solomon by portraying all the kings of Israel. According to St. Matthew's genealogy, these numbered fifteen from David to Jechonias, king at the time of the Babylonian captivity, which brought an end to the rule of the descendants of David. Jechonias' son, Salathiel (Shealtiel), who is portrayed in the sixteenth flute as a king, was in the Genealogy of Christ, but it is doubtful that he was ever anointed, for the puppet ruler, Sedecias, an uncle or brother of Jechonias, was placed on the throne in his stead. It may well be, therefore, that the northern dome was constructed with sixteen flutes to accommodate the fifteen royal ancestors of Christ, Salathiel being added as a space filler and given royal vestments to conform to the others. Again the dome followed the architectural practice, mentioned above, that the number of segments in a dome should be a multiple of four.

In the following section the individual items of mosaic will be taken up for descriptive and analytical purposes in the order in which they fall within the framework of the iconographic program that has been outlined above. As the Preface explains, a number is assigned to each item of mosaic whether it be a figural composition standing alone in an individual panel, or one of a

37

series of figures that comprise an iconographic category, or a scene within a series of pictorial compositions that constitute a narrative cycle. The order in which these items are numbered and discussed in the text and illustrated in the plates of Volume 2 is intended to correspond to the sequence in which the iconographer of the Kariye Djami wished for the mosaics to be viewed so that the beholder might grasp the significance and unity of the themes that comprise the iconographic program as a whole. The reader should observe that the key numbers assigned to the individual units appear with the text entries, with the illustrations of Volume 2, and on the diagrammatic plans and sections that accompany each of the volumes.

DEDICATORY AND DEVOTIONAL PANELS

[1]

Christ Pantocrator PL. 17–19

᾽Ι(ησοῦ)ς Χ(ριστὸ)ς | ἡ χώρα τῶν ζώντων
Jesus Christ, the dwelling-place of the living

The first of the mosaics confronting the beholder when he enters the church of the Chora is the monumental bust image of Christ above the entrance to the inner narthex on the axis of the building. The type of the image is that of Christ Pantocrator, but the accompanying inscription designates him as the *chora ton zonton* (the dwelling-place, or land, of the living), a phrase taken from the Psalms as a play upon the name of the monastery.[1] It will be seen that the same epithet accompanies other images of Christ at important positions in the church ([3] and [186]) and that the word *chora* also figures in the epithet inscribed on two images of the Virgin ([2] and [187]) that were placed in confrontation with those of Christ. The inference to be drawn from the use of ἡ χώρα as the common denominator of these epithets is that in the fourteenth century the Chora monastery was consecrated to both Christ and the Theotokos in the qualities ascribed to them by their respective epithets, that is, as the embodiment of life and as the instrument of the Incarnation (see no. [2], below), even though in that period it was said by some to have been consecrated to Christ and by others to the Virgin.[2] The figure of the Pantocrator and that of the Virgin Blachernitissa [2], which faces it, should therefore be regarded as dedicatory images; this conclusion is further supported by their positions at the entrance to the church.

In the mosaic Christ clutches the Book of the Gospels to his bosom with his left hand. The curious delineation of the hand, with thumb raised vertically and index finger widely separated from the others, which come to a point, is peculiar to the Pantocrator. His right hand, extended somewhat to the left, emerges from folds of the himation, as from a sling, and is turned toward the Gospels in a gesture of blessing. The figure appears to be turned slightly toward the left and is noticeably unsymmetrical. The right sides of the head and body are rendered at a considerably larger scale than the left, and it is in part through this device that a degree of foreshortening on the left is achieved to give the figure the appearance of being turned in that direction.

Dimensions	*Condition*
Greatest breadth within borders, 3.63 m.; height from border to top of cornice over door, 2.15 m.; height of head, including beard, .78 m.	Gold tesserae in areas of background at sides had been removed, but original plaster of setting bed, painted red, was found largely preserved. These areas were

1 Ps. 116:9: "I will walk before the Lord in the land of the living."
2 See above, pp. 27–28.

cleaned and consolidated, and patches of new plaster were introduced, wherever necessary, and painted to harmonize. Plaster between lower edge of mosaic and top of cornice is original setting bed, painted red but never set with tesserae. Inscriptions are largely intact, but there are a few areas of lost tesserae, in which the black underpainting was preserved.

Colors and Materials

FACE flesh tones, small tesserae of pink and white marbles; highlights, mat white stone; shading of left side of face from top of forehead to bottom of ear, yellowish green and pale gray-blue glasses; shading of right side of forehead and face, greenish brown glass along outer edge and two zones to left in checkered pattern, the outer of yellowish green glass alternating with pink marble, the inner of greenish yellow glass alternating with pink marble; shadow on right side of neck cast by chin, light brown glass. HAIR OF HEAD executed in rows of glass ranging from black through three values of brown and in stones of light brown and white. BEARD AND MUSTACHE principally of glass in several values of brown into which, near upper edges, small glass tesserae of greenish brown, yellowish green, and greenish yellow are mingled. HANDS upper edges of fingers, outlined with two rows of glass, brown above and gray-blue below; bottom of hand at right, outlined by single row of glass, dark brown half way and then continued in black; above this, fingers are shaded by single rows of light brown stone; principal area of shading in hand at right, executed in checkered pattern of pink marble and green glass.

GARMENTS tunic and himation, both executed in blue glass tesserae of ultramarine color in four principal values; contours and principal drapery folds, delineated in black glass; clavus over left shoulder of tunic, gold with folds indicated by rows of greenish brown glass. BOOK golden cover, adorned by cruciform design outlined in red glass, in the center a red terra cotta disc surrounded by a golden band studded with small round stones of mat white representing pearls. Above are triangular gems of green glass, a lozenge-shaped gem of blue glass, and two leaf-shaped ornaments of dark red glass at upper corners. Symmetrically distributed over field of cover are large circular stones of mat white (pearls). Book is provided with two dark red glass clasps, which are unfastened, tipped with gold glass (one gold tip missing). Edge of book, rendered in alternate rows of gold and greenish brown glasses. All major outlines of book, dark red glass. NIMBUS cross-inscribed, drawn with double row of dark red glass; fields of cross arms, rows of gold glass parallel to direction of arms; fields between arms, rows of gold glass concentrically laid. INSCRIPTION black glass.

[2]

The Virgin Blachernitissa and Angels

PL. 20–25

Μ(ήτ)ηρ Θ(εο)ῦ | ἡ χώρα τοῦ ἀχωρήτου
The Mother of God, the dwelling-place of the uncontainable

Opposite the mosaic of the Pantocrator [1], in the lunette above the entrance door of the church, is the figure of the Virgin with the Christ Child between two angels. The lunette itself is reduced by the intrusion of the arch above the door to a rather narrow semicircular zone. For want of space the Virgin, at the center, is rendered as a half-figure but in the pose of a full-length standing orant whose lower half is cut off by the arch; the green zone of ground in which she would have stood appears at each side of the open arch. Admirably fitted into the sloping sides of the arc, above the ground zone, are two flying angels, in near-profile view, their hands covered with the folds of their garments as they approach the Mother of God in adoration.

The Virgin is of the type of the Blachernitissa, so called because its prototype is believed to have been an icon in the chapel of the Soros (i.e., reliquary) at the church of the Theotokos of Blachernae, where the most prized relic of the Virgin—her maphorion, or veil—was venerated. The type is characterized by the orant attitude of the Virgin and, in one variant, by the bust figure of the Christ Emmanuel which appears in an aureole of ovoid shape on her breast. The latter detail, it is evident, was meant to recall the prophecy of Isaiah 7:14, repeated in Mat-

40

thew 1:23, that in the womb of the Virgin the Emmanuel, that is, God with us, should be conceived. Iconographically, therefore, the type symbolizes the Incarnation. This meaning is made explicit by the inscription in the mosaic. The immediate source of the inscription was probably an epithet of the Virgin found in the celebrated Akathistos hymn, Θεοῦ ἀχωρήτου χώρα;[1] but the origins of the epithet go back at least to the fifth century, for in one of his homilies St. Cyril of Alexandria hails Mary as τὸ χωρίον τοῦ ἀχωρήτου.[2] The word *chora* is used in our inscription, as in the hymn, in a sense that is antithetical to ἀχώρητος (uncontainable): the Godhead, who could not be "contained" or encompassed as a finite being, was, nevertheless, "contained" through the mystery of the Incarnation and the union of the two natures of Christ.

As was explained in the description of Christ Pantocrator [1], the two confronting images at the entrance to the church are to be regarded as dedicatory images. Iconographically, the two should be considered in conjunction with the scenes in the domical vault between them. Together they epitomize the central dogma of salvation through the Incarnation and through the sacrifice of the Logos, which is shared by all through the two elements of the Eucharist. The latter are typified in the scenes of The Miracle at Cana [117] and The Multiplication of Loaves [118] in the vault above.

Dimensions

Greatest breadth within borders, 3.60 m.; height of figure of Virgin, including nimbus, .69 m.; zone of green ground below, .38 m. high at left, .33 m. at right.

Condition

A break in the masonry through the lunette to right of center caused some losses of mosaic tesserae in the right side of the Virgin. Other areas of loss occur in ornamental borders and background. In the inscription, the letter theta, the upper half of the left stroke of the upsilon, and the abbreviation mark in the word *theou* were found to have been painted black on the setting bed, but no tesserae had ever been inserted.

Colors and Materials

GARMENTS OF THE VIRGIN   blue glass of three principal values with outlines and drawing of folds in black glass; ornaments on cuffs, gold bordered by dark red glass; edging of mantle and of maphorion around face, gold glass; edge of kerchief beneath maphorion, executed in small tesserae of light blue and gray-blue glass and white stone.

HALO   typical of style used throughout the mosaics, a single row of red glass surrounding a field of concentrically laid gold glass tesserae.
MANDORLA   field of light blue glass is surrounded by two rows of bluish gray glass and a single row of very light gray stone, highlighted along left side by a single row of white stone.   GARMENTS OF CHRIST CHILD gold glass with contours, interior drawing of folds, and shading at right side in violet glass of several values.
ANGEL AT LEFT   tunic, visible at shoulder and over left knee, blue glass in three values highlighted in gray and white stones; himation, including drapery over hands, green glass of three values extensively highlighted with gray and white stones; outer parts of wings, brown glass of several values and brownish stone, shaded along outer edges by deep violet glasses and highlighted by gold glass; under parts of right wing, blue glasses highlighted by gray and white stones.   ANGEL AT RIGHT tunic, visible at bent knee, blue glass; himation, brown glasses and yellowish stones, highlighted with white stone and shaded, along left edge of straight leg, by single row of blue glass, dark blue along thigh and light blue from knee downward.

1 See Egon Wellesz, *The Akathistos Hymn* (Monumenta Musicae Byzantinae, Transcripta, Vol. IX, Copenhagen, 1957), p. LXXV, stanza xv, line 8; for the date and authorship of the hymn, idem, "The 'Akathistos,' a Study in Byzantine Hymnography," *D. O. Papers*, 9 and 10 (Cambridge, Mass., 1956), 143 ff.

2 Homily XI, Migne, *Pat. Gr.*, 77, col. 1032 D. I am indebted to Professor James H. Oliver for calling this passage in the writings of St. Cyril to my attention. See his forthcoming work, *A Peplos for Athena*.

[3]

The Enthroned Christ and the Donor

PL. 26–29, AND FRONTISPIECE

'Ι(ησοῦ)ς Χ(ριστὸ)ς | ἡ χώρα τῶν ζώντων
Jesus Christ, the dwelling-place of the living

Ὁ κτή|τωρ λο|γοθέ|της τοῦ γε|νικοῦ. Θεό|δωρος | ὁ Μετο|χί|τη|ς
The Founder, the Logothete of the Genikon, Theodore Metochites

On entering the inner narthex on the axis of the church the spectator is confronted by the donor panel, filling the lunette above the main door leading into the nave. In the center is the figure of Christ, seated in nearly frontal pose on a jeweled throne with two cushions, a footstool at his feet. Resting on his left thigh is the closed Book of the Gospels, which he holds upright with his left hand; he raises his right hand before him in blessing. In near-profile at the left, kneeling and offering his church to Christ, is Theodore Metochites, "founder" of the monastery and Logothete of the Genikon,[1] to whom we are indebted for the reconstruction of the church of the Chora and for all the mosaics and frescoes it contains, with the exception of those which appear in the wall tombs.[2]

Both as statesman and as scholar, Metochites was one of the outstanding men of his time. A few years after completion of his work at the Chora, his emperor, Andronicus II, elevated him to the office of Grand Logothete, a position in which he served as the emperor's chief minister. So closely was he associated with the policies and family of Andronicus (his only daughter married the emperor's nephew, John Palaeologos, the Panhypersebastos and later Caesar) that he suffered exile and impoverishment on the overthrow of Andronicus' government. Near the end of his life, under the monastic name Theoleptos, Metochites was confined as a monk in the Chora, where he died on March 13, 1332, and where he was buried.

Metochites is portrayed with a square-cut brown beard of moderate length and wavy hair that falls to his collar behind. He is dressed in the costume of his office, which according to a contemporary source consisted of a hat known as the *skiadion* (literally, sunshade) and an outer garment called the *kabbadion*.[3] The latter is a kind of caftan, or long, loose coat, gathered at the waist by a girdle. The one Metochites wears is ornamented with borders of gold at the collar, cuffs, and hem and along the edges of the front opening. The material is dark bluish green with an all-over pattern composed of two leaf forms arranged in alternating horizontal rows. The *skiadion*, the most striking feature of the costume, seems to be constructed of a light but rigid armature covered with a fabric. It is characterized by a high and widely spreading crown that rises in a double curvature to a rim of great diameter. The white fabric of the crown, probably meant to be silk, is decorated with horizontal stripes, which perhaps represent a series of pleats; wide golden stripes edged with red run up the crown, and the rim is bound by a roll of gold and gray with diagonal lashings of red.

---

1 Controller of the general treasury.
2 See Vol. 4 for a biographical study of Metochites.

3 Codinus Curopalates, *De officialibus palatii Constantinopolitani*, Ch. IV; Bonn ed. (1839), p. 20.

The model of the church held by the founder is a somewhat simplified version of the structure itself (PL. 1). The principal dome, over the nave, the two smaller domes at the ends of the inner narthex, and the arched façade of the outer narthex correspond to the salient features of the actual structure.[4] The parecclesion along the right side, which renders the church itself asymmetrical, has been omitted, and the number of bays of the outer narthex has been reduced to three.

Dimensions

Greatest breadth within borders, 2.30 m.; height at center of panel within borders, 1.62 m.; height of figure of Christ from top of head to toes, 1.40 m.; head of Christ including beard, .22 m.; height of figure of Metochites from top of hat to knees, 1.13 m.

Colors and Materials

CHRIST   *Head:* flesh tones, pink marbles; hair, alternating rows of greenish yellow and greenish brown glass; beard, greenish brown glasses. *Garments:* tunic (right sleeve, shoulder, and breast and hem visible), violet glass in three values with some drawing in black glass, and clavus over sleeve in gold and red glasses; himation, blue glass in three values. *Book:* gold with red outlines for cross and borders; studded with white stones (pearls) and green and red glass gems; clasps, red; edges of book (top and left), alternating rows of gold and blue. *Cushions:* front cushion, red with gold ornaments at ends; rear cushion, green glass with gold ornaments at ends. *Throne and footstool:* fronts and tops, gold studded with gems of red, blue, and green glass and with pearls of mat white stone; panels on front of throne, brownish green and brown glasses; receding faces, greenish brown glasses studded with pearls and gems; panel in right side of throne, violet.

METOCHITES   *Head:* flesh tones, pink marbles; hair and beard, brown glasses with gray stone highlights. *Hat:* light gray stone with narrow stripes of bluish gray stone; wide vertical stripes, gold edged with red; rim, gold and gray with lashings of red. *Caftan:* dark bluish green glass decorated with pattern of gold leaves of two forms and with gold dots; collar, cuffs, and borders, gold and red. *Model of church:* walls, gray stone in two values with drawing in brownish green glass; roofs, blue glass of two values with highlights of light gray stone and cross on top of dome in white stone; door, gold and brownish green.

GOLD BACKGROUND   laid in scale pattern except in area of inscription to far left.

4 The model reflects the fact that in the original façade the roof line of the first five bays broke up in a series of lunettes above the arches of the windows and door. To simplify the roof, the existing spandrels (Turkish masonry) were constructed as can be seen in PL. 1. For the original appearance of the external lunettes see the lithograph published in A. G. Paspates, Βυζαντιναὶ μελέται τοπογραφικαὶ καὶ ἱστορικαὶ μετὰ πλείστων εἰκόνων (Constantinople, 1877), opp. p. 326.

[4], [5]

St. Peter and St. Paul

PL. 30–35

[4] Ὁ ἅγ(ιος) Πέτρος

[5] Ὁ ἅγ(ιος) Παῦλος

At each side of the door leading into the nave, above which is the figure of the Founder of the Chora presenting his church to Christ, are the full-length standing portraits of the two "princes" of the apostles, Sts. Peter and Paul. In this context they too, as it were, assume the character of "founders," inasmuch as they, of all the apostles, were most instrumental in bringing Christ's Church into being; and in late Byzantine church decoration they not infrequently take their place, as here, at each side of the door to the nave. Peter, the vigorous, natural leader—the "Rock" on which the Church was to be founded, and Paul, the great teacher and formulator of Christian doctrine—the Lord's "chosen vessel," are inseparably linked in joint commemoration by the Church on June 29.

The tall, round-headed panels are framed with multicolored marbles set into the system of marble revetments which covers the walls of the inner narthex. In the panel at the left, the more honored position of the two since it is at the right hand of the figure of Christ above, the forceful character of Peter is captured in his commanding bearing, his erect posture, and the movement of the drapery below his left arm. He stands in three-quarters pose, facing the door and his companion to the right. With his right hand he firmly grips the scroll containing his epistles; his right arm is held stiffly at his side. From his upraised left hand two keys—the "keys of the kingdom of heaven"—hang from the ends of a short cord that is twined around the first two fingers. As is usual in representations of the apostles, he wears a blue tunic with a red clavus, and the classical himation that is draped over the shoulders and right arm and around the waist and lower part of the body; this garment is yellow, as always in the case of Peter at the Kariye Djami. Sandals are on his feet.

Paul, whose pose is reversed, is dressed in similar garments, but his himation is violet. The profound intellect of the theologian is expressed by the long, ovoid head, which contrasts with Peter's round one, the lofty brow furrowed with wrinkles, the scant hair, the rather long, pointed beard, and the hooked nose, all of which are traditional in the portrayal of Paul. The hair and beard are dark blue-violet lighted with blue. With his right hand raised before him he makes a gesture of teaching—the tip of the ring finger touching the tip of the thumb. In his left hand he holds the closed codex of his numerous epistles.

Dimensions

ST. PETER [4] height of panel within frame, 2.05 m.; breadth of panel within frame, .76 m.; height of figure from head to foot, 1.845 m.; diameter of nimbus, .45 m. ST. PAUL [5] height of panel within frame, 2.05 m.; breadth of panel within frame, .72 m.; height of figure from head to foot, 1.83 m.; diameter of nimbus, .445 m.

Condition

Paspates (pp. 331 f.) wrote that in the course of repairs in the building in 1876 these two mosaic panels, and those of Christ [186] and the Virgin [187], were discovered under coatings of plaster and were uncovered and found to have suffered damage. As can be seen in Plate LIX of Feodor Shmit's work,[1] photographed about 1901, which records the condition in which the Byzantine Institute also found the panels in 1947, the areas of lost tesserae surrounding the lower parts of the figures were later covered anew with plaster. In addition to cleaning and repairing the preserved areas of mosaic surface, the staff of the Byzantine Institute removed the patching plaster that covered the areas of preserved setting bed. These areas were cleaned and repaired, and the paint on the setting bed was revealed, with imprints of the tesserae that had long since been picked out by souvenir hunters. The areas of exposed setting bed now provide excellent evidence of the medieval techniques of mosaic work, the extent to which the wet plaster was painted in color before the tesserae were inserted, and the amount of detail which was used.

Colors and Materials

St. Peter

HAIR brown, brownish green, and light blue glasses with white stone highlights. NECK shaded areas at right checkered in pink marbles and brown and yellow glasses. FEET shod with sandals fastened by thongs of very dark violet glass; originally had rather wide shadows (3 rows) under them in very dark brown glass. GARMENTS tunic, visible at left sleeve and breast—and suggested at hem, where it is preserved in painted setting bed—blue glass in three values with lights in gray and white stones; clavus of red glass in two values bordered by single row of dark violet; himation, largely yellow and tan stones with brown and greenish brown glasses for shading and white stone for highlights. KEYS AND SCROLL blue glass and gray and white stones; keys hanging from cord of black glass and scroll tied with cord of dark red glass.

St. Paul

HEAD one of finest and most colorful among mosaics of Kariye Djami; forehead shades from light pink to almost white marbles, then enters area of shadow in checker technique, with alternating bluish gray and orange-yellow glasses, then, toward upper right, alternating bluish gray and green glasses, and finally, a solid zone of graded greenish brown glasses that darken until the outer row of blue-violet glass is reached; hair and beard, three values of dark blue-violet, with which are

1 *Kakhrie-dzhami* (Izvestiia Russkago Arkheologicheskago Instituta v Konstantinopole, XI; text, Sofia, album of plates, Munich, 1906).

mingled several strands of light blue and light bluish gray glasses and accents of black or very dark violet; a good deal of orange-yellow glass is used to outline right side of beard, in and around eyelids, in shaded side of nose, and again in checker work in left side of neck. GARMENTS tunic, visible at breast and sleeve at left and at hem, blue glass in three values and bluish gray and white stones, with clavus of red glass in two values bordered by single rows of dark violet; himation, mainly of violet glass of five values with highlights of bluish gray and white stones. CODEX cover in two values of red glass with terra cotta used in lightest parts of design; lozenge and triangles of gold glass; edges of book, pink marble, terra cotta, and white stone; clasps, black.

[6]

The Deesis

ʼΙ(ησοῦ)ς Χ(ριστὸ)ς | ὁ χαλκίτης *Jesus Christ of the Chalke*

Μ(ήτ)ηρ [Θεοῦ] *The Mother of God*

ʽΟ υἱὸς τοῦ ὑ|ψηλοτάτου | βασιλέως | ʼΑλεξίου | τοῦ Κομνηνοῦ, | ʼΙσαάκιος | ὁ πορ|φυρο|γέννη|το|ς
The son of the most high emperor Alexius Comnenus, Isaac the Porphyrogenite

[. . . ʼΑ]νδ[ρον]ίκου τοῦ Πα|λαιολόγου ἡ κυρὰ τῶν | Μουγουλίων, Μελάνη ἡ | μοναχή
. . . of Andronicus Palaeologos, the Lady of the Mongols, Melane the nun

The cornice and the marble revetments which decorate the walls of the inner narthex were omitted from the eastern wall of the fourth bay to provide space for the huge mosaic panel devoted to a representation of the Deesis,[1] in which the Virgin, in supplication before Christ, intercedes on behalf of mankind and in particular of the two imperial personages, Isaac Comnenus and Melane the nun, who are represented in the lower corners. Standing on a footstool near the left margin of the panel is the colossal figure of the Virgin, who turns in three-quarters view toward her son, her head bowed and her hands extended in the usual attitude of *deesis*. In the right side of the panel but near the center, where he could be drawn on a still larger scale, is the figure of Christ, of a type (the *Christos Chalkites*) that is unusual, if not unique, in a Deesis composition. In the more frequent version, where he is flanked by the Virgin and John the Baptist, Christ is seated on a throne and holds the Book of the Gospels in his left hand while his right is slightly raised in an outwardly directed gesture of blessing. Here, however, Christ stands in frontal pose upon a footstool, his right hand held before him in a blessing that is perhaps directed toward the small figure in the lower right; his left hand clutches the folds of his garment at the waist. His weight rests on his right leg; the left leg is bent slightly at the knee. Like the composition itself, the figure is unsymmetrical, for both head and body are noticeably larger on the right than on the left. By this means the figure, though essentially frontal, appears to be turned toward the beholder who approaches it from the left on entering the narthex.

According to the accompanying inscription, Christ is portrayed in the manner of the famous

1 This mosaic was previously discussed by the author in "The Deisis Mosaic in the Kahrie Cami at Istanbul," *Late Classical and Mediaeval Studies in Honor of Albert Mathias* *Friend, Jr.*, ed. Kurt Weitzmann (Princeton, 1955), pp. 254–60, and in reports on the work of the Byzantine Institute in *D. O. Papers*, 9 and 10 (1956), 295 f., and 12 (1958), 284–87.

icon that stood above the Chalke Gate, the principal gateway and ceremonial entrance to the Great Palace of the Emperors in Constantinople.[2] In that position, the *Christos Chalkites* became the insigne, as it were, of the Christian empire, and as a type it appears to have acquired imperial connotations. Few examples of the *Chalkites* with the inscribed epithet have survived. The version here used reproduces the type rather faithfully, except that typically the left hand would hold the codex of the Gospels. Its use in the Deesis panel may well have been motivated by the portrayal of the two imperial figures.

The mosaic as a whole is more than a representation of the Deesis; it is at the same time a commemorative panel. The only portraits of historic personages, other than his own, that came within the scope of Metochites' original program of decoration [3] are the two in the lower corners of the Deesis. At the lower left, with an identifying inscription, is the figure of Isaac Comnenus, son of the Emperor Alexius I Comnenus (1081–1118) and younger brother of the Emperor John II (1118–1143). His commemoration in the church is to be explained through his family's and his own connection with the monastery of the Chora. Isaac's grandmother, Maria Ducaena, had constructed an earlier church, whose ruins are incorporated in the present building. The remains which have been identified as those of Maria's church indicate that by the early twelfth century the church was so seriously damaged that rebuilding became necessary; the builder was probably her grandson Isaac.[4] In any case, in his youth Isaac had set up his tomb in the church of the Chora, and with it a portrait of himself. Late in his life he ordered the removal of the tomb to another of his monasteries but requested that his portrait remain at the Chora. The existing portrait is not, however, the one he commissioned.

Although the figure of Isaac Comnenus is fragmentary, it can be seen that he was portrayed as a standing figure bent slightly forward with hands extended in prayer and head turned upward toward Christ. Only the head, the right shoulder, the hands, and a bit of the lining of the outer garment, below the hands, now remain in mosaic tesserae. Other parts of the costume, however, can be distinguished in the painted plaster of the setting bed where the tesserae have been lost. Isaac wears a jeweled blue-violet (representing purple) crown and a heavy, sleeveless blue-violet mantle fastened at the throat but open down the front. The garment is decorated with gold-bordered lozenges containing fleurs-de-lis and with a square patch, or tablion, near the right hand; its lining is rendered in a conventional representation of fur.

The nun portrayed in the lower right corner cannot be identified with certainty. The fragmentary inscription indicates that she was in some way related to the Emperor Andronicus Palaeologos (probably Andronicus II), that she bore the title Lady of the Mongols, and that her name in religion was Melane. There are two Byzantine princesses who best fulfill these conditions. The first is Maria Palaeologina, illegitimate daughter of Michael VIII Palaeologos and half sister of Andronicus II, known as the Despoina of the Mongols because of her marriage to, and conversion of, the Great Khan, Abaga, in 1265. She is known also as a *ktetorissa* ("foundress") of the Constantinopolitan convent of the Theotokos Panaghiotissa, whose church was called, as it is to this day, St. Mary of the Mongols. The second possibility is that the nun

2 For the history and iconography of the Chalke mosaic, see Cyril Mango, *The Brazen House, a Study of the Vestibule of the Imperial Palace of Constantinople* (Det Kongelige Danske Videnskabernes Selskab: Arkaeologisk-kunsthistoriske Meddelelser, IV, 4; Copenhagen, 1959), pp. 108–42; André Grabar, *L'Iconoclasme byzantin, dossier archéologique* (Paris, 1957), pp. 130 ff.

3 The tombs that were later incorporated into the walls of the Chora contained other portraits, illustrated in Vol. 3 (PL. 534, 553).

4 On these matters see above, Introduction, pp. 11–13. See also David Oates, "A Summary Report on the Excavations of the Byzantine Institute in the Kariye Camii: 1957 and 1958," *D. O. Papers*, 14 (Washington, 1960), 223–31.

Melane was the princess Maria, illegitimate daughter of Andronicus II, who married Tuktai, the Mongol Khan of the Golden Horde, in the last decade of the thirteenth century.[5]

The figure of Melane has suffered very severe damage. Only the face, part of the black headdress, and the hands are preserved to any degree in mosaic tesserae; but the general form of the figure emerges from the painted setting bed, which still exists in several areas.

Before the discovery of the two portraits there had been disagreement among scholars regarding the date of the Deesis panel; the inscription accompanying the figure of Isaac, part of which had been known before the removal of the covering materials, had led some to date it in the eleventh or twelfth century. For technical reasons,[6] and because the portrait of the Palaeologan princess is an integral part of the panel, the entire mosaic should be regarded as a Palaeologan work executed in conjunction with Metochites' decoration in the second decade of the fourteenth century.

Dimensions

Height of panel from wave border above to top of dado beneath, 4.81 m.; width of panel at lower edge, 4.32 m.; height of figure of Christ from top of head to upper edge of footstool, 4.20 m.; head of Christ including beard, .75 m.; height of Virgin from top of head to level of upper edge of Christ's footstool, 3.67 m.; head of Virgin from top of head to point of chin, .55 m.

Condition

Before work of restoration was begun, plaster covered almost all parts of the panel where mosaic tesserae had been lost, as well as the two imperial figures in the lower corners, PL. LX of Shmit, *Kakhrie-dzhami*, illustrates conditions in the upper half of the panel as they continued to exist until May of 1953, when work on the panel was begun. The condition of the lower half, which was completely covered with plaster, can be assessed from Fig. 1 in the author's article of 1955, cited above in n. 1, which illustrates the early stages of the work. Further information can be found in the other publications cited in the same note. All that was visible was the upper parts of the two principal figures and their identifying inscriptions (but not the epithet *Chalkites*), a few letters of the inscription at the far left that still survived in mosaic tesserae, and almost all the fragments of gold background that had survived. These areas had been covered with a lime wash, which was still lodged in all interstices.

The removal of all covering plaster revealed that most of the painted setting bed was still extant and that it too had been whitewashed before being covered with plaster. The principal areas where even the setting bed was destroyed are the following: in the upper right, a large and very irregularly shaped piece of the background extending from below the inscription to the right of Christ down to the preserved parts of the in-

scription above Melane, filling near its bottom the entire space between Christ's waist and the right edge of the panel; beneath this, a large strip which included the back of the nun's headdress and continued irregularly downward to the bottom of the panel but within which were small pieces of original setting bed pertaining to the costume of the nun; a number of rather minor areas within the figure of the Virgin (one quite large, extending in an irregular course from her wrist downward past the front of Isaac's head almost to the hem of her garment; a small one between and below her two hands; another somewhat larger one above her knees in the right part of her garments; and two small ones at about the level of her knees); a large area in the lower left part of the panel which included the lower parts of the figures of Isaac and the Virgin and most of her footstool; and a number of relatively small areas where plaster was lost in the background in the upper part of the panel.

The next stage in the restoration, some of which was carried out as the removal of covering plaster was proceeding, was the consolidation of the setting bed wherever it was broken up or crumbled. Many of the smaller areas where original plaster was lost were immediately filled with new white plaster to a level slightly lower than that of the surrounding original setting bed, but some of the larger areas that came at structurally important points in the wall were left open for a time to permit the study and recording of the eleventh-century masonry and of some alterations in the wall that were probably made in the twelfth century. The edges of the areas which still retained their mosaic tesserae were secured by narrow retaining walls of new plaster to prevent further losses. Next, the painted setting bed was carefully cleaned to restore as much of the brilliance of the original underpainting as possible. A large, rounded area of setting bed near the bottom of the panel, between the figures of Christ and the Vir-

---

5 See Underwood, "Notes on the Work of the Byzantine Institute in Istanbul: 1955-1956," *D. O. Papers*, 12 (1958), pp. 286 f. and n. 49, 50; and "The Deisis Mosaic," pp. 258 ff.

6 See Underwood, *D. O. Papers*, 12, p. 285.

gin, had been covered by plaster containing brick dust, and this had left a stain on the setting bed of a different hue from that of the earth-red pigment with which all areas to receive gold tesserae had been painted. In consolidation of the setting bed all the hundreds of minor cracks and fissures in the original plaster were carefully filled. The areas of mosaic surface were then cleaned by brushing and the interstices cleared of all deposits of lime and dirt by means of hand dental instruments. At the same time all loose tesserae were reset. Finally, after the large areas of lost plaster had been filled the new surfaces were carved in a schematic way to suggest rows of imprints, to harmonize with the surfaces of original plaster, which still retained the imprints of the lost tesserae. These areas were then tinted with colors that were different either in value or in hue from the surrounding areas of original paint.

Colors and Materials

CHRIST *Face:* cheeks and beard constructed of rows of cubes which radiate from points at inner corners of eyes, and forehead of rows which tend to divide diagonally from center line; flesh tones are of pink marbles with very few whites; shading along right side of forehead, a checker pattern of pink marble and greenish yellow and greenish brown glasses; shading of left edge of face, two rows of gray stone along outer edge, and within, one row of alternate gray and pink cubes. *Beard:* mainly of brown glasses with a few black glass lines at right side and greenish yellow glass near mouth. *Hair of head:* mostly brown glasses with highlights of light tan stone and a few lines of black glass for accents and for drawing contours of hair. *Neck:* pink marbles with shading at right in glasses of yellow, greenish yellow, yellowish green, green, and brown. *Halo:* bordered by two rows of dark red glass; arms of cross, silver glass outlined by dark red; arms drawn in perspective as if seen from below and right. *Garments:* tunic (visible only in sleeve at left and at breast) in three values of blue-violet glass with drapery accents in black; clavus in lines of gold, amber (reversed gold tesserae), and black, bordered by single lines of dark red, all laid in plaster painted yellow; himation, five values of blue glass with accents and drawing in black.

THE VIRGIN *Face:* constructed quite differently from that of Christ, for the rows tend to parallel curved outlines of face, and in cheek at left curves tend to surround darker pink area of cheek bone; same colors and materials used as in face of Christ except for absence of darker colors used in his beard; shading of jaw and cheek at left, in greenish brown glass shifting to light grayish blue glasses, which, at transition to pink flesh, are arranged in checker pattern with pinks. *Garments:* same blue colors and color values as in Christ's himation; tunic has tight sleeves of blue with ornamented cuffs of gold and dark red; maphorion edged across upper arm by border of gold (2 rows) trimmed by single rows of amber color, from which hangs a fringe of gold; around neck opening and edge of headdress are borders of gold and dark red; golden stars appear at both shoulders and at center of head covering; edge of kerchief (visible between face and headdress), light blue glass and gray stone.

ISAAC COMNENUS *Face:* flesh areas white and pink marble and most of drawing (for nose, wrinkles, upper eyelids) in darker pink marble, while contour line at right side of brow and cheek is executed in terra cotta; glass tesserae are used in face only for indicating eyebrows, eyelashes, irises and pupils of eyes, all of which are greenish brown except pupils, which are black. *Mustache:* two hues of brown glass underlined by row of very small black glasses. *Beard and hair:* greenish brown and two values of dark brown glass with short lines of black. *Crown:* the stephanos is gold bordered at top and bottom by rows of red and studded with gems, alternately red (lozenge-shaped) and green (circular), with four pearls in the space between each two; above front of stephanos is a semicircular projection of gold bordered with red and studded with alternate red and blue gems with two pearls between and at center a semicircular green gem; the covering above, which probably represents cloth, forms a semicircle of blue-violet glass the color of his mantle. *Mantle:* decorated with large diaper pattern of same blue-violet glass as cover of crown; lozenges outlined with double rows of gold; within each lozenge a simplified fleur-de-lis of gold; mantle originally held together at throat by two horizontal rectangles of gold trimmed with red, separated by circular object (fibula?), all of which are now indicated only in setting bed; below the hands the two edges of the mantle are parted to reveal the lining, in part preserved in mosaic tesserae, of gray marble with a grid work of lines and ornaments of light blue glass set into the field of gray stone as a means of indicating fur; traces in setting bed, to left of hands, of a large ornamental rectangle, probably a tablion.

MELANE THE NUN *Face and hands:* flesh tones of pink marbles, drawing of features in red and eyebrows and edges of eyelids in greenish brown. *Vestments:* dull black glass except for outlines, which are glossy black glass.

THE GENEALOGY OF CHRIST [1]

PL. 42–64; 66–84

SOUTHERN DOME, *medallion*

[7] 'Ι(ησοῦ)ς Χ(ριστό)ς   *Jesus Christ (Pl. 44, 45)*

SOUTHERN DOME, *upper zone*

From Adam to Jacob [2] (Luke 3:34–38)

[8] 'Αδάμ *Adam (1)* Pl. 46, 47	[20] Σερούχ *Saruch (17)* Pl. 52	
[9] Σή[θ] *Seth (2)* Pl. 46	[21] Ναχώρ *Nachor (18)* Pl. 52	
[10] Νῶε *Noah (10)* Pl. 48	[22] Θαρά *Thara (19)* Pl. 53	
[11] [Καϊνά]ν *Cainan (4)* Pl. 48	[23] 'Αβραάμ *Abraham (20)* Pl. 53	
[12] Μαλελεήλ *Maleleel (5)* Pl. 49	[24] 'Ισαάκ *Isaac (21)* Pl. 53, 54	
[13] 'Ιάρεδ *Jared (6)* Pl. 49	[25] 'Ιακώβ *Jacob (22)* Pl. 54, 55	
[14] Λάμεχ *Lamech (9)* Pl. 50	[26] Φάλεκ *Phalec (15)* Pl. 56	
[15] Σήμ *Sem (11)* Pl. 50	[27] 'Ραγαῦ *Ragau (16)* Pl. 56	
[16] 'Ιάφεθ *Japheth (11)* Pl. 51	[28] Μαθουσάλα *Mathusala (8)* Pl. 57	
[17] 'Αρφαξάδ *Arphaxad (12)* Pl. 51	[29] 'Ενώχ *Enoch (7)* Pl. 57	
[18] Σάλα *Sala (13)* Pl. 51	[30] 'Ενώς *Enos (3)* Pl. 57	
[19] "Εβερ *Heber (14)* Pl. 52	[31] "Αβελ [3] *Abel (2)* Pl. 46	

SOUTHERN DOME, *lower zone*

The Sons of Jacob, [4] Two Sons of Judah, and the Son of Pharez

[32] 'Ρουβείμ *Reuben (1)* Pl. 58
[33] Συμε(ών) *Simeon (2)* Pl. 58
[34] Λευί *Levi (3)* Pl. 59
[35] 'Ιούδας *Judah (4)* Pl. 59   } *by Leah (Gen. 35:23)*
[36] Ζαβουλών *Zebulun (10)* Pl. 59, 60
[37] 'Ισσάχαρ *Issachar (9)* Pl. 60

[38] Δάν *Dan (5)* Pl. 60   *by Bilhah (Gen. 35:25)*
[39] Γάδ *Gad (7)* Pl. 61
[40] 'Ασήρ *Asher (8)* Pl. 61   } *by Zilpah (Gen. 35:26)*
[41] Νεφθαλείμ *Naphtali (6)* Pl. 62   *by Bilhah (Gen. 35:25)*
[42] 'Ιωσή(φ) *Joseph (11)* Pl. 62   } *by Rachel (Gen. 35:24)*
[43] Βενιαμίν *Benjamin (12)* Pl. 63

---

1 The Greek spellings are those of the mosaics; the English equivalents are taken from a variety of spellings used in the King James version.

2 Numbers accompanying the English versions of the names from Adam to Jacob record the generations, hence

the chronological sequence of the Genealogy.

3 Shmit, *Kakhrie-dzhami*, p. 67, read this as [Καιν]άν.

4 Numbers accompanying the English versions of the names of the sons of Jacob refer to the chronological order of birth.

[44] Φαρές *Pharez* *Pl. 63*
[45] Ζαρά *Zarah* *Pl. 64* } *sons of Judah (Gen. 38)*
[46] Ἐσρώμ *Esrom* *Pl. 64* *son of Pharez* *(Matt. 1:3)*

NORTHERN DOME, *medallion*

[51] Μ(ήτ)ηρ Θ(εο)ῦ *Mother of God (Pl. 68–70)*

NORTHERN DOME, *upper zone*

Kings of the House of David: David to Salathiel (Matt. 1:6–12)

[52] Δα(βί)δ *David* *Pl. 71*
[53] Σολομών *Solomon* *Pl. 72*
[54] Ῥοβοάμ *Roboam* *Pl. 72*
[55] Ἀβιά *Abia* *Pl. 73*
[56] Ἀσά *Asa* *Pl. 73*
[57] Ἰωσαφάτ *Josaphat* *Pl. 74*
[58] Ἰωράμ *Joram* *Pl. 74*
[59] Ὀζίας *Ozias* *Pl. 75*

[60] Ἰωάθαμ *Joatham* *Pl. 75*
[61] Ἄχαζ *Achaz* *Pl. 76*
[62] Ἐζεκίας *Ezekias* *Pl. 76*
[63] Μανασσῆς *Manasses* *Pl. 77*
[64] Ἀμμών *Amon* *Pl. 77*
[65] Ἰωσίας *Josias* *Pl. 78*
[66] Ἰεχωνί(ας) *Jechonias* *Pl. 78*
[67] Σαλαθιήλ *Salathiel* *Pl. 71*

NORTHERN DOME, *lower zone*

"Other Ancestors outside the Genealogy"

[68] Ἀνανίας *Hananiah* *Pl. 79*
[69] Ἀζαρίας *Azariah* *Pl. 79*
[70] Μισαήλ *Mishael* *Pl. 80* } *(Dan. 1:7)*
[71] Δανιήλ *Daniel* *Pl. 80*
[72] Ἰ[ησοῦς υἱὸς] Ναυή *Joshua* *Pl. 81*
[73] Μωϋσῆς *Moses* *Pl. 81, 82*
[74] Ἀαρών *Aaron* *Pl. 82*
[75] Ὥρ *Hur* *Pl. 83 a* *(Exod. 17:12)*
[76] Σαμουήλ *Samuel* *Pl. 83 b*
[77] Ἰώβ *Job* *Pl. 84 a*
[78] Μελχισεδέκ *Melchizedek* *Pl. 84 b*

Among the most splendid features of the Kariye Djami are the two fluted domes that cover the end bays of the inner narthex. Their inner surfaces are decorated with mosaics representing the ancestors of Christ, surrounding the medallions of Christ, depicted in the type of the Pantocrator [7], in the summit of the southern dome, and of the Mother of God, that is, the Virgin and Christ Child [51], in a corresponding position in the northern dome.

The domes provide the major source of illumination in the narthex. Structurally, they are of the highly decorative variety known as fluted, or melon, domes. They are raised on drums in which windows are placed; the flutes, however, descend in sweeping curves from medallion to cornice without interruption. While they are very much alike in construction, the domes differ perceptibly in size,[5] in the number of flutes and windows, and in the patterns and prevailing colors of their mosaic ornaments.

The southern dome, the larger of the two, was constructed with twenty-four flutes and nine windows; the northern dome, with sixteen flutes and five windows. The small number of windows, which appear only in alternate flutes in the western sides, is accounted for by the fact that the domes are not entirely free-standing; on their eastern sides the drums are incorporated in the masonry of the nave clerestory, which rises on the eastern wall of the inner narthex. In plan, the flutes form arcs of circles. In the southern dome, where their larger number required them to be quite narrow, the flutes are nearly semicircular; in the northern dome, where they are fewer, they are proportionally wider and shallower. In the masonry construction, behind the mosaics, the flutes adjoin one another in sharp edges, or arrises, but because of the thickness of the covering plaster and mosaic the arrises on the surface resemble rounded ribs; they are decorated with ornamental borders from 13 to 15 cm. in width.

The arrises of the flutes in the southern dome are marked by two patterns of mosaic decoration, which alternate in pairs. One is a double pattern, predominantly green in color, divided down the center by a row of gold tesserae; it is composed of green leaf-like forms accented with red, black, and gold. The second, predominantly blue, is composed of a succession of connected three-lobed leaves of blue, edged with gold and black; these are flanked by half-leaves as space fillers. In the northern dome, on the other hand, the ribs of the upper zone are all ornamented with golden vine scrolls on a field of red. In the lower zone the mosaics of the ribs simulate a colonnade supporting the ribs above. The columns are represented with golden capitals and gray shafts, the latter highlighted down the center by a band of gold and entwined with red ribbons. To separate the two zones within each of the domes, and to provide niche-like settings for the figures of the lower zones, mosaic borders span the flutes from rib to rib as though they were arches. The arched borders in the southern dome repeat the foliate motifs of the bull's-nose borders, of green, red, gold, and black, which frame the heads of the windows; those in the northern dome, which spring from the capitals of the imitation columns, consist of a running motif of light blue in a field of white.

The figural decorations that are accommodated to these forms constitute a unified iconographic theme, the Genealogy of Christ, which encompasses both the domes. The bust of Christ, Son of God, of the type of the Pantocrator, presides at the summit of the larger, southern dome, where his genealogy begins. In the summit of the other dome, to the north, is the instrument of the Incarnation, the Mother of God, also a bust representation, with the infant Christ in her arms.

The two domes are so constructed that flutes occur at the eight points that correspond to their cross and diagonal axes. However, the figures in each dome are placed in such a way as to establish an "iconographic axis" for each of the domes that deviates slightly from the system of the structural axes, though still retaining a generally east-west orientation. The eastern axis of the southern dome passes through the flute in which Abel is placed, but the axis of the medallion of Christ, above, is turned one flute to the right and falls above Adam, who

5 See below, "Dimensions," and above, pp. 35–37.

is iconographically the important figure in the upper zone. In a similar manner, the structural axis of the northern dome passes through the figure of Solomon whereas that of the medallion of the Virgin in the summit of the dome is turned one flute to the left, the opposite direction from that in which the axis of the medallion of Christ is turned. It lines up with David, who is iconographically the important figure in the upper zone. The medallions and the figures beneath them thus share common "iconographic axes," for Adam and David, it will be seen, are the initiating figures in the genealogies of the two domes. It seems likely that the "iconographic axes" were shifted from the structural axes in opposing directions for the sake of the spectator, who enters the narthex midway between them, approaching the southern dome from the left and the northern dome from the right.

With the mosaics in these two domes the iconographic program of the decoration as a whole begins to reveal itself. As Metochites himself said, in Homeric verse, his purpose in the decoration of the church was, first, "to relate, in mosaics and paintings, how the Lord Himself . . . became a mortal man on our behalf." [6] Appropriately, the opening theme in the depiction of the manner in which the divine plan of salvation was carried out, first through the mystery of the Incarnation, is that of the Ancestry of Christ. Sixty-six full-length portraits of the ancestors find their places in the flutes of the two domes. Thirty-nine of these, in the two zones of the southern dome ([8]–[46]), represent the genealogy from Adam to Esrom, who serves as a link, after an omission of seven generations, with sixteen of the kings of Judah, beginning with David, who are portrayed in the upper zone of the northern dome ([52]–[67]). The group of figures in the lower zone of this dome ([68]–[78]) are not, strictly speaking, within the lineage of Christ, but they were, nevertheless, regarded as "other ancestors who are outside the genealogy." [7]

The immediate textual source for the genealogy, as illustrated in the mosaics, is liturgical. Authority for the inclusion of Abel, Japheth, the sons of Jacob other than Judah, Judah's son Zarah, and the eleven "other ancestors" does not come from the genealogies recorded in Matthew and Luke. All those who appear in the mosaics, and others as well, are to be found in the synaxarion of the service for the Sunday before the Birth of Christ, in the distichs composed in the middle of the eleventh century by Christopher of Mytilene, which had been incorporated by the thirteenth century into the Menaion for December. [8] A very similar list, with iconographic instructions, is found in the *Hermeneia*, the painters' manual of the monk Dionysius of Fourna, [9] and this too probably had its source in the distichs of Christopher.

The order in which the early ancestors are placed in the upper zone of the southern dome ([8]–[31]) does not consistently follow the chronological sequence of the distichs and the genealogies of Luke and Genesis. The mosaicists appear to have vacillated between two conflicting systems of composition—a system of pendants around the central figure of Adam and a clockwise chronological arrangement. In the eastern side, near the eastern axis of the dome and exactly on that of the medallion of Christ above, is Adam [8], between two of his sons: to the left his slain son, Abel [31], and to the right Seth [9], of whom God said that he was

6 Treu, p. 30, lines 1087–92.

7 Ἕτεροι προπάτορες ἔξω ἀπὸ τὴν γενεαλογίαν, as the painters' manual of Dionysius of Fourna (Papadopoulos-Kerameus, p. 75) captions the list, which almost exactly corresponds to the series of figures in the lower zone of the dome.

8 Gabriel Millet, *La Dalmatique du Vatican* (Paris, 1945), p. 83. They are still to be found in the modern Menaion (cf., for example, the edition of M. Saliberos, Athens, 1904, pp. 199–204).

9 Papadopoulos-Kerameus, pp. 73–77. The manual is considerably later in date than the mosaics.

"another seed instead of Abel, whom Cain slew" (Gen. 4:25). By placing Enos [30] to the left of Abel, the mosaicist seems to have begun with a system of pendant figures alternating between left and right about the figure of Adam. But he has interrupted this system by bringing the important figure of Noah [10] onto the diagonal axis of the dome, so that he is to the right of Seth far out of chronological order. There follows, to the right of Noah, a correctly chronological series of three — Cainan, Maleleel, and Jared ([11]–[13]), who are balanced, as a group, by their two immediate successors, Enoch [29] and Mathusala [28], in the left side of the dome. The next six in the genealogy (excluding Noah) are placed in the right side ([14]–[19]), and the following two ([26], [27]), in inverted order, appear opposite. The six figures who make up the last group, from Saruch to Jacob ([20]–[25]), are arranged in sequence in clockwise order.

Aside from the sequence of figures, the genealogy in the mosaics of the upper zone differs in only one respect from its liturgical source and the genealogies of Luke and the painters' manual: only one of the two Cainans is depicted. This can be explained by the fact that while the verses of Christopher list twenty-five ancestors in the group from Adam to Jacob (by including Abel and Japheth, who do not properly belong), the dome contained only twenty-four flutes in which to put them.[10] The only change necessary was to have one Cainan serve for both.[11]

The figures in the lower zone are separated from those above by a series of narrow arched borders, which form a continuous arcade around the dome. These borders frame the windows and the fifteen figures, most of whom are sons of Jacob. Only Judah, Pharez, and Esrom rightly belong in the Genealogy. However, the very same figures that are in this zone, and in precisely the same order, are found in the verses of Christopher, who followed the order in which, according to Genesis 49:1–27, Jacob blessed his sons. Their order does not correspond to the chronology of their births, as given in the Book of Genesis, nor are the brothers consistently grouped to bring together all sons of each of the four mothers.

The genealogy in the northern dome is in good part calculated to exhibit the royal and priestly ancestry of Christ, the royal above and the priestly below; six of the eleven figures below wear priest's miters. The ultimate authority for portraying the kings of Judah in the genealogy of Christ is the Gospel of Matthew (Ch. 1), and both the verses of Christopher and the list in the painters' manual [12] follow Matthew rather than Luke for this part of the genealogy. Beginning with David,[13] the sixteen kings are arrayed in chronological order in a clockwise direction around the dome. The mosaicists have placed David [52] just to the left of the eastern axis of the dome but directly upon the axis of the bust of the Virgin above, in the pre-eminent position at the head of his royal descendants, to emphasize that Christ is "born of the seed of David" (Rom. 1:3) and to accentuate his role as the progenitor of the Messiah, or the anointed of God. Limited as they were by the number of flutes in the dome, the mosaicists could carry the royal lineage only as far as Salathiel. All the kings wear crowns, and two of them, Solomon [53] and Roboam [54], are even accorded the *loros* of the Byzantine emperors. As setting for these royal personages the mosaicists appropriately made red and gold the pre-

---

10 The segments in Byzantine fluted or ribbed domes were constructed in multiples of four and, where possible, of eight, in order that symmetry could be achieved along the cross and diagonal axes. See above, pp. 35–37.

11 In the Hebrew texts of Genesis there is no authority for the second Cainan, son of Arphaxad, although he appears in the Septuagint version.

12 Papadopoulos-Kerameus, pp. 74, 75.

13 It is interesting to note the omission of Jesse in view of his prominence, especially in Western iconography, in the genealogy of Christ.

vailing colors in the ornaments of the ribs, and to a great extent in the vestments of the figures.

The eleven figures of the lower zone do not belong, in any strict genealogical sense, to the ancestry of Christ. However, included in this group are priests (Samuel and Aaron); prophets and righteous who foretold the Advent of Christ or, in some instances, even prefigured him (Moses, Daniel, the three Hebrew children, Joshua and Melchizedek); and some individuals who personify the institutions of Christian kingship or priesthood (Melchizedek, Aaron, Hur). Perhaps these qualifications led the group to be accepted as "other ancestors who are outside the genealogy." They are commemorated, as ancestors, on the Sunday before the Birth of Christ. In the verses of Christopher of Mytilene this category of the ancestry consists of twelve persons; of these only Nathan was not represented in the mosaics, probably because only eleven places were available. The list in the painters' manual is in very near agreement with the distichs but, remarkably enough, omits the key figure, Daniel. Daniel and the three Hebrew children play a very important part in the commemorations of the feasts of the Sunday of the Holy Ancestors (Κυριακὴ τῶν Ἁγίων Προπατόρων) and of the Sunday before the Birth of Christ, the two Sundays preceding Christmas. In the mosaics the youths and Daniel are placed in sequence in the east side. Daniel is accorded the position of honor on the eastern axis.

Among the figures in the genealogy some bear iconographic attributes or are otherwise endowed with particular iconographic significance. Adam [8] stands in triumph upon the serpent, and in his right hand he holds a tree as a king might hold a scepter. As Luke says in his genealogy, Adam was the son of God; he was also a type of Christ — "a type of him who was to come," according to St. Paul (Rom. 5:14) — and Christ, in turn, was the second, or new, Adam. The two attributes of Adam refer, of course, to the serpent that was the instrument of Man's fall in Eden, and to the "tree of life" in the Garden, the prototype of Christ's Cross, through which mankind could triumph over the serpent and death.

Noah [10] carries the ark, a symbol from the beginnings of Christian art which recalls the hope of salvation from the deluge of sin. Literature abounds in metaphors likening the ark to the Virgin, hence to the Incarnation.

Judah [35] is distinguished from his brothers by the fact that only he is given an attribute — the sword. Although he was the fourth son of Jacob, he received the firstborn's privilege (Gen. 49:8 ff.), and of him Jacob prophesied, "thy hand shall be in the neck of thine enemies; thy father's children shall bow down before thee. . . . The sceptre shall not depart from Judah . . . and unto him shall the gathering of the people be." The sword is appropriate to him as founder of the conquering tribe of Judah, and as the son of Jacob who figures in the genealogy of Luke he has been marked by an attribute.

While a number of the figures in the southern dome conceal one hand beneath their robes, there is a peculiarity about the way Zarah [45] draws his left hand back deep into the sleeve of his tunic, which may well be in reference to the circumstances of his birth as recounted in Genesis 38:27-30. It was Zarah's twin, Pharez [44], who was the firstborn, but it is said that first Zarah put forth his hand, the midwife bound it with a scarlet thread, and Zarah withdrew it; his brother was the first to come out.

There are two major iconographic themes in the mosaics of the lower zone of the northern dome. First, the group of four figures representing the three Hebrew youths and Daniel ([68]–[71]) express an analogy to the Incarnation: when placed in the fiery furnace the youths were not consumed. The first few chants in the service of Vespers of the Sunday of the Ancestors —

54

"the *stichera* of the Ancestors," as they are designated [14]—are devoted mainly to the three Hebrew youths and Daniel. They state that the three youths symbolize the Trinity and the Incarnation of Christ. In the mosaic, Daniel holds the open book of his prophecy, the inscription in which quotes from Daniel 2:35: "and the stone [i.e., the stone cut out of the mountain without hands] that smote the image became a great mountain, and filled the whole earth," a text that was universally interpreted by Christian exegetes as a prophecy of the Incarnation. These four Israelite youths, princes of the house of Judah and thus related to the kings depicted in the zone above, were taken to the court of Nebuchadnezzar, where they distinguished themselves in all matters of wisdom and were found "ten times better than all the magicians and astrologers that were in all his realm;" they are represented as μάγοι, that is, priests and wise men who, according to classical Greek sources, came from the East and were able to interpret dreams. They wear the oriental priest's hat that the painters' manual calls the μίτρα and that the Septuagint version of Exodus 29:6 says was also worn by the Jewish priesthood. In the Kariye Djami and in late Byzantine art in general, Jewish priests, the Magi, the three Hebrews, and Daniel all wear the same type of headdress.

The second theme, which seems to be the main preoccupation of the decoration of the dome, is concerned with priesthood and kingship. Joshua, Moses, Aaron, and Hur ([72]–[75]) follow immediately to the right of Daniel. These four were the leaders of the Israelites in their journey to the promised land. In the battle against Amalek, Joshua went out with his men to fight, while Moses, Aaron, and Hur went to the top of a hill. So long as Moses held up his hands Israel prevailed, and to gain the victory "Aaron and Hur stayed up his hands, the one on the one side, and the other on the other side" (Exod. 17:8–13). This incident was interpreted by the fifth- and sixth-century exegetes, Severian of Gabala and Timothy of Antioch, as signifying that Moses' outstretched arms prefigured the Cross, which was supported by Royalty (Hur) on the one hand, and by the Priesthood (Aaron) on the other.[15] In the mosaics Moses stands between Joshua, his successor (who, according to the painters' manual, should wear a crown), and Aaron, his brother—between a leader of his people (and in this sense a king) and the founder of the Israelite priesthood. To the right of Aaron is Hur, who in many respects shared with Moses the secular leadership of the Israelites. Joshua, whose portrait is all but destroyed, was depicted as a warrior, a spear in his right hand and a shield, probably supported by a belt, suspended at his left side, but it is impossible to say whether he also wore a crown. The prophet Moses, in whom were combined many functions of the king and priest, wears priestly vestments (compare the mantle worn by Melchizedek [78]) and holds in his hands a holy vessel, on which one can see the image of the Virgin. The vessel may be likened to that which appears in the scenes known as the Tabernacle of Witness (Lev. 9:1–7), where it represents the stamnos, or pot of manna (Exod. 16:33). In late-Byzantine hymnography the Virgin is repeatedly called the golden stamnos that contained the manna,[16] the latter being regarded as the prototype of the bread of the Holy Eucharist. Aaron, attired in the short mantle of a priest, bears the flowering rod in his right hand. Both the pot of manna and the rod of Aaron were kept before the ark of

14 See the Menaion for December (ed. Saliberos, p. 112).

15 Severian, *De serpente*, in Migne, *Pat. Gr.*, 56, col. 504; Timothy of Antioch, *In crucem et in transfigurationem*, in Migne, *Pat. Gr.*, 86, col. 257. These references I owe to my colleague Professor S. Der Nersessian.

16 Cf. S. Eustratiades, Ἡ Θεοτόκος ἐν τῇ ὑμνογραφία

(Paris, 1930), p. 73, where many instances are cited, among them one that plays upon the name of the monastery of the Chora, in which the Virgin is likened to "the *stamnos* that has contained (χωρήσασα) the giver of manna"—i. e., Christ.

55

testimony. The incident of the flowering rod (Num. 17:1–11) revealed Aaron's divine authority and was evidence that the tribe of Levi should forever be the possessors of the priestly prerogatives. The rod (ῥάβδος) of Aaron was recognized by Christian writers as a prefiguration of the Virgin and was closely associated with the "stem" (ῥίζα) of Jesse, as in the words with which Andrew of Crete hails the Virgin: Χαῖρος, ἡ ῥάβδος Ἀαρών, ἡ ῥίζα τοῦ Ἰεσσαί.[17] The idea of the stem of Jesse originates in the words of Isaiah (11:1–3), "And there shall come forth a rod out of the stem of Jesse, and a Branch shall grow out of his roots," the passage that gave rise to the representation of the ancestry of Christ in the form of the Tree of Jesse, in which the rod is the Virgin and the branch is Christ.

David, the son of Jesse, was anointed by Samuel [76] the priest (I Sam. 16:13), who is shown next in the series of figures in the mosaics. He wears the vestments of a priest and holds in his hands the horn of anointing.

Job [77], whose portrait comes next, is shown as a king, a crown on his head and a scroll in his left hand. The authority for his kingship is not to be found in the versions of the Bible in common use today, nor in the Hebrew or the Vulgate. It is contained, however, in a section added to the last chapter of the Book of Job in the Septuagint version, which says that Job was originally known as Jobab and identifies him with the Jobab of Genesis 36:33, who reigned as King of Edom.[18]

The final figure in the series is Melchizedek [78], King of Salem (Jerusalem) and "priest of the most high God," who received Abraham, offered him bread and wine, and blessed him (Gen. 14:18–20). He is often cited as the εἰκών or τύπος of Christ, the one foreshadowing the other.[19] In the mosaic he is shown in priest's vestments holding a paten on which are three small loaves.

The mosaics of the two domes are unusually rich both in the beauty of their execution and in their iconographic content. While their main purpose is to commemorate the ancestors of Christ and the Virgin, who preside at the summits of the domes, as the lineage through whom the Word was made flesh, they also prepare the way for the story of the Virgin, the instrument of the Incarnation, which begins in the vaults immediately beneath the dome, whose center is occupied by her medallion.

Medallions containing busts of angels were placed above the supporting arches of the domes of the inner narthex, where they serve to accent the axes of the bays and fill the spaces between the pendentives. The eastern and western medallions of the southern dome ([47] and [49]) are perfectly preserved, but the head of the angel in the southern medallion [48] and the lower part of the bust in the northern medallion [50] have perished. Of the four medallions beneath the northern dome, the eastern one [79] has suffered slight damage, the western [81] is intact, and the southern [80] is preserved only in small fragments, while the northern one is entirely destroyed. The medallions differ from one another in size, and the angels are differentiated in their attitudes and in the colors of their garments. All outlines of medallions and halos are of red glass; the angels wear fillets about their heads, are depicted with outspread wings, and raise their right hands before them with palms outward.

---

17 Migne, *Pat. Gr.*, 97, col. 865.
18 Cf. O. Kurz, "An Alleged Portrait of Heraclius," *Byzantion*, 16 (1944), 162–64.

19 See Hebrews 7:1–16, which says that Christ is a priest "after the order of Melchizedek," and that "after the similitude of Melchizedek there ariseth another priest."

Dimensions

Diameter of domes near cornice level, between opposite ribs (excluding depth of flutes) on E-W axes: south dome, 3.74 m.; north dome, 3.40 m. Heights of domes from crown to cornice: south dome, 3.79 m.; north dome, 3.10 m. Heights of domes from crown to floor: south dome, 10.54 m.; north dome, 10.10 m. Diameter of medallion of Christ [7], south dome, including border, 1.24 m. Head of Christ from top of head to tip of beard, .42 m. Diameter of medallion of Virgin [51], north dome, including border, 1.14 m. Head of Virgin, .35 m. high. Average heights of figures, south dome: upper zone [8]–[31], ca. 1.38 m.; lower zone [32]–[46], ca. 1.48 m.; north dome: upper zone [52]–[67], ca. 1.40 m.; lower zone [68]–[78], ca. 1.30 m.
Diameter of medallions: South dome, [47] .565 m.; [48] .44 m.; [49] .395 m.; [50] .41 m. North dome, [79] .39 m.; [80] .38 m.; [81] .385 m.

Condition

Conditions prevailing when restoration work began in 1952 were much the same as those recorded in 1906 by Shmit (*Kakhrie-dzhami*, PL. III–XX). Most losses are attributable to fractures in the fabric of the domes resulting from severe earthquakes. The paths of the fractures are clearly visible in PL. 42 and 66. Greatest losses have occurred in the southeastern quadrant of the southern dome (PL. 48, 49, 61, 62) and in the northeastern quadrant of the northern dome (PL. 78, 71, 72, 80, 81). Especially in the southern dome, a number of smaller areas of loss are attributable to the rusting and consequent expansion of some of the large-headed iron nails, anchored in the masonry, which served to bond the plaster beneath the mosaic surfaces to the masonry; this practice was limited to the more horizontal areas of the vaults and not followed on their more nearly vertical areas or on the walls. The mosaics in the domes seem never to have been covered with plaster (except as a result of crude patching of cracks in lost areas); but extensive areas around the heads, hands, and feet of all the figures were heavily daubed with yellow paint. In the restoration, all patching plaster and paint were removed, the fissures in the masonry were cleared out and consolidated, and all areas of lost mosaic were carefully covered with new plaster, which was then given a mottled tone of grayish yellow. Many structural repairs were required, and special attention was given to the windows and their setting.

Colors and Materials

Henceforth the notes on colors and materials will usually be more summary than they have been in the preceding descriptions, which, for the most part, concerned figures that were relatively large and therefore permitted the mosaicists considerable scope in both color and technique. The figures in the series of ancestors and in the narrative scenes that are to be described below are so small that the heads, which range in height from about 10 to 20 cm. (about 4 to 8 in.) excluding beards, and in the case of infants are as small as 6 cm. (about 2½ in.), are of necessity much simplified in their construction, coloring, and shading. Considering the large number of color plates in Vol. 2, which supply specimens of most if not all types of treatment of the heads, garments, and settings (although the colors are not always entirely faithful), and considering the detailed descriptions that have been supplied above, it seems unnecessary to dwell in detail on the colors used in most of the remaining mosaics. Except in representations of Christ and the Virgin, garments are not generally executed in a single type of material or in a single color but employ two or more colors, each in more than one value, and two or three types of materials, as has already been seen in such figures as those of Peter [4] and Paul [5]. Nevertheless, it is meant to be understood that each garment is of one solid color, the shading or highlighting being achieved by means of tesserae of different colors. The intended color of each garment, except for those of yellow, is usually to be found in the areas that are executed in glass and in the middle or darker ranges of the color. Often the intended color of a garment is very limited in extent and its highlighted areas, usually in gray and white stones, are by far the greatest. The most frequently used colors in the garments (aside from gray and white, and the blacks that are used for drawing) are blue, green, red, violet, and yellow. In those garments that are intended to be red, red glass, terra cotta, and pink marbles are used to give the impression of the garment's color, and the highlights are usually of white stone. The yellow garments are generally executed in various yellow stones (light grayish yellow, yellow ochre, and sienna), with greenish brown or umber-colored glasses for the shadows. The garments of the Virgin are entirely of glass in several values of a blue which resembles ultramarine; in the scenes where Christ appears, his outer garment, or himation, is, with few exceptions, of the same blue glass while his tunic is generally of violet glasses throughout. Hair and beards are treated in so many ways that they cannot all be individually described; the color plates will convey an impression of their colors and treatment. In the luxuriant hair and beards of some of the ancestors of Christ in the south dome, and again of some of the saints in the medallions of the outer narthex, there is a contrast of colors that should be pointed out. In a number of instances ([8], [9], [14], [15], [18], for example), the hair of the head has a strong admixture of violet, or even blue, glasses, along with gray and white stones, while the gray of the beard contains much yellow, both stone and glass, or yellowish green and greenish brown glasses. In a few instances, [10] for example, the contrast is reversed and it is the beard that assumes the violet cast while the hair is predominantly of the yellow and green that are used most frequently throughout the mosaics for rendering both hair and beards. In the following color notes for each of the ancestors in the domes, only the intended colors of the garments are stated, first of the undergarment, or tunic, and then of the outer garment, or himation.

Southern Dome

MEDALLION *Border:* seven zones of lozenge-shaped tesserae in the following sequence of colors from outer to inner edge: black (half-lozenges), red, pink (marble), gold, light bluish green, dark emerald green, black (half-lozenges). *Christ Pantocrator* [7]: hair and beard, greenish brown and brown glasses in darker parts, greenish yellow glass in highlights; garments, blue-violet glass tunic, with highlights of grayish lavender stone and clavus of gold, red, and silver glass, and blue glass himation; book cover, gold with borders and ornaments of red; cross in nimbus, silver bordered with red.

UPPER ZONE *Garments of ancestors:* [8] tunic of blue, himation of green; [9] yellow (blue and gold ornaments), blue; [10] blue (dark blue clavus), violet; [11] blue (red clavus), green; [12] destroyed; [13] tunic invisible, himation of red-violet; [14] green, blue; [15] blue (blue and gold ornaments), dark brownish green and brown; [16] blue (red clavus), red-violet (blue and gold ornaments); [17] blue (red clavi), green; [18] blue (red clavus), dark brownish green and brown; [19] dark brownish green and brown (blue ornament), blue; [20] blue (dark blue ornaments), yellowish green and brown; [21] blue, red-violet; [22] blue (red clavi), dark brownish green and brown; [23] blue (dark blue clavi), green; [24] blue (red clavi), dark brownish green and brown; [25] red-violet, blue; [26] blue, red-violet; [27] blue (red clavi), yellow; [28] green (red clavus), blue and dark violet; [29] blue (dark blue clavi), red-violet; [30] blue, green; [31] red-violet, blue.

LOWER ZONE (figures stand in zone of green) *Garments of ancestors:* [32] blue (red clavi), violet; [33] blue (red clavi), brownish yellow; [34] brownish yellow, blue; [35] blue (red clavi), yellowish green and brown; [36] blue (red clavus), green; [37] wears only a tunic of violet with ornaments and scapular of gold and red; [38] yellows and browns, yellowish greens and bluish greens; [39] yellows and browns, blue; [40] blue (gold hem and dark green girdle), violet; [41] blue (red clavus), green; [42] blue (gold and red ornaments), yellows and browns; [43] blue (red clavus), green; [44] blue (dark blue clavi), red-violet; [45] blue (dark blue ornaments), red (black border lines); [46] blue (gold and clear glass ornaments), green.

UNDERGARMENTS OF ANGELS [47] tan with gold and red clavus; [48] blue with gold and red clavus; [49] blue with red clavus; [50] blue with dark blue clavus; [79] blue with gold and greenish translucent glass clavus; [81] white (yellowish) with gold and red clavus. OUTER GARMENTS [47] blue; [48] brown; [49] green; [50] violet; [79] green; [81] blue. WINGS

of all angels executed in brown amber translucent glasses, some of which are gold tesserae set in reverse, and in light transparent glasses.

Northern Dome

MEDALLION *Border:* a conventionalized golden wreath bordered within and without by black and divided in the center by a row of silver; zig-zag bindings are indicated in black and brown glass; within the wreath are borders of gold and red. *Virgin and Christ Child* [51]: garments of Virgin, blue with borders and stars of gold, edge of head kerchief of alternate stripes of blue and white; nimbus, rimmed in red; inscription, black; garments of Christ Child, gold with highlights of silver, shading of brown glass; scroll, white outlined with red; cross in nimbus, gold outlined with red.

UPPER ZONE *Garments of royal ancestors* (the following color notes refer to the intended color first of the tunic, which is ornamented at the collar, hem, and cuffs with golden embroideries studded with gems, and then of the garment worn over the tunic, either the chlamys, a mantle fastened at the breast, or the loros, a long golden scarf adorned with gems which is wound around the body; the crowns and footwear are not individually described, but the former are basically of gold studded with gems, and the latter is red with ornaments of various colors): [52] red, blue (with gold tablion, white lining); [53] red, loros is worn instead of chlamys; [54] violet, loros is worn instead of chlamys; [55] blue, red (gold tablion ornamented in blue); [56] violet, green (gold tablia); [57] green, violet (gold and red tablion); [58] blue, red; [59] green, blue (white lining); [60] red, green (gold and red tablion); [61] blue, violet; [62] violet, blue (white lining); [63] blue, red; [64] yellow and brown, violet (gold and red tablia); [65] red, blue (white lining); [66] blue, green (gold and red tablia); [67] green, red.

LOWER ZONE (figures stand in two zones of green: upper, dark green glass; lower, light green stone) *Three Hebrew Youths and Daniel* [68]–[71]: all wear: *a)* tight-fitting pantaloons, *b)* short, tight-sleeved tunics ornamented at neck and hem, *c)* short, sleeveless tunics, *d)* sashes tied around chests, *e)* short, loose mantles, *f)* spiral leggings or soft boots. The miters, or priests' hats, have red crowns, gray and blue brims, and gems of green or blue set at centers. The intended colors of the garments are as follows: [68] *a)* tan, *b)* green, *c)* gray, *d)* red, *e)* blue, *f)* pink; [69] *a)* tan, *b)* blue, *c)* violet, *d)* blue, *e)* green, *f)* upper half blue, lower half violet; [70] *a)* blue, *b)* bluish green, *c)* tan, *d)* red, *e)* violet, *f)* violet; [71] *a)* pink and greenish brown, *b)* blue, *c)* green, *d)* blue, *e)* red, *f)* upper half gray, lower half blue. *Joshua* [72]: enough remains to indicate that he was dressed in military garb and that his pose and arms were arranged like those of St. Demetrius [253] in the fresco in the parecclesion; tunic, red; mantle, blue; armored sleevelet, gold and silver; shield, green with gold; spear shaft, violet and black. *Moses*

[73], *Aaron* [74], *Hur* [75], *Samuel* [76], *Melchizedek* [78]: all wear priests' vestments which are essentially alike, though only the last two wear miters like those of [68]–[71]: *a*) long tunic (ornamented at hem), *b*) short tunic (ornamented at hem), *c*) short mantle fastened at breast and either cut away in front (as in [73] and [78]) or cut nearly square (as in [74], [75], [76]). The intended colors are: [73] *a*) blue, *b*) green, *c*) blue with lining of gray and designs of blue; [74] *a*) yellowish gray, *b*) green, *c*) red; [75] *a*) blue, *b*) green, *c*) violet with white lining; [76] *a*) red, *b*) blue, *c*) green; [78] *a*) blue, *b*) red, *c*) green. *Job* [77]: royal garb consisting of blue tunic, red chlamys, and gold and red crown.

THE CYCLE OF THE LIFE OF THE VIRGIN

[82]

Joachim's Offerings Rejected

PL. 86, 87

(Protevangelium 1:1–2; Pseudo-Matthew 2) [1]

'Η προσέν[εξις τῶν δώρων](?)   *The presentation of the offerings(?)*

Having presented the Genealogy of Christ and the Virgin in the domes of the inner narthex, the program of decoration next takes up the story of the life of the Virgin in the remaining spaces beneath the dome of the first bay and in the vaults and lunettes of the second and third bays. The cycle of the Life of the Virgin, the first of three narrative cycles into which the mosaic scenes of the two narthexes are divided, originally consisted of twenty scenes. Of these, fifteen are largely, if not completely, intact, four are preserved in part, and only one is entirely destroyed. The events they depict are derived from the Apocryphal Gospel of James—the so-called Protevangelium—and those versions of the Virgin's life which are based upon it.

Of the first scene, which was divided between the two pendentives at the northern end of the narthex, only the left half is preserved. The scene depicted the incident of the rejection of Joachim's offerings, with which both literary and pictorial narrations of the life of the Virgin normally begin. To quote from the first two verses of the Protevangelium: "In the histories of the twelve tribes of Israel it is written that there was one Joachim, exceeding rich. . . . Now the great day of the Lord drew nigh and the children of Israel offered their gifts. And Reuben stood over against him [Joachim] saying: It is not lawful for thee to offer thy gifts first, forasmuch as thou hast gotten no seed in Israel."

In the part of this scene that is preserved, we find the high priest Zacharias, father of John the Baptist, standing within the golden gates of the sanctuary enclosure. Behind him is the altar beneath its ciborium. Nimbed and wearing priestly vestments, he turns somewhat toward the right, his hands held before him with palms turned outward (in a gesture of rejection?) as he looks toward the pendentive at the right, where Joachim and Anne once stood with their offerings in their hands. The center of the triangular pendentive has been admirably filled by

1 References to the Apocrypha give the divisions into chapters and verses found in such standard editions of the Greek texts as that of Constantinus Tischendorf, *Evangelia Apocrypha* (Leipzig, 2nd ed., 1876). English translation used here in quoting from the Protevangelium is that of M. R. James, *The Apocryphal New Testament* (Oxford, 1924), pp. 39–49. See also the edition of the Protevangelium, with French translation and commentary, of Emile Amann, *Le Protévangile de Jacques* (Paris, 1910), and the recently discovered fourth-century manuscript, with French translation and commentary, published by Michel Testuz, *Papyrus Bodmer V: Nativité de Marie* (Cologny [Geneva], 1958). English translations of the major New Testament Apocrypha are also assembled in *Fathers of the Third and Fourth Centuries*, ed. A. Cleveland Coxe (The Ante-Nicene Fathers, eds. Alexander Roberts and James Donaldson, VIII, Buffalo, 1886), pp. 361 ff.

the polygonal form of the sanctuary, and at the sides architecture and trees have been used to fill out the angles, a compositional device that one often finds in the pendentives. Connecting the two parts of the scene was the inscription, of which only the first seven letters still exist, at the extreme right edge of the fragment. The extant letters of the second word, its gender, and the position of the accent suggest that the inscription began with the words ἡ προσένεξις ² (the presentation), in reference to the offerings of Joachim and Anne.

Condition

Since the construction and decoration of the inner narthex the church of the Chora has been subjected to a number of severe earthquakes, any one or more of which may have caused the extensive damage that is very conspicuous in the northern bay. It would be surprising if the earthquakes of October 1343, the first violent ones after the completion of the mosaics, had not caused much damage. They lasted twelve days, were accompanied by tidal waves, and severely affected the nearby land walls.³ In any case, the eastern part of the scene of Joachim's Offerings Rejected and the scenes contiguous to it in the northern lunette (PL. 88) and in the northern half of the eastern lunette (PL. 92) have been almost entirely destroyed. The great fissure in the dome above extends downward through the eastern and northern walls of the bay, severing connection between the northeastern quadrant of the bay and the rest of the narthex. In the course of repairs made here by the Byzantine Institute in 1954 the walls were reinforced by the insertion of heavy steel bars, which run the length of the narthex within the channels left by the rotting of timber chains built into the walls above the cornices. The steel bars now tie the north-

eastern quadrant of the bay to the rest of the structure. Where the mosaics were lost the exposed masonry was consolidated and covered with new plaster, which was toned with a mottled grayish yellow color; new marble revetments were installed to replace those which had been destroyed in the eastern wall of the bay. In the surviving fragment of scene [82] some damage occurred in the gates and barrier of the sanctuary and in the architecture at the left.

Colors and Materials

ZACHARIAS   long tunic, violet; short tunic, green; mantle, red; hat, red crown and gray brim.   SANCTUARY gates of gold, silver, and greenish brown; barrier (in imitation of veined marble), yellowish and dull brown stones outside, dark brown stones inside; altar cloth, red; ciborium columns, green shafts and gold capitals; canopy, gray and white stones in lighted areas and violet glasses in shaded areas.   ARCHITECTURE lighted faces, gray stones; shaded faces of building at left, brownish green glass; shaded faces of building at right, grayish green glass; roof at left, blue glass and gray stones; door openings, dark violet; drapes on building, red.

---

2 An alternative spelling is possible: προσένεγξις. Shmit, *Kakhrie-dzhami*, p. 74, completed the inscription as ἡ προσευχή τοῦ Ζαχαρίου, that is, the Prayer of Zacharias (Luke 1:8–22).

He would not have read it in that way had he known that the final letter preserved in the mosaic was nu and not upsilon.

3 V. Grumel, *La Chronologie* (Traité d'études byzantines, I, Paris, 1958), p. 481.

[83]

An Unidentified Scene from the Life of the Virgin

PL. 88, 89

The lunette in the northern wall of the inner narthex (PL. 88) contains a triple window, which was deliberately placed to the left of center to provide sufficient space at the right for the major figures and action of a narrative scene. The mosaic has suffered destruction save for a fragment at the far left, which depicts a genre element of a scene whose subject must remain uncertain.

The fragment (PL. 89) represents a maidservant peering out from a doorway of a house; she stands, partly emerged, on the stoop and holds the knotted curtain with her left hand while she looks to the right toward the missing parts of the scene. On the flat decks of the roof are two partridges, and to the right appears some foliage of a tree that once rose above the top of a wall.

The position of this scene in the sequence of events from the Life of the Virgin is also uncertain, for it could be either the second or the fourth in the series, that is, after the rejection of the offerings [82], which is above it, or after the scene of Joachim in the Wilderness [84], in the southeastern pendentive. The text of the Protevangelium says that after the rejection of his offerings Joachim searched the records of the twelve tribes to learn if he alone had begotten no seed. This subject, however, is very rarely represented and if it appeared here would be unique among extant fresco or mosaic cycles. In the monumental pictorial tradition the scene of rejection is very often followed by an incident for which there is no specific textual motivation, namely, Joachim and Anne departing from the temple. While the mosaic fragment seems to indicate a domestic setting, rather than a temple, the departure from the temple is so commonly a part of the pictorial cycle as to make its omission unusual. The genre theme of the maid peering from a door need not rule out this subject as a possibility; a similar motif occurs in the mosaic of the meeting of Joachim and Anne at the gate [86]. Another possibility, as Jacqueline Lafontaine-Dosogne suggests in Volume 4, is that the scene illustrated Joachim and Anne returning to their house after the rejection of their offerings.

The possibility remains, however, that the lost mosaic represented a scene following upon Joachim's retirement to the wilderness—Anne's lament, or her reproof by her maidservant, Judith, for her lamentations upon the day of the Lord (Protevangelium 2:1, 2). Despite the fact that the fragment provides a suitable setting, these subjects are rather unlikely to have been included in the cycle; they do not occur in extant Byzantine monumental paintings or mosaics, although they are to be found in manuscript illumination.

Dimensions
Total height of fragment, ca. 1.85 m.

Colors and Materials
MAIDSERVANT dress, cool gray and white stones with important lines of drapery and shaded areas in blue glass; arm band, red and gold glasses. BUILDING lighted faces, yellow-gray stones with outlining in yellow-brown stone; background of open door, black glass; curtain, red; roofs, yellow-gray and white stones. BIRDS backs and wings, violet glasses; underplumage, alternate bands of yellow-gray stone and black glass; legs, terra cotta; eyes and beaks, red.

[84]

Joachim in the Wilderness

PL. 90, 91

(Protevangelium 1:4; Pseudo-Matthew 2)

['Ο ἅγιος] 'Ιωακεὶμ προσευχόμ(εν)ος ἐν τῷ ὄρει μετὰ τῶν | ποιμένων
Joachim praying on the mountain with the shepherds

The account of this incident in the Protevangelium reads: "And Joachim was sore grieved, and showed not himself to his wife, but betook himself into the wilderness, and pitched his tent there, and fasted forty days and forty nights, saying within himself: I will not go down either for meat or for drink until the Lord my God visit me, and my prayer shall be unto me meat and drink." Both the inscription and the mosaic representation conform somewhat more closely to the version of the Pseudo-Matthew, which specifies that Joachim retired to the mountains in the company of his shepherds: "Being therefore put to shame in the sight of the people, he retired from the temple of the Lord weeping, and did not return to his house, but went to his flocks, taking with him his shepherds into the mountains to a far country."

Although the text of the Protevangelium and the inscription speak of Joachim's prayer, the scene in the southeastern pendentive of the first bay, like the Pseudo-Matthew, emphasizes his shame and weeping by showing him seated with his head resting upon his hand in an attitude of dejection. The rather puzzling foliage that surrounds him is to be interpreted as a poorly executed representation of a primitive shepherd's hut, made of branches of shrubs lashed together at the top, such as is convincingly rendered in the scene of the Annunciation to Joachim in the mosaics of the narthex of the church at Daphni, Greece.[1] The huts in the two mosaics have precisely the same shape, but the version at Daphni clearly shows the lashings at the top and has succeeded in suggesting a hollowed space, within which Joachim is seated.

The nimbus, head, and torso of Joachim are somewhat distorted because of structural damage in the pendentive. As is the case throughout the mosaics, Joachim is portrayed with a dark head of hair, a relatively low forehead, and a short but wavy beard. As he does with only one exception, [87], he wears a blue tunic and violet himation. The first of the two shepherds carries a staff in his right hand and a sack strapped to his back; his left hand points toward Joachim, and what appears to be a leash, which may have been attached to an animal, hangs from his left forearm. The younger shepherd, at the right, has placed his right hand on the shoulder of his companion and gesticulates toward Joachim with his left; he, too, carries a sack strapped to his back. The shepherds, in solicitous consultation, approach Joachim from the mountain which fills the upper right angle of the pendentive. Other mountains and a tree fill the left angle.

Condition

Much of the gold background in the upper left, including parts of the inscription, is lost. The original painted setting bed still retained the traces of those letters no longer preserved in glass; the letters have been reconstituted, on the basis of positive evidence, on the new plaster by means of short strokes of black paint. A considerable area of mosaic and plaster in the lower right, which included the border separating the scene from that in the adjoining arch, was also destroyed and has been filled with new plaster. Lesser damage was caused by a fissure in the masonry, which runs through the center of the pendentive and causes displacement in the head and body of the figure of Joachim.

Colors and Materials

JOACHIM tunic, visible only at breast, blue; himation violet, with gray and yellowish stones in highlights. SHEPHERD AT LEFT tunic, red; shoulder strap, black; staff, verd antique marble along left side and dull gray stone along right; headband, white and gray stones and blue glass; leash, brown glass along left, black along right. SHEPHERD AT RIGHT tunic, green; shoulder strap, black; sack, yellowish gray and brown stones. HUT dull grayish green (two values), light bluish green, blue, and black glasses. GROUNDWORK OF MOUNTAINS (to left and right) areas of gray stone ranging from warm yellowish gray to cool and dark bluish gray, with dark contour lines in violet glass. MOUNTAIN PEAKS gray stones enlivened by short strokes of green, blue, and red glasses. LOWER GROUND ZONE two horizontal bands of dark and light green glasses.

1 Cf. Ernst Diez and Otto Demus, *Byzantine Mosaics in Greece* (Cambridge, Mass., 1931), Fig. 109; also, the hut in the painting (possibly ninth century) of the same subject in S.

Maria de Gradellis (Fortuna Virilis), Rome, in Jacqueline Lafontaine-Dosogne, *Peintures médiévales dans le temple dit de la Fortune Virile à Rome* (Brussels and Rome, 1959), PL. II and III.

[85]

The Annunciation to St. Anne

PL. 92–95

(*Protevangelium 2:3–4:1; Pseudo-Matthew 2*)

Ἡ Ἁ(γία) Ἄννα προσευχομέ|νη ἐν τῷ παραδείσῳ
St. Anne praying in the garden

The lunette in the eastern wall of the northern bay (PL. 92) originally contained two scenes. The surviving scene in the right side, The Annunciation to St. Anne, fills somewhat more than half of the total area (PL. 93). The only surviving remains of the missing scene at the left consist of three letters of its inscription pertaining to an unknown word ending in οφὴ. These are found at the left edge of the remaining mosaic between the upper border and the architecture; they align with the first line of the inscription of the existing scene at the right. It is rather unlikely that the cycle of mosaics would depict Joachim in the Wilderness [84] but omit the more important incident of the angel's appearance before Joachim announcing that his prayers had been answered (Protevangelium 4:2; Pseudo-Matthew 3). For this reason the missing scene may be assumed to have represented The Annunciation to Joachim. If it did, the lunette contained the two annunciations, resembling in this respect the lunette in the narthex at Daphni.

In the extant scene of annunciation, Anne stands in the midst of her garden, between her house and a fountain of flowing water. She turns toward the right, her hands held up before her in an attitude of prayer, as she looks upward at the angel, who is represented as a half-figure—a common convention in the depicting of angels in flight. Before her also are trees, in one of which is a nest containing two young birds; at the right the mother bird flies toward her young. In the doorway of the house at the left a young boy is seated, although one would have expected to find Anne's maidservant, Judith, who is prominent in the account of the Protevangelium.

The scene illustrates best the text of the Protevangelium, although in all essential details it agrees also with the Pseudo-Matthew account. These texts agree that Anne lamented and bewailed her barrenness after Joachim's departure; that she, like Joachim, determined to pray that the Lord visit her; that the prayer took place in the garden; and that, while praying, she espied a bird's nest in a laurel tree. That sight inspired her lamentations, which are quoted by the Protevangelium. Four times she asks, "Unto what am I likened?" She answers that she is not likened to the fowls of the heaven, nor to the beasts of the earth, nor even "unto these waters" (the phrase that accounts for the presence of the fountain in the pictorial versions), nor to the earth, for all these are fruitful before the Lord. The two texts agree also that when the angel appeared, saying that the Lord had heard her prayer, he also foretold that her seed should be spoken of through the whole world. It was then, according to the Protevangelium, that Anne vowed that if she were granted a child, whether male or female, she would give it to the Lord's service.

The house, a very prominent feature of the mosaic, is unusual in its scale and fantasy. A monumental exterior staircase leads to an upper-story portico that rests on consoles. The ter-

64

raced roof is sheltered by a fanciful shell-like canopy and by a great swag of red drapery supported by a little column that is mounted upon a turret. Among the extant scenes in the cycle the figure of Anne is introduced here for the first time. Throughout the mosaics she is clad, as here, in a long, tight-sleeved dress of blue beneath a red mantle that covers most of her figure, including the head.

Dimensions
Original width of lunette, within its mosaic border, ca. 3.30 m.; height within borders, ca. 1.78 m.

Colors and Materials
ANNE   see above.   ANGEL   blue undergarment, violet outer garment.   BOY   blue tunic, green himation wrapped about legs.
HOUSE   dominant color, used on dark faces of walls, is a fine-grained stone of mat brown the color of lightly roasted coffee, a material and color extremely rare among the mosaics of the Kariye Djami; lighted walls, yellowish gray stone; steps, drawn and shaded in blue glass, remainder in gray and white stone; roof canopy, columns of green glass with shell motif of violet glass and yellowish gray stones and dome of blue glass and gray stone.   FOUNTAIN   shaded faces of violet glass; lighted vertical faces, reddish gray stone; upper faces, gray and white stones.   GROUND   horizontal zones in two values of green glass; triangular area to right of fountain is of verd antique stone, an unusual material to use in mosaics, which has badly crumbled.   FOLIAGE   mainly green glasses, black glass, and white stone.

[86]

The Meeting of Joachim and Anne   PL. 96, 97

(*Protevangelium 4:4; Pseudo-Matthew 3*)

Ἡ σύλληψις τ(ῆς) Θ(εοτό)κου   *The conception of the Theotokos*

Immediately to the right of The Annunciation to St. Anne, in the eastern soffit of the transverse arch between the first and second bays, is the rather badly damaged mosaic which represents the embrace of Joachim and Anne upon Joachim's return from the mountain, the subject that in western iconography is commonly called The Meeting at the Golden Gate.[1] The scene, however, has a higher significance than that of the mere return of Joachim, for the inscription marks it as the prelude to one of the momentous events in the Incarnation, namely, the conception of the God-bearer, which is commemorated in the calendar of the church on the ninth day of December as the feast of Ἡ σύλληψις τῆς Ἁγίας Ἄννης τῆς μητρὸς τῆς Θεοτόκου.[2] As is often the case in Byzantine art, the scene of the embrace is adopted as the illustration for that feast, not necessarily because of a wish to indicate a miraculous conception but probably because of the words spoken by Anne on that occasion: "Now know I that the Lord God hath greatly blessed me: for behold the widow is no more a widow, and she that was childless shall conceive."[3]

---

1 Derived from the Latin version, the Pseudo-Matthew, which embroidered the account of the Protevangelium by having Anne go to meet her husband at the city gate that was called "Golden." The Protevangelium simply says that Anne went to the gate, or door—presumably the door of their house.

2 i. e., the Conception of St. Anne, the Mother of the Theotokos. The word σύλληψις is used both actively, as in the Menaion, and passively, as in the inscription.

3 Protevangelium 4:4. Pseudo-Matthew 3: "I was barren, and behold I *have now conceived*" (italics mine). The past tense was also used by the angel, according to one of the MSS of the Protevangelium (4:2), in speaking to Joachim. See Amann, *Le Protévangile*, pp. 17 ff., for evidence that this reading existed in the earliest MSS and for a brief discussion of the position of the Protevangelium with regard to the question of the Immaculate Conception of the Virgin. For the date of the text and the earliest MSS, see chapter of J. Lafontaine-Dosogne in Vol. 4.

Despite its damaged condition, the main elements of this mosaic are preserved. Joachim and Anne, dressed in the costumes and colors we have already encountered as theirs, embrace one another before a narrow, tower-like structure of three stories, typical of a number of the architectural compositions in the mosaics. Two parallel walls, their front ends placed parallel to the picture plane, recede at an angle toward the right and are viewed as though from above. The second-story ceiling is supported at the front by two mottled columns. A piece of red drapery hangs down the left side of the building, and nearby are the head and shoulders of a young woman, possibly Anne's maidservant, Judith, peering over a low wall. At the left this vertical composition was framed by a cypress tree, which is now all but destroyed.

Dimensions

Approximate original width between borders (now missing), 1.03 m.; approximate height, on the curved surface, from top of inscription to top of mosaic border (now missing) above the cornice, 2.02 m.

Condition

The mosaic surface of this scene was found covered by a calcareous incrustation attributable to seepage of water, over a long period of time, which brought with it, through breaks in the masonry, concentrations of lime from the mortar and the lime plaster renderings in which the mosaic tesserae are set. The removal of these exceedingly hard deposits required much time and the use of chisels, carborundum, and other abrasives. Most of the losses of mosaic and plaster were caused by decomposition of the plaster support for the mosaic surface and by the loss of adhesion between plaster and masonry which resulted from water seepage. Concealed copper cramps, placed close together around the edges and within the area of mosaic, now assure the attachment of the mosaic to the masonry of the arch. New plaster was added surrounding the mosaic and was toned a mottled grayish yellow.

Colors and Materials

JOACHIM himation, violet. ANNE dress, blue; mantle and headdress, red. MAIDSERVANT dress, red; mantle, blue.
BUILDING shaded walls of two upper stories, terra cotta with outlines, designs, and window openings of dull black glass; lighted faces of two upper stories, yellow and light gray stones; shaded face of lower story and low wall at far left, dark and light gray stones; column shafts, green glasses and white stone producing mottled appearance of verd antique marble; column capitals and decorative bands on shafts, gold glass and gray stone; drapery, red. GROUND ZONE (preserved in small area between feet of figures) green glass.

[87]

The Birth of the Virgin

PL. 98–103

(*Protevangelium 5:2; Pseudo-Matthew 4*)

'Η γέννησις τῆς Θ(εοτό)κου *The birth of the Theotokos*

The Birth of the Virgin, like her Conception, is celebrated as a feast of the church (September 8); it is the second of five events in her life which are commemorated, all of them depicted in the mosaics of the Kariye Djami.[1] The scene is placed in the eastern lunette of the second bay, one of a number of wide panels, each framed above by a rather flat, multicentered arch, which gave the mosaicists considerable scope for a developed composition. Portrayed as a single incident, in contrast to renditions of the nativities of Christ (such as [102]) and of John the Baptist, which usually combine two or more events from the narratives of their births, the scene, as

1 The remaining three are The Presentation of the Virgin in the Temple [91], The Annunciation [98], and The Dormition of the Virgin [185].

here, generally borrows the motif of the bathing of the infant from the iconography of Christ's nativity.

The composition, which is of a type that will recur several times ([94], [96], [101]), uses the architectural background as a compositional aid by supplying two vertical accents at right and left, in the form of tower-like structures, connected by a low wall that acts as a backdrop in the center. The principal personages and accessories of the narrative are placed before the vertical elements: Anne, sitting upright in her bed, is at the left, relieved against one tower, and the newly born infant, about to be bathed by the midwife and a servant, is placed before the doorway at the right, from which Joachim, the sole male in an event that is otherwise reserved for women, peers out solicitously. The other persons in the scene are disposed rhythmically between, and for them the low wall acts as a backdrop. It is characteristic, in those panels that are framed, as this one is, by rather flat arches, that of the two vertical structures the one at the left is viewed from above while the one at the right is viewed from below. In this way the slopes of their receding sides are made to respond, in each case, to the direction of slope in the frame above, and the general configuration of the architecture to some degree parallels that of the border.

In most versions of this scene, one of Anne's maids is shown raising her into a sitting position. Here, this action has already taken place and the attendant stands nearby with folded arms. Another maid, at the right, wields a triangular fan of peacock feathers on a long pole. Between these two maids a group of three young women approach the mother bearing gifts for the occasion. The first holds a small blue phial of glass with a pointed bottom and a long neck, perhaps containing some precious fluid. The second carries a large bottle with a long neck, also of blue but decorated with gold and red bands. The last of the visitors holds a flat dish of food, which she is about to place on the golden table standing near the foot of the bed. On the table are other presents—a bowl with a high foot, containing food, and a round object, probably a loaf of bread.

In the lower right corner, seated on a low stool, is the midwife, holding the infant Mary in her hands as one of the maids prepares the bath. The diminutive figure of Mary, while not a very accurate portrayal of a newly born child (one does not expect to find such realism in medieval art), is nevertheless charmingly and skillfully rendered. It is perhaps worthy of note that the heads of the midwife and of the maid who swings the fan are rather successfully drawn in profile; the technique is one in which medieval artists, including those of the Kariye Djami, very often failed. In the lower left corner is a delightful genre theme: a very young maidservant is busily engaged in preparing the cradle, which she has placed close beside the mother's bed.

Dimensions

Width between borders, measured at bottom, 2.485 m.; height between borders, 1.645 m.

Condition

A continuous fissure, with a number of secondary ones stemming from it, runs diagonally through the center of the lunette. The amount of separation between the two halves is indicated by the wide joint in the cornice; the separation has caused distortions that are particularly noticeable in the large bottle, the head of the woman who carries it, and the left side of the table. Moisture, which caused decomposition and considerable loss of stone tesserae, has badly affected many areas, especially in the lower right quadrant.

Colors and Materials

ANNE dress, blue; mantle and headdress, red.   BED cover, green; side, violet with borders of gold; end, dark violet with borders of yellow stone, brown glass, and a little gold.   FIVE ATTENDANTS AT BACK (left to right) *1*): Dress, bluish green and yellowish green glass and yellow stone with gold and red collar and cuffs. *2*): Dress, pink with blue collar, cuffs, and hem. *3*): Dress, blue with gold and red collar, cuffs, and hem; mantle, brown and yellow. *4*): Dress, green with gold and red collar. *5*): Dress, blue; mantle, violet; triangular fan, blue and light green. TABLE gold, violet, and brown. JOACHIM tunic, blue; himation, green (elsewhere his himation is violet). CRADLE gold with outlining of reversed gold tesserae; cover, red. MAID AT CRADLE dress, light blue with dark blue collar and hem. MAID AT BATH dress, light blue with gold and red collar and hem. INFANT MARY flesh, pink and white marbles with outline drawing of red glass; hair and outlining of eyes, very small tesserae of greenish brown glass; eyes, black glass; nostrils and lips, red glass. MIDWIFE dress, medium and light blues with gold and red collar and sleeve bands; mantle, covering lower part of figure, violet; headdress, light blue. WATER BASIN gold with greenish brown outlines and ornaments; water, blue. WATER JUG gold with drawing of reversed gold tesserae.

ARCHITECTURE low wall and pavilion at far left, gray stone with windows of violet and roof canopy of blue; wall in center and pavilion at right, grayish yellow stone in both light and shade; roof tiles, blue; shadows in door, violet. AWNING red. GROUND ZONE mixed green glasses.

[88]

The First Seven Steps of the Virgin

PL. 104–107

(Protevangelium 6:1)

'Η ἑπταβηματίζουσα   *She who takes seven steps*

The Protevangelium is the only one of the Apocryphal Gospels that recounts the charming incident of Mary's first steps: [1] "And day by day the child waxed strong, and when she was six months old her mother stood her upon the ground to try if she would stand; and she walked seven steps and returned unto her bosom. And she caught her up, saying: As the Lord my God liveth, thou shalt walk no more upon this ground, until I bring thee into the temple of the Lord. And she made a sanctuary in her bedchamber and suffered nothing common or unclean to pass through it. And she called for the daughters of the Hebrews that were undefiled, and they carried her hither and thither." Just as the story of the conception and birth of the Virgin was calculated to demonstrate that the circumstances of the birth were more miraculous and holy than those of the birth of John the Baptist or certain Old Testament personages whom God had destined to perform his will, so the purpose of the author of the Protevangelium, at this point in the story, was to show the miraculous precocity of the Virgin and to indicate the means by which her purity was to be protected until the vow taken by Anne could be fulfilled and the Virgin could be presented, spotless, to the service of the Lord in his temple.

The mosaic representation of this incident was placed in the eastern soffit of the transverse arch between the second and third bays. In a simple but effective composition the mosaicists have captured the more human sentiments evoked by the subject and have fully expressed them by means of gestures, lines, and movements. The postures of the beautifully drawn maidservant at the left and the mother at the right, as they bend all their attention upon the infant, produce an outer circular configuration that revolves about an internal circle of extended arms and hands expressing so admirably the theme of filial and maternal love. As in most of the mosaics, the movement of the composition is from left to right. It is initiated in the upper left in the figure of the attendant, whose head is beautifully framed by the circular form of a wind-blown veil of red. It passes in a curve through her long, bare arms to the eagerly outstretched arms of the

---

[1] Not to be confused with Mary's ascent of the fifteen steps of the temple on the occasion of her presentation (Pseudo-Matthew 4; Gospel of the Nativity of Mary 6).

child, as she haltingly advances toward her mother, and then it inclines upward and finally to the left, through the great curve formed by the posture of Anne. Even the bench on which the mother is seated is made to contribute to the movement by its position and its curved form, and the sweep of the composition is heightened by the wind, which blows the veil and the trees in the background toward the right.

The scene is laid before the perfectly symmetrical façade of a building placed parallel to the picture plane. A stage-like niche is formed in the center by two projecting wings, whose orthogonals recede in a pseudo-perspective toward a central vanishing axis. Where the building joins the ground, however, its depth is denied, for the green zone, which signifies but does not depict a horizontal ground plane, cuts off the base of the building in a straight line and does not penetrate into the niche. It will be observed throughout the mosaics and paintings of the Kariye Djami that in this respect, as in many others, the artists still adhered to many of the conventions of medieval art.

The motif of the billowing scarf worn by the maidservant is a particularly interesting one to find in the Kariye Djami, as it illustrates a renewed interest on the part of artists and patrons of the Palaeologan era in motifs and styles that were in vogue in pagan art of late classical antiquity;[2] the scarf motif often appears there as an attribute of various personifications. In our mosaic it seems to have been employed not with allegorical or symbolic connotations but as a device whose beauty of line and form could be exploited as a decorative feature.

Dimensions

Width between borders, 1.08 m.; height, on curved surface, from top of inscription to top of mosaic border above cornice, 1.81 m.

Colors and Materials

This mosaic represents one of only two instances in the Kariye Djami in which the mosaicists changed the natural color of their stones by the application of pigments after the mosaic was completed (see also [118]). The broad surfaces of the building in the background are made of gray stones. In the upper story all surfaces, except the cornices, ornaments, and window, were toned with a flat, dull, reddish brown pigment of a single value for the faces parallel to the picture plane and of darker values for the receding planes. In the lower story the receding faces only were toned with the same pigment that was used above; the gray stones of the faces parallel to the picture plane were left in their natural colors.

MAIDSERVANT dress, blue with gold and red hem; scarf, red. MARY dress, blue; shoes, red. ANNE dress, blue; mantle and headdress, red. FURNITURE lighted faces, gold with brown glass outlines; shaded faces, brown stones and glass. BUILDING see above; fill of window, blue and black; outlines, blue and violet. TREES green and black.

2 This is not to say that art of the Palaeologan era was unique in this respect; such "revivals" had occurred intermittently throughout the history of Byzantine art.

[89]

The Virgin Blessed by the Priests   PL. 108–113

(*Protevangelium 6:2*)

Ἡ εὐλόγησις τῶν ἱερέων   *The blessing of the priests*

The rather flat domical vault (PL. 108) that covers the second bay of the inner narthex is devoted to two scenes: The Virgin Blessed by the Priests [89], in the western half, and The Virgin Caressed by Her Parents [90], in the eastern half. By a skillful arrangement of architectural elements a framework for two scenes is provided which yet creates a unified composition for the vault as a whole. Four tower-like structures, which diminish in scale as they ascend, rise from the pendentives to provide strong accents on the diagonals of the square. Between these, other, lower architectural elements combine with the radially disposed figures and trees to transform the composition from a square at the base of the vault to a continuous circular zone suitable to the domical structure. The circularity of the zone of figures and buildings is enhanced by the large ornamental medallion in the center (PL. 331 *a*), by the disposition of the inscriptions that surround it, and by the fact that the rows of tesserae in the gold background are laid concentrically around the central point of the vault.

Mary's first anniversary, according to the Protevangelium, was celebrated by Joachim with a feast to which he invited the priests, scribes, and all Israel. During the festivities "Joachim brought the child to the priests, and they blessed her, saying: O God of our fathers, bless this child and give her a name renowned for ever among all generations. And all the people said: So be it, so be it. Amen. And he brought her to the high priests, and they blessed her, saying: O God of the high places, look upon this child, and bless her with the last blessing which hath no successor." Mary's blessing, it is inferred, was performed in Joachim's house, first by priests of the lower rank and a second time by the "high priests." It is the second, highest blessing that is illustrated in the mosaic. With this incident Mary's divinely appointed role is being manifest to all people and an exceptional religious rite is performed whereby Mary, though a female, is sanctified by the priests. According to Jewish religious practice anniversaries were not celebrated and only first-born males, on the fortieth day after birth, received the priestly blessing, in the temple. In contrast to the great majority of representations of the subject, but literally in accordance with the text of the Protevangelium, Joachim alone presents the infant Theotokos to the priests; her mother is thus excluded from the rite. Joachim, at the left, advances to receive the benediction from three high priests sitting on a long bench behind a table. In one of the finest details anywhere in the mosaics, he strides forward vigorously with a great flutter of drapery. The child's position, nestled in the drapery that completely covers Joachim's hands, symbolizes her sacredness and likens her to a holy vessel borne toward the altar. The analogy between the table and an altar must not be pressed too far, but on the table are three vessels, two that might be designated as chalices and one in the form of a paten; scattered about the table are six round objects apparently representing loaves of bread.

In the architectural background we find a device that has been used elsewhere—two pylons erected near the ends of the composition with the leading actors placed in relief before them; Joachim and Mary are at the left, and the most venerable of the high priests is at the far right. The other priests are equidistantly spaced between them. The center of the scene is partly screened off from the gold "sky" by a low wall, a colonnade, the back of the bench, and some trees.

Dimensions of Vault

Between mosaic surfaces of inner faces of arches, on E–W and N–S axes, ca. 2.56 m.; on curved surface between arch faces, dimension is considerably greater.

Colors and Materials

JOACHIM tunic, blue; himation, violet. MARY clad entirely in blue. PRIEST AT LEFT tunic, yellow with gold and red hem and cuffs; mantle, blue with gold and red ornaments. PRIEST AT CENTER tunic, blue with gold and red cuffs; mantle, red with gold and red ornaments. PRIEST AT RIGHT tunic, blue with gold and red hem and cuffs; mantle, green with gold and red ornaments.

BENCH gold outlined with brown glass. TABLE bluish gray stone with moldings and openings in front of blue glass.   WALLS lighted faces, brownish gray stone with outlines of dark brown and white stone; shaded faces, brownish gray of darker value than lighted faces.   COLUMNS blue shafts with capitals of gold and brown glass.   GROUND ZONES upper zone, gray stones darkening at top; middle zone, greenish gray stone; lower zone, in pendentives, green glass.

[90]

The Virgin Caressed by Her Parents

PL. 108, 114–118

ʿΗ κολακεία τῆς Θ(εοτό)κου   *The fondling of the Theotokos*

The textual sources of the infancy of Mary do not refer to a specific incident in which Joachim and Anne fondle their child, yet the scene appears quite regularly in the monumental cycles of the Life of the Virgin from the thirteenth century onward. Its presence must therefore be accounted for as the adaptation of a traditional motif from infancy cycles in general. While its chronological position in the story is thus rather vague, it was probably intended to come immediately after the birth of Mary and before the incidents of her first steps, at six months, and her blessing by the priests, when she was a year old. In any case, in the Kariye Djami it was placed in the eastern half of the vault of the second bay, the vault which also contains the scene of the priestly blessing [89].

To a remarkable degree the scene is consistently depicted in Byzantine art in the general form in which it appears here. Joachim, at the left, and Anne, at the right, seated symmetrically on a bench or throne and turned toward one another, hold the child between them and bend over her. Usually the child faces toward the right, as here, but inclines toward her mother for the parental kiss. In our mosaic, however, the child is about to be kissed by Joachim, while she, in turn, places her hand on the face of her mother. A young woman attendant stands gracefully at the left before one of the four towers that radiate on the diagonals of the vault, and another emerges from the house at the right.

The two eastern pendentives are occupied by exceptionally fine representations of peacocks, which serve to give an eastward orientation to the composition of the vault as a whole. It will be seen that in the next vault, where the single scene [91] is also oriented to the east, the equivalent positions are occupied by a pair of pheasants. Thus, all the vaults of the inner narthex are composed along east-west axes. In contrast, the compositions in the first three vaults of the outer narthex are centered on the north-south axes of the vaults and are thus designed to be viewed along the axis of the narthex.

Dimensions of Vault
See no. [89].

Colors and Materials
JOACHIM   tunic, blue; himation, violet.   ANNE dress, blue; mantle and headdress, red.   MARY clad entirely in blue; shoes, red.   ATTENDANT AT LEFT dress, blue with gold and red collar, cuffs, and hem; mantle, wound around body, red.   ATTENDANT AT RIGHT dress, red with gold collar and cuffs.

FURNITURE lighted faces, gold with brown glass outlining and lighter brown stone panel; shaded faces, brown stones.   LOW WALL (extending from tree at left to house at right) brown and dark gray stones with shadows of coping in violet glass.   PAVILION AT LEFT (above wall) shaded faces, blue glasses; lighted faces, gray stones; under side of flat wooden roof, violet glass, brown and gray stone; curtain at door, pink.   HOUSE AT RIGHT narrow front side, yellow stone with outlines of gray; reveal of door, violet glass;

reveal of window, brown stone; steps, gray treads and risers, blue drawing and shaded face; shaded side of house, brownish yellow stone with brown and white drawing; fill of large door, dull black, clinker-like glass in left reveal, the rest jet black glass; roof tiles, blue with highlights of gray.   DRAPERY   red.

PEACOCK AT RIGHT   neck, breast, and underparts as far back as tail, primarily of blue glass (4 values) with small highlights in gray stone; wings, dark violet glass as background on which feathers of light blue glass

(below) and yellowish gray stones (above) are outlined with black; two red feathers project from beneath wing; tail, green glass as background with feathers and "eyes" outlined in black and highlighted with gold; legs and feet, violet and black. (Peacock at left similarly executed.)

TREES   foliage, green and black; trunks and branches, violet and brownish green glass and brown stones.

GROUND ZONE IN PENDENTIVES   green glasses.

[91]

The Presentation of the Virgin in the Temple

PL. 119–125 b

(Protevangelium 7:2; Pseudo-Matthew 4; Gospel of the Nativity of Mary 6)

Τὰ ἅγια τῶν ἁγίων   *The Holy of Holies*

The principal entrance to the nave opens from the third bay, where the inner narthex intersects the axis of the church. In contrast to all the other vaults in the narthexes, which contain two or more scenes, the domical vault of the axial bay is devoted to a single scene, depicting the entry of the Virgin into the Holy of Holies of the temple. This event in the life of the Virgin was purposely chosen to crown the entrance to the nave because of its appropriateness in that position and because of its importance as a feast of the church (Nov. 21). Much of the poetic imagery contained in the liturgy of the feast of the Virgin's presentation derives from the following passage of the Protevangelium, which is also the textual source for the mosaic:

"And the child became three years old, and Joachim said: Call for the daughters of the Hebrews that are undefiled, and let them take every one a lamp, and let them be burning, that the child turn not backward and her heart be taken captive away from the temple of the Lord. And they did so until they were gone up into the temple of the Lord.

"And the priest received her and kissed her and blessed her and said: The Lord hath magnified thy name among all generations: in thee in the latter days shall the Lord make manifest his redemption unto the children of Israel. And he made her to sit upon the third step of the altar. And the Lord put grace upon her and she danced with her feet and all the house of Israel loved her."

Like that of the mosaics in the other domical vaults of the Kariye Djami, the composition of this mosaic consists of a circular zone of figures and architecture in the lower slopes of the vault, but, perhaps because a single scene is represented, the ornamental medallion found at the center of the other vaults has here been omitted; its place and to some extent its function are taken over by the domical canopy that covers the Holy of Holies. The latter, as the principal element in the narrative, is placed in the eastern side of the vault so that the scene will conform in its orientation to that of all compositions in the domes of the inner narthex. The procession, however, begins in the western side, where the last of the daughters of the Hebrews emerge from a building which may represent the house of Joachim. From opposite sides these beautifully portrayed maidens, each holding a lighted torch, converge upon the sanctuary; before the gate,

Joachim and Anne urge the child Mary onward toward the high priest, who is ready, with hands extended, to receive her.

Although the mosaic is composed as a single subject, another incident from Mary's life in the temple — Mary receiving food from an angel — has been merged with the Presentation in the Temple even though it is repeated as an independent scene in the arch to the right [92]. This conflation was customary in depicting the Presentation and served as a means of illustrating its most significant points, namely, that the Virgin actually entered the Holy of Holies and sat upon "the third step of the altar," where she was divinely nurtured. In the mosaic the child is enthroned not on the altar itself but, as usual, on a stepped platform behind the altar but still within the ciborium, into which the angel enters to offer the bread.

The literary source does not name the high priest, but in Byzantine pictorial tradition he was identified, often by means of inscriptions, as Zacharias, prophet and father of John the Baptist, as he was also in the liturgy of the day. There is a certain poetic justification for this assumption, for the circumstances under which Zacharias and Elizabeth begot their child were so like those of Joachim and Anne. In the mosaic the priest has a halo, as he has in the scene of Joachim's offerings [82] and in the two scenes of the betrothal of Mary to Joseph, [95] and [96], where the textual source identifies him as Zacharias.

Attention should be called to the two pheasants represented in the eastern pendentives, the male bird at the left and the female at the right. As a means of further accentuating the orientation of the composition, they are comparable to the peacocks in corresponding positions in the eastern pendentives of the second bay of the narthex [90].

Dimensions of Vault

Between mosaic surfaces of inner faces of arches, on E–W and N–S axes, ca. 2.50 m.

Colors and Materials

JOACHIM tunic, blue; himation, violet. ANNE dress, blue; mantle and headdress, red. MARY clad entirely in blue. ZACHARIAS tunic, blue with richly ornamented hem of gold studded with rectangular gems (red, green, red) and pearls; mantle, red edged with gold and ornamented with a gold tablion studded with red and green gems and with pearls, with a lining of white and gray stones.

DAUGHTERS OF THE HEBREWS (counterclockwise starting at right of sanctuary) *1*): Dress, blue with red girdle and gold and red collar and cuff; mantle, grayish yellow stone. *2*): Dress, grayish yellow stone; mantle, green ornamented with gold and red. *3*): Dress, red with golden collar, cuffs, and hem; mantle, blue; headdress, light blue, gray, and white. *4*): Dress, violet with gold hem; mantle and headdress, green. *5*): Dress, blue with gold and red hem; mantle, red; headdress, violet. *6*): Dress, violet with gold hem; mantle, green ornamented with gold and red. *7*): Sleeveless dress, red with gold hem; short sleeveless tunic, violet with gold and red collar and gold hem bordered by red and blue; mantle, blue. *8*): Dress, blue with gold collar, cuffs, and hem; mantle, red. *9*): Dress, blue with gold cuff; mantle, green.

HOLY OF HOLIES *Barrier:* exterior face, yellow stone background with imitation veining of dull brown and dark violet glasses; interior face, background of yellow stone and dull brown glass with veining of dark violet. *Base of sanctuary:* blue riser and gray stone tread. *Altar cloth:* red. *Throne and steps:* risers and exterior face of throne, blue; treads, bluish gray stone; interior face of throne, violet. *Ciborium:* canopy, bluish gray stones in lighted face, violet glass in shaded face; columns, mottled green and black; capitals, gold. *Low wall of background:* yellowish gray stones.

BUILDING IN WEST SIDE shaded faces, greenish brown glass; lighted faces, yellowish gray stone; roof tiles, blue; door at right, black; curtain, red.

MALE PHEASANT *Tail and body, to base of neck:* ground of light violet glasses and gray stone; feathers outlined in dark violet glass except in narrow part of tail, where cross-lines are light blue; individual cubes of light blue and green spotted over fore and upper parts of body. *Triangular wing:* blue in lower part, green, greenish yellow, and yellow glasses in upper part, with some gold cubes in center. *Ring at base of neck:* blue with a few green cubes; outlining of feathers in dark violet. *Neck:* feathers of mixed green and blue glasses and gray stone with outlining in medium violet. *Head:* blue ground with drawing in violets; eye, greenish yellow iris and violet pupil, with red terra cotta area around eye; beak, green and greenish yellow. *Legs and feet:* violet.

FEMALE PHEASANT *Breast and front part of wing:* gray

73

stone background with red terra cotta feathers outlined in dark red glass. *End of wing:* feathers, brownish green and brown glasses; two wing bars of yellow stone. *Rump:* gray and white stone ground, violet feathers with blue cube at center of each. *Long, thin tail:* green

glasses with drawing in violet. *Neck:* ground of red terra cotta; feathers indicated by gray stone and dark violet glass. *Beak:* green outlined with violet. *Legs and feet:* violet.

[92]

The Virgin Fed by an Angel

PL. 126–128

(Protevangelium 8:1; Pseudo-Matthew 6; Gospel of the Nativity of Mary 7)

Ἡ Θ(εοτό)κος δεχομένη τ(ὸν) ἄρτον παρὰ τοῦ ἀγγέ(λο)υ
The Theotokos receiving bread from the angel

Μ(ήτ)ηρ Θ(εο)ῦ   *Mother of God*

In the eastern soffit of the transverse arch between the third and fourth bays of the narthex, the incident of Mary being fed by an angel is illustrated for the second time. It was introduced as a minor motif in the mosaic of Mary's Presentation in the Temple [91], as was usual in the iconography of that subject; its representation as an independent subject is most uncommon in the monumental cycles of the Life of the Virgin.

The text of the Protevangelium that is here illustrated reads: "And Mary was in the temple of the Lord as a dove that is nurtured: and she received food from the hand of an angel." According to the accounts of her life, Mary continued to dwell in the Holy of Holies from her third to her twelfth (or fourteenth) year and was daily fed the heavenly bread by an angel. Thus, from the sanctuary of Anne's bedchamber, where she had been kept from contact with anything unclean, she was removed to the service of the temple, where her purity was now safeguarded both by the holiness of the place and by the heavenly food with which she was nurtured.

In the mosaic Mary is seated on a golden throne beneath a ciborium, her feet resting on a three-stepped podium. An angel in flight appears from the left and offers the bread. Seated on a footstool in the lower left is one of the company of daughters of the Hebrews who had, from her early infancy, served as guardians and attendants of the Virgin.

Dimensions

Width between borders, 1.00 m.; height, on curved surface, from top of inscription to top of mosaic border above cornice, 1.82 m.

Colors and Materials

MARY dress, blue; shoes, red. ANGEL garment, violet; upper parts of wing, transparent glasses of greenish, yellowish, and amber color and some gold, with glittering dark red glass along lower edge and at ends of long feathers; lower part of wing, blue glasses and white stone; staff, red with 7 pearls at top. MAIDEN dress, blue with gold and red collar and sleeve band; sleeveless short tunic, violet; mantle, red. THRONE gold with violet drawing and transparent glass panels; cushion, red. CIBORIUM canopy, blue glasses, gray and white stones; column shafts, green glasses with black veining in imitation of verd antique; capitals and bases, gold with amber (reversed gold tesserae) drawing; base of ciborium, blue riser, gray and white stone floor. STEPS vertical faces, violet; treads, gray. FOOTSTOOL gold with amber drawing. WALL yellow-gray stone; shadow on tower, violet. DRAPERY red. FOREGROUND mixed green glasses.

[93]

Instruction of the Virgin in the Temple   PL. 129

ἡ Θ(εοτό)κος διδασκομένη ἐν τῷ ἱερῷ
The Theotokos receiving instruction in the temple

The mosaic in the western side of the arch between the third and fourth bays, entitled "The Theotokos receiving instruction in the temple," has been seriously mutilated; Shmit, in his work published in 1906, states it as a fact that this mosaic had only recently been damaged by some "lover" of art who had unsuccessfully attempted to remove it and thus "preserve" it.[1] This is the more to be regretted because the subject is otherwise unknown in Byzantine art. No such event is mentioned in the Protevangelium, and only in Western apocryphal sources are there even phrases that might suggest that the Virgin had received instruction in the temple.

It is evident that the attempt was made to remove the portions of the mosaic which contained the figures. The shape of the lost area suggests that the figures were concentrated in two places —at the left, where fragments of the Virgin and one of her attendants still remain, and lower down at the right, where, we may presume, a figure once stood before the Virgin, at the base of her footstool.

What now remains permits us to say that the Virgin was seated on a high bench at the left, on a red cushion, and faced toward the right. Her feet rested on the second step of a two-stepped footstool, and within her reach, to the right, was a lectern of the type with two sloping faces; on it, facing the Virgin, was an open book. Behind the Virgin, between her and the wall at the back of the aedicula, stood one or more daughters of the Hebrews; at the far left, partly concealed behind the support of the aedicula, can still be seen the back of the head, the right shoulder, the left hand, and a large part of the dress of one of the "daughters."

The inscribed title of the scene implies the presence of an instructor. It would be most interesting to know whether the instructor was a priest or, perhaps, an angel. The sole remaining physical evidence of this figure, who must have been placed at the right facing the Virgin, consists of a group of four dark blue tesserae at the very edge of the destroyed area where it cuts across the tread of the otherwise entirely golden lowest step. The figure did not necessarily stand on the step; it is more likely that he stood to the right of it and that the tesserae in question pertained to a piece of drapery or perhaps the tip of a wing.

The Latin Apocryphal Gospel of Pseudo-Matthew devotes a chapter to Mary's special virtues and describes her daily life in the temple in terms of monastic practices. As regards her intellectual accomplishments, which might presuppose instruction, it is said only that there was "no one more learned in the wisdom of the law of God" and that Mary "was always engaged in prayer and in searching the law." While no instructor is mentioned, it should be noted that the same source twice speaks of the daily visitations of the angels of God, who "were often seen

1 *Kakhrie-dzhami*, p. 72. N. P. Kondakov, in *Vizantiiskiia Tserkvi i Pamiatniki Konstantinopolia* (Odessa, 1886), published a watercolor sketch (PL. 29) of the inner narthex which indicates that the mosaic was already damaged in his day.

75

speaking with her." Mary's precocity is described as being so great, and her life so fully ordered by divine rather than human means, that instruction, it would seem, could be given only through the angels of God. (Pseudo-Matthew 6.)

The scene is placed in a setting of symmetrical architecture consisting of an open gable, covered by billowing awnings, which rests upon corbels supported, in turn, on narrow mullions. Behind this structure a wall extends across the picture, and above the wall the tops of two cypress trees are visible. It is interesting to find the modified classical egg and dart motif used in the gable, not, as it should be, as the decoration of the bed moldings of the raking cornice but on the cyma.

In view of the principle of convergence of orthogonals toward a central vanishing axis which was adopted for the only other pictures in the Kariye Djami where symmetrical architecture provides the background (nos. [88] and [97]), it is curious that in this picture the situation is reversed and the orthogonals diverge toward two vanishing axes at the sides.

Dimensions

Width between borders, 0.98 m.; height, on curved surface, from top of inscription to top of mosaic border above cornice, 1.88 m.

Colors and Materials

MARY garments, blue. MAIDEN dress, red. BENCH AND FOOTSTOOL receding faces at left, brown stone with square panels of gold tesserae set in reverse; risers of steps and front of bench, light brown stone; upper surfaces, gold. ARCHITECTURE raking cornice, violet drawing, eggs half gray, half yellow stone; corbels, gray, yellow, and white on front, violet on receding faces; mullions, gray and yellow; wall, gray with drawing of blue. DRAPERY red with bands of blue and edgings of gold.

[94]

The Virgin Receiving the Skein of Purple Wool

PL. 130–134

(*Protevangelium 10; Pseudo-Matthew 8*)

Ἐνεγκόντες οἱ ὑπηρέται ταῖς παρθένοις | τοῦ λαβεῖν ἔρια ἔλαχε τῇ Μα|ριὰμ τὸ πορφυροῦν.

The servants having brought the wool for the virgins to take, the purple fell to Mary's lot.

The Virgin Receiving the Skein of Purple Wool is a rarely illustrated subject, and the mosaic version of it in the Kariye Djami is by far the most impressive one that has come down to us. The panel containing it is far out of its proper place in the sequence of events, for according to the textual sources the incident took place after Mary's betrothal to Joseph and before the Annunciation. More precisely, it should be placed immediately after the scene of Joseph Taking Leave of the Virgin [99]; instead, it has been placed in the lunette above the door from the outer narthex, where it is grouped with incidents from Mary's life in the temple, even though Mary had, by then, left the temple to live in the house of Joseph.

The mosaic depicts the events described by the Protevangelium, Chapter 10: "Now there was a council of the priests, and they said: Let us make a veil for the temple of the Lord. And the priest said: Call unto me pure virgins of the tribe of David. And the officers departed and sought and found seven virgins. And the priests called to mind the child Mary, that she was of the tribe of David and was undefiled before God: and the officers went and fetched her. And they brought them into the temple of the Lord, and the priest said: Cast me lots, which of you shall weave the gold and the undefiled (the white) and the fine linen and the silk and the hyacinthine, and the scarlet and the true purple. And the lot of the true purple and the scarlet fell unto Mary, and she took them and went unto her house. . . . But Mary took the scarlet and began to spin it." With this incident, the Protevangelium demonstrates that Mary, although she had departed from the Holy of Holies to live in the house of Joseph, was still pure and undefiled at the time of the Annunciation. The Virgin Birth was to be attested by the fact that God allotted to Mary, alone among the virgins of the tribe of David, the purple and the scarlet (the royal colors) as a sign that the long-prophesied Messiah, who was to be King and Savior of his people, was about to spring from the seed of David.

As are so many of the panels in the Kariye Djami, this one is composed of two confronted groups of figures, each group singled out and given distinction by a prominent architectural element rising behind it—a curved apsidal structure at the left, behind the priests, and a kind of pylon at the right, behind the group of virgins of the tribe of David. The three priests are seated on a curved, two-stepped synthronon, or priests' bench, a piece of furniture that was commonly found against the curved wall of the apse of an early Christian church. While the synthronon in the mosaic is placed outside the apse, it is meant to be understood as within it. The architecture and furnishings in the scene are thus used not only as compositional elements but as symbols to indicate the nature of the setting. In this case the temple is suggested by the two principal elements of the Christian sanctuary—the apse and the synthronon. The priest at the right, nearest the center of the panel, is depicted as he is about to present the skein of "purple" [1] wool to Mary, who stands, a little detached from the other virgins, in the center at the focal point of the composition.

There appears to be a contradiction in the text between the number of tasks that were to be allotted to the virgins and the number of virgins called to perform them. Seven materials or colors were to be woven into the veil, but the text implies that there were eight virgins in all— the seven who were originally called and Mary, whose inclusion was an afterthought. The confusion is heightened, after the allotting, when Mary is given two colors to spin and weave. The fact that the number seven is mentioned has caused our artist, perhaps inadvertently, to resolve the difficulty by depicting only six companions for Mary and by presenting Mary, according to both the picture and its inscription, with only one color—the purple.

In the mosaic the contrast between Mary and the other virgins is marked. She is a slight and youthful figure, exhibiting humility as she receives the skein of purple. The others appear to be older and more stately in both stance and attire; some of them, at the far right, display attitudes of agitation as they comment among themselves, and there is no note of reverence toward Mary, who is receiving the highest award. In these particulars the mosaic would seem to draw upon the version of the Pseudo-Matthew, which says: "And when . . . [Mary] had got it [the skein of purple], those virgins said to her: Since thou art the last, and humble, and younger than all, thou hast deserved to receive and obtain the purple. And thus saying, as it were in words of annoyance, they began to call her queen of virgins. . . . the angel of the Lord appeared . . .

1 In the mosaic the skein is red, not purple.

saying: These words shall not have been uttered by way of annoyance, but prophesied as a prophecy most true."

Dimensions

Width between borders, measured at bottom, 2.36 m.; height between borders, 1.635 m.; height of Mary, .62 m.; height of virgin to right of Mary, .71 m.

Colors and Materials

PRIESTS *Left:* tunic, blue with gold and red hem; mantle, red with borders of violet and gold; hat, red crown and blue and white brim; shoes, red ornamented with blue and gold. *Center:* tunic, violet with gold and red ornaments; mantle, completely in blue glass with gold and red borders and white lining; hat, red crown and blue and white brim; shoes, blue with gray and red ornaments. *Right:* tunic, mainly gray stone with some blue glass, ornamented with gold and red; mantle, red bordered with gold and violet; hat, red crown and blue and white brim; shoes, blue with gray and white stripes; skein of wool, red glass, terra cotta, pink and white stone.

MARY clad entirely in blue, mantle and headdress edged in gold; shoes, red.

VIRGINS OF TRIBE OF DAVID (left to right) *1)*: Dress, blue with red and gold hem; short tunic with long sleeves, green with gold ornaments; mantle, red; skein of wool, blue. *2)*: Dress, red with gold and red ornaments; mantle, blue; skein of wool, blue. *3)*: Dress, gray with blue and white vertical stripes and gold and red hem and collar; mantle, yellow. *4)*: Dress, green with gold and red hem and collar and gold and blue cuffs; mantle, red. *5)*: Dress, violet with gold and red ornaments; mantle, yellow. *6)*: Dress, blue; mantle, green. (All shoes black.)

PRIESTS' BENCH vertical faces, yellowish brown stone; horizontal faces, gold. ARCHITECTURE vertical surfaces, stones of various values of yellowish gray to brownish gray; drawing, violet glass; window opening at left, violet; window at right, violet glass and brown stone. GROUND ZONE green glass.

[95]

Zacharias Praying before the Rods of the Suitors

PL. 135–137

(Protevangelium 8:2–9:1; Pseudo-Matthew 8; Gospel of the Nativity of Mary 7, 8)

Ἡ πρὸς τὰς ῥάβδους προσευχή *The prayer before the rods*

The story of what might be termed the Virgin's "marriage" to Joseph is depicted in two scenes. The first of these, Zacharias Praying before the Rods of the Suitors [95], occupies the western soffit of the arch between the second and third bays, while the second, The Virgin Entrusted to Joseph [96], is to the right in the adjoining lunette of the second bay.

To explain the circumstances of the "marriage" and the role of Joseph in these and later events, it will be necessary to quote at some length from the account of the Protevangelium. The passage on which the first incident of the betrothal is based reads:

"And when she was twelve years old, there was a council of the priests, saying: Behold Mary is become twelve years old in the temple of the Lord. What then shall we do with her? lest she pollute the sanctuary of the Lord. And they said unto the high priest: Thou standest over the altar of the Lord. Enter in and pray concerning her: And whatsoever the Lord shall reveal to thee, that let us do.

"And the high priest took the vestment with the twelve bells and went in unto the Holy of Holies and prayed concerning her. And lo, an angel of the Lord appeared saying unto him: Zacharias, Zacharias, go forth and assemble them that are widowers of the people, and let them bring every man a rod, and to whomsoever the Lord shall show a sign, his wife shall she be. And the heralds went forth over all the country round about Judaea, and the trumpet of the Lord sounded, and all men ran thereto.

"And Joseph cast down his adze and ran to meet them, and when they were gathered together they went to the high priest and took their rods with them. And he took the rods of them all and went into the temple and prayed."

It is this last incident, the prayer before the rods, that is illustrated in the mosaic now to be described. Mary stands in prayer behind the altar in the Holy of Holies. Beside her is a three-stepped structure, rather like an ambo, similar to the structures found in the other scenes depicting her in the sanctuary. Neatly arrayed on the altar before her are twelve "rods" — the walking sticks of the widower-suitors. The altar is enclosed by a low barrier of horseshoe shape, with a closed gate at the right, and is covered by a ciborium consisting of four columns surmounted by a domical vault. Before the gate the high priest Zacharias kneels as he prays that a sign may be given by the Lord in designation of Mary's future husband. In answer, Joseph's rod, the fourth one from the right, has sprouted three small leaves from the knob at the upper end. The leaves are not readily apparent in black and white photographs, but the green glass in which they are executed renders them prominent in the mosaic itself or in a color photograph. It will be seen, from the discussion of the next panel, that this is not the sign, according to the text, by which the Lord designated Joseph to be Mary's husband; the mosaicists have deliberately followed another tradition in this detail, and this for definite iconographic purposes.

Dimensions

Width between borders, 1.08 m.; height, on curved surface, from top of inscription to top of mosaic border above cornice, 1.86 m.

Colors and Materials

MARY clad entirely in blue. ZACHARIAS tunic, blue; mantle, red, ornamented with gold tablion studded with blue gems (center and two corners), red gems (other corners), and pearls; hair, largely violet glasses; beard, largely yellow stone.

HOLY OF HOLIES barrier, imitation of veined marble, mottled in light yellowish gray stones in a background of dark reddish gray stones of various values; gates, gold with designs drawn in greenish brown glass; altar cloth, red; rods, gold on upper side and blue on lower; three-stepped throne, blue of slightly lighter value than garments of Mary, outlined in darker blue glass and white stone; columns, green with golden capitals; canopy, cool gray and white stones and violet glass; platform before gates, bluish gray and white stones and blue glass.

WALL (in background at left) warm yellowish gray stone. BUILDING (in background at right) lighted vertical faces, light gray stone at left and yellow stone at right, outlined in blue glass; shaded vertical faces, dull gray stone with drawing in violet glass; openings in receding face, violet; roof, light gray. DRAPERY red with gold and blue ornament.

[96]

The Virgin Entrusted to Joseph

PL. 138–142

(Protevangelium 9:1–2; Pseudo-Matthew 8; Gospel of the Nativity of Mary 8)

Ἡ πρὸς τὸν Ἰωσὴφ παράδοσις   *The handing over to Joseph*

The text of the Protevangelium, describing this second of the two incidents of the betrothal of Mary to Joseph, reads: "And when he [Zacharias] had finished the prayer he took the rods and went forth and gave them back to them: and there was no sign upon them. But Joseph received the last rod: and lo, a dove came forth of the rod and flew upon the head of Joseph. And the priest said unto Joseph: Unto thee hath it fallen to take the virgin of the Lord and keep her for thyself. And Joseph refused, saying: I have sons, and I am an old man, but she is a girl: lest I became a laughing-stock to the children of Israel. And the priest said unto Joseph: Fear the Lord thy God, and remember what things God did unto Dathan and Abiram and Korah, how the earth clave and they were swallowed up because of their gainsaying. And now fear thou, Joseph, lest it be so in thine house."

In this scene, which is illustrated in the western lunette of the second bay, the sanctuary is placed at the left; the eleven rods of the rejected suitors lie tightly bunched upon the altar. Zacharias, his left hand placed on Mary's head and Joseph's flowering rod held out before him in his right hand, presents Mary to Joseph, who advances from the group of widower-suitors at the right; all the suitors are portrayed as old men.

The two mosaic representations at the Kariye Djami of the betrothal differ from the principal textual sources in the sign by which Joseph was designated as Mary's husband. The Protevangelium and Pseudo-Matthew speak only of the dove that issued from Joseph's rod. The Gospel of the Nativity of Mary, on the other hand, says that the Virgin should be entrusted to him "whose rod . . . should produce a flower, and upon the end of whose rod the Spirit of the Lord should settle in the form of a dove." The mosaic version represents a conflation of the story as told in the Protevangelium and Pseudo-Matthew and the story of the rebellion of Korah and the budding of Aaron's rod (Num. 16 and 17) to which all three texts allude. In art, three methods are used to indicate the Lord's choice of Joseph: sometimes only the dove appears; at other times the dove and the flowering rod occur together; and occasionally, as in the Kariye Djami, only the flowering rod is used as the sign. When the scene depicts the flowering of Joseph's rod rather than the dove, it is for purposes of iconographic analogy to Aaron's rod, to indicate that the latter was a prefiguration, or Old Testament prophecy, of the Virgin. This analogy is made evident in the two Kariye Djami mosaics of Mary's betrothal by the fact that twelve rods are depicted, in allusion to the twelve rods, one for each of the twelve tribes of Israel, which the Lord had demanded of Moses (Num. 17:2). The analogy between the Virgin and the rod of Aaron is made explicit by the high priest's act of holding the rod in one hand and firmly placing his other hand upon the head of the Virgin. This analogy, in turn, is commonly associated with the "rod out of the stem of Jesse" (Is. 11:1), which was universally interpreted as a prefiguration of the advent of Christ: "And there shall come forth a rod out of the stem of Jesse, and a Branch shall grow out of his roots." The Gospel of the Nativity of Mary quotes this very passage in relating the circumstances of Mary's betrothal to Joseph. It is evident, therefore, that the incidents of the rods of Aaron and Joseph and the prophecy concerning the "rod out of the stem of Jesse" were to be regarded as manifestations of the Incarnation.

Dimensions

Width between borders, measured at bottom, 2.425 m.; height between borders, 1.69 m.

Colors and Materials

ZACHARIAS tunic, blue with gold and red hem studded with gems (alternately red and blue) and pearls; short tunic with long sleeves, yellow with gold and red hem studded with pearls; mantle, red with gold and red border and gold and blue tablion studded with one blue and four red gems and pearls; hat, red crown and gray and blue brim; Joseph's rod, dark violet and greenish brown glass with green leaves. MARY clad entirely in blue. JOSEPH tunic, blue; himation, yellow. FOUR SUITORS OF FRONT RANK (to right of Joseph) *1*): Blue tunic and green himation. *2*): Blue tunic with red clavus, and violet himation. *3*): Yellow tunic and pink himation. *4*): Blue tunic and green himation. HOLY OF HOLIES like that of [95] in corresponding parts. WALL like that of [95]. BUILDING AT RIGHT stones of various values of warm gray; drawing of blue and violet; curtain, red; door and window openings, black; left jamb of door, light blue. DRAPERY red, with ornamental band of gold and blue. GROUND ZONE green glasses.

[97]

Joseph Taking the Virgin to His House   PL. 143–145

(Protevangelium 9:2)

'Ο 'Ιωσὴφ παραλαβὼν τὴν Θ(εοτό)κον ἀπέρ|χεται ἐν τῷ οἴκῳ αὐτοῦ.
Joseph, taking the Theotokos, goes to his house.

The scene of Joseph taking Mary to his house is in the western half of the transverse arch between the first and second bays. On this subject, which is rarely depicted, the Protevangelium merely says: "And Joseph was afraid, and took her to keep her for himself." In the mosaic the figures of Mary, Joseph, and one of Joseph's sons are placed before a symmetrically composed building, one of the few symmetrical representations of architecture in the Kariye Djami (see also [88] and [93]). This example differs from the others, however, in that the station point is high up so that one looks down upon the top of the building.

As in the two preceding scenes, Mary is represented with her covered hands held up before her. The artist has endeavored to indicate the rapid pace of her movements, and those of Joseph, by the agitated drawing of the drapery fluttering around their feet. Joseph, striding toward the right, is curiously, and most unsatisfactorily, drawn with his head not only in profile but turned completely around as he looks back over his shoulder at Mary. The youthful son of Joseph, at the right, also turns to look back toward the Virgin.

Judging from the inscription, one might suppose that the scene represents the arrival before the house of Joseph. There are several points, however, that serve to identify the building as the temple and the scene as representing the beginning of the journey rather than the arrival. The figures are moving briskly toward the right; all the gestures point in that direction and away from the building in the background. Furthermore, the building is an apsidal structure; though depicted from an entirely different point of view, it is to be compared with the apsidal building in the scene of the skeins of wool [94], which represents a temple. It is presented, however, not merely as an indication of setting for the narrative, but also as a symbol identifying the Virgin with the Temple of the Lord. Evidence for this identification is found in the center of the apse, above the curtained doorway, where there is a lunette containing a haloed bust that should be interpreted as an icon of the Virgin. This little image is the counterpart of one that appears in a similar setting above the closed gate of the city of Jerusalem in the Kariye Djami fresco of the Angel Smiting the Assyrians before Jerusalem [235]. It will be seen that that incident was used as an Old Testament prefiguration of the Virgin, in which the city of Jerusalem typified the Virgin. The two images may also be compared with the equally small representation of the Virgin on the vase held by Moses [73], in the mosaics of the northern dome, where the intention was to liken the Virgin to the stamnos that contained the manna.

Dimensions

Width between borders, 1.03 m.; height, on curved surface, from top of inscription to top of mosaic border above cornice, 2.04 m.

Colors and Materials

MARY clad entirely in blue, with red shoes. JOSEPH tunic, blue with red clavus; himation, yellow. SON OF JOSEPH pantaloons, yellow with red ornamental

bands; short tunic with long sleeves, blue with gold and red collar, cuffs, and sleeve band; mantle, violet.
ARCHITECTURE curved inner surface of wall, violet; columns, green with capitals of reddish violet stone and gold; imposts, warm gray stone with drawing of violet stone; top surface of apse wall, cool gray stone; bases of towers, lighted faces, cool gray stone with slits and drawing of light blue glass; bases of towers,

shaded faces, blue glass with slits of dark blue; pyramidal roofs of towers, three values of blue with white stone highlights; floor of porch, cool gray stones with drawing of light blue glass; low wall at sides, warm gray stones. CURTAIN IN DOOR red and gold. DRAPERY SWAG red with edgings of gold and shadings and shadows of dark violet glass. GROUND in two zones of green glasses.

[98]

The Annunciation to the Virgin at the Well

PL. 146–147

(Protevangelium 11:1; Pseudo-Matthew 9; Gospel of the Nativity of Mary 9)

Ὁ εἰς τὸ φρέαρ εὐαγγελισμὸς   *The annunciation at the well*

The scene of the Annunciation at the Well, in the southwestern pendentive of the northern bay, is wedged between the scene of Joseph Taking the Virgin to His House [97] and that of Joseph Taking Leave of the Virgin [99]. This position in the cycle makes the chronology of events differ from that recorded in the Protevangelium, the basic textual account of Mary's life. The Annunciation should come after Joseph takes leave of Mary [99], and even after Mary's summons to the temple to receive the purple wool [94] and her return to Joseph's house to spin the wool (unillustrated). It will be seen in the discussion of the next two scenes [99] that the mosaicist had an iconographic purpose in representing the Annunciation as an event that preceded Joseph's departure.

According to the Protevangelium, it was while Mary was engaged in spinning the wool that "she took the pitcher and went forth to fill it with water: and lo a voice saying: Hail, thou that art highly favoured; the Lord is with thee: blessed art thou among women. And she looked about her upon the right hand and upon the left to see whence this voice should be."

It is this moment that the mosaicist has attempted to depict. Filling the lower angle of the pendentive is the open well, which is surrounded, as though in a courtyard, by Joseph's house. With one foot on the second step of the well and a golden pitcher in her right hand, Mary appears to have been stooping over the well when she was startled by the voice. The artist has succeeded in capturing the movements of Mary's surprise; she turns sharply toward the right, raising her left foot far behind her and her left hand toward the flying angel, who appears from above and from the right.

Colors and Materials

MARY clad entirely in blue; gold edging on mantle and headdress; shoes, red; pitcher, gold tesserae, some set on sides, and clear amber-colored glass; cord attached to pitcher, red. ANGEL tunic (right sleeve visible), blue; mantle, green; wings, violet glass in dark areas, light brownish stones in middle tones, short strokes of gold for highlights; staff, red capped by three pearls.

WELL curved vertical faces, violet with light brownish stone highlights; opening of well, violet and black; horizontal faces, cool gray and white stones. WALL IN CENTER BACKGROUND dull light yellow stone with coping of dull brownish and white stones.
BUILDING AT LEFT narrow front faces, violet; receding face at left of two lower stories, dull reddish brown stone; other receding walls, violet with slashes of gray and white to indicate highlights; doorway of

82

lower story, black; column shafts of green glass, capitals of gold, clear green, and amber; drapery on roof, green.

BUILDING AT RIGHT   narrow front of first story, brownish gray stone, doorway black, and drawing of gold and clear glasses; receding side at right, mixed clear glasses (greens and ambers) with some gold; flat roofs

of two lower stories, gold; column shafts and bases, green; column capitals, blue, white, and gray; curved roof of upper story, red glass, terra cotta, and white stone; drapery, red.

TREES   branches, greenish brown and violet glasses and yellowish gray and white stones; leaves, green bordered with blue.

[99]

Joseph Taking Leave of the Virgin   PL. 148–150

(*Protevangelium 9:2*)

Ἰδοὺ καταλιμπάνω σε ἐν τῷ | οἴκῳ μου. Ἐγὼ γὰρ ἀπέρχο|μαι οἰκοδομεῖν
Behold, I am leaving thee in my house while I go away to build.

Μ(ήτ)ηρ Θ(εο)ῦ   *Mother of God*

Joseph Reproaching the Virgin   PL. 148, 151

(*Protevangelium 8; Pseudo-Matthew 10; Gospel of the Nativity of Mary 10*)

Μαρία, τί | τὸ δράγμα [sic; δρᾶμα?, πρᾶγμα?] τοῦτο   *Mary, what is this thy deed?*

Μ(ήτ)ηρ Θ(εο)ῦ   *Mother of God*

The two scenes of Joseph Taking Leave of the Virgin and Joseph Reproaching the Virgin, the last of the illustrations of the life of Mary in the mosaics of the inner narthex, are placed together in a single lunette on the western wall of the northern bay. According to the literary accounts, two important events that were depicted out of their proper sequence (the distribution of skeins of wool [94] and the Annunciation [98]), and one that was not illustrated at all in the mosaics (the Visitation), intervene between the two subjects. It would seem, therefore, that the scenes were placed side by side in one lunette for reasons of iconographic content and antithesis of subject matter, Joseph's departure at the left and Joseph's return at the right. On the subject of Joseph taking leave of the Virgin, the Protevangelium says: "And Joseph said unto Mary: Lo, I have received thee out of the temple of the Lord: and now do I leave thee in my house, and I go away to build my buildings and I will come again unto thee." This text, it is clear, was used, with modifications, as the source for the inscription in the mosaic.

In the scene of Joseph's departure, the Virgin stands at the left in an attitude whose meaning is not evident from a reading of the text; her head bent over to rest on her shoulder, and her hands crossed in front of her at the waist, she appears to be greatly troubled and perhaps humiliated. Beside her in the lower left corner of the lunette is a tree stump, its main branches dead or cut off, from which one new stem, laden with foliage and fruit, has sprouted. The stump is repeated at the opposite corner of the lunette, again beside the figure of the Virgin. In the gold of the background, above and to the left, is the inscription, "Mother of God." Joseph, to the right, speaks the words of farewell that are inscribed above and turns to follow his young helper, one of his sons, who has already set off on the journey that is to keep Joseph away for some six months. The youth, with a basket of carpenter's tools on his back, looks back toward Mary and Joseph as he strides away toward the right. The scene is laid before two houses that are connected by a wall and a piece of billowing drapery stretching from roof to roof. Mary and the youth stand before the houses; Joseph stands before the wall in the center.

Despite the testimony of the narrative texts that the Annunciation to Mary, and her conception, occurred after the departure of Joseph, there are a number of indications, in addition to the sequence in which the scenes occur, that the mosaicist deliberately represented the Virgin as having already conceived prior to Joseph's departure. The Virgin's attitude of humiliation strongly suggests this, as does the fact that Mary is now designated, for the first time in the cycle except for the isolated instance in scene [92], as "Mother of God," as she will be from this point onward through the scenes of Christ's infancy. There may be some significance, also, in the apparently dead root of a tree that has put forth a living branch, a motif not used before in the cycle but in this lunette placed close beside the Virgin each time she is represented. Indeed, a similar motif will appear in the next two lunettes, which present other events during the pregnancy of Mary. In the first example of this motif, in the scene of departure, the mosaicist has taken an unusual measure in representing what may be blossoms and fruit on the living branch of the tree; he has used for this purpose white stones and specially cut pieces of fine white ware with a brilliant turquoise glaze on both sides, a material that is used nowhere else in the mosaics of the Kariye Djami.

In these scenes the motif of the living root might be interpreted, therefore, as a reference to the prophecy (Is. 11:1): "And there shall come forth a rod out of the stem of Jesse, and a Branch shall grow out of his roots." The rod signifies the Virgin, and the branch out of his roots is interpreted as Christ. Such an analogy would be a culmination of the iconography developed previously in the mosaics in the analogies between Joseph's rod and the rod of Aaron (see above, [96]) as symbols of the Incarnation.

In the scene of Joseph Reproaching the Virgin, in the right side of the lunette, the upper halves of the figures of Joseph and Mary and parts of the architectural background have been destroyed. On his return after a lapse of six months, according to the Protevangelium, Joseph "found her great with child. And he smote his face, and cast himself down upon the ground on sackcloth and wept bitterly." On arising from the ground, Joseph likens himself to Adam, and, quoting from the words the Lord had addressed to Eve (Gen. 3:13), he asks in accusation of the Virgin, "What is this that thou hast done (τί τοῦτο ἐποίησας)?" In view of the dependence of the inscription in the preceding scene upon the text of the Protevangelium, it is probable that the inscription for this scene, in its intended meaning, would have paraphrased that source and the words of Genesis. For that reason it is here suggested that the mosaicist was in error in using the word *dragma* (sheaf) instead of *drama* (deed) or *pragma* (in the sense of matter, or business).

For the sake of balance and symmetry in the lunette as a whole the sequence of the figures is the reverse of that in the left side; Joseph is at the left and Mary, with the tree stump in mirror reversal beside her, is at the far right. Joseph stands with his staff in his hand before the entrance portico of his house and confronts Mary, who is placed before another vertical element of the architectural background. Between the two structures is the inscription, "Mother

84

of God." Above the house a second piece of drapery is stretched from a tree at the left to the roof of the building at the right.

Dimensions

Width of lunette at base, within borders, 3.15 m.; height at center, within borders, 1.715 m.; area of lost mosaic, ca. 94 cm. by 57 cm.

Colors and Materials

Joseph Taking Leave of the Virgin (*left*)

MARY clad entirely in blue; gold edging on mantle and headdress; shoes, red.   JOSEPH tunic, blue with dark blue clavus; himation, yellow.   SON OF JOSEPH short tunic, red with gold cuff; mantle wrapped about body, blue; pantaloons, yellow; boots, violet; braided basket, yellow and white stones with darks in alternating strokes of clear violet and clear greenish glasses; opening of basket in same clear glasses.

HOUSE AT LEFT lighted faces, grayish yellow stone; shaded faces, grayish brown stone; opening of door and dark borders around it, violet glass; roofs, blue glass with gray and white stone; stoop, bluish gray stone with drawing of blue glass and white stone.   HOUSE AT RIGHT lighted faces, predominantly bluish gray and elsewhere grayish yellow stone; drawing in violet glass; shaded faces, violet glass highlighted by gray and white stone; flat roof areas, light bluish gray stone; curved roof, blue glass and gray and white stones.   DRAPERY red with ornaments of blue and gold.   TREE AT LOWER LEFT stump, greenish brown glass at left and violet at right; foliage, green and black; fruit, white stone, and on lower right branch cut pieces of fine white ware (ca. 4.5 mm. thick) with turquoise glaze on both front and back sides.

Joseph Reproaching the Virgin (*right*)

JOSEPH tunic, blue; himation, yellow; staff, gray stone at left and green glass at right.   MARY clad in blue mantle with gold edging; shoes, red.

HOUSE AT LEFT lighted faces, brownish yellow, bluish gray, and white stones; shaded faces, mat brown stone like that used in house in [85], but of slightly lighter value; flat roofs, bluish gray and white stone.   HOUSE AND WALL AT RIGHT lighted faces, grayish yellow stone with drawing in brownish yellow stone; shaded faces, violet; window, black.   DRAPERY red with ornaments of blue and gold.   TREE AT LOWER RIGHT similar in materials and colors to tree at lower left in preceding scene, but glazed ware is omitted.

85

THE CYCLE OF THE INFANCY OF CHRIST

[100]

Joseph Dreaming

(Matthew 1:20; Protevangelium 14:2; Pseudo-Matthew 11; Gospel of the Nativity of Mary 10)

Ἰδοὺ ἄγγελος Κυ(ρίου) κατ᾽ ὄναρ ἐφάνη αὐτῷ λέγων, | Ἰωσὴφ υἱὸς Δα(βί)δ, μὴ φοβηθῇς παραλαβεῖν Μαριὰμ | τὴν γυναῖκά σου, τὸ γὰρ ἐν αὐτῇ γεννηθὲν ἐκ πν(εύματό)ς ἐστιν ἁγίου.

Behold, the angel of the Lord appeared unto him in a dream, saying, Joseph, thou son of David, fear not to take unto thee Mary thy wife: for that which is conceived in her is of the Holy Ghost. (Matt. 1:20)

The Virgin and Two Companions

PL. 152–154

Μ(ήτ)ηρ Θ(εο)ῦ *Mother of God*

The Journey to Bethlehem

PL. 152, 155–158

(Luke 2:4; Protevangelium 17:2; Pseudo-Matthew 13; Gospel of the Nativity of Mary 10)

Ἀνέβη δὲ καὶ Ἰωσὴφ ἀπὸ τῆς Γαλιλαίας, ἐκ πόλεως | Ναζαρὲτ εἰς τὴν Ἰουδαίαν εἰς πόλιν Δα(βί)δ, ἥτις καλεῖται | Βηθλεέμ,

And Joseph also went up from Galilee, out of the city of Nazareth, into Judaea, unto the city of David, which is called Bethlehem . . . (Luke 2:4)

To take up the narrative at the point where it breaks off in the inner narthex, it is necessary to turn to the mosaics of the outer narthex, where succeeding events in the lives of the Virgin and Christ are depicted in the series of lunettes that makes a complete circuit of the walls. This part of the narrative forms a cycle that begins where the canonical Gospels take up the story of the birth and infancy of Christ and that may be called the Infancy Cycle. It will be seen that, while most of the events depicted in this cycle are recounted both in the Apocrypha and in the Gospels, the inscriptions, in most cases, will be found to quote directly from the Gospels. In a number of instances, however, the iconography will appear to be closer in detail to the apocryphal sources than to the narrative of the Gospels.

The cycle of the Infancy begins in the lunette on the wall at the northern end of the narthex, in which three scenes are merged within a single landscape setting. At the left is the scene of Joseph Dreaming. He lies asleep on his pallet, his himation drawn about him in sharp folds and

86

his head resting on his right hand. Above, hovering in flight, the angel extends his right hand toward Joseph in a gesture of speaking; in his left hand he holds a scepter. Above the angel, the first of the two lengthy inscriptions quotes the words addressed to Joseph as they are recorded in the Gospel of Matthew. In the lower left corner, serving as a space filler, is a gnarled tree trunk with foliage on one branch. Another, much like it, appears in the opposite corner of the lunette.

The second scene in the lunette is depicted in the background above and to the right of the first. Partly concealed behind a hill are the tightly grouped figures of Mary, who is inscribed as Mother of God, and two women companions; the scene was previously thought to represent the Visitation. The woman in profile at the left is dressed in red; Mary stands in frontal pose at the right and is dressed, as usual, in blue. Between Mary's nimbus and the woman at the left there is visible a small part of a third woman, whose headdress and garments are green. The three women appear to be engaged in conversation as they approach the foot of a steep hill at the right, toward which Mary points. In the background, and partly obscured from view by the hill, are the walls and houses of a town, probably Nazareth, from which the women may be thought to have emerged.

The identification of this subject is somewhat problematical in view of the absence of an inscription. It seems clear, however, that it cannot represent the Visitation. According to the Protevangelium (15 and 16), immediately after Joseph had dreamed he and Mary were summoned to the temple in Nazareth to undergo the trial by water, an event that has been omitted from the mosaics of the Kariye Djami. First Joseph drank of the water and was sent to the hill country to die if he were judged by the Lord to have been guilty of adultery. When Joseph returned whole, Mary was likewise given to drink and sent to the hill country, and she too was vindicated by the Lord and returned whole. It seems most probable that the motif of Mary and her companions before Nazareth, and at the foot of the hill, is the only recognition of the apocryphal story of the trial by water to appear in the mosaics and represents the departure of Mary to the hill country. The Protevangelium, like the mosaic, places this event between Joseph's Dream and The Journey to Bethlehem.[1]

At the right is the major scene in the composition, The Journey to Bethlehem, which occupies somewhat more than half of the lunette. In response to the decree of Caesar Augustus that all should be taxed, the family of Joseph journeyed from Nazareth to Bethlehem to be enrolled. The mosaic depicts the journey in more literal conformity to the text of the Protevangelium, although the inscription quotes from Luke. The apocryphal source says: "And . . . [Joseph] saddled the she-ass, and set . . . [Mary] upon it, and his son led it and Joseph followed after." The movement of all three figures, in the prescribed order, is toward the right; an unusual composition is thus produced, in which all figures appear to be walking out of the picture and toward the scene of the enrollment itself, in the adjoining lunette at the right. This first composition of the

1 Several of the frescoes in the monastic church at Kalenić appear to have been copied from the mosaics of the Kariye Djami or from another source, either a sketch book or a wall painting, which drew directly from them. Among these is a painting which in composition and details closely resembles our mosaic [100] and depicts the same three incidents, including that of Mary and a companion leaving a walled town. This is the only other example of this subject known to me. See V. R. Petković and A. Ž. Tatić, *Manastir Kalenić* (Na-rodni muzej u Beogradu, Srpski spomenici, IV, Belgrade, 1926), Figs. 42, 43. Other paintings at Kalenić which may have been modeled on mosaics at the Kariye Djami are The Enrollment for Taxation (Petković and Tatić, Fig. 44), The Adoration of the Magi (Fig. 45), and The Return of the Magi to the East (Fig. 46); the last two paintings may provide a basis for reconstructions of their counterparts at the Kariye Djami. See discussion of mosaic [105], below.

series in the lunettes of the outer narthex thereby serves as a signpost indicating the starting point and the direction that the spectator is to pursue in viewing this cycle of mosaics.

Joseph, with the slight stoop and the mincing gait of an old man, follows behind the donkey on which Mary is seated. His gaze is directed toward Mary, who turns her head toward him. It is characteristic that she and the animal should be centered before the mountainous background, the most commanding element of the composition. Leading the way at the far right is one of Joseph's sons, his billowing mantle and a bundle of provisions for the journey slung from the end of a staff across his shoulder.

Dimensions

Width of lunette at bottom, within borders, 3.58 m.; height of lunette within borders, 1.715 m.

Colors and Materials
Joseph Dreaming (*left*)

JOSEPH tunic, blue; himation, yellow; halo, gold with border of light blue (with few exceptions borders of haloes are red; blue was used here to contrast with red pallet behind it). PALLET pink and white stones above and red glasses below figure of Joseph. ANGEL tunic, blue; himation, violet; wings, red, tan, and translucent glasses in left sides and blue glass and gray and white stones in right sides; scepter, red glass with three white stones (pearls) at top.

The Virgin and Two Companions

WOMAN AT LEFT clad entirely in red. MARY clad in blue garments with gold edging. WOMAN AT CENTER (part of headdress, lower left side of chin, and part of shoulder are visible between heads at each side) headdress, very dark green at top; chin, small yellowish green glass tesserae such as are used in modeling faces; dress at shoulder, two values of green.

The Journey to Bethlehem (*right*)

JOSEPH tunic, blue; himation, yellow. MARY clad entirely in blue garments with gold edging. DONKEY four values of cool gray stones, with white stone highlights; bridle, red glasses; saddle, pink and white stones, terra cotta, and red glasses. JOSEPH'S SON loose-sleeved tunic, yellow with blue hem; mantle, red; leggings, blue glass and gray stone with black drawing; staff, green glass; bundle, blue.

Landscape and Architecture

TREES AT FAR LEFT AND RIGHT trunks, green, greenish brown, and black glasses; foliage, green of two contrasting hues and black. WALL BEHIND JOSEPH DREAMING warm yellowish gray stone. MOUNTAIN (beginning at lower left, below Joseph Dreaming, and extending across remaining width of lunette) mainly in one of lighter values of violet glass, but with outlines and shaded parts of darker violet; highlights, white stone. TOWN lighted faces of fortress walls, warm yellowish gray stone; shaded faces of fortress walls, light violet glass; houses, walls of gray stones and roofs of red glass, pink marble, and white stone; two trees at left, blue; two trees at right, green.

[101]

The Enrollment for Taxation

PL. 159–165

(*Luke 2:4–5; Protevangelium 17:1; Pseudo-Matthew 13*)

διὰ τὸ εἶναι αὐτὸν ἐξ οἴκου καὶ πατριᾶς Δα(βί)δ, ἀπο|γράψασθαι σὺν Μαριὰμ τῇ μεμνηστευμένῃ | αὐτῷ γυναικὶ οὔσῃ ἐγκύῳ.

. . . because he was of the house and lineage of David . . . To be taxed with Mary his espoused wife, being great with child. (*Luke 2:4–5*)

Μ(ήτ)ηρ Θ(εο)ῦ *Mother of God*

The scene of enrollment in Bethlehem occupies the first of the lunettes along the eastern wall of the outer narthex, adjoining the Journey to Bethlehem. Its inscription continues the text of Luke that was quoted in the preceding scene.

At the far left a fully armed military guard stands beside Cyrenius, the governor of Syria, who supervises the enrollment decreed by Caesar Augustus (Luke 2:1–2). The governor sits on a cushioned golden throne, his feet resting on a footstool. He wears a military cape, or chlamys, attached at the right shoulder by a fibula, and on his head is a hat which in some respects resembles that of Theodore Metochites [3] but which curves forward to a sharp point. In his right hand he holds a white cylindrical object (not a scroll), apparently a badge of authority. Standing a little apart and in the center of the scene are a scribe and a second military guard. The scribe, who wears a short, long-sleeved tunic over a full-length garment, holds an unfurled scroll, on which he inscribes the names. The second guard, an older man, holding a sheathed sword vertically beside him in his left hand, takes part in the interrogation. All these representatives of the military authority face toward Mary, who stands somewhat isolated from all the others at the right but on whom all attention is focused. An unusually tall figure, Mary stands erect, her head bowed toward the officers, and draws her maphorion modestly about her shoulder. Above and to the left of her nimbus is the inscription "Mother of God." At the far right, with his four sons behind him, stands the nimbed figure of Joseph, leaning forward to assist and sustain the Virgin.

As the two important persons in the confrontation, Cyrenius and Mary are given special prominence in the composition by their greater proportions and dignity and by their placement symmetrically, and alone, before two tower-like structures. A low wall runs across the entire width of the panel, separating the figures and architecture in the foreground from a more distant building at the far left and a gnarled tree with a single living branch that rises behind the wall to the left of the Virgin.

Dimensions

Width of lunette at bottom, within borders, 2.51 m.; height of lunette within borders, 1.705 m.; height of guard at far left, .93 m.; height of guard at center, .90 m.; height of Virgin (without nimbus), .94 m.

Colors and Materials

GUARD AT FAR LEFT trousers, green; leggings, gray and white stones and blue glasses; short tunic, red with gold cuffs; armor, gold and translucent amber-colored glasses; girdle, breastband, and collar, gray stones and blue glass; mantle, blue; spear, violet and black shaft and blue and gray head; shield, bluish gray and white stones with ornaments of blue glass; sword, blue scabbard ornamented with gold, gold and brown hilt, and red thong. CYRENIUS tunic, blue, decorated at hem, breast, and cuffs with gold and red bands; chlamys, red with red and gold fibula centered with blue gem; hat, white and tan stones with red bindings; cylindrical object in right hand, white stone; boots, red; throne and footstool, gold in all lighted faces and translucent amber-colored and green glasses in shaded faces; cushion, green. SCRIBE long tunic, red with gold and red hem; short tunic with long sleeves, blue ornamented with gold and red hem and collar and gold and amber-colored cuffs; boots, blue; scroll, white and tan stones with black simulated writing; inkwells above hand, one square and one small and round, gold, translucent, and black glasses. GUARD AT CENTER trousers, blue; leggings,

yellow and white stones and greenish brown glass; short tunic, armor, and sword, similar to those of other soldier.

MARY clad entirely in blue; gold edging on headdress; shoes, red. JOSEPH tunic, blue; himation, brownish yellow stone with deepest shadows of very dark violet glass and an unusual brown stone and highlights of bluish gray and white stone. JOSEPH'S SONS *Son at far right:* trousers of green glass and bluish gray stone ornamented with bands of gold and red; leggings, blue glass and gray stone; short tunic, blue with gold and red hem and collar; mantle, red. *Son in background:* tunic, green with gold and red collar and hem. THE BACKGROUND *Colonnaded building at left:* lighted faces, light greenish brown glasses with green, gray, and white drawing; shaded faces, green glasses; flat roof, tiles of blue glasses highlighted with gray stone; floor of upper portico, bluish gray stone; column shafts, dark green glasses; capitals and bases, gold. *Structure at right:* lower story and two-stepped podium, bluish gray stone in lighted faces, blue glass in shaded faces; upper story, warm gray stones in lighted faces, light violet glass with cast shadows of dark violet in shaded faces. *Horizontal wall:* yellowish gray stone; drawing in brown stone; small window at far left, dark violet and black. *Small building at far left:* lighted faces, bluish gray stones; shaded faces, blue glass. *Drapery:* red with gold and blue band. *Tree at center:* branches, brown stones and violet glasses; foliage, green and black; fruit (?), white.

89

[102]

The Nativity

PL. 166–172

(Luke 2:6–14; Protevangelium 18–20; Pseudo-Matthew 13)

Ἡ Χ(ριστο)ῦ γέ|ννησις   *The birth of Christ*

Μὴ φοβεῖσθε, | ἰδοὺ γὰρ εὐαγγελίζομαι | ὑμῖν χαρὰν μεγάλην ἥτις | ἔσται
παντὶ τῷ λαῷ.
*Fear not: for, behold, I bring you good tidings of great joy, which shall be to
all people.*   *(Luke 2:10)*

As is usual in monumental Byzantine versions of the subject, the mosaic of the Nativity, in the
eastern lunette of the second bay of the outer narthex, is a composite of a number of incidents
connected with the birth of Christ. Mary and the Child in the cave, the annunciation to the
shepherds, the heralding angels, the bathing of the Child, and the seated Joseph are distinct
themes that are distributed over a single hilly landscape. It is noteworthy that the theme of the
Magi approaching Bethlehem has been omitted, probably because their role in the Nativity was
to be fully depicted in the four succeeding lunettes.

Mary reclines on a pallet at the foot of the highest hill, in the center of the composition. In a
small cave above her [1] the newborn infant, wrapped in swaddling cloths and bearing a cross-
nimbus, lies in a stone manger. The ox and the ass peer at the Child from behind the manger, and
a ray of light shines directly down upon him from a golden star in an arc of heaven at the top of
the lunette.

In the right side of the composition, the angel of the annunciation, partly concealed by the
central hill, leans forward with outspread wings and addresses the shepherds in the words that
are inscribed above. He carries a jeweled staff in his left hand and makes a gesture of speaking
with his extended right hand. On the slope of a lower hill at the right, three shepherds, diagonally
aligned, react in various ways to the appearance of the angel. At the left, the standing shepherd,
with a bundle on his back and a stick in his left hand, seems to recoil with fear; he raises his right
hand in a defensive gesture. Seated near him and holding a shepherd's pipe in his right hand is
another youth, who leans back and touches an old shepherd at his left as though seeking or giving
reassurance. Unlike his young companions, who are simply dressed in short tunics and leggings,
the old man wears a fur mantle over a long tunic; in his left hand he holds a gnarled stick. The
jutting head, hunched posture, and hands resting passively on the knees are all expressive of
feebleness and old age. Lying and standing before the shepherds, and partly concealed by the
central hill, is the flock which they have been tending.

Emerging from behind the hill, at the upper left behind the Virgin, is a group of four angels,
their heads and hands raised toward the glory of the heavens as though in praise. These are the

---

1 In Byzantine art the place of Christ's birth is always a cave (the grotto of the Nativity),
as is specified by the Protevangelium, 18:1.

heavenly host who appeared after the annunciation to the shepherds, saying: "Glory to God in the highest, and on earth peace, good will toward men" (Luke 2:13–14).

The bathing of the Child, or rather, the preparation for the bath, fills the lower left foreground of the composition. At the far left a midwife stands facing toward the right and pours water from a golden vessel, rather like an oenochoë in form, into a large golden basin, or font, raised on a pedestal. A second midwife, facing the basin from the opposite side, holds the nude infant on her lap in the folds of her mantle, which she has slipped from her shoulders; her hair is covered by a cloth wound around her head in the manner of a turban.

The solitary figure of Joseph is seated on a small mound in the foreground at the right. Drawn in near-profile, with his chin resting on his right hand and his elbow on his right knee, he gazes pensively toward the Christ Child in the scene of bathing at the left and contemplates the significance of the events he has witnessed.

As do all the mosaics that deal with events between Christ's conception and his birth ([99] to [102]), the scene of the Nativity includes, in close proximity to the Virgin, the stump of a tree, from which a single living branch has sprouted. It appears here on the axis of the composition, directly beneath Mary and the manger, in the very midst of all the events connected with the birth of Christ. As was suggested above in the discussion of the first of the mosaics [99], this motif seems to refer to the prophecy concerning the branch that was to grow out of the root of Jesse, that is to say, to the Incarnation.

Dimensions

Width of lunette at bottom, within borders, 2.59 m.; height of lunette within borders, 1.73 m.; figure of Mary, from head to toe, .76 m.

Colors and Materials

MARY   clad entirely in blue with gold edging on mantle and headdress; shoes, red; halo, gold outlined with single row of blue glass; pallet, red glass, terra cotta, and pink stone.   CHILD AND MANGER   swaddling cloths, gray and white stones and blue glasses; halo, gold, with cross outlined in red; interior of manger, violet; rim of manger, white and gray stones; exterior of manger, greenish brown glasses and gray and white stones.   OX   yellow and gray stones and greenish brown glass; horns and shadows, violet; area within ray of light, bluish gray and white stones and blue glass.   ASS   bluish gray and white stones.   CAVE INTERIOR   black glass.   ARC OF HEAVEN (exterior to interior)   one row white stone, three rows light bluish gray stone, five rows dark bluish gray stone, five rows light blue glass; star, gold.
ANGEL OF ANNUNCIATION   tunic, blue; clavus, red edged with violet; mantle, green glasses in darks, gray and white stones in lights; staff, red bordered at right with black; head of staff, decorated with four pearls and one green gem; wings, underfeathers of blue glass and gray and white stones and main feathers of mixed translucent glasses (amber, light greens, violets).
SHEPHERDS (left to right)   1) short tunic, blue; sash,

red glass, pink and white stone; bundle, yellowish brown; fur boots, blue glasses and gray stone; stick, green glasses.   2) short-sleeved tunic, red; leggings, green glasses and gray and white stones; pipe, light yellow and brownish gray glass with holes of black.   3) long tunic, yellow; fur mantle, blue glass, gray and white stones; shoes, terra cotta and red glass; stick, green and grayish brown glasses.   FLOCK   blue-gray and white stones and greenish brown, violet, and black glasses.
HERALDING ANGELS (left to right)   1) mantle, yellow; wings like those of angel of annunciation (see above).   2) tunic, blue; mantle, violet.   3) tunic, blue with red clavus; mantle, green.   4) tunic, blue; mantle, yellow.   MIDWIFE, LEFT   sleeveless garment, blue; outer garment, red; water jug, gold with designs of translucent glasses (amber, violets, greens).   MIDWIFE, RIGHT   short-sleeved garment, blue with dark blue collar bordered with gold and red and gold and red cuffs; sleeveless garment, yellow; mantle over lower parts of figure, green; turban, blue.   NUDE CHRIST CHILD   body, pink and white marbles; hair, light brownish glass; drawing and outlining, red glass; halo, gold with red border and cross.   BASIN   gold with designs of translucent glasses (amber, violets, greens).   JOSEPH   tunic, blue with red clavus; himation, grayish yellow and white stones, with shadows of raw-sienna-colored glass.   TREE STUMP   green glasses, a few gray stones; foliage, green and black.
LANDSCAPE   *Main hill, at center:* upper slope, light yellowish gray stone with bluish gray and white stone highlights and contour outlines in blue glass at upper

left and violet glass elsewhere; steep slopes, left and center, darker grayish yellow stone in two values used alternately in facets of hill; shading of right contour, three values of violet glass. *Hill at right* (with shep-

herds): treated like upper parts of main hill. *Foreground:* low mounds of bluish gray stone outlined and shaded with green glasses; narrow zone at base of panel, green.

[103]

The Journey of the Magi

PL. 173, 176

(Matthew 2:1–2; Protevangelium 21:1, 3; Pseudo-Matthew 16)

Κ(αὶ) ἰδοὺ μάγ(οι) ἀπὸ ἀνατολ(ῶν) παρεγένοντ(ο) | εἰς Ἱ(εροσό)λυμ(α) λέγοντ(ες). Ποῦ ἐστὶν ὁ τεχθεὶς | βασιλεὺς τῶν Ἰουδαίων.

And behold, there came wise men from the east to Jerusalem, Saying, Where is he that is born King of the Jews? (Matt. 2:1–2)

The Magi before Herod

PL. 173–175

(Matthew 2:7, 8; Protevangelium 21:2; Pseudo-Matthew 16)

The Journey of the Magi, an incident that is sometimes included in compositions of the Nativity, is combined here with the appearance of the Magi before Herod, in the eastern lunette of the fourth bay. These are the first of five events dealing with the quest of the Magi and Herod for the King of the Jews which were originally represented in the mosaics of the Infancy Cycle in the Chora. Of the other three, two (Herod Inquiring of the Priests and Scribes [104], and The Return of the Magi to the East [105]) are preserved in fragmentary state and one (in all probability The Adoration of the Magi) has been totally destroyed.

At the left, the three Magi, mounted on spirited horses, ride over a mountainous trail in pursuit of the star of Bethlehem, which is shown within a circle in the upper center of the panel. The first Magus, a beardless youth drawn in profile, mounted on a gray horse, points to the star. Behind him, the second Magus, riding a dun horse, is also drawn in profile but is represented as a middle-aged man with a short, dark beard, while the third, on a black horse, is an old man with a long, gray beard. The costumes of the three Magi in certain respects resemble those of the priests and the Three Hebrew Youths and Daniel in the mosaics of the inner narthex. They include the anaxyrides (tight trousers), boots, a long tunic, a mantle, usually fastened by a small fibula at the neck, and a small sacerdotal hat, or miter, such as is worn by the Hebrew priests throughout the mosaics.

In the scene of The Magi before Herod, the three wise men stand in a row at the left facing the enthroned king. They are arranged in the order in which they appeared in the Journey: the youth at the left, the middle-aged wise man in the center, and the old wise man at the right. The first, who is shown in an attitude of walking, his hands extended before him, appears to be speaking to Herod. The old man holds a golden casket with a gabled cover—the container for their precious gifts—in the folds of his mantle. Herod, seated on a cushioned throne with his feet on a footstool, turns toward the Magi and extends his right hand in a gesture of speaking. An armed guard stands at the far right behind the throne. The costumes of the Magi are like those worn in the preceding scene. Herod wears a richly decorated tunic, a chlamys fastened by a fibula at the right shoulder and ornamented with a tablion, and a crown, and in his left hand he holds a sword.

This second scene in the lunette is out of its proper chronological order, for according to the texts Herod consulted his priests and scribes (an incident illustrated in the next lunette, [104]) before soliciting the Magi for information regarding the birthplace of Christ, whom he secretly wished to destroy.

Dimensions

Width of lunette within borders, 1.925 m.; height within borders, 1.65 m.

Colors and Materials

The Journey of the Magi

YOUNG MAGUS trousers, violet with ornamental band of gold and red; boots, red; tunic, blue with gold and blue cuff; mantle, red; hat, red and gold; horse, cool gray stones (3 values) with white stone in highlights; saddlecloth, gold and red; saddle, red glass, terra cotta, pink and white stones; girth and headstall, gold and red; all other harness, red. SECOND MAGUS tunic, violet; mantle, blue and black; hat, red crown and white and blue brim; horse, light yellow and brown stones with outline drawing in very porous, dull black stone. OLD MAGUS trousers, yellow; boots, red; tunic, green, with gold and red embroidery on breast; mantle, red; fibula, blue; hat, red crown and white and blue brim; horse, black clinker-like stone and dark gray stones, and in darkest parts black glass; girth and headstall, gold and red; other harness, red. STAR eight points and circular center, gold; circular background, blue; border of circle, two rows of bluish gray stone and one row of white stone. INSCRIPTION mixed blue glasses (the usual material is black glass).

The Magi before Herod

YOUNG MAGUS long tunic, green with gold and red hem and cuffs; mantle, red with edgings of gold and red; fibula, blue; hat, red crown and blue and white brim; boots, red. SECOND MAGUS trousers, violet; boots, blue; tunic, blue with gold and red hem and collar; mantle, green with gold and red edging and ornament; hat, red crown and blue and white brim. OLD MAGUS tunic, blue with gold and red hem; mantle, red with gold and red edging; hat, red crown with blue and white brim; boots, red with gold ornament; casket, gold, with gabled lid drawn in violet glass and lower parts drawn in greenish brown.

HEROD *Tunic:* solid blue glass with hem of gold and red studded with red lozenge-shaped gems flanked by pairs of pearls; cuffs, gold and red; collar and rectangular ornament at breast, gold and red studded with red lozenge-shaped gem and pearls. *Mantle:* red with gold and red edging and gold and red tablion studded with red lozenge-shaped gem and pearls; fibula, a single large, round piece of gold glass. *Crown:* gold and red studded with a lozenge-shaped blue gem and pearls and on top a free-standing red gem, one large piece of glass. THRONE AND FOOTSTOOL lighted faces, gold with drawing in greenish brown glass; shaded faces, dull, porous brownish yellow stone with drawing in greenish brown glass; cushion, green. MILITARY GUARD cuirass, dull, porous yellowish brown stone with scales drawn in red; skirt, gold and greenish brown glass; collar, blue glass and bluish gray and white stone with border at neck of gold and red; mantle on shoulder, green; shield, blue at center surrounded by wide area of bluish gray and white stone; spear, red shaft and white stone head.

ARCHITECTURE lighted faces, light yellow stone with outlines of blue glass and white and gray stone; shaded faces, yellowish brown stone; shadows of doorways, dark brown porous stone; gabled roof, red glass and pink and white stone.

Landscape

TRAIL dark yellowish brown stone. GROUND AREAS to left of trail, light yellow stone; between trail and left edge of architecture, cool gray stones; middle ground below building, light yellow stones. HORIZONTAL ZONE OF FOREGROUND three values of green glass in horizontal bands.

[104]

Herod Inquiring of the Priests and Scribes

PL. 177-179

(*Matthew 2:4–6; Protevangelium 21:2; Pseudo-Matthew 16*)

Κ(αὶ) συναγα[γὼν πάντας τοὺς ἀρχιερεῖς καὶ γραμματεῖς τοῦ λαοῦ
ἐπυνθάνετο] παρ᾽ αὐτῶν ποῦ [ὁ Χριστὸς γεννᾶται.]
*And when he had gathered all the chief priests and scribes of the people together, he
demanded of them where Christ should be born.* (*Matt. 2:4*)

When Herod heard of the Magi's search for the newborn King of the Jews, we are told, he was troubled, and, secretly desiring to destroy the Child, he inquired of the priests and scribes where it was that Christ should be born; he then called the Magi to ask that they inform him when they had found Christ. As already mentioned, the mosaics depicting these two incidents are arranged on the wall in reverse order.

Approximately a third of the mosaic of Herod Inquiring of the Priests and Scribes, in the eastern lunette of the fifth bay of the outer narthex, has survived. The extant fragment, in the left side of the lunette, presents the enthroned Herod and behind him a military guard, at the far left. The missing parts of this mosaic are known, since the scene is duplicated among the frescoes of the upper zone of the south, west, and north walls of the nave of the Church of Saint Nicholas at Curtea-de-Argeş, Rumania,[1] which reproduce with considerable accuracy a selection of scenes from the mosaics of the outer narthex of the Kariye Djami. It can be seen from the painted version of this scene that the priests and scribes, some ten or a dozen in number, stood in a compact group at the right, some, in animated conversation, gesticulating toward the king; in the background behind them was a two-storied building that balanced the structure behind King Herod.[2]

In the mosaic the military guard is represented in an unusual pose; he stands with his back turned to the beholder and with his head turned toward the right, but not quite in profile, so that one sees the back of the head and the right cheek but not the mouth, nose, or eyes. Slung over his shoulder is a shield of elliptical shape that may have been intended as a foreshortened circle; in his right hand he holds a spear. Herod, too, is unusual in his pose. The head is drawn in sharp profile, the upper part of the body in three-quarters rear view, and the lower part, again, in profile. He extends his right hand toward the group with whom he speaks, and in his left hand he holds a sword. The throne and footstool, on the other hand, are turned in pseudo-perspective toward the right front, parallel with the architecture in the background.

1 O. Tafrali, *Monuments byzantins de Curtéa de Arges* (Paris, 1931), Atlas, PL. LXXI bis, 1; I. D. Stefanescu, *La Peinture religieuse en Valachie et Transylvanie* (Paris, 1930), Album, PL. 7 (upper right). See also V. Draghiceanu, "Curtea Domnească din Argeş, Note Istorice şi Arheologice," *Buletinul Comisiunii Monumentelor Istorice*, Anul X–XVI (Bucharest, 1923), pp. 9–76.

2 The subjects in the upper zone of paintings at Curtea-de-Argeş which to an amazing degree correspond to their counterparts at the Kariye Djami are: on the south wall, The Journey to Bethlehem, The Enrollment for Taxation, The Magi before Herod, Herod Inquiring of the Priests and Scribes; on the west wall, The Return of the Holy Family from Egypt, Christ Taken to Jerusalem for Passover; and on the north wall, The Multiplication of Loaves. See Stefanescu, PL. 6, 8, and 7, for proper sequence. Two of these paintings—Herod Inquiring of the Priests and Scribes, and especially The Multiplication of Loaves—are of great importance, for they enable us to reconstruct their fragmentary counterparts in mosaics [104] and [118] at the Kariye Djami.

Dimensions

Width of lunette from masonry at right to outer edge of red and gold inner border at left, 2.115 m.; height of lunette from soffit of masonry arch to cornice, 2.075 m.; maximum width of mosaic fragment, without border, .84 m.; maximum height of mosaic fragment within borders, 1.68 m.

Colors and Materials

MILITARY GUARD trousers, green with gold ornamental band; boots, blue; short tunic, visible at hem and sleeve, red; armor, brown stone and gold and greenish brown glass; collar, girdle, and other ornamentation, blue glass and gray and white stones; shield, red glass, terra cotta, pink and gray stones; spear, black and red shaft and gray stone head. HEROD tunic, blue with gold and red hem, studded with small green gems and pearls, and gold and red cuff; mantle, red with gold tablion edged in red and studded with green gems and pearls; crown, gold edged in red and set with pearls; sword, dark red scabbard ornamented with gold.

THRONE AND FOOTSTOOL cushion, green; lighted faces, gold with drawing in brownish green glass; shaded faces, brown stone with drawing in greenish brown glass. ARCHITECTURE lighted walls, light yellowish gray stones with drawing in light yellowish brown stone; shaded walls, light yellowish brown stones with drawing in greenish brown glass; roofs, light gray and white stones.

[105]

The Return of the Magi to the East

PL. 180 *b*, 181

(Matthew 2:12; Protevangelium 21:4; Pseudo-Matthew 16)

From their interview with Herod in Jerusalem the Magi were led by the star to Bethlehem, where they worshiped the Child, presented their gifts, and then, being warned in a dream not to return to Herod, "departed into their own country another way." To find where these subjects are depicted, and pursue the chronological sequence of events, we must turn the corner into the eastward extension of the outer narthex and consider the northern and eastern lunettes of the seventh bay. The northern lunette (PL. 180 *a*), which comes after that containing the fragment of Herod Inquiring of the Priests and Scribes [104], now lacks any trace of its mosaics, but a small fragment of the Return of the Magi to the East [105] is preserved in the eastern lunette (PL. 180 *b* and 181). The lost mosaic of the northern lunette, therefore, must have depicted an event that occurred after Herod's inquiries and before the return journey of the Magi. We are limited to two subjects: The Adoration of the Magi, and The Dream of the Magi. Of these, The Adoration is the more likely; it is the principal and culminating event in the narrative of the Magi, and it was omitted from the mosaic of the Nativity [102], where it is often to be found in Byzantine art.

The fifteenth-century frescoes of The Adoration and The Return of the Magi in the Serbian monastery of Kalenić quite possibly reflect, in composition and detail, the lost mosaics of these two lunettes, for several of the monastery's paintings dealing with the Infancy of Christ are remarkably like their extant counterparts at the Chora.[1] In The Adoration of the Magi at Kalenić [2] the Virgin, with the Child in her lap, is seated at the far left on a throne with a high polygonal back; only the head and shoulders of Joseph appear above the back of the throne. In the mosaic, this part of the composition would well fit the narrower space to the left of the arched window

---

1 Other scenes at Kalenić that show a striking similarity in composition to their counterparts at the Kariye Djami are: Joseph Dreaming and The Journey to Bethlehem, and The Enrollment for Taxation.

2 Petković and Tatić, Fig. 45; Gabriel Millet, *Recherches sur l'iconographie de l'Évangile* (Paris, 1916), Fig. 105.

that penetrates the lunette. At the right, in the fresco, the three Magi advance, one behind the other, toward the throne; holding their offerings before them, all bend forward in obeisance. The old Magus, who leads his comrades, presents a gabled casket, while the middle-aged and the youthful Magi, in that order, offer covered, chalice-like vessels. These three figures, in the mosaic, would probably have filled the remaining space in the lunette, to the right of the window.

The lunette at the east side of the seventh bay (PL. 180 *b*) and the two columns that support it serve to screen the end of the outer narthex from the western end of the pareclesion, which lies beyond. The lunette is pierced at the bottom by three stilted arches resting on the columns and above, in the center, by a fourth arch. On this discontinuous wall surface the mosaicists placed The Return of the Magi, a composition that must have been unusual owing to the peculiar distribution of the spaces available to it. Only two fragments of mosaic still survive. One, at the far left between the curved border of the lunette and the first of the three arches, retains a blank background of gray stones above a horizontal band of green, indicating a landscape. Between the first and second arches is the youthful Magus on his gray horse. He rides, from right to left, up a very steep and winding trail entering, at the top of the fragment, into a narrow and rocky defile, through which he must pass. He holds his body quite straight, as though standing erect in the stirrups; with his stiffly extended left arm he points upward.

There is an extraordinary resemblance between this figure and the lowest of the three Magi in the fresco version of the subject at Kalenić.[3] The poses of the horse and rider in both are identical, and in both the rider is about to enter a narrow defile in the mountains. Indeed, it is altogether possible that the entire frieze composition at Kalenić, which contains, from left to right, The Adoration, The Return of the Magi, and the second Dream of Joseph (instructing him to flee to Egypt with his family to escape the wrath of Herod), all combined in a single mountainous landscape, is based upon the Chora mosaics or upon an intermediary that was so based. The composition of The Return of the Magi and the second Dream of Joseph, which at Kalenić are interwoven in a common setting, could very well have been adapted from that created by the peculiar conditions of the lunette at the Chora. One might suppose, then, that the second horseman was placed above and to the left of the first and turned from left to right, as at Kalenić. This would have put him above and slightly to the right of the left-hand arch, in the direction toward which the first horseman is pointing. The third would have been still higher and immediately to the left of the arch in the upper center of the lunette. The highest mountain, on which sits what appears to be a mountain fortress, near the upper right of the Kalenić version, could have been placed to the right of the upper arch. The rest of the lunette could have depicted Joseph's Dream — the spandrel to the right of the central arch of the arcade would have held the reclining figure of Joseph, while the angel would have been placed above the right-hand arch. If the various elements were so disposed in the lunette, the composition of the scenes would correspond to, and account for, the unusual distribution of figures in the frieze at Kalenić.

Dimensions

Total width of lunette at cornice level (corresponding to the span of the relieving arch), ca. 4.60 m.; height from soffit of arch to cornice level, ca. 2.35 m.; width of mosaic fragment on spandrel above N capital, between ornamental surrounds of arches, ca. .62 m.; height of same mosaic fragment above geometric border, ca. 1.08 m.

Colors and Materials

YOUNG MAGUS trousers, violet with ornamental band of gold and red; tunic, green with cuff of gold and red; sash around waist (possibly his mantle tied about him),

---

3 Petković and Tatić, Fig. 46, and Millet, Fig. 105.

red; hat, red crown and blue and white brim; horse, cool gray stones with white stone highlights; saddle-cloth, red with wide gold border; saddle, gold and red; headstall, noseband, and bit, red and gold; all other harness, red. LANDSCAPE background, yellowish gray stones; winding trail, light violet glasses; shadows of rocky defile, darker violet glasses; horizontal zone of foreground, mixed green glasses.

[106]

The Flight into Egypt

PL. 182, 183

(*Matthew 2:13–14*)

Ἡ πρὸς τὴν Αἴγυπτον φυγή   *The flight into Egypt*

The lunette in the southern wall of the seventh bay is pierced by a large window placed to the right of the center, so that its mosaic decoration is divided into two areas of unequal width. At the left, in the larger of the two sections, are the fragmentary remains of the scene depicting the journey of the Holy Family to Egypt, which is recorded in Matthew; represented in the narrow space to the right is the apocryphal incident of the fall of the idols from the walls of an Egyptian city at the approach of the Holy Family.

Of the journey to Egypt, only the inscription and the merest fragments of the youth, the animal on which Mary rode, and the landscape setting have survived, but they are sufficient to make it evident that the Flight was probably of the well-known type in which the young James, the youngest of Joseph's sons, leads the donkey on which Mary is seated while Joseph, behind the animal, carries the infant Jesus astride his shoulders as he does in the mosaic of the Return from Egypt [111]. Often, in those examples in which Joseph and the Child follow behind the animal, Mary turns about in the saddle and extends her arms to the Child, who responds in like manner. It is not certain that this was the case in the mosaic or that any of the other sons of Joseph were represented, for only the forelegs of the donkey and the legs of James, who wore a short tunic, tightly fitting trousers stopping above the knees of his bare legs, and spiral leggings around his ankles, are now preserved near the right edge of the scene.

The mosaic of the Falling Idols, to the right of the window, is nearly intact. The available space is almost solidly filled by the representation of turreted city walls enclosing a number of houses; in the center of the forward wall is the city gate, with its doors slightly ajar. From the top of the walls and turrets four idols, represented as nude figures in simple silhouette, the uppermost with a short upturned tail, are casting themselves down with outstretched arms.

The incident of the idols is not mentioned in the Gospel account nor in the Greek text of the Protevangelium, which in its original form ended with the story of the Magi. The theme, however, was well known to Byzantine artists, and the incident is alluded to in various Greek sources, including the famous Akathistos hymn, which hails many events in the life of Mary and provides the themes for cyclical illustration in late-Byzantine art. Versions of the story are recounted in several of the oriental paraphrases of the Protevangelium, and it appears in considerable detail in the Latin Pseudo-Matthew. In the latter, which was probably not the source for the Byzantine representations, it is said that when the family entered the temple in a city called Sotinen, the three hundred and fifty-five idols that were worshiped there prostrated them-

97

selves before the Virgin and Child and broke into pieces in fulfillment of the prophecy of Isaiah 19:1. The miracle led to the conversion of the inhabitants, including one Affrodosius, the governor. The Kariye Djami mosaic lacks the richly clad personage who kneels or bows before the Virgin and Child at the gate of the city in many representations of the subject. This figure is often interpreted as Affrodosius; in most instances, however, it is a female figure, who should be regarded as a personification of the city or of Egypt.[1]

Dimensions

Width of lunette at top of ornamental mosaic base, from soffit of masonry arch at left to soffit mosaic at far right, 4.525 m.; height of lunette at center from mosaic soffit above to top of cornice, 2.31 m.; width of scene at left, above lower ornamental border, from masonry soffit at far left to ornamental border surrounding window, 2.01 m.; width of scene at right, at same level, from right edge of ornamental border surrounding window to soffit mosaic at far right, .81 m.

Colors and Materials

LEGS OF DONKEY gray stones with accents drawn in blue glass. BOY legs, flesh-colored marbles; leg-gings, blue; short trousers, blue with green band at bottom; short tunic, probably red since outline drawing is red glass, but only the lining, of blue-gray and white stones, is visible. LANDSCAPE foreground, horizontal band of green glass; middle ground, light yellowish brown stone; distant background above, darker brownish stone becoming very dark at upper edge. CITY fortified walls, light yellowish brown stones; drawing and shaded faces of turrets, darker yellowish brown stone with highlights of very light yellowish gray stone; gates, blue glass, bluish gray and white stones; walls and roofs of buildings within city walls, gray and white stones and blue and red glasses. IDOLS very light yellowish gray stones.

1 See Lafontaine-Dosogne, in Vol. 4 of this work.

[107], [108]

The Massacre of the Innocents

PL. 184–193

(Matthew 2:16; Protevangelium 22:1; Pseudo-Matthew 17)

[107] Herod Ordering the Massacre (left); The Soldiers Go Forth to Slay the Children (right)

PL. 184–189

Τότε Ἡρώδης ἰδ(ὼν) ὅτι ἐνεπαίχθη ὑπὸ τ(ῶν) μάγων ἐθυμώθ(η) | λίαν, κ(αὶ) ἀποστείλας ἀνεῖλε πάντ(ας) τοὺς παῖδας τοὺς ἐν Βηθλεὲμ | κ(αὶ) ἐν πᾶσι τοῖς ὁρίοις αὐτῆς ἀπὸ διετοῦς κ(αὶ) κατωτέρω.
Then Herod, when he saw that he was mocked of the wise men, was exceeding wroth, and sent forth, and slew all the children that were in Bethlehem, and in all the coasts thereof, from two years old and under (Matt. 2:16)

[108] The Soldiers Slaying the Children

PL. 190–193

The theme of The Massacre of the Innocents, and events that are closely related to it, has received an unusually expansive treatment at the Kariye Djami; no fewer than four of the lunettes of the Infancy Cycle are devoted to its various parts. Three phases in the execution of Herod's command that all children of Bethlehem up to two years of age should be slain are illustrated in the two large lunettes, [107] and [108], in the southern and western walls of the sixth bay, and the two succeeding lunettes, [109] and [110], in the western walls of the fifth and fourth bays depict other incidents from the narrative.

The mosaics in the first two lunettes ([107] and [108]) are described together here, for in reality they form one subject, normally a single composition; it has been arbitrarily separated at a point where there is no distinguishable break in the narrative. The subject can be subdivided into three succeeding phases. At the left in the southern lunette [107], Herod issues his command to the executioners; in the center the executioners depart in search of the infants; and in the lower right corner the massacre begins. The lunette in the western wall [108], which has suffered extensive losses above the window, was apparently devoted in its entirety to a demonstration of the various methods employed by the executioners in slaying the children. Thus, the break between the second and third parts of the narrative actually occurs within the first of the lunettes; it is marked by the narrow slit window, near the right side, which provides light for the spiral stairs of a roof turret on which the Turkish minaret was later erected. The small rectangular opening is original fourteenth-century construction, and the mosaics were adapted to it when they were put in place.

The narrative begins at the left in the southern lunette with the rather symmetrically balanced group of Herod and his soldiers in the throne room of his palace, a columnar building in the background with a central niche. Herod, on his throne before the niche, turns to the soldiers at the right and, holding out both hands, gives the command. While he bears no arms, he wears a golden cuirass; a fanciful crown is on his head. His mantle, probably the chlamys, has fallen in folds about his hips. Behind him, at the left, are two soldiers. One, standing in a nearly frontal pose near the enthroned king, is doubtless his personal guard. He is dressed in full armor and holds a spear in his right hand; his left forearm is concealed by a shield with a highly decorated outer face, whose form seems to be derived from that of the ancient *pelta*, a shield carried by spearmen of the light infantry and by Amazons. In this version the face is decorated with a shell motif. At the far left another soldier, his face in profile, advances toward Herod; he too is in full armor, including a helmet with a noseguard and a crest that imitates the wings of a bird. His mantle and sword hang from his left shoulder. To the right of Herod, and facing him, is a group of three soldiers, to whom the command is being given. The first, who gesticulates with both hands, is drawn in profile; he wears a cuirass but no helmet, and a sword hangs at his left side. Behind him, at the right, another fully armored soldier turns toward Herod, in three-quarters pose. In the background between these two is a third soldier, who turns his back; his head is turned somewhat to the left, and one sees the left cheek and brow but no other parts of the face.

In the right half of the lunette, in a landscape of rolling hills, the soldiers have turned away from Herod and begin to put their orders into effect. In the foreground to the left of the small window is a soldier in full armor with a sheathed sword at his side, advancing toward the right. Over the brow of the hill, above the window, another soldier, with drawn sword, is in pursuit of a mother who holds a small child in the folds of her mantle and cringes behind a tree. In the foreground to the right of the small window a soldier, drawn in profile, has snatched a naked infant from its mother; leaning forward toward the mother, he holds the child by one leg as he pierces its breast with a short sword or dagger. The mother, who is seated on the ground at the right, raises her hands in a tragic gesture. Her head is turned away in sharp profile; her disheveled hair suggests the struggle she has had with the soldier or, perhaps, indicates that she has pulled at her

99

hair in despair and grief. The mosaicist has sought to achieve a concentration of dramatic effect in this figure not only through pose and gesture but through the voluminous aspect of the garments and the spectacular contrasts of their colors, which are unmatched in any of the mosaics.

All the lunettes in the western wall of the outer narthex are crescent-shaped, because of the encroachment of the large arched windows, which rise from the floor to a height well above the cornice level. The compositions in these lunettes are fitted around the tops of the arches. In the western lunette of the sixth bay [108], where The Massacre of the Innocents is continued, an extensive area of mosaic above the window was lost because of the shattering of the arch, but two large fragments, at left and right, are in an excellent state of preservation.

A landscape of two ranges of barren hills, one above the other, provides the only setting for the scene. At each side of the arch, silhouetted against a low hill, is a group of three figures, more or less symmetrically disposed. A single, larger hill above forms the background for other figures, a number of whom are partly obscured by the lower hills of the foreground.

In the group at the lower left, a soldier stoops over a child lying flat on its back on the ground; he has placed his right foot on its body and is about to thrust his sword into its neck. Behind him, to the right, another soldier brandishes a sword over his head and with his left hand snatches at the head of an infant held in the arms of its mother, standing in profile at the right, while she resists the attack. In the corresponding group at the lower right, at the broken edge of the mosaic, a soldier whose features are particularly brutal holds an infant, head downward, by one leg with his left hand and, with his right hand raised, is presumably about to pierce the child with his sword. Partly obscured by a small hillock to the right, a mother turns her back to a soldier attacking from the right, and to the beholder, in an attempt to shield her child, whose head is partly visible over her left shoulder. Of her face only the outline of the right cheek and brow are visible. The soldier from whom she tries to escape is drawn in profile; with his left arm he reaches out toward the woman, while he attempts to draw the long sword at his left side from its scabbard by reaching around with his right arm to grasp the hilt.

In the upper zone of the left fragment are two soldiers; the legs of a third and the outstretched arms of a mother are to be seen at the broken edge of the mosaic. The legs of the first two soldiers are hidden from view by the brow of the hill in the foreground. The first soldier, drawn in profile, rushes toward the right with arms outstretched, perhaps in a gesture of admiration for the diabolical manner in which his companion has slain a child. The latter stands with his back turned to the beholder, but with his head turned to the left in profile as he looks up at the infant impaled on the end of his long spear and silhouetted against the gold of the sky. A comparably gruesome detail is to be seen in the upper zone of the right-hand fragment, where another soldier, again drawn in profile and again partly obscured by the lower hill, has transfixed a child on the point of his sword, which he raises aloft.

A striking feature of the two mosaics of The Massacre of the Innocents is the attempt of the artist to represent figures in unusual poses. Here and there in the preceding scenes we have observed a few figures whose heads are drawn in profile and one figure presented in rear view. In these two panels, however, the frontal or three-quarters view is the exception; the heads, and often the bodies, of the great majority are drawn in profile, near-profile, or rear view. To some extent this approach is perhaps attributable to the mosaicist's models and to existing traditions in the representation of this scene of violent action. It may well be, also, that Byzantine painters were disinclined to represent the faces of evil persons, who were not supposed to be depicted in the iconic manner of sacred persons. Nevertheless, the interest in the representation of motion that is evident at the Kariye Djami and in Palaeologan art in general was given freer rein here than in many of the mosaics and to a great extent accounts for the predominance of profile figures in the scenes of the Massacre.

Dimensions

SOUTHERN LUNETTE [107] width between borders, measured at bottom, 3.71 m.; height between borders, 1.97 m.; rectangular window, within its plaster surround of unset setting bed, .385 m. wide and .86 m. high. WESTERN LUNETTE [108] width between borders, measured at bottom, 4.40 m.; height at center, from masonry of relieving arch to level of top of cornice, 2.43 m.; width of mosaic at left of window, at level of bottom of green zone and between borders, 1.155 m.; width of mosaic at right of window, at level of green zone and between borders, 1.225 m.

Colors and Materials

Southern Lunette [107]

HEROD tunic, blue with accent drawing in black and cuffs and hem of gold and red; mantle, red; boots, red with gold ornaments; cuirass, gold, light yellow stone, and greenish brown glass, adorned at neck and waist with gold and red; armored sleevelets, gold and violet; collar, blue and gray; crown, gold and greenish brown glass with highlights in silver and outlining at left and top in red glass and in front in dull black stone. THRONE AND FOOTSTOOL lighted faces, gold glass and light brownish stone; shaded faces of throne, translucent amber and green and gold glasses with drawing in dark violet glasses; shaded face of footstool, light brownish stone with drawing in violet glass; cushion, green. GUARD (to left of Herod) tight trousers, green; boots, blue; short tunic, red, with gold and red cuff; armored skirt, gold glass and brown stone; cuirass, gold and greenish brown glass; armored sleevelets, gold and terra cotta; girdle at waist, sash at chest, and collar, blue glass, gray and white stone; mantle, blue; helmet, violet glass and gray and white stone on top, with ear pieces of blue, gray, and white; spear, red and black shaft and gray and white head; shield, green, gray, and white. SOLDIER AT FAR LEFT tight trousers, yellow, with ornamental bands of gold and red; boots, green and gray; armored skirt, gold glass and brown stone; cuirass, light green with white highlights; armored sleevelets, gold and terra cotta; girdle and fringe of cuirass, blue, gray, and white; helmet, plumed crest of gold outlined in brown and black glass and brim and nose guard of blue, gray, and white; mantle, red; scabbard, dark bluish violet. FOUR SOLDIERS TO RIGHT OF HEROD (left to right) 1): Tight trousers, red; boots, blue; short tunic, blue; armored skirt and cuirass, gold glass and grayish yellow stones; armored sleevelets, gold and terra cotta; girdle and collar, blue and bluish gray; mantle, red; scabbard, red; sword hilt, blue. 2) (partly visible with head in rear view): Tight trousers, green; boots, blue; short tunic, terra cotta; cuirass and armored skirt as in no. 1; mantle, violet; helmet, gold crest outlined in red, and blue brim and neck armor. 3): Tight trousers, dark violet; boots, green; armored skirt and sleevelets as in no. 1; cuirass, green with fringe, sash, and collar of blue and gray; helmet, blue crown, with gold and brown armor covering neck and ears; scabbard, dark blue; sword hilt, light blue. 4) (facing toward right at left of window): Tight trousers, green; boots, red; armored skirt, armored sleevelets, and girdle as in no. 1; cuirass, violet and gray; sash at chest, white with terra cotta and red lines; sleeve of short tunic, green with gold and red cuff; helmet, gold crest with blue and gray brim; scabbard, red; sword hilt, blue; shoulder strap, black. SOLDIER ABOVE WINDOW armored skirt, sleevelets, and cuirass, gold and greenish brown; fringe and sash around chest, blue and gray; collar, violet; helmet, crest of gold, greenish brown, and violet and brim of blue and gray; mantle, red; scabbard, violet; sword, blue, gray, and white. WOMAN AT UPPER RIGHT dress and outer headcovering, green; veil beneath outer headcovering (visible above brows), blue and white; infant's dress, pink and white marble with outlining in terra cotta and red glass. SOLDIER AT RIGHT OF WINDOW (slaying child) tight trousers, green; boots, blue; short tunic, blue; armored skirt and cuirass, gold glass and brown stone; helmet, like that of soldier no. 4, above; mantle, red; scabbard, blue; child, white and pink stones with drawing in terra cotta and red glass. WOMAN AT LOWER RIGHT dress and headcovering, blue glass in four values with highlights of bluish gray and white stones; mantle, dark areas in four values of brown lusterless glass, the darkest of which is nearly black, and lighted areas (almost equal in extent with the browns) in two values of highly reflective glasses, one a middle yellow and the other a brownish yellow; shoes, black. ARCHITECTURE walls and arch, bluish gray stone with white highlights and shadows of blue glass; column shafts and capitals, green glasses; column bases, bluish gray stone; draperies, red. LANDSCAPE lower hill in foreground, from architecture at left to far right, yellowish gray stone outlined above in yellowish brown stones; distant hill, above at far right, bluish gray stone outlined in blue glass; tree, trunk of brown and brownish green glass and foliage of green and black glasses and light gray stone.

Western Lunette [108]

THREE FIGURES AT LOWER LEFT (left to right) *1)* (soldier slaying infant): Tight trousers, blue; boots, red; short tunic, red; cuirass, gold, brownish yellow stone, and brown glass; armored sleevelets, gold and terra cotta; helmet, same as cuirass with outlining in red; sword, blue and white stone; infant, pink marbles with drawing in red glass and hair and shadows of greenish brown glass. *2)* (soldier): Tight trousers, red; boots, violet; short tunic, blue; armored skirt, gold glass and brown stones; cuirass, violet glass and white stone with blue fringe, sash, and collar; armored sleeve-lets as in no. 1; helmet, gold and brown glass with red outline and blue brim; sword, blue and white; scabbard, dark violet. *3)* (woman): Undergarment, blue; mantle and headdress, red.

THREE FIGURES AT LOWER RIGHT (left to right) *1)* (soldier slaying infant): Tight trousers, red; boots, green; short tunic, blue, with gold and red cuff on sleeve; armored skirt, gold glass and brown stone; cuirass, green with blue fringe, sash, and collar; armored sleevelets, gold and terra cotta; helmet, gold and brown glasses with red outline and blue brim; infant, pink and white marbles with drawing in red and hair in brown glasses. *2)* (woman): Garments, green. *3)* (soldier): Tight trousers, green; boots, blue; short tunic, blue with gold and red cuff; armored skirt and cuirass, violet glasses and white stone; sleevelets as in no. 1; helmet, blue glass and bluish gray and yellowish gray stones; scabbard, red.

THREE SOLDIERS AT UPPER LEFT (left to right) *1)*: Armored skirt and cuirass, gold glass and brown and yellow-brown stones with fringe at waist of blue glass and gray stone; armored sleevelets, gold and terra cotta; mantle, red; helmet, gold glass and brown stones with outlines of black and red glass and brim of bluish gray and white stone; scabbard of dagger, green; hilt of dagger, blue and gray. *2)*: Tight trousers, red; short tunic, visible at sleeves, brown and yellowish gray stones with gold and red cuff; armored skirt, gold glass and brown stones with outlines in very dark red glass; cuirass, green glasses and white stone with fringe and sash of blue, gray, and white; sleevelets as in no. 1; mantle, red; helmet, gold glass and brown stone with blue and gray brim; spear, black shaft and blue and gray head; infant, like others. *3)* (fragment, facing right): Tight trousers, green; boots, blue; short tunic, blue. FRAGMENT OF FIGURE OF A MOTHER (preserved only in arms; facing left) sleeves, blue and gray with gold and red cuffs.

TWO SOLDIERS AT UPPER RIGHT (left to right) *1)* (fragmentary figure): Tight trousers, brown; boots, blue; short tunic, green; armored skirt, gold, greenish brown, and brown glasses; scabbard, red. *2)*: Short tunic (right sleeve visible), green; armored skirt, cuirass, and helmet, gold glass and brown stones, cuirass with blue and gray fringe and collar; armored sleevelets, gold and terra cotta; mantle, red; sword, blue and gray; scabbard, blue; infant, like others.

LANDSCAPE hill in lower left, bluish gray stone with heavy outline of blue glasses; hill in upper left, light yellowish brown stone with outline and shading in violet glasses and highlights in white stone; hills in lower right, light yellowish brown stone with shading in light brown and outline in dark brown stones; hill in upper right, to right of broken edge of mosaic, bluish gray stone shaded and outlined with dark brown stones.

[109]

The Mothers Mourning Their Children

PL. 194–196

(*Matthew 2:18*)

[Φωνὴ ἐν ῾Ρα]μᾶ ἠκούσθη, θρῆνος κ(αὶ) κλαυθμὸς κ(αὶ) ὀδυρμὸς πολύς.
In Rama was there a voice heard, lamentation, and weeping, and great mourning

(*Matt. 2:18*; cf. *Jer. 31:15*)

In Byzantine iconography, the theme of the mothers mourning their dead children often finds a place, as a motif, within the composition of the Massacre itself, where it is sometimes inscribed as "Rachel Weeping for her Children." It is inspired by the text of Matthew (2:17,18), "Then was fulfilled that which was spoken by Jeremy the prophet, saying, In Rama was there a voice heard, lamentation, and weeping, and great mourning, Rachel weeping for her children, and would not be comforted, because they are not," from which the inscription in the mosaic of the Kariye Djami quotes.

When the motif is included in the scene of the Massacre, it usually takes the form of a soldier with drawn sword holding an infant head-downward by one leg above a pile of dismembered infants, while a single mother nearby tears at her hair or otherwise expresses her grief. This motif was adapted in the lower right corner of the first Massacre mosaic [107], but the pile of slain children was omitted. It is to be noted, indeed, that in neither of the two mosaics of the Massacre are the dead shown heaped or scattered on the ground.

At the Kariye Djami the theme of the mourning mothers was reserved for a separate and more elaborated treatment, in the western lunette of the fifth bay, but unfortunately only the right half of the mosaic still exists. The fragment presents a group of the mothers huddled together on the ground in various attitudes of sorrow. Seated in the front row at the center of the fragment is one whose face and shoulders are twisted to the left while the lower parts of her body are turned toward the right. With her left hand she clutches the severed head of her child to her breast; her right hand is raised to her face. She is flanked by two women who turn their backs to the beholder; one of these, at the right, holds her dead child before her. At the broken edge of the mosaic another woman appears to be rising to her knees. Of the others, only the faces or the shrouded heads are visible.

The heads of all the women are inclined toward the left and the missing parts of the mosaic, and all eyes are focused on what must have been the source of the mothers' grief. Since no close parallel for this treatment of the subject exists, one can only speculate that the center of attention in the left part of the composition was the pile of dead children and perhaps an executioner, or even the enthroned Herod.

Dimensions

Width of lunette from soffit of arch at left to and including the wider of two ornamental borders at right, 2.13 m.; height at center, including mosaic borders at top and bottom, .855 m.; height at center, from top of mosaic border at top to cornice level, 2.00 m.

Colors and Materials

WOMAN IN FRONT ROW, LEFT garments, blue; left cheek, green glasses with 2 pink stone tesserae.

WOMAN IN FRONT ROW, CENTER dress, blue with green and gold cuff; mantle and headdress, red; shoes, dark gray stone. WOMAN HOLDING CHILD, FAR RIGHT garments, yellow and brown stones. WOMAN AT FAR LEFT, BACK ROW garments, red. FIVE HEADS IN BACKGROUND (left to right) 1, 2, and 5, violet headdresses; 3 and 4, green headdresses.

LANDSCAPE hillock in foreground (in spandrel), bluish gray stone outlined above by four rows of brown stone; hillock in background, yellowish gray stone outlined above by one row of grayish brown stone.

[110]

The Flight of Elizabeth and John
PL. 197–199

(*Protevangelium 22:3*)

Ἡ φηγὴ [sic] τῆς Ἐλισάβετ   *The flight of Elizabeth*

The western lunette of the fourth bay, containing The Flight of Elizabeth and John, is the last of the series of four lunettes devoted to various episodes in the story of The Massacre of the Innocents. A representation of a purely apocryphal incident, the mosaic depicts the means of

John the Baptist's escape from the wrath of Herod as it is narrated in the Protevangelium: "But Elizabeth when she heard that . . . [the executioners] sought for John, took him and went up into the hill-country and looked about her where she should hide him: and there was no hiding-place. And Elizabeth groaned and said in a loud voice: O mountain of God, receive thou a mother with a child. For Elizabeth was not able to go up. And immediately the mountain clave asunder and took her in."

Like the preceding incident, The Mothers Mourning Their Children [109], this one often forms a minor motif in monumental compositions of the Massacre, but here it is assigned a panel to itself. At the right Elizabeth has already found sanctuary in the mountain. At the left, in a splendid attitude of running, one of Herod's executioners is in close pursuit, his sword drawn and ready to strike and his mantle blown out behind him; he wears no helmet and his legs are bare, but otherwise he resembles the soldiers in the preceding scenes of the Massacre. In the opening of the mountain, which we can presume is about to close, or at any rate conceal her from the soldier, stands Elizabeth, holding the child, wrapped in swaddling cloths, in her arms.

Dimensions

Width within borders, 1.91 m.; height at center, within borders, .90 m.; height at center, from lower edge of border at top to cornice level, 1.965 m.

Colors and Materials

SOLDIER boots, violet; armor, primarily of porous yellowish brown stone with scales outlined in gold or greenish brown glasses; fringe of cuirass, collar, and sash, blue; mantle, red; sword, blue glass and gray and white stones; scabbard, blue-violet glass with ornaments of gold bordered by greenish brown glass. ELIZABETH dress (visible at lower right), blue; outer garment and headdress, four values of green glass with some drawing in black; kerchief worn beneath headdress, blue. INFANT JOHN swaddling cloths, blue glass and gray and white stone.

LANDSCAPE hills, grayish yellow stones with white highlights; outlines of tops, at right, of dark yellowish brown stones shading to greenish brown and dark violet glasses at outer edges; interior of mountain, very dark blue; tree, trunks of greenish brown, outlined at right in violet, and foliage of green and black glasses and gray stone; foreground in spandrels, green glasses outlined above, in right spandrel below tree, in two values of blue glass and above left spandrel in violet glass.

[III]

Joseph Dreaming; The Return of the Holy Family from Egypt PL. 200–205

(Matthew 2:19–23)

Χρηματισθεὶς δὲ κατ' ὄναρ ἀνεχώρησεν εἰς τὰ μέρη τῆς Γαλιλαίας, κ(αὶ) ἐλθὼν κατῴκησεν εἰς πόλιν λεγομένην Ναζαρέτ.

Being warned of God in a dream, he turned aside into the parts of Galilee: and he came and dwelt in a city called Nazareth   *(Matt. 2:22–23)*

Μ(ήτ)ηρ Θ(εο)ῦ   *Mother of God*

'Ι(ησοῦ)ς Χ(ριστό)ς   *Jesus Christ*

The western lunette of the second bay of the outer narthex continues the narration of the infancy of Christ in two scenes. It is uncertain whether the Dream of Joseph at the far left was intended to represent the first or the second of his two dreams concerning the return to Israel from Egypt.

In the first, which is the third recorded dream of Joseph, the Angel of the Lord commanded him while he was in Egypt to take Mary and the Christ Child back to Israel, since those who had sought to take the Child's life were dead. This was followed by another dream when Joseph, after entering Israel, feared to proceed because he had learned that Archelaus, son of Herod, had succeeded his father in Judaea and was engaged in quelling a rebellion in the land. In the latter dream Joseph was warned to turn "aside into the parts of Galilee" and thus avoid the soldiers of Archelaus. The inscription refers to this dream. The second scene, in the center and far right of the lunette, depicts the Holy Family approaching the Galilean city of Nazareth, where they were to dwell.

The two subjects are skillfully adapted to the crescent form of the lunette. The axial group, above the center of the window, consists of one of Joseph's sons (probably James), Mary, and Joseph carrying the Child on his shoulders. At the left, the dreaming Joseph, the angel, and the donkey in the background balance the city of Nazareth, at the right, while the low corners are filled by a stunted tree, below Joseph, and a small gabled building, before the walls of Nazareth.

As in his first dream [100], Joseph is stretched out on a pallet in a rocky, barren setting. His chin rests on his right hand; his legs are crossed and his left hand rests on his knee. The fluttering half-figure of an angel with right hand raised in a gesture of speaking is above his head.

In the Return from Egypt, the movement of all figures is toward the right. The donkey, laden with a bundle of provisions, emerges from behind the small hill that forms the background for the Dream. The rein in his right hand, Joseph's youthful son leads the animal, turning to look back at it; over his left shoulder he carries a staff. He wears tightly fitting trousers and boots, a short tunic, and a mantle arranged across his shoulder and chest like a sash. Mary walks close behind Joseph and the Child, her gaze directed toward her son and her right hand raised in a speaking gesture. The Child, astride Joseph's shoulders, turns his head back to look at his mother and grasps Joseph's hair with both hands. Joseph leans forward, his head tilted upward, and with his right hand he holds the Child by the right ankle; his left hand is concealed beneath a fold of his himation. A small hill in the background separates the family from the town of Nazareth, which seems to be nestled in a valley at the far right. The houses and trees are clustered together behind a battlemented wall. In the foreground, before the town, is a gabled building raised on a two-stepped base; between it and the town is a group of small trees and shrubs.

Dimensions

Width of lunette, at level of top of window, within borders, 2.62 m.; height at center, from lower edge of border at top to cornice level, 1.89 m.

Colors and Materials

Joseph Dreaming (left)

JOSEPH tunic, blue with dark blue clavus; himation, yellow. PALLET red. ANGEL tunic, blue; outer garment, violet; wings, blue below and violet above with gold highlights.

Return from Egypt (center and right)

DONKEY gray and white stones; saddlecloth and harness, red; saddle, red and gold; drapery of bundle, green. SON OF JOSEPH trousers, blue; boots, red; short tunic, green with hem and collar of yellowish gray stones; mantle, red; staff, brownish green and greenish brown glasses. MARY garments entirely of blue with gold edging on mantle and headdress; shoes, red. JOSEPH tunic, blue; himation, yellow. CHRIST CHILD short tunic, light blue with collar of red outlined in dark violet.

NAZARETH *Wall:* grayish yellow stone; coping outlined at top in blue and green glasses and white stone and at bottom in blue glass; lighted faces of turrets, grayish yellow stone with copings and left sides outlined in blue glass; shaded faces of turrets, brownish green outlined at right sides in dark violet. *House at left:* lighted walls, brownish gray stones; windows, doors, and shaded surfaces, violet glasses. *House at far right, front:* lighted wall, light green; shaded wall, dark green; roofs, red. *Third house from left* (with gabled roof): lighted wall, gray; shaded wall, green; roof, red. *Gabled house in center, rear:* lighted wall, light pink; shaded wall, darker pink and red; roof, blue. *Other houses:* combine gray and greenish brown walls with blue or white roofs. *First, third, and fourth trees* (behind town): green and black glasses. *Second tree:* blue glasses with white stone highlights. *Gabled building in front of town:* front wall, light violet glass with white stone outlines and darker violet glass door; side wall, medium violet; roof, red tiles with white highlights, outlined in red and black; two-stepped podium, medium violet glass risers and light violet glass and white stone treads. *Trees to left of building:* blue and black glasses and gray

stones. *Trees behind and to right of building* substitute green for blue. *Foreground around building:* green.

Landscape

TREE AT LOWER LEFT branches, greenish brown glasses with black and green outlines; foliage, green and black; mound at base of tree, dark green. BACKGROUND BEHIND TREE AT LOWER LEFT yellow stones bordered above by three rows of light gray stone above which is a heavy outlining of green glasses. HILLOCK BEHIND SLEEPING JOSEPH light gray stones with shading above in light green glasses. HILLS BEHIND HOLY FAMILY light gray stones which become progressively bluer toward right, with shading at right of Joseph in grayish brown stones and at far right in graded blue glasses.

[112]

Christ Taken to Jerusalem for Passover

PL. 206–210

(*Luke 2:41, 42*)

Κ(αὶ) ἐπορεύοντο οἱ γονεῖς αὐτοῦ κατ' ἔτος εἰς Ἰ(ερουσα)λὴμ | τῇ ἑορτῇ τοῦ πάσχα

Now his parents went to Jerusalem every year at the feast of the passover. (*Luke 2:41*)

Μ(ήτ)ηρ Θ(εο)ῦ   *Mother of God*

Ἰ(ησοῦ)ς Χ(ριστό)ς   *Jesus Christ*

Although the mosaic is inscribed with verse 41 of the second chapter of the Gospel of Luke, it illustrates the particular journey to Jerusalem for the celebration of Passover, when Christ had reached the age of twelve, that is described in verses 42–50. This is the last scene from the cycle of Christ's Infancy; it occupies the lunette in the western side of the first bay and thus completes the circuit of scenes in the lunettes in the outer narthex. Its subject, however, is merely the first of a series of incidents relating to the journey to Jerusalem. Events that occurred after the arrival of the Holy Family are depicted immediately above it, in the northern half of the vault [113]; they inaugurate the cycle of Christ's Ministry.

In composition the journey to Jerusalem resembles the journey to Nazareth [111] in the adjoining lunette: in both the Holy Family, at the left, advance on foot toward a walled town, at the right. In the scene of the journey to Jerusalem, since much more space was available and the animal was omitted, it was possible to draw the figures and the town at much larger scale.

Making the journey with the Holy Family are two of Joseph's sons. They and the youthful Christ, who is now richly dressed in cloth of gold, form a compact group between Mary, at the left, and Joseph, at the right. Mary, Christ, and Joseph are aligned in a front plane, and they assume similar postures of walking, each with left leg thrust forward, right leg extended behind, and right arm held out as though pointing to the city. Mary and Christ look forward; Joseph turns his head to look back at Christ; and Joseph's sons, in a rear plane behind Christ, are in frontal poses with heads turned toward Mary.

At the far right, a turreted wall, with what appears to represent an open gate between two turrets, encloses the buildings of the city. In the midst of the city is a rotunda consisting of a central dome surrounded by a low circular wall and roof. Before it and slightly to the right is a gabled building, possibly a basilica, of greater proportions than other structures in the representations of Jerusalem or of Nazareth in the Kariye Djami. The forms of these buildings and their proximity to one another may be intended to recall the great Christian shrines of Jerusalem — the rotunda of the Church of the Holy Sepulchre and the Martyrion basilica. The other houses are much like those in the representation of Nazareth [111]. A tree at the lower right, before the walls of the city, balances the figure of the Virgin at the far left.

Dimensions

Width of lunette, at level of top of window, within borders, 2.555 m.; height at center, from lower edge of border at top to cornice level, 1.95 m.

Colors and Materials

MARY garments entirely of blue with gold edging on mantle and headdress; shoes, red. YOUNGER SON OF JOSEPH (left) tight trousers, dark green; spiral leggings, violet glass and gray and white stone; short tunic, blue with gold hem bordered with reddish brown stone and cuffs and collar of gold and red glass; mantle worn about shoulders and down the back, red with lining of pink and white stone. OLDER SON OF JOSEPH tunic, blue; outer garment, yellow. CHRIST tunic and himation, exactly alike in materials and colors, gold shot with silver, with folds and outlines drawn in greenish brown glass; clavus on shoulder, green, silver, and blue. JOSEPH tunic, blue; himation, yellow.

JERUSALEM *Walls:* two values of grayish yellow stone with highlights of white stone; openings, dark violet glasses and some black glass; turrets, lighted faces like main field of wall, outlined at both sides by lines of translucent amber glass, and shaded faces of red. *Rotunda:* walls of grayish yellow and white stone; roofs of blue glass. *Gabled building:* lighted face, warm gray stone outlined at left in brownish green glass; shaded face, brownish green outlined in brown glass; roof, red. *House at far left:* walls of blue-gray stone and roofs of blue glass. *Other houses* have gray or grayish yellow walls and roofs of gray and white or of red. *Trees within city:* green, blue, and black.

TREE AT LOWER RIGHT trunk, green glasses, greenish brown stone, and black glass; foliage, bluish green and black glasses. LANDSCAPE BEHIND FIGURES uniform grayish yellow stone. FOREGROUND IN LOWER CORNERS dark green glasses.

[113]

Christy among the Doctors PL. 211–214

(Luke 2:43–49)

With this subject a new phase in the narrative of the life of Christ is begun. The cycle of the Infancy in the lunettes around the perimeter of the narthex has been completed, and the story is continued in the domical vaults with the public appearances and acts of Christ, which we can call the cycle of Christ's Ministry. The first of these, illustrated in the northern half of the vault of the first bay, was his appearance in the temple in Jerusalem in the midst of the doctors, "both hearing them, and asking them questions." Without Joseph's and Mary's knowledge, the boy Jesus had remained in Jerusalem when they departed after the Passover, and after a day's journey they returned seeking him and found him in the temple. Christ's words of explanation on that occasion, "I must be about my Father's business," indicate his purpose to begin his mission among men.

The mosaics of the vault of the first bay (PL. 211) are largely destroyed. Fortunately, however, the lower slopes, though there are two lacunae, in the eastern and southern sides, are sufficiently preserved to permit identification of the two principal subjects into which the vault is divided. The scene of Christ among the Doctors, and possibly two incidents associated with it, occupied somewhat more than the northern half of the vault (left in PL. 211). It begins on the axis of the western side (top in PL. 211; see also left in PL. 212) and ends three fourths of the way along the eastern side, near the southeastern pendentive (lower right in PL. 211; see also left in PL. 214). The identification of the subject is definitely established by the nature of the architectural setting, whose lower portions are preserved along the whole of the northern side (left in PL. 211; see also details in PL. 212 and 213). What now remains represents the lower parts of an imposing synthronon, or curved priests' bench, which extended from one pendentive to the other. The synthronon consisted of two steps, which are visible at the far left and again at the far right in the northern side, and would probably also have had a back. Figures must have been seated on the second step, for the feet of one dangle over the edge of that step near the left end of the synthronon (PL. 212, right). In the center of the synthronon, on the northern axis of the vault, there was a smaller, stepped, throne-like structure, also curved, which may have been standing free in front of the synthronon. Such architectural elements as the setting for a scene occurring at this point in the narrative can only mean that the subject was Christ among the Doctors. An indefinite number of doctors would have been represented, to left and right, on the synthronon itself, while the youthful Christ would doubtless have been seated "in their midst" on the central throne.

Exactly in the angle of the northwestern pendentive (PL. 212, center), immediately to the left of the end of the synthronon, there are still preserved the lower parts of three standing figures; it is uncertain whether these are doctors, who normally sit on the synthronon, or merely spectators in the temple. The man at the right is partly obscured by the end of the synthronon, while to the left of the group there is a corner of another piece of architecture—an indication that there was a narrow space between the back of the synthronon and architectural elements in the background. Still further to the left, partly obscured by the background structure, was the standing figure of the Virgin, identifiable because of her blue garments and because the figure beside her, to the left, is attired exactly as Joseph is throughout the mosaics. As in a number of other examples of this subject, Joseph and Mary are about to enter the temple from the left to find the boy Jesus after their discovery that he has tarried in Jerusalem. The architectural treatment suggested by these remains must have made an imposing and fitting axial motif at the northern end of the narthex and by its prominence have called attention to the beginning of the cycle of Christ's Ministry.

A little to the right of the right end of the synthronon, in the left half of the eastern side of the vault, is an extensive area of lost mosaic, which includes part of the soffit of the eastern relieving arch (lower left in PL. 211). In its lower perimeter, therefore, there is a rather wide and complete lacuna in the scene. To the right, and extending almost to the southeastern pendentive, there are further remains of mosaic that pertain to the subject of Christ among the Doctors (see PL. 211 and 214). At the left end of this fragment an area of gold background comes down to the bull's-nose border that separates the mosaics in the vault from those in the soffit of the arch. The right edge of the gold coincides with the left corner of a building that extends to the right to the curved line, near the southeastern pendentive, where the next scene in the vault [114] begins. The building rests on an area of green ground in which stand the lower parts of a figure and some trees. In its details, the preserved portion at the left end of the structure closely resembles the corresponding part of the open screen, or portico, that appears between the infant Mary and the first priest in the scene of The Virgin Blessed by the Priests (PL. 109). On the basis of this analogy, it seems probable that the figure stood before an opening in a portico, through which the gold of the background was visible.

The small, bare-footed figure standing before this building is to be identified as the boy Jesus. He is clad in cloth of gold. Indeed, his lower extremities are exactly like those of the youthful Christ in the scene of the journey to Jerusalem [112]—and he must have been represented in a similar fashion on his throne among the doctors. He stands facing left, toward the other parts of the scene in the northern half of the vault, and is therefore to be associated with it rather than with the scene in the southern half of the vault. (It will be seen that the latter represents an event that occurred when Christ was about to acquire disciples, at which time he was a grown man and would be shown wearing blue garments.) There is a considerable unoccupied distance between the youthful Christ and the left edge of the fragment, and we may suppose, therefore, that the incident was one in which the boy Jesus stands alone. A very rarely illustrated incident that fits these conditions is that of Christ tarrying in Jerusalem after permitting his family to depart without him. In a similar form it is illustrated on folio 106v of MS. Plut. VI.23 in the Laurentian Library, Florence, and again on folio 165r [1] of MS. gr. 510 in the

---

1 Reproduced in Henri Omont, *Miniatures des plus anciens manuscrits grecs de la Bibliothèque Nationale* (Paris, 1929), PL. XXXV.

Bibliothèque Nationale, Paris. If this identification of the mosaic fragment is correct, the incident was placed out of chronological order with regard to the Christ among the Doctors, for it occurred before Christ's discovery in the temple.

There is such a great space between the right end of the synthronon and the fragment of the young Christ—almost half of the eastern side of the vault—that it seems likely that another incident, now completely lost, was placed here. A possibility is an incident, very rarely illustrated, which appears in conjunction with those of Christ tarrying in Jerusalem and his discovery in the midst of the doctors in the miniature of Paris, gr. 510, mentioned above. It represents Joseph, at the left, and Mary, at the right, in the act of embracing the young Christ. The inscription in the miniature indicates that the scene was motivated either by the words of Mary, "behold, thy father and I have sought thee sorrowing," or by Christ's words, "How is it that ye sought me?" (Luke 2:48, 49). This incident is again illustrated to the right of Christ among the Doctors in the Brontochion at Mistra, Greece, and it is physically possible, though not certain, that it was also represented in the Kariye Djami mosaic.[2]

Dimensions of Vault

Between mosaic surfaces of inner faces of arches, on E–W axis, 2.75 m.; on N–S axis, 2.775 m. Rise in vault above highest level of mosaic surface on soffits of transverse arches, .70 m.

Colors and Materials

SYNTHRONON vertical face of lower step, on curved surface, transparent glasses (amber, green, and violet) with ornamental designs of gold and dark violet; vertical face of upper step, on curved surface, transparent glasses (same colors) with ornamental designs of gold and blue; vertical faces of ends of steps at far left and right, light violet, with outline drawing in transparent glasses and ornamental designs of gold and transparent glasses, mostly amber; horizontal faces of steps, gold. CENTRAL EXEDRA OR THRONE vertical faces of steps, on curved surface, violet, with darker violet ornamental designs; vertical faces of ends of steps, light violet glass and gray stone; horizontal faces of steps, bluish gray stone with outline drawing in white stone. FRAGMENTARY FIGURE (seated on synthronon at left) hem of garment, similar to those on garments of three men grouped to left, gold and red; boots, blue. FRAG-MENTARY GROUP OF THREE MEN (standing behind left end of synthronon) Left figure: tunic, blue with hem of gold and red; outer garment, green; boots, red. Central figure: only tunic of blue with red and gold hem is visible; boots, red. Right figure: tunic, green with hem of gold and red; outer garment, violet glasses; boots, red.

CORNER OF STRUCTURE TO LEFT OF GROUP OF THREE MEN shaded face, to right, light violet glasses; lighted face, to left, yellowish gray stone. FRAGMENTARY FIGURES OF JOSEPH AND MARY (at far left) Joseph: yellow stone garments with gray and white highlights. Mary: garments of blue with gold edging. FOREGROUND (throughout scene of Christ among Doctors) green.

FRAGMENT OF CHRIST TARRYING IN JERUSALEM (at right in eastern side of vault) Christ: garments, gold shot with silver. Building behind and to left of Christ: lighted face, bluish gray stone; receding face of post at left, darker bluish gray stone. Background (visible to left of building and in opening in building to right of corner post): gold. Foreground: dark green. Trees: yellowish gray stone and violet glass branches; foliage, blue and black glasses.

2 As was suggested by Millet, *Recherches sur l'iconographie de l'Evangile*, p. 651.

[114]

John the Baptist Bearing Witness of Christ (I)   PL. 211, 214, 215

(John 1:19–28; Matthew 3:7–12; Mark 1:5–8; Luke 3:15–17)

The scene in the southern half of the domical vault in the first bay of the outer narthex is preserved in two rather widely separated fragments in the southeastern and southwestern pendentives (right in PL. 211; see also PL. 214, right, and 215). The identification of the subject of these fragments is based on several points of evidence. First of all, the scene is laid on the bank of the Jordan, which flows along the entire lower margin of the southern side of the vault. Standing at the very edge of the river, near the right-hand side of the composition, was the figure of John the Baptist (PL. 215, left); still preserved are the emaciated legs and the lower fringe of the camel's-hair raiment (Matt. 3:4) which are characteristic of John in such a scene. Enough of the mosaic surface exists to both left and right of John to make it evident that he was not depicted in the act of baptizing but was, in all probability, addressing a number of persons standing at the water's edge at the far left (PL. 214, right) and near him at the far right (PL. 215, right). The composition and iconography of this scene, therefore, closely resemble those of the next mosaic [115], in the northern side of the vault of the second bay, which is still intact.

According to the first chapter of the Gospel of John, John the Baptist publicly testified, on three successive days, that Christ was the son of God. Since it is the second of these "witnessings" (John 1:29–34) that is depicted in the second vault of the narthex [115], the very similar scene in the first vault would most probably have represented the first one (John 1:19–28). This occurred when the Pharisees sent priests and Levites from Jerusalem to ask malicious questions. When asked why he baptized if he was not Christ or one of the prophets — for he had denied being either, John replied, "I baptize with water: but there standeth one among you, whom ye know not; He it is, who coming after me is preferred before me, whose shoe's latchet I am not worthy to unloose" (John 1:26, 27).

The final evidence in support of this identification is the close iconographic resemblance between the mosaic and the fresco in the Protaton, Mount Athos, which depicts the first occasion on which John bore witness of Christ;[1] the inscription of the latter paraphrases John's reply to the priests and Levites, which has just been quoted. As in the mosaic, John the Baptist stands at the right and addresses the priests and Levites, at the left; he holds a long crossed staff in his left hand and makes a speaking gesture with his right. In the midst of the group of priests and Levites the figure of Christ, who is unknown to them, stands out prominently. Again as in the mosaic (PL. 214), there is a group of young boys at the water's edge. In the fresco this genre-like motif, appearing at the lower center, consists of a small bridge with three boys on it holding hands, arms outstretched; in the mosaic, the motif consists of two boys in close struggle on a small promontory, at the lower left, at the edge of the water. Perhaps because of its crowded position, to the left of Christ's Baptism, the fresco has omitted the two figures that appear at the far right in the mosaic version. In all likelihood these two figures are Christ's future disciples, Andrew and John, who overheard the Baptist's testimony; they appear again in the next mosaic [115], where their features conform to those of the types of Andrew and John and where their presence has some textual motivation.

Dimensions of Vault

See no. [113].

Colors and Materials

TWO YOUNG BOYS (in SE pendentive) *Boy with back turned:* short tunic, blue; mantle, red; boots, green. *Second boy:* short tunic, violet; boots, blue.   THREE FIGURES OF PRIESTS AND LEVITES (left to right) *1*): Tunic, blue with gold hem; outer garment, white and light yellowish gray stones, spotted with large single tesserae of gold, with some folds drawn in violet; boots, blue, green, and gold.   *2*) (only right foot and lower parts of garment visible): Tunic, violet with gold hem; boot, blue.   *3*): Hem of tunic, gold; outer garment, red; boots, blue and gold.   JOHN THE BAPTIST (only bare legs and fringe of garment preserved) legs, white and pink marbles with left

1 Millet, *Monuments de l'Athos* (Paris, 1927), PL. 7,2; 11,2 (far left); 14,1; and 14,3.

contours drawn in light blue glass and right contours in red; fur garment, brown and bluish gray glasses.

FIGURES AT FAR RIGHT *1)* (cf. description of Andrew in [115]): Tunic, blue, with red clavus; himation, green. *2)* (cf. description of John in [115]): Tunic, blue; himation, violet.

LANDSCAPE main slopes of land, grayish yellow stones; narrow vertical face of land at water's edge, violet glasses; water, blue glasses, bluish gray stone, and white stone; bits of near bank of river in fragment at right (SW pendentive), yellowish gray stone and violet glasses; narrow zone at bottom, above border of arch, green.

[115]

John the Baptist Bearing Witness of Christ (II)

PL. 216–221

(John 1:29–34)

Οὗτος ἦν ὃν εἶπον, ʿΟ ὀπίσω μου | ἐρχόμενος ἔμπροσθέν μου γέγονεν | ὅτι πρῶτός μου ἦν.

This was he of whom I spake, He that cometh after me is preferred before me: for he was before me.

(John 1:15; cf. John 1:30)

ʿΟ ἅ(γιος) ᾿Ιω(άννης) | ὁ πρ(ό)δρ(ο)μος   *Saint John, the Forerunner*

᾿Ι(ησοῦ)ς | Χ(ριστό)ς   *Jesus Christ*

In the decoration of all the domical vaults of the Kariye Djami the basic compositional formula was that of a continuous, circular frieze of scenes surrounding an ornamental medallion at the summit. In the two domical vaults of the inner narthex (PL. 108, 119) the application of this type of composition encountered difficulties and had to be compromised. The uniform scale of figures and architecture adopted for all scenes proved too large for the small dimensions of these vaults, and its use resulted in a loss of rhythmic flow, overcrowding, and distortion, especially in the architecture. The scenes had to be forced, for want of space, into the pendentives, with the result, in the second bay of the inner narthex (PL. 108), that the two scenes have essentially rectangular formats reflecting the squareness of the bay rather than the intended circle of the composition. However, in the mosaics of the larger second vault of the outer narthex (PL. 216) we find the type of composition employed more successfully and under nearly ideal circumstances. Indeed, all but two of the vaults of the outer narthex are large enough for its successful use, and although the mosaics of the vaults of the still larger third, sixth, and seventh bays are no longer intact, they would have provided the best examples of this type of composition in the church (cf. PL. 228, 250, 258).

The annular frieze of scenes in the second vault (PL. 216) is divided into two subjects by inconspicuous caesuras at the centers of the eastern and western sides; there the gold of the background descends to the ornamental borders of the mosaic, giving the decoration a north-south orientation like that of the vault of the first bay. In the north side (left in PL. 216) is the scene of John the Baptist Bearing Witness of Christ (II), and in the south (right in PL. 216) is The Temptation of Christ. The first of these scenes illustrates John 1:29–34, the passage immediately following the verses that were suggested as the textual source of the fragmentary mosaic, John's first testimony of Christ's divinity [114], in the adjacent vault to the north.

The inscription of John's second "witnessing" quotes from John 1:15. This verse occurs in the prologue of the Gospel and does not refer to a specific event. But the same statement, with only minor differences in wording, is repeated in verse 30; it is the significant assertion in the second testimony. The artist would have been more correct had he used the latter verse as the inscription.

The scene is composed of two opposing groups of figures placed on the diagonals of the vault above the two northern pendentives. As the principal figure, placed slightly to left of center and somewhat apart from the others, John the Baptist stands at the very edge of the river Jordan. His body turned in three-quarters view toward the right, he holds a crossed staff in his left hand, points toward Christ, at some distance to the right, and turns his head to address the priests and Levites, who stand close together behind him at the left. He wears a short tunic of brown fur, which stops at the knees and exposes his slender legs. As an outer garment he wears a brown and yellow mantle wrapped about his body. The priests and Levites, who are twelve in number, are men of various ages and types dressed in a variety of costumes, but none wears the traditional "classical" garb, which is here reserved for Christ and two of his disciples-to-be in the opposing group.

This second group, above the northeastern pendentive, is composed of just three figures. At the left, but standing back on higher ground, is Christ, shown here for the first time in the narrative mosaics (except as he would have appeared in the now-lost area of the preceding scene) as a mature man and in the type which will be repeated over and over again in the remaining mosaics. Turning in three-quarters view toward John the Baptist, he extends his right hand in blessing and holds a scroll in his left.

In the foreground to the right of Christ are two figures, dressed in the traditional tunic and himation of Christ's disciples, who are identifiable, by their head types, as the youthful, beardless John and the elderly Andrew with his unruly hair. The same disciples, in reverse order, seem to have been represented in the preceding scene [114], for in both mosaics their respective outer garments are violet and green, as they are whenever they appear among the disciples in later scenes. While the immediate textual source for the scene does not mention any of Christ's future disciples, the succeeding passage (John 1:35–42), which refers to events on the following day, describes in these words the defection of two of the Baptist's disciples to follow Christ: "One of the two which heard John [the Baptist] speak [saying "Behold the Lamb of God"], and followed him [Christ], was Andrew" (John 1:40). The traditional interpretation of this enigmatic statement is that the unnamed disciple was the author of the Gospel, John himself. It seems probable, therefore, that the mosaic represents a conflation of two incidents: the second witnessing of John the Baptist and the calling of John and Andrew.

The youthful John, after the manner of the angels in scenes of the Baptism, veils his extended hands with the folds of his outer garment. His body turned toward the left in a three-quarters view, he looks back at Andrew, who advances, in near-profile, with left hand extended in a speaking gesture and part of his himation billowing out behind him.

Near the base of the vault the river Jordan flows across the entire width of the scene, widening at the ends to fill the two pendentives. In the water in the right pendentive is a wading bird of the heron family in the act of attacking a snake. This space-filling motif, related as it is to the group of Christ and his disciples rather than to John and the priests and Levites, may possess an iconographic significance. In the general context of baptism in which the entire scene is laid, one thinks of the serpent as the agent of sin and man's downfall, and of the waterfowl as a symbol of baptism and immortality through the cleansing from sin.

From the jagged edge of the far bank of the river the landscape setting rises behind each of the two groups to craggy peaks. The slope behind the priests and Levites contains a cave; and at the opposite side Christ stands relieved against the gold of the sky between two natural bridges of rock, through which gnarled trees can be seen.

Dimensions of Vault

Between mosaic surfaces of inner faces of arches, on the two axes, 2.72 m. Rise in vault above highest level of mosaic surface on soffits of transverse arches, .73 m. Diameter of ornamental medallion at summit, .735 m.

Colors and Materials

JOHN THE BAPTIST fur garment, brown and bluish gray glasses, with white stone highlights; mantle, brown and yellow glasses; cross, black glass and dark gray stone.

THE PRIESTS AND LEVITES (5 in front rank, left to right) *1*): Long tunic, pink (mostly terra cotta, pink marble, and white stone, and very little red glass) with gold hem and cuff; mantle, blue; headdress, violet and blue glasses and yellow and white stones; boots, blue. *2*) (partly concealed): Long tunic, violet with gold hem; mantle, green; kerchief around neck, pink; boots, green. *3*): Long tunic, blue with gold hem and cuff; mantle, dark pink; kerchief around neck, blue; boots, blue. *4*): Short tunic, yellow with gold and blue hem, girdle, and collar, the last ornamented with large white stones; tight trousers, green with red and gold ornamental bands; leggings, violet, black, and white; hat, red. *5*): Long tunic, pink with gold hem and cuff; mantle, green; headdress, blue; boots, blue.

CHRIST tunic, dark reddish violet glasses with two red clavi; himation, blue; scroll, gray and white stones tied with red cord; cross-nimbus, gold outlined in dark red. CHRIST'S DISCIPLES *John*: tunic, blue; himation, violet glasses and bluish gray and white stones. *Andrew*: tunic, blue; himation, green glasses and bluish gray and white stones.

LANDSCAPE *River*: dark streaks in water, blue glass; middle tones, bluish gray stone; lights, white stone. *Heron*: body, bluish gray and white stones with violet glasses in darks; legs, black and dark violet; eye, pink encircled by red, with black pupil. *Snake*: bluish gray and white stones and greenish brown glass. *Narrow vertical face of land* at water's edge: yellow-brown stones and dark violet glasses. *Strip of land* on which all figures stand and *rocky peak* at far right: light brownish yellow stone with lights in light yellow and gray stone and crevices in light violet glass. *Peaks* at far left and between Baptist and Christ: bluish gray stones, with shaded faces in violet glasses. *Interior of cave at far left*: black. *Tree at far left*: trunk, green; foliage, green and black. *Tree between Baptist and Christ*: trunk, brown and grayish yellow stones, with violet glass on shaded side; foliage, green and black. *Tree at right*: trunk, gray stones; foliage, green and black. *Near bank of river*: yellowish gray stone cooler in value than that of far bank, outlined in dark violet glass; in angles of pendentives, two bands of dark green glass.

[116]

The Temptation of Christ

PL. 216, 222–227

(*Matthew 4:1–11; Mark 1:12–13; Luke 4:1–13*)

1. FAR LEFT, *Below:*

Εἰ υἱὸς εἶ τοῦ Θ(εο)ῦ, εἰπὲ | ἵνα οἱ λίθοι οὗτοι | ἄρτοι γένωνται.
If thou be the Son of God, command that these stones be made bread. (*Matt. 4:3*)

Above:

Γέγραπται, Οὐκ ἐπ' ἄρτ(ῳ) | μόνῳ ζήσεται (ὁ) ἄνθ(ρωπο)ς, ἀλλ' ἐπὶ | παντὶ ῥήματι (ἐ)κπορευο|μένῳ διὰ στόματο(ς) Θ(εο)ῦ.
It is written, Man shall not live by bread alone, but by every word that proceedeth out of the mouth of God. (*Matt. 4:4*)

114

2. LEFT OF CENTER, *Below:*

Ταῦτα πάντα σοι | δώσω, ἐὰν πεσὼν | προσκυνήσῃς μοι.
All these things will I give thee, if thou wilt fall down and worship me.   (*Matt. 4:9*)

Above:

Ὕπαγε ὀπίσω μου, | Σατανᾶ   *Get thee behind me, Satan*   (*Matt. 4:10*)

3. RIGHT OF CENTER, *Above:*

Τότε παραλαμβάνει | αὐτ(ὸν) ὁ διάβολο(ς) εἰς | τ(ὴν) ἁγίαν πόλιν.
Then the devil taketh him up into the holy city   (*Matt. 4:5*)

4. FAR RIGHT, *Below:*

Εἰ υἱὸς εἶ τοῦ Θ(εο)ῦ, | βάλε σεαυτὸν | κάτω.
If thou be the Son of God, cast thyself down   (*Matt. 4:6*)

Above:

Γέγραπται, Οὐκ ἐκπειρά|σεις Κ(ύριο)ν τὸν Θ(εό)ν σου.
It is written . . . Thou shalt not tempt the Lord thy God.   (*Matt. 4:7*)

ACCOMPANYING EACH REPRESENTATION OF CHRIST:

Ἰ(ησοῦ)ς Χ(ριστό)ς   *Jesus Christ*

In the mosaics of the Temptation, in the southern half of the second vault (PL. 222), Christ and the devil confront one another four times, as though in four distinct incidents: *1*) at the far left, over a box filled with stones; *2*) above the southeastern pendentive, in which the "kingdoms of the world" are represented; *3*) to the right of center, ascending a steep mountain; and *4*) above the southwestern pendentive, in the scene at Jerusalem on the "pinnacle of the temple." In all but one of the four scenes, the inscriptions quote from the dialogue of Christ and the devil, the words of the devil being placed below, in the zone of the landscape, and those of Christ in the gold of the sky, above.

Christ's temptation is recorded in the three Synoptic Gospels, but only in Matthew and Luke is it described. Both accounts agree that there were three, not four, incidents but disagree on the order in which they occurred. According to Matthew, Christ was challenged to prove his divinity first by changing stones into bread and then by casting himself down unharmed from the pinnacle of the temple, and finally was offered the kingdoms of the world in return for worshiping at the feet of the devil. The sequence of the last two incidents is reversed in Luke, and in this respect the mosaic version agrees with Luke, although the inscriptions, with one minor exception, are drawn from Matthew. The scene of the ascent of the mountain that has been added in the mosaic is inscribed with a verse (Matthew 4:5) that is preliminary to the description of the temptation in Jerusalem on the pinnacle of the temple. As a picture, however, it illustrates Matthew 4:8, "Again, the devil taketh him up into an exceeding high mountain, and sheweth him all the kingdoms of the world." As a scene, therefore, it pertains to, and should precede, the second incident, but its inscription and position within the series make of it a transition to the final scene on the pinnacle of the temple.

In all four images the devil is portrayed as a dark, winged creature, thin and intensely animated; his sharp features and streaming hair give him a wild and furious aspect. In all but one instance his features are drawn in profile, the pose that is so often given to evildoers. He is scantily clad in a dark mantle that reveals his slender legs and arms. In contrast to the devil, Christ appears as a figure of great dignity and calmness; he is dressed, as usual, in the purple tunic and blue himation, holds a scroll in his left hand, and is marked by the cross-nimbus.

In the first scene, at the far left, the devil stands at the left in profile view, arms extended toward Christ; in his left hand he holds a stone from the chest filled with stones at his feet. Christ stands erect in three-quarters view at the right, facing the devil, and raises his right hand in speech.

In the second scene, the devil stands, or hovers, within the walls that enclose the "kingdoms;" his pose is a spiral twist, his legs and hips in profile facing left, shoulders turned in three-quarters view to reveal his back, and head turned backward in profile toward the right, toward Christ, who stands behind him. Satan's arms point stiffly downward to a row of six kings seated on a common throne within the turreted walls. The kings wear richly decorated vestments and fancifully shaped crowns; across the right shoulders of four of them lie white staffs, held in the right hand. Placed in the sharp angle of the pendentive as they are, the row of kings and the fortress walls are necessarily much deformed. Christ, who again stands in three-quarters view at the right, and at a somewhat higher point in the vault than before, leans forward slightly and extends his hands, directing his speech toward the devil.

In the third scene, Christ, at the left, follows the devil up the steep side of a mountain. His body in near-profile, but his head in three-quarters view, he looks upward and raises his right arm toward the devil. These gestures, as well as his striding pose and the billowing drapery behind him, convey a sense of rapid and strenuous upward motion despite the loss of the lowest parts of the figure. No less impressive in this respect is the little figure of the devil, near the top of the jagged peak, who seems about to take flight in the same upward direction. His lithe body, partly obscured by the rocks, faces right, in near-profile, in the direction of his extended right arm. His wings are outspread symmetrically, and his head, hair streaming upward, is turned in near-profile so that he looks back at Christ.

The final scene, on the pinnacle of the temple, receives the greatest space and the most elaborate setting. Although some of the mosaic at the lower left has been lost, including the lower half of the devil, the scene is intact in all its essentials. Filling the pendentive are the walls of Jerusalem, which parallel the lower edge of the vault toward the left, and the "pinnacle" of the temple, which rises at an angle toward the right. It is evident that the devil stood on a now-destroyed section of the walls at the lower left. Facing right and again drawn in near-profile, he raises his left arm toward Christ, and his right arm points downward and to the right in indication of his command to Christ to cast himself down. Christ stands erect, in three-quarters view and with right hand extended, on the flat, square roof, supported on square piers, of an open-sided tower at the center. The tower is seen as if from above; its piers descend into the pendentive and are cut off by the border of the arch. Filling out the remainder of the scene, and indicating that the setting is the temple, is an altar, standing on a platform to the right of the "pinnacle." The altar is supported by a pedestal, partly visible beneath the altar cloth, and covered by a ciborium, which consists of four slender columns carrying trefoil-arched spandrels and a small pyramidal roof.

The rocky landscape spread out behind the figures in the scenes of the Temptation is composed of three peaks of fantastically jagged form, which, with the ciborium and a gnarled tree, break up the field of the gold background at quite regular intervals with recurring accents arranged like the spokes of a wheel and provide the framework for the disposition of the figures. In the first three scenes Christ is relieved against the first two peaks; the devil in the second scene is aligned with the tree above him, and the devils of the third and fourth scenes are carefully placed on a line with the third peak. The first devil, at the far left, Christ atop the tower, and the ciborium, at the far right, complete the series of compositional elements that radiate from the center of the vault.

Dimensions of Vault
See no. [115].

Colors and Materials
CHRIST tunic, dark reddish violet, with red and gold clavus; himation, blue; scroll, gray and white stones; cross-nimbus, gold outlined in dark red glass. DEVIL flesh, brown glasses with black drawing; hair, brown glass and dark brownish gray stone; wings and mantle, dark brownish gray and bluish gray stones.
BOX OF STONES front side, green glass with gray stone designs; receding side, dark green glass with black and light green glass designs; stones, dark gray, brown, and brownish green in shadows, and light blue-gray, light yellow, and white in highlights.
KINGDOMS OF WORLD *Walls:* bluish gray stone, with blue glasses in shadows and white highlights. *Kings:* vestments, alternately blue and light red with gold and red ornamentation; crowns, gold and red; staffs, white stone.
JERUSALEM AND TOWER OF TEMPLE *Wall at left:* bluish gray stones with shadows of blue glass. *Tower:* lighted faces, light gray stone outlined with white; shaded faces and ornaments of piers, green glasses; curtain within tower, red.
CIBORIUM AND ALTAR *Ciborium:* lighted faces of superstructure, light gray stone with wide borders of green glass; shaded faces of superstructure, green glasses with black outlining; columns, shafts of green highlighted with white and capitals of gold, brown, and black; ornamental bands on shafts of columns, gold and red. *Altar:* cloth, red with ornamental borders at top and bottom of gold and blue; pedestal of altar, light gray stones and blue glass. *Platform:* floor, light yellowish gray stone with white stone borders; vertical faces, two values of yellowish brown stone with ornaments of brown glass.
LANDSCAPE *Mountain peak at left:* bluish gray stones with highlights of warm light gray and white stones and shaded faces of blue glasses; crevices, lines of pink stone and terra cotta. *Second and third mountain peaks:* gray stones in lighted areas, warm grayish yellow and brown stones in shaded areas, blue and violet glasses in outlines. *Ground of middle zone:* at left, in scene one, cool bluish gray stones with blue glass shadows; to left of kingdoms, below scene one, and as main background of scene two, light yellow stone; at feet of Christ in scene two and as background for scenes three and four, light brown stones with outlining of hillocks in dark violet glasses. *Tree:* trunk and branches, gray stone in lights, brown stones in shading; foliage, green glasses with black accents.

[117]

The Miracle at Cana

PL. 228–237

(*John 2:1–11*)

In recognition of its position on the longitudinal axis of the church and its function as the principal entrance, the third bay of the outer narthex was made larger than those at the sides. The scenes that were chosen to decorate its domical vault also set it apart from the other bays, for they convey an iconographic significance beyond that deriving from their context within the series of narrative scenes of Christ's public ministry. As was pointed out in the description of the mosaic of the Virgin Blachernitissa [2], all the mosaics of this bay, those in the lunettes above the doors as well as those in the vault, were intended as an exposition of the divine plan of Salvation, whereby man is to attain union with God, and achieve Life, through the mysteries of the Incarnation and the sacrament of the Eucharist. With the latter theme in mind, the mosaicist confronted The Miracle at Cana (PL. 228, left) and The Multiplication of Loaves (PL. 228, right) in the two halves of the vault, the first in the northern half and the second in the southern.

These mosaics, which must have been among the most impressive in the church, have suffered very extensive losses in the central part of the vault, where a large ornamental medallion and appropriate inscriptions were most probably set in the gold background. Fortunately, large parts of the mosaics around the periphery of the vault, where the scenes themselves were placed, are still extant, and most of the essential elements are present. We are also fortunate that much detailed knowledge of the missing parts of the scenes can be supplied from the frescoes of the Rumanian church of St. Nicholas at Curtea-de-Argeş, which reproduce, in almost exact form, the scene of The Multiplication of Loaves at the Kariye Djami and, somewhat less closely, the scene of The Miracle at Cana.[1]

Christ's first miracle, the turning of the water into wine, is also the first of an extensive series of miracles which are the subjects of the remaining mosaics of the narthexes. It begins on the western axis of the vault, above the lunette of the Virgin Blachernitissa [2], with a representation of the marriage feast itself and continues in a semicircle to the opposite side, above the head of Christ, the Land of the Living [1], ending with the performance of the miracle.

Relatively little now remains of the scene of banqueting (PL. 230, 232) above the northwestern pendentive. It doubtless represented Christ, one or more disciples, the bride and groom, and the steward seated at table while servants performed their duties. At its far left edge a narrow strip of gold background, which separates it from The Multiplication of Loaves, rises from the border of the lunette. To the right is a vertical line of blue that defines the left edge of a piece of architectural background. Seated on a low stool, or bench, at the far left is the fragment of a figure turned to the right and dressed in the yellow garments which Peter always wears. In front of him, one sees the lower parts of Christ, who was seated on a somewhat higher golden bench with a red cushion, facing in near-profile to the right. He is clad in his blue himation, his legs are extended, and his feet rest on a golden footstool. Before him are the lower parts of a golden table, which separated the scene of feasting from the motif that occupies the triangular area of the pendentive beneath it. To the right of the table, at the very edge of the fragment, is a small piece of a blue, gray, and white garment with a hem of gold and red. The banqueting scene seems to have extended still further to the right, to the center of the transverse arch; there it probably ended with the bit of architectural background at the far left edge of the large fragment, containing the miracle, which fills the northeastern quadrant of the vault (PL. 231).

As a suitable motif to fill the triangular space beneath the banqueting table, the mosaicist has depicted the slaying of a white bullock in preparation for the feast. Crouching astride its back, in the manner of Mithras slaying the bull, a young man bends the animal's head up by grasping one of its horns with his left hand, while he pierces its throat with a knife held in his

1 Tafrali, *Monuments byzantins de Curtéa de Arges*, Text, pp. 128 f., Atlas, PL. LXVIII, 1 and 2. These are details; for a complete illustration see *Buletinul Comisiunii Monumentelor Istorice*, Anul X–XVI, Fig. 260. For references to illustrations of Multiplication of Loaves see [118], n. 1.

right; streams of blood gush forth from the wound. This incident has no textual authority in the account of the marriage at Cana and was surely borrowed from a composition of the parable of the Prodigal Son. Among representations of the marriage feast of Cana, this detail is found only in the mosaic at the Kariye Djami and in the fresco at Curtea-de-Argeş, where it occurs to the right of the table but in the same form as in the mosaic.[2] At the Kariye Djami it was introduced not only as a space filler but for iconographic purposes, for it recalls the blood of the sacrifice, thus becoming analogous with the wine in the next pendentive and the bread in the scene of The Multiplication of Loaves in the southern side of the vault. At Curtea-de-Argeş the introduction of this motif into the scene of the marriage feast did not have the iconographic motivation, nor was it required for compositional reasons. The appearance of the motif there is a strong indication of the direct dependence of the work at Curtea-de-Argeş on the Kariye Djami mosaics; the dependence appears not alone in this instance but in the paintings that occupy the upper zone of the three walls of the nave, where close copies, with some compositional adaptation, of the corresponding subjects in the Kariye Djami are to be found.

The feasting scene at Curtea-de-Argeş corresponds with the mosaic in those details that are preserved and supplies the following information for the missing parts. Seated to the left of Christ is Peter (as in the mosaic); other figures, possibly disciples, stand in the background behind Christ. To the right, behind the table, are the standing figures of a richly dressed young man, probably the groom; the bride in elaborate attire, wearing a crown; and a second man. Standing at the right end of the table and facing Christ is a man, probably the "ruler" or "governor" of the feast, whose head is covered by a hood; he raises a glass in his right hand. (In the mosaic this person appears, in like costume and pose, in the scene of the Miracle at the right, and he may well have been present, in the same pose, at the feast.) At a higher level, in the architectural setting behind those at table, stand two young male servants; one of them holds a platter, and the other, carrying a vessel (empty?) in his left hand, seems to address Christ, with right arm extended in a gesture of speech.

Miraculously the scene of the changing of the water into wine at the Kariye Djami has remained intact. At the left Christ and his mother, with Peter and John behind them, look on as the servants, at the right, pour water into great jars and the "governor of the feast" offers a tumbler of water (?) to Christ.

Peter, at the far left, makes his first appearance here as one of Christ's disciples; his features are unmistakable, and he is clad, as usual, in yellow. He stands calmly looking at Christ, his arms resting in the folds of his himation, as in a sling, and his hands folded before him. The young, beardless disciple between Peter and Christ should be identified as John; his type is that of John in the scenes of John the Baptist Bearing Witness ([114] and [115]) and his garments are of the same colors: the tunic blue and the himation violet. He has turned his head far over toward Peter, to whom he seems to speak, and his right hand is raised, palm outward. Christ stands with his left foot forward, a scroll in his left hand and his right hand extended toward the tumbler held by the governor of the feast. Mary, who stands close to Christ at his left side, is partly obscured by his halo and figure. Her role in the miracle was an important one, for it was she who instigated it and instructed the servants to obey her son's commands.

Grouped together in the pendentive are six pithoi, or earthenware jars; tesserae of terra

2 See illustration in *Buletinul*.

cotta—the material of which the jars themselves would have been made—are the main material used in their representation. A young man dressed in a simple, short-sleeved tunic pours water into the second of the three jars in the back row from a golden vessel with a long neck and a low foot, which he supports with his left hand and shoulder; in his right hand he grasps what may be a slender handle. At the far right another youth approaches, a clay or stone amphora with golden handles supported on his left shoulder and held with both hands. The governor of the feast stands behind the first youth, faces Christ, and presents the tumbler; a bearded old man, he wears a blue, tight-sleeved tunic ornamented with gold and red at the cuffs (and presumably at the hem), a red mantle, and a blue scarf, which covers his head, in the manner of a hood, and is wrapped around the base of his neck and shoulders.

The architectural background consists of a low wall behind the group of figures at the left, a two-storied house behind the servants and the jars, and another wall at the right, extending to the limits of the scene. The façade of the house is pierced at the left by a rectangular opening; in the center is an arched doorway, which is recessed between two projecting piers surmounted by a pair of corbels and a square tower with openings in the sides.

The ornamental motif immediately above the arched door, illustrated in nearly full size on Plate 237, has been mistakenly thought to represent the Arabic number 6811, and interpreted as the date of the mosaics in terms of the number of years from the Creation, corresponding to the year A.D. 1302–03. For a refutation of this interpretation the reader should turn back to the Introduction (pp. 14–16), where the dating of the mosaics is discussed in detail.

Dimensions of Vault

Between masonry surfaces of inner faces of arches, on E–W axis, 3.92 m.; on N–S axis, 3.84 m. Rise in vault above highest level of soffits of transverse arches, .79 m.

Colors and Materials

The Marriage Feast (NW quadrant)

FRAGMENT OF SEATED FIGURE (at far left) garment, gray, tan, and yellow stones; bench, gray and tan stones. FRAGMENT OF FIGURE OF CHRIST himation, blue; cushion, red; bench, gold glass on exposed end and grayish brown stones with drawing in very dark gray on receding face; footstool, gold glass with drawing in brown stones on top and left side, and brown stones with drawing in very dark gray on right side. TABLE gold glass with drawing in brown stones on long side, and brown stones with drawing in gold and dark gray on right end. FRAGMENTARY FIGURE (to right of table) piece of garment blue, with gold and red hem.

YOUTH SLAYING BULLOCK short tunic, blue; boots, green; scarf around neck, red. BULLOCK light yellowish and light brownish gray stones with shading in brown stones and drawing in very dark gray stone; blood, red. BACKGROUND arranged in zones, from top to bottom, of light yellowish gray stone, dark gray stone, light green glass, and dark green glass.

The Miracle (NE quadrant)

PETER tunic, blue; himation, yellow. JOHN tunic, blue; himation, violet. CHRIST tunic, dark reddish violet with gold and silver clavus; himation, blue; scroll, white stone; shadows under feet, very dark blue-violet glass. MARY garments, blue; cuff of sleeve, gold and red; point of shoe, warm gray stone used in background.

GOVERNOR OF FEAST tunic, visible only at sleeve, blue with gold and red cuff; mantle, red; scarf on head and shoulders, blue; tumbler, exterior of gray stone above and blue glass below and interior of blue glass. SERVANT POURING WATER tunic, blue; scarf around neck, yellow; vessel, gold with brown stone outline and shading, ornamental bands and handle of red glass; water, gray and white stones and a few blue glass tesserae. SERVANT CARRYING WATER short tunic, green; scarf around neck, yellow; mantle, red; boots, blue; amphora, brownish yellow and brown stones with shading of violet glasses and handles of gold and violet glasses. EARTHENWARE JARS terra cotta in right sides; pink stones and white stone highlights in left sides, outlined by a row of red glass; right sides outlined by a row of red and one of dark violet glass.

Background

FRAGMENTARY STRUCTURE AT FAR LEFT blue glasses and bluish gray and white stones. LOW WALL AT LEFT light yellowish gray stones. BUILDING AT CENTER lighted faces, brownish gray stones with outlines in violet glass and bluish gray stone; shaded faces, some in violet glass, others in light brown stone; corbels, gray stone in carved ends and blue glasses in receding sides; drapery over roof, red; darkest parts of openings, black. LOW WALL AT RIGHT brownish gray stones. ZONES OF LOWER FOREGROUND zone in which jars are set, bluish gray stones; zones below, medium green glass above and very dark green glasses below.

[118]

The Multiplication of Loaves

PL. 228, 238–245

(*Matthew 14:15–21; Mark 6:35–44; Luke 9:12–17; John 6:5–13*)

The Miracle of the Multiplication of Loaves, or the Feeding of the Five Thousand, forms the counterpart to The Miracle at Cana in the vault of the entrance bay of the narthex. The dogmatic significance of the juxtaposition of these subjects and their relation to the mosaics of the two lunettes beneath them has been pointed out above ([2] and [117]). The Multiplication of Loaves, even more than its companion, is a subject that lends itself to an episodic presentation. In describing the performance of this miracle, the four Gospel accounts agree upon the following episodes: *1*) Christ took the five loaves, and, looking up to heaven, he blessed them (John says he gave thanks); *2*) Christ broke the bread and gave it to his disciples; *3*) the disciples, in turn, distributed the bread to the multitudes (five thousand men, besides women and children), who had been instructed to sit on the grass in companies of fifty or one hundred; *4*) after the multitudes had eaten, the disciples "took up of the fragments that remained twelve baskets full" (Matt. 14:20). From a comparison of the existing parts of the mosaic with the almost identical version in the frescoes of Curtea-de-Argeş,[1] it is clear that these four episodes were literally and chronologically represented at the Kariye Djami.

The first episode, The Blessing of the Five Loaves (PL. 240), was put at the center of the east side of the vault, almost directly above the head of the great iconic mosaic of Christ, the Land of the Living, in the lunette above the door leading to the inner narthex; it was thus prominently displayed to those entering the church. The upper parts of the figures are destroyed, but one sees that two of the disciples, standing side by side at the left, face their master, at the right, over two large, empty baskets which are on the ground between. The disciples veil their hands, which they extend toward Christ, in the drapery of their mantles in the manner of the Apostles in scenes of their Communion. Christ, standing with slightly bent knees, holds both arms upward before him. The complete scene, as represented at Curtea-de-Argeş, shows the disciples looking directly at Christ, who holds in his left hand a stack of five round, flat loaves. He steadies the loaves against his vertically raised right forearm. His head is turned upward toward an arc of heaven, from which rays of light shine down upon the bread.

The second episode (PL. 241), to the right of the first, depicts Christ breaking the bread, two disciples about to receive it, and a company of the multitude sitting on the grass as they await its distribution (PL. 242). In the group of Christ and the disciples, the composition of the first episode was used in reverse. Christ, facing right, stoops over three baskets, now filled with broken pieces of bread. In each hand he holds bread; he is about to give it to the disciples,

---

1 The best published reproduction of the entire scene at Curtea-de-Argeş is in *Buletinul Comisiunii Monumentelor Istorice*, Fig. 266, pp. 229, 230. See also Stefanescu, *La Peinture religieuse en Valachie et Transylvanie*, Album, PL. 6; Tafrali, Atlas, PL. XLIV, XLV, XLVI.

who stand to the right of the baskets, facing him with hands extended to receive it. The two disciples are the same ones who appeared in the first episode; their features and the colors of their garments are identical with those of the disciples in both episodes in the Curtea fresco. The older disciple, who leans closer to Christ, is identifiable as Andrew; his features, his hair, and the green color of his himation are those of Andrew in the second scene of John the Baptist Bearing Witness [115]. Perhaps Andrew is here represented in a favored position, as he was also in the preceding episode, because he and Philip are the only disciples to be mentioned by name (John 6:5–9) in the narrative accounts of the miracle. However, the second disciple in this scene is not Philip, who is universally represented as a beardless young man, but an older man with short beard. In all particulars except the number of baskets this group is closely duplicated at Curtea-de-Argeş. The fact that the mosaicist's mistake with regard to Philip (who is correctly represented in the cathedral at Monreale) is repeated by the Curtea painter is another indication that the mosaic itself served as his model. To judge from the fresco, about one third of the first company of the multitude has been lost at the right side of the mosaic fragment. In this group also the fresco can be trusted for information regarding the mosaic, for it repeats the existing parts with great accuracy. The two are alike in such details as the small child standing on his mother's lap at the left and even in the details of the drapery, especially that of the men in the front row. Pertaining to this episode is a detail lost from the mosaic which is supplied by the painting. Partly concealed behind the left slope of a jagged, two-pronged mountain peak, which rises quite high behind the company, and at a point just above the broken edge of the mosaic, a youth holds up a round loaf of bread as he peers down upon the scene of The Breaking of the Bread. This is, perhaps, the lad from whom the five barley loaves were obtained (John 6:9).

The third episode, The Distribution of the Bread, received a rather extended treatment in the mosaic. Two additional companies of the multitude were arranged in succession to carry on the annular frieze of scenes. The episode began to the right of the company shown in The Breaking of the Bread, in the area of lost mosaic; passing above the curved contour of the hillock that forms the background of the final episode, in the southwestern pendentive, it ended with another company of seated figures (PL. 245), which is partly preserved, near the center of the west side of the vault. As in the Curtea fresco, therefore, three companies of the multitude were represented in all: the first company witnesses the breaking of the bread but has not yet been served; the second, as the painted version shows, receives bread from the disciples but has not yet eaten; and the third, as can be observed in the mosaic itself, has been served and has begun to eat.

Except for a small fragment at its right end, the mosaic version of the second company and the disciples who distribute the bread is destroyed. In the fresco, a disciple in the foreground with a full basket resting on his back, held in place by his upraised right arm, strides toward the right, filling the space between the first and second groups. Above, and partly obscured by him, is a disciple, possibly Peter, who leans far forward toward the right with his mantle blowing out behind him. He stretches out both arms to pass bread to a man standing at the back of the company, who reaches for it with one arm. To the left, behind the reaching disciple, one of the younger disciples emerges from behind the mountain holding a basket before him in both arms. The small mosaic fragment of the one surviving figure in the second company appears above the upper left edge of the final episode, in the southwestern pendentive; it consists of the upper body and part of the head of a bearded man facing left; he wore a scarf over his head and around his shoulders (PL. 244). A little further to the right, after a lacuna in which one of the disciples may have stood, is a bit of a basket, and partly concealed by its right side is the fragmentary figure of a small boy. At the right, the undestroyed part of the third company is seated on the ground; two men in the front row, at the left, the first with his back to the beholder, face one another, holding pieces of bread near their mouths. In the fresco, this group is placed at the far right, after the episode of the twelve baskets rather than above it. It has been modified in its details but retains the essential features of the mosaic: a disciple at the left; the basket on the ground; two small boys instead of one; and the third company of the multitude, who are standing instead of sitting.

The final episode in The Multiplication of Loaves (PL. 244) was used by the mosaicist at the Chora to fill the southwestern pendentive with an iconographically important motif—that of the twelve baskets—that would serve as pendant to the six great jars of wine in the pendentive diagonally opposite. Christ is seated at the left, his feet on a footstool. In his left hand he holds the scroll and with his right he blesses the baskets of bread, which are arranged in the foreground in four rows to fit the sharp angle of the pendentive. To the right, behind the baskets, are three of the disciples. Nearest Christ is Peter, looking at Christ and gesticulating with both hands. He and the second disciple have dispensed with their himatia and are clad in short-sleeved tunics, Peter in yellow, as usual, and the other in blue. The third disciple, one of the three beardless disciples, is probably intended as John, since he wears a violet himation as he did in scenes [114] and [115]. This suggests the probability that the second disciple is James, since Peter, James, and John formed an inner group among the disciples.

In its physical relation to The Distribution of the Bread, the scene of the twelve baskets in the pendentive forms a lower zone, centered below the interval between the second and third companies. At this point in his composition the Curtea painter misunderstood the sequence of incidents in his model, the mosaic of the Kariye Djami. Since he was composing in a continuous horizontal frieze, he simply raised the scene of the pendentive mosaic, rearranging the baskets to suit his conditions but otherwise copying it quite accurately, and inserted it into the midst of the scene of the Distribution, between the two companies. A look at this part of the painting shows how artificially the episode was fitted in; the outlines at both sides cut off the flanking groups in a manner that is comprehensible only if it is regarded as an attempt to force the pendentive into the composition at the point beneath which it occurred in the mosaic.

In composing the various incidents of the two subjects which share the domical vault, the mosaicist coped very successfully, in three out of the four instances, with the problem of filling the triangular spaces at the corners with appropriate and iconographically significant motifs (the slaying of the bullock, the six jars of wine, the twelve baskets of bread) while still retaining, as the major compositional element, the annular frieze that encircles the vault. In the fourth pendentive, at the southeastern corner, he was less successful. Here he introduced a genre-like scene of a group of small children scrambling about on the ground and snatching up pieces of bread (PL. 243).

Dimensions of Vault

See no. [117].

Colors and Materials

CHRIST (3 figures) tunic, dark reddish violet glass in shaded areas only and blue glass of two values in middle tones and highlights (one of few instances in the mosaics where anything but violet is used in Christ's tunic); clavus, gold bordered with red except in second figure, where border is dark blue; himation, blue; shadows under feet, very dark blue (cf. Christ in Miracle at Cana [117]; only in this vault does detail of heavy shadow beneath feet of Christ appear; a similar device was used, however, in one or two of the frescoes of the parecclesion).

DISCIPLES *Episode 1*. Left figure: tunic, blue with dark blue clavi; himation, tan and violet. Right figure: tunic, blue; himation, green. *Episode 2*. Figure in foreground: tunic, blue with dark blue clavus; himation, violet. Andrew: tunic, blue with dark blue clavus; himation, green. *Episode 4* (in pendentive). Peter: short-sleeved tunic, yellow. Second disciple: short-sleeved tunic, blue. Third disciple: tunic, blue; himation, dark violet shadows, tan and gray lights.

BASKETS exterior wickerwork, tan and brown stones with reinforcing bands of dark brown stones and short diagonal bindings of black glass; interiors of empty baskets, light tan stone; bread, light tan and brown stones. FIRST COMPANY OF MULTITUDE old man at front left, gray and tan garment, red scarf about neck; man at front center with back turned, red garment, blue scarf at neck; man at front right, green garment, red scarf and headdress; woman at left holding child, green garment; child, pink garment. CHILDREN (in southeastern pendentive) three boys at left and in foreground, short tunics respectively yellowish gray and blue, red, blue; three children seated at right, blue tunic, red mantle around neck; green tunic and headdress, red garment at shoulder, and yellow mantle; red garment.

FRAGMENTARY FIGURE FROM SECOND COMPANY (above

Christ in Episode 4) red garment, yellow scarf over head and shoulders. THIRD COMPANY OF MULTITUDE (above and to right of pendentive; front row, left to right) small boy to right of basket, green garment; men, brown and tan garment, red scarf; blue undergarment, red mantle, brown headdress; brown undergarment, blue mantle, red headdress; green mantle, red scarf. Between first two men at left, a figure dressed in solid blue is to be seen.

LANDSCAPE *Background of Episode 1 and area to left of baskets in Episode 2:* blue-gray stone hill outlined at top with band of white stone and at left with band of white stone and row of blue glass. *Background to right of baskets of Episode 2* (in SE quadrant): brownish yellow stones above fringe of grass and light yellowish stone below fringe, extending to top of triangular area of green glass in pendentive. *Background of third company* (above Episode 4 in SW quadrant): blue-gray stone outlined at top right with band of light bluish gray stone. *Background hill in Episode 4:* brownish gray stones outlined at top with band of light gray stone. *Background of zone containing twelve baskets:* dark green glass.

TECHNICAL NOTE

When the mosaic representations of the baskets were cleaned, brown pigment was found to have been applied, after the tesserae had been set, to certain parts of the wickerwork in order to make the baskets stand out more prominently from the similar brown color of the background and to sharpen the contrast between the pieces of bread and their background. This is one of the few instances of color correction by the use of pigments to have been found in the mosaics of the Kariye Djami.

[119]

Christ Healing a Leper

PL. 246, 247

(*Matthew 8:1–4; Mark 1:40–44; Luke 5:12–14*)

[120]

An Unidentified Scene

PL. 246, 248

The domical vaults of the fourth and fifth bays are considerably smaller than the others in the outer narthex and even slightly smaller than the two in the inner narthex. The fourth vault (PL. 246) retains fragments of its mosaic decoration, but all mosaics in the fifth (PL. 249) are now lost. In contrast to the mosaics of the first three vaults, which were composed on the north-south axes, those in the fourth, and probably those in the fifth as well, were given an east-west orientation.

The identification and the composition of The Healing of the Leper, in the eastern side of the fourth vault, are clearly evident despite the loss of the upper parts of the scene. As in all but one of the numerous scenes of healing at the Kariye Djami, Christ and a number of his disciples are at the left and the afflicted, with accompanying bystanders, are at the right. The two groups stand radially disposed at the corners of the vault, with the result that they are widely separated from one another. In the background a low wall containing a series of rectangular niches, a pier rising above it at the center, joins the two groups of figures.

Of the group at the left, the fragment still retains the lower half of the figures of Christ and a disciple standing behind him at the left. A bit of garment of still another disciple appears at the left edge, and it seems likely that the group originally continued to the left with additional disciples. Christ is turned toward the right in near-profile, his right arm extended horizontally before him; in his left hand, which is concealed in a fold of his himation, he holds a scroll.

At the opposite side, the leper's bare, spotted legs and the lower parts of his short garment are preserved. Close behind him, to the right, are the lower parts of three richly dressed men, and still further to the right another section of the low wall of the background is exposed to view, an indication that the composition ended there and that the group behind the leper never contained more than the three figures.

All that now remains of scene [120], in the western side of the fourth vault, is a narrow strip of mosaic (PL. 248) that adjoins and parallels the ornamental border of the arch at the west side. It represents waves of the sea and is executed in blue glass and bluish gray and white stones. At the top edge of the fragment, almost exactly in the center of the western side and thus in the center foreground of the picture, is a short interval between waves that is solidly filled with violet tesserae. In all likelihood this small area of violet represents a bit of what was once the hull of a boat set in the midst of a stormy sea.

Christ performed two miracles that involved a boat in a rough sea, either one of which might have been the subject of this mosaic: Christ Stilling the Tempest (Matt. 8:23–27; Mark 4:35–41; Luke 8:22–25); and Christ Walking on the Water (and rescuing Peter) (Matt. 14:22–33; Mark 6:45–51; John 6:16–21). One factor might seem to favor the latter subject. In the three Gospels which describe it, Christ Walking on the Water follows immediately after The Multiplication of Loaves; the order of the mosaics corresponds to this sequence, for the western side of the fourth bay, the setting of the fragmentary mosaic, could be thought to follow the southern side of the preceding bay, where The Miracle of the Loaves is depicted. However, it will become evident that the mosaicists at the Kariye Djami did not attempt a chronological treatment for the miracles as a whole, which in the Gospels themselves are only loosely ordered.

Dimensions of Vault

Between mosaic surfaces on inner faces of arches on E–W axis, 2.37 m.; between masonry surfaces of inner faces of arches on N–S axis, 2.175 m.; rise in vault above highest level of soffits of transverse arches, .61 m. Mosaic fragment of scene [120], ca. .15 m. high, and ca. 1.45 m. long.

Colors and Materials

Christ Healing a Leper [119]

CHRIST tunic (visible only at sleeve and hem), violet; himation, blue; scroll, gray and white stones. LEPER legs, pink and white marbles in flesh tones outlined at left sides in light greenish brown glass and at right sides in very dark greenish brown glass, with spots in dark greenish brown; short tunic, blue.

DISCIPLES   disciple to left of Christ, tunic (visible at hem), blue; himation, violet; evidences of a second disciple at left edge of fragment, toes of a foot and gray stone from a garment.   THREE COMPANIONS OF THE LEPER *Central figure:* long tunic, blue with hem of greenish brown and brown glasses; mantle (held out to left), yellowish and dull reddish brown stones with drawing in greenish brown glass; boots, blue. *Figure to left:* long tunic, red with blue hem; mantle, violet; boots, blue. *Figure to right:* long tunic, blue with darker

blue hem; mantle, green; boots, blue.
ARCHITECTURE   lighted faces, greenish gray stone; shaded face of turret and reveals in left sides of niches, brownish green glass; soffits of lintels of niches, brownish green glasses in light areas and brown glass in dark areas.   ZONE BELOW WALL dark green.   BACKGROUND ABOVE WALL   gold.

An Unidentified Scene [120]

WAVES   shaded parts at right sides, blue glasses; lighted faces at left, bluish gray stone highlighted with white stone.   HULL OF BOAT (?)   violet glass.

[121], [128]

Christ Healing the Paralytic at the Pool of Bethesda[1]   PL. 250, 251 *a*, 251 *b*

(John 5:2–15)

['Ο Χριστὸς ἐπὶ τῇ προβατικῇ κολυμβήθρᾳ ἀπὸ τῆς] | κλίνης ἐγείρει τὸν παράλυτον λόγῳ

Christ at the sheep pool raises the paralytic from his bed by his word.

Christ Healing the Paralytic at the Pool of Bethesda is the first of a series of scenes in the large domical vault of the sixth, or corner, bay of the outer narthex. Before it is described, it is important that the compositional treatment and distribution of all the scenes in the vault (PL. 250) be explained. In individual descriptions of the other scenes, a number of which are fragmentary and unidentifiable, the reader will be referred to this section, and to the accompanying diagram (text Fig. B), for their positions, for their relation to each other, and for evidence regarding their original limits since the points of separation between them are not always apparent at first glance.

Three very irregularly shaped areas of mosaic are still *in situ*. The largest fragment is in the southern side; it comprises the great ornamental medallion at the center (PL. 331 *c*), most of the southwestern quadrant, including its pendentive, and portions of the southeastern pendentive. The other two fragments occupy the northern pendentives and limited areas above them. Fragmentary though these mosaics are, the original layout of the decoration in the vault can still be discerned.

Around the central ornamental medallion six scenes were placed in succession, in an annular frieze whose perimeter was defined by a continuous band of green representing in a general way a zone of ground, or a base for the scenes. The green band inscribed a circle within the square formed by the supporting arches and separated the scenes in the frieze from those below in the pendentives at the corners of the vault. In effect, the composition imitated arrangements in a true dome with structurally separate pendentives. Two of the pendentives (NW and SE) were filled with complete and individual scenes; another (NE) with a second episode of the

---

1 For the iconographic relationship between this scene and the two in the NW and SE pendentives of the sixth vault, see the discussion of scene [129], below.

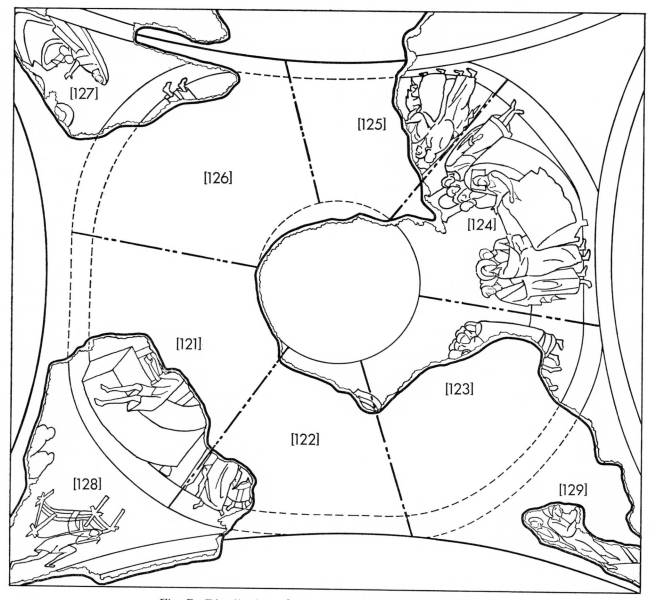

Fig. B. Distribution of scenes in the vault of the sixth bay

subject that lies above it in the circular frieze; and the fourth (SW) with an ornamental motif. Thus, there were eight subjects in the whole vault: six in the annular frieze (one expanded into a second zone in the pendentive beneath) and two in the pendentives. The accompanying diagram,[2] when compared with the general view looking up into the vault (PL. 250), will serve to identify the scenes by number and indicate the points of separation between them.

In contrast to the compositions in the preceding vaults, the six scenes of the annular frieze appear to have contained no landscape; in this vault landscape was limited to the scenes in the pendentives. Nor does the gold of the sky appear to have been brought down at any point to the lower margin of the frieze as a means of indicating separation between scenes. Instead, a continuous background, which further emphasizes the circular form of the composition, is provided by a wall, which seems to shift in height, and sometimes in color, from scene to scene

2 The reader should be warned that in the general view of the sixth vault (PL. 250), and in its diagram, the sequence of the scenes is counterclockwise, while in the diagrammatic plan of the narthexes at the end of the volumes of text and plates the sequence is clockwise. This discrepancy is due to the fact that one is a view looking upward, which reverses the points of the compass, and the other is a reflection of it, in which the positions of the scenes are projected downward, as though onto the floor, and are correctly related to the compass points.

but in most places is so low that the upper parts of the figures are relieved against the gold of the sky. In addition, the composition was punctuated at intervals, sometimes at one edge of a scene, by small structures rising into the gold background; evidences of three buildings still exist in the mosaic. Finally, the circular form of the composition was further enhanced by the inscriptions, which seem to have been placed in circular alignment above the scenes; two of these and the merest fragment of another are still to be seen.

It should be mentioned here that in the general view (PL. 250) and its diagram the western side of the vault is at the top and the northern side at the left. The number of segments, or scenes, into which the frieze was divided and the points at which the divisions occur can be determined as follows: The division points at the edges of scene [124], in the southern side, are clearly visible. At the left of the scene, near the center of the southern side, there is a gap between two groups of figures standing back to back: a group of bystanders in scene [123] at the left, and Christ and his disciples in scene [124] at the right. The right-hand edge of a building in scene [124] is the boundary which separates the bystanders in [124] from another group of disciples (Christ is missing) at the left edge of scene [125]. In the eastern side (bottom in the diagram), the point of separation between scenes [122] and [123] is suggested by the space between the ending of the fragmentary inscription of scene [122] and the beginning of the one pertaining to scene [123]. Between these two, moreover, is a bit of a pointed arch from a structure that in all probability stood at the right edge of scene [122]. Proceeding now a little to the left in the eastern side, we find the lower extremities of two disciples standing in frontal pose; to the right of them are small bits of blue from the lower parts of the garments of Christ, who must have been facing right. It can be assumed that these figures stood at the left edge of scene [122], since in the miracle scenes at the Kariye Djami Christ and his disciples, with only one exception, are at the left and the afflicted are at the right. The division between scenes [122] and [121] thus coincides with the corner of a wall and the lower part of a colonnette to the right of the paralytic on his bed in scene [121]. With the limits of these three scenes ([122]–[124]) established, we find that the scenes were about equal in size and that exactly half of the frieze has been accounted for. The remaining spaces in the vault can safely be assumed to have contained an equal number of scenes. One of these, whose right side is in good part preserved and whose left margin can be approximated, is Christ Healing the Paralytic at the Pool of Bethesda [121]. A second, well preserved at its left edge, is scene [125]. A small fragment of another, [126], stands in isolation from the others. The division of the annular frieze in this way makes it evident that the mosaicist had established a distinctly east-to-west axis for the vault as a whole, more or less centering scenes [122] at the east and [125] at the west on that axis.

It was Feodor Shmit [3] who first identified the subject of the fragmentary scene [121] above the northeastern pendentive as Christ Healing the Paralytic at the Pool of Bethesda and who observed that the scene [128] beneath it was, in reality, a second episode of the same subject. He also remarked upon the close similarity between these two mosaics and the miniature on folio 377v of the Gospel manuscript, Iviron 5, of Mount Athos, which illustrates the text of John 5:2–15. The inscription above the lower mosaic is intact, or nearly so, but it is obviously not the complete inscription, which must have been divided, like the scene itself, into

---

3 *Kakhrie-dzhami*, pp. 199 f.

two parts, the first of which, originally placed above the upper scene, is now missing. Shmit's reconstruction of the missing line is transcribed in the heading of this section.

Of the first episode (PL. 251 a), there is preserved only the headless figure of the paralytic, sitting in three-quarters view on the edge of his bed with arms and legs held out stiffly toward the left. Rising in the background behind the bed are two colonnettes and a wall; a third colonnette is seen at the right, partly obscured by a figure in scene [122]. To complete the composition one should compare the fragment with the Iviron miniature. In the miniature the paralytic and the bed are much the same as in the mosaic, and the bed is placed beneath, or in front of, a vaulted canopy supported by a series of slender columns. In the mosaic Christ must have stood to the left of the foot of the bed, as he does in the miniature, probably at the very point where the mosaic is broken off, with right arm outstretched toward the afflicted. Close behind Christ, and also facing right, the miniature shows Peter with a youthful disciple behind him.

The scene dealing with the second episode [128] depicts the now healed paralytic carrying his bed (PL. 251 b). Two bystanders are at the left; both are bearded men, their heads covered with scarfs. The one at the right holds up both hands in amazement. The paralytic, dressed in his short tunic, carries a simple wooden bedstead totally unlike the luxurious draped affair in the scene above. His head turned back toward the bystanders, he strides toward the right, grasping the ends of the ropes which secure the bed to his back. The scene is laid before a hilly landscape. Essentially the same composition, but with a background of architecture, is found in the miniature, immediately to the right of the first episode. For the hole in this and other pendentive scenes, see the discussion of scene [127].

Dimensions of Vault

Between masonry surfaces of inner faces of arches, on E–W axis, 4.14 m.; on N–S axis, 4.59 m. Rise in vault above highest level of soffits of arches, 1.29 m. Diameter of ornamental medallion, 1.715 m.

Colors and Materials

No. [121]

PARALYTIC short tunic, yellow. DRAPERY OF BED top surface, light grayish yellow stones with white stones at edge; sides, red with gold and red border at bottom. COLONNETTES green glasses with white stone for veining. WALL IN BACKGROUND bluish gray stones. GROUND ZONE dark green glass.

No. [128]

PARALYTIC short tunic, red; bed, brown glasses and brown and yellowish gray stones; ropes, dark red glass. MAN AT FAR LEFT mantle, green with gold and red armband; scarf over head and around neck, blue. SECOND MAN undergarment (visible at sleeves), blue; mantle, red; scarf over head and around neck, blue. LANDSCAPE slopes of hills, grayish yellow stones; shading at top in brown stones with parts outlined above in dark red glass; ground zone in three bands, light brown stone above, greenish gray stone in center, and dark green glass below.

[122]

An Unidentified Scene [1]

PL. 250, 251 a, 252

Scene [122] occupied the axial position at the eastern side of the sixth vault of the outer narthex (PL. 250); remnants of it still exist in two widely separated fragments. Its lower left

---

1 For a discussion of the relation of this scene to the others in the same vault, and for a diagram illustrating its original limits, see the section dealing with scene [121], [128].

corner (PL. 251 *a*, at right), adjoining the right side of The Healing of the Paralytic at the Pool of Bethesda [121], is part of the fragment in the northeastern quadrant of the vault. A bit of architectural setting and traces of the end of the inscription, remains of the upper right area of the scene, may be found at the broken edge of the mosaic just to the east of the ornamental medallion at the center of the vault (above the medallion in PL. 250 and upper left in PL. 252).

In the remnant from the lower left corner there are portions of three figures. At the left is the lower half of one of Christ's disciples, possibly St. Peter, wearing a blue tunic with dark blue clavi and a yellow himation. He stands in a nearly frontal pose but seems, in the existing parts of his body, to turn slightly to the left. His position at the left edge of the composition, and probably his pose, are repeated in scene [124] (PL. 253), where he turns his head toward the left. At the right edge of the fragment are bits of the dark blue glass drapery of Christ, specifically the end of the train that sometimes hangs down his back, the curve at the back of the thigh which one finds in profile figures of Christ, and below it a piece of the hem. These bits of drapery resemble, for example, the corresponding parts of the figure of Christ in the second episode of the mosaic of The Multiplication of Loaves (PL. 241), or in the fresco of The Raising of the Daughter of Jairus (PL. 363). Between Peter and Christ are the lower parts of a second disciple standing in frontal pose and wearing a blue tunic, with dark blue clavi, and a violet himation.

The remnant from the upper right background of the scene contains the upper part of a structure (PL. 252, upper left) that marked the scene's right edge and separated it from the scene to the right [123]. All that remains of this building is part of a sharply pointed arch. The ogee form of the arch may be compared to that of the pediment at the right in Plate 98. Very fragmentary traces of a line of the inscription occur to the left of the arch along the broken edge of the mosaic. These consist of a few black tesserae, the illegible remains of letters, and, at the end, the abbreviation marks (two parallel diagonal strokes) designating the letters omicron and nu.

Colors and Materials

DISCIPLE AT LEFT tunic, blue with dark blue clavi; himation, yellow. SECOND DISCIPLE tunic, blue with dark blue clavi; himation, violet. CHRIST drapery, blue.
BACKGROUND between figures, light salmon-pink stone like that of wall in scene [123]; ground zone, dark green glass. ARCH OF BUILDING a band of brown stone flanked by rows of bluish gray stone and again by rows of white stone; soffit of arch, brown stone flanked by rows of dark blue-gray stone; fill of arch, alternating rows of brown and bluish gray stone.

[123]

Christ Healing the Dropsical Man[1]

PL. 250, 252

(*Luke 14:2–5*)

ʽΟ Χ(ριστὸ)ς ἰώμ(εν)ος τ(ὸν) ὑδρωπηκ(όν)   *Christ healing the dropsical man*

Of the scene of Christ Healing the Dropsical Man there now remain the following parts: the titular inscription, which is intact; the heads and most of one figure from the group at the right,

---

1 See discussion of [121], [128] for layout of scenes in the vault of the sixth bay.

representing the afflicted man, his companion, and the lawyers and Pharisees that are mentioned in the Gospel text; the abbreviation marks and bits of the iota and two sigmas from the inscription $\overline{\text{IC}}$ $\overline{\text{XC}}$; and at the lower right a small portion of the low wall, or background, above the zone of green ground.

The lost group of Christ and some of his disciples, who would have stood at the left facing right, was doubtless very much like others in the series of mosaics illustrating Christ's healing miracles. Much can be inferred regarding the rest of the scene from the existing remains and from a number of manuscript illuminations of the twelfth to fourteenth centuries. In some of these miniatures the dropsical man stands near the center of the scene wearing only a loincloth. Often his bare torso is bent far back toward the right and is supported by a companion who stands behind him. In these instances Christ sometimes reaches out to touch the man's greatly swollen belly.

It seems likely that the fragment preserves, in whole or in part, all the heads of the compact group at the right. Five heads are aligned in a horizontal row and the tops of three others are visible above them; at a lower level, in the forefront of the group, still another head is partly preserved at the broken edge of the mosaic. This may well be the head of the dropsical man. If his upper body leaned far back, as, for example, in the Mount Athos Gospel manuscript, Iviron 5, folio 299v, his posture and position would put the man within reach of the hand of Christ, who stood beneath his now-fragmentary inscription, and would account for the head's being placed at a considerably lower level than the others. The figure whose head and shoulder appear above and in close proximity to the fragmentary head may well be the companion supporting the dropsical man from behind, as in Iviron 5.

The intention of the mosaicist seems to have been to place the figures before a low wall, as he did in other scenes of the annular frieze. However, the men's feet rest at a level almost halfway up from the bottom of the wall, far above the zone of green "ground" beneath. Along a straight diagonal line that passes just to the right of the feet of the old man at the far right there is a change in color in the wall. To the left of this line, behind the group, light salmon-pink stones are used and to the right, in the next scene, tesserae of bluish gray stone.

Colors and Materials

OLD MAN (at far right) tunic, green with gold and red hem; mantle, red; scarf over head and around neck, blue; boots, blue. YOUNG MAN (at center) collar of garment, gold and red; boots, red. MAN AT FAR LEFT collar over shoulder of garment, blue; toe of left boot, blue.

BACKGROUND in which figures stand (wall?) light salmon-pink stone (representing marble?), which terminates along diagonal line at right edge of scene. GROUND ZONE dark green glass.

[124]

Christ Healing the Paralytic at Capernaum[1]

(Matthew 9:1–2; Mark 2:1–5; Luke 5:18–20)

Ὁ Χ(ριστὸ)ς λέγων τῷ παραλυτικῷ ἀφέωνταί [σοι] | αἱ ἁμα[ρτία]ις [sic] σου.
Christ says to the paralytic, "Thy sins are forgiven thee."

Ἰ(ησοῦ)[ς] Χ(ριστό)ς   *Jesus Christ*

The scene of Christ Healing the Paralytic at Capernaum is the only one in the annular frieze of the sixth bay (PL. 250) that has suffered relatively little destruction. Some loss has occurred in the roof of the building at the right edge of the scene. Most of the first line of the inscription is intact; in the second, although some letters are incompletely preserved in mosaic tesserae, their traces in the painted setting bed warranted their reconstruction in hatched, painted lines. Only the last three letters of the first line are totally missing. Otherwise, the scene was found to be in a remarkably good state of preservation.

The miraculous healing of the paralytic is recounted in the Synoptic Gospels with only one variation of any importance. Mark and Luke dwell on the manner in which the paralytic was brought to Christ's attention: by means of ropes he was let down in his bed through the roof of the house where Christ was, because of crowds gathered within. Matthew, on the other hand, makes no mention of the action. This discrepancy may well account for two of the variant picture-types in which this miracle is depicted in Byzantine art: in one, the bed is being lowered by ropes; in the other, as in the mosaic at the Kariye Djami, this aspect of the story is not alluded to. Whereas the mosaic illustration would seem to reflect Matthew's version of the miracle, its inscription, in quoting Christ, follows the words of Luke.

In the mosaic (PL. 253), Christ stands in three-quarters view at the foot of the bed, facing the paralytic. His right hand is extended at arm's length in blessing and his left, as usual, holds the scroll. Five disciples, all facing left, stand close together around Christ. Peter, at the left, though his body faces slightly to the right, turns his head in the opposite direction to gaze pensively downward and out of the picture. His right arm rests in a fold of his himation, as in a sling. To the right of Christ is a youthful disciple raising his right hand, palm outward, in reverence or surprise; his left arm and hand are covered by his himation. Parts of the heads of three other disciples are crowded into the space between the head of Peter and the halo of Christ.

The paralytic lies on a richly draped bed, his head resting on a rectangular pillow and his legs covered by a red blanket. He is dressed in a tunic with tightly fitting sleeves; a hood covers his head and shoulders and exposes only his bearded face. His right arm raised from the elbow, he stretches his hand toward Christ. The bed, like that of the other paralytic [121] and that of the daughter of Jairus [203] in the frescoes of the parecclesion, curves upward into a rounded head; drapery covers the sides, and a mattress rounded at the head lies on top.

Mark states that the paralytic "was borne of four" when he was brought to Christ. His four

1 See discussion of [121], [128] for layout of scenes in the vault of the sixth bay.

132

bearers are drawn up in a row behind the head of the bed, all facing toward Christ. The man at the left makes the same gesture of awe that the young disciple makes; the others stand in stiff, disciplined attitudes.

The background at the left consists of a wall low enough that the upper parts of Christ and the disciples are relieved against the gold of the sky. Behind the bearers is a gabled, towerlike structure that breaks the monotony of the wall tying the annular frieze together and marks the right-hand limits of the scene. It might be noted, in passing, that on the dark receding face of this building is a design whose left half closely resembles the decorative motif over the door in The Miracle at Cana [117], which some have interpreted as a date in Arabic numerals (see Introduction, pp. 15–16).

Colors and Materials

CHRIST tunic (unusual), violet glass in shaded areas, light blue glasses in middle lights, and gray stone in highlights; clavus, gold and red; himation, blue. PETER tunic, blue; himation, yellow, indicated in the usual way but with a few strokes around knee and one above right forearm in light blue glass. ONE OF THREE DISCIPLES IN BACKGROUND green garment. YOUNG DISCIPLE tunic, blue; himation, green. PARALYTIC tunic, yellow, with upper outline of right sleeve and folds at elbows of both sleeves in light blue glass; hood, red; blanket, red; pillow, green; mattress, gray and yellow stones; drapery at sides of bed, violet, with gold and red border at bottom. BEARERS (left to right) 1) Loose tunic, yellowish pink (almost salmon) stones, white lights, and some drawing in red glass; mantle, green. 2) Outer garment, red; headdress, blue. 3) Tunic, green with blue collar; mantle on right shoulder, violet. 4) Tunic, green with gold and red hem; mantle, red; scarf around neck, yellow; boots, blue.

LOW WALL bluish gray stone with coping indicated by blue glass lines. BUILDING lighted faces, bluish gray stone of two values outlined in blue glass and white stone; shaded faces, mixed blue glasses with drawing and ornamental motif in dark blue glass; roofing tiles (visible at right end of gable), red. GROUND ZONE narrow upper band, medium green glass; wide lower band, dark green glasses.

[125]

An Unidentified Scene[1]

PL. 250, 253, 256

To the right of the small building in the preceding scene and in the same fragment is still preserved a tightly compressed group of Christ's disciples. Some of the nine figures appear to emerge from behind the building, and with only one exception they face toward the right. Only the two who stand in the front rank are fully visible; the remaining seven are crowded together in the background behind and between them, and in all but one instance these are represented merely as heads. The bearded disciple at the left in the front rank wears a blue tunic and a violet himation; he holds his hands before him in the manner of a suppliant. Despite the destruction of the face, the disciple at the right is identifiable as Peter because of his yellow himation and his prominent position; he too held both hands before him. Between these two is a young, beardless disciple wearing a blue tunic and a green himation.

In the lower right part of the fragment there is a considerable area of the low background wall, an indication that Christ, who must have stood still further to the right, was more than usually detached from his disciples; but it can be assumed that he, too, faced right to confront at

---

1 See discussion of [121], [128] for layout of scenes in the vault of the sixth bay.

least one other figure, at the far right, in a scene which was probably a miracle but whose subject cannot be identified.

While it is not possible to fix the position of the right-hand margin of this scene, it is reasonable to say that the isolated fragment numbered [126] is too far to the right to have pertained to the scene. The position of the fragmentary figure of scene [126] would suggest, however, as illustrated in text Fig. B, p. 127, that scene [125] was somewhat narrower than the others in the annular frieze. Only a relatively small space would have been left, therefore, to the right of the disciples, in which little more than the figures of Christ and an afflicted person could have been represented.

Colors and Materials

DISCIPLE IN LEFT FOREGROUND   tunic, blue; himation, violet.   PETER   tunic, blue; himation, yellow.

YOUNG DISCIPLE   tunic, blue; himation, green.
BACKGROUND WALL (rising approximately to shoulder height): light grayish yellow stone.   GROUND ZONE three bands of green glasses.

[126]

An Unidentified Scene[1]

PL. 250, 257 *a*

A small area of mosaic pertaining to a scene in the annular frieze of the sixth vault forms the upper edge of the fragment in the northwestern pendentive (PL. 257 *a*). In this area one sees the feet and the lower parts of the legs of a figure that stood in the zone of green ground before a background composed of two zones: the upper light grayish yellow stone and the lower a band of darker grayish yellow stone. The figure was clad in "pajama" trousers extending to the ankles. The trousers are executed in light yellowish gray and light bluish gray stones shaded on the right sides with blue glasses, the intention being to represent a white garment. The position of the feet indicates that the figure faced the left and, therefore, that Christ and a number of his disciples were at the left, as usual.

Because of the costume worn by the man, who is surely the subject of a healing miracle, it is probable that the scene illustrated one of the numerous passages in the Gospels which describe Christ's healing of a demoniac or a lunatic.[2] The two most frequently illustrated miracles of this sort are The Healing of the Gadarene Demoniac, sometimes represented without reference to the swine, and The Healing of the Blind and Dumb Demoniac of Capernaum.

In the representations of Christ healing a demoniac or a lunatic [3] the afflicted man is sometimes nude and sometimes wears only a loincloth; in a number of examples, however, he is dressed in long white trousers, very much like those represented in the mosaic, sometimes knotted at the waist. In these examples his torso is bare and he is depicted in an attitude of mad violence, his body bent forward and his arms bound behind his back, or body bent backward and

1 See discussion of [121], [128] for layout of scenes in the vault of the sixth bay.

2 The principal passages are Matt. 4:24, 8:28–34, 12:22–30; Mark 3:22–30, 5:1–20; Luke 8:26–40, 11:14–26.

3 See, for example, the demoniacs wearing white trousers in the facsimile publication, *The Rockefeller McCormick New Testament* (Chicago, 1932), folio 42 (for an especially close

parallel to the trousers in the mosaic) and folios 15v, 19v, 63v. See also Leningrad, MS. 105, in Harold R. Willoughby, *The Four Gospels of Karahissar*, II (Chicago, 1936), p. 143 and PL. LXXV. For a lunatic wearing white trousers, see the frescoes of the Catholicon of the Lavra and the Trapeza of Dionysiou in Mount Athos, in Millet, *Monuments de l'Athos*, PL. 127,2 and 212,1.

arms wildly flung out; nearly always his rather long hair streams upward. The demon is not always represented.

Colors and Materials

See the general description of the fragment, above.

[127]

Christ and the Samaritan Woman at the Well[1]

PL. 250, 257 a

(John 4:4–27)

Ὁ Χ(ριστὸ)ς διαλεγόμενος τῇ Σαμαρείτι[δι]
Christ conversing with the Samaritan woman

Ἰ(ησοῦ)ς Χ(ριστό)ς   *Jesus Christ*

In the northwestern pendentive, below the zone of scenes that encircles the vault of the sixth bay, is the scene of Christ conversing with the Samaritan woman at Jacob's well. The woman stands at the left, close to the wellhead, and faces Christ, who was seated at the right. In the background is a mountainous landscape. Over her head the woman wears a long mantle that hangs down evenly at both sides, partly concealing a dress with ornamental bands at collar, hem, and sleeve. Her right arm, bare to the elbow, is extended in a speaking gesture. Over the opening of the well she holds, in her left hand, a golden pitcher, which is attached to the well by a rope. Most of the figure of Christ is destroyed; his head and the larger part of the halo, his right hand, raised in blessing, and his right knee are all that now remains. To the right of Christ, where the mosaic is destroyed, there is enough space to have held one or two of Christ's disciples. Ample precedent exists in Byzantine art for representing the subject with as well as without disciples present. The cylindrical wellhead, drawn as though seen from above, is built on a projecting triangular base. The well was designed to fit the lower point of the pendentive, and it thus resembles the one in the scene of The Annunciation at the Well [98], which is also in a pendentive.

The hole in the side of the wellhead should be mentioned. An original part of the structure, it is the end of a cylindrical terra-cotta tube that penetrates into the masonry of the pendentive; it is believed to have been placed there for reasons of acoustics. Similar holes occur in the other pendentives of this bay and in those of the seventh bay and the nave of the church.

Colors and Materials

CHRIST tunic (visible at sleeve), violet; himation, blue. SAMARITAN WOMAN dress, blue with gold and red ornaments at collar, hem, and sleeve; mantle, red; pitcher, gold glass and brown stones, green glass rope. WELL grayish yellow stones with outline drawing in light yellow, brown, and white stones; water, dark brown and nearly black stones. LANDSCAPE bluish gray stones; shading and outlining of hills in violet glasses; foreground zone, green glasses.

1 For the iconographic relationship between this scene, the one in the SE pendentive of the sixth vault, and the one in the NE pendentive and just above it, see [129], below.

[128]

Christ Healing the Paralytic at the Pool of Bethesda: Second Episode

See [121], above.

[129]

Christ Healing the Blind Born

(*John 9:1–7*)

The final scene in the vault of the sixth bay is preserved in fragmentary condition in the south-eastern pendentive. The existing parts of its figures make it plain that the scene represents Christ healing a blind man; it will be shown in the chapter dealing with the cycle of Christ's Ministry in Volume 4 that when the scene is placed in context with the others in the pendentives—Samaritan Woman [127], Paralytic at Bethesda [128] (and [121] above it)—it becomes virtually certain that its subject was Christ anointing the eyes of the Blind Born as described in John 9:6. The reasons for placing the three scenes in context with one another, it will be seen, are liturgical.

At least two disciples stood at the left behind their Master. The hand at the left edge of the fragment belongs to a disciple (Peter?), otherwise entirely destroyed, who wore a yellow himation; the edge of that garment runs parallel to the broken edge of the mosaic both above and below the hand. The second disciple is young and beardless. He is drawn in three-quarters view, striding toward the right behind Christ, but his head is turned toward his lost companion at the left. His left hand is carried in the folds of his green himation and his right is concealed beneath the himation. Christ also is drawn in three-quarters view, in an attitude of walking. His right hand is extended, at shoulder height, toward the blind man, who stood facing him at the right. All that now remains of this latter figure is his legs below the knees and the lower part of the walking stick, held vertically, on which he leaned. His feet and ankles are wrapped with leggings, but above them the legs are bare.

In most respects the mosaic is very similar to the miniature of The Healing of the Blind Born on folio 405v of Iviron 5, Mount Athos, a manuscript of the Gospels whose two preceding miniatures (371r and 377v) illustrated the scenes of The Samaritan Woman and The Paralytic at the Bethesda Pool; it was observed earlier that the miniature of the Paralytic is exceptionally like its equivalent in mosaic, number [121]. In the miniature of the Blind Born, which probably supplies some of the lost details of the mosaic, Christ stands in an attitude very much like that of the mosaic with his blessing hand just above the top of the stick of the blind man. The latter, bare-legged but with feet and ankles wrapped in leggings, wears a short tunic over short white trousers that reach not quite to the knees. Leaning on his stick, holding it with both hands close to its

136

top, he stoops forward from the hips, so that his face is very near, and on a level with, Christ's blessing hand. The miniature, unlike the mosaic, also depicts the episode of the Blind Born washing himself at the pool of Siloam in obedience to Christ's command. The pool is represented in the form of a font surmounted by a ciborium.

Colors and Materials

CHRIST Unusual representation in that both tunic and himation are blue glass, the tunic being slightly lighter in color value; clavus, gold and red. YOUNG DISCIPLE tunic, blue; himation, green. SECOND DISCIPLE (right hand and small part of garment preserved at left edge) himation, yellow and brown stones.

BLIND MAN (only lower parts of legs and lower end of stick preserved) legs, pink and white marble, outlined at right in red glass and at left in brown stone; leggings, white stone with drawing in blue glass; stick, greenish brown glass.

BACKGROUND yellowish gray stone bordered at upper right with light brown stone and outlined by single row of dark brown stone; ground zone, mixed green glasses and some blue glasses.

[130]

Fragmentary Inscription of an Unidentified Scene

PL. 258, 259 *a*, LEFT

The vault of the seventh bay (PL. 258), an eastward extension of the outer narthex, is very similar to that of the sixth bay (PL. 250) in its dimensions and form, the two obviously having been designed as twin elements of the narthex. The evidence offered by the surviving mosaics indicates that in their compositional arrangement the decorations of the two vaults were also similar: that is, a large decorative medallion at the center was surrounded by an annular frieze of scenes, perhaps six in number as in the preceding vault; the pendentives, like those of the sixth vault, must surely have been treated as separate units devoted either to scenes or, less probably, to ornaments. There are differences, however, between the two. In the annular frieze of the sixth vault there seems to have been no landscape; low walls and small buildings rest upon a more or less uniform zone of green ground, which provided a continuous base for the frieze. On the other hand, in the one scene of the seventh vault where the foreground is preserved, landscape is represented and there is no trace of an encircling zone of green ground.

The accompanying diagram (text Fig. C), made from a tracing of Plate 258, identifies by letter the six fragments scattered about the southeastern quadrant of the vault. The points of separation of the four scenes of which fragments still remain, all from the annular frieze, are indicated by broken lines, and the scenes are designated by number.

Of the two surviving fragments of the medallion, that marked *a* in the diagram belongs to one of the inner zones, or borders, and seems to represent an architectural dentil band; it is of blue glasses surrounded by a narrow band of gold. The second fragment, marked *b*, contains motifs from zones that were exterior to those of *a*: a continuous wave pattern in red glass on a narrow band of white stones, surrounded by a zone of foliate designs, perhaps a wreath, in green, red, and blue glasses set in a ground of gold. In general character the medallion recalls the one preserved at the summit of the sixth vault (PL. 250 and 331 *c*).

Of the scene numbered [130] (diagram, fragment *c*), the only surviving evidence consists of the last three letters of a line of the inscription and two converging rows of black tesserae beneath the second letter which are certainly not parts of letters nor of a piece of architecture. All

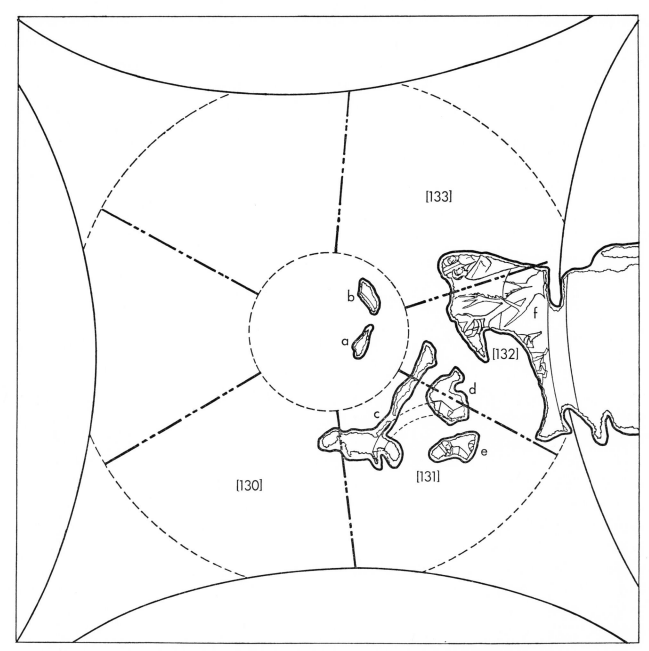

Fig. C. Distribution of scenes in the vault of the seventh bay

these traces appear at the left end of fragment *c* and can best be seen at the extreme left in Plate 259 *a*. The three letters in question are, first, an upsilon (Y) that has lost the upper part of its left stroke; second, a kappa (K); and finally, an eta (H). The last two letters have lost some of their black glass tesserae; the places are now filled with new plaster toned with gray. To the right of the eta the gold of the background is preserved in an interval of about 23 cm. between the inscriptions of scenes [130] and [131]. The point of separation between these two scenes would have occurred approximately at the center of this interval. The three surviving letters suggest the word [C]YKĤ (fig tree) and the possibility that the miracle here represented was that of Christ cursing the fig tree and causing it to wither (Matt. 21:19; Mark 11:13, 14). Another factor reinforces this identification: A listing of all those miracles and public acts of Christ not present among the extant mosaics or not belonging to the cycles of the "great feasts" or the Passion reveals that the only theme whose subject noun terminates with the three letters of the inscription is ἡ συκῆ, as in the words of Matthew 21:19: Καὶ ἐξηράνθη παραχρῆμα ἡ συκῆ ("And presently the fig tree withered away"). Were this to be accepted as the subject of scene [130] the seemingly inexplicable lines in black tesserae beneath the inscription, high up in the scene within the gold of the sky, could be interpreted as traces of a sharply pointed leaf of the fig tree, which in most representations of the subject is placed at the right side with Christ and a few disciples standing under it at the left.

Dimensions of Vault

Between masonry surfaces of inner faces of arches, on E–W and N–S axes, 4.58 m. Rise in vault above highest level of soffits of arches, 1.29 m.

[131]

An Unidentified Scene[1]

PL. 258, 259 *a* CENTER

Various parts of scene [131] (PL. 259 *a*) appear in three fragments of mosaic in the seventh vault. Fragment *c* (see text Fig. C) contains illegible portions of the inscription and the upper left corner of an exedra, which is viewed as if from above. The corresponding right end of the exedra is found in fragment *d*. The curve of the structure, as seen in these two fragments, appears to be symmetrical. In the right end is still preserved a small rectangular opening, and below it is the flat roof of an extension; it can be presumed that these additional features were repeated at the left side of the exedra. At a lower level, the center of the exedra wall was pierced by an opening, showing at the left in fragment *e*; the fragment also retains parts of the wall and bits of three figures. Within the opening, or door, which is rendered in dark blue glasses, there is a bit of the left shoulder of a figure clad in red, at the broken left edge of the fragment. A little lower and to the right of the opening, relieved against the wall of the exedra, can be seen the bearded head and the shoulders of an old man facing left. Part of the head of a third figure, who also faced left, appears at a still lower level at the right end of the fragment. The forehead, eyes, nose, and part of the scarf which covered his head are still preserved. The back of his head intrudes into a dark area of the architectural background which is in vertical alignment with the dark vertical face of the end of the exedra above. The existence of this dark area indicates that another opening occurred in the extension to the right of the exedra proper.

A line of the inscription for this scene (PL. 259 *a*, fragment *c*) began above and somewhat to the left of the exedra and to the right of the interval of gold ground that followed the inscription of number [130]. The first letter is probably an eta (H) whose vertical strokes are broken off above the horizontal bar. This is followed by the lower parts of two vertical strokes from an unidentifiable letter or letters, and by a rather long hiatus. The lower parts of an omega (ω) and another letter appear above the center of the exedra, followed by illegible fragments of accents, breathings, and abbreviation marks and the upper parts of letters which seem to continue to the

---

1 For comments on the relation between the vaults of bays six and seven and on the composition of their mosaic decoration, see the descriptions of [121], [128] and of [130] above.

legible parts of the inscription pertaining to the next scene, at the right. The point at which the inscription for scene [131] ends cannot be precisely determined.

Although the subject of the scene represented in these fragments must remain in question, the forms of the architectural setting and the placing of the figures in relation to the architecture suggest certain possibilities. The setting is an exedra, which is seen as if from above in a frontal, and apparently symmetrical, view. In its right side, beginning to right of center, were at least three figures, none of whom was Christ or a disciple. All three faced inwards toward the left, and each succeeding figure, from left to right, was placed at a lower level than the preceding one. The most likely explanation of these features is that the figures were placed in a curve to fit the curvature of the exedra and, since they were to appear to be seen from above, at successively lower levels. If, as might be assumed, there were corresponding figures in the left side of the exedra, there would have been a row of men seated in a semicircle on curved priests' benches; such a composition recurs in certain scenes in the temple — that of the young Christ among the Doctors, for example. From its context in the seventh vault the scene must be one from the public ministry of Christ, and from its form it should be one in which the adult Christ is in the temple, or the synagogue, surrounded by priests. Such subjects are very limited in number. For reasons of composition, the scene of Christ Driving the Money-Changers from the Temple can be eliminated. The subject of Christ's Authority Being Questioned in the Temple (Matt. 21:23–27; Mark 11:27–33; Luke 20:1–8) would be highly suitable in this position in the vault, for its textual sources in Matthew and Mark are in the same chapters as those of Christ Cursing the Fig Tree (in all probability the subject of the preceding scene), and in Luke the scene occurs in the chapter preceding the account of Christ Calling Zacchaeus (the succeeding scene in the mosaics). The questioning of Christ's authority was very rarely illustrated in manuscript illuminations; and no example in extant monumental painting is known to me. In MS. Plut. VI.23 in the Laurentian Library in Florence, where the three Gospel sources are illustrated, the version for Luke (fol. 151v) presents Christ seated in the center beneath a ciborium while the priests and scribes stand in tight groups at each side. The fact that the mosaic presents a different composition, however, need not eliminate the subject as a possible one. Another subject, and one which occurs in late-Byzantine monumental art in a composition that is very much like that of the mosaic, is Christ Reading in the Synagogue from the Prophecy of Isaiah (Luke 4:16–20). In the Serbian fresco at Dečani,[2] Christ stands in the center of an exedra reading from a book which rests on a lectern to his right; at each side three priests or scribes are seated on curved benches, and a young attendant stands in the left background. At each end of the exedra is an extension pierced by an opening; the flat roofs of these extensions slope downward from small openings in the ends of the exedra proper. Even in such precise architectural details the mosaic is like the fresco of Dečani. A somewhat different version is found in the frescoes of the Catholicon of Chilandari, Mount Athos.[3]

Colors and Materials

EXEDRA   inner face of wall, gray stones; left end, light blue glass; right end, dark blue glass; opening in right end, darker blue glass; flat tops of walls, white stone.

REMNANTS OF THREE FIGURES IN FRAGMENT E (left to right)   *1*): Red glass garment at shoulder.   *2*): Green garment, gray scarf at neck and shoulder.   *3*): Gray scarf on head.

2 Vlad. R. Petković and D. Bošković, *Dečani* (Belgrade, 1941), Album, PL. LXXXII.
3 Millet, *Monuments de l'Athos*, PL. 75,3.

[132]

Christ Calling Zacchaeus[1]

PL. 258, 259 a, 259 b

(Luke 19:1–5)

. . . [λέγω]ν Ζακχαῖε σ[πεύσας κατάβηθι] . . .
. . . saying, Zacchaeus, make haste and come down . . .

Fragment *c* (see text Fig. C, p. 138) contains part of the inscription and fragment *f* recognizable portions of the scene of Christ calling to Zacchaeus to come down from the sycamore tree, the only clearly identifiable scene in the annular frieze of the vault of the seventh bay. The remains of the inscription appear at the far right in Plate 259 *a*, those of the scene itself in Plate 259 *b*.

At the lower left in Plate 259 *b* can be seen, at the broken edge of the mosaic, the left and right feet of a figure that is otherwise destroyed; a little to the right is the left foot and then the right foot and part of the hem of the blue garment of Christ. Both Christ and the disciple who stood behind him seem to have been striding toward the right. In front of Christ, and apparently turned slightly toward the left to face him, are the lower parts of another disciple, wearing a blue tunic and a green himation. The himation is draped over his left shoulder, visible in the sharp point of the fragment to the left of Zacchaeus, and billows out to the right. Zacchaeus stands on an overhanging branch of his sycamore tree. The tree, which separates the scene from another to the right, is old and gnarled, with sharp and barren branches near its base. Only the lower half of the very short figure of Zacchaeus is still preserved. He is richly dressed in a blue undergarment with a wide hem of gold and red, and over it a red mantle, which falls into loops at the knees. His right hand and foot are missing, but his left hand, grasping a branch of the tree, remains.

The remnants of inscription in fragment *c* which definitely pertain to this scene (PL. 259 *a*, far right) consist, first, of the upper parts of three letters, possibly lambda, epsilon, gamma, followed by a well-preserved nu and the name of Zacchaeus. The letter that may be a lambda has a left-hand serif at the top of two converging strokes: a sloping one at the left and a vertical one at the right. This is followed by the top of a letter that could be a sigma or, preferably, an epsilon. The presumed gamma retains only its upper, or horizontal, stroke, now separated into two parts by the loss of one of its tesserae. Under this stroke, and between the lost vertical stroke of the gamma and the relatively complete nu at the right, is space enough for the insertion of a small omega; this juxtaposition occurs frequently in inscriptions where an omega follows a gamma or a tau. If the extant nu is combined with these conjectured letters, a word becomes identifiable: [λέγω]ν, that is, "saying." A comparison of these fragmentary letters with the letters in the same word (λέγων) as it appears in the inscription of Joseph Dreaming (PL. 152) will confirm the above reconstruction.

Most of the name of Zacchaeus is intact. The fragment of its final letter (the next to last letter in the inscription), which could be interpreted as the lower part of a sigma or of an epsilon,

---

1 See [121], [128] and [130] above for comments on the composition of the mosaic
decorations of the vaults of the sixth and seventh bays.

should be read as epsilon to provide the vocative that is required by the λέγων. The fragment of the very last letter, apparently the start of a new word, is very much like the fragment which precedes it and might also be part of a sigma or epsilon. Since the evidence suggests that Christ's words to Zacchaeus are about to be quoted, one should, perhaps, interpret the letter as a sigma, so that the inscription will be in conformity with Luke 19:5, which quotes Christ as saying, Ζακχαῖε, σπεύσας κατάβηθι . . . ("Zacchaeus, make haste, and come down").

Colors and Materials

FRAGMENT OF CHRIST'S GARMENT blue (usually the tunic is violet, but see the blue tunic of Christ in scene [129]). DISCIPLE TO RIGHT tunic, blue; himation (visible in billowing fold at right and again at shoulder, above), green. ZACCHAEUS undergarment, light blue with gold and red hem; mantle, red. TREE trunk and large branches, greenish brown glass; foliage, green and some black. BACKGROUND LANDSCAPE rolling hill, yellowish gray stones which darken in hue near top, with outline in large gray stones.

[133]

An Unidentified Scene[1]

PL. 258, 259 b

To the right of Zacchaeus' tree is a fragment of another of the scenes of the seventh vault: two of Christ's disciples, their lower parts destroyed, stand in front of a piece of architecture (PL. 259 b and fragment f in text Fig. C, p. 138). The first disciple, broken off on a diagonal line from left hip to right knee, bears the features of Peter; he faces to the right in three-quarters view. As he so often does in other representations in the mosaics, he rests his right arm in a fold of his yellow himation. To the right, head inclined toward Peter, is a young, beardless disciple, whose head and right shoulder and upper arm are all that remain; he appears to have been in a frontal pose. In the absence of any portion of its inscription, and with the evidence so insufficient, it is not possible even to suggest an identification of this subject.

Colors and Materials

PETER himation, yellow. YOUNG DISCIPLE tunic, blue with dark blue clavus. ARCHITECTURE violet glasses in the darker areas and yellowish gray and white stones in the lighter areas.

1 See numbers [121], [128] and [130] above for comments on the composition of the mosaic decorations of the vaults of the sixth and seventh bays.

[134]

Christ Healing a Blind and Dumb Man

PL. 260, 261

Ὁ Χ(ριστὸ)ς ἰώμενος τὸν τυφλὸν κ(αὶ) κωφόν
Christ healing the blind and dumb man

Ἰ(ησοῦ)ς Χ(ριστό)ς *Jesus Christ*

From the seventh bay of the outer narthex a door leads into the southern end of the inner narthex, and there the cycle of Christ's Ministry, which fills the successive domical vaults of the outer narthex, is brought to a conclusion with a series of eight healing miracles. These are placed in the pendentives, vaults, and lunettes beneath the dome containing the early ancestors of Christ (PL. 16, 42), which is the point of origin of the four successive cycles (Genealogy, Life of the Virgin, Infancy of Christ, and Christ's Ministry) into which the narratives of the narthexes are divided. Thus, the four cycles are finally linked up to form, as it were, a single continuing illustration of the unfolding, from the beginning of time, of the divine plan of salvation; its culminating phase, the Passion, was undoubtedly depicted among the lost mosaics of the nave, to which the spectator would logically proceed through the nearby door.

The first four healing miracles, in the pendentives of the dome of the Ancestors, form a compositional group of their own. It begins with a pair of scenes that mirror one another in the two western pendentives—the one at the left [134] has a leftward compositional direction with Christ and his disciples at the right facing left (a quite exceptional feature in the miracles), while its pendant at the right [135] is directed toward the right with Christ and his followers (as usual) at the left. In other words, the two scenes are placed back to back, facing away from one another, so that they both converge, from opposing directions, upon the pair of miracles in the eastern pendentives ([136] and [137]). The latter, on the other hand, are contrived to face each other. Thus, the four pendentive compositions take cognizance of the eastward orientation of the mosaics in the dome above. The same compositional device will be found in the pendentives of the parecclesion. In subject matter, also, the scenes are grouped in opposing pairs: the two miracles at the west concern the healing of men; those at the east, of women.

In the first of these scenes [134], which the inscription, perhaps erroneously, calls The Healing of the Blind and Dumb Man, the afflicted stands at the left in nearly frontal pose, his left hand resting on the end of his walking stick and his right arm raised in a pointing gesture that seems to be directed toward his obviously blind eyes. He wears a knee-length tunic, gathered at the waist, and tightly fitting trousers and boots; at his right hip is a sack, or pouch, hanging by a thong from his left shoulder. At the right is Christ, in three-quarters view, blessing with his right hand and holding a scroll in his left. He is flanked by Peter on the left and a young disciple on the right, both of whom extend their left hands toward the afflicted. The scene takes place in a landscape that slopes to a rocky peak at the right. At the left is a piece of architecture containing a column with a piece of drapery knotted about it. A great canopy of drapery, which shelters the figures below, is stretched from the building to a tree at the right. Low in the center background are the fortified walls of a city.

There is an inconsistency between the inscribed titulus of this scene and the actual representation which makes the identification uncertain. In the only miracle in which Christ healed a man who was both blind and dumb (Matt. 12:22), the more essential fact is that he was a demoniac, a fact that is neither mentioned in the inscription nor illustrated in the mosaic. In the manuscript illustrations of Matthew 12:22, the artists indicated the fact that the afflicted was a demoniac either by showing him in a strait jacket or partially nude or by representing a demon issuing from his mouth. Moreover, since Pharisees were present when the miracle was performed, they are nearly always depicted, but not in the mosaic.

The mosaic clearly represents a blind man, but not necessarily one who is also dumb. From this point of view it corresponds more closely to some illustrations of The Healing of the Blind Bartimaeus (Mark 10:46–52; Luke 18:35–43), which took place outside the city of Jericho. Byzantine manuscript illuminations present Bartimaeus either sitting by the road begging or standing before Christ to be healed. In the latter situation Bartimaeus wears a costume similar to the one in the mosaic (short tunic, tight trousers, and boots), and in one instance (Athens, MS. gr. 93, fol. 74r) a rectangular object is strapped at his hip. Were this the subject of the mosaic the relation between it and its counterpart in the northwestern pendentive [135]would be even closer than indicated above, for the fortress walls that appear in both would represent Jericho and both miracles would have been performed on blind men who hailed Christ as the son of David.

Dimensions

From bottom of inscription to top of blue field filled with ornament below ground zone, 1.28 m.

Colors and Materials

BLIND MAN undergarment, blue; short outer tunic, red; trousers, green; boots, pink; pouch, yellow and yellow-brown stones; thong, black; stick, yellowish brown stones. CHRIST tunic, violet with gold and red clavus; himation, blue (as in all four pendentives, the blue is deeper and warmer than elsewhere in mosaics). PETER tunic, blue; himation, yellow. YOUNG DISCIPLE tunic, blue; himation, green. LANDSCAPE hill, yellowish gray stones; shading of peak at right, violet glasses; ground zone (as in remaining pendentives of dome), green glasses. ARCHITECTURE *Tower at left:* base, gray stones; lighted faces above base, gray stones; receding face, brown stones; column, green shaft and golden capital and base. *Draperies:* red, decorated with gold and red band and fringe. *Fortress walls:* yellowish brown stones. TREE trunk and branches, green glasses; foliage, blue and black glasses; fruit, white stone.

[135]

Christ Healing Two Blind Men

PL. 262, 263

(Matthew 20:29–34)

ʽΟ Χ(ριστὸ)ς ἰώμενος τοὺς δύο τυφλούς   *Christ healing the two blind men*

ʼΙ(ησοῦ)ς Χ(ριστό)ς   *Jesus Christ*

The second healing miracle in the pendentives of the southern dome is placed at the northwest. From the left, followed by two of his disciples, Christ approaches two young blind men seated beneath an overhanging tree outside the walls of Jericho. Drawn in profile at the far left, part of his himation fluttering behind him, is a young disciple. To the right and partially obscuring him is Peter, standing in three-quarters view, his right arm resting in a fold of his garment and his left gesturing toward Christ or the blind men. Christ, also in three-quarters view, advances with his right arm fully extended in blessing; his left hand, which holds a scroll, emerges in front of him from a great cascade of flying drapery. The first blind youth, who sits upright on the ground, holds the end of a long staff in his left hand and gestures toward Christ with his right; the second, seated near the base of the tree, extends both hands in supplication to the "son of David" (Matt. 20:30, 31). Both youths are dressed in simple tunics that reach their ankles. Corresponding to the horizontal elements (the tree and awning) that shelter the figures in the preceding scene [134] is a gnarled tree springing out almost horizontally from the right above the blind men. Like its counterpart in [134], this tree bears small white fruit and its foliage is rendered in blue glasses. At the far left, incompletely shown in Plate 262, is another blue tree, and at the far right, behind the wall, are two cypress trees.

Dimensions

From bottom of inscription to top of blue field filled with ornament below ground zone, 1.37 m.

Colors and Materials

YOUNG DISCIPLE tunic (visible at neck), blue; himation, green. PETER tunic, blue with red clavus; himation, yellow. CHRIST tunic, violet, decorated with gold and red clavi; himation, blue (see color note for Christ in [134]). FIRST BLIND MAN (left) long tunic, red; staff, brown. SECOND BLIND MAN (right) long tunic, blue.

LANDSCAPE hills and foreground, yellowish gray stone with shading in violet glass; shadow in cleft between peaks at left, green glass; other shading of peaks, blue glass; highlights, gray and white stones. WALLS slightly lighter shade of yellowish gray stone used in hills. TREES *Tree at far left:* blue foliage. *Large tree at right:* trunk and main branches, green glasses; foliage, two values of blue glass, with greenish gray in light areas; fruit, light gray stone. *First cypress tree at right:* foliage, medium green, with darks in blue glass and lights in gray stone. *Second cypress tree at far right:* green and black glasses.

[136]

Christ Healing Peter's Mother-in-Law

PL. 264–267

(Matthew 8:14–15; Mark 1:29–31; Luke 4:38–39)

Ὁ Χ(ριστὸ)ς ἰώμενος τὴν πενθερὰν τοῦ Πέτρου   *Christ healing Peter's mother-in-law*

Ἰ(ησοῦ)ς Χ(ριστό)ς   *Jesus Christ*

The mosaics of the two eastern pendentives of the southern dome are confronting compositions. The first, at the northeast, illustrates the healing of Peter's wife's mother, who lay "sick of a fever," according to Matthew and Mark, and was cured when Christ touched her hand. Mark also states that the miracle was performed in the presence of four disciples: Peter, his brother Andrew, and James and John. The mosaic, however, depicts only three disciples: a beardless youth, who must be John, and the two brothers.

John, who stands at the far left, is drawn in a rather grotesque profile view, facing to the right. It is curious that in nearly all the miracle scenes at the Kariye Djami one of the three young disciples (John, Philip, or Thomas) is present, is very often placed at or near the far left or right, and is usually drawn in profile. Indeed, without exception, the only disciples to be drawn in sharp profile are the young ones. In this instance, John is engaged in conversation with Andrew; both hands are raised before him, and with both he points to himself. Although Andrew is turned in three-quarters view toward the right, he looks back at John; his hands are folded before him and his right arm rests in a fold of his outer garment. Christ, at the center of the mosaic, leans forward toward the right and, fully extending his right arm, grasps the wrist of the woman; from his left arm hangs a great fold of his himation, and in his left hand he holds a scroll. Peter's mother-in-law is at the right facing Christ. She sits with a violet coverlet over her legs on her richly draped bed, which is placed at an angle to parallel the slope of the arch below it. Peter, also facing Christ, stands close beside her but is partly obscured by her. Serving to accentuate the group of Peter and the woman, and to indicate an interior setting, is a rectangular, flat-roofed house, placed behind them in the upper right. This is balanced at the left by another building. A low wall connects the two buildings and forms a background for the three center figures.

145

Dimensions

From bottom of inscription to top of blue field filled with ornament below ground zone, 1.26 m.

Colors and Materials

JOHN tunic (visible as a triangular bit at bottom of figure), blue; himation, brown stones, outlined at left side and below elbow with one row of blue glass. ANDREW tunic, blue with dark blue clavus; himation, green. CHRIST tunic, violet with gold and red clavus; himation, blue (see color note for Christ in [134]).

THE MOTHER-IN-LAW tunic (visible at wrist), red with golden cuff; mantle and headdress, green; coverlet, vio- let; drapes at sides of bed, red bordered at top and bot- tom with gold and dark red; mattress, white and gray stones with two blue stripes; pillow at head of bed, dark green glass with corner tabs of gold and red. PETER tunic, blue with red clavus; himation, brown stone (unusual).

BUILDING AT LEFT bluish gray stone in two values with shadows and outlines of blue glass and lines of white stone for highlights. WALL IN CENTER yel- lowish gray stone outlined above with blue. BUILD- ING AT RIGHT reddish brown stone in two values; large opening at right, dark violet glass; soffits of opening in front, light violet; curtain, showing in a dark blue in- terior doorway, red and gold.

[137]

Christ Healing the Woman with the Issue of Blood   PL. 268–271

(Matthew 9:20–22; Mark 5:25–34; Luke 8:43–48)

Ὁ Χ(ριστὸ)ς ἰώμ(εν)ο(ς) τὴν αἱμορροοῦσαν
Christ healing the woman with the issue of blood

Ἰ(ησοῦ)ς Χ(ριστό)ς   *Jesus Christ*

The scene of Christ Healing the Woman with the Issue of Blood is found in the southeastern pendentive of the southern dome. Compositional considerations in the laying out of the mosaics of the four pendentives required that this scene should read from right to left, counter to the usual practice (see comments on mosaic no. [134] above). On the other hand, custom dictated that wherever possible the figures of Christ and his disciples should be at the left, an arrangement that normally resulted in a composition reading from left to right. These seemingly irreconcil- able demands were harmonized in the mosaic by the choice of subject, for the narratives state that while Christ was on the way to the house of Jairus the woman with the issue of blood pressed through the crowd behind him and touched the hem of his garment. The mosaicist, therefore, was able to represent Christ and the disciples at the left moving toward a confronta- tion with the pendant scene in the northeastern pendentive.

Peter, a young disciple, and Christ walk briskly toward a house at the far left. All three turn the upper parts of their bodies and look back with expressions and gestures of surprise at the woman on the ground. Head raised and knees far apart, as though crawling on hands and knees, the woman grasps the hem of Christ's tunic with both hands. At the right is a group of men, some of whom emerge from a building in the background, led by a bearded old man, his head covered by a scarf; one hand is exposed and the other concealed beneath his mantle, but he raises both in an attitude of surprise. His prominence in the scene and the type in which he is represented (see the fresco of The Raising of the Daughter of Jairus, PL. 363) suggest that he is to be identified as Jairus, a ruler of the synagogue, who had come to fetch Christ to heal his dying daughter.

The principal figures are placed in a landscape of rolling hills between the two buildings. An unusual feature of this mosaic is the pronounced undulation of the zone of green "ground" at the base of the scene, reflecting the configuration of the kneeling woman and the contours of the hills above.

Dimensions

From bottom of inscription to top of blue field filled with ornament below ground zone, 1.26 m.

Colors and Materials

PETER tunic, blue; himation, yellow stone with drawing of dark brown glass. YOUNG DISCIPLE tunic, blue; himation, green. CHRIST tunic, blue (unusual) with gold and red clavus; himation, slightly darker blue than tunic, but cooler and lighter than blue (of an unusual hue) in himation of Christ in other three pendentives of southern dome; feet, unlike those of other three figures of Christ in pendentives, are bare.
WOMAN mantle and headdress, dark violet with lighted areas of blue. JAIRUS tunic, light blue with wide hem of dark blue; mantle, red; headdress, light blue. MAN AT FAR RIGHT mantle, dark blue; headdress (slipped off head onto shoulders), red. YOUTH AT CENTER OF CROWD mantle, green; headdress (on shoulders), yellow.
BUILDING AT LEFT bluish gray stone; column shaft, green; column base and capital, gold and greenish brown glass; curtain, red. BUILDING AT RIGHT lighted face, greenish gray and yellowish gray stones; receding face, darker grayish green (verd-antique marble); door opening, dark blue; drapery on roof, red with gold border. LANDSCAPE ground and background hills, yellowish gray stone shaded at contours with brown stones; mountain peak at far left, same, but with drawing in green, pink, violet, and brown. TREE AT FAR RIGHT branches, brown; foliage, green and black.

[138]

Christ Healing the Man with the Withered Hand

PL. 272, 273

(Matthew 12:9–13; Mark 3:1–5; Luke 6:6–10)

ʽΟ Χ(ριστὸ)ς ἰώμενος τ(ὸν) ξηρὰν ἔχοντα τὴν χεῖρα
Christ healing the man with the withered hand

Ἰ(ησοῦ)ς Χ(ριστό)ς   *Jesus Christ*

The soffit of the southernmost arch, like those of the other arches spanning the inner narthex, is decorated with two scenes; the one in the eastern side illustrates Christ Healing the Man with the Withered Hand. It is laid in an architectural setting indicating the synagogue where the miracle is said to have been performed. Followed at the left by three disciples, Christ approaches the afflicted man, a beardless youth, who stands at the right facing him. The youth is dressed in a short-sleeved, knee-length tunic and spiral leggings covering the ankles of his otherwise bare legs. His stiff right arm, supported by his left hand, is extended horizontally toward Christ, who, as usual, blesses with his right hand and holds a scroll in his left. Silhouetted against an area of gold sky that shows through an opening at the center of the building, the "withered" hand and arm and Christ's healing hand are made the focal point of the composition.

The three disciples are probably Peter, James, and John. Peter stands at the far left, turned slightly to the right; as usual, his right arm is slung in the folds of his himation. Beside him, and partly obscured by the figure of Christ, is a young disciple, probably John, who tilts his head to-

147

ward Peter as though in conversation. Between these two appears little more than the head of the third disciple, who wears the short, dark beard attributed to James and one or two other disciples.

Dimensions

Width between borders, 1.28 m.; height, on curved surface, from top of inscription to top of mosaic border above cornice, 1.85 m.

Colors and Materials

PETER tunic, blue; himation, yellow. SECOND DISCIPLE tunic, blue. YOUNG DISCIPLE tunic, blue; himation, green. CHRIST tunic, violet with golden clavus bordered by rows of inverted gold tesserae; himation, blue. MAN WITH WITHERED HAND short tunic, blue; leggings, dark blue. ARCHITECTURE low wall, yellowish gray stone; lighted face of tower at left, yellowish gray stone with outline drawing in blue glass; receding faces, dull brown stone with outline drawing in violet glass; soffit of lintel, light yellowish gray stone; drapery on roof, red with outlines of gold. TREE AT FAR RIGHT green and black. GROUND ZONE green.

[139]

Christ Healing the Leper

PL. 274, 275

(Matthew 8:1–4; Mark 1:40–44; Luke 5:12–14)

'Ο Χ(ριστὸ)ς ἰώμενος τὸν λεπρὸν   *Christ healing the leper*

'Ι(ησοῦ)ς Χ(ριστό)ς   *Jesus Christ*

The mosaic in the western side of the southern arch of the inner narthex illustrates Christ Healing the Leper, a miracle that was also depicted in the vault of the fourth bay of the outer narthex (see above, no. [119]). In this second version Christ and two disciples stand at the left confronting the leper, at the right. The upper parts of the disciples and Christ are now destroyed, but the figure at the far left, in near-profile, wears a yellow himation, which identifies him as Peter. The second disciple is clad in a himation of green, the color adopted, with only two exceptions, in the other miracles of the inner narthex for the youthful disciple who may be John. Except for the right hand, the figure of the leper is intact. His only garment is a loincloth tied in front; his emaciated body is rendered in light gray and yellow stones and his spots in a dull brown porous stone. The background consists of a horizontally disposed building extending from border to border, its roof at several levels. The figures stand well above the "ground" zone in a horizontal band, representing the foreground, that is barely distinguishable in color from the wall above it.

Dimensions

Width between borders, 1.125 m.; height, on curved surface, from top of inscription to top of mosaic border above cornice, 1.80 m.

Colors and Materials

PETER tunic, blue; himation, yellow. SECOND DISCIPLE tunic, blue; himation, green. CHRIST tunic, violet with gold and red clavi; himation, blue. LEPER loincloth, blue; flesh, warm light gray and reddish yellow stones with drawing and spots in dull brown scoriaceous stone.
GROUND ZONE a band of dark green glass above another of dark blue. FOREGROUND a horizontal zone of yellowish gray stone slightly darker than lighted face of building above. ARCHITECTURE lighted face, yellowish gray stone; receding faces, brown stones; openings, black glass and dark purplish scoriaceous stone; flat roofs, light yellowish gray stone; roof tiles on tower, blue glass and dark and light bluish gray stones.

[140]

An Unidentified Scene (a Miracle of Healing)

Ὁ Χ(ριστὸ)ς ἰώμενος   *Christ healing . . .*

Ἰ(ησοῦ)ς [Χ(ριστό)ς]   *Jesus [Christ]*

The mosaic in the southern lunette of the inner narthex (PL. 15) represents still another of Christ's miracles of healing, as the incomplete inscription informs us. A window in the center divided the composition into two parts. The figures of Christ and one of the two disciples who stood behind him, in the left side of the lunette (PL. 276), are severely damaged; in the right side, all mosaic, including the portion of the inscription that would have identified the scene, is now destroyed.

The bodies of the three extant figures are turned in near-profile toward the right. Peter, at the far left, raises his hands to his breast. Partly obscured by Christ, a young disciple turns his head in sharp profile to look back at Peter. Near the window, Christ extends his right hand in a gesture of blessing toward the figures that once stood in the far side of the lunette; his left hand, which holds a scroll, emerges from a great fold of drapery before him. The upper part of his body, except the blessing hand, and the right shoulder of his young disciple fall within the area of destroyed mosaic. The background consists of a simple wall, about waist-high, that extends from border to border; the ground zone is composed of two horizontal bands, a green one above a blue one.

Dimensions

Total width of lunette, 3.19 m.; height at center within ornamental borders, 1.48 m.

Colors and Materials

PETER tunic, blue; himation, yellow.   YOUNG DISCI-PLE tunic, blue; himation, green.   CHRIST tunic, violet glasses with clavus of gold and red; himation, blue.   WALL stones of light violet color; drawing at top in violet glass and white stone.   GROUND ZONE a band of dark green glass above another of dark blue.

[141]

Christ Healing a Multitude

Ὁ Χ(ριστὸ)ς ἰώμενος τὰ ποικίλα πάθη τῶν νοσημάτων
Christ healing those afflicted with various diseases

Ἰ(ησοῦ)ς Χ(ριστό)ς   *Jesus Christ*

The series of eight healing miracles in the southern bay of the inner narthex, and with it the cycle of Christ's Ministry, comes to a close with a scene in the western lunette entitled Christ Healing Those Afflicted with Various Diseases—one of the largest of the scenes and in many ways one of the finest compositions among the mosaics. The scene as a whole and the inscription above fail to designate a specific miracle; nor can a definite identification be made by comparison with other representations, for no close parallels exist. The inscription suggests that for the close of the series of healing miracles the intention was to illustrate one of the numerous instances of Christ's healing large numbers of people. The afflicted are described in such general terms as the "lame, blind, dumb, maimed, and many others" (Matt. 15:30) or as those who suffered from "all manner of sickness and all manner of disease" (Matt. 4:23) or "every sickness and every disease" (Matt. 9:35), or again, as those who "were sick of divers diseases" (Mark 1:34).

In the left side of the lunette is Christ, followed by three disciples; they are looking to the right, toward the afflicted, who fill the larger part of the space. All face left to receive Christ's blessing. The scene is laid in a hilly landscape; one hill rises behind each of the three groups into which the figures are composed. A tree grows near the center background between Christ and the crowd, and in the right background are two houses.

At the far left a young disciple, whose head is much too small for his body, stands in profile view, his himation billowing out behind him. The second disciple, an elderly man with pointed beard, turns his body toward the left but faces right. Peter, his right arm resting in a fold of his garments and his left concealed under another, stands in nearly frontal view beside his Master. The disciples stand in the foreground close to the bottom of the ground zone. Christ is farther back, on a plane with those he is healing. He stands in three-quarters pose and stoops forward, his right arm extended in the sign of blessing; in his left hand he holds a scroll.

Seated on the ground at Christ's feet is the first of the afflicted; a blind cripple, bearded and dressed in a long tunic, he leans back, raises his head toward Christ, and gestures in supplication with his right hand; in his left hand he holds a hand crutch. Behind him, to the right, are two other seated men, both in simple, short tunics which expose their legs; they make similar gestures of supplication with their right hands as they lean intently forward. The first is a blind man with a short beard. The second is beardless; his affliction, a greatly distended growth or tumor visible between his knees, is not one recorded as being among those which Christ healed.

In the background, behind the group of seated men, there stands the most prominent figure among the crowd—a mother, leaning forward and holding her sick child out toward Christ. Compositionally she and the figure of Christ are pendants, both in configuration and in the symmetry that the two establish around the tree in the center of the lunette. The woman is dressed in a dark green mantle and headdress; the child, whose bare legs seem to be deformed, stretches his hands out at both sides and turns his head slightly toward her. Still further in the background, and partly obscured by the first mother and by a low hillock, is a second, her child held close to her breast; the child's head and shoulders emerge from the folds of the mother's mantle.

Behind the first group of the afflicted is a second, made up of three figures standing in the nearer foreground at the far right. The first figure is that of a bearded man; he leans slightly forward, his left hand holding a heavy stick for support while with his right hand he entreats Christ's healing. He is clad in a short tunic over rather tight trousers that reach his feet. His affliction is not apparent. The stick may signify lameness, but the fact that he wears trousers may indicate that he is a demoniac (cf. above, no. [126]); in a number of miniatures illustrating the healing of multitudes a demoniac is among the prominent figures, although he is usually nude. At the far right are two women, both clad in very long dresses and in mantles that cover their heads. The one in the forefront, standing in profile, is represented after the manner of the "bent woman" as she appears in numerous illustrations of the miracle described in Luke 13:11– 16—the healing of the woman who for eighteen years "was bowed together, and could in no wise lift up herself." In the mosaic, bent into a right angle at the hips, she leans on a short stick, which she holds in her left hand; her head is so low that she must tilt it back sharply to look toward Christ. The second woman, who is partly concealed by the first, is blind; both her right hand and her left, which is covered by her mantle, are extended in a gesture of supplication, and she leans forward in reverence.

Dimensions

Width between borders, measured at bottom, 3.48 m.; height between borders, 1.57 m.

Colors and Materials

YOUNG DISCIPLE AT FAR LEFT tunic, blue; himation, violet. SECOND DISCIPLE tunic, blue; himation, green. PETER tunic, blue; himation, yellow. CHRIST tunic, violet with gold and red clavus; himation, blue. BLIND CRIPPLE (at feet of Christ) tunic, gray and white stones with shadows and drawing in blue glasses; hand crutch, yellow stone outlined with brown stone. SEATED BLIND MAN short tunic, red. SEATED MAN WITH GREAT SWELLING BETWEEN KNEES short tunic, yellow stones with shadows of brown stones and some outlines of black glass, and a few folds at elbow drawn in blue glass. WOMAN HOLDING CHILD IN HANDS outer garments, dark green; edge of kerchief below headdress, white; child's undergarment (visible above waist), blue; child's outer garment, yellow. WOMAN WITH CHILD IN THE BACKGROUND tunic (visible at shoulder), blue; mantle and headdress, red; edge of kerchief below headdress, blue; child's dress, yellow. MAN LEANING ON STICK trousers, yellow; short tunic, blue; stick, brown. BENT WOMAN undergarment (visible at hem), blue; mantle and headdress, yellow; stick, brown. BLIND WOMAN undergarment, blue; mantle and headdress, red.

LANDSCAPE *Tree at center:* trunk, gray stone highlights, olive-green porous stone in shaded side, and green glass outlines; foliage, light green, blue, and black glass; fruit, white stone. *Hill at left:* grayish yellow stone outlined with violet glass. *Hill at center:* yellow stone outlined with violet glass. *Hill at right:* bluish gray stone outlined with blue glass.

ARCHITECTURE *Large building:* lighted wall, yellow stone with shadows of warm brown stone; door opening, dark violet glass above area of warm brown stone; receding wall, brown stone, with dark violet window; roof, red. *Small building:* walls, grayish yellow stone in two values; door and window, dark violet glass; roof, blue.

PORTRAITS OF SAINTS

[142]-[178]

Martyrs in the Arches

BAY 1, EASTERN ARCH, MEDALLIONS *(left to right facing east)* (PL. 282 *a*)

[142] Ὁ ἅγ(ιος) Μαρδάριος	*Mardarius of Sebaste*	*Dec. 13*	*Pl. 284*
[143] [Ὁ ἅγ(ιος)] Αὐ[ξ]έντιος	*Auxentius of Sebaste*	*Dec. 13*	*Pl. 285*
[144] Ὁ ἅγ(ιος) Εὐστράτιος	*Eustratius of Sebaste*	*Dec. 13*	*Pl. 286*
[145] Ὁ ἅγ(ιος) Εὐγένιος	*Eugenius of Sebaste*	*Dec. 13*	*Pl. 287*
[146] Ὁ ἅγ(ιος) Ὀρέστης	*Orestes of Sebaste*	*Dec. 13*	*Pl. 288*

BAY 1, WESTERN ARCH, MEDALLIONS *(left to right facing west)* (PL. 282 *b*)

[147] Ὁ ἅγ(ιος) Ἀνεμπόδιστος	*Anempodistus of Persia*	*Nov. 2*	*Pl. 289*
[148] Ὁ ἅγ(ιος) Ἐλπιδηφόρος	*Elpidephorus of Persia*	*Nov. 2*	*Pl. 290*
[149] Ὁ ἅγ(ιος) Ἀκίνδυνος	*Acindynus of Persia*	*Nov. 2*	*Pl. 291*
[150] Ὁ ἅγ(ιος) Ἀφθόνιος	*Aphthonius of Persia*	*Nov. 2*	*Pl. 292*
[151] Ὁ ἅγ(ιος) Πηγάσιος	*Pegasius of Persia*	*Nov. 2*	*Pl. 293*

BAY 1, SOUTHERN TRANSVERSE ARCH, 1 MEDALLION AND 2 FULL-LENGTH FIGURES

[152] Ὁ ἅγ(ιος) [. . .]	*Medallion of unidentified martyr (Probus of Cilicia?)*	*Oct. 12*	*Pl. 294, 295*
[153] [Ὁ ἅγ(ιος)] Ἀνδρόνικος	*Andronicus of Cilicia*	*Oct. 12*	*Pl. 294*
[154] Ὁ ἅγ(ιος) Τάραχος	*Tarachus of Cilicia*	*Oct. 12*	*Pl. 295*

BAY 2, EASTERN ARCH, MEDALLIONS *(left to right facing east)* (PL. 282 *c*)

[155] Ὁ ἅγ(ιος) Φιλήμων	*Philemon of Egypt*	*Dec. 14*	*Pl. 296*
[156] Ὁ ἅγ(ιος) Λεύκιος	*Leucius of Nicomedia*	*Dec. 14*	*Pl. 297*
[157] Ὁ ἅγ(ιος) Ἀγαθόνικος	*Agathonicus of Nicomedia*	*Aug. 22*	*Pl. 298*
[158] Ὁ ἅγ(ιος) Θύρσος	*Thyrsus of Nicomedia*	*Dec. 14*	*Pl. 299*
[159] Ὁ ἅγ(ιος) Ἀπολώνιος [sic]	*Apollonius of Egypt*	*Dec. 14*	*Pl. 300*

BAY 2, WESTERN ARCH, MEDALLIONS *(left to right facing west)* (PL. 282 *d*)

[160] Ὁ ἅγ(ιος) Λαῦρος	*Laurus of Illyria*	*Aug. 18*	*Pl. 301 a*
[161] Ὁ ἅγ(ιος) Φλῶρος	*Florus of Illyria*	*Aug. 18*	*Pl. 301 b*

[162] ῾Ο ἅγ(ιος) Μηνᾶς   *Menas of Phrygia*   *Nov. 11*   *Pl. 302 a*
[163] ῾Ο ἅγ(ιος) Βίκτωρ   *Victor*   *Nov. 11*   *Pl. 302 b*
[164] ῾Ο ἅγ(ιος) Βικέντιος   *Vincentius*   *Nov. 11*   *Pl. 303*

BAY 2, SOUTHERN TRANSVERSE ARCH, EAST SIDE, FULL-LENGTH FIGURE

[165] *Inscription lost. Probably George of Cappadocia*   *Apr. 23*   *Pl. 304*

BAY 3, SOUTHERN TRANSVERSE ARCH, EAST SIDE, FULL-LENGTH FIGURE

[166] *Inscription lost. Probably Demetrius of Thessalonica*   *Oct. 26*   *Pl. 305*

BAY 2, SOUTHERN TRANSVERSE ARCH, WEST SIDE, FULL-LENGTH FIGURE

[167]   *An unidentified martyr*   *Pl. 306 a*

BAY 3, SOUTHERN TRANSVERSE ARCH, WEST SIDE, FULL-LENGTH FIGURE

[168]   *An unidentified martyr*   *Pl. 306 b*

BAY 4, EASTERN ARCH, MEDALLIONS (*left to right facing east*)   (PL. 283 a)

[169] ῾Ο ἅγ(ιος) Ἄβιβος   *Abibus of Edessa*   *Nov. 15*   *Pl. 307 a*
[170] ῾Ο ἅγ(ιος) Γουρίας   *Gurias of Edessa*   *Nov. 15*   *Pl. 308*
[171] ῾Ο ἅγ(ιος) Σαμων(ᾶς)   *Samonas of Edessa*   *Nov. 15*   *Pl. 307 b*

BAY 4, WESTERN ARCH, MEDALLIONS (*left to right facing west*)   (PL. 283 b)

[172] ῾Ο ἅγ(ιος) Ἔγγραφος [sic]   *Eugraphus of Alexandria*   *Dec. 10*   *Pl. 309 a*
[173] ῾Ο ἅγ(ιος) Μηνᾶς   *Menas of Alexandria*   *Dec. 10*   *Pl. 309 b*
[174] ῾Ο ἅγ(ιος) Ἑρμογένης   *Hermogenes of Alexandria*   *Dec. 10*   *Pl. 310*

BAY 4, SOUTHERN TRANSVERSE ARCH, FULL-LENGTH FIGURES

[175]   *An unidentified martyr*   *Pl. 311*
[176]   *An unidentified martyr*   *Pl. 312*

BAY 5, EASTERN ARCH, MEDALLION (*left side of arch*)   (PL. 283 c)

[177] [῾Ο ἅγ(ιος) . . .]λ   *An unidentified martyr*   *Pl. 313 a*

BAY 5, WESTERN ARCH, MEDALLION (*right side of arch*)   (PL. 283 d)

[178] ῾Ο ἅγ(ιος) [Σέργιος
or Βάκχος]   *Sergius or Bacchus*   *Oct. 7*   *Pl. 313 b*

Portraits of martyr saints were placed in the soffits of the arches of the outer narthex. There were originally fifty, of which thirty-seven still exist in whole or in part. They are of two kinds: busts in medallions, and full-length standing figures. The busts decorate the relatively narrow soffits of the eight relieving arches at the east and west ends of Bays 1, 2, 4, and 5. The only bays of the outer narthex with oblong plans, they are covered by square domical vaults, so that the relieving arches at the two ends of the bays are exposed. Bays 3, 6, and 7, being square in plan, are vaulted to their full extent and have only slightly projecting relieving arches at the closed sides. Medallion portraits were placed also, in all probability, in the summits of the transverse arches that span the narthex. Evidence of their presence at these points exists only in the arch between Bays 1 and 2 (no. [152], PL. 294, 295), where two short segments of a circular border and a bit of the inscription are still preserved.

Each of the four relieving arches of Bays 1 and 2 contains five medallion portraits; in the smaller arches of Bays 4 and 5, however, there is space for only three medallions per arch. Originally, therefore, the relieving arches contained a total of thirty-two medallions; there would have been six more in the summits of the transverse arches. Of the thirty-two portraits in the relieving arches, twenty-five are now intact and three others exist in fragments; a fragment of only one of the six medallions in the transverse arches has survived.

The standing figures, of larger proportions than those in the medallions, were placed in the haunches of the six transverse arches, one in each side of each arch. Of the original twelve, only three are completely preserved (one of these has lost its inscription), but the lower parts of five others have survived. The massive, slightly pointed reinforcing arches built within the two transverse arches at the open sides of the sixth bay, at the southwestern corner of the building (PL. 11), have obscured all evidence of the four standing figures (and the two medallions) that were once there.

With only a few exceptions the martyrs' attributes in the Kariye Djami are a small cross, which is held in the right hand, and princely attire. They are portrayed not as martyrs in terrestrial form but in their state of beatitude in triumph over death. The cross does not denote the manner in which they met death but is held in witness to their own passion and as a symbol of Christ's cross of victory, which becomes the trophy of their own victory over death.

Most of the martyrs wear a costume that recalls the sumptuous attire of the imperial courtier. The typical costume consists of the tunic and the chlamys. The tunic, which is gathered in at the waist by a cord, is richly embroidered at the collar and cuffs and, in the full-length figures, at the hem as well. It can be seen that some of the full-length figures ([153], [154], [175]) wear, under the tunic, the anaxyrides (tight-fitting trousers); some also wear richly decorated boots. Over the tunic most wear the chlamys, a sleeveless mantle that hangs over the shoulders. It is normally worn so that the opening falls at the right side, leaving the right arm exposed, in which case it is held together with a fibula at the right shoulder; in a majority of these portraits, however, it is fastened below the chin, so that it falls symmetrically, with the opening, either parted or closed, at the center. It is also worn in various other ways: unfastened and hanging open [153]; wrapped diagonally about the body [155]; or hanging over the left shoulder and held together at the hip by the left hand [168]. With few exceptions the chlamys is decorated with tablia, large, richly ornamented patches of embroidery at the two edges near waist level; it is sometimes also decorated with an all-over pattern ([165]–[168], [176]). In two instances, [146] and [147], it is dispensed with and only the tunic is worn. Instead of a chlamys one of the full-length figures wears, slipped around his shoulders, a long, loose coat unfastened at the throat, its long sleeves hanging empty [175]. This type of garment seems to have been in vogue among the Palaeologan nobility of Constantinople; we encounter such a garment, for example, in the portraits of deceased members of the dynastic family in Tombs C and F (PL. 535 and 547).

154

A few of the martyrs, however, are attired differently and are given other attributes in addition to their crosses. Mardarius [142], as he does in other portraits elsewhere, wears a hat with a wide, upturned brim of fur and a rounded red crown. Because they were deacons Vincentius [164] and Abibus [169] are dressed in clerical garb, the long white tunic (sticharion) and scarf (orarion) of the deacon. Each also seems to wear a black garment, visible only at the neck, beneath the sticharion. The orarion, worn vertically over the left shoulder, is of gold bordered with red, and on it is inscribed the word ἅγιος. However, Apollonius [159], who also is said to have been a cleric, possibly a deacon, has no clerical attribute. Another cleric, Hermogenes [174], who is said to have been a bishop, holds a book of the Gospels in veiled hands but lacks the more obvious attributes by which bishops are designated; he is, however, distinguished from the other martyrs in wearing what appears to be a simple, undecorated yellow tunic. A number of the saints are said to have been soldiers, but in only three instances do their costumes recall this fact. The two full-length figures, [165] and [166], in the eastern sides of the arches flanking the entrance to the inner narthex, whose inscriptions are lost but who are to be identified as Sts. George and Demetrius, hold sheathed swords in their left hands in recognition of their pre-eminence among the military saints. George, in addition, wears the short, sleeveless tunic of the warrior beneath his chlamys. Possibly another allusion to the military calling is found in the fragmentary medallion [178] in the western arch of Bay 5, in which the saint wears around his neck the maniakion (a metal necklace, or torque) usually worn by Sts. Sergius and Bacchus. The Constantinopolitan Synaxarion lists this as one of the badges of their military office which were taken from these two saints on their martyrdom; in their portraiture, as saints, this military insigne is usually restored to them.

In four of the medallions the martyr does not carry the cross. Hermogenes holds a book, but Eustratius [144], Acindynus [149], and Victor [163] have no attribute at all; in fact, even their hands are omitted. The mosaicist seems to have based his portraits of the first two, which are placed in the centers of their respective arches, on a single model and made only slight modifications; Eustratius has a knotted scarf around his neck, but his chlamys lacks the round shoulder patches that appear on that of Acindynus. It is possible that all three were modeled on full-length figures which held their hands, and crosses, too low to be encompassed in bust medallions.

The list of inscriptions at the head of this section, arranged in the order in which the portraits of the martyrs appear in the arches of the successive bays, records the dates of the feasts according to the Constantinopolitan calendar and the place (geographic region, or city) of their martyrdom. It illustrates at a glance some of the principles that were followed in the grouping and distribution of the portraits in the various arches. First of all, it is evident that in so far as possible each arch was devoted to a group who were companions in martyrdom, usually compatriots, and whose feasts were celebrated, as a group, on the same day. The groupings correspond to those that appear in the synaxes for those days. Examples of this arrangement occur in the three arches of Bay 1 ([142]–[146]; [147]–[151]; [152]–[154]) and the eastern and western arches of Bay 4 ([169]–[171]; [172]–[174]). In the first of these (the eastern arch of Bay 1) is the group known as "the five martyrs;" all came from Sebaste in Lesser Armenia and all are jointly commemorated on December 13. Opposite them, in the western arch of the same bay, are five martyrs of Persia (Nov. 2), and in the first transverse arch are the full-length figures of Andronicus and Tarachus ([153], [154]), Cilician martyrs, who are commemorated with their chief companion, Probus of Anazarbus in Cilicia, on October 12. Although the medallion between the two full-length figures is destroyed, there is little doubt that it portrayed Probus. In the eastern arch of the fourth bay are the three companion-martyrs of Edessa ([169]–[171]), commemorated on November 15, and opposite them are the three martyrs of Alexandria ([172]–[174]), whose feast comes on December 10.

It was not always possible to fill an arch with a single group of companions or with martyrs whose feasts fell on the same day, but in every arch where they are identifiable the portraits are ordered in groups of two or more companions commemorated on the same day or martyrs of the same city, whose feasts may or may not be celebrated jointly. A case in point is the eastern arch of the second bay (PL. 282 c), in the center of which are three martyrs of Nicomedia ([156], [157], [158]); the centermost (Agathonicus, Aug. 22), however, does not share the feast of his two neighbors (Leucius and Thyrsus, Dec. 14). At the two ends of the same arch are the companion-martyrs from Egypt, Philemon [155] and Apollonius [159], whose feast coincides with that of the two Nicomedian martyrs who adjoin them. In the western arch of the same bay (PL. 282 d), in the center and at the right side ([162]–[164]), are three saints (Menas of Phrygia, Victor, said to be from Italy, and Vincentius) who met martyrdom in different places but share a joint commemoration on November 11. The two saints ([160], [161]) in the left side of that arch (Laurus and Florus, Aug. 18) were twin brothers from Byzantium martyred together in Illyria.

In the transverse arches that flank Bay 3, at each side of the door leading into the inner narthex, there is still another system of pairing saints, one that is based not on the dates of their feasts, or on their being companions or compatriots (they were not), but simply on the fact that they stand at the head of the hierarchy of all the martyrs, rather as Peter and Paul are so often paired as chiefs of the Apostles. In the eastern side of the arch to the north of the door is the full-length figure of a saint [165] whose inscription is destroyed but whose features identify him as St. George of Cappadocia (Apr. 23). Countless portraits, over many centuries of time, demonstrate that St. George's features were perhaps more consistently delineated than those of any other martyr. As was pointed out above, a number of the saints in the arches were soldiers, but only George and his pendant [166] on the other side of the door are given a military attribute — a sheathed sword. The military saint who is normally paired with George and who shares with him the chief position among military saints is St. Demetrius of Thessalonica, whose feast is celebrated on October 26, and it is logical to suppose that these two, as the pre-eminent martyrs, were assigned positions in the arches at each side of the door to the inner narthex, much as Peter and Paul ([4] and [5]) were placed at each side of the door beyond it, into the nave.

It is evident that in arranging the portraits of a single group within the same arch the mosaicist was influenced by the protocol, or order or precedence, that is established in the text of the Constantinopolitan Synaxarion. He consistently followed the principle that the first martyr to be named should have the position of honor at the summit of the arch and that his portrait should be turned at right angles to the curve of the arch, whereas the others in the group should be placed parallel to the curve, one above the other. His ideal arrangement, which he did not or could not always follow, was to place the succeeding martyrs on alternate sides beginning at the central figure's right hand and proceeding back and forth at successively lower levels. To illustrate this system: the order in which the saints in the eastern arch of the first bay are listed in the Synaxarion is reproduced in the arch in the following pattern, from left to right: 4, 2, 1, 3,

5. The western arch of the same bay follows the system of alternating sides but places the second and third saints at the lower ends of the arch: 3, 5, 1, 4, 2. The three saints in the transverse arch of the first bay are listed in the Synaxarion as Probus, Tarachus, and Andronicus. Looking at the arch from the south, the direction from which one approaches it, one sees them in the order 2, 1, 3, with Tarachus at Probus' right hand.

In the eastern arch of the second bay the mosaicist was dealing with three different groups: Agathonicus, the single representative from a group of six fellow martyrs commemorated on August 22; two fellow martyrs of Nicomedia (Dec. 14); and two martyrs of Egypt (also Dec. 14). He placed Agathonicus in the center; then, first at his left and then at his right, his fellow Nicomedians; and finally, at the two opposite ends, the two Egyptians; the four saints with the same feast day were honored in the order in which their commemorations occur in the Synaxarion: 4, 3, 1, 2, 5. The western arch of the second bay presented another problem, since it was to have two groups, one of three fellow saints and the other of two. In this instance the first saint listed from the group of three was placed at the center, with the other two at his left, and the second group side by side at his right: 5, 4, 1, 2, 3. Finally, a group of three fellow saints fills each of the two smaller arches of Bay 4, the first listed in each instance being placed in the center, the second to his left, and the third to his right: 3, 1, 2.

The portraits are not highly individualized; rather, they represent a limited number of head types. Each type is arbitrarily assigned to more than one saint, but when the heads are compared individually with their equivalents in other monuments it becomes evident that a number of the saints, more especially the "great martyrs," as they are called in the Synaxarion, tend to conform to traditional types. The thirty heads that are still preserved at the Kariye Djami can be divided as follows into eight or ten types, the number depending on whether one regards certain heads as variants of a single type:

1) Middle-aged; a heavy head of hair that falls in three waves at each side almost to the shoulders; a rather straight hairline across a medium-height brow; a few strands of hair curling to left or right at center of brow; a rather short, dark beard parted at the center ([142], [145], [154], [156]).

2) Middle-aged; similar to no. 1, but with two waves at each side of the head; beard parted into two lobes, one longer than the other ([150], [151], [174]).

3) Middle-aged; similar to nos. 1 and 2 but with a still shorter beard not parted ([159], [163], [171]).

4) Middle-aged; dark hair falling in two or three waves at each side; a rather straight hairline across a moderately high brow; a few strands of hair curling to right at center of brow; a rather long, pointed beard ([144], [149]).

5) Elderly; hair in small, tight curls; a rather straight hairline across a low brow; a short beard of the type worn by St. Peter ([162]).

6) Old; thin, bony face; gray hair falling in waves at each side; a rather straight hairline across a moderately high brow; a few strands of hair curling to right at center; long, pointed gray beard ([148], [155], [170]).

7) Old; very little hair on top of head; what is left above ears clings to temples in a leaf-like form; a high, domed brow with a tuft of hair at the top; a medium-length beard, parted in lobes below the point of the chin ([158], [173]).

8) Young; beardless; long, oval face; hairline either relatively straight across a medium-height brow or sloping down from a center part; hair falling more or less to shoulders in waves ([146], [147], [153], [157], [164], [169], [172], [178]).

9) Young; beardless; similar to no. 8, but with a shorter face ([160], [161]).

10) Young; beardless; a heavy head of hair, short, tightly curled, and circular in contour (St. George [165]; [175] may be of the same type and may therefore represent St. Panteleimon, whose portraits often resemble those of St. George).

Dimensions

MEDALLIONS (diameter) [142]: .47 m. [144]: .47 m. [145]: .47 m. [146]: .485 m. [147]: .515 m. [148]: .53 m. [149]: .555 m. [150]: .56 m. [151]: .485 m. [152]: ca. .87 m. when complete. [155]: .50 m. [156]: .48 m. [157]: .505 m. [158]: .515 m. [159]: .51 m. [160]: .49 m. [161]: .485 m. [162]: .485 m. [163]: .49 m. [164]: .48 m. [169]: .565 m. [170]: .60 m. [171]: .60 m. [172]: .61 m. [173]: .61 m. [174]: .61 m. [177]: .61 m. [178]: .62 m.

STANDING FIGURES [153]: height, head to foot, 1.72 m.; diameter of halo, .42 m.; height of green zone, .59 m.; width of soffit, including wave borders, measured at center of figure, .92 m. [154]: height, 1.72 m.; diameter of halo, .415 m.; height of green zone, .57 m.; width of soffit, including wave borders, .935 m. [165]: height, 1.87 m.; diameter of halo, .44 m.; height of green zone, .44 m.; width of soffit, including wave borders, .88 m. [166]: height of fragment from top of cornice to high point of figure, 1.78 m.; height of green zone, .54 m.; width of soffit, including wave borders, .925 m. [167]: height from foot to high point of fragmentary figure, 1.70 m.; height of green zone, .48 m.; width of soffit, including wave borders, .96 m. [168]: height of fragment from top of cornice to high point of figure, 1.66 m.; height of green zone, .485 m.; width of soffit, including wave borders, .91 m. [175]: height of fragment from top of cornice to high point of figure, 2.10 m.; height of green zone, .435 m.; width of soffit, including wave borders, .87 m. [176]: height of fragment from top of cornice to high point of figure, 1.70 m.; height of green zone, .485 m.; width of soffit, including wave borders, .84 m.

Colors and Materials

[142]: tunic, green, with gold and red collar; chlamys, blue, with gold and red borders and tablia, latter ornamented with pearls and green gems; hat, brown glasses in brim, red glass in crown; cross, white stone; hair and beard, brown glass and black stone. [143]: fragment of chlamys, green. [144]: chlamys, violet; rectangular fibula, gold and red; scarf, blue glasses and gray stone; hair and beard, dark violet. [145]: tunic, green, with gold and red collar; chlamys, red, with gold and red borders and tablia, latter ornamented with pearls and green gems; fibula, green; cross, white stone; hair and beard, brown glasses, with yellow glass highlights in hair. [146]: tunic, blue, with gold and red collar ornamented with pearls and red and green gems; cross, dark blue; hair, brown with highlights in yellow.

[147]: tunic, blue, with gold and red collar ornamented with pearls and green and red gems; cross, blue and white; hair, brown with orange highlights at top of head and yellow elsewhere. [148]: tunic, blue, with gold and red collar; chlamys, bluish green, bordered at edges and ornamented at shoulders with gold and red; rectangular fibula, gold and red, set with yellowish green gem; cross, white; hair, light violet, gray, and white; beard, gray and light blue, with brown shadows. [149]: chlamys, dark violet, bordered at edges and decorated at shoulders with gold and red; fibulae, gold and red; hair and beard, dark violet with highlights in light blue. [150]: tunic, green, with gold and red collar; chlamys, blue, with gold and red borders and tablion, latter ornamented with pearls and red and green gems; cross, white and blue; hair and beard as in preceding medallion. [151]: tunic, blue, with gold and red collar; chlamys, red, with gold and red borders and tablion, latter ornamented with pearls and green gem; hair and beard, brown, with yellow and green lights; cross, white and blue.

[153]: tunic, red, with gold, red, and blue collar, cuffs, and hem, all ornamented with pearls and green and red gems; belt, gold and blue; chlamys, blue, with gold and red borders and tablia, latter ornamented with pearls and blue and red gems; chlamys lining of white stone decorated with geometric pattern in blue glass; trousers, violet; boots, red, with bands of gold and red and foliate greaves of green; cross, white and light blue; hair, brown and yellow. [154]: tunic, blue, with gold and red hem ornamented with pearls and green and red gems; chlamys, red with white lining, borders and tablia of gold and red, latter ornamented with pearls and green and red gems; fibulae, gold and red; trousers, black; boots, red, with bands of gold and brownish glass; cross, white and blue; hair, brown with yellow lights; beard, brown.

[155]: tunic, blue, with gold and red collar containing a design in translucent amber glass; chlamys, red, ornamented with gold and red band; cross, red; hair, gray and white, shaded in violet; beard, white, bluish gray, and greenish brown. [156]: tunic, green, with gold and red collar; chlamys, blue, with borders and tablia

of gold and red; fibula studded with green gem; cross, white and gray; hair and beard, light brown. [157]: tunic, blue, with gold and red collar ornamented with pearls and green and red gems; chlamys, green, with gold and red bands; cross, white and blue; hair as in preceding figure. [158]: chlamys, blue, with gold and red borders and tablia, latter ornamented with pearls and green and blue gems; cross, white; hair and beard, gray, brown, and blue. [159]: chlamys, red, with gold and red borders and tablia, latter ornamented with pearls and red gems; fibula studded with blue gem and pearls; cross, white; hair and beard, brown and yellow.

[160]: tunic, green; chlamys, red, with gold and dark blue borders and tablia, latter ornamented with pearls and red gems; fibula studded with red gem; cross, white; hair, brown and yellow. [161]: tunic, yellow, with gold and red collar ornamented with pearls; chlamys, green, with gold and red borders and tablion, latter ornamented with pearls and red gem; fibula, red and gold; cross, white; hair, brown and yellow. [162]: tunic, gold and red; chlamys, blue, with gold and red borders and tablia, latter decorated with pearls; fibula studded with blue gem; cross, white; hair, light brown, gray, and white; beard, same as hair but with some light blue lines. [163]: chlamys, green, with gold and red borders; fibula, gold and black with pearls at corners and green gem; hair and beard, brown and yellow. [164]: undergarment (visible only at neck), black; sticharion, white, with collar outline in gray stones and folds in light yellow stones; orarion, gold and red, with lettering in black; cross, red; hair, brown and yellow.

[165]: tunic, blue, with over-all trefoil pattern of gold, and with gold and red collar (studded with pearls), hem (studded with pearls and red and green gems), and cuffs; short, sleeveless tunic, green glass in shadows and white and gray stones in lights, with over-all pattern of gold lozenges and with gold and red hem; chlamys, red, with over-all gold pattern of leaves surrounded by inverted hearts and with gold and blue borders and tablion, latter ornamented with pearls and green and red gems; fibula, gold, with red gem and two red cords tipped with gold; boots, red, with gold bands; sword hilt, green, with gold bands; scabbard, same, with black and violet thongs; cross, white and blue; hair, brown and yellow.

[166]: tunic, red, with same over-all pattern in gold that appeared on chlamys of preceding figure and cuffs and hem of gold and red ornamented with pearls and green and red gems; chlamys, green, with over-all pattern of golden four-pointed stars and with gold and black borders and band, latter ornamented with pearls and green gems; boots, red; sword hilt, blue with gold band; scabbard, dark blue-violet, with bands of gold and thongs of red and white; cross, white and blue.

[167]: tunic, red, with over-all pattern of golden trefoils and with gold and red shoulder disc and hem, latter ornamented with pearls and green and red gems, and gold and brown cuff ornamented with pearls and red gem; chlamys, violet, with over-all pattern of golden "spades" and with gold and red borders and tablion, latter ornamented with pearls and green and red gems; boots, blue, with gold and red bands; cross, white and blue.

[168]: tunic, red, with over-all pattern of golden "spades" and with gold and red cuff and hem, latter ornamented with pearls and green and red gems; chlamys, blue, with over-all gold pattern of large fleurs-de-lis enclosed within inverted hearts and with gold and red borders and tablion, latter ornamented with pearls and green and red gems; boots, blue, with dark blue stripes; cross, white and blue.

[169]: colors and materials like those of [164] above. [170]: chlamys, red, with borders and tablia of gold and red; cross, blue; hair, mainly greens and greenish brown with gray and white lights; beard, mainly yellow with blue outlines and brown and green shadows. [171]: chlamys, blue, with borders and tablia of gold and red; fibula, studded with green gem and surrounded by pearls; cross, white; hair and beard, brown and brownish green with yellow highlights.

[172]: chlamys, green, with borders and tablia of gold and red; cross, black; hair, greenish brown glass and brown stone, with orange-yellow stone for highlights. [173]: chlamys, red, with gold and red borders and tablia; fibula, blue, surrounded by pearls; cross, blue; hair and beard, much blue and greenish blue in modeling and in hair, with greenish brown shadows and lights in white stone. [174]: tunic, yellow, warm gray, and white stones; book, golden cover with greenish brown border, outlined in red and ornamented with pearls and green gems; hair, brown, greenish brown, and green glasses and gray stones; beard, dark violet and blue glasses and gray stones. [175]: tunic, blue, with gold and red collar and hem, former decorated with pearls and green gem, latter with pearls and red gems; coat, red, with over-all pattern of golden fleurs-de-lis and with gold and red borders; trousers, green; spiral leggings, violet; cross, blue. [176]: tunic, green, with gold and greenish brown cuff and gold and red hem, latter ornamented with pearls and green and red gems; chlamys, red, with over-all pattern of golden number signs (#) alternating with small golden lozenges, and with gold and red borders and tablion, latter ornamented with pearls and green and red gems; boots, blue, with bands of red and gold; cross, blue.

[177]: chlamys, green, with borders and tablia of gold and red; fibula studded with green gem and surrounded by pearls; cross, white. [178]: chlamys, green, with gold and red borders; fibula studded with blue gem; maniakion, gold outlined in red and ornamented at center front with a vertical row of three blue gems; cross, white; hair, brown with orange-yellow highlights.

159

[179]-[184]

Saints in the Wall Panels

The walls of the outer narthex, whose masonry construction is now exposed, were originally faced with marble revetments. On each of the pilasters that receive the transverse arches a mosaic panel, semicircular at the top and framed with marble, was set into the revetments, just as the panels of Sts. Peter and Paul ([4] and [5]) were let into the marbles of the inner narthex at either side of the door to the nave. There were originally twelve mosaic panels on the walls of the outer narthex, but only six ([179]-[184]) still exist, in fragmentary form; their nearness to the floor has resulted in severe damage. Parts of the marble frames of two others, without any traces of their mosaics, are also preserved; these occur on the western pilaster between the third and fourth bays and on the eastern pilaster between the fourth and fifth.

The mosaics, within their frames, averaged about 1.75 m. in height and about .68 m. in width. The mosaic area was framed first by a narrow, projecting molding, of white marble, with a beveled inner edge. In those cases where the outer parts of the frames, surrounding the semicircular heads of the panels, still exist they consist of an archivolt of simple wedge-shaped voussoirs, about .15 m. high, of alternating pink and gray marbles ([179], [183], [184]), or of fan-shaped voussoirs of the same colors ([181], [182]). As a finishing touch the marbles were enclosed within a narrow bull's-nose molding.

The six panels of the first, second, and third bays would seem to have been devoted to portraits of those who, by divine intervention, were precursors of the Incarnation, that is, members of what might be termed the three holy families. Thus, facing one another across the narthex on the pilasters between the first and second bays are St. Anne with the infant Mary in her arms [179] and her husband Joachim [180]; between the second and third were Mary and the infant Christ [181] and, in all probability, her husband Joseph, although the latter is entirely destroyed. On the eastern pilaster between the third and fourth bays is a small fragment of St. John the Baptist [182]. His pendant, across the narthex, would most probably have been his father, the Prophet Zacharias, although it is possible that Elizabeth, his mother, was represented there. The panels on the six other pilasters probably also portrayed saints; one of the two remaining fragments [183] depicts a military saint and the other [184], St. Euthymius, the Palestinian hermit.

In its form, the standing figure of St. Anne holding the infant Mary [179] imitates the type of the Virgin Eleousa, a particularly fine example of which is found on the wall of the bema in the parecclesion ([249], PL. 486). In contrast to the figures in the other panels, which assume a nearly frontal pose, St. Anne is turned rather sharply to the right; this brings her into relation with the figure of the Virgin and the Christ Child [181], which is to the right, on the next pilaster. In accordance with the type, St. Anne's head juts forward from the base of the neck so that her left cheek may touch the right cheek of her infant daughter, who bends her head back to receive her mother's affection.

As in her representations in the narrative scenes, St. Anne wears a blue tunic and over it a red mantle, which also covers her head. The mantle hangs down her back and around her shoulders and is draped between her arms in a curved fold beneath the child. Between her brow and headdress can be seen the edge of a light blue and white headcloth, which covers her hair. Owing to the fragmentary condition of the mosaic, the only parts of the tunic now visible are the tightly fitting blue cuff and a triangular area below the cuff, at the gathered waist.

Very little remains of the small figure of Mary; fortunately, however, most of her face is preserved. Otherwise, only her clenched left hand and a small area of her blue mantle, above the curving fold between her mother's hands, still exist. Her head was covered with a violet headdress, instead of the blue one found in the other representations of the infant Mary. In the absence of inscriptions, the identification of this panel as a representation of St. Anne and Mary rather than Mary and Christ rests on the colors of the garments, the fact that the child's head is covered, the absence of a cross in the nimbus of the child, and the context in which the panel appears, pendant to the figure of Joachim and adjacent to the representation of the Virgin and Christ.

The panel facing that of St. Anne and the Virgin contains a fragmentary figure [180] whose position, features, and colors identify him as St. Joachim. Sts. Joachim and Anne are often paired in a similar way among the saints that adorn a narthex. A comparison with other mosaic representations of Joachim in the cycle of the Life of the Virgin in the Kariye Djami, especially with his image in the scene of the priests blessing the Virgin ([89], PL. 110, 111), will show the same type of face and beard and garments of the same colors: a blue tunic and a violet himation.

Although the upper right side of his head is destroyed, the upper part of the figure of Joachim is otherwise still rather well preserved to a point somewhat above the knees. He stands in a frontal pose, his head turned slightly toward the left. He holds his right hand before him, palm outward, a little above waist-level, and his left hand clutches at a fold of his himation, which is wrapped around his waist so that his right sleeve and shoulder are exposed.

The panel of the Virgin and the Christ Child [181] is on the pilaster to the left of the door leading into the inner narthex. Although it was doubtless pendant to a figure of St. Joseph on the opposite pilaster, it is also to be regarded as pendant to the figure of St. John the Baptist, to the right of the door. These two panels, together with the great bust of Christ Pantocrator that is between them, above the door, thus comprised a kind of Deesis. The icon of the Mother and Child is a reversed variant of the templon mosaic of the Virgin, of the Hodegetria type, on the southeast pier of the nave ([187], PL. 329, 330). The Mother is designated by the inscription [Μήτηρ] Θ(εο)ῦ, and it is likely that the Child also was accompanied by his usual inscription. Mary is turned slightly toward the right (toward the axis of the Deesis group); her head is erect and her glance is directed straight at the beholder. She holds the Child in the crook of her left arm, her left hand grasping his thigh and her right hand pointing toward him. The Child sits upright, in three-quarters view, facing toward the left, and with his right hand he makes a gesture of blessing, directed not toward his mother but toward all who come before him; in his left hand he holds a scroll.

Mary, as usual, is clad entirely in blue. Her maphorion, which covers her head, falls at her sides and is draped across her arms in a curved fold beneath the Child; its edges are bordered with gold, and on the right shoulder and again where it covers the brow is a small golden star. Across the brow, beneath the edge of the maphorion, can be seen the light blue and white edge of the headcloth. The Child wears a golden tunic, decorated with two red clavi, and a golden outer garment.

The mosaic of St. John the Baptist [182], to the right of the door leading to the inner narthex, is preserved in a small fragment at the top of the panel. Despite the loss of the inscription (save for the rough breathing at the upper right) the figure can be identified, owing to the distinctive hair and garments which are accorded to John's portraits. The face and all but the tip of the beard are lost, but the disheveled hair at the top and right side of the head, the long locks at the shoulder, the fragment of camel's hair garment at the breast, and the brownish green color of the himation, preserved at the right shoulder, are all characteristic features of St. John when he is depicted as the Forerunner of Christ.

Of the mosaic of the military saint [183] on the western pilaster between the fourth and fifth bays, there now remains only a fragment of the torso. The inscription, the head, and most of the neck are destroyed, but it can be seen that the saint wore a cuirass, bound together above the waist by a metal girdle, and a green mantle, which seems to have been pinned at his right shoulder and is thrown back over his left to hang freely down his back. He also carried a shield, which hung at an angle at his left side; a segment of its rim, touching his shoulder, remains. These elements of his costume can be better understood if the mosaic is compared with the parecclesion frescoes of Sts. Demetrius, Mercurius, and Artemius or Nicetas ([253], [256], [264]), for the metal girdle; of St. Eustathius [261], for the manner in which the mantle is worn around the neck; and of Sts. George and Mercurius ([250], [256]), for the position of the shield.

The mosaic of St. Euthymius [184], on the southern pilaster between the sixth and seventh bays, can be seen only at an angle; a column now rises in front of it to support the masonry with which the transverse arch is reinforced. Although some areas of mosaic tesserae in the lower part of the figure and most of the gold-glass cubes of the background have been extracted by souvenir hunters, the figure still remains largely intact and is by far the most completely preserved mosaic in the series on the walls of the outer narthex.

St. Euthymius, one of the Palestinian Desert Fathers, is represented in the vestments of a monk. In accordance with his traditional type he is depicted as an old man, with bald head and an exceedingly long beard descending almost to his knees. He stands in nearly frontal pose, his head turned slightly to the left, holding a scroll before him in both hands. His attire consists of a long tunic and the scapular and mantle in which monks are usually represented. The apron of the scapular hangs down to his knees; a hood, which is attached to the neck opening of this garment and hangs down the back, is visible at his shoulders. The mantle is fastened below his chin, under the beard, and two cords, with which he could draw the lower parts of the mantle around him, are attached to its lining at the level of the knees.

The monk is identified by the fragmentary inscription to the right of his head; the first four letters of his name are preserved in mosaic and the remaining characters in the painted setting bed: ['Ο ἅγ(ιος)?] Εὐθύ[μιος].

Dimensions

[179]: area within frame, .675 m. x 1.725 m.; maximum height of mosaic fragment, .89 m. [180]: area within frame, .67 m. x 1.72 m.; maximum height of mosaic fragment, .885 m. [181]: area within frame, .70 m. x 1.76 m.; maximum height of mosaic fragment, 1.03 m. [182]: area within frame, .71 m. x 1.80 m.; maximum height of mosaic fragment, .58 m. [183]: area within frame, .645 m. x 1.725 m.; maximum height of mosaic fragment, .30 m. [184]: area within frame, .69 m. x 1.58 m.

Condition

The general view of the outer narthex in the Russian publication on the Kariye Djami (Shmit, *Kakhrie-*

dzhami, PL. LXXV) shows that in 1906 parts of the frames of seven of the original eight wall panels in Bays 1–5 were still attached to their pilasters (five now exist) but the mosaics were invisible beneath a covering of plaster. The same view shows the plaster rendering with which the walls had been covered after removal of the marble revetments. In 1929 workmen of the Evkaf of Istanbul (the authority in charge of the mosques of Istanbul) superficially uncovered the mosaics that still survived; [1] it was not until 1958 that thorough cleaning and repair were completed by the Byzantine Institute. In 1953 the Institute removed all modern plaster from the walls, and it subsequently repointed and repaired those areas of masonry that needed attention. At that time the original positions of the marbles that had framed the icons were discovered, and it became evident that the lower parts of all the panels except [184] had been destroyed and that the proportions had been altered (cf. Shmit, PL. LXXV). In conjunction with the restoration of the mosaics the existing marbles of the frames were reset by the Byzantine Institute and the original proportions of the inner frames were restored.

Colors and Materials

[179]: Panel bordered by a row of green glass within a row of red glass. *St. Anne:* tunic, blue; mantle and headdress, red; edge of headcloth, alternate stripes of blue glass and white stone. *Mary:* dress, blue; headdress, violet with narrow border of gold. [180]: hair and beard, dark violet, blue, and black glasses and gray stone; tunic, blue with dark blue clavus; himation, violet.

[181]: Panel bordered by two rows of dark red glass. *Mary:* garments, blue with gold borders and gold stars at shoulder and center of forehead; edge of headcloth, light blue; cuffs, gold and red. *Christ Child:* garments, gold glass with shadows of brown and greenish brown glass and clavi of red glass. [182]: Panel bordered by two rows of dark red glass. Hair, dark brown glasses and light brown stones; fur garment, blue glasses, bluish gray and white stones; himation, brown, dull greenish brown, and light yellow glasses.

[183]: cuirass, violet stone ground with ornaments of dark violet and white stones; collar, blue glass with ornaments of blue and gray stones; girdle, blue glass, gray and white stones; mantle, green glasses. [184]: Panel bordered by two rows of blue glass. Hair, gray and white stones and greenish brown glass; beard, yellow stones with shadows of brown stone and greenish brown glass and highlights of white stone; tunic, light blue; scapular and hood, dark blue; mantle, violet with highlights of yellowish brown stone.

1 See illustrations and comments by Jean Ebersolt, "Trois Nouveaux Fragments de mosaïques à Kahrié-Djami," *La Revue de l'art*, LVI (1929), 163–66.

THE MOSAICS IN THE NAVE

[185]

The Dormition of the Virgin

PL. 320–327

ʹΗ [Κοίμ]ησις τῆς Θ(εοτό)κου   *The dormition of the Theotokos*

ʹΙ(ησοῦ)ς Χ(ριστό)ς   *Jesus Christ*

By the end of the eleventh century the scene of The Dormition of the Virgin had begun to appear in representations of the cycle of the Great Feasts which decorated the walls and vaults in the naves of Byzantine churches. As in the Kariye Djami (PL. 5), it usually took its place on the west wall of the nave above the entrance door, and by the thirteenth century it was frequently spread out over the entire wall in a number of episodes that tended to become a cycle of their own. The remarkably well preserved and beautifully executed panel at the Kariye Djami, however, shows the restraint and much the same iconography found in the earlier examples, which were limited to one episode illustrating the moment of the Virgin's death.[1]

The Dormition at the Kariye Djami is the only scene left from the cycle of the Great Feasts that once adorned the tympana and the soffits of the arches in the nave. Its survival is attributable to the fact that it was set into the midst of the marble revetments, which have been preserved, and was covered with heavy coatings of plaster.

As in so much of Christian art, the iconography of the Dormition derives from literary sources. The most important one in the development of the Byzantine version is the Greek apocryphal text, of fourth- or fifth-century origin, entitled "The Discourse of St. John the Divine Concerning the *Koimesis* of the Holy Mother of God."[2] Briefly, the essential points in the narrative are these: Mary, who lived in Bethlehem with three other virgins after the ascension of Christ, prayed that she might depart to join her Son in heaven. On a Friday the Apostle John, in Ephesus, was caught up in a cloud and placed at Mary's bedside, where he and the three virgins worshiped her. On the same day the Holy Ghost commanded all the apostles, both living and dead, to "mount up upon clouds" and gather from the ends of the earth at Mary's house in Bethlehem. (According to the narrative of Joseph of Arimathaea, however, all but Thomas reached Bethlehem before her death, but Thomas, arriving later at the Mount of Olives, witnessed the Assumption of the Virgin, and she threw down her girdle to him.) When the apostles had assembled about the Virgin the Holy Ghost transferred them all on a cloud to the house of

---

1 On the development of the iconography of the Dormition, see L. Wratislaw-Mitrovic and N. Okunev, "La Dormition de la Sainte Vierge dans la peinture médievale orthodoxe," *Byzantinoslavica*, III (1931), 134 ff.

2 For the Greek text see Tischendorf, *Apocalypses Apocryphae* (Leipzig, 1866), pp. 95 ff.; for an English translation, see James, *The Apocryphal New Testament*, pp. 201 ff.

the Virgin in Jerusalem, where they might escape the plotting of the Jews. For five days the apostles sang praises without ceasing. On the Lord's day Christ appeared, sitting upon the throne of the cherubim and accompanied by a host of angels. The time having come for her death, "the Lord spread forth his unstained hands and received . . . [Mary's] holy and spotless soul;" according to some other Apocrypha Christ gave the soul to Michael, or to one of the angels, to be taken to heaven. There follows the account of the funeral procession to her tomb in Gethsemane; the incident of Jephonias the Jew, whose hands were cut off when he attempted to destroy the body of Mary; and, after three days, the translation of Mary to Paradise.

In the highly symmetrical composition of the mosaic a great inner triangle provides the framework for the arrangement of the figures. The horizontal mass of the bed with the figure of the Virgin recumbent upon it forms the base. From the figures of Peter and Paul, at the lower angles, the sides of the triangle move up through the figures stooping over the bed. The apex is formed by the double mandorla, with its outer zone of angels, and the seraph above. All other figures are fitted into the lesser triangles at the sides.

In the center foreground is the richly draped bed, with its curved head at the left; below it, on the floor, is a footstool. Mary, who is nimbed and clad in her usual blue garments, lies stretched out on the bed, her eyes closed and her hands folded at the waist. Behind the bed, at the center of the panel, stands Christ in a double mandorla; two angels, treated in grisaille, stand at each side within the outer aureole, and a six-winged seraph hovers above it. Dressed entirely in cloth of gold, his head surrounded by a golden cross-nimbus, Christ turns slightly toward the right, but his face is turned in the other direction, toward that of his mother. He holds out his hands, covered by the folds of his himation, to the right; in them, marked by a small golden nimbus, sits the figure of the soul of Mary, represented as a new-born infant wrapped in swaddling cloths.

Grouped at the sides are the apostles, bishops, and several women. In the group at the left, behind the head of the Virgin, are six apostles and two bishops, and in the background is a curiously shaped structure resembling an exedra, surmounted at the center by a turret and pierced by two openings which are separated by a column. At the right are five apostles, one bishop, two women behind the apostles at the far right, and another group of women in the door of a house in the right background. Two flying angels approach from the upper right, perhaps to take the soul of Mary from Christ and transport it to heaven.

Most, if not all, of the individual apostles can be identified. As usual, Peter and Paul are placed most prominently in the foreground, Peter at the left and Paul at the right. Peter bends slightly forward, swinging a censer; Paul, at the foot of the bed, also bends forward, his right hand at his breast and his left extended. Again according to iconographic tradition, John the Evangelist, who was charged by Christ with the care of Mary, is placed closest to her head; he stands directly behind the head of the bed, both hands resting on its edge, and bends forward with gaze fixed upon her face. These three apostles are easily identified both because of their traditional positions in the scene and because of their distinctive types: Peter has the usual short, curly beard, banged hair across a low brow, and pugnacious jaw; Paul, the short, dark hair, domed brow, and black, pointed beard; and John (as he has when represented as Apostle-Evangelist), the nearly bald and rather massive head, lofty brow, and long, curly gray beard.

Also identifiable by his type is the Evangelist Matthew, who stands erect at the left edge of the panel looking upward, his hand raised toward his face; he has gray hair arranged in wavy locks and a beard, partly destroyed, of moderate length. To the right of Matthew another apostle, probably Simon Zelotes, turns his head downward and to the left; he wears a beard similar to Peter's but a little longer. The two apostles above Matthew and Simon are hardly distinguishable from one another. The one at the far left, who turns his head to look away from the scene, is probably Bartholomew, and the one in front of him with a dark clavus on the shoulder of his tunic is probably James Alphaeus.

The apostles at the right side, gathered at the foot of the bed, are quite easily distinguished from one another. The apostle behind the foot of the bed, to the left of Paul, is the Evangelist Luke; he is characterized by the double fringe of hair that surrounds the tonsure on the top of his head. He bends very low and holds his right hand to his chin while touching the edge of the bed with his left. Immediately above him is the Apostle Andrew, who stoops forward to gaze directly at the face of the Virgin. He is distinguished by his unruly locks of gray hair and his rather long, pointed beard. At the right edge of the panel stands the Evangelist Mark, nearly erect, his head slightly bowed and his left hand extended toward the Virgin; his black hair is more abundant, and his brow is less lofty, than those of Paul, whom he somewhat resembles.

To the left of Mark is the eleventh and final apostle to be represented in this version of the Dormition. He raises his right hand, palm upward, to his beardless face. Only two apostles, Philip and Thomas, are ever represented without beards; and in view of the fact that only eleven apostles, but one of whom is beardless, are present, it must be assumed that the mosaicist included Philip but not Thomas, taking account of the tradition that Thomas was absent when the Virgin died, despite the fact that the narrative of the Pseudo-John and others name Thomas as being among the apostles who were present.

In the upper tier of figures, close to the left and right sides of the mandorla, are three bishops. Each is marked by a halo and wears around his shoulders the omophorion, a scarf adorned with large crosses. The one farthest to the left, holding in his covered hands a closed book, seems to be glancing toward Christ and the soul of Mary. The second supports an open book on his extended left arm and directs his glance at the imitation writing on the pages as though officiating at a divine liturgy. The draped arm and the book encroach into the area of the mandorla, and like the angels they are rendered in grisaille. The third bishop, on the opposite side of the mandorla, immediately in front of the women in the door of the house, seems younger than the others; he wears a short beard.

The principal authority for the inclusion of bishops in scenes of the Dormition is a passage in "De Divinis Nominibus" of Dionysius, Pseudo-Areopagite,[3] which was interpreted by John of Damascus to mean that the four bishops there named were in attendance at the death of the Virgin. Three of the four were converts or disciples of Paul: Dionysius himself, who was thought to be an early bishop of Athens; Timothy, Paul's most faithful disciple and first bishop of Ephesus; and Hierotheus, also a bishop of Athens. The text also states that James, the Brother of Our Lord, first bishop of Jerusalem, was present. The identification of each bishop in the mosaic cannot be firmly established, since the features of the four bishops in question vary considerably from one monument to the next. However, a comparison of the bishop who reads from an open book with certain representations of John, the Brother of the Lord (in the minia-

---

3 In Migne, *Pat. Gr.*, 3 (Paris, 1889), col. 681. See also John of Damascus, "Homilia II in dormitionem B. V. Mariae" (Migne, 96 [Paris, 1891], col. 749), and the translation into French of Pierre Voulet, S.J., in *S. Jean Damascène: Homélies sur la nativité et la dormition* (Paris, 1961), p. 173.

ture on folio 131 of the Menologion of Basil II,[4] in the mosaics of the monastic church of Hosios Loukas and the Cappella Palatina at Palermo, and in the fresco in the apse at Nereditsa), shows a similarity of characteristics — gray hair that covers the top of the head and a rather long beard with two points — which strongly suggests that the bishop is James, one of Christ's brethren and founder of the See of Jerusalem. It is most probable that one of the two remaining bishops is meant to be Dionysius.

The women in the doorway of the house in the upper right are probably the virgins referred to in the texts. There are two other women, however, who stand with the group of apostles at the right. The one nearest the Virgin is represented in the same manner and colors as St. Anne is throughout the mosaics. The text of Pseudo-John, in describing events after the burial of Mary's body in the tomb at Gethsemane, says that Anne, the mother of Mary, and Elizabeth, the mother of John the Baptist, appeared with Abraham, Isaac, Jacob, and David and all the choirs of saints, singing praises and worshiping the body of the Mother of the Lord. It is possible that the two women in the mosaic derive from this textual source.

Dimensions

Width within marble frame, 1.91 m.; height within frame, 2.02 m.; distance from floor to bottom of mosaic, 3.37 m.

Condition

A continuous crack rises in an arc from the level of the shoulders of the lowest apostles, at the two edges, and passes through the top of the inner aureole of the mandorla; it has been carefully filled with new plaster and rendered as unobtrusive as possible by tones of gray. The crack corresponds to the curve of a concealed masonry relieving arch, behind the mosaic, which was filled with horizontal courses of brick resting on wooden beams above the marble lintel of the door. When the beams rotted the masonry fill of the concealed arch slipped downward a few centimeters and the break in the mosaic was produced. The only other areas of lost mosaic occur at the upper left, where part of the inscription was destroyed; at the lower right, in the lower parts of the figures of Paul and Mark; and along the lower edge, above the top of the carved lintel. In 1929 the mosaic, which had been concealed from view by heavy coatings of plaster, was uncovered by the Evkaf of Istanbul.[5] However, the Byzantine Institute found it in need of repairs and further cleaning, for plaster and yellow daub still adhered here and there to the surface.

Colors and Materials

MARY *Garments:* entirely of blue with gold edges and cuffs; edge of kerchief over hair, light blue and white; shoes, red. *Halo:* gold with no border. *Bed:* top cover, red; square cushion behind halo, green glass, corners ornamented with gold glass and brown stone; side drapes, violet glasses, ornamented at top and bottom with wide gold borders and on front side with roundels and lozenge of gold and red; feet of bed, gold glass, yellowish brown and brown stones. *Footstool:* top and front, gold, outlined in yellowish brown stone; receding face, yellowish brown stone, outlined in violet glass. CHRIST garments, gold, with shadows and drawing in transparent glasses of violet, amber, and green; halo, gold, with red outlines. SOUL OF MARY swaddling cloths, blue glass, bluish gray stone, and white stone; halo, gold outlined in red.

MANDORLA inner aureole, bluish gray stone, bordered at left by narrow zone of light bluish gray stone and single row of white stone, and at right by three rows of light blue glass and one row of darker blue glass; outer aureole, bluish gray stone bordered at left by row of white stone and at right by row of light blue glass. ANGELS IN GRISAILLE (in outer aureole) bluish gray stone with highlights of white stone and drawing in light blue glass. SERAPH *Parts outside mandorla:* brown stone with highlights of gold and outlines in dark violet glass; feathers along lower edges of outspread wings, blue glasses. *Parts within mandorla:* treated like angels within mandorla.

FIGURES AT LEFT *Peter:* tunic, blue with dark blue clavus; himation, yellow; censer, golden bowl outlined with transparent dark violet glass, and chains of white stone. *John:* tunic, blue; himation, violet. *Matthew:* tunic, blue; himation, green. *Apostle above Peter (Simon?):* tunic, blue; himation, brown with bluish gray and white highlights. *Apostle at far left,* above Matthew (Bartholomew?): himation, brownish green.

4 Codex Vaticanus, MS. graec. 1613; published in facsimile in *Il Menologio di Basilio II* (Codices e Vaticanis Selecti, VIII, Turin, 1907), Vol. II.

5 Ebersolt, "Une Nouvelle Mosaïque de Kahrié-Djami," *La Revue de l'art,* LV (1929), 83–86, and "Trois Nouveaux Fragments . . . ," LVI (1929), 163–66; and H. E. Del Medico, "La Mosaïque de la Κοίμησις à Kahrie Djami," *Byzantion* VII (1932), 123–41, with illustrations.

James: tunic, blue with dark blue clavus; himation, violet. *First bishop, at left:* chasuble, yellow; omophorion, gray ornamented with black crosses; book cover, gold and red; halo, gold bordered with red. *Second bishop* (James, the Brother of the Lord?): chasuble (visible at neck), greenish blue; omophorion, yellow with black crosses; book, grisaille (bluish gray with white highlights and imitation writing in black); halo, gold bordered with red except in mandorla, where it is grisaille.

FIGURES AT RIGHT   *Paul:* tunic (visible below chin and in a fragment above his right foot), blue; himation, violet. *Luke:* tunic, blue with dark blue clavus; himation, red. *Andrew:* tunic (visible below chin), blue; himation, green. *Philip:* tunic, blue; himation, yellow. *Mark:* tunic, blue; himation, green. *Bishop:* chasuble, pink; omophorion, white and gray with blue outlining and black crosses; halo, gold bordered with red except in mandorla, where it is grisaille. *Woman between Philip and Mark* (Anne?): outer garment and headdress, red; edge of kerchief covering hair, blue and white. *Woman at far right* (Elizabeth?): garments entirely of blue glass. *Women in doorway* of house at upper right: first woman, dressed entirely in green; second woman, dressed entirely in blue; headdress of a woman to left of second, yellow; headdress of a woman to right of second, red.

TWO ANGELS AT UPPER RIGHT   *Angel at right:* garments, green; hair, brown glasses with yellow stone highlights; wings, violet glasses with gold highlights; halo, gold bordered with red. *Angel at left:* garments, violet; hair and halo, like those of angel at right; wing at left, brown stone with gold highlights.

BACKGROUND   *Sky:* gold. *Curved building at left:* inner face of walls, green glasses with bluish gray stone highlights; upper faces, bluish gray stones with white highlights; capital, blue, gray, and white; openings, black. *House at right:* lighted front face, grayish yellow stone with drawing and outlining in light grayish yellow and brown stones; shaded receding faces, light brown stone with outlining in transparent glasses of amber and green; door openings, black; roof tiles, blue. THREE ZONES OF FOREGROUND   three shades of green, the darkest zone, very narrow and mostly lost, being at the bottom.

THE HEADS are, on the whole, more colorful than most others on this small a scale in the mosaics of the Kariye Djami. The flesh tones range from light to dark pink with touches of light blue in the shading as well as the usual yellows, greens, and browns.

[186], [187]

The Templon Mosaics: Christ; the Virgin Hodegetria   PL. 328–330

['Ιησοῦς Χριστὸς ἡ χώρα τῶν] ζών|των
Jesus Christ, the dwelling-place of the living

Δεῦτε | πρός με | πάντες | οἱ κοπι|ῶντ(ε)ς κ(αὶ) | πεφορ|τισμένοι | κἀγὼ ἀ⟨ναπαύσω ὑμᾶς⟩
Come unto me, all ye that labour and are heavy laden, and I will give you rest.

(*Matt. 11:28*)

Μ(ήτ)ηρ Θ(εο)ῦ | ἡ χώρα τοῦ ἀχω|ρήτου
The Mother of God, the dwelling-place of the uncontainable

'Ι(ησοῦ)ς Χ(ριστό)ς   *Jesus Christ*

Set into the marble revetments on the western faces of the northeastern and southeastern corner piers of the nave, at a height of about 1.75 meters from the floor, are the two mosaic panels of Christ and the Virgin Hodegetria (PL. 4). In this position they served as monumental "icons" flanking the structure of the templon that once rested on the step of the bema, somewhat more than a meter and a half to the east, where there were undoubtedly other, portable icons, attached to the iconostasis that screened the sanctuary from the main body of the nave. Such monumental representations of Christ and the Virgin, in a comparable relation to the templon, were a common feature of Byzantine churches of the Comnenian and Palaeologan periods.

Each of the mosaics was originally surrounded by sculptural and architectural elements that contributed to its prominence and to its compositional relationship with the now missing templon. The mosaic area itself is bordered by a narrow marble frame similar to those that surround all the other mosaics set into the revetments of the walls. Carved corbels at the lower corners, now mutilated, once supported coupled, knotted colonnettes, which framed the sides of the panels; fragments of these were found in the excavations of the apse. The knotted columns supported richly carved and painted slabs, which formed the upper elements of the frames, but only that above the mosaic of the Virgin [187] still remains *in situ*, the corresponding slab above the figure of Christ [186] having been destroyed (see PL. 4).

In the great majority of churches where such templon images still exist, the figure of the Virgin is at the left of the bema, from the point of view of the beholder, and Christ at the right. In the Kariye Djami, as in a few other monuments, this arrangement is reversed and Christ takes his place at the left, a position that in the normal "protocol" of an iconographic program takes precedence over the right. Although most of Christ's inscription is lost, enough remains in the painted setting bed to show that he bore the epithet *chora ton zonton* (the dwelling-place of the living); the Virgin's inscription, which is completely legible, reads *chora tou achoretou* (the dwelling-place of the uncontainable). These are the same epithets inscribed on their images in opposing lunettes of the entrance bay of the outer narthex ([1] and [2]), which are to be regarded as dedicatory panels both because of their position and because their inscriptions, as here, employ the name of the monastery (Chora) in a mystical sense that is relevant to both personages. It is possible that the two panels in the nave, besides being the traditional figures to flank the templon, may again reflect a dual dedication of the church; their reversed positions could be accounted for by the precedence which the dedication gave to Christ.

Although the mosaic of Christ [186] has suffered severe damage, it still gives an accurate impression of the qualities which made it the finest of all existing representations of Christ among the mosaics of the Kariye Djami. A beautifully proportioned figure, Christ stands in frontal pose on what was once a jeweled footstool; his head is turned slightly to the right. He holds up an open book, at hip level, in his left hand; its pages are inscribed with the verse, "Come unto me, all ye that labour and are heavy laden, and I will give you rest" (Matt. 11:28). It is this verse that motivates the gesture of his right hand toward himself. The hand emerges from a sling-like fold of his blue himation, which supports his right elbow and forearm. The arrangement of the drapery draws the himation away from his right shoulder and breast to expose a dark violet tunic adorned with a golden clavus.

Like its companion, the panel of the Virgin [187] is severely damaged, but the figures of the Mother and the Child are nearly intact. The image is of the type known as the Hodegetria, which derived from the celebrated portable icon of that name that at times played such an important role as the palladium of Constantinople and its empire. According to tradition the original was painted from life by the Evangelist Luke; obtained in the fifth century by the Empress Eudocia, it was placed in the Constantinopolitan church of the Theotokos Hodegetria by the Empress Pulcheria. It is of interest to note that at the final attack on the city in 1453 the icon was brought to the Chora, where prayers were offered before it in the vain hope of saving the city. In the original icon, it is believed, the Mother supported the Child on her left arm so that he was at the right from the point of view of the beholder. The mosaic at the Kariye Djami, like some others of the type, would thus represent a reversal of the original composition. The Mother, standing on a jeweled footstool, is turned slightly toward the left, her head inclined in the same direction so that she can contemplate her Son. The latter, seated in three-quarters pose on his Mother's right forearm, looks up to return her glance; his right arm is extended in a gesture of blessing, and in his left hand he holds a scroll. His left leg is bent to pass under his right, so that the sole of his bare left foot is exposed; the Mother holds his right ankle lightly in her left hand.

The Virgin is clad in blue garments. Her mantle is so arranged that it hangs at her sides, exposing her tunic in its entire width up to the fold of the mantle, near the waist, that passes from arm to arm beneath the Child. Over her head and shoulders is the maphorion, bordered in gold around the face and decorated with a golden fringe, which shows below her left shoulder. Golden stars appear at her shoulders and above her forehead. The Child is dressed in garments of gold with highlights of silver; two rows of red mark the clavus at the shoulder.

Dimensions

CHRIST [186] height of mosaic panel within frame, 2.52 m.; width within frame, 1.01 m.; height from floor to bottom of frame, 1.77 m.; height of figure from top of head to level of right toes, 2.15 m. VIRGIN [187] height of mosaic panel within frame, 2.53 m.; width within frame, 1.05 m.; height from floor to bottom of frame, 1.72 m.; height of figure from top of head to toes, 2.20 m.

Condition

The condition of the two mosaic panels prior to the cleaning and repairs executed by the Byzantine Institute in 1956 (the Virgin) and 1957 (Christ) is illustrated in Shmit, *Kakhrie-dzhami*, PL. LXVIII. (See also Paul A. Underwood, "Notes on the Work of the Byzantine Institute in Istanbul: 1955–1956," *D. O. Papers*, 12, p. 283 and Fig. 16, for a description and illustration of the panel of the Virgin prior to its restoration.) In general, all areas where mosaic surface or plaster support had been lost were covered with lime plaster, painted a dark blue, which to a considerable extent encroached upon the still existing areas of mosaic surface. The mosaics themselves were obscured by lime washes and an accumulation of grime. The original plaster support for the mosaic above the head and shoulders of Christ had been destroyed; here new plaster was applied to the masonry by the Byzantine Institute and given a suitable surface texture and a neutral color tone. Most of the Virgin's figure was dimly visible, but only the hands and legs of the Child could be discerned, even on close examination. His head and shoulders were found to have been covered by a thin coating of concrete made of fine sand and Portland cement, which presented great difficulty in cleaning; the remaining parts of his image were covered with lime plaster. While the building was still in use as a mosque these two panels were covered with wooden shutters.

Colors and Materials

Christ [186]

GARMENTS tunic, four values of violet glass with clavus of gold (only yellow paint on setting bed exists) bordered by red; himation, five values of blue glass with black glass for drawing of principal folds; thongs of sandals, very dark brown glass and an occasional black glass tessera, highlighted with a row of small gold glass tesserae. FACE pink and white marble for flesh tones; shading in checkered technique, pinks alternating with yellow and green glasses, shading into brown at the edges of the face. HAIR rows of small brown glasses alternating, near face and in wavy lock at left, with rows of yellow glass.
BOOK cover, red (visible only in outlines at sides and bottom); pages, light gray stone with letters of black glass, each line of lettering bordered at top and bottom by single row of bluish gray glass; edges of book, alternate rows of bluish gray and silver; two clasps at left and one at bottom, gold. FOOTSTOOL no tesserae exist, but evidence of footstool of Virgin and some traces of paint on setting bed indicate a gold upper surface and gems, probably blue and red, on sides.

Virgin [187]

GARMENTS five values of blue glass with black glass for drawing of principal folds; mantle, edged by single row of gold and also bordered at bottom of folds hanging at left by two rows of gold between single rows of red glass; maphorion, ornamented below left shoulder with golden fringe edged above with one row of red glass, and bordered around face by two rows of gold between single rows of transparent amber and violet glasses; at each shoulder is a golden star composed of seven pointed rays radiating from a single round glass; above forehead is a golden star with eight angular rays that form a square; kerchief covering hair, blue glass, bluish gray and white stones; shoes, red glass.   FACE flesh tones, pink and white marbles; shading at right side, checkered technique, with inner zone of alternating pink marble and bluish gray glass followed by zone of alternating bluish gray and yellowish green glasses and zone at edge of greenish brown glass; shading on neck below chin, alternating dark pink marble and yellowish green glass in checkered technique.

CHRIST CHILD *Garments:* gold with highlights of silver and shadows of brown and brownish green glass; cla-

vus, represented by two rows of red glass. *Face:* very small tesserae of pink and white marble in flesh tones. *Hair:* tight curls of brown glasses and a few short strokes of black with highlights of greenish yellow.

FOOTSTOOL upper surface, gold (as indicated by one tessera and yellow paint of setting bed); front edge, gold with tall rectangular gems of blue and green alternating with pearls; receding edge at right, background of transparent green and violet glasses with pearls and green and blue gems.

The Technique of the Mosaics

A description of the technique that was used in creating the mosaics of the Kariye Djami, or any other medieval mosaics, must inevitably be somewhat speculative on many points concerning the procedures of the mosaicist, for on this subject no medieval treatises exist that are at all comparable to the various manuals of instruction in the art of fresco painting. We must therefore depend, on the one hand, upon observations made in the course of the Byzantine Institute's work on the mosaics of the Kariye Djami and other monuments in Constantinople and, on the other hand, upon the few reliable reports of others who have had similar opportunities to observe the construction of mosaics elsewhere.[1] Some of the problems that are inherent in the creation of a mosaic, however, are also present in the creation of a fresco, and a number of the procedures are similar in the two media. The reader would do well, therefore, to consult the chapter on the technique of the mural paintings,[2] where we are on surer ground, before proceeding with the following comments on the technique of the mosaics. In many respects the two arts are related, and it is probable that the real masters of mural decoration in the Middle Ages were equally proficient in both media. It is my conviction that the artisans who produced the mosaics at the Kariye Djami were also responsible for its fresco paintings.

As a broad generalization it may be said that up to its final stage a wall mosaic is essentially a type of true fresco, painted *in situ* on freshly laid plaster, into which small colored tesserae of various durable materials, such as glasses and stones, are inserted while the painted plaster is still soft. The painted surface is thus covered and largely obscured by a new surface, quite different in character, which reproduces the design and to some extent the colors of the painting beneath. With this generalization in mind, we can see that with only limited modifications the early stages of the creation of a fresco could be adapted to those of the creation of a mosaic. It is also important to realize that all procedures in the making of a mosaic, including the setting of the tesserae in all parts of the composition, were performed *in situ* and not in a studio. All evidence indicates that techniques such as *mosaico al rovescio* (or *a rivoltatura*), a process in which the tesserae are first attached to reversed, full-size cartoons laid out on a horizontal surface in a

1 For recent discussions on the techniques of Byzantine mosaics, see E. Kitzinger in *Enciclopedia Universale dell' Arte*, Vol. IX (Venice and Rome, 1963), "Tecnica del mosaico," cols. 673–75, and for a brief bibliography see col. 702, "Tecnica;" idem, *The Mosaics of Monreale* (Palermo, 1960), pp. 64–68 (in the Italian edition, *I Mosaici di Monreale*, see pp. 66–69). See also A. V. Vinner, *Materialy i Tekhnika Mosaichnoi Zhivopisi* (Moscow, 1953), reviewed by B. Rubin in *Byzantinische Zeitschrift*, 47 (1954), 439 ff.; V. N.

Lazareff, *Nouvelles Découvertes à la cathédrale Sainte-Sophie de Kiev* (Moscow, 1955); G. Bovini, "Notes techniques sur la préparation des mosaïques anciennes de Ravenne," *Les Cahiers techniques de l'art* (1955), pp. 51–54; G. Tschubin-aschwili, *Georgische Baukunst*, II (Tiflis, 1934), 94–112 (on the mosaics at Tsromi) and especially n. 2, pp. 109 and 110, Fig. 46, and PL. 42, 43. References to reports on some other mosaics will be given below.

2 Pp. 300–309.

studio, and then set into position on the freshly plastered wall, were not practiced by the Byzantine mosaicists. We possess evidence, also, that the heads, hands, and feet of figures were executed *in situ* and not prepared elsewhere, as has sometimes been suggested.

Unlike the frescoes, where two layers of plaster with a combined thickness of about 3 cm. underlie the painting, the mosaics of the Kariye Djami, and all others that are extant in Constantinople, are composed of three layers, the mosaic tesserae being inserted into the surface of the third. The combined thickness of the three layers measures from 4 to 5 cm. The plaster in the first two, as in the two layers that support the frescoes, is a simple mixture of lime and chopped straw; the first coat is about 1.75 cm. thick, and the second about 1.5 cm. The mixture for the final layer (called the setting bed), which is about 1.25 cm. thick, consists of lime and marble dust; the straw is omitted.

In part, at least, the greater number and thickness of the plaster renderings in the mosaics is attributable to the fact that all angles formed by the masonry structure, whether salient right angles (e.g., along the edges of arches) or re-entrant angles (such as occur along the junctures of intersecting masonry surfaces), had to be rounded to convex or concave forms so that the mosaicist could construct the ornamental borders (which are usually about 15 cm. wide) with which he framed all the structural units, such as the arches or lunettes. To provide for the softly rounded bull's nose borders at the edges of the arches, or the concave borders at re-entrant angles, it was necessary to build up the plaster beds to a considerable thickness, and this was in good part achieved with the first of the three layers. Whereas it is entirely feasible, and normal, in fresco to paint flat borders along sharp corners, mosaic tesserae cannot be set where sharp angles occur; this is especially the case at salient right angles along the edges of the arches.

Although the first two renderings of plaster were alike in composition, each of the two received a distinctive surface treatment. While the plaster of the first coat was soft its surface was keyed to receive the second layer by being impressed with an allover pattern of rather deep gouges, or indentations, which are roughly oblong in shape and measure some 6 cm. in height by 8 to 10 cm. in length. These indentations were pressed into the plaster quite close to one another in rather irregular, but generally horizontal, rows. Although one cannot be certain, this first coat may at times have been applied in one operation over a much larger area than the coats which were to be laid over it would be, possibly over an entire vault or bay if it was accessible from a scaffolding set up as an individual work area. If this was the case, the first coat would surely have solidified before being covered by the two subsequent coats, which were to be laid upon it in smaller areas, one after the other, as each area in turn was brought to completion.

The surface of the second coat in the mosaics was treated like that of the first coat in the frescoes. That is, while it was soft the plaster was keyed to receive the setting bed by means of a series of rather narrow indentations from 8 to 10 cm. long and less deep than those of the first. They tend to be arranged parallel to one another and in rows of opposing directions, as in a herring-bone pattern. They appear to have been made with the slightly curved edge of a trowel impressed at an angle, so that they are v-shaped in cross-section. The second coat was applied over an area which the mosaicist thought he could complete before the plaster of this coat, as well as the setting bed, which was to be quickly laid over it, should begin to solidify. It corresponded, therefore, to the first rendering coat in a fresco in that one of its functions was to provide a reserve of moisture to retard the drying of the setting bed, which was to be painted and set with its tesserae while it remained pliant.

In addition to keying the surfaces of the undercoatings of plaster to assure adhesion between the coats, the mosaicist took special precautions in the vulnerable, nearly horizontal surfaces at the tops of the vaults and arches to secure the adherence of the mosaics to the masonry itself. In most of these areas it was found that iron nails with large flat heads measuring up to about 4 cm. in diameter had been driven into the masonry before the plastering began. The nails were placed at random distances from one another but seldom less than 30 to 40 cm. apart. The heads projected some 3 to 3.5 cm. from the surface of the masonry so that the first coat and most of the second could be squeezed in beneath them and yet they would be covered over by the setting bed and its tesserae. Thus, the nail heads acted as concealed cramps to support the heavy weight of the plaster and its mosaic surfacing should any cleavage occur between the masonry and the first rendering of plaster. While they may have been effective in this regard for a period of time, the nails eventually caused considerable damage to the mosaics, for the iron heads rusted and gradually expanded as the amount of corrosion increased; in many places their expansion caused the plaster around them to shatter and consequently to disrupt the mosaic surface itself.

In a number of the mosaics of Constantinople extensive areas of mosaic tesserae have been pried loose from their setting with the result that the painted surfaces of the setting beds were exposed to view. A few examples in the Kariye Djami are the panels of Sts. Peter and Paul (PL. 30, 31), the Deesis (PL. 36–41), and the templon mosaics (PL. 328–330). In Hagia Sophia, there is exposed setting bed in the lower parts of the Zoe panel[3] and particularly extensive areas in the vault mosaics of the room at the southern end of the west gallery.[4] Additional examples are to be found in Fethiye, Kilisse, and Fenari Isa Djamis.[5] An examination of all such areas leads to the conclusion that prior to the insertion of the tesserae the setting bed had been covered by a rather fully developed painting, not a mere sketch—albeit a painting of a special kind. It was executed in considerable detail, in various colors, and with some degree of shading; in it no areas of the plaster were left unpainted. All the colors have the transparency that is characteristic of paints the pigments of which have been mixed exclusively in water; nowhere do they present the opaque qualities of colors that are mixed with lime, as would the painting of the later stages of a fresco that was to be left exposed. The painting beneath a mosaic figure also possesses a pronounced linear quality, for its purpose was to serve as an accurate guide to the mosaicist in the delineation of his forms, drapery folds, and contours, as well as to indicate the colors of the tesserae to be inserted in given areas and to some extent even the values of those colors. There was at least one convention in the use of color. The areas of the background that were to be set with gold tesserae were painted an earth red, although in a few of the mosaics of Hagia Sophia yellow ochre was used instead.

The painting of the setting bed served still another function. Obviously, the painting of the background, which was to be covered rather mechanically with gold tesserae, was not done

3 Thomas Whittemore, *The Mosaics of Haghia Sophia at Istanbul: Third Preliminary Report, The Imperial Portraits of the South Gallery* (Oxford, 1942), PL. 3, 13, 16, 17.

4 Underwood, "A Preliminary Report on Some Unpublished Mosaics in Hagia Sophia," *American Journal of Archaeology*, 55 (1951), pp. 367–70 and drawing, PL. 17. Fuller publication of these mosaics is planned for the future.

5 For the Kilisse Djami, see Aziz Ogan, "Bizans mimari tarihinde Istanbul kiliseleri ve mozaikler," in *Güzel Sanatlar*, 5 (Istanbul, 1944), figs. on pp. 12 and 13. The few remnants of painted setting bed in the south church of the monastery of Constantine Lips (Fenari Isa Djami) are discussed and illustrated by Feridun Dirimtekin, "Remains of Mosaics in the Church of the Monastery of Lips," in *Ayasofya Müzesi Yılliği* (Annual of Ayasofya Museum), 2 (1960), pp. 44–46 and Figs. 17 and 18; concerning the same fragments of setting bed see also Cyril Mango and E. J. W. Hawkins, "The Monastery of Lips, Additional Notes," *D. O. Papers*, 18 (Washington, 1964), Mango-Hawkins Figs. 2 and 3. The specimens of painted setting bed at Fethiye Djami (Pammakaristos) are as yet unpublished but will be described below.

for the guidance of the mosaicist in the insertion of the gold tesserae, for here he could easily have dispensed with painting of any kind. However, since the tesserae in a mosaic are seldom, one might say never, in full contact with one another, interstices of various widths always exist between them, through which the color of the painting is often visible. To have left the white plaster untoned would therefore have had a most adverse effect on the general tonality of a given area of mosaic.

One of the more troublesome problems in attempting to reconstruct the techniques of mosaic is to ascertain whether preliminary sketches exist on one or another of the undersurfaces beneath the setting bed, and in those instances where sketches have been observed to determine what their purpose may have been and what their relation was to the painting on the setting bed and hence to the finished, tesselated product. With only one exception, which will be discussed below, no sketches have been found at the Kariye Djami on any of the undersurfaces, masonry or plaster renderings, beneath the setting bed, nor have any drawings, other than unintentional or casual markings, been found on such surfaces in any of the mosaics of Constantinople despite the fact that we have seen many exposed areas of all undersurfaces. However, it has often been assumed, with little or no evidence, that the sketch of an entire composition was always drawn on an undersurface and that the undersurface was then covered by a succession of small areas of setting bed, each of which was then immediately painted and set with its mosaic tesserae before the next small area was applied. In this way, it has been assumed, the mosaic fairly accurately reproduced the preliminary sketch. Such a technique would resemble that of *buon fresco*: the coat of plaster beneath the setting bed would correspond to the *arriccio* on which the *sinopia*, or fully sketched composition, was drawn when the plaster was dry, and the setting bed would correspond to the *intonaco*, laid on in a succession of small areas (the *giornate*) which were individually painted and, in the case of a mosaic, set with tesserae. In at least one mosaic, far removed in time and distance from the mosaics of Constantinople, a technique very similar to this does seem to have been used, as will be pointed out below, but it represents the exception rather than the rule.

Some of the difficulty concerning the use of preliminary sketches lies in the fact that there seems to have been more than one method of constructing a mosaic. Distinctions should be made, for example, between mosaics that were constructed with only two layers of plaster, that is, a thin first rendering and a painted setting bed, and mosaics, such as those of Constantinople and others elsewhere, which consist of three layers. Distinctions should also be made between casual, isolated markings that may appear on one of the undersurfaces; a rough sketch made as a compositional tryout but not necessarily to be reproduced on the setting bed; and a true sketch, which was intended for the guidance of the painter of the setting bed.

There are at least two authentic instances in which sketches appeared on the masonry surface beneath mosaics. At the summit of the rotunda of St. George at Salonika a very rough sketch of a medallion with figures was found on the brickwork,[6] but it bore no real relation to the fifth-century mosaic that was laid over it, and the sketch should be regarded as a compositional study, perhaps as a tryout to establish the proper scale for the mosaics, and not as a guide to the mosaicist. Another example was found beneath the seventh-century mosaics at Tsromi, in Georgia.[7] An entire composition was sketched in the conch of the apse, in part on the surface

---

6 This sketch still remains unpublished.   7 G. Tschubinaschwili, loc. cit.

of the cut stone masonry and in part on the very thin applications of plaster that occur here and there to correct slight irregularities in the masonry surface. The setting bed, laid over this, appears to have been fully painted and closely reproduced the preliminary sketch; it was applied in relatively small pieces ranging up to 50 x 50 cm. The technique at Tsromi thus seems to bear a relation to that of *buon fresco*. It may be that this technique was found to be feasible in structures built of cut stone because such masonry was less absorbent of moisture than brickwork, as the *Hermeneia* of Mount Athos implies.[8] It is possible that such a technique may have been used also in the sixth-century mosaics of the church of St. Catherine on Mt. Sinai, where the masonry is of carefully dressed blocks of granite and the total thickness of plaster and tesselated surface is hardly more than 2 to 3 cm.[9] However, the extant mosaics of Constantinople, which are later in date and are constructed with three layers of plaster applied to brick masonry, have little in common with the Tsromi mosaics in matters of technique.

It is said of certain mosaics—such as those of San Marco, Venice; Hosios Lucas, in Phocis; Cefalù and other places in Sicily—that they were constructed with two renderings of plaster: a rough coat, and the painted setting bed.[10] It may be that some observers had no opportunity to distinguish between the first and second coats beneath the setting bed; at any rate, at San Marco there is at least one mosaic that was definitely constructed with two layers.[11] The first was applied directly to the brick masonry, and its surface was keyed in a herring-bone pattern similar to that of the second rendering in the Constantinopolitan mosaics. It received a sketch that does not correspond closely to the painting on the setting bed and the design of the finished mosaic. It is not known, however, whether this was normal practice throughout the mosaics of San Marco.

Mosaics constructed with three coats of plaster are far more numerous than those with only two. For this major category there are only a few reports that definitely establish the presence of preliminary sketches on one of the undercoatings. One mosaic so handled is in the tomb of Demetrius at the Kariye Djami (PL. 550–553) where the sketches in the soffit of the arch seem not to have been made for the guidance of the painter of the setting bed, as part of the normal procedure in mosaic work, but rather as a study, *in situ*, to help the painter or his client decide at an early stage what should be repersented in that place. They are rather crude linear brush drawings of the contours of saints painted in rather faint black lines on the very thin first rendering. It is evident that the decision was made not to represent those figures but to decorate the soffit with the purely ornamental designs that are still partly preserved in mosaic. Another instance is in the fifth-century mosaics on the triumphal arch of Santa Maria Maggiore, Rome, where sketches were found on the first of three layers, but these occur only in the upper register

---

8 See Didron's translation of the *Hermeneia* of Dionysius of Fourna, *Manuel d'iconographie chrétienne* (Paris, 1845), p. 57.

9 This fact was observed during conservation work performed by the Byzantine Institute in January 1959, but it was not possible to observe other technical features of the construction of the mosaics. The Alexandria-Michigan-Princeton expeditions to Mt. Sinai are soon to prepare a publication dealing with these important mosaics.

10 For St. Mark's, see G. Musolino, *La Basilica di San Marco in Venezia* (Venice, 1955), p. 45; for Hosios Lucas see R.W. Schultz and S. H. Barnsley, *The Monastery of St. Luke of Stiris, in Phocis*, etc. (London, 1901), p. 42; and for

Cefalù (and apparently for all other mural mosaics in Sicily), see the statement of G. Riolo, *Dell' artificio dei musaici antichi e moderni* (Palermo, 1870), p. 7. The reliability of Riolo on this point is open to question since he depended on information passed on to him from his father. One might also question the accuracy of Musolino on the mosaics of San Marco, and of Schultz and Barnsley on those of Hosios Lucas; it is possible that they failed to distinguish two coats beneath the setting bed. On the other hand Millet, *Le Monastère de Daphni, histoire, architecture, mosaïques* (Paris, 1899), p. 165, correctly identified three layers of plaster at Daphni.

11 F. Forlati, "La Tecnica dei primi mosaici marciani," *Arte Veneta*, III (1949), p. 85 and Figs. 82–84.

176

and not in other parts of the arch.[12] The sketches were quite rough and did not correspond closely to the mosaic as it was finally executed. In this instance, too, the sketching should be viewed as a tryout and not as a guide to the painter of the setting bed. There is also the statement of Thomas Whittemore, in his report on the mosaic panel in the southern vestibule of Hagia Sophia,[13] that he observed traces of a sketch on the second of the three layers of plaster. However, the mosaic figures in question are so nearly intact that he could not have seen whether they were sketched on a layer of plaster that was separated from the tesselated surface by the setting bed, which was also nearly intact. We do not know in what part of the panel his observations were made, what the purpose of the brush lines may have been, or what their relation was to the mosaic as it was actually executed.

However, much more positive evidence is at hand in Hagia Sophia to indicate that when mosaics were constructed with three coats of plaster preliminary sketches were not normally used on surfaces beneath the setting bed. The fragmentary mosaics of the late ninth century in the room at the south end of the west gallery constitute the only extensive works in Constantinople where large areas of masonry, first and second renderings, setting bed, and tesselated surfaces are exposed to view.[14] On none of the surfaces beneath the setting bed are there traces of drawings of any kind. Had preliminary sketches been consistently employed some trace of them would have been found. On the other hand, all the areas of setting bed which were exposed when the tesserae were deliberately scraped off, possibly for reuse elsewhere, still preserve their paintings; the imprints of the missing tesserae show how accurately the painting was reproduced in the tesselated surface.

In the great Deesis panel of the Kariye Djami (PL. 36–41) huge areas of painted setting bed are exposed. In the entire panel there exists only one suture in the setting bed; it runs vertically, from top to bottom, dividing the setting bed into two nearly equal parts. Thus, in each half of the panel the setting bed, and probably also the second rendering beneath it, was laid in one continuous operation, and, incredible though it may seem, the figures and the background were painted and the tesserae were inserted before the plaster hardened. However, if we bear in mind that in the parecclesion considerably larger areas of fresco were painted, from sketch form to nearly final state, while the plaster was still moist, it becomes rather more credible that the virtuosity of these artists was great enough to enable them to complete such mosaic areas before the plaster of the setting bed hardened.[15] If we assume that the second coat (if not also the first) was freshly laid and still moist when the final coat was applied, as was certainly the case in the frescoes, we can understand how the drying of the mosaic setting bed would be retarded and the plaster of the bed would remain pliant long enough to enable the painter-mosaicists to carry out their work over a rather large area. We should recall the testimony of Didron, cited below in the section dealing with the technique of the paintings, that he saw a painter on Mount Athos sketch in a complete scene in the course of one hour, without the aid of models of any kind, and prepare it for the application by one of his assistants of the more opaque layers of paint on the draperies. The painting on a mosaic setting bed, of course, was not as detailed as a completed

---

12 See B. Biagetti in *L'Illustrazione Vaticana*, Mar. 15, 1931, pp. 26–32 (especially p. 29 and Fig. 5); and Mar. 31, 1931, pp. 27–33 (especially p. 30 and Figs. 13 and 14).
13 *The Mosaics of St. Sophia at Istanbul: Second Preliminary Report, The Mosaics of the Southern Vestibule* (Oxford, 1936), p. 10.

14 Underwood, "A Preliminary Report."
15 The right-hand portion of the Deesis panel, which was laid first and is slightly larger than that at the left, has an area of approximately nine square meters. The largest work area of fresco in the parecclesion measures about fourteen square meters.

fresco painting and did not involve numerous superimposed layers of paint; it could, therefore, be executed with considerably greater speed than a fresco of comparable size. The setting of the tesserae was a rather lengthier process, and the area of mosaic that could be undertaken at one time could never be as large as the individual work areas in fresco painting.

Whereas it is relatively easy to discern the sutures when a sufficiently large area of the setting bed is laid bare, it is seldom possible to detect the joints between the individual work areas when the mosaic surfaces are intact, for at these points the mosaicists of the Kariye Djami took great care to maintain continuity from one area to the next in the alignment of the rows of tesserae. In two of the domical vaults, however, a line of juncture between two major work areas can be seen on close inspection or even in good photographs. In the scene of The Presentation of the Virgin in the Temple, which occupies the entire vault of the third bay of the inner narthex (PL. 119), the joint in the gold background runs across the center of the composition in a nearly straight line from north to south, indicating that the scene was executed in two major sections. A similar joint appears in the gold background of the vault in the second bay of the outer narthex (PL. 217), this time running east and west, and marks the dividing line between scenes [115] and [116], which appear to have been executed in two successive operations. The sutures in the mosaics of these vaults may be compared to the joint that is so clearly visible in the much larger fresco painting of The Last Judgment (see PL. 368), in the domical vault of the parecclesion, which will be described below in the section dealing with painting technique. It is an open question, however, whether the setting beds within such relatively large work areas were indeed continuous or whether they were laid, painted, and set with their tesserae in still smaller units, in such a way that the sutures would occur at the contours of individual figures, or groups of figures, where they could be easily concealed. At the Kariye Djami no evidence of such smaller subdivisions within the larger work areas has been observed, nor have such subdivisions been seen in the mosaics in the room at the south end of the west gallery in Hagia Sophia, where very large areas of bare setting bed exist.

In a few places in the mosaic surfaces of the Kariye Djami there is evidence that the borders which frame the scenes and the structural units of the narthexes were executed in separate operations after the scenes were finished. A case in point is the bull's nose border surrounding the window that penetrates the lunette containing the scene of Christ being taken to Jerusalem for Passover (PL. 208). Here there is an irregular suture within the area of the lunette at varying distances from the exterior edge of the border. It would seem that when the scene itself was executed, the edge near the opening of the window did not coincide with the exact contour that was to be given to the ornamental border but fell somewhat short of it. Proof that the border was constructed after the scene in the lunette was finished lies in the fact that the green glass tesserae of the ground zone adjoining the border at the left of the arch were laid in rows which parallel the curve of the border and thus run in a direction counter to the horizontal rows of the main area of the green ground. Similar instances can be found elsewhere in the mosaics of the Kariye Djami. Apparently the execution of borders as a separate operation, carried out after the mosaics at either side had been completed, was common practice, for in Hagia Sophia most convincing evidence exists in the mosaic fragments of the room off the south end of the west gallery and in the mosaics in the immediate vicinity of the Alexander portrait.[16]

16 Underwood and Hawkins, "The Mosaics of Hagia Sophia at Istanbul: The Portrait of the Emperor Alexander," D. O. Papers, 15 (Washington, 1961), 203, 204, 206.

In my discussion of the technique of the paintings I will show that the actual painting of a composition was carried out in the following sequence of operations on the surface of the freshly laid final coat of plaster: the composition was sketched in lightly; the contours of the figures, the principal folds of their drapery, and the other elements of the composition were more precisely established in a firm brush drawing; the background was then painted; the ground color for the drapery of the figures was applied and the principal lines were incised with a sharp instrument in preparation for the detailed overpainting of the garments by an assistant. The heads, and possibly also the hands and feet (the latter if they were to be bare or shod with sandals), were reserved for the master painter, who fully painted these parts only after the drapery was completed. The question arises whether the procedures in the execution of the mosaics followed a somewhat similar sequence. It is my opinion that there is a relation between the procedures in mosaic work and fresco painting with respect to the sequence of operations as there is in so many other aspects of the work in the two media. For example, the practice of leaving the heads, hands, and feet for the last may be observed in some of the mosaics of the parecclesion of the Fethiye Djami (Pammakaristos) in Constantinople. The evidence to this effect also proves conclusively that the setting of the tesserae in the heads was done *in situ* and that the heads were not prepared in a studio as separate pieces of mosaic to be put into position as finished products, as some, including myself, had previously supposed.[17]

Among the extant mosaics in the parecclesion of the Fethiye Djami there are four small panels, each containing a single standing figure, which were left in an unfinished state.[18] In the panel of St. John the Baptist, on the south wall of the bema, the gold background, including the inscription, the garments, and the head, is finished work and still exists in a nearly perfect state of preservation. The feet of the figure, however, are only partly set with glass and stone tesserae; much of the setting bed, painted in great detail and with considerable modeling, was left unset. The hands contain not a single tessera, but they were fully painted on the setting bed. The condition of the feet reveals a great deal about the method of the mosaicist in the setting of the tesserae. The main outlines, which are set with single rows of small black glass tesserae, are complete and seem to have been done first; the thongs of the sandals, set with black glasses, are also complete, as are the lines, in red glass tesserae, that are drawn between the toes. Single rows of greenish yellow glass provide the shading along the arch of one foot and along the bottom edge of the other. The only other tesserae that were pressed into position are of white stone and occur in the areas that were to be highlighted. The mosaicist had just begun to set the pinkish marble tesserae with which the local color of the flesh was to be represented when he halted work, and only one row of these stones was put in position. In the setting bed, areas that were to be represented in flesh tones are painted in brownish yellow shading off into yellow but are left devoid of tesserae. The implications of this evidence are that in this panel the background and the garments of the figure, in whatever sequence, were set first, followed by the head and the feet; the hands were to come last, but in this instance they received none of their tesserae. In the panel containing the fragmentary portrait of a church Father, possibly to be identified as St. Clement, the

17 Professor Kitzinger, in his work on the mosaics of Monreale, p. 129, n. 101, correctly reported that I held this view in 1959. The subsequent discovery of the unfinished mosaics at the Fethiye Djami has proved that my earlier opinion was incorrect.

18 The uncovering and cleaning of the existing mosaics in the Fethiye Djami, which are nearly contemporaneous with those of the Kariye Djami, has only recently been completed. Their publication is planned for the near future.

background and the garments, so far as they exist, as well as the hands and feet were completed, but the head was left in an unfinished state. In this instance, the hair and beard, the features (nose, eyes, ears, and mouth), all the white highlights on the face, and the shaded areas in greenish yellow glasses had received their tesserae, but only a few small areas of the flesh had been set with pink marble tesserae. Large areas of the flesh, painted in yellow, remained unset in the setting bed. Finally, in the portrait panels of St. Cyril of Alexandria and St. Athanasius all parts excepting the hands were completed in mosaic tesserae; the hands were left bare of stones of any kind, but again the setting beds were painted.

Although it can be seen from this evidence that the heads (as well as the hands and feet) were the last parts of a mosaic to receive their tesserae, it is still a question whether the draperies within the contours of the figures were the first parts to be set or whether the mosaicist began by filling in the background, as was done in the frescoes. It is my impression, which I am unable to prove, that after the contours of the figures were firmly established in the brush drawing and the various areas of the background were quickly painted in their appropriate colors, the procedure may have been as follows: First, the mosaicist carefully surrounded the contours of the figures or objects (buildings, trees, etc.) with two or three rows of tesserae, set parallel to the contour lines, which were of the materials and colors to be used in the immediate background. Once this "trim," which became part of the background, had been laid down, the rows of tesserae in the remainder of the background could be set in directions that were totally independent of those of the "trim" without destroying the precise line of demarcation between figures and background. One or more mosaicists could then be assigned to the rather mechanical task of setting the tesserae in the background while another, perhaps the master himself, could concurrently proceed, within the area surrounded by the "trim," to the painting of the draperies and the setting of their tesserae.

The tesserae in Byzantine mosaics were never fully inserted into the plaster; from one fourth to one third of their thickness projects from the surface of the setting bed. At the Kariye Djami the tesserae themselves vary greatly in size and, therefore, in thickness. In the representations of flesh and hair, where very small tesserae of marble and glass are used, their thickness may be as little as 2 mm., but the gold tesserae of the background, which normally have surface dimensions of from 7 to 10 mm., are usually from 6 to 7 mm. thick.

In the mosaics at the Kariye Djami the tesserae were made of the following materials, listed here in the order of their prevalence: glass, stone, marble, and red terra cotta (brick). The use of a few small pieces of glazed pottery, of a turquoise color, amidst the foliage of the trees in panel [99] is most exceptional.

Glass is by far the most important and predominant material, for it was through vast areas of gold and variously colored glass tesserae that mosaics achieved the highly prized qualities of brilliance and richness, as the light was refracted from their glittering surfaces in ever-changing effects. Since the tesserae were inserted individually by hand, their surfaces were not all on a uniform plane but varied slightly in their inclinations, a condition that always produced a glitter, whatever position the mosaic was viewed from. The glass tesserae are of two principal kinds: those covered with gold and, infrequently, with silver leaf; and those which are pigmented throughout. Slight use was made of translucent, nearly colorless glass having a slight greenish or pinkish tinge. The pigmented glasses, of all colors, could be opaque, translucent, or transparent.[19]

The glass from which the tesserae were cut seems to have been formed as plates of varying thicknesses whose edges were unconfined by a mould of any kind, for one often finds tesserae with a rounded edge on one side, which came from the edge of the plate. The shapes of these tesserae often indicate that the contours of the plates from which they came were not rectangular but curved; possibly they were roughly circular in shape. The plate was fractured into rectangular shapes to form the tesserae, but their sizes depended upon the thickness of the plate and whether they were to be used in the backgrounds, in the draperies of the figures, or in the heads, hands, and feet. In an individual tessera one can distinguish the upper and lower surfaces of the plate as well as the fractured sides. To attain a particular effect when using pigmented tesserae, the mosaicist could expose the upper surface, but for other purposes he might expose a fractured side, which was more glossy than the others, or even reverse the tessera, exposing its bottom side.

Metallic glass was produced by covering a plate of transparent glass, usually of a light greenish cast and normally about 6 mm. thick, with gold or silver leaf; this, in turn, was coated with a thin layer of clear glass about 1 mm. thick. The "sandwich" was then heated until all its elements fused, and it was thereupon fractured into tesserae. Fusion was not always fully obtained and very often in a field of gold background one finds that the thin covering layer has come away and sometimes that the metal foil has come with it. When used in the backgrounds or in the representation of golden objects, such as book covers or cloth of gold, the upper surfaces of the gold tesserae were exposed, but for special purposes they were sometimes set on their sides to obtain a transparent amber color. Since apparently the plate for the manufacture of gold glass was poured on a surface covered with a red substance, the under surface of a gold tessera was often of a dull reddish color and had a pebbled texture. For special effects the gold tesserae were set in reverse and sometimes can be mistaken for cubes of reddish terra cotta.

Although a wide range of colors and hues are represented in the pigmented glass tesserae of the Kariye Djami, the basic colors, in the order of their prevalence, are blue, green, violet, red, yellow, and black. Whereas the red and black glasses tend to be of a single value, the basic blue, green, and violet glasses, which were used primarily in the draperies of the figures, were manufactured in a range of from four to five values. Variant types of blue, green, and yellow, which give the appearance of mixed colors, are numerous, but these appear, for the most part, among the smaller tesserae used in the modeling of faces and in the hair and beards of figures; the variant greens, however, also appear as large tesserae in the ornamental borders and in the zones of solid-green foreground at the bases of the panels. Thus, in the modeling of the heads of figures one

19 There are a number of Greek and Latin alchemical treatises in which the methods of manufacturing glass of various colors are described. Some of the Greek texts have been assembled by M. Berthelot, *Anciens Alchemists grecs*, II (Paris, 1888), 338 ff. Another medieval source is *Compositiones ad tingenda musiva*, which was published in Latin by L. A. Muratori in *Antiquitates italicae medii aevi*, II (Milan, 1739), cols. 365–92, and in a German translation with commentary by H. Hedfors, *Compositiones ad tingenda musiva* (Uppsala, 1932); a study of the sources of this text was made by R. P. Johnson, *Compositiones variae* (Urbana, Ill., 1939). Still other treatises in which glass and its coloration are

discussed: *Mappae clavicula*, in *Archaeologia*, 32 (1847), 187–244; Heraclius' *De coloribus et artibus Romanorum*, text and translation by A. Ilg (Vienna, 1873); Theophilus' *De diversis artibus*, translated by C. R. Dodwell (London, 1961). Two of the more important secondary sources are Cabrol-Leclerc, *Dictionnaire d'archéologie chrétienne et de liturgie*, Vol. 12, Part 1 (Paris, 1935), s. v. "Mosaique," cols. 70–75; and M. G. Chesneau, "Contribution à l'étude de la technique des vitraux du moyen age," *Bulletin Monumental*, 92 (1933), 265–95. For bibliographical assistance on this subject I am much indebted to Dr. Herbert Kessler.

finds cerulean and grayish blue, yellowish green, and greenish yellow tesserae, and in the green zones a great variety of greens as well as the basic green.

The basic blue may be characterized as ultramarine. This is used primarily in the blue draperies. With very few exceptions, only the blue garments of Christ and the Virgin are made entirely of glass tesserae; in other situations, for example in the blue tunics of all figures of the disciples, the ultramarine-blue glass is rather sparingly used and is greatly supplemented by bluish gray stones. The violet glasses are generally of the bluish rather than reddish variety. They appear in a wide range of values and are sometimes used in the tunic of Christ (as the exclusive material), in the himatia of many other figures, where stones as well as glass occur, and in outlining elements of landscape and architecture. The basic green glass is on the order of viridian, and when it appears in the green garments it is seldom employed over large areas. The red glass can best be described as the color of red sealing wax. It appears in all red garments, greatly supplemented by red terra cotta and pink marbles, and it was extensively used in the outlines of haloes, in the delineation of faces, hands, and feet (in tesserae of very small sizes), and in the ornamental borders. Yellow glass tesserae were seldom made in the larger sizes and almost never appear in the yellow garments, an exception being the garment of the seated woman in the lower right corner of panel [107] (PL. 186).

In most, if not all, of the colored glasses, the tesserae of the very darkest values tend to be glossy and are relatively free from the small air holes, or bubbles, that are especially noticeable on the surfaces of the glasses of lighter values. Indeed, the lighter the value of a glass of any given color the larger and more numerous the air holes; in the lightest values the surfaces of the tesserae sometimes have a granular or crystaline appearance.

I have already mentioned that glass is the principal material in the rendering of the garments of figures. However, except in the garments of Christ and the Virgin, which are exclusively of glass tesserae, extensive use was made of gray and white stones and red terra cotta in representing the half lights and highlights of garments. To understand the manner in which these materials were combined in the garments, the reader is referred to the color plates of Volume 2 and to the discussion of materials and colors that follows the description of the mosaics of the Genealogy ([7]–[78]).

There is no need here to discuss in detail the numerous types of stones that were cut into tesserae; the color plates illustrate the appearance of the stone and terra-cotta tesserae, their extent, and the particular elements of the compositions in which they were employed. The notes on colors and materials which accompany the descriptions of the individual mosaics are also useful in this respect. As a general summary, however, it can be said that stones, mainly of cool and warm grays, tan, brown, and yellow, were by far the major materials used in depicting the landscapes and architecture that provide the settings for the narrative scenes; that very small pink marbles are used primarily for the flesh of heads, hands, and feet; that red terra-cotta tesserae appear extensively, in conjunction with pink marbles and red glass, in the representation of red draperies; and that a white, finely textured stone, distinct from all other stones, is used for the brightest highlights and in the representation of pearls. In representing yellow garments, little if any glass is used; instead a yellow stone, available in several values and resembling yellow ochre in color, was the primary material used, in combination with stones of brown for the drawing and shading and white for the highlights.

In several of the mosaics of Hagia Sophia, earlier in date than those of the Kariye Djami, tesserae dipped in paint, most often of a vermilion color, were very sparingly used whenever such colors were not obtainable in glass or as the natural color of stones. This device has not been observed at the Kariye Djami. On the other hand, in a very few instances certain areas of stone tesserae which were found to be of an undesirable color or value after they had been set were painted over to obtain a more suitable color. Instances of this were found in two of the walls in the background of mosaic [88], The First Seven Steps of the Virgin, and in the baskets of scene [118], The Multiplication of Loaves (see PL. 244).

PART TWO

The Frescoes

The Program and Layout

The fresco paintings of the Kariye Djami, described below and illustrated in Volume 3, are dealt with under the following groupings, which have been made with one exception on the basis of location in the church: the paintings of the parecclesion ([201]–[269], PL. 335–520), that is, the chapel-like annex attached to the south side of the nave; the paintings of the pastophoria (PL. 521–529), the rooms flanking the bema of the church, which are known as the prothesis and the diaconicon; the painted ornaments in the northern passageway, connecting the prothesis with the inner narthex (PL. 530, 531), and the passageway between the nave and the parecclesion (PL. 532); and finally, the sepulchral monuments (PL. 533–553), wall niches or arcosolia constructed in the walls of the parecclesion and the narthexes. For descriptions of the structural features of most of these parts of the church the reader is referred to the Introduction to this volume.

The frescoes in the parecclesion, which comprise the major part of the painted decorations in the church, were uncovered by the Byzantine Institute between 1951 and 1958 and published, as they were brought to light, in a series of four preliminary reports.[1] The fragmentary remains of the paintings in the pastophoria were cleaned and repaired in 1958 and were partially described and illustrated in the Fourth Report.[2] Work on the fragments of painting and mosaic in the arcosolia was conducted from time to time between 1956 and 1959 and the results were published in a preliminary manner in a series of "Notes on the Work of the Byzantine Institute in Istanbul."[3]

For the convenience of the reader it will be necessary to repeat much that was published earlier about these paintings, but some of the detailed information contained in the Reports and the Notes, particularly discussion of the methods employed in the cleaning and repair of the paintings and descriptions of the prior condition, will not be included here. Although it does not entirely supersede them, the present publication revises the earlier Reports at a number of points and has the merit of bringing together, within a single compass and in a systematic manner, the description and illustration of all the frescoes and of examining the fresco program in relation to the decoration of the church as a whole. The plates of the frescoes, many in color for the first time, will be found to be more numerous and of better quality than those previously published.

All the paintings in the Kariye Djami, with the exception of those contained in the wall

---

1 D. O. Papers: First Report, Vol. 9–10 (Cambridge, Mass., 1956), pp. 253–88 and Figs. 61–105; Second Report, Vol. 11 (Cambridge, 1957), pp. 173–220 and Figs. 1–51; Third Report, Vol. 12 (Cambridge, 1958), pp. 235–65 and Figs. 1–39; Fourth Report, Vol. 13 (Washington, 1959), pp. 185–209 and Figs. 1–30.

2 Pp. 209 and 210 and Fig. 31.

3 D. O. Papers, Vol. 12 (1958), pp. 271–78 and Figs. 5–15; and Vol. 13 (1959), pp. 216–28 and Figs. 1–12.

tombs, were executed under the patronage of Theodore Metochites. Stylistic and practical considerations lead to the conclusion that the frescoes of the parecclesion were painted after the mosaics of the nave and the narthexes had been completed, that they comprise one of the last stages in the decoration, and that they should be dated in 1320–21.[4] It is not possible to say at what stage in Metochites' program of decoration the paintings of the pastophoria and the ornaments in the passageways were executed, but the portraits of the deceased in the wall tombs were painted, one by one and over a lengthy period of time, after the completion of Metochites' restorations and as need arose for funerary monuments in the church.[5]

To understand the underlying purpose of the iconographic program that was chosen for the decoration of the vaults of the parecclesion it is important first that the question of the function of this impressive structure be clarified. It was proposed by Feodor Shmit[6] that the parecclesion should be identified as the *trapeza*, or refectory, of the monastery. His view was based on two passages in Metochites' poems. Beginning at line 334 in Poem B[7] Metochites says that "in addition, alongside, and nearby" other parts of the church which he had previously mentioned, he built "a common sanctuary of the *trapeza*," which he adorned throughout with paintings that recount "the mysteries and miracles of Christ;" these, he says, were very pleasing to the monks who ate there. Because this is the only passage in which Metochites speaks of a structure that was decorated throughout with paintings, as opposed to mosaics, Shmit assumed that the reference was to the parecclesion, which, indeed, is the only existing part of the church that could possibly serve such a purpose and that was so decorated. The *trapeza* was also equated by Shmit with one of the two annexes that Poem A, lines 1053–54,[8] says lay at the sides of the nave just as the *pronaoi*, or narthexes (mentioned in the same poem beginning at line 1047), extended across the front of the church. The question is whether the *trapeza* is, in fact, to be identified as the southern annex (the parecclesion), which lies alongside the nave.

The following points militate against such an assumption. The description of the refectory follows upon comments that refer to the church as a whole (the nave, narthexes, and lateral annexes),[9] a fact that tends to differentiate the *trapeza* from either one of the lateral annexes and to indicate that the refectory was a separate structure built "in addition" to (though alongside) the structures previously mentioned; in this it would have conformed with the common practice of the period—for monastic refectories were usually separate buildings, entirely detached from the church. Moreover, the paintings of the parecclesion, which are extant, can hardly be said to depict "the mysteries and miracles of Christ,"[10] as will be seen below when the iconographic program is described. The great majority of the scenes in the parecclesion depict various elements of the Last Judgment and Old Testament subjects, and somewhat more than half of the paintings in the vaults are devoted to the role of the Virgin in the divine plan of salvation.

Certain structural elements that were built into the chapel itself indicate that the parecclesion

---

4 For evidence concerning the date, see above, pp. 15–16, and for the stylistic considerations that indicate that the frescoes were painted at the end of operations in the church see the chapter of Otto Demus in Vol. 4 of the present publication.

5 The dates of the paintings in the arcosolia will be discussed below in connection with their descriptions.

6 *Kakhrie-dzhami* (Izvestiia Russkago Arkheologicheskago Instituta v Konstantinopole, XI; text, Sofia, album of plates, Munich, 1906), pp. 92 ff.

7 *Dichtungen des Gross-Logotheten Theodoros Metochites*, ed. M. Treu (Programm des Victoria-Gymnasiums zu Potsdam, Ostern 1895, Potsdam, 1895), p. 47.

8 Treu, p. 29.

9 Poem B, lines 310 ff. (Treu, p. 46).

10 The resurrection of the Widow's Son and that of the Daughter of Jairus ([202], [203]) are miracles, and the Anastasis ([201]) could be called either a mystery or a miracle, but these form only a small part of the program as a whole.

was in reality the mortuary chapel of the church. Four wall tombs, in the form of arcosolia, were built within the thickness of the walls and were actually used for sepulchral purposes (see below: The Sepulchral Monuments), and in addition two long vaults were built parallel to one another beneath the floor of the parecclesion, probably to serve as the ossuaries of the monastery. Finally, it will be seen that the iconographic program of the paintings reflects this funerary function and the inscriptions in the paintings of hymnographers in the pendentives ([224]–[227]) quote from funerary hymns.

For all these reasons it seems very unlikely that the parecclesion was the refectory. If this is the correct conclusion it means that Metochites' *trapeza*, along with all the paintings it contained, has long since been destroyed.

In plan, it will be recalled, the parecclesion is composed of an apse, at the east end, and two square bays, separated from one another by transverse arches.[11] The apse and the arch immediately before it comprise the bema, which, as in the main body of the church, served a liturgical function; it should be considered a unit distinct from the two bays to the west, the equivalent of the nave. The superstructure throughout its length is divided horizontally by a continuous cornice into two structural zones: the vertical walls below, and the arches, lunettes, and vaults above. In addition, there is a third zone in the western bay, a lofty dome raised on a drum. Although all these areas of the superstructure are decorated with fresco paintings, narrative scenes are to be found only in the second zone, that is, in the arches, lunettes, and vaults. In the third zone (the dome in the western bay), and in the lower zone (the walls), the painted decoration consists of figural representations.

In the iconographic program of the parecclesion, the greatest importance, from the point of view of thematic content, was attached to the narrative paintings in the zone of the vaults and to the figures in the dome which rises above them. Here we find that two broad themes of nearly equal prominence and extent, which were distinct from one another yet in some respects interrelated, were developed for specific purposes. In our discussion of the program and its layout, and in the descriptions of the individual paintings which will follow, we begin with these parts of the iconographic program.

Of the two general themes in the vaults, one is devoted primarily to Christ, the other to the Virgin, as was true also in the mosaic decorations of the narthexes. It might be said, however, that the two themes of the vaults of the parecclesion share the purpose of attesting to the redemptive powers of both Christ and the Virgin whereas the intent in the cycle of the Virgin and those of Christ in the mosaics of the narthexes was to exhibit the roles of the Virgin and Christ in the Incarnation. The redemptive aspect of the program made it eminently appropriate to the function of the parecclesion as a mortuary chapel.

The paintings in the eastern half of the parecclesion possess a thematic unity, for they illustrate Christ's victory over death and his power to bestow eternal life upon the righteous or to condemn the wicked. The conch of the apse and the arch of the bema contain scenes of resurrection—the Anastasis [201] and two resurrection miracles of Christ ([202], [203]), and the adjoining domical vault of the eastern bay and its two lunettes are devoted to the numerous scenes and elements that together comprise a Last Judgment ([204]–[210]). While the re-

---

11 See the Introduction for a description of the structure of the parecclesion; also Figs. 1, 9–12 and PL. 336–339.

demptive implications of these paintings and their relevance to the functions of a funerary chapel are obvious, the program that was laid out in the vaults of the western bay touches in only a minor way upon the redemptive aspects of the program as a whole.

The paintings in the dome that towers above the western bay ([211]–[223]) announce that the program in this portion of the chapel will be principally devoted to the Virgin; with her attendant angels she presides, as it were, over the events that are depicted in the vaults below. In the pendentives of the dome four hymnographers ([224]–[227]) compose hymns which, as will be seen below in the description of the paintings, are relevant both to the iconography of the Virgin, as it is depicted in the rest of the western bay, and to the funerary nature of the chapel.

The remaining areas of the western bay, the vaults and lunettes, with the exception of the western tympanum and the crowns of the transverse arches, are devoted to a series of frescoes of Old Testament events ([228]–[236]) selected because they were allegorically interpreted as prophecies, or prefigurations, of the Virgin. In these frescoes, for example, are Jacob's Ladder, the Burning Bush seen by Moses, the sacred vessels that were deposited in the Holy of Holies of Solomon's temple, the closed gate of Jerusalem, and the altar of Moses, all interpreted as typifying the Virgin Mary. And it will be seen also that the Biblical texts on which these paintings are based appear in the pericopes that were read at one or another of the feasts celebrating the important events of Mary's life. Yet even among these Old Testament subjects there is one that reflects the role of the Virgin as mediatrix between earth and heaven and thus relates her to the redemptive theme. One of the most prominent of her Old Testament prefigurations is Jacob's Ladder, which is interpreted in the hymns being composed by two of the hymnographers in the pendentives as alluding to Mary as the ladder between earth and heaven or the bridge leading all who praise her from death to life.

Finally, at the west end of the upper zone, above the principal entrance to the parecclesion, there is one theme that, as it were, bridges the Mariological themes of the western bay and takes us back to the redemptive themes of the eastern half of the chapel: it is The Souls of the Righteous in the Hand of God, which was painted in two parts, in the crown of the western arch [237] and in the western tympanum [238]. It illustrates a verse from the Book of Wisdom, which reads, "But the souls of the righteous are in the hand of God, and the tortures of death shall not touch them." This subject, which so clearly reverts to the themes at the east, was, like them, selected for its aptness in the iconography of a funerary chapel.

The walls of the parecclesion (PL. 474–476), from floor to cornice, are divided into two horizontal zones. At the base of the walls a continuous dado, about 1.32 m. high, is painted, in imitation of marble paneling, and above the dado is a frieze, about 2.30 m. high, which originally contained thirty-four figures; of these twenty-seven are still preserved in whole or in part (see Fig. 10). Most of the figures were depicted at full length, but because of the arcosolia and doors that were let into the walls of the two square bays some were depicted as bust figures in medallions.

The figures on the walls may be divided into three categories: a series of six church Fathers, dressed in bishop's vestments, on the semicircular wall of the apse ([243]–[248], PL. 476–485); the Virgin Eleousa ([249], PL. 486, 487), on the south wall of the bema, which undoubtedly faced a figure of Christ, now lost, on the opposite wall; and an array of twenty saints and martyrs ([250]–[269], PL. 488–520), on the remaining walls of the chapel. A majority of the figures in the last category were soldier-saints portrayed at full length, dressed in military garb and carrying their weapons.

So many of the paintings that adorned the pastophoria [12] are now lost and those remaining are in such fragmentary state that the iconographic programs developed for these two rooms cannot be fully determined. In the prothesis, however, enough remains to indicate that the program was appropriate to the special rites which were performed there at the table of oblation (PL. 521–524). Less can be learned from the extant fragments of paintings in the diaconicon; all that can be said regarding the program of the diaconicon is that standing portraits of the apostles occupied the segments of the ribbed dome (PL. 525–528). For further comments on the iconography of the pastophoria the reader is referred to the section below describing the frescoes (see The Paintings of the Pastophoria).

With the exception of those that have been found in eight sepulchral monuments in the parecclesion and the narthexes, which are described below (see The Sepulchral Monuments; also PL. 533–553), no other figural or narrative paintings now exist in the Kariye Djami. However, some purely ornamental painting is found in the lower story of the northern annex and in the narrow passageway leading from the nave to the parecclesion; this also will be described below (see The Painted Ornaments in the Passageways; also PL. 530–532).

12 For a description of the structure of the pastophoria see the Introduction, pp. 22–23.

1 *The Paintings of the Parecclesion*

THEMES OF RESURRECTION AND JUDGMENT

[201]

The Anastasis

'Η 'Ανάστασις   *The resurrection*

'Ι(ησοῦ)ς Χ(ριστό)ς   *Jesus Christ*

When the spectator enters the parecclesion at the west his attention is led, by a series of medallions along the axis of the vaults, to the figure of Christ in the Anastasis, the composition that fills the semidome of the apse at the east (PL. 336, 338). Depicted here is Christ's triumph over Death through his descent to Hell and his redemption of the Righteous of the old dispensation, symbolized by his act of raising Adam and Eve, progenitors of all mankind. The scene sums up in pictorial form the principal elements of the doctrine of the *descensus ad inferos*, which had been expressed in several of the early creeds of the church and in patristic writings and was later elaborated in narrative form in the Apocryphal Gospel of Nicodemus of the fourth or fifth century.[1]

Briefly, the essential points of the Greek version of the narrative, as they relate to the picture, are the following. Preceded by a great light, John the Baptist enters Hell and announces to the Righteous (that is, to the forefathers and prophets, among whom Abraham, Isaiah, Adam, Seth, and David are mentioned by name) that Christ has sent him to proclaim his coming that they may be saved. Satan commands Hades, lord of the underworld, to hold Christ fast when he comes, and he warns of Christ's power to raise the dead and deprive him of all his captives. A great voice of thunder announces that the "King of Glory" (Christ) shall come in, and Hades orders his devils to make fast the gates of brass and the bars and locks of iron. Again a great voice speaks, commanding: "Lift up the gates," whereupon the gates are broken and the dead are loosed from their bonds. Christ, in the fashion of a man, enters, and all the dark places of Hell are enlightened. He commands angels to bind Satan's hands, feet, and neck and charges Hades to hold Satan prisoner until his Second Coming. With his right hand Christ raises Adam as a sign of the redemption of all the Righteous; holding Adam by the hand, he leads them all to Paradise unto Michael the Archangel.

In the traditional representation of the Anastasis prior to the late thirteenth century, when the type of composition used here was introduced, it is only Adam who is seized by the hand and raised from the dead; Eve merely stands or kneels at his side, and both are placed either at

---

1 See the translations of Greek and Latin versions by M. R. James, *The Apocryphal New Testament* (Oxford, 1924), pp. 117 ff.

the right or at the left of Christ. In this respect the traditional composition followed the texts more closely than the type adopted by the painter of the Kariye Djami, in which Christ, standing between the two, simultaneously raised Adam with his right hand and Eve with his left. The decision to put the Anastasis in the conch of the apse, where it was seldom placed, may in part account for the adoption of the symmetrical type, which is so admirably suited to a semidome and to the aesthetic requirements of the decoration of the chapel as a whole.

In a most skillful manner the painter has focused attention upon the action and the principal elements and figures of the composition by use of a great central triangle: the splendid figure of Christ in a pointed mandorla, at the center and apex, performs the act of resurrection above the abyss of Hell—a great curved area of darkness at the base of the composition, in which are the broken gates and the shackled figure of Satan; Adam and Eve form the sloping sides of the triangle, and the sarcophagi from which they are being raised provide strong accents at the lower angles. Balancing each other at the sides of the conch are two groups of the Righteous. They are placed before barren mountain peaks, whose fantastic rocky forms reach out to one another at the top as though to engulf all figures save Christ, whose mandorla nearly fills the open sky between them. In each group a single figure is somewhat detached from his companions: to the left, above Adam, John the Baptist is depicted, in his capacity as forerunner, announcing Christ's coming; at the head of the group at the right and standing in the tomb with Eve, his mother, is Abel, the young shepherd who was the first to meet Death.

The figure of Christ and the mandorla behind him incline perceptibly to the left, the direction taken by the vigorous movements of his body. These directional forces are depicted by various means; a foreshortening and reduction of scale in the left parts of the body, the wide stance, the strong diagonal line of thrust that is given to the leg at the right all combine to heighten the movement. At the same time Christ seems to pull Adam toward him from the left with his slightly flexed right arm, while his raised, rather massive left shoulder and arm seem to lift Eve out of her tomb with great force. Contributing also to the sense of movement are the prominent fluttering draperies of all three figures. The idea that life resides in Christ, the vanquisher of Death, is expressed through the contrast between Christ's figure, the active source of movement, and the passive, listless attitudes of Adam and Eve.

Christ's garments and the mandorla, so slightly contrasting in color, are of extraordinary luminosity (PL. 343); they are so painted to accord with the statements of the narrative that a great light accompanied Christ's entry into the darkness of Hell. Tunic and himation are identical in their very light, warm grays, in three values, brilliantly highlighted with pure white. Even the clavus at the right shoulder is of the darker gray that appears in the shadows of the drapery folds. The only other color in the garments is found in the narrow brush strokes of light blue applied over the gray along the outer contour of the thigh at the right. The three zones of the mandorla are of approximately the three values of color employed in the garments, and the distinction between them and the garments is produced not through differences of color value but mainly through the use of blues, which lighten in hue from the inside to the outside zone. The radiance that was so consciously sought by the painter was enhanced by the halo and by the stars that are scattered over the surface of the mandorla; these were originally executed in gold leaf, which is now preserved only in small fragments.

In a long and sweeping curve that is paralleled by the curve of his sarcophagus, the contours of Adam lead to his limp and lifeless left hand, which is so expressively contrasted to the firm grasp with which Christ draws him from the tomb (PL. 350). Adam's right hand is hesitantly extended in a gesture of supplication. His head is a particularly fine example of a venerable, patriarchal type, with strong modeling in the features and in the long, wavy locks of hair and beard boldly highlighted with white. He is dressed in a blue tunic, visible only in his left sleeve and the tortured folds of the hem between his feet; a white outer garment covers most of his body. The warm gray colors in the upper parts of the outer garment, similar to those of Christ's garments, tend further to unify the central element of the composition and to direct the movement toward the left.

Eve, on the other hand, is enveloped in a great red mantle, which all but conceals a tight-sleeved tunic worn beneath. Her pose reverses that of Adam, but her extended left arm and hand are entirely covered by her mantle.

Beneath Christ's feet and partly covered by the overhanging rocky ledge on which he stands are two leaves of the broken gates of Hell. These are formed of coffered panels and are painted in orange-yellows to simulate the brass gates described in the text. Innumerable pieces of iron ware—hinges, locks, keys, nails, bolts, and so forth—are strewn about the black areas of the abyss; these are the "bars and locks of iron" referred to in the text. The small figure of Satan lies prone at the bottom of Hell; painted in very dark monochrome, he is represented in human but grotesque form, wearing only a loincloth. His feet are tightly fettered, and his wrists are bound behind him in manacles joined to an iron collar around his neck by a long bar of iron.

Given special prominence at the head of the group of Righteous at the left is the nimbed figure of John the Baptist, who turns his head to speak to his companions while pointing to Christ with his left hand. He is dressed in a loose-sleeved tunic of a brownish yellow and a still more somber himation of a dull brownish green, which covers his right shoulder and wraps around his waist. In accordance with the accepted canon, his ascetic features are lined and weathered; his unruly hair falls over his shoulders in twisting locks, and his rather long beard is equally disordered.

The mass of figures at the left is composed of two categories of the Righteous. To the left of John stand several kings. In so far as the poor condition of their colored haloes permits one to judge, the artist intended to suggest the presence of six kings, but only the three in the front rank are delineated. Fully exposed to view are David, who faces toward Christ, and Solomon, who turns his head to look back at David; between them only parts of the crowned head and garments and the feet of another king are to be seen. Their royal attire, like that of most of the kings in the northern dome of the inner narthex ([52]–[67]), consists of a crown, a tunic richly embroidered at collar and hem and gathered by a belt at the waist, a chlamys adorned with a tablion, fastened at the right shoulder and thrown back over the left to expose the tunic, and royal boots of red and gold. The second category of the Righteous, at the far left, is composed of six anonymous figures of various types, who wear the classical tunic and himation, but only one of these, at the very edge of the composition, is fully exposed to view. Like the kings with whom they are grouped they hold out their hands in supplication to Christ.

The right side of the painting in the semidome is in a nearly perfect state of preservation, unlike the left side, where much surface paint has been lost. Here is the youthful Abel, set somewhat apart from his companions to serve as pendant to John the Baptist. He stands in the sarcophagus of his mother and holds his shepherd's crook vertically in his right hand while gesturing with his left. He is further distinguished from the others by his unique costume—a long, green tunic that is adorned at the collar, cuffs, armbands, and hem with representations of richly patterned embroidery. This garment is made to appear tubular by the drawing of the hem *di sotto in sù*, that is, as though seen from below at a sharp angle, a device that is to be observed elsewhere in the frescoes and in the mosaics as well. Abel's legs are covered by purple trousers, and over these spiral leggings enwrap his ankles and feet. With the exception that he wears no chlamys his costume resembles that of some of the martyrs in the outer narthex (PL. 294, 311). Six other Righteous are clustered at the right; like their counterparts at the far left they wear the tunic and himation and represent prophets and forefathers.

Dimensions

Width of conch at cornice level, 4.35 m.; width of painting on curved surface at cornice level, 6.78 m.; height of painting on curved surface at center, 3.40 m.; Christ, from top of head to level of feet, 1.63 m.; head of Christ including beard, .245 m.; maximum width of mandorla, 1.39 m.; average height of figures in group at left, ca. 1.37 m.; average height of figures in group at right, ca. 1.45 m.

Colors

CHRIST tunic, white (light, warm gray) with gray clavus, and with light blue shading along outer edge of thigh at right; himation, same as tunic; mandorla, three successively lighter zones of very light blue covered with stars originally in gold leaf over a dull red; halo, yellow ochre originally covered with gold leaf, bordered in brown and white.

ADAM tunic, blue; himation, white (light, warm gray); sarcophagus, pinkish brown (red-violet pigment mixed with umber?).   EVE tunic, blue; mantle, red; shoe, brown and black; sarcophagus, like that of Adam.

JOHN THE BAPTIST tunic, brownish yellow with black clavus; himation, dull brownish green (terre-verte with brown or black?); halo, yellow ochre (originally covered with gold leaf?).

GROUP OF KINGS *David* (left): tunic, red-violet with red belt and golden ornaments (yellow and red) studded with pearls at collar, down the front, and at hem; chlamys, dark blue with golden tablion; boots, red decorated with gold (yellow) and with pearls; crown, now largely yellow and red; halo, originally pale violet (now largely underpainting). *Solomon* (right): tunic, green, decorated like that of David; chlamys, red with golden tablion; boots and crown, like David's; halo, originally light green (now largely yellow underpainting). *Third king* (between David and Solomon): tunic, red; chlamys, green; boots and crown, like others; halo, now largely yellow. *Segments of haloes of three*

kings in background (otherwise not represented): light green and light violet.   GROUP OF SIX RIGHTEOUS TO LEFT OF KINGS clad in blue tunics and himatia of various colors: fully exposed figure at far left, light violet "shot" here and there with light blue; partly obscured figure to right (behind David), yellow.

ABEL (to right of Eve) tunic, green (malachite?) ornamented at collar, armbands, cuffs, and hem with embroideries of yellow (to represent gold?) decorated with designs of red; tight trousers, violet; leggings, gray; shepherd's crook, black shaft and white crook (latter now pale green owing to transformation of azurite in sky into malachite).   GROUP OF SIX RIGHTEOUS TO RIGHT OF ABEL clad in blue tunics and himatia of various colors: fully exposed figure in center, red-violet; figure to left (partly concealed by Abel), yellow; figure at far right, yellow; figure to his right, green; figure in center of rear rank (head and shoulders visible above fully exposed figure in front rank), yellow.

ABYSS IN FOREGROUND *Satan:* flesh, dark, warm brown, with drawing of brown deepened with black (?) and brown lightened with white for highlights; loincloth, white with shadows of black and shading of gray; shackles, gray. *Gates:* yellow and orange-yellow. *Ironware:* gray. *Background:* dull charcoal black.

LANDSCAPE rocks at left and center, warm greenish yellow; facets of rocky peaks detailed in terre-verte or blue, with warm brown shadows and light yellow and white highlights; rocks at right side, cool greenish gray highlighted with white, with shaded facets in dark greenish brown and upper contour in reddish yellow. SKY now a slightly bluish black (charcoal) but originally covered with a thin application of azurite blue, which, in the upper right side of the conch, had been transformed into malachite green owing to humid conditions and had to be removed; in all probability all areas of sky in the paintings were originally painted in azurite over the black.

[202]

The Raising of the Widow's Son

(Luke 7:11–15)

ʿΟ Χ(ριστὸ)ς ἀνιστά[νων τὸν υἱὸν] τῆς χήρας
Christ raising the son of the widow

The theme of resurrection, inaugurated with the scene of Christ's descent into Hell in the conch of the apse, extends into the adjoining arch of the bema in two confronted paintings of Christ's earthly miracles of resurrection. In the Anastasis Christ raises the forebears of mankind, male and female, represented by Adam at the left and Eve at the right; in the two miracle scenes, the two sexes similarly disposed, he resurrects the widow's son, in the left side of the arch, and the daughter of Jairus, in the right.

The first of these two scenes, the resurrection of the son of the widow of Nain (Luke 7:11–15), is in a very poor state of preservation; much of the surface paint is eroded and at the bottom of the panel is a large area of total destruction, which has been replaced with new plaster painted in flat, neutral tones of color.

The composition is basically like that employed in the series of miracles in the mosaics of the outer narthex: Christ, followed by a group of his disciples, stands at the left confronting the object of the miracle and his attendants. In pose and colors the figure of Christ also conforms to his representations in the mosaic miracles. He stands in three-quarters view, his right arm extended, his left arm supporting a great fold of hanging drapery, and his left hand holding a scroll; his tunic is blue-violet with a golden clavus at the right shoulder, and his himation is blue. Behind him are at least three of his disciples, all but one partly obscured in the background. The disciple in the foreground, nearest to Christ, is probably Peter, who so often occupies this position in the mosaics; he wears the short beard and the yellow himation that are characteristic of his representations throughout the Kariye Djami.

At the head of the funeral procession, which has just emerged from the gate of the city in the right side of the panel, the widow's son sits upright on his bier as it is carried toward the right on the shoulders of four men; by implication Christ has spoken and the dead has come to life. The youth is wrapped in a winding sheet and his head is covered by a hood, so that only his face is exposed to view. The rectangular bier is covered with a red cloth. The green pall that lay over him has been thrown back over his legs. The widowed mother stands in the very center of the panel, at the far side of the bier between Christ and her son. She bends toward Christ with outstretched hands; her face is extraordinarily dark and wrinkled and her eyebrows are drawn together in an expression of grief. Behind her stands an old man in frontal pose, his right hand raised in wonder as he turns his head to look at the resurrected youth.

In the farther background a crowd of mourners is grouped before the gate of the city of Nain, which, as is usual in such representations, consists of a turreted wall enclosing a jumble of small buildings, some of them gabled, and several tall cypress trees. Seemingly as an afterthought, the cypress were painted out and replaced by deciduous trees; the surface paint in these areas has now nearly vanished and the original forms of the trees predominate. Finally, as a counterbalance to the towering walls of the city, a sharp mountain peak, reminiscent of the peaks in the adjacent scene of the Anastasis, occupies the background at the far left.

Dimensions

Average width, 1.57 m.; height from top of inscription to cornice, 2.37 m.

Condition of Inscription

The thin and discolored white impasto in the omicron, chi, sigma, alpha, and nu at the beginning of the inscription is still largely original paint, though somewhat fortified. The impasto in the letters of the words τῆς χήρας, at the end of the inscription, had fallen away, but the letters were plainly legible on the black of the background because the black paint as long as it was covered by the impasto had been protected from the decomposition that affected the surrounding areas. The iota and the combined form of the sigma and tau in the word ἀνιστάνων were less clearly legible, and only small parts of other letters could be established. To preserve the traces of these letters from further deterioration and ultimate total loss, lime paint was newly laid on them. The iota of ἀνιστάνων was at first wrongly interpreted as an alpha, and it so appears in illustrations of this scene in the First Preliminary Report (*D. O. Papers*, Vol. 9–10, Figs. 63 and 82).

Colors

CHRIST tunic, blue-violet with yellow clavus; himation, blue. DISCIPLES tunics, blue; himation of disciple in forefront (Peter?), yellow; himation of disciple at far left edge, light red-violet. SON winding sheet and hood, light red-violet; covering of bier, red; pall over foot of bier, brownish green. BEARERS (left to right) blue-violet outer garment; red outer garment and blue headdress; blue outer garment.
WIDOW garments, very deep blue-violet. MAN BEHIND WIDOW red garment with green collar.
MOURNERS (in background) painting badly effaced; only red, green, and blue can be seen among various garments.
CITY OF NAIN city walls, light and dark blue-violet; roofs of houses, bluish gray and red; walls of houses, greenish brown. MOUNTAIN greenish yellow.

[203]

The Raising of the Daughter of Jairus

PL. 363–367

(*Matthew 9:18–19, 23–25; Mark 5:22–24, 35–43; Luke 8:41, 42, 49–56*)

The second of Christ's miracles of resurrection depicted in the arch of the bema is The Raising of the Daughter of Jairus. We are told by the three Gospel accounts that the miracle was performed in Jairus' house and by Mark and Luke that it was witnessed by three of Christ's disciples — Peter, James, and John — and by the maiden's parents.

The relatively tall and narrow proportions of the arch soffit have led to a composition in which the figures are compactly grouped and in which the architectural setting is emphatically vertical and rather larger in scale than usual. As in most of the miracle scenes, two groups of figures confront one another: Christ and his followers at the left, and the object of the miracle and her attendants at the right. At the same time, the principals involved in the event — Christ, the daughter, and the parents — comprise a second compositional grouping, circular in form, with the figure of the young girl in the center; this form is achieved by the disposition of the figures and by the directions given to the lines of Christ and the mother of the girl, in relation to the curvature of the bed.

Behind each of the lateral groups rises a tall, tower-like structure, set at an angle in bird's-eye perspective. The forms and colors of the two are deliberately contrasted: the tower at the left is covered by a flat roof, has rectangular openings in the sides, and is painted in red-

197

dish violet; the building at the right is gabled, all its openings are arched, and its walls are yellow. Both are richly ornamented with friezes and carved imposts, and the main arch of the gabled structure rests on classical consoles. Stretching from roof to roof is a great swag of red drapery adorned at the center by a wide yellow stripe in imitation of gold. The vista between the buildings is closed off by a low wall, capped by a curious form of stepped crenelation, which provides a degree of horizontality to this predominantly vertical composition.

At the far left, partly concealed by Christ, is a tight group of six disciples — not three as Mark and Luke say there were. Peter stands in full view at the far left; next to him in the front rank, but partly obscured by Christ's back, is a disciple whose features may be those of James. The beardless head in sharp profile nearest the halo of Christ probably represents John. The features of a fourth disciple appear in the background between the heads of Peter and James; the tops of two other heads complete the group of six disciples.

Christ stands at the foot of the bed in near-profile, but with his head in three-quarters view, and bends forward, grasping the wrist of the maiden with his right hand. The fact that so many details, and even artistic idiosyncrasies, that appear in this figure of Christ, and in that in the Anastasis, are also to be found among his representations in the mosaics, especially in The Multiplication of Loaves [118], strongly indicates that the painter of these scenes was also responsible for some parts of the mosaics. Allowing for the differences in the media, one should compare the general configuration, the treatment of drapery, the features of the head and its relation to the thrust of the neck, and the little "tail" of drapery at the back with its upturned point. And the peculiar shadows under the feet of Christ in the mosaic just cited are repeated in fresco beneath the left foot of Christ in the Anastasis [201] and under the feet of some of the Righteous in the right side of that composition.

The daughter of Jairus, now restored to life, sits upright on her bed. She is clad in a tight-sleeved red tunic adorned at the cuffs and on bands around the upper parts of the sleeves with golden embroideries. Over her head and arranged around her neck like a collar is a light blue hood, pushed far enough back to reveal two long curls falling over the collar, one at each side. Draped over the lower parts of her body is a deep blue-violet robe. Christ grasps the wrist of her outstretched right arm. The bed slopes upward toward the right to a curved head; around the sides it is covered with red-violet drapes bordered at top and bottom with bands of golden yellow embroidery. On the bed is a yellow mattress cushioned at the head, ornamented across head and foot with three slightly diagonal grayish blue stripes.

Jairus, represented as an old man with a long, pointed beard, stands in the background at the very center of the scene, between Christ and the girl and partly obscured by the bed and the building at the right. He faces Christ and holds out his hands in either respectful thanks, supplication, or surprise. As a "ruler of the synagogue" he wears a hood over his head and shoulders, and a loose mantle hangs from his shoulders and drapes over his raised arms.

At the right, behind the head of the bed, is a group of three women. The first, who is the mother, leans forward over her daughter in a hovering pose, her hands raised in a gesture of startled surprise. She is dressed in a heavy dark green mantle and headdress. The other two women, standing to the right behind the mother, are similarly clad. The color treatment of the mantle of the woman at the far right is worthy of note. The darker areas are painted in reddish and yellowish browns, the fully lighted areas in a near-complementary light blue, to give the effect of a garment of "shot" or changeable colors.

198

Dimensions

Average width including red borders, 1.60 m.; height at center from upper guideline of lost inscription to top of cornice, 2.43 m.

Condition of Inscription

Two roughly drawn guidelines, about 4 cm. apart, were scratched onto the background at the top of the painting after the painted plaster had completely hardened. At scattered points between these lines traces of only three incomplete letters in white lime paint now remain; one of the letters is either a sigma or an omicron. The inscription may have read: Ὁ Χ(ριστὸ)ς ἀνίστάνων τὴν θυγατέρα Ἰαείρου.

Colors

CHRIST tunic, dark blue-violet with yellow and red clavus; himation, blue. DISCIPLES all tunics, blue; himation of Peter, yellow; of James, green; of John, dark blue-violet. DAUGHTER tunic, red with red and yellow armbands and cuffs; hood over head and shoulders, very light blue; robe over lower part of body, dark blue-violet; drapes around sides of bed, red-violet strongly highlighted in white and bordered at top and bottom with yellow; mattress, yellow with blue stripes. JAIRUS mantle, dark red-violet; cuffs of tunic, light blue; hood over head and shoulders, light blue. WOMEN mantle of mother, dark green; mantle of woman to right of mother, light red-violet. Woman at far right wears a dull gray-blue tunic. Her mantle was first completely painted in light blue, then overpainted in parts—the medium lights in yellowish brown and the shaded areas in reddish brown. ARCHITECTURE *Building at left:* walls, dull red-violet in light and dark values; flat roof, yellow. *Building at right:* walls, yellow ochre in light and dark values; shaded areas and drawing of ornament in yellow-brown; roof tiles, blue-gray; consoles at imposts of main arch, blue-gray. *Wall across background:* painted in the darker values of yellow and yellow-brown of the building at right. *Drapery* (suspended from roofs of buildings): dark red ornamented with a stripe of yellow. FOREGROUND a zone of dark green.

[204]–[210]

The Last Judgment

PL. 368–407

TITULI:

Ἡ δευτέρα | τοῦ Χ(ριστο)ῦ παρουσία   *The Second Coming of Christ*

Χορὸς ἱεραρχῶν   Χορὸς ὁσίων   Χορὸς γυναικῶν   Χορὸς μαρτύρων   [Χορὸς] ἀποστόλων   [Χορὸς] προ[φ]ητῶν
Choir of hierarchs   Choir of holy men   Choir of (holy) women   Choir of martyrs Choir of apostles   Choir of prophets

CHRIST'S WORDS OF JUDGMENT

[Δεῦτε, οἱ εὐλογημένοι τοῦ πατρός] μου | κλ[ηρο]νομήσατε τ(ὴν) ἡτοιμασμένη(ν) | ὑμῖν βασιλείαν ἀπὸ κατα|βολῆς κόσμου
Come, ye blessed of my Father, inherit the kingdom prepared for you from the foundation of the world   (Matt. 25:34)

Πορεύεσ[θε ἀπ᾽ ἐμοῦ, οἱ] κατηραμένοι, εἰς τὸ πῦρ τὸ αἰώνιον τὸ ἡτοιμασμ(έ)νον τῷ διαβόλῳ | κ(αὶ) τοῖς ἀγγέλοις αὐτοῦ
Depart from me, ye cursed, into everlasting fire, prepared for the devil and his angels   (Matt. 25:41)

The iconographic program of Christ's triumph over death and redemption of the righteous that was assigned to the decoration of the eastern vaults of the parecclesion most fittingly concludes with the Last Judgment—the Second Coming of Christ, as it was known in Byzantine art and is inscribed in the main titulus of the scene. All the traditional elements that make up this complex subject are distributed in a well-conceived order in the domical vault and lunettes that envelop the eastern bay.

The middle-Byzantine version of the subject, on which this painting is based, embraced as much as possible of the Christian doctrine of "the last things" — death, final judgment, immortality in the heavenly kingdom or condemnation to the fires of hell. It was a composite of a number of motifs drawn from Christ's teachings, most importantly his eschatological discourse recorded in Matthew 24 and 25 and Mark 13, or adapted from the imagery of such other Biblical sources as the Prophets, the Psalms, or the Apocalypse of John. The iconographic motifs which comprise the Last Judgment in the parecclesion, together with indications of their position in the composition and the key numbers under which they are discussed below, may be tabulated as follows:

[204] The composition in the domical vault:

    1   *The Scroll of Heaven*, at the center of the vault.

    2   *Christ in Judgment* accompanied by the Virgin and John the Baptist, the Twelve Apostles, Angels, and Archangels, in a zone the full width of the vault to the east of center.

    3   Clouds bearing the *Choirs of the Elect*, arranged in an incomplete circle around the periphery of the vault:
       A) *Hierarchs, or Bishops;* B) *Hosioi, or Holy Men;* C) *Holy Women;* D) *Martyrs;* E) *Apostles;* F) *Prophets.*

    4   *The Etimasia*, flanked by Adam and Eve, at the center of the eastern side of the vault beneath the mandorla of Christ.

    5   *The Weighing of Souls*, beneath the Etimasia and immediately above the center of the eastern arch.

    6   *The Fiery Stream and the Lake of Fire*, in the area of the vault above the southeastern pendentive.

[205] *The Land and Sea Giving Up Their Dead*, in the southwestern pendentive.

[206] *An Angel and a Soul*, in the northwestern pendentive.

[207] *Lazarus the Beggar in Abraham's Bosom*, in the northeastern pendentive.

[208] *The Rich Man in Hell*, in the southeastern pendentive.

[209] *The Torments of the Damned*, in the eastern half of the southern lunette:

    1   *The Gnashing of Teeth* (?), upper left.

    2   *The Outer Darkness*, upper right.

    3   *The Worm That Sleepeth Not*, lower left.

    4   *The Unquenchable Fire*, lower right.

[210] *The Entry of the Elect into Paradise*, in the northern lunette.

By adopting the domical vault as the setting for these traditional themes the painter has been able to create a Last Judgment that in its composition is unique and that is peculiarly effective in depicting the celestial character of the apparition of "the Son of man in heaven." Using the angel rolling up the scroll of heaven and Christ in glory with his attendants as the central motifs, the painter has arranged the other celestial elements — the clouds of the elect, the Etimasia, and the fiery stream that issues from the feet of Christ — in a circle about the lower slopes of the vault, making the vault, as it were, a "dome of heaven." The remaining motifs are placed in a lower zone, around the circle of heaven, in the four pendentives and the lunettes at the sides. Disposed in this manner the composition forms a three-dimensional canopy enclosing the beholder within it.

Such a composition stands in marked contrast to all other examples of the Last Judgment in Byzantine art. In manuscript illumination and in icon painting the various elements are arrayed in superimposed horizontal zones in a rectangular format; they lack the illusion of a supernatural apparition in a heavenly setting. In other instances where the Last Judgment was used in the decoration of churches it was placed within a large panel on a wall, in a composition like that of an enormous icon, or its components were dispersed in a series of compositions on the walls, vaults, and piers, so that the unity and the "scenic" quality that are evident in the Last Judgment of the Kariye Djami are totally lacking.

[204]–1 The Scroll of Heaven PL. 368, 370–372

At the very center of the vault is an angel in full flight, rolling up the scroll of heaven as though to announce and reveal the drama of final judgment. The theme, usually included in Last Judgments, was doubtless inspired by the imagery of Apocalypse 6:14, "And the heaven departed as a scroll when it is rolled together;" it was used as a means of illustrating Christ's statement that as a sign of his Second Coming "the sun shall be darkened, and the moon shall not give her light, and the stars shall fall from heaven, and the powers of the heavens shall be shaken" (Matt. 24:29).

The still-unfurled portion of the scroll is beautifully formed into a spiral, like an Ionic volute, and on it are depicted the sun, the moon, and the stars. The sun is represented at one side as a disc bearing the features of a face, from which rays are emitted; at the opposite side is the crescent moon. Scattered over the field of the volute are eight-pointed stars, much like those on the mandorla of Christ in the Anastasis. At its western side, the tightly furled portion of the scroll is held in the extended hands of the flying angel, whose pose is like that of the angels supporting the mandorla of Christ in scenes of the Ascension. The curve of the angel's body reverses that of the scroll, providing a continuity of line and movement and a graceful union between the two forms. As a compositional device to give stability and a sense of direction to the whole, the angel's wings are spread wide in a shallow curve, an extension of the attitude of the arms and shoulders, and this line is paralleled below by the angel's legs at the right and the train of flying drapery that balances the legs at the left.

Again, it was probably the selection of the vault as the setting for the Last Judgment and the painter's obvious intention to exploit the possibilities of the vault in rendering it as a "dome of heaven" that inspired this unique and most effective version of the Scroll of Heaven. In other examples the motif produces little if any illusion of reality, the scroll being usually a narrow strip, loosely rolled and often strung out horizontally before a standing, not a flying, angel.

[204]–2 Christ in Judgment

Occupying the most prominent position in the composition, commensurate with its thematic importance, is the Parousia itself, which extends the full width of the vault in a slightly curved zone a little to the east of center. Here is illustrated Christ's description of his Coming, as stated in Matthew 25:31: "When the Son of man shall come in his glory, and all the holy angels with him, then shall he sit upon the throne of his glory." With him also are his twelve apostles, as he promised them that they would be: "ye which have followed me, in the regeneration when the Son of man shall sit in the throne of his glory, ye also shall sit upon twelve thrones judging the twelve tribes of Israel." (Matt. 19:28.) Finally, the Virgin and John the Baptist stand one at each side of Christ as intercessors on behalf of mankind, so that a Deesis is created at the center of the composition. Christ's words of blessing (Matt. 25:34) to the elect who approach his right hand are quoted in the inscription below and to the left of the mandorla, while his condemnation of the cursed (Matt. 25:41) is inscribed to the right.

The great fissure in the structure, which runs completely across the vault, and the consequent loss of plaster and paint at each side have destroyed much of the lower parts of Christ and the mandorla in which he sits. The mandorla was originally perfectly circular; his "throne" was a narrow arc, or rainbow, now destroyed in the right side but visible in the left, and his "foot-stool" was another, smaller arc, of which only a small portion is preserved at the right of the toes of his left foot (PL. 374). The mandorla is composed of four concentric zones of blue, the darkest at the center and the lightest, which is almost white, at the outer edge. Very little larger than the figures that accompany him, Christ turns slightly to his right, a wounded hand extended at each side to make the gestures of acceptance and rejection. His open right hand, palm outward, is relaxed; it is held at a higher level than his left, which, by contrast, has its back outward and its fingers, like talons, fiercely tensed and pointed downward. He is clad in a "golden" tunic and himation; hatched lines radiate from the yellow highlights, once covered with gold leaf, which overlie the reddish yellow areas of the middle lights. The yellow halo, to which small bits of gold leaf still adhere, is inscribed with a cross and bordered with dark red and with white. In the case of the inscription, $\overline{\text{IC}}\ \overline{\text{XC}}$, half of which appears at each side of the halo, most of the gold leaf with which the letters were covered still adheres to its mordant.

Completing the Deesis at the center of the Parousia are the standing figures of the Virgin, at Christ's right, and John the Baptist, at his left; they face inward, in three-quarters view, with heads bowed and hands held out in attitudes of entreaty. Like the figure of Christ between them, they are rather slight in proportions. The Virgin is dressed in an enveloping mantle and head-dress over a tunic with tightly fitting sleeves; John the Baptist wears a tunic and himation of the same somber colors he wore in the Anastasis.

Symmetrically disposed in two groups to the left and right of the Deesis are the twelve apostles. Each group is seated on a synthronon, or bench, and each of the twelve holds an open book on his lap. Within each group of six the postures of the individual apostles are arranged in an ordered rhythm of repeats and variations, which avoids monotony while it assures composi-tional unity. The first and last figures in each group are turned sharply inward toward Christ and are much more nearly in profile than the others. The second and fourth figures, counting from the center outward, sit in a very nearly frontal pose but turn their heads inward toward Christ. The third and fifth, bodies turned moderately toward the center and torsos inclined in that direction, turn their heads backward to look at their immediate companions, as though conversing with them. The third and fourth, and the fifth and sixth, are thus pairs whose members turn toward each other; the first and second constitute pairs with heads turned in common toward the center.

The individualization of the apostles is not quite as clear in this painting as it was in the mosaic of the Dormition, where most could be distinguished by type. However, because their types are so well established and because of the conventions of protocol, the figures at the ends of each of the two groups can readily be identified: Peter and Paul, as usual, are nearest to Christ, the former at his right, the latter at his left; the two beardless apostles farthest removed from Christ are Philip and Thomas. It is surely John the Theologian who sits to the left of Peter, and to the right of Paul is probably James, followed, to the right, by Andrew and Matthew. The third figure from the left in the left-hand group, who is represented with black hair, short beard, and a tuft of hair over his forehead, may be Mark; the apostle to his left, with whom he converses, may possibly be the Evangelist Luke. If these identifications are correct, the two remaining figures, who sit next to the young apostles at the two ends, can be assumed to be Simon and Bartholomew. The apostles thus tentatively identified may be numbered as follows, from left to right across the vault: *1*) Philip or Thomas;   *2*) Simon or Bartholomew;   *3*) Mark?;   *4*) Luke?;   *5*) John;   *6*) Peter;   *7*) Paul;   *8*) James?;   *9*) Andrew;   *10*) Matthew;   *11*) Simon or Bartholomew;   *12*) Philip or Thomas.

The host of attendant angels, holding pearl-studded scepters, stand in the background, filling the entire width of the composition. Those behind the Deesis are tightly grouped in three ranks, while those behind the apostles are more widely spaced and in a single row. Like the apostles, they tend to be represented either looking toward one another in pairs or facing inward in pairs toward Christ in glory. Two archangels stand somewhat apart from the other angels, one at each side of the Deesis, between it and the first apostles; and like the apostles they hold open books before them. They are further distinguished from their companions by the costume they wear: the long, red tunic of an imperial courtier, possibly the divitision, adorned with wide collar, strip down the front, armbands, and cuffs, all studded with pearls and dark red gems.

[204]–3 Choirs of the Elect   PL. 368, 370, 384 *a*–385 *b*

Four clouds, so disposed as to form three-fourths of a circle around the vault, on its lower slopes, contain six "choirs" of the elect, shown in kneeling or standing postures in reverence before the King of Heaven. They represent the elect from all "nations," or categories, of men, who are to be on the King's right hand and to whom he addresses the words of acceptance inscribed at his right. Three of the clouds are placed symmetrically in the western half of the vault. The two at the north and south are small and support only one choir each; between them, on the western axis, is a long cloud containing three choirs. On the fourth cloud, leading all the other choirs, are the prophets; they are placed below the enthroned apostles at Christ's right, literally "on his right hand," where they are pendant to the damned, "on his left hand." The choirs begin at the south and are arranged in a counterclockwise direction, in ascending order of precedence; they are identified, both by the inscriptions above them and by their costumes, as hierarchs (bishops), hosioi (holy men), women, martyrs, apostles, and prophets. The figures in most of the choirs have suffered severe loss of surface paint; many details remain only in the preparatory sketch, while others are totally obliterated.

The choir of the hierarchs, or bishops, was composed of about twenty-four figures, if one counts the heads, but the vestments of only three in the front rank and a few others behind them are exposed to view. The vestments consist of the white phailonion, or chasuble, on which are variously formed patterns of red or black crosses and gammas; the omophorion, or collar, also of white with red or black crosses; and beneath these the white sticharion, a long tunic visible below the knees, adorned at each side with wide vertical stripes, again of red or black. All the bishops kneel and face toward the left, as do the figures in the other choirs to the south of the main axis of the vault.

The choir of the hosioi is on the southern end of the long cloud in the western side of the vault. All figures appear to be dressed in monk's habit: tunic, scapular, and mantle, and a hood drawn over the head or hanging down at the back of the neck. Next to them is an area of new plaster that replaces a great loss at the center of the cloud, very nearly coinciding with the choir of women. Traces of the lower and upper parts of the first woman at the left in the front rank show that she stood upright facing left, wore a blue tunic and a dull green mantle and headdress, and may have carried a book. The faintest traces of the paint and underdrawing of the heads of several of her companions, all facing left, are still visible. Among them is a woman, possibly a royal personage, who wore a tall hat, or crown, widest at the top. The choir of martyrs, at the northern end of the same cloud, has three figures in the front rank, dressed in courtiers' costumes, and numerous others are behind. Of the three in front, the one at the center stands in a frontal pose but turns his head toward the right; the two flanking him, shown in profile, stride vigorously toward the right, stooping forward with hands extended. At this point the direction of movement has shifted from leftward to rightward—from clockwise to counterclockwise as the spectator looks from below facing eastward.

The apostles kneel on their cloud and face the right. Again, three figures are placed in the front rank; the others are partly visible between and above them in the background. The beardless apostle at the right, holding out his hands, is dressed in a green himation. The central figure, possibly Peter, wears a yellow himation. The apostle at the left, with head turned sharply upward, wears a violet himation; the shape of his head resembles that of Paul's.

In the front rank of the final choir, that of the prophets, are four kneeling figures with hands extended, all dressed in the usual himation. Near the right end, but in the background behind the leading figure, are two kings, doubtless David and Solomon, who rank as prophets; they are distinguished by their crowns.

[204]–4 The Etimasia PL. 368, 369, 386

On the eastern axis of the vault, below the mandorla of Christ, is depicted the preparation of the throne—the Etimasia. The sources of the theme, as it appears in illustrations of the Second Coming, are Psalm 88 (89):15, "Justice and judgment are the habitation of thy throne" (ἑτοιμασία τοῦ θρόνου σου), and Psalm 102 (103):19, "The Lord hath prepared his throne in the heavens [ἐν τῷ οὐρανῷ ἡτοίμασε τὸν θρόνον αὐτοῦ]; and his kingdom ruleth over all."

The throne itself, and its footstool, are simple rectangular blocks, not adorned in any way. On the seat, and hanging down the front, is a folded piece of black drapery. On it is placed the Book of the Gospels, and behind it are displayed the instruments of Christ's passion: a double-armed cross; a crown of thorns, looped around the upper arms of the cross; a spear, at the right; and, at the left, a sponge, tinged with red, attached to a hook at the end of a pole. Behind the throne, and partly concealed by it, are two cherubim, guardians of the throne, and in front of it at either side are Adam and Eve in attitudes of *proskynesis*, their hands covered by the folds of their garments.

[204]–5 The Weighing of Souls

PL. 368, 369, 386–390

The scene in which the records of the souls are weighed in the balance is placed below the throne of the Etimasia in the sharply curved rise of the vault above the crown of the eastern arch. Here space limitations have caused a considerable reduction in scale, which extends also to all elements of the damnation crowded into the lower right angle of the vault (PL. 369).

A balance is suspended from the foot of the throne, and under it stands a single nude soul, with arms folded, awaiting judgment. At the left are two angels, their arms filled with bundles of scrolls—the records of souls about to be judged. Below the right-hand scale, which is piled high with evil records, is a black devil, of whom very little more than the legs now remains; he attempts to add weight to his side by pulling the scale downward with a hooked stick. In the scale at the left there are now no traces of objects which could account for the seemingly greater weight on that side, for much of the paint in the area has been lost. A group of about nine nude souls (PL. 386), standing huddled together at the right, lends symmetry to the composition. They seem to be souls already found wanting and condemned, for around the neck of the one at the right is the same rope that binds together the necks of four other souls, still farther to the right (PL. 389), who are being conducted by black devils into the lake of fire at the far right. The devil who leads the string of captive souls has entered into the fire. The devils are now little more than sketches deeply incised into the plaster in very expressive and energetic strokes. Here and there a few brush strokes of a thin white paint indicate that originally the figures were more completely detailed in paint than they are now.

[204]–6 The Fiery Stream and the Lake of Fire

PL. 368, 369, 390, 391

Descending from the feet of Christ is a narrow stream of fire, which widens in the area above the southeastern pendentive into a body of flame engulfing all those who have been condemned. The imagery here derives not only from the words of judgment inscribed above the scene but also from other Biblical sources. The idea of a stream issuing from Christ's feet is found in the prophecy of Daniel (Dan. 7:10): "A fiery stream (ὁ ποταμὸς πυρός) issued and came forth from before him . . . the judgment was set, and the books were opened." Also relevant to the iconography of the theme are various passages in the twentieth chapter of the Apocalypse (20:10, 15), where the body of fire is described as a lake inhabited by the devil, the beast, and the false prophets, into which those who were not enrolled in the book of life were to be cast.

The red paint of the narrow stream, to the point where it widens into the lake, is relatively well preserved and retains details of the tongues of flame. The main body of fire, however, is so seriously impaired that very little now exists of the large number of figures, painted over the red, that were once depicted in the midst of the flames.

Where the stream approaches its full width (near center on PL. 390), faint traces of an angel can be seen. One of the principal figures in the fire, the angel seems to have been painted full length and at a somewhat larger scale than most of the other figures in this part of the composition. His head, in three-quarters view, faced downward and to the right; his right arm was raised high behind his head and held a lance, which in places is still faintly visible. The lance, directed downward and to the right, prodded a figure, now lost, toward a monstrous beast in the center front of the lake of fire. Only the front quarters of the beast, which face toward the left, are still preserved, and most of the head is lost; it seems to have had a sharply pointed beak, or lower jaw, long, white whiskers, and paws like those of a lion. Immediately above the beast are traces of black paint indicating that it may once have carried on its back a black, semihuman figure, possibly representing Hades, similar to those found on the backs of such monsters in other representations of the Last Judgment.

Along the upper edge of the lake of fire a number of other heads and parts of bodies can still be seen. Among these are the head and shoulders of what appears to be a second angel, looking down and to the left, and close by, to left and right, are other fragmentary heads. Of the two just to the right, one wears what seems to be a court official's widely flaring hat, similar to that of Metochites the Logothete [3], and the second wears a white, round-topped hat. In the upper right, to the right of an arm that seems to belong to the wearer of the second hat, are the remnants of seven or eight figures; one of these wears a hat similar to that of Cyrenius in The Enrollment for Taxation [101] and may therefore be another official, and below him is an old man wearing a tall, round-topped hat of white such as was worn by still other officials. To the right are three who seem to be attired in the black hoods and vestments of monks. In the only reasonably well preserved portion of the lake of fire, at the far right along the border of the arch, is the bust of an old man holding his hand over his mouth as the leaping flames threaten to engulf him; on his head is a large, white turban with bindings of black. In the lower left part of the sea of flames, immediately to the left of the devil who leads the souls into the fire, is the bust of a man wearing a sharply pointed hat. Another man, similar to him and more clearly visible, is found to the right of the devil; he overlaps still another of the same type near the paws of the monster. These may possibly represent the Jews.

In its iconography the portrayal of the fires of hell follows the precedent of mid-Byzantine Last Judgments, where one usually finds two angels goading the damned within the fires; many devils in the service of Hades, who sits on the back of a monster as on a throne; and a wide variety of categories of the damned: kings, queens, court officials, bishops, monks, barbarians, Jews, and infidels. In our painting the condemned seem to have been loosely distributed in groups according to categories.

Above the body of fire is a group of figures of the damned only half submerged in the flames (PL. 390). The right half of this group is very poorly preserved, and little more than the preparatory sketch can be seen. The figures in the left half are predominantly old, bearded men with scarfs worn over their heads and shoulders.

206

[205] The Land and Sea Giving Up Their Dead

PL. 368, 370, 392

Although the compositions in the four pendentives form entities in themselves, with one exception they are treated as continuations of the paintings in the domical vault and are not dissociated from them by borders of any kind, although the joints where the painted plaster of the pendentives overlaps the previously executed paintings above are now rather noticeable. The one pendentive composition that is distinctly separated from the vault painting is the northeastern one [207], whose background contrasts in color with that above.

The composition in the pendentive at the southwest (PL. 392), illustrating Apocalypse 20:13, depicts two angels blowing trumpets as the land and sea give up their dead. Across its center is the jagged shore line dividing the land above from the sea below. The land rises in a hill at the top center, and at the sides half-length flying angels, relieved against the sky, emphasize the symmetry of the composition. With both hands each angel holds a trumpet, a long, slightly curved instrument that resembles the Roman military tuba. The trumpet of the angel at the left extends downward to the edge of the sea and sounds the command for the creatures of the sea to disgorge their dead. The second angel directs his instrument toward the land, where three groups of the dead are being resurrected. The group at the left, barely distinguishable because of extensive loss of surface paint, rise out of the ground; the other groups stand erect in two sarcophagi. Some of the dead are shrouded and bound, while others seem to wear tunics, some with hoods.

The largest of the creatures of the sea, at the center of the triangular composition, is a dolphin-like fish, from whose mouth emerges the torso of a human body. On its back is what appears to be a shell with serrated edge, and from this rises a three-quarters-length nude female figure, probably Thalassa, the personification of the sea; her right arm is raised and her left, held down at her side, grasps the edge of the shell. Although her head is badly damaged, she can be seen to wear a headdress from which project two horns or crustacean's claws. To the left of the largest fish, and slightly above, are two smaller fish; a human head projects from the mouth of one, while the second disgorges a foot. Above the tail of the large fish is a fish of another type, giving up a human hand. Below, in the point of the pendentive, are four more fish, each disgorging parts of human figures: a long, slender fish with a long, pointed nose, and another fish beneath it, give up human feet; the other two give up heads.

[206] An Angel and a Soul

PL. 368, 370, 393

In the pendentive at the northwest are an angel and a small soul, both of whom stand in a rolling landscape in three-quarters view, facing to the right toward the throne of judgment. The angel, with his wings spread wide, stoops forward slightly and rests his right hand on the head of the nude soul; his left arm, now partly destroyed, was fully extended toward the right, and the palm of his hand was turned upward, as though in a gesture of offering; his head is tilted back. The soul, half the height of the angel, stands erect with both hands raised, palms upward, in supplication.

This theme has no known parallel in compositions of the Last Judgment, and it might well be an interpolation on the part of the painter; its identification and precise meaning are, therefore, uncertain. In the Third Preliminary Report on the frescoes in the Kariye Djami [1] it was proposed that the painting should be placed in context with the two subjects in the eastern pendentives, which relate to the parable of the Rich Man and the Beggar Lazarus, and interpreted as the soul of Lazarus being carried to Abraham's bosom in illustration of Luke 16:22. The attitudes of the figures, however, do not accord well with the text, for the soul is not being carried by a number of angels, as the narrative requires. It seems, rather, that the soul is being presented for final judgment under the protection and with the blessings of an angel. So it may be, as Professor Der Nersessian will suggest in Volume 4, that at the behest of Theodore Metochites the artist has here represented the Archangel Michael interceding on behalf of Metochites before the seat of judgment, as Metochites had requested in one of his literary compositions addressed to the Archangel.

[207] Lazarus the Beggar in Abraham's Bosom

PL. 368, 369, 394–396

The painting in the northeastern pendentive, representing Abraham in paradise with Lazarus the beggar at his bosom and other souls grouped about, is a continuation, in accordance with the iconographic traditions of the Last Judgment, of the scene of The Entry of the Elect into Paradise [210], which fills the lunette immediately to the left. However, just as in the parable the fate of Lazarus is contrasted with that of the rich man (Luke 16:19–31), the scene has been placed in antithesis to the scene of The Rich Man in Hell [208], which occupies the southeastern pendentive, at the opposite side of the arch of the bema.

The background of the painting, like that of the portrayal of paradise adjoining it at the left, was originally white but has now become a yellowish gray. Abraham is seated on a throne in the midst of trees and plants, his feet resting on a footstool. He faces the spectator, but his body turns somewhat to the right. His left hand is extended; his right holds the small figure of Lazarus the beggar, who sits in his lap. Represented as a young child in finest attire, Lazarus faces frontward, his right hand clutching a sprig of a plant, his left hand held palm outward before his breast. In the background behind the throne a group of souls, also represented as children, stand in serried ranks; they are dressed in short tunics with embroidered collars, cuffs, and hems. Some turn their heads toward their neighbors, and some in the front row hold sprigs in their right hands and gesticulate with their left.

[208] The Rich Man in Hell

PL. 369, 397

In the southeastern pendentive, separated from Abraham and Lazarus by the span of the bema arch, is the scene of the rich man suffering the torments of Hell. The nude rich man, seated amidst the swirling flames, turns to the left to face Abraham and raises his right hand to his mouth as he beseeches Abraham to send Lazarus "that he may dip the tip of his finger in water, and cool my tongue" (Luke 16:24). His left arm is stretched across his well-filled stomach in

1 D. O. Papers, 12, 257–59.

allusion to the daily sumptuous fare to which he was accustomed on earth. Below him in the sharp angle of the pendentive, at the very bottom of Hell, are two moneybags, and spilled out at his feet are a large number of golden coins.

While the flames surrounding the rich man extend upward to the very bottom of the Lake of Fire without being separated from it by a border, the two are quite separate iconographic elements of the Last Judgment and are distinct in both color and form. Where the two meet there is a joint in the painted plaster which indicates that the scene of The Rich Man in Hell was executed after the paintings above it.

In placing Abraham and the rich man at opposite sides of the arch of the bema, the artist has cleverly taken advantage of spatial relationships to illustrate both the statement that the rich man "seeth Abraham afar off" (Luke 16:23) and Abraham's reply to the plea of the suffering man: "between us and you there is a great gulf fixed: so that they which would pass from hence to you cannot; neither can they pass to us, that would come from thence" (Luke 16:26).

[209] The Torments of the Damned   PL. 398–403, 453

In the eastern side of the southern lunette, immediately to the right of the pendentive containing the figure of The Rich Man in Hell [208], are four monochromatic paintings depicting the torments of the damned, in which standing, nude men in tightly crowded groups are drawn in a variety of contorted poses. The panels are arranged in checkerboard fashion in two zones; they have no borders of any kind between them, their contrasting colors establishing their individual limits.

Both the background and the figures in the triangular painting at the upper left, now nearly effaced, were painted in yellow with some highlighting of the figures in white. A few bare legs and feet in the lower parts of the panel, especially in the corners, and an arm or two near the center can still be distinguished.

In the painting at the upper right the figures and the background are entirely black, without any traces of highlights. The figures are brush drawings rather carefully executed in deep black lines on the thinner, lighter black that is used in the backgrounds throughout the chapel. The modeling of the figures is hatched in with brush strokes of the deeper black. The heads are indistinct, but the three figures in the front rank, and the legs and feet of many others behind them, are clearly visible. Of the three who are fully exposed, the bearded old man at the left and the beardless man in the center are in nearly frontal pose, while the figure at the right turns his back to the spectator and his head to the left in profile.

Again, the painting at the lower left is executed in black and in the same technique. Here, however, the figures and the ground beneath their feet are covered with innumerable squiggles of white paint, which, it will be seen, represent worms. Four figures in the front rank are fully exposed to view: at the far left a youth, facing right in near-profile; in the center a bearded man and another youth, both frontally posed; and at the right a young man with his back turned to the spectator. The head of this last figure is drawn upside down, face outward, to indicate that he is bent violently backward.

The fourth painting, at the lower right, is executed throughout in very hot colors; there are several values of yellowish red, and the principal contours are rendered in deep red and the highlights in white. In contrast to its handling in the other paintings, the muscular structure of the figures is detailed, and it is so emphatically modeled that the men appear to be flayed.

Together the four panels comprise an element that usually appears in typically Byzantine compositions of the Last Judgment which date from the eleventh century onward. A series of usually rectangular, but sometimes round-headed, panels is placed in close proximity to the Lake of Fire; it sometimes includes representations of The Rich Man and Tartarus. Most of the early examples merely depict heads or skulls in small panels, usually in two zones, although half- and full-length figures are sometimes substituted; very seldom, however, are the subjects given such prominence or painted in such anatomical detail as they are in the Kariye Djami.

Some representations of The Torments of the Damned bear inscribed tituli which enable us to identify the analogous panels in the Kariye Djami as follows: at the upper left, in all probability, is "The Gnashing of Teeth" (ὁ βρυγμὸς τῶν ὀδόντων); at the upper right, "The Outer Darkness" (τὸ σκότος τὸ ἐξώτερον); at the lower left, "The Worm That Sleepeth Not" (ὁ σκώληξ ὁ ἀκοίμητος); and at the lower right, "The Unquenchable Fire" (τὸ πῦρ τὸ ἄσβεστον). These subjects are derived from Christ's descriptions of the penalties awaiting those who do iniquities in this world. According to Matthew (chapters 8, 22, 24, 25) such persons are to be "cast into outer darkness" where there shall be "weeping and gnashing of teeth." In Mark (chapter 9), on the other hand, there recurs, like a refrain, the dictum that they will be cast "into the fire that never shall be quenched: Where their worm dieth not, and the fire is not quenched."

[210] The Entry of the Elect into Paradise   PL. 368, 404–407

The Entry of the Elect into Paradise, the final element in the composition of the Last Judgment, was assigned the entire northern lunette and the pendentive adjoining it to the east. The painting in the lunette is divided into two equal parts. To the left, led by St. Peter, is the crowd of the Elect approaching the gate of paradise, at the center of the lunette, which is guarded by a cherub with drawn sword. The setting of the right half, plus that of the episode of Lazarus and Abraham in the pendentive to its right [207] — a luxuriant garden relieved against a white sky — represents paradise. Immediately to the right of the gate stands the figure of the Good Thief holding a wooden cross; he points the way to the enthroned Virgin, attended by two angels, in the space at the far right.

In the front rank of the Elect, where they are more or less fully exposed to view, are eight figures, moving in procession from left to right. Crowded into the background behind them are many others, some with garments partially exposed and others simply indicated by heads. As in so many of the paintings of the chapel, all that remains in the area of the heads is traces of the underpainting; and to the left, in the upper parts of some of the figures, is an area of total destruction, filled in by a patch. The figures of the Elect at the left can be classified, by means of their costumes, as follows: from left to right, there are a woman; a martyr; a holy monk; two bishops, one fully exposed and the other visible only at the shoulders; and two kings, probably David and Solomon in their role as prophets, one fully exposed and the other only partly visible. At the right end of the crowd, in the front rank, are three men clad in tunic and himation; three others, similarly clad, are partly visible between them. This group, headed by Peter, who is preparing to insert a key into the lock of the gate, represents the apostles and, in all probability, more prophets. Thus, all the groups of the Elect that were depicted in the composition of the domical vault, where they rode their own clouds, are here assembled to make their entry into paradise.

The gate of paradise is in the form of a stele, with molded base and coping in veined gray marble and a yellow shaft, which is meant to be understood as a door, since it has a lock near the left edge. The nimbed cherub, centered on the shaft, is painted in monochrome in earth reds; held vertically in his right hand is a sword, pointed downward.

The Good Thief, clad only in a loincloth, holds a simple wooden cross in his right hand. He stands in frontal pose with his head turned to the left toward the approaching figures of the Elect, and with his left hand he gestures toward the Virgin at the right.

The symmetrical composition of the enthroned Virgin flanked by two angels is severely marred by a wide area of total destruction, which was created by a great fissure in the wall passing vertically through this part of the lunette. Enough remains, however, to show the Virgin facing outward, with her hands raised before her, palms exposed, in an orant attitude similar to the one she assumes in other compositions of the Last Judgment. She sits on two cushions on a straight-backed throne, and her feet once rested on a footstool. The attendant angels at her sides are partially concealed by the back of the throne; each extends a hand and inclines his head toward the Queen of Heaven. All three figures bear yellow haloes.

The background of the left half of the lunette is black down to the level of the knees of the Elect, where it meets a zone of green, representing the ground. In the right half, the white of the background descends to the level of the base of the gate, a point well beneath the feet of the figures in paradise. Here it meets a narrow zone of green, which coincides with a strip of plaster added across the full width of the lunette in a secondary operation after completion of the painting above. Over the white background of paradise, trees, plants, and vines, some of the last bearing red blossoms, were painted in brownish greens of several values.

Dimensions

[204]–[208] (the composition in the domical vault). On longitudinal axis, from crown of eastern arch to crown of western arch, 4.77 m. (before the vault was fractured by earthquakes and its eastern part was displaced by 8 cm., this dimension was 4.69 m.). On transverse axis, from crown of northern arch to crown of southern arch, 4.69 m. Rise of vault including its pendentives, from cornice level to summit of vault, 4.22 m. Diameter of unfurled scroll of heaven, north to south, .86 m.; width of scroll in hands of angel, .75 m. Original diameter of mandorla of Christ, .98 m.

[209]: height of lunette from summit of arch to cornice, ca. 2.50 m.; width of paintings at base of lunette from arch at left to left side of window, including red borders, 1.51 m.

[210]: greatest height from top of red border to cornice, 2.50 m.; width at base including red borders, 4.74 m.

Colors

[204]–1. *Scroll:* light gray with stars of yellow originally gilded; sun, earth reds; moon, yellow. *Angel:* tunic, blue; himation, yellowish browns; halo, yellow bordered with brown and white.

[204]–2. *Christ:* tunic and himation, imitation cloth of gold—reddish yellow with dark red drawing and highlights of yellow ochre (originally gold leaf was applied over highlights); stigmata, black; halo, yellow (originally gold leaf) with borders of dark red and white; mandorla, concentric zones of blue, darkest in center and lightest at outer edge; arcs of "throne" and "footstool," pink. *Virgin:* tunic, blue; mantle and headdress, deep blue-violet. *John the Baptist:* tunic, yellowish brown; mantle, dark greenish brown. *Apostles:* all tunics blue except that of no. 3, which is red-violet; himatia, from left to right, *1*) red-violet, *2*) yellow, *3*) blue, *4*) green, *5*) red-violet, *6*) yellow, *7*) red-violet, *8*) green, *9*) yellow, *10*) red-violet, *11*) yellow, *12*) green; haloes, yellow bordered with dark red and white. *Archangels:* outer garments, red with yellow embroidery studded with pearls and dark red gems. *Angels:* tunics, blue; himatia, red-violet, blue, green, or yellow. *Benches of apostles:* yellow with dark red drawing, except front edges of footstools and receding ends of benches, which were red.

[204]-3. All clouds were originally yellowish gray. HIERARCHS *First and third bishops in front rank:* tunics, white with dark red clavi; chasubles, white with black crosses and gammas; omophoria, white with dark red crosses. *Bishop at center in front rank:* tunic, white with black clavi; stole (nearly effaced), ornamented in yellowish red; chasuble, white with dark red crosses and gammas; omophorion, white with black crosses. HOSIOI (left to right in front rank) violet tunic, brown mantle (effaced), and gray turban; gray tunic, brown mantle (effaced), black scapular and hood. WOMEN colors of surviving fragments lost. MARTYRS (left to right in front rank) red tunic with gold hem, blue chlamys over back, red boots; blue tunic with gold hem and collar, red chlamys bordered with gold, red boots; blue tunic visible at sleeves, red chlamys bordered with gold, red boots. APOSTLES (right to left in front rank) green himation; blue tunic and yellow himation; red-violet himation. Of two others in background, one at right wears violet himation, one at left, green himation. PROPHETS (right to left in front rank) himatia of red-violet; light green; red-violet; and yellowish green. *David* (in background at right): wears a crown and a blue chlamys.

[204]-4. *Throne and footstool:* yellow ochre, upper planes lightest, frontal planes medium, and receding planes darkest. *Drapery:* black. *Book:* covers, yellow; front and left edges, red. *Instruments of the Passion:* brown, except sponge, which is pink. *Cherubim:* wings, reddish brown with outlines of red. *Adam:* garments, yellow. *Eve:* garments, red.

[204]-5. *Souls:* reddish yellow with drawing in red and highlights in white. *Angel at left:* tunic, blue; himation, red-violet. *Second angel:* tunic, blue; himation, yellow. *Devils:* black with white-line drawing (incisions exposing white plaster) and a few highlights in white paint.

[204]-6. *Fire:* medium red with individual flames of a darker red and highlights of pink. See main text above for description of figures in the fire and indications of color.

[205]. *Angel at left:* tunic, blue; himation, red-violet; trumpet, brown. *Angel at right:* tunic, blue; himation (nearly destroyed), yellow; trumpet, brown. *Sarcophagi:* red-violet. *The dead:* monochromatic painting in yellowish green (perhaps terre-verte). *Land:* yellow. *Sea:* bluish gray, with waves indicated in very light blue. *Fish:* bellies, lavender and white; backs, yellow and brown; shell carried on back of largest fish, lavender outside and brown inside; Thalassa, yellow and

brown underpainting; parts of human figures in mouths of fish, flesh-colored.

[206]. *Angel:* tunic, blue with brown clavus; himation, yellow; wings, brown; nimbus, yellow. *Soul:* flesh colors. *Landscape:* yellow and brown.

[207]. *Abraham:* tunic, blue with dark blue clavus; himation, blue-violet; cushion, red; throne and footstool, yellow upper faces and red vertical faces. *Souls:* short tunics, gray (with allover pattern of tiny blue and red fleurs-de-lis and in some cases clusters of three red dots) with yellow and red collars and hems in imitation of gold embroidery; boots, blue. *Background:* white. *Trees and plants:* dark green and brown.

[208]. *Fire:* slightly bluish red, with flames highlighted in pink and white. *Rich man:* monochromatically painted in browns over red, with some white highlights. *Moneybags:* yellow highlighted in white, with brown thongs. *Coins:* yellow ochre.

[209]. See main text above for indications of color.

[210]. THE ELECT (from left to right) *Woman at far left:* garments, red. *Martyr:* tunic, dark red with gold embroidery; chlamys, blue with gold-embroidered edges. *Monk:* tunic, black (blue?); mantle, dark brownish green with yellow highlights. *First bishop:* sticharion, light yellow; chasuble, light violet with patterns of crosses and gammas in dark red-violet; omophorion, yellow with black crosses. *Second bishop* (mostly concealed): chasuble, light yellow; omophorion, light red-violet with dark violet crosses. *First king-prophet:* tunic and boots, dark red ornamented with gold; chlamys, green with gold tablion and borders. *Second king-prophet* (mostly concealed): chlamys, dark red. *Three apostles or prophets in front rank:* tunics, blue; himatia (from left to right), yellow, red-violet, and yellow. *Three others* (partly exposed between them): himatia, yellow, green, and violet. PARADISE *Gate:* base and coping, blue-gray; door, yellow. *Cherub and sword:* monochromatically painted in reds with white highlights. *Good Thief:* flesh, yellow, green, brown, and red; loincloth, very light brown with highlights of gray; cross, brown; halo, yellow. *Virgin:* tunic, blue; mantle and headdress, dark red-violet, latter decorated with golden star at forehead; halo, yellow. *Throne:* back, red; seat and footstool, yellow and brown; cushion, red, in front of another that may have been green originally. *Angel at left:* tunic, blue; himation, yellow; wings, brown; halo, yellow. BACKGROUNDS left half of lunette, black above a wide band of green; right half of lunette, white above a narrow band of green.

THE COMPOSITION IN THE DOME

[211]–[223]

The Virgin and Child and Attendant Angels   PL. 408–425

IN THE MEDALLION:

M(ήτ)ηρ Θ(εο)ῦ *Mother of God*

ABOVE EACH OF THE TWELVE ANGELS:

῎Αγγελ(ος) Κ(υρίο)υ *Angel of the Lord*

The major themes in the upper zones of the western half of the parecclesion deal with the Virgin and Old Testament subjects which prefigured her role in the divine plan of salvation. They are centered on the crowning feature of the chapel, the great dome of the western bay, in which are represented the Mother of God and the Christ Child and their celestial court of angels and archangels.

The dome spans the full width of the parecclesion. It sits on a high drum pierced by twelve windows; between the windows rise twelve ribs, which converge in the summit of the dome on a medallion with a rainbow border, containing busts of the Virgin and the infant Christ. Above the windows, in the triangular spaces between the ribs, are twelve "Angels of the Lord." The ribs are brilliantly ornamented with a variety of motifs and patterns, no two alike, and the faces of the window openings, their reveals, and a narrow base around the dome, immediately above the cornice, are decorated with ornaments that differ in character from those of the ribs. All these ornaments are described below.

The medallion of the Virgin and Child [211] is very similar in type to the mosaic medallion in the summit of the northern dome of the inner narthex [51]. The Virgin supports the half-length figure of the Christ Child, who must be thought of as seated on her lap; her left hand rests on his shoulder, and she holds her right hand before his breast. Holding out his hands nearly symmetrically at both sides, the Child makes a sign of blessing with each. Both figures are in frontal pose, but the heads are turned slightly to the left.

The Virgin is clad in a deep blue-violet tunic and mantle, and her head is covered by a maphorion of the same color. The maphorion is ornamented by a narrow golden border at the Virgin's face and neck; the mantle, where it drapes over her left shoulder, is likewise bordered with gold but also has a golden fringe. At each shoulder, and again in the center of the headdress, is a golden eight-pointed star with a dot at the center. Beneath the headdress the Virgin wears a very light blue kerchief, which covers her hair and frames the upper part of her face. The

213

Christ Child wears a tunic and a himation, both represented as cloth of gold; a considerable amount of gilding still remains in a strip at the bottom of the medallion.

The frame around the medallion is so executed as to produce a remarkable prismatic effect and a sense of plastic modeling so strong that it gives the false impression of a molded surface. The frame is constructed of five concentric, interlocking rows of diamond shapes, with rows of half-diamonds along the two edges. The colors used are detailed below, in the color notes.

The twelve angels and archangels, the courtiers in attendance upon the heavenly queen, stand in a variety of poses in a zone of green above the windows of the dome. In his right hand each angel but one holds a staff studded at the top with five pearls; the archangel in the center of the east side [212] holds a staff surmounted by a small labarum, on which the trisagion is inscribed. The four archangels, in addition, hold orbs in their left hands. Two of the orbs ([212], [222]) are transparent, support a small cross, and are inscribed with a small letter chi. The other two orbs ([217], [218]) are less transparent — [217] is nearly opaque — and each has a large chi within four bars that form a square; originally they, too, were probably surmounted by crosses.

The angels are clothed in brilliantly colored court attire, consisting in part of garments of a ceremonial, military origin which are suitable to the angels' function as a royal guard of honor. Six items make up their costumes. Each wears a fillet bound around the hair, ornamented red boots as an imperial badge, and as an undergarment a long, tight-sleeved tunic richly embroidered at cuffs, collar, and hem. The tunic is always partly exposed in the right sleeve and in its lower parts, below the knees; sometimes it is also visible at the neckline. As an outer garment, all angels wear the imperial chlamys. Over the long tunic and beneath the chlamys, seven angels ([212], [214], [216]–[219], [222]) wear the knee-length military tunic, with loose, elbow-length sleeves or no sleeves at all ([217]), which is usually ornamented at the collar and hem. The outermost tunic, long or short, is gathered at the waist by a concealed girdle and in all but two instances is also bound by a sash that passes around the body under the arms.

The chlamys is worn by the angels in a variety of ways but is nearly always fastened with a knot instead of the usual fibula. It may be tied at the right shoulder, so that the right arm and breast are left free; it often is draped over the left shoulder, falls diagonally across the left arm, and is brought around the right thigh to be held by the left hand. In other cases it is knotted at the center of the breast, and it may have been slipped around to hang almost entirely down the back.

The ornaments of the ribs are fully as colorful and varied as the angels and demonstrate the painter's great invention and versatility in avoiding repetition. Even within a single rib, which may appear to be composed by the rhythmical repetition of a single motif, the painter did not limit himself to mechanical duplication but altered the forms slightly from unit to unit, varied the rhythm of the color repeats, or rearranged the coloring of different parts of the plant or flower forms which constitute the motif. There is abundant evidence that stencils were not used. As is noted below in the technical discussion (p. 301), the plastering and painting of the dome was carried out in three horizontal zones. In some of the ribs the colors of one zone fail to match exactly those above or below; there are also subtle changes in the rhythm of the repeats from zone to zone within a single rib.

The ribs average about 25 cm. in width; the continuous bands of ornament on them, about 19 cm. wide, are bordered at each side by a narrow white line and by the earth-red border that frames all the structural forms of the vaults. The ornamental motifs fall into several general categories. By far the most prevalent are those whose composition was inspired by plant and flower forms (e.g., the ribs to the right of [213], [215]–[217], [221], [222]). Others intersperse flower forms in an interlacing of vines [212], or within the square frames provided by an angular interlacing of ribbons [220]; still another motif combines masks with forms derived from plants and flowers [219]. Three ribs employ variants of scale patterns combined with foliate or floral forms ([214], [218], [223]). The forms that are based on plant life are, in a sense, abstractions, for no individual plant or flower is clearly recognizable, and, indeed, it is often difficult to determine whether it is a leaf or a flower that is the source of inspiration of a given motif. Partly because of the marked differences in character of the motifs but also because of variations in the colors of the backgrounds on which they were painted, some of the ribs stand in striking contrast to the others. The colors used in the backgrounds and in the motifs of all the ribs are recorded below in the color notes.

The arched openings of the windows (PL. 409, 410) are framed by rather wide ornamental bands in grisaille, which contrast strongly with the colorful decoration of the ribs between them. The type of ornament is that used in the mosaics for decorating the reveals of the windows in the outer narthex (PL. 334), in the domes of the inner narthex (PL. 58, 61–64, 67), and in the tympana of the nave (PL. 8), that is, a running pattern of strapwork-like interlaces. These bands are painted in yellow on a gray background and are outlined in red. While the motifs differ in detail from one window to the next, all are composed of interlacing scrolls or rinceaux, and in some a rinceau is interlaced with a zigzag strip. This type of ornament is used again in the reveals of the windows in the southern lunettes of the parecclesion; in fact it seems to have been the favored type for window reveals, as is further evidenced by its use in the windows of other parts of the Kariye Djami as well as other Byzantine churches of the period. Its use as a facing around the windows of the dome is exceptional.

In the reveals of the dome windows variations of the ribbon meander pattern used on the face of the conch of the apse (PL. 340, 341) were substituted for the strapwork interlaces. The basic design was given a different treatment from window to window, either in pattern, in color arrangement, or in scale of parts. Originally the dome was girdled by a chain of oak tie beams at the springing line of the arches. These beams were cut at a later date, but their stumps are still visible where they emerge from the masonry. The original window frames, later replaced by the existing reinforced-concrete frames, were placed against the outer faces of the tie beams. Thus the original reveals of the windows were much shallower than they are now; the meander pattern extended only to the line of the outer faces of the tie beams.

Finally, around the base of the dome just above the cornice, where it is quite invisible from the floor, is a continuous ornamental band composed of a running motif of gray and white fleurs-de-lis painted on a black background.

Dimensions

Diameter of dome, ca. 4.70 m.; height of dome from top of dome to floor, 11.18 m.; width of ribs, ca. 25 cm.; diameter of medallion including border, 1.10 m.; average height of angels from top of head to level of feet, ca. 1.45 m.

Colors

[211]. VIRGIN all garments, dark blue-violet; maphorion, bordered with gold; mantle, bordered and fringed with gold over left shoulder; stars at shoulders and above forehead, gold. CHRIST tunic and himation, yellow paint highlighted with gold leaf, and drawing in reddish brown. BORDER successive concentric rows of diamonds colored, from inner row to outer, in *1*) very dark blue-violet (half-diamonds); *2*) dark earth red; *3*) a light value of the same red; *4*) white (center row); *5*) light green; *6*) a dark value of the same green; *7*) very dark blue-violet (half-diamonds).

[212]–[223]: fillets bound around heads, light blue;

wings, dark brown outer feathers highlighted with yellow, and blue under feathers highlighted with white; staffs, dark red; boots, red and yellow; haloes, yellow fields, originally gilded, and brown and white borders. [212]. *Undertunic* (visible in lower sleeve at left and below knees): blue; gold-embroidered cuff and hem, latter set with pearls and red and green gems. *Short tunic:* light red-violet with light blue hem; gold embroidery down front, set with pearls and red and green gems. *Sash:* gold bordered with red. *Chlamys:* green with gold tablion. *Orb:* transparent, showing colors behind it; surmounted by small gold cross; inscribed with chi. *Labarum:* red, inscribed with trisagion and fringed at bottom in white. [213]. *Undertunic* (visible only in lower sleeve at left): blue; cuff, gold. *Long outer tunic:* very light yellow with shadows of dull brownish green; gold at hem and in wide collar. *Sash:* dark blue. *Chlamys:* dark blue-violet shot with light blue; gold tablia. [214]. *Undertunic* (visible in sleeve and breast at left, and below knees): earth red; cuffs, collar, and hem, gold. *Short tunic:* light red-violet with stripe and fringed hem embroidered in gold. *Chlamys:* green, with gold stripe.
[215]. *Undertunic* (visible in lower sleeves and hem): blue; cuffs and hem, gold. *Short tunic:* green; gold collar. *Sash:* blue. *Chlamys:* red-violet with gold tablion (visible under arm at left). [216]. *Undertunic* (visible in lower sleeve at left, below neck, and below knees): earth red; cuff, collar, and hem, gold. *Short tunic:* light red-violet with gold collar and hem. *Sash:* light blue. *Chlamys:* blue (lapis lazuli) field ornamented with gold fleurs-de-lis and gold tablia. [217]. *Undertunic* (visible in sleeve and shoulder at left, and below knees): light blue; cuff, wide collar over shoulder, and hem, gold. *Short, sleeveless tunic:* light green; hem, white ornamented with blue figures; exposed ends of narrow green girdle at waist terminate in red tassels. *Sash:* red. *Chlamys:* earth red with gold tablion. *Orb:* light bluish gray; inscribed with yellow chi framed on four sides by yellow bars; originally surmounted by small cross (?). *Anaxyrides* (visible above boots): blue.
[218]. *Undertunic* (visible in lower sleeve at left and below knees): dark earth red; cuff and hem, gold. *Short tunic:* light red-violet with lighter red-violet hem and gold cuff and collar. *Chlamys:* dull earth green with blue tablion. *Orb:* like that of [217] but giving effect of greater translucence. [219]. *Undertunic* (visible in lower sleeve at left, at neck, and below knees): dark blue; cuff, hem, and collar, gold. *Short tunic:* light greenish yellow; hem, lighter value of same color; cuff and collar, gold. *Sash:* blue. *Chlamys:* dark blue-violet with gold-embroidered tablia. [220]. *Undertunic* (visible only in lower sleeve at left): earth red; cuff, gold. *Long outer tunic:* dark yellow; collar and hem, gold. *Sash:* red. *Chlamys:* dark blue with gold tablion. [221]. *Undertunic* (visible only in lower sleeves): blue; cuffs, gold. *Long outer tunic:* light red-violet; collar and hem, gold. *Sash:* blue. *Chlamys:* light green with gold

tablia. [222]. *Undertunic* (visible in lower sleeve at left, around neck, and below knees): dark blue-violet shot with light blue; cuff and hem, gold; collar, gold and light blue. *Short tunic:* light green with gold hem and collar. *Sash:* blue. *Chlamys:* earth red with gold tablion. *Orb:* transparent; like that of [212]. [223]. *Undertunic* (visible only in lower sleeve at left): light blue; cuff, gold. *Long outer tunic:* like that of [213] but with brown shadows. *Sash:* blue. *Chlamys:* dark blue-violet shot with light blue; decorated with gold tablion.

THE ORNAMENTS OF THE RIBS (each number refers to the rib to the right of the angel bearing that number):
[212]. *Background:* black with some azurite overlaid. *Intertwining vines:* lighter of two sets, yellow and dark violet; darker set, green. *Flower forms:* red, yellow, and green. [213]. *Background:* yellow. *Plant forms:* blue, red, and green. [214]. *Background:* light gray. *Plant forms:* green, red, blue, dark violet, and occasionally yellow. Although there is a tendency to repeat in groups of three, repeats are not consistent. *Large scales between plant forms:* painted in three concentric zones; each scale is in three different values of one color, darkest at center, lightest at outside. Scales are in red, a color like raw sienna, and green.
[215]. *Background:* black. *Leaf forms:* mostly red and green, occasionally blue. Greens tend to be shaded with blue. [216]. *Background:* yellow. *Plant forms:* colored as in [213], but forms are different. [217]. *Background:* black overlaid with azurite. *Plant forms:* red, green, yellow. Note that decoration of this rib begins at top with mask like those of rib [219] (see PL. 411). [218]. *Background:* black. *Plant forms:* red and green. *Scales:* two-lobed; each represented in either three or four values of a single color. Scales repeated in groups of four in the sequence green, red, yellow, red. [219]. *Background:* black overlaid with azurite. *Masks* (connected by plant forms that issue from their mouths): yellow. *Plant forms:* green, red, blue, and yellow. Note: all masks were damaged by yellow daub, which has been removed. [220]. *Background:* yellow. *Two ribbons* run length of rib and cross one another repeatedly, forming the sides of squares. They are seen in perspective: one ribbon is light blue on one side and light green on reverse; the other ribbon is red on one side and light green on reverse. *Flower forms* (in centers of squares): some parts red, others green or blue.
[221]. *Background:* black. *Pattern:* similar to but not exactly like that of [215], where motifs are on a larger scale. *Plant forms:* red, green, yellow, and, to a lesser extent, blue. [222]. *Background:* yellow. *Plant forms:* red, green, blue. [223]. *Background:* black. *Pattern:* similar to but not exactly like that of [218]. Double-lobed scales intended to be alternately red and green, but scheme not consistently carried out. Zones of each scale in three values of one color. *Leaf forms:* red, green, and blue, but not in consistent repeats.

[224]–[227]

Four Hymnographers

[224] Northeastern pendentive

TITULUS:

ʿΟ ἅγ(ιος) ʼΙω(άννης) ὁ Δαμασκηνός   *St. John Damascene*

ON SCROLL:

Ποία τοῦ | βίου τρυ|φ[ὴ δι]|αμένει | λύ[πης] ⟨ἀμέτοχος⟩ . . .
*What joy of life remains without its share of sorrow . . . (John Damascene,
incipit of "Idiomela for the Funeral Service," Migne, Pat. Gr., 96, col. 1368)*

[225] Southeastern pendentive

TITULUS:

ʿΟ ἅγ(ιος) Κοσμᾶς ὁ Ποιητής   *St. Cosmas the Poet*

[226] Southwestern pendentive

TITULUS:

ʿΟ ἅγ(ιος) ʼΙωσὴφ ὁ Ποιητής   *St. Joseph the Poet*

ON SCROLL:

ʿΙλαστήρι|ον τοῦ κόσ|μου χαῖρε, | ἄχραντε | Δέσποινα . . .
*Propitiation of the world, hail, spotless Virgin . . . (Joseph Hymnographer,
from Ode 4, "Canon for the Akathistos Hymn," Migne, Pat. Gr., 105, col.
1021)*

[227] Northwestern pendentive

TITULUS:

ʿΟ ἅγ(ιος) Θεοφάνης   *St. Theophanes*

ON CODEX:

Εἰς γῆν | ἀπεστρά(φημεν,) | παρα|βάντες | (τοῦ) Θ(εο)ῦ ⟨τὴν ἐντολὴν
τὴν ἔνθεον⟩ . . .
*We were turned back to the earth after having transgressed God's divine com-
mandment . . . (from the* Theotokion *of Ode VI of the "Canon for the Funeral Service for Laymen,"* Εὐχολόγιον τὸ Μέγα, *ed. N. P. Papadopoulos
[Athens, 1927], p. 305)*

In the pendentives below the dome of the western bay four poet-hymnographers are portrayed
in the act of composition: St. John Damascene (northeast); St. Cosmas the Poet (southeast);
St. Joseph the Poet (southwest); and St. Theophanes (northwest). In their poses and in the
settings in which they are placed they are strongly reminiscent of the seated portraits of the
Four Evangelists which are so frequently found in pendentives. Each poet, dressed in monastic

garb, bends toward his work amidst the furnishings and materials of a scriptorium. Fanciful architecture of a kind that appears in many of the scenes in the Kariye Djami to suggest interior settings is used at each side, together with an occasional tree, to fill out the upper angles of the pendentives. The figures, slightly larger than life-size, are arranged so that St. John Damascene and St. Cosmas are paired in the eastern pendentives and face inward toward one another, while the two at the west turn their backs on one another but face toward their companions at the opposite side. Thus the entire group is given an eastward orientation in conformity with the structural and iconographic orientation of the parecclesion as a whole. The arrangement is meaningful also in regard to historical considerations, for it places at the east, in the more honored positions, the two earlier monks, who were not only close friends and contemporaries but even foster brothers.

Before the individual paintings are described in detail, something should be said about the four poets and especially about their inscriptions, for it is through the texts of the works they are composing that we find an explanation of their contribution to the iconographic program of the parecclesion.

John of Damascus occupies the most favored of the four positions as befits his great fame as a theologian, defender of orthodoxy during the first phases of iconoclasm, and writer of hymns. The hymn he is writing can be identified from the five lines inscribed on the narrow piece of parchment that lies before him on the lectern. While the inscription (PL. 436 *a*) is imperfectly preserved, its first and second lines, above the upper fold in the parchment, and its fourth line, above the second fold, can be deciphered with certainty on close inspection; the third line retains only its initial letter and the fifth only the first two letters. This evidence is sufficient to establish the text of the inscription as the *incipit* of John's "Idiomela for the Funeral Service," which reads: "What joy of life remains without its share of sorrow . . . ."

Cosmas the Poet, who occupies the southeastern pendentive, should be identified as the St. Cosmas who is also known as *o Melodos, Hierosolymitanus,* and bishop of Maiuma. He was the younger of two men named Cosmas who bore close relationships to John Damascene and who are sometimes confused with one another in the literary sources. The elder Cosmas was a learned monk from Sicily who was redeemed from Saracen slavery in Damascus by the father of John Damascene; the father entrusted Cosmas with the education of his son John and of his adopted son, the younger Cosmas. The younger Cosmas and his foster brother John are said by the Constantinopolitan Synaxarion to have embraced the monastic life together at the monastery of St. Saba in Jerusalem, where both were inspired to sing of the Godhead and the Theotokos in many troparia and canons. In the painting, Cosmas, who is about to dip his pen and begin a composition, holds an open, uninscribed codex in his lap (PL. 436 *b*).

In the southwestern pendentive, facing toward the pair at the east, is the ninth-century monk-hymnographer Joseph. Of Sicilian origin, he fled from the Arabs to the Peloponnesus and found his way, via Thessalonike, to Constantinople; sent to Rome on a mission, he was captured by pirates and taken to Crete, whence he went to Jerusalem; there he is said to have written most of his hymns. In the painting, he holds a scroll before him and reads the lines he has written. The five-line inscription (PL. 436 *c*), which is entirely legible though now effaced to a considerable extent, records one of the verses from the fourth ode of his "Canon for the Akathistos Hymn." In translation it reads: "Propitiation of the world, hail, spotless Virgin . . . ."

The last of the hymnographers, active, like Joseph, in the ninth century, is Theophanes Graptos, so called because he was branded on the face, along with his brother Theodore, in 836 in the renewal of iconoclastic persecutions under the Emperor Theophilus. With his brother he had taken orders in his youth at the monastery of St. Saba in Jerusalem, where he became a pupil of Michael Syncellos. In 813 he set out with his master and his brother on a mission to Constantinople; there the three received the hospitality of the monastery of the Chora (Kariye Djami), which was traditionally granted to Palestinian monks on their visits to the city. Upon the triumph of orthodoxy in 843, Theophanes was appointed Metropolitan of Nicaea. Two years later, at the age of 67, he died; he was buried in the monastery of the Chora, where his old master, Michael Syncellos, presided as abbot. Theophanes is depicted in the act of writing in an open codex, which rests on his left knee. On the verso he has written two lines, and he is finishing a three-line inscription on the recto (PL. 436 d). These correspond to the first two verses of the *Theotokion* that follows the sixth ode of his "Canon for the Funeral Service for Laymen": "We were turned back to the earth after having transgressed God's divine commandment . . . ."

The three poetic works which the inscriptions identify for us appear to establish a two-fold relationship between the hymnographers and the iconographic program of the parecclesion, with respect, first, to the function of the chapel and, second, to the scenes in the vaults around the dome of the second bay. It is noteworthy that two of the inscriptions—those of John Damascene and of Theophanes—quote from works composed for funeral services and thus remind us of the mortuary character of the chapel. The third inscription, taken from Joseph's "Canon for the Akathistos Hymn," hails the spotless Virgin and thus relates to the cycle of Old Testament scenes ([228]–[236]) allegorically prefiguring the Virgin, which fills the areas surrounding the dome and the four hymnographers. The text of Theophanes, even though it derives from a funeral hymn, makes explicit reference to one of these scenes—that depicting Jacob's Ladder [228], which is situated immediately to the right of his portrait; if the inscribed portion of the hymn were to be extended to include the succeeding verses the significance of the Ladder as a means of typifying the Virgin would be made clear. The pertinent verses read as follows: "But through thee, O Virgin, we have been raised from earth to heaven, having shaken off the decay of death" (διὰ σοῦ δὲ Παρθένε πρὸς οὐρανόν, ἐκ γῆς ἀνυψώθημεν, τὴν φθορὰν τοῦ θανάτου ἐκτινάξαντες). Similarly, were we to consider the verses that succeed those inscribed on the scroll of the hymnographer Joseph, we would again find the Ladder of Jacob interpreted as a type of the Virgin—the link between earth and heaven: "Hail, O Ladder that hast raised us all from earth through Grace; hail, veritable Bridge leading all that praise thee from death to life" (Χαῖρε, κλίμαξ γῆθεν πάντας ἀνυψώσασα χάριτι. Χαῖρε, ἡ γέφυρα ὄντως ἡ μετάγουσα ἐκ θανάτου πάντας πρὸς ζωὴν τοὺς ὑμνοῦντάς σε).

[224] St. John Damascene   PL. 426, 427, 436 a

The monk's habit worn by John Damascene consists of a tunic, scapular, and mantle and a turban-like headdress, which distinguishes him from his companions; he is also unique in being unshod. The tunic is long and loose and has wide sleeves. The scapular, which is visible only above and below the extended right arm, is a sleeveless, knee-length garment, open at the sides, which is put on over the head and falls from the shoulders in front and behind. Two black cords, with which he could draw his mantle about him, hang loose in great loops around his knees; they are understood to be attached to the lower corners of the mantle, on which he sits, and they converge at a point behind his right arm, pass through a series of ringlets, and disappear under the mantle, presumably passing then around his neck. The turban, wound in folds around his head, is so arranged that a notched end emerges and hangs down over his right ear.

He is seated in a chair with a high, curving back, resembling the kind so often assigned to the Evangelist John in portraits of the seated Evangelists, and his feet are firmly planted on a low footstool. He concentrates on sharpening the reed pen in his left hand with a knife whose blade curves at the point. Beside him is a low work table with rather wide rails showing faint traces of openings that give access to a lower shelf. On the table is a double lectern which has a curiously formed base; beside the lectern is a box without a lid, divided into unequal compartments — a container for red and black inks. Two other scribe's instruments are faintly visible on the table: a pair of dividers and a flat blade, one side curved and sharpened for making erasures and the other straight, with a long, pointed extension used for pricking the blank pages in preparation for the ruling of guide lines.

[225] St. Cosmas the Poet

PL. 428, 429, 435, 436 b

The portrait of the poet Cosmas is rather well preserved, especially in the area of the head; the features retain most of their surface colors. Cosmas wears a rather long, heavy beard, of very dark brown highlighted with blue, which divides at the end into two points. He is clad in a tunic of the type worn by the others. The front of his scapular emerges from beneath his mantle at the chest, is hidden under the codex in his lap, and reappears between his knees. It is not clear whether his headdress is the conventional cowl of a monk or whether it is a large scarf drawn over the head and wound about the neck to form a collar. In any case, it differs from the scapular in color and seems not to be attached to the scapular as the usual cowl is. On his feet Cosmas wears pointed black slippers.

Unlike the other hymnographers, who sit on chairs, Cosmas is seated on a low bench, resembling a work table, with openings in the visible rail giving access to a lower shelf; his feet rest on a low footstool. Beside him is a table with a lower shelf. On the table is a long box with two compartments, the larger one containing a pen and the smaller one, into which the hymnographer is about to dip his pen, filled with ink. There are also on the table a round ink pot, perhaps for red ink, a knife similar to the one held by John, and an instrument with a wooden handle and a semicircular blade, perhaps used for scraping, like one that lies on Theophanes' table. On the shelf beneath the table is a flask partially filled with red ink.

[226] St. Joseph the Poet

PL. 430, 431, 436 c

Although the head of Joseph, like much of the rest of the figure, is preserved only in the underpainting, it can be seen that his beard and hair are rather short. Unlike his companions, he has dispensed with his mantle, so that his scapular and tunic are revealed. The two aprons of the scapular fall from his shoulders in front and behind and are held together under the arms by straps. Attached at the back of the neck opening and hanging down his back is a hood, of the same color as the scapular. His pose is such that only one foot is visible; on it he wears a pointed black slipper.

He sits on a cushioned chair with a low, straight back and curved arms; under the seat is a shelf accessible through small rectangular openings at the side. His feet rest on a polygonal footstool. Rising from the table at the left is a lectern, on which lies an open codex; on the pages of this book there was once an inscription, but it is now entirely illegible. On the lower right corner of the table, partly concealed by Joseph's scroll, is a box with two compartments, one for pens and the other for ink. Nearby is a knife with a slightly curved and pointed blade. To the left is a round ink container, and beyond this is a pair of dividers. Just above the tightly curled end of the scroll, and now barely visible, are the traces of two quill pens, and to the right of the vertical support for the lectern are a large curved blade and another pair of dividers. Finally, at the right end of the table two doors of a cupboard below the table top stand open to reveal two scrolls, one partly furled, the other open; in the opening in the long side of the table are two flasks.

[227] St. Theophanes

PL. 432, 433, 434, 436 d

The best preserved of all four paintings in the pendentives is that of Theophanes. He is given a rather massive head with blond hair and a wavy, pointed beard of moderate length. Like his companions, he wears a long, loose-sleeved tunic; a scapular, to which a hood is attached; a mantle, which is fastened with a button at the breast; and pointed black slippers.

He sits on a cushioned chair with a low, straight back, and his feet rest on a footstool. The table beside him is much like that of St. Cosmas, but larger. On the table top is a pen-and-ink box with three compartments, the long central one containing a pen and the two smaller ones at the ends filled with black ink. Another box, with two compartments, is at the upper right corner, its small compartment filled with red ink. A circular inkwell is at the lower right corner. Between these last two containers lies a scraping knife with a short semicircular blade and a wooden handle, similar to one that appears on the table of St. Cosmas. The table has a lower shelf accessible through two openings in the long side and one in the end. In the latter is a flask partly filled with red ink. In one of the side openings is a bundle of tightly furled scrolls, and another scroll, partly open, lies on the table.

Dimensions

The circumference of the circle formed by the tops of the four pendentives measures ca. 15.40 m. Each pendentive measures ca. 3.85 m. along the curve of each of its three sides, and the height along its axis is ca. 3.18 m. The seated figures average ca. 1.33 m. in height from head to foot.

Colors

[224]: tunic, light red-violet; scapular, lapis lazuli; mantle, yellowish green with yellow highlights; draw cords, black; headdress, light blue; furniture, yellow on lighted and reddish brown on shaded faces; inkwell, brown; knife blades, blue-gray; architecture, grays and browns with columns of red-violet (in building at left) and brownish green (in building at right); draperies over roofs, red.

[225]: tunic, blue-gray; scapular, originally light red-violet, now showing much of blue-gray underpainting of tunic beneath it; mantle, yellowish green with gray highlights; headdress, lapis lazuli; shoes, black; codex, gray pages and red edges; furniture, writing instruments, and architecture, similar to those of [224].

[226]: tunic, now largely underpainting of brown umber, but this was originally covered with greenish brown (as in area on hip at right where surface paint is preserved); scapular and hood, now largely black, but

traces of lapis lazuli indicate they were originally blue; shoe, black; scroll and pages of codex, gray, latter edged with red; furniture, writing instruments, and architecture, similar to those of [224].

[227]: tunic, blue-gray with drawing and shadows in black and highlights in white; scapular and hood, dark yellowish brown; mantle, dark blue-violet with drawing in black; shoes, black; furniture and writing instruments, similar to those in other three pendentives but in much better state of preservation; building at left, bluish violet of a value comparable to lightest colors in mantle of Theophanes, with bluish gray column, reddish yellow cap and base, dark green and dark red curtains, and two yellow and brown corbels on roof;

building at right, dark bluish gray with red draperies hanging from roof.

N.B. Furniture in all four pendentives is set in a zone of green, and lower points of pendentives, below footstools, are ornamented with foliate motifs similar to some that appear in ribs of dome (e.g., [217]). Above crowns of northern and southern arches, between pendentives, cross-axis of bay is marked by two pin-wheel ornaments, each ca. 30 cm. in diameter, composed of a star pattern of sixteen points, painted in yellow, green, and red, in three concentric zones, all within a white circle; above arches on longitudinal axis are medallions containing busts of Melchizedek [239] and Christ [240].

OLD TESTAMENT PREFIGURATIONS
OF THE VIRGIN

Five Old Testament subjects, some in more than one episode, are illustrated in nine pictorial units in the arches and lunettes below the dome of the western bay. The subjects depicted in these areas were selected from a larger number of Old Testament events that were traditionally interpreted as divine manifestations symbolizing, or prefiguring, the Incarnation through the instrumentality of the Virgin Mary. Thus, the objects through which God made manifest his presence—for example, Jacob's ladder reaching to heaven; the bush that burned but was not consumed; the ark of the covenant, in which the God of Israel dwelt; etc.—were regarded as types of the Virgin. Analogies and interpretations of this kind abound in the liturgy, hymnography, and homilies of the church, and in these was found the literary authority for the development of an iconography that would illustrate the typology of the Virgin, as exemplified by the group of paintings listed below.

The cycle starts with the northern lunette of the western bay and proceeds in a clockwise direction along the soffits of the arches and the lunettes beneath the dome; the paintings will be described in that order, under the following headings:

[228] Jacob's Ladder; Jacob Wrestling with the Angel
[229], [230] Moses and the Burning Bush:
    [229] Moses before the Bush; Moses Removes His Sandals
    [230] Moses Hides His Face
[231]–[234] The Dedication of Solomon's Temple:
    [231] The Bearing of the Ark of the Covenant
    [232] The Bearing of the Sacred Vessels
    [233] Solomon and All Israel
    [234] The Installation of the Ark in the Holy of Holies
    [235] Isaiah Prophesying; The Angel Smiting the Assyrians before Jerusalem
    [236] Aaron and His Sons before the Altar

These paintings are closely related to the liturgy of the feasts of the Virgin, for with only one exception one or another of the Biblical texts on which the paintings are based appears among the pericopes that are read at one or more of the feasts celebrating the Virgin's Birth, the Presentation, the Annunciation, and the Dormition. It will be seen that in the one instance where the text is not read the artist has related the subject to the typology of the Virgin by inserting her image and by endowing the scene with a special meaning that was more commonly expressed in another text read at all the Marian feasts. Moreover, he has made the typological analogy explicit in several of the paintings by depicting the bust of the Virgin on an object of which she is the antitype. Two instances of the same phenomenon have been observed among the mosaics of the inner narthex: an image of the Virgin on the stamnos held by Moses [73], and another above the door of the temple in the scene of Joseph taking Mary to his house [97]. Indeed, the mosaics of Mary's life in the temple, four scenes ([91]–[94]) in the axial bay of the inner narthex, are complementary to some of the Old Testament paintings in the pareeclesion and in a sense reverse their typological analogies, for they make use of incidents in Mary's life to indicate the fulfillment of that which is foretold in the paintings.

[228]

Jacob's Ladder; Jacob Wrestling with the Angel

PL. 437–443

LOWER LEFT:

K(αὶ) ἔλαβ(εν) ᾽Ιακὼβ | ἀπὸ τῶν λίθ(ων) | τοῦ τόπου κ(αὶ) ἔ|θηκε πρ(ὸς) κε|φαλῆ(ς) αὐτοῦ | κ(αὶ) ἐκοιμήθη

And Jacob took one of the stones of the place and put it at his head, and lay down to sleep . . .

(Gen. 28:11)

LOWER RIGHT:

ἐν τῷ τόπῳ ἐκείνῳ | κ(αὶ) ἐνυπνιάσθει [sic]

. . . in that place, and dreamed, . . .

(Gen. 28:11, 12)

UPPER RIGHT:

κ(αὶ) ἰδοὺ κλίμαξ ἐστηριγμένη ἐν | τῇ γ[ῇ] ἧς ἡ κεφαλὴ ἀφικ[νεῖ]το εἰς τ(ὸν) οὐρανόν | κ(αὶ) οἱ ἄγγελοι τοῦ Θ(εο)ῦ ἀνέβαιν(ον καὶ) κατέβαιν(ον) | ἐπ᾽ αὐτήν. ὁ δὲ Κ(ύριο)ς ἐπεστήρι|κτο ἐπ ᾽αὐτῆς

. . . and behold a ladder fixed on the earth, whose top reached to heaven, and the angels of God ascended and descended on it. And the Lord stood upon it

(Gen. 28:12–13)

ABOVE:

M(ήτ)ηρ Θ(εο)ῦ   *Mother of God*

In the western half of the northern lunette two theophanies to Jacob are illustrated in a single composition: Jacob's vision of the ladder that reached to heaven, on which angels ascended and descended and above which stood the Lord (Gen. 28:10–17), and his struggle with the angel, in the course of which he saw "God face to face," was touched in the hollow of his thigh, and was renamed Israel (Gen. 32:24–30). The first of these is the more important in the iconography of the prefigurations of Mary; all the inscriptions in the painting refer to it, and the text describing Jacob's vision is read at the Great Vespers of the Birth of the Virgin (Sept. 8), the Annunciation (Mar. 25), and the Dormition (Aug. 15). Moreover, as has been pointed out above, the hymns that are being composed by Sts. Joseph and Theophanes in the paintings of the pendentives ([226], [227]) clearly draw the analogy between the Ladder of Jacob and the Virgin. The struggle with the angel, which neatly fills the space to the right of the ladder, can be justified in this context on genealogical grounds, for the renaming of Jacob as Israel signified that he was the preordained progenitor of God's chosen people, so that through Mary, his descendant, the messianic expectations of the children of Israel would finally be fulfilled.

In the lower left corner of the lunette lies the youthful, beardless Jacob, asleep on the ground, propped up on his right elbow and supporting his head on his right hand; his left hand clutches a great fold of his himation. The upper part of his body leans against a pile of jagged stones, and his gnarled stick lies before him on the ground.

Rising from behind the rocks in a sweeping curve that nearly parallels the contour of the lunette is the ladder, or more accurately a great curved flight of stairs, complete with treads, risers, and ornamented stretchers. Four angels are on the stairs. The lower two descend but glance back at the angel above them, who mounts upward with left arm outstretched while turning his head and body toward the first two; the uppermost angel, near the top of the ladder, advances with hands extended toward the half-length figures of the Virgin and the Christ Child, who are contained within a large arc of heaven at the crown of the lunette. The arc, composed of four concentric zones, and the garments of the Virgin and Child are rendered in grisaille, but the haloes are now yellow and the faces and hands are painted in the usual flesh colors.

The figures of the angel and Jacob, locked in their struggle, fill the triangular space between the foot of the ladder and an arched opening in the center of the lunette. One of the angel's wings is lowered and the other raised; his arms nearly surround the shoulders of his opponent, and his nimbed head rests on the right one. Jacob, who has no halo in this episode, braces himself with his left leg as he tries to gain a firm hold around the angel's body; his left hand emerges from beneath the arm of the angel, and his head is pressed against the latter's shoulder. Flying out behind his back and contributing to the impression of lively movement is the billowing loose end of his himation, which is otherwise wound around his waist. In the background a rocky hillock rises to the right of the wrestlers.

Dimensions

Height at center of lunette, from soffit of arch to cornice level, 2.68 m.; total width of lunette, including scene [229], 4.67 m.

Colors

SLEEPING JACOB tunic, visible only at breast, green; himation, red-violet; stick, brown and red-violet; rocks, yellow ochre, with light yellow highlights and shadows of reddish brown. LADDER side rails, light pinkish brown with dark pinkish brown ornaments and drawing; treads, light gray; risers, dark gray. ANGELS (left to right) _1_): tunic, blue with red-violet clavus; himation, red-violet. _2_): tunic, blue; himation, yellow. _3_): tunic, blue; himation, green. _4_): tunic, blue; himation, red-violet. _Wings of all angels:_ brown outer feathers and blue and white under feathers. ARC OF HEAVEN four concentric zones of gray deepening in value toward center. VIRGIN AND CHILD garments, gray; faces, the usual flesh colors; hair, brown; hands, gray.
JACOB WRESTLING tunic, dark green with yellow and brown hem; boots, same as hem; himation, red-violet. ANGEL WRESTLING tunic, blue; himation, reddish yellow and yellowish brown; wings, brown outer feathers and blue under feathers. LANDSCAPE greenish grays in a light and a dark value; undulating slopes near bottom, now greenish gray.

[229], [230]

Moses and the Burning Bush

[229] Moses before the Bush; Moses Removes His Sandals   PL. 437, 444–449 b

ABOVE:

Εἰσῆλθε Μωσῆς εἰς τὸ ὄρος τοῦ Θ(εο)ῦ Χωρηβ | ὤφθη δὲ αὐτῷ ἄγγελος Κ(υρίο)υ ἐν φλογὶ | πυρὸς ἐκ τοῦ βάτου

Now Moses came to the mountain of God, even to Horeb. And the angel of the Lord appeared unto him in a flame of fire out of the midst of the bush   (*Exod. 3:1–2*)

LOWER LEFT:

Λῦσ(αι) τὸ ὑπόδημα | ἐκ τ(ῶν) ποδῶν σου ὁ [γὰρ] | τόπ(ος) ἐν [ᾧ σὺ ἕ]σ[τηκας γῆ ἁγία ἐστίν]

. . . Put off thy shoes from off thy feet, for the place whereon thou standest is holy ground   (*Exod. 3:5*)

Ὁ Προφήτης Μ[ωσῆς]   *Moses the Prophet*

The theophany to Moses in the burning bush is illustrated in two distinct compositions, one in the eastern half of the northern lunette [229] and the other to the right in the soffit of the adjoining arch [230]. In the first of these there are two episodes: the angel in the flaming bush appearing to Moses, and Moses obeying God's command to remove his shoes because the ground on which he stands is holy.

Like the Ladder of Jacob, the Burning Bush was traditionally interpreted as a type of the Virgin. Here it signifies the Virgin Birth, for as the bush burned but was not consumed, so Mary conceived and gave birth but remained a spotless Virgin. It is to convey this analogy that the image of the Virgin is depicted in the bush and that the text of Exodus 3:1–8 is read at the Great Vespers of the Annunciation (Mar. 25); parts of this text are inscribed on the two compositions.

In the first episode (PL. 444), to which the principal inscription refers, Moses, standing at the left, bends slightly toward the right as he beholds the angel. His left hand is raised, palm upward; his right grasps a fold of his himation. Rising behind him in a sharp peak is Horeb (Sinai), the "mountain of God." The half-figure of the angel, painted in grisaille, now appears at first glance to be flying in the open sky. In reality it was placed within the bush, which is now ill-defined, being nearly effaced. However, some of the flames and tendrils are still visible between the angel and Moses, proof that in this regard the composition originally resembled the one in the arch (PL. 450, 452), which shows the angel in "the midst of the bush." Also within the bush is a medallion containing a bust of the Virgin and Child, painted in grisaille like the angel (PL. 448, 449).

The second episode, Moses removing his sandals (PL. 446), is placed below the bush at the bottom of the lunette. (It should be pointed out that when the carved tomb facing (PL. 533 *a*) was installed below the lunette a horizontal strip of painting, about 32 cm. high, behind the cornice was destroyed.) Moses, in illustration of the text inscribed in red paint to the left, sits on the ground removing his sandals; he has already removed one, which lies before him. Although the painting is poorly preserved, parts of one hand can be seen, loosening the laces of the other sandal. His left leg is drawn up close to his chest, and his head, which is nearly destroyed, bends over it. On the ground behind him, near the inscription, is his stick. Before and above him, filling the lower right angle of the lunette, is the flock he has been tending. A number of the animals, especially those above the seated Moses, are barely distinguishable. To the left in this area a ram with curved horns lies on the ground facing right. Closer to the bush and partly obscured by a goat is another sheep, which faces the ram. The goat, with straight, vertical horns and a pointed beard, turns away from the bush and lowers his head. More clearly discernible are the six sheep, including a ram, in the lower right corner; some of these are eating tendrils of the bush. Finally, at the very bottom edge of the painting, bodies destroyed behind the cornice of the tomb, are the rather well preserved heads of a black goat and a brown dog.

Dimensions

See [228].

Colors

STANDING MOSES tunic, visible at his left shoulder and at hem, blue; himation, yellow ochre in lighter parts, ranging to slightly greenish yellow and umber in the darker parts. SEATED MOSES garments, same as those of preceding figure; stick, blue-black and violet.

THE BUSH nearly destroyed except in small area of upper left beneath angel, where tendrils are greenish brown, leaves are green, and tongues of flame are red. ANGEL AND MEDALLION OF VIRGIN AND CHILD entirely in grays and white. ANIMALS (in order of reference in text, above) *Ram:* fleece, reddish yellow; horns, brown and yellow. *Goat:* gray and black. *Another ram:* gray and black. *Sheep:* reddish yellow; legs, gray and black. *Goat:* black. *Dog:* brown. LANDSCAPE grayish yellow and brown.

[230] Moses Hides His Face

PL. 450-452

Ἀπέστρεψε δὲ Μω(σῆ)ς τὸ πρόσωπ(ον) αὐτοῦ εὐλαβεῖτο γὰρ κατεμ|βλέψαι ἐνώπιον τοῦ Θ(εο)ῦ
And Moses hid his face; for he was afraid to look upon God (*Exod. 3:6*)

The second composition dealing with the subject of Moses and the Burning Bush is adapted to the tall, narrow proportions of the soffit of the arch adjoining the preceding episodes, in the lunette to the left. According to the inscription the painting illustrates Moses hiding, or turning away, his face from fear of beholding God. Moses stands at the left; his body, in three-quarters view, is turned slightly to the right, toward the bush and the figures of the angel and the Virgin and Child again depicted within it, but his head is turned away. He raises his right hand as though to cover his face, and in his left he holds the small end of his rod. These details are to be found in representations of yet another miraculous sign revealed to Moses while he conversed with God before the burning bush, namely, the transformation of the rod of Moses into a serpent, which again became a rod when, as God commanded him, Moses picked it up by the tail (Exod. 4:1–5). It seems likely, therefore, that the painter's model represented the moment when the serpent became a rod in Moses' hand, or that the painter wished to combine the essential features of the two episodes within one composition.

The bush in this composition is better preserved than its counterpart in the lunette at the left and can well serve as a guide to the latter's reconstruction. The angel and the medallion containing the Virgin are again in grisaille, and except for the proportions of the medallions the two sets of images are much alike (compare PL. 448 and 452), as are the two representations of "the mountain of God."

Dimensions	*Colors*
Width including borders, 1.025 m.; height from top of inscription to cornice, 2.69 m.	MOSES tunic, blue with blue-black clavus; himation, brownish yellow; stick, brown. THE BUSH greens, browns, and black; flames, red. LANDSCAPE as in [229].

[231]–[234]

The Dedication of Solomon's Temple

[231] The Bearing of the Ark of the Covenant
PL. 453–455

[Καὶ ἐγένετο] ὡς συνετέλεσε Σολομ(ὼν) [sic] τοῦ οἰκοδομῆσα[ι τὸν ο]ῖκ[ον
Κ(υρίο)υ | τότε ἐξ]εκκλησίασε(ν) πάν(τας) τοὺς πρεσβυτέρους 'Ι(σρα)ὴλ ἐν
Σιὼν τοῦ ἀνενεγκ[εῖν | τὴν] κιβωτ(ὸν) διαθήκ(ης) Κ(υρίο)υ ἐκ πόλε(ως)
Δα[βίδ] αὕτη ἐ[στὶν Σ]ιὼν   [Καὶ ἦραν] | οἱ ἱεροῖς [sic] τ(ὴν) κιβω(τὸν) τῆς
διαθήκης Κ(υρίο)υ κ(αὶ) τὸ σκή|νωμα τοῦ μαρτυρίου
And it came to pass when Solomon had built the house of the Lord, then he assembled the elders of Israel in Sion that they might bring up the ark of the covenant of the Lord out of the city of David, which is Sion. And the priests took up the ark of the covenant of the Lord and the tabernacle of testimony (excerpted from III Kings 8:1–4 [Septuagint], i.e., I Kings 8:1–4 [English])

On the feast of the Presentation of the Virgin in the Temple (Nov. 21), one of the lessons read is III Kings 8:1–11, which describes the dedication of Solomon's temple. Four episodes of the dedication, each inscribed with the pertinent verses from this passage, are depicted in sequence in the southern lunettes of the parecclesion and the arch between them. Although no image of the Virgin now appears in any of these paintings, it is evident that the actions of bringing the ark of the covenant and the holy vessels into the temple are illustrated as prefigurations of Mary's presentation and life in the temple. The implication is that Mary, "the dwelling place of the uncontainable," was the antitype of the ark, the abode of God, through her role in the Incarnation (see Part One: The Mosaics, [1]).

Before the construction of Solomon's temple the ark and the holy vessels had been kept in the tabernacle within the fortress of Sion, known also as the city of David. The first of the four scenes in the parecclesion illustrates the removal of the ark from Sion and the beginning of the procession that is to take it to the new temple. The scene is in the right-hand side of the southern lunette of the eastern bay; although it encroaches on areas otherwise devoted to the Last Judgment, it nevertheless adjoins the other episodes of the dedication, which are to the right, in the arch and lunette of the western bay.

In the foreground four priests carry the ark of the covenant on their shoulders; they are dressed in the classical tunic and himation and not in the usual priestly vestments, such as we find in the temple scenes of the inner narthex ([82], [91], [94], etc.) or in the fresco of Aaron and His Sons before the Altar [236]. The ark and its bearers appear to have emerged from a great cleft in the mountainous background, through which the battlements of the city of David are to be seen. The ark is borne toward the right, the direction in which the procession moves from episode to episode of the dedication.

The ark, depicted as a gabled structure with sloping top, resembles the lid of a gabled sarcophagus. The long side and top are divided into vertical strips whose color and texture make them seem to represent slabs of porphyry and veined marble bound by straps of yellow metal, perhaps gold. In the center of the gable is a yellow roundel, or disc, in which there may have been an image of the Virgin.

Dimensions

Height at center of lunette, ca. 2.50 m.; width of painting at base of lunette from window opening at left to arch at right, including borders, ca. 1.50 m.

Colors

ARK gable, red-violet with yellow disc and yellow band at bottom; stripes on side and top (left to right), mottled red-violet, yellow, gray and white veining as in marble, yellow, mottled red-violet, yellow. PRIESTS tunics, blue; himatia (left to right), yellow, red-violet, green, yellow. LANDSCAPE zone at bottom, green; slopes of mountain, warm grays; rocks at top of mountain, warm gray with full lights in yellow, shadows in brown, and a few highlights in white. BATTLEMENTS OF CITY AND TREE warm gray in lights and brown in shadows.

[232] The Bearing of the Sacred Vessels   PL. 456, 457

The scene in the soffit of the southern half of the arch between the two lunettes continues the procession begun in the preceding scene and represents the bearing of the sacred vessels to Solomon's temple. The painting has suffered severe effacement and, in the area at the top where the inscription must have been placed, even total loss. Enough remains, however, to show that it illustrates the last half of the fourth verse of III Kings, chapter 8, and the inscription, continuing that of the preceding scene, probably read as follows: καὶ πάντα τὰ σκεύη τὰ ἅγια τὰ ἐν τῷ σκηνώματι τοῦ μαρτυρίου, that is, "and all the holy vessels that were in the tabernacle of testimony." The suggested reading of the inscription is confirmed by the fact that the painting corresponds precisely to this otherwise missing section of the text, which is continued in the inscription of the next episode in the lunette to the right [233].

The narrow space assigned to this composition is filled by two priests, one bearing the seven-branched candlestick described in Exodus 25:31–36 and the other a large vase, the stamnos in which the manna was kept (Exod. 16:33). The priest at the left, dressed in a tight-sleeved tunic, a mantle, and a headcloth, strides forward in near-profile, head raised, and holds the golden candelabrum aloft with both hands. At the lower end of the shaft of the candelabrum one of the feet of the base can be seen; the others are covered by the priest's forearm. The shaft is composed of alternate beads, or rounded knobs, and elongated reels. A shallow bowl of large diameter is attached to the top of the shaft, and in the center of the bowl is a rounded element, now partly destroyed, from which the seven branches radiate. Each branch, composed of two reels separated by a round bead, terminates in a small bowl; from each bowl projects a sharp spike, to which a candle could be attached.

The second priest is dressed like the first, but his headcloth has fallen around his neck and shoulders. Facing toward the onlooker, but with hips and legs turned considerably toward the right, he raises both arms above his head to support the heavy golden stamnos that rides on his shoulders. The vessel has a rather large, covered bowl, a low foot, a long neck, and two handles. The priest's head obscures the lower right part of the bowl and all but the left edge of the foot. The bowl, cylindrical in shape, with a rounded bottom, is surmounted by a domical cover, which seems to have been fluted. From the center of the cover projects the long neck, flaring out in the manner of a trumpet; the top of the neck is linked with the rim of the bowl beneath by two gracefully curved handles, which terminate at each end, where they attach to the vessel, in tightly curled spirals. A white cylindrical object, wrapped with a crossed white, red-bordered ribbon, rises vertically above the back of the neck. The cylinder appears to be a scroll; it is possible that it originally extended down into the neck of the vessel, but the deterioration of the yellow underpainting has caused the paint in that part of the scroll to flake off completely. The scroll, if such it was, may be identified as the Torah scroll.

The only place on either of the holy vessels where an image of the Virgin could have been placed is on the rounded element from which the seven branches of the candlestick radiate, but no evidence of such an image now exists. It clearly was intended, however, that both these objects should be interpreted as types of the Virgin, for they both figure prominently among her epithets in Byzantine hymnography and exegesis.

Dimensions
Width including borders, ca. 1.03 m.

Colors
PRIEST AT LEFT tunic, originally red with gold-embroidered hem and cuffs; mantle, green; headdress, violet; boots, originally red. CANDLESTICK original sketch, in thin black, can be seen at various points; extant overpainting is yellow with drawing in reddish brown. PRIEST AT RIGHT tunic, green with gold-embroidered hem and cuffs; mantle, red; headdress (around shoulders), blue; boots, red. STAMNOS same as candlestick; scroll(?), gray and white with red and white ribbon. LANDSCAPE zone at bottom, green; slopes of mountain, yellow with brown shadows.

[233] Solomon and All Israel PL. 458, 459

Κ(αὶ) ὁ βασιλεὺς κ(αὶ) πᾶς Ἰ(σρα)ὴλ ἔμπροσθ(εν) τῆς κιβωτοῦ
And the king and all Israel (were assembled) before the ark (III Kings [I Kings] 8:5)

The third episode in the dedication of Solomon's temple occupies the eastern half of the southern lunette beneath the dome. It represents King Solomon leading the elders of Israel in procession before the ark and the holy vessels. Its inscription, III Kings 8:5, is a continuation of the text inscribed above the two preceding scenes.

In the background is a cleft mountain, which rises to a rocky peak; a tree emerges from behind the peak. A nimbed Solomon stands in the right foreground, his body, in three-quarters view, turned toward the right and his head turned the other way so that he looks back at the group of six or seven figures following him at the left. He wears the vestments of a Byzantine emperor: a red divitision, or long, richly decorated ceremonial robe, a golden loros, or heavily embroidered scarf that is wound about the body, a crown, and red boots. In his right hand he holds a slender, lighted taper, and with his left hand he swings a censer. The divitision is decorated at the hem and in a strip down the front with golden embroidery studded with pearls. The loros is also encrusted with pearls, and where it is folded back to reveal the reverse side it shows a green lining. Solomon's feet were destroyed when the plaster was cut away for the installation of the cornice of the wall tomb below, but a remaining bit of ankle, painted red, indicates that he wore the imperial boots. The censer, bowl-shaped and provided with a low, flaring base, is adorned with gems and pearls; it is suspended on three chains, each of which has a small cross midway between the bowl and the handle.

The elders of Israel are represented by three full-length figures and, crowded in behind them, several heads, all severely damaged. Those in front, at least, wear tunics, visible only below their mantles, and all seem to have been provided with headcloths, in some cases loosely draped around necks and shoulders.

Dimensions

Total width of lunette including scene [234], 4.67 m.; height at center of lunette, from soffit of arch to cornice level, 2.34 m.

Colors

SOLOMON divitision, red, ornamented with gold embroidery at hem and collar, and down front (cuffs were originally blue); loros (wrapped around shoulders, crossed on chest, wrapped around back, brought forward over hip, and draped over left arm), gold-embroidered, studded with pearls, lined with green; boots, red, ornamented with pearls; crown, golden, ornamented with pearls; taper (badly flaked where painted over divitision), green, yellow, and reddish brown; censer, yellow with outlines and drawing in reddish brown, encrusted with pearls.

ELDERS OF ISRAEL (front rank, left to right) *1*): tunic, invisible save in gold-embroidered hem; mantle, yellow with cruciform violet patch near shoulder; headdress, around shoulders, blue-violet; boots, blue-violet. *2*): tunic, blue-violet with blue hem; mantle, dark green with blue band at arm; headdress, gold-embroidered; boots, originally red. *3*): tunic, blue with gold-embroidered hem; mantle, blue-violet with horizontal band of gold embroidery; headdress, green.

LANDSCAPE traces of green zone at bottom; slopes of mountain, gray; shaded faces of rocks, grayish terre-verte; crevice at center of mountain, very dark greenish brown; tree, trunk and branches of grayish terre-verte, with greenish gray and white foliage.

[234] The Installation of the Ark in the Holy of Holies

PL. 458, 460

K(αὶ) εἰσφέρουσιν οἱ ἱερεῖς τὴν κιβωτ(ὸν) τῆς διαθήκης | εἰς τ(ὸν) τόπον αὐτῆς εἰς τὸ δαβὴρ [sic] τοῦ οἴκου εἰς τὰ ἅγια | τ(ῶν) ἁγίων ὑπὸ τ(ὰς) πτέρυγας τῶν χερουβίν

And the priests brought in the ark of the covenant into its place, into the oracle of the house, even to the holy of holies, under the wings of the cherubim (III Kings [I Kings] 8:6)

The final scene in the dedication of Solomon's temple fills the right half of the southern lunette beneath the dome. Here the priestly bearers bring the ark of the covenant into the Holy of Holies of the temple and are about to deposit it on the altar before two cherubim. In the upper left are the elders of Israel, crowding through a gateway into the temple, and in the upper right is an arc of heaven containing a cusped mandorla.

The bearers, grouped at the lower left and dressed in tunic and himation as they were in [231], place the ark on the altar. The bearer in the foreground is about to step up onto the low platform on which the altar, a rectangular table with single supporting pedestal, rests. The altar is covered by an altar cloth ornamented with golden borders at the bottom and where it hangs over the edge. In the center of each of the two exposed sides is a gold-embroidered ornament: on the front a roundel and on the receding side a lozenge. Neither in the roundel, where one might expect to find an image of the Virgin, nor in the lozenge are there any traces of painted designs.

The ark of the covenant is of the same gabled type that appeared in the first scene of the dedication [231]; it is again divided into varicolored vertical stripes, and as before there is a small disc in the center of the gable. On close inspection one can see within the disc the faint trace of a segment of a circle, which may be part of a halo and therefore of a tiny image of the Virgin, such as exists in the next scene [235].

Behind the altar and the ark, and seen as if from above, is a low structure, Π-shaped in plan, which creates within its walls a rectangular niche, or sanctuary, similar to the one behind the altar in scene [236]. The front ends of the two receding walls rest on coupled columns, one of which, with its capital, is seen in its full length at the far right; parts of the two capitals of the columns at the left are barely visible above the ridge of the ark. Spanning the niche is a thin roof in the form of a barrel vault, its exterior covered with semicircular slates similar to those on the roof of the building at the left.

Partly obscured by the left edge of the sanctuary wall is one of the cherubim mentioned by the inscription. The other, more fully exposed, is directly behind the ark; the upper pair of crossed wings and the upper part of one of the lowered wings can be seen. At the juncture of the upper wings faint traces of the cherub's face are still visible.

A low wall with a single turret separates the foreground of the composition from the group of elders of Israel emerging from a gabled portico in the background. The elders appear to be dressed as they were in the preceding scene. A voluminous red drape extends from the roof of the portico to the roof of the sanctuary to the right.

To indicate that "the glory of the Lord" filled the temple after the installation of the ark and the holy vessels (III Kings 8:11), the painter has placed a large arc of heaven above the scene. Within the arc is a cusped mandorla, or glory, from which a ray of light once descended to shine on the ark of the covenant. Although the ray is now nearly effaced, its path, widening as it descends, can be traced from a point to the left of the right-hand prong of the mandorla through the left corner of the sanctuary and onto the top of the ark.

Dimensions

See [233].

Colors

ARK gable, blue-violet with yellow disc (containing image of Virgin?) at center and yellow band at bottom; stripes on top and side (left to right), yellow, blue-violet, yellow, gray and white (veined like marble), yellow, blue-violet. PRIESTS tunics, blue; himatia, red-violet (left), and yellow (right). ALTAR pedestal, blue-violet; altar cloth, red with yellow ornaments. CHERUBIM (left to right) reddish brown; yellow underpaint with reddish-brown drawing. ELDERS OF ISRAEL elder in front, bluish gray tunic and yellow himation; elder at left, green mantle and violet headdress; elder in background at left, bluish gray garment; elder in background at right, red garment. FLOOR veined red marble, visible at far left, below, and at right. PLATFORM light gray upper surface; darker bluish gray sides with dark bluish gray ornaments. SANCTUARY NICHE walls, greenish gray; column at right, bluish gray; capitals, yellow; curved roof, gray and white on exterior surface and yellow inside. WALL AND TURRET AT LEFT light gray. BUILDING IN BACKGROUND walls, gray; column capitals, bluish gray; roof, bluish gray exterior face and yellow interior. DRAPERY CONNECTING ROOFS red. ARC OF HEAVEN AND MANDORLA each in three concentric zones of gray, lightest at outer edge.

[235]

Isaiah Prophesying; The Angel Smiting the Assyrians before Jerusalem

PL. 461–465

In the southern soffit of the western arch is a scene depicting the fulfillment of Isaiah's prophecy that the forces of Sennacherib, King of the Assyrians, would not enter the city of Jerusalem but would be smitten by the angel of the Lord (Is. 37:21–36; IV Kings [II Kings] 19:20–35). In the absence of a titulus or a superscription, the identification of the subject can be established from the painting itself and from several key words that can still be deciphered on the scroll of the figure at the left. It must be supposed that above the painting there was originally a principal inscription which, like the others on the series of paintings of the Virgin's prefigurations, quoted from the Old Testament text describing the event; but the plaster in the area where the inscription would have been placed is now destroyed, owing to structural damage in the arch. In all probability the inscription quoted from IV Kings 19:35 ("And it came to pass at night that the angel of the Lord went forth, and smote in the camp of the Assyrians"), or from Isaiah 37:36, which is worded much the same way.

The poor condition of the paint and the extreme use of abbreviations make it impossible to reconstruct the entire five-line inscription on the scroll held by the prophet (text Fig. D), but there can be little doubt that it paraphrases the significant passage of the prophecy, derived from Isaiah 37: 21 and 33. A close inspection reveals seven letters at the beginning of the first line, τάδε λέγ[ει], and bits of three letters in the second; these letters, which occur in verse 21, are evidence that the passage could be an excerpt therefrom: "Thus saith the Lord God of Israel, Whereas thou hast prayed to me against Sennacherib". The third line contains a much abbreviated continuation of the same verse:

Fig. D. Inscription on scroll of Isaiah, scene [235]

βασι[λέως] τ(ῶν) 'Ασ(σ)υρί(ων), "king of the Assyrians". The fourth and fifth lines, quoting from verse 33, are more nearly complete and can be transcribed as: οὐ [μὴ (?) εἰσ]έλθ(η) εἰς τ(ὴν) πό(λιν) ταύτ(ην), that is, "he [Sennacherib] shall not come into this city".

The nimbed figure at the left, holding the inscribed scroll, must therefore be the prophet Isaiah. Dressed in the classical tunic and himation, he stands in three-quarters view, facing the right. With his left hand he holds one side of the open scroll; the other side rests against his hip. In an attitude of speech he fully extends his right arm, pointing with it toward the figure of the angel at the right.

The angel is caught in a pose of vigorous action. All lines and forms contribute to expressing the power and direction of the blow that is about to fall upon the Assyrians. The angel stands in a frontal pose, but he turns his head in near-profile to look down on his foes, at the lower right; his right hand holds aloft his drawn sword, and his left, in which he holds, at arm's length, the empty scabbard, is aimed in the direction of his blow. His spread wings and the drapery of his himation, billowing out behind him, also contribute to the air of violent action. Because the paint has flaked it can be seen that the painter altered the position of the sword, which inclined more steeply downward originally than in the final version.

The area containing the group of fallen warriors has suffered much loss of detail. In the center of the group, however, one can see the rear half of a white horse, whose rider is huddled behind his shield as though in an attempt to ward off the blow. Between the left foot of the angel and the horse is a crouching, wounded soldier, clad in gray mail like the others, who has lost his helmet. Above him are three slain warriors; one has blood spurting from his outstretched arm. The arm is relieved against a dappled pink area representing the haunches of another horse. Another pink area below the white horse may represent a fallen mount. Here and there in the lower parts of the chaotic group are scattered shields and helmets.

These three elements of the composition—the prophet, the angel, and the fallen Assyrians—are placed in a rocky foreground above a zone of green. Nearly filling the background is the fortress city of Jerusalem with its crenelated walls, towers, and gate. The most prominent of the buildings within the walls is a basilica with a gabled roof and a lower side aisle; before the gabled end of this building is a construction that may represent its apse or, perhaps, a separate domical structure.

The most significant details in the painting, however, are the gate of the city and the words inscribed on the scroll of the prophet, for it is these which convey the meaning of the scene and place it in iconographic context with the other prefigurations of the Virgin. The gate is placed at the focal point of the scene, between the scroll and the angel. The doors, slightly ajar, are painted an orange-red; above them is a recessed tympanum containing a tiny bust of a nimbed figure with arms extended at the sides. This image, comparable in size and general configuration to the one on the stamnos held by Moses in the mosaic of the northern dome of the inner narthex [73] or that above the door of the temple in the mosaic of Joseph Taking the Virgin to His House [97], must be regarded as a representation of the Virgin. Her image is used here to signify that Holy Sion (Jerusalem), the city inviolate, is a type of the Virgin and that the words of the prophet, "he shall not come into this city," foretell the virgin birth of the incarnate God. The motif of the closed gate of Jerusalem is the iconographic counterpart of representations of Ezekiel's vision of the closed door (Ezek. 44:1–4), a theme that was frequently used in late-Byzantine art to express the same idea and illustrates the only lesson that is read at all the Marian feasts. The essential passage in that text is: "This gate shall be shut, it shall not be opened, and no man shall enter in by it; because the Lord God of Israel hath entered in by it . . . it is for the prince; the prince, he shall sit in it." The closed door is, of course, the Virgin, who, though a virgin, bore the Son of God, and the "prince" is Christ. Perhaps because the door is reserved for the prince, in the Kariye Djami painting it has been made red, the royal color.

Dimensions

Width including borders, 1.72 m.; height from broken edge of original plaster above scene to cornice level, 2.51 m.

Colors

ISAIAH tunic, blue; himation, yellow highlighted with white, but main folds drawn in blue and shaded areas painted orange-yellow and drawn in reddish brown; scroll, yellow with black outlining and lettering. ANGEL tunic, blue; himation, greenish yellow-gray with white highlights, decorated with pink tablion;

wings, yellow and brown outer feathers and blue-gray under feathers. ASSYRIANS described in text above. CITY WALLS lighted faces, slightly reddish yellow; drawing and shaded faces, warm yellow-browns; doors, red. BUILDINGS WITHIN WALLS *Basilica at center:* walls, same colors as city walls; roof tiles, bluish gray. *Small basilica to left:* walls, grayish green; roofs, red. *Colonnade in front of small basilica:* entablature, violet; column shaft, dark green; capital, yellow. *Low, flat-roofed building to right of central basilica:* grayish green. *Other buildings:* walls, yellow; roofs, bluish gray. TREES retain traces of green.

[236]

Aaron and His Sons before the Altar

PL. 466–468

The painting in the northern soffit of the western arch completes the cycle of paintings of the Virgin's Old Testament prefigurations that fills the vaults and lunettes below the dome of the western bay. Owing to the almost total disappearance of the inscription above it, we are unable to identify a specific text, and it is even uncertain that the painting can be related to any specific event. When the overlaid whitewash was first removed from the area of the inscription it was discovered that the heavy lime white in which the letters had been painted had disappeared entirely. A series of scratched guidelines indicated that the inscription had contained four lines. Here and there between the guidelines the "ghosts" of a number of letters were recognizable where the black paint of the background had been preserved somewhat under the original lime-white letters from the corrosion that had affected the exposed surface around them. Most of the legible characters were isolated or in such short sequences as to offer no basis for a reconstruction, but in two of the lines they were sufficiently continuous to suggest the words "altar" (. . . τ[ὸ] θυσιαστήρ[ιον] . . .) and "burnt offering" (. . . [ὁ]λοκαύτωμ[α] . . .). To prevent their total disappearance these and a few other recognizable letters were lightly drawn in with a white, water-soluble pigment.

The essential features of this rather enigmatic scene are three priests, each bearing an offering, the altar toward which they advance, and an arc of heaven in the upper right, from which a ray of "glory" descends to shine on the head of the priest nearest the altar.

Each of the priests is given a halo and wears vestments of the same types that appear on the priests in some of the mosaics dealing with the life of the Virgin ([89], [91], [94], etc.), that is, anaxyrides, or tight trousers, boots or spiral leggings, a rather short, tight-sleeved tunic, a short or long chlamys fastened in front by a brooch, and a small miter, or priest's hat. Although the heads of the two priests at the left are considerably effaced, it can be seen that all three priests wear rather short, pointed beards; but, unlike the others, the priest at the right, who stands nearest the altar and on whom the light shines, has long locks of gray hair, which mark him as the most venerable of the three. The first and third priests stoop far forward; the second is more nearly erect. The first holds out in both hands a small, rectangular golden casket; the second, in hands covered by his mantle, holds out a gabled casket, also of gold; and the third not only offers a square golden casket but also swings a censer. In pose and dress the priests are strongly reminiscent of the three Magi in adoration before the Virgin.

The priests stand on a large platform of veined marble, below which the usual green band stretches across the bottom of the painting. At the far right two smaller platforms, one resting on the other, are placed on the large one. On these is a structure of richly veined marble, forming in plan a narrow rectangular niche, or sanctuary; the two receding walls, low at their front ends, are stepped up part way back to the full height of the rear wall, so that the structure has the shape of the letter pi. Within the sanctuary is an altar, resting on a single pedestal, which is covered by a red altar cloth; the corners of the cloth are adorned with golden gammas, and in the center of the front panel is a golden leaf-shaped motif.

Behind the priests there rises a high podium, which supports a small gabled building with an apsidal structure at the back and a flight of steps at the front leading to a porch flanked by corbeled pillars. At the far left is a free-standing columnar monument, which rests on a two-stepped pedestal. From the monument a great swag of drapery stretches across the top of the scene to a tower-like structure in the background at the right. A low wall cuts off the vista between the two buildings, and behind the wall rises a tree. Finally, an arc of heaven is placed above the building at the right, and from it emerge two flame-like "glories" and a ray of light that slants downward toward the priest nearest the altar.

In identifying and interpreting the subject of the painting [1] it is necessary to bear in mind the clues offered by its inscription and the formal similarities that exist between this composition and the fourth episode in the dedication of Solomon's temple [234]. Both paintings depict interior settings, as is evident from the marble floors, the platforms, and the low walls in the background. Priests, bearing an object or objects, approach altars that are alike in design. In each case the altar is placed within a structure that forms a rectangular, niche-like sanctuary, and finally, in each case "the glory of the Lord" shines down upon the scene. Since one of these paintings represents the dedication of Solomon's temple, can it be that the other has to do with the consecration of its predecessor, the first sanctuary where God dwelt, the tabernacle which God commanded Moses to build, to equip with altars, and to fill with the sacred objects which would be a witness of God to his people?

The Lord's instructions to Moses concerning the tabernacle and its furnishings, the establishment of the priestly office, and the sacrifices to be performed are all detailed in the book of Exodus, chapters 25 through 31. The manner in which all this was accomplished is described in chapters 36 through 39, and the dedication of the tabernacle is recounted in chapter 40. Aaron and his four sons were appointed by the Lord to be consecrated as his priests, and they alone (even Moses was excluded) were to serve before his altars. But after the consecration two of the sons, Nadab and Abihu, perished because they had taken "strange fire" in their censers in violation of God's command (Lev. 10:1–2). Only Aaron, Eleazar, and Ithamar remained as priests before the Lord.

The inscription refers to an altar, and it is an altar that is the focal point of the painting. A burnt offering also appears to be mentioned, but such an offering seems to play no part in the scene. However, the two terms of the inscription are brought into conjunction several times (especially in verse 7) in Leviticus, chapter 9, part of a passage that deals with the rites of

---

[1] For some points in the following interpretation I am indebted to Professor Serarpie Der Nersessian; in her chapter in Vol. 4 she will discuss the subject in greater detail. See also my earlier comments in *D. O. Papers*, 11, 205 ff.

consecration of Aaron and his sons and their first performance of priestly duties and reproduces much that is said in Exodus 29. There can be no doubt, therefore, that while the scene may not depict a specific event it nevertheless refers to the altar erected by Moses and served by Aaron and his sons.

Although the painting fails to provide a specific, visual analogy with the Virgin it should be interpreted as another of her prefigurations, for one of the pericopes read on the Feast of the Presentation of the Virgin is excerpted from Exodus 40, in which the sanctification of the altars and other furnishings of the tabernacle of testimony is described; the lesson ends with the words, "and the glory of the Lord filled the tabernacle." It was remarked above that the garb and the attitudes of the priests in this painting recall those of the three Magi in adoration of the Virgin; it is perhaps not unreasonable to suggest that the creator of this iconography consciously sought these means to establish the altar of Moses as the type of the Virgin.

When this painting was first discovered and published it appeared to be a unique representation, related to a subject known as The Tabernacle of Testimony which appears in the repertory of Serbian cycles of Marian prefigurations (Lesnovo, Gračanica, Dečani) but quite different in form from those examples of the subject. The latter are rather heraldic compositions showing Moses and Aaron standing at the sides of an altar on which the holy vessels—the ark, stamnos, candelabrum, etc.—are placed, each object bearing a small image of the Virgin. More recently, however, a second example of the scene of Aaron and His Sons, very much like that of the Kariye Djami but combined with the theme of the Virgin as the Closed Door, was discovered, in the southern narthex of the Fethiye Djami (Pammakaristos) in Istanbul. This painting, moreover, was found to be a part of a Marian cycle, probably painted in the late thirteenth century, of which fragments of two other scenes were discovered.[2] It is quite possible, therefore, that the scene of Aaron and His Sons before the Altar, as part of a Marian cycle, may have been peculiar to Constantinopolitan iconography.

Dimensions

Width including borders, 1.72 m.; height from upper scratch mark of inscription to cornice level, 2.525 m.

Colors

PRIESTS (left to right) *1*): tunic, blue with gold cuffs, hem, and stole; mantle, red with narrow golden border at bottom and white lining; spiral leggings, blue; anaxyrides, dark blue-violet; miter, now retains only the yellow underpainting; casket, yellow. *2*): tunic, blue with golden hem; mantle, dark blue-violet; miter, red crown (cubical) and narrow light blue brim and button; boots, red-violet with band of light blue around top; casket, yellow. *3*) (Aaron): tunic, very light blue with golden cuffs, collar, and hem; mantle, which is lined with pink, was originally green, now largely effaced; miter, red crown (domical) and narrow light blue brim and button; boots, red-violet with gold bands around tops; anaxyrides, dark blue ornamented with narrow violet band; casket, yellow; censer, yellow. FLOOR orange-yellow with red veining. DAIS up-

per stage, dark greenish gray on riser and lighter value of same color on horizontal surface; lower stage, bluish gray on riser and lighter value of same color on tread. SANCTUARY NICHE imitation of Dokimion marble, light gray with veins of red-violet. ALTAR pedestal base, blue and gray; altar cloth, dark red ornamented with gammas, borders, and leaf motif in yellow. ARCHITECTURE *Low wall:* color of raw umber. *Building in right background:* shaded faces, color of raw umber; lighted faces, yellow ochre; cornice, yellow with red fret pattern; consoles, bluish gray. *Podium for structures at left:* vertical wall, yellow-brown; horizontal surface, yellow ochre. *Gabled building:* shaded faces, grayish green; lighted faces, light yellow ochre; steps and roof, bluish grays. *Columnar monument at left:* pedestal, bluish grays; shaft, greenish brown; capital, yellow; impost block, gray. *Drapery swag from building to building:* red. ARC OF HEAVEN AND MANDORLA each in concentric zones of gray, lightest at outer edge. TREE grayish green leaves and stems over black background. ZONE AT BOTTOM OF PAINTING green.

2 See Cyril Mango and Ernest J. W. Hawkins, "Report on Field Work in Istanbul and Cyprus, 1962–1963," *D. O. Papers*, 18, pp. 323–28, Figs. 10 and 11, and Section D (in pocket at end of vol.).

237

[237], [238]

THE SOULS OF THE RIGHTEOUS
IN THE HAND OF GOD

The fragmentary painting in the top of the western arch, between scenes [235] and [236], in all probability formed part of an iconographic theme that included the paintings beneath it on the western tympanum of the parecclesion. In these areas very little original painted plaster now survives, but the subject of the fragment in the arch is clearly evident and suggests an identification for the little that remains in the tympanum [238]. These paintings, which occur immediately above the western entrance to the parecclesion, bear no iconographic relation to the others in the vaults of the western bay, which up to this point have been devoted to an iconography of the Virgin. Instead, they revert to the theme of the redemption of the Righteous, which occupies the vaults of the eastern bay, at the opposite end of the chapel.

The fragment in the arch consists of a small segment of an arc of heaven (PL. 470 a, upper right) and, emerging from it, a small part of the palm of a colossal right hand, which holds within it three infants wrapped in swaddling cloths. The composition, as is evident from the position of the infants, was designed to be viewed from the east; the chord of the arc of heaven lay along the eastern edge of the arch, and the fingers of the hand, now lost, were in the western side. Of the hand there survives part of the outer edge of the palm, between the wrist, which adjoins the arc, and the base of the little finger. The complete painting would have consisted of the following parts: at the top, an arc with at least three concentric zones; the palm of a hand with the thumb at the left, the existing fragment at the right, and the fingers, curled up, at the bottom; and, finally, a large number of souls, represented as newly born infants, filling the hollow of the hand. This reconstruction is based on a comparison of the fragment with fully preserved examples of the theme in other late-Byzantine monuments.[1]

The painting is an illustration of a verse from the Book of Wisdom, attributed to Solomon (Sapientia 3:1, of the Septuagint), which reads: "But the souls of the righteous are in the hand of God, and the tortures of death shall not touch them." In one of the examples referred to above (monastery of Manasija, in Serbia), the Hand of God is flanked in its arch by standing figures of the prophets David and Solomon, each holding a scroll; the scroll of Solomon is inscribed with the verse from Sapientia and David's scroll with Psalm 43 (44):23, which reads, "Awake, why sleepest thou, O Lord? arise, cast us not off for ever." It is most probable, therefore, that Solomon at least, if not David also, was portrayed in the western tympanum of the parecclesion [238] and that he held a scroll inscribed with the verse from which the motif of the Hand of God derived.

The tympanum [2] is penetrated by four arches — three spanning the intercolumniations of the lower zone and a fourth above the central arch. Originally glazed window frames, now lost,

---

1 See Second Preliminary Report (*D. O. Papers*, 11), p. 186, n. 27, and chapter by Prof. Der Nersessian in Vol. 4.
2 See PL. 469.

238

occupied the arches, dividing the mosaic decoration of the reveals in the west, or narthex, side of the tympanum from their fresco decoration in the east side. Owing largely to settlement in the foundation of the southernmost column, and severe shattering of the masonry, about three fourths of the original painted plaster and an even greater amount of mosaic have been dislodged from the faces of the tympanum. Only three areas of original painted plaster survive, in the lower right side of the tympanum, but sufficient evidence exists to make it possible to determine the general nature of the decoration — evidence, moreover, which strengthens the case for linking the paintings of the tympanum with the theme of the Hand of God in the soffit of the arch above them [237].

A zone of green ran across the bases of the spandrels immediately above the antae and the column capitals. The area at the right side of the tympanum, where the paint is preserved to a considerable height, and presumably also the corresponding area at the opposite side, contained no representation of any kind; above the green zone there is only black background. In the small area of fresco on the impost above the right-hand column, the background is again black, but above the green zone is the lower part of a standing figure, whose feet indicate that he was turned toward the left to face the center of the tympanum. The painted plaster on the corresponding impost to the left is broken off at a considerably lower level, but it would seem certain that another figure once stood here, facing his companion on the opposite side of the arch. Judging from the proportions of the existing fragment, the head of the figure on the right, as well as that of his assumed companion, was at a level somewhat above the sill of the uppermost arch, so that not enough space was left in the tympanum for other representations.

The figure on the right-hand impost (PL. 470 *b*) now appears to have three feet, because flaking of the paint has uncovered a foot that the artist had painted out in a correction of his work and replaced with the foot at the right, to give the figure a wider stance. The feet are clad in red buskins of the type worn by kings, as are the feet of David and Solomon in the Anastasis [201] and of Solomon in the procession to his temple [233]. The hem of the garment, which is badly effaced, was basically yellow, apparently in representation of golden embroidery of the type that usually decorates the garments of the kings.

As was suggested above, it is most probable that the figures in the tympanum represented the prophets who usually accompany representations of The Souls of the Righteous in the Hand of God, holding scrolls that display their own words regarding the redemption of the souls of the Righteous. Since Solomon is credited with the text of Sapientia, on which the subject is most literally based, one can suppose that he was portrayed in the tympanum. He may, however, have been accompanied by David, and either one of these kings may have been the fragmentary figure dressed in royal vestments.

Dimensions

[237]: total breadth of arch soffit, ca. 1.70 m.; height of painted fragment, ca. .86 m. [238]: total width of tympanum, ca. 4.67 m.; total height of tympanum, ca. 2.42 m.; width of impost with fragmentary figure, ca. .74 m.

Colors

[237]: arc of heaven, three zones of light blue, second one darkest; hand, flesh colors; souls, swaddling cloths, greenish grays; faces, flesh colors. [238]: feet, clad in red buskins; garment, ornamented with a yellow hem in imitation of gold embroidery.

MEDALLION PORTRAITS IN THE ARCHES

[239], [240]

Melchizedek and Christ

PL. 471 *a*, 471 *b*

[239] ['O] Δίκα[ι]ος Μελχισεδέκ   *Melchizedek the Righteous*

[240] 'Ι(ησοῦ)ς Χ(ριστό)ς   *Jesus Christ*

The only paintings of the vaults remaining to be described are the four medallion portraits in the crowns of the transverse arches. The first two, which portray Melchizedek and Christ, will be described together since they are pendant figures placed in a typological relationship to one another (PL. 471 *a* and *b*).

The medallion of Melchizedek is placed at the center of the vertical face of the western arch, in the narrow space below the dome cornice; it faces the medallion of Christ, in the corresponding position on the arch at the eastern side of the dome. The shattering of the western arch caused the destruction of a wide area through the medallion of Melchizedek; the head is missing in its entirety, and of the hair only one long curl exists, lying on the shoulder at the right. Melchizedek wore a garment of a very dark gray color, almost black, which was adorned by a wide gold-embroidered collar. The background of the medallion is painted in three concentric zones, in three values of pink, the darkest at the center.

Although the medallion of Christ also suffered losses of paint and plaster as a result of the shattering of its arch, most of the essential features are still preserved. In his left hand Christ holds a scroll, the rolled ends slightly separated; on the surface between the two rolls are some small scribbles, imitations of writing. In a particularly crumbled area at the breast faint traces of his right hand can be seen on close inspection; the hand makes a gesture of blessing, the ring finger bent to touch the thumb. The head, though severely damaged, possesses the usual traits of Christ. The right eye is preserved, but the mouth and parts of the beard are lost. Christ's tunic and himation are of yellow covered with a fine network of bright-yellow highlights and deep blue-violet shadows, in indication of golden garments. The background is painted in three concentric zones of green, the darkest at the center. Where the yellow mordant of the nimbus has disappeared the green of the background is exposed.

These two portraits were placed in confrontation to illustrate that Melchizedek the Righteous, king of Salem and priest of the most high God, who offered bread and wine to Abraham and blessed him (Gen. 14:18–19), was the εἰκών, or τύπος, of Christ, the one foreshadowing the other. In Christian thought and literature Melchizedek has often been compared to Christ, and even in the Psalms (109(110):4) it was said that the future Messiah would be a priest "after the order of Melchizedek." In the epistle to the Hebrews, chapter 7, the priesthood of Melchizedek is held to have foreshadowed the new, eternal priesthood of Christ, transcending that of Aaron and the Levites, which was a priesthood of men subject to man's imperfections. Early theologians—St. Cyprian, Origen, St. Epiphanius, St. Ambrose, and others—drew similar analogies, and some regarded Melchizedek's encounter with Abraham as a theophany, in which it was the Son of God himself who appeared to Abraham and offered the bread and wine, in prefiguration of the holy Eucharist.

Dimensions

[239]: diameter, .635 m.   [240]: diameter, .60 m.

Colors

[239]: garment, dark gray-black with collar of gold embroidery; background, three concentric zones of pink, darkest at center (same as [242]).   [240]: tunic and himation, yellow with network of bright-yellow highlights and shadows of deep blue-violet in imitation of cloth of gold; scroll, white with imitation letters in black; background, three concentric zones of green, darkest at center.

[241]

Christ

’Ι(ησοῦ)ς Χ(ριστό)ς   *Jesus Christ*

A second medallion portrait of Christ occurs on the same arch as the preceding one, this time on the horizontal surface in the center of the soffit. Since the head is at the west side of the arch, the spectator is expected to view the medallion while facing eastward. Except for a small area of hair at the right side, the head is destroyed, and the surface of the garments and the hands is so badly effaced that little more than underpainting now exists in the bust, but the background, again in three concentric zones, and the inscription are well preserved.

The fragment suggests that the head and shoulders were turned slightly toward the left and that in his left hand Christ held a tightly rolled scroll. While it is impossible to make a positive identification of the type of Christ that was here represented, the painting of the hair indicates that the portrait was of neither Christ Emmanuel nor Christ as the Ancient of Days, but probably possessed the usual features of the historic Christ.

Dimensions

Diameter, .76 m.

Colors

GARMENTS surface badly effaced; remaining yellow and brown underpainting probably indicate that cloth of gold was imitated.   BACKGROUND three concentric zones of green, darkest at center.

[242]

The Archangel Michael

PL. 472, 473

Ο Α(ρχάγγελος?) Μιχ(αήλ)   *The Archangel (?) Michael*

X̄ | Δ̄ K̄ [*on the globe*]

In a position of special honor and importance, at the center of the arch of the bema, is a large medallion containing the bust of the Archangel Michael. Here he is placed in the midst of the scenes of the eastern vaults of the chapel, which deal with the theme of man's redemption and final judgment; for to the east, in the conch of the apse, is the Anastasis, to the west is the vault of the Last Judgment, and at his sides in the soffit of the arch are two of Christ's miracles of resurrection. His portrait is the fourth and last in the series of medallion portraits in the crowns of the transverse arches, but being at a larger scale than the others, and in the arch of the bema, it is the most important of all.

The inscription to the left of the medallion, which should record Michael's category, or rank, is somewhat enigmatic; it consists simply of an omicron and an alpha without breathings or accents. The alpha might stand for ἄγιος, ἄγγελος, ἀρχάγγελος, ἀρχιστράτηγος, or ἄρχων, all of which appear as appellations of Michael. The archangel, as he is most commonly known, wears a tunic and himation and bears a scepter and a globe, the emblems of royal authority, in his right and left hands respectively; around his head is a fillet. Filling the spaces beside him are the upper parts of his wings. The background is composed of three concentric zones, the darkest at the center. In general the right half of the figure is in good condition but the left is badly effaced. Although the condition of the face is imperfect, it is evident that the features were given great beauty and elegance.

The himation is draped over the angel's left shoulder and across his back and is brought forward under his right arm, so that his tunic is exposed at his right breast and shoulder. The hand that holds the scepter is now defined only in the underpainting, and except for its upper part the scepter exists only in the outlines of the preliminary sketch; the upper end of the scepter is shaped like a spool and decorated along the edges with pearls. The globe, which rests in the palm of the angel's left hand, is rendered as a semitransparent sphere; some of the drapery behind it shows through. Near the top of the sphere is the letter chi, and below it are the letters delta and kappa. Above each letter is a mark of contraction indicating that it is an abbreviation of a word.[1]

There are several reasons for depicting Michael in his prominent position in the arch of the bema of the parecclesion. In the Christian hierarchy of the celestial beings Michael was the chief of the four major archangels, and by some exegetes he was placed above all other angelic beings who were created to be intermediaries between God and man. By long tradition, images of archangels, Michael most prominently, were placed in the arch of the bema (witness, for ex-

---

1 For an explanation of the sigla X Δ K on the globe, see the chapter of Prof. Der Nersessian on the iconogra- phy of the paintings of the parecclesion, in the forthcoming Vol. 4 of this work.

ample, the apse mosaics of Hagia Sophia, where he occupied the position of honor in the left side of the arch). In late-Byzantine art archangels were almost always placed within the conch at each side of the Virgin (the chief mediatrix on behalf of mankind), as I observed above in speculating upon the lost mosaics in the nave apse at Kariye Djami. But it was especially fitting that the medallion of Michael should be placed between the Anastasis and the Last Judgment, for that position calls attention to the most important of his functions. He played the preponderant role in the destiny of the Christian soul at the threshold of the future life, and it was he, par excellence, who served as the conductor of souls to judgment and the righteous to paradise. At the Anastasis, for example, the righteous whom Christ redeemed from the dominion of Hades were taken to paradise by the Archangel Michael, and at the Assumption of the Virgin it was he who bore the soul of Mary to heaven. It has been seen above, in the discussion of scene [206], that Theodore Metochites himself directed a plea to the Archangel to intercede on behalf of his soul and that the scene, in one of the pendentives of the vault of the Last Judgment, might well represent Michael with the soul of Metochites. It is entirely possible that this special interest of the founder in Michael may have led him to dedicate his funerary chapel to the Archangel; this would account for the special honor accorded to him in portraying him above the bema. There was good precedent for such a dedication, for among the burial chapels that were placed under Michael's patronage was the heroön of the Comnene emperors, which was attached to the church of the Pantocrator by the Emperor John II.

Dimensions

Diameter, 1.21 m.

Colors

TUNIC   faint traces of yellow on sleeve at left; clavus, black.   HIMATION   red-violet with half-lights of blue and highlights of pale blue and white.   WINGS   underpainting of dark greenish brown.   FILLET   blue with white highlights.   SCEPTER   reddish brown.   ORB   rendered in bluish grays; letters, now yellow and reddish brown, were probably gilded.   BACKGROUND   three concentric zones of pink, darkest at center (same as [239]).

PORTRAITS ON THE WALLS

[243]–[248]

Church Fathers

PL. 476–485

[243] *An unidentified church Father* *Pl. 477*
[244] [῾Ο ἅγ(ιος) ᾿Αθαν]άσιος *St. Athanasius* *Pl. 477*
[245] ῾Ο ἅγ(ιος) ᾿Ιω(άννης) ὁ Χρισόστομος *St. John Chrysostom* *Pl. 478, 482*
[246] ῾Ο ἅγ(ιος) Βασίλειος *St. Basil* *Pl. 479, 483*
[247] ῾Ο ἅγ(ιος) Γρηγόριος ὁ Θεολόγος *St. Gregory the Theologian* *Pl. 480, 484*
[248] ῾Ο ἅγ(ιος) Κύριλλος *St. Cyril of Alexandria* *Pl. 481, 485*

Having completed the description of the paintings in the vaults of the parecclesion, we turn now to the frieze of portraits that encircles the chapel on the walls below the cornice. The first of these portraits are the series of church Fathers, or Patriarchs, arrayed on the wall of the apse. These imposing figures, all dressed in bishops' vestments, have so many points of similarity that they can be discussed together.

By the fourteenth century it had already become customary in churches that were decorated with frescoes to portray the principal Fathers of the church on the wall of the main apse, behind the high altar. There they usually were placed beneath the scene of the Communion of the Apostles, in which Christ officiates in the administration of the sacred elements. When appearing in this context, the Fathers also are depicted as officiants, bending forward reverently toward the center of the apse and holding open scrolls inscribed with texts relevant to the rites they perform. However, in churches where the vaults of the nave were decorated with mosaic and the walls below the cornice with marble revetments, as at the Chora, no space was available for figures on the wall of the main apse. In the Chora, where they are placed on the apse wall of the parecclesion, far removed from the sanctuary and from proximity to the altar, the Fathers are depicted not as officiants but as the chief representatives of the ecclesiastical hierarchy; they are the great church Fathers, some of whom formulated the liturgy, all of whom participated in the definition of Christian doctrine and as Patriarchs or Bishops held high ecclesiastical office. They are present as one of the categories of the saints. Their images are essentially portraits; they stand in almost complete frontality, holding closed books of the Gospels and, with one exception, making a gesture of blessing.

In the apse the wall has a height of 3.61 m. from floor to cornice. The frieze of figures, above a dado about 1.32 m. high painted in imitation of marble incrustations, has a total height of about 2.29 m., including the red borders, which are each about 5 cm. wide. The figures, as usual, stand in a band of green foreground, about .56 m. high; above this the background is now black. A triple-arched window on the axis of the apse divides the frieze into two symmetrical groups. Over the window are two pin-wheel ornaments, placed above the spandrels of the arches.

The paintings in the northern half of the apse wall, to the left of the window, have suffered considerable damage. At the far left the loss of a large area of plaster and the corroding effects of water seepage have caused the disappearance of all but the lower parts and the right arm and hand of an unidentifiable Father [243]. The second Father [244], who can be identified as St. Athanasius from the surviving part of his inscription, has fared somewhat better, despite the complete destruction of an area of plaster through the middle of the figure and the corrosion of much of the existing painting; the head is preserved only in the underpainting, but the essential details of gesture and costume are still clearly discernible. The condition of the third figure from the left, St. John Chrysostom [245], and of the remaining figures, Sts. Basil [246], Gregory [247], and Cyril [248], is excellent, and it improves with each succeeding figure.

The six austere figures wear precisely the same types of bishops' vestments, and all are bare-headed, except St. Cyril of Alexandria, who wears his usual miter. The principal under-garment is a white sticharion, or long tunic, decorated at each side with two vertical stripes, or clavi, which contrast starkly with the white. Over this each wears an epitrachelion, or richly embroidered stole, studded with pearls, fringed at the bottom, and hanging down the front al-most to the feet. Like the stoles, the epimanikia, sleevelets that cover the wrists and forearms, and the epigonation, the lozenge-shaped, tasseled ornament of stiff material that hangs from the bishop's girdle at his right side, are richly embroidered and adorned with pearls. Worn over all these is a strikingly ornamented phailonion, or chasuble—a sleeveless, enveloping mantle with a small opening for the head. The chasubles are white like the tunics, and they bear patterns of large crosses, usually combined with gammas or checkers, which, like the stripes on the tunics, stand out in bold contrast. Finally, over the chasuble is draped a long scarf, the bishop's omophorion; it is folded in a right angle at the breast and passes over the shoulders, one end be-ing brought back to hang down the front and loop over the left arm, and the other end hanging down the back. This element of the costume is also white; it is always decorated with a large, dark cross at each shoulder and with stripes and fringe at the ends.

A degree of symmetry about the central axis of the apse is discernible in the arrangement and composition of the six Fathers. The order in which they are placed seems to follow an accepted, though not invariable, rule of protocol. Perhaps the two who were most highly honored by the Eastern Church are Sts. Basil and John Chrysostom, after whom the two most important liturgies of the Byzantine rites were named. In the apse they are paired at the center, St. Basil at the right and St. John at the left. On the principle that positions of relative honor alternate between right and left as one moves away from the central axis, a principle that was observed several times in the arches of the outer narthex, the arrangement in the apse corre-sponds exactly with the sequence in which the first five Fathers are listed in the *Hermeneia*: first Basil, then John Chrysostom, Gregory the Theologian, Athanasius, and Cyril. The *Hermeneia* lists Nicholas, bishop of Myra, in the sixth position, and it seems most probable that the unidentified Father at the far left in the apse was St. Nicholas. Thus, the order of precedence among the figures in the apse would be, from left to right, 6, 4, 2, 1, 3, 5.

In pose and gesture also some symmetry exists, although it is far from complete. The two figures at the far ends of the row hold their right hands out to the side, free of the body, in a gesture of blessing; the two in the centers of the two groups of three hold their right hands

245

before them but turned toward the Gospels, which they seem to bless. The inner two, however, are not mated in pose: Basil holds his book in his left hand, which is concealed beneath his chasuble, and blesses those before him with his right, which is turned palm outward; whereas John Chrysostom grasps his book firmly with both hands.

The patterns on the three white garments, the tunics, chasubles, and omophoria, are either black or red: when the tunic has black stripes, the pattern on the chasuble is red and the crosses and stripes on the omophorion are black. But to avoid monotony, in view of the similarity of all the costumes, this alternation of colors in the garments is reversed in adjacent figures. Thus, for Sts. Athanasius, Basil, and Cyril (alternate figures) the order is black, red, black, but for the others it is red, black, red.

The figures are plastically modeled in a sense; for their stiff vestments, especially the chasubles, provide broad planes, which have been folded or curved this way and that and thus put into perspective—notice especially the treatment of the chasubles of Basil and Gregory. The large-scale patterns on these planes could likewise be put into perspective to accentuate the directions of the folds and facets of the garments. The white vestments are modeled to a degree, in addition, by the sparing use of shading for the folds. The shading in the first and third figures in each group of three is done in warm but rather pale gray; in the central figure of each group, however, it is in a grayish yellow.

All the chasubles are of the type universally adopted in Byzantine art by the thirteenth century, which is known as the polystaurion because its geometric pattern develops around a regular distribution of many crosses. The most complicated patterns, which are also at a smaller scale than the others, appear on the chasubles of Athanasius and Basil. Perhaps because of their intricacy, the painter, in these two instances, first incised into the plaster a grid of guidelines for the pattern in each individual fold, the direction of the lines being adapted to the direction in which the folds were to hang. For the other chasubles, where the patterns were simpler and at a much larger scale, incised guidelines were not used, and consequently their patterns are less accurately painted and the effect of perspective is less successful. Because of its fragmentary state and the complexity of its ornament the exact form of the pattern on the garment of St. Athanasius is difficult to determine; it is not clear, for example, whether the crosses were left in the white of the ground or were formed of the dark red. The chasuble of Chrysostom has a pattern of simple interlocking rows of crosses. That of Basil is composed of square units, each consisting of a large cross framed by four small gammas, drawn in rather narrow lines, which form the corners of the square. Gregory's chasuble has the same design, but the crosses are much larger and the lines of the gammas and crosses are of equal thickness. Still another pattern was used on Cyril's chasuble—a gridwork of aligned checkers with large crosses interspersed at regular intervals.

As has already been noted, St. Cyril is the only one of the figures whose head is covered. This distinction often, though not invariably, occurs when Cyril is represented among the church Fathers. The great church of Hagia Sophia had mosaics (late 9th or early 10th century, now destroyed) showing both Cyril and Methodius with tightly fitting hoods drawn over their heads and tied under the chin. But most often in thirteenth- and fourteenth-century representations of the Fathers all are bare-headed but Cyril; he wears a white cloth miter that is usually decorated with crosses and gammas, like the one in the Kariye Djami fresco. According to a late-Byzantine tradition, Cyril and his successors in the See of Alexandria were the only bishops who officiated with heads covered; this is explained on the dubious grounds that St. Cyril received the miter of Pope Celestine I when the Pope charged him to preside in his absence at the Council of Ephesus.

In portraying the features of the individual Fathers, our painter adhered to the types that were in current use in his day. Some of these types had undergone little or no change from the earliest examples that survive, but rather abrupt changes had been introduced in others before the Palaeologan artists took them over or formulated their own versions.

Judging from what can now be seen in the underpainting of the features of St. Athanasius he was given a very high, domed forehead, thin hair, and a squared beard of moderate length. Traces of color indicate that the beard was gray and yellow and that it may have been curly. In coloration and general form it would therefore have resembled that of St. Gregory, as was usually the case in Palaeologan representations.

Portraits of the choleric, irritable, but wonderfully eloquent orator, John Chrysostom, acquired increasing individuality from preiconoclastic times onward, and although a degree of resemblance continued to exist between the earliest versions and those of the late twelfth century and later, the Palaeologan type seems to be based principally upon the literary descriptions of Chrysostom's person. He was said to have been emaciated and small of stature; his forehead was unusually high and bulging and was deeply furrowed; his eyes were piercing, his cheeks sunken; and his chin was pointed and almost beardless. At times, especially from the late fourteenth century onward, these features were caricatured in the extreme, but the Kariye Djami portrait reproduces them with restraint.

The portraiture of St. Basil underwent less change in the course of time than that of some of the others. He is shown here with a high brow. His head is long and narrow and covered with thick black hair. His spade-like beard is quite long, black, and pointed.

The type of Gregory that is represented here began to appear ever more frequently during the course of the eleventh and twelfth centuries. In the ninth and tenth centuries his type resembled that of Basil except in the color of the hair and beard, which in Gregory were blond, tending to gray; this is the only feature that was retained in later centuries. In our portrait his features are unusually severe; his yellow hair, above a broad, furrowed brow, is thin; and the wavy locks of his beard are neatly parted at the center and shaped to a rectangle.

St. Cyril is characterized by a pointed beard slightly shorter than Basil's. In the present painting his beard is very dark brown with fine highlights of blue. As was pointed out above, he is usually represented with his head covered by either a tightly fitting hood or a cloth miter, as here. Except for the color and length of the beard, in which there is some variation, this is the type of the earliest extant portraits of Cyril.

Dimensions

Average height of figures from top of head to level of feet, ca. 1.90 m.

Colors

[243], [245], [247]: tunics, white with red stripes; chasubles, white with black crosses and geometric designs; omophoria, white with red crosses at shoulders.

[244], [246], [248]: tunics, white with black stripes; chasubles, white with red crosses and geometric designs; omophoria, white with black crosses at shoulders.

All stoles, sleevelets, epigonatia, and book covers, reddish yellow with designs drawn in dark reddish brown, studded with pearls and with gems of red and green.

[249]

The Virgin Eleousa

PL. 486, 487

M(ήτ)ηρ Θ(εο)ῦ   *Mother of God*

Ἰ(ησοῦ)ς Χ(ριστό)ς   *Jesus Christ*

Beneath the arch of the bema life-size figures of Christ and the Virgin originally confronted one another; the portraits occupied rectangular panels on the piers at opposite sides of the bema. The figure of Christ, and indeed the plaster of the entire panel on the north wall, in which he was portrayed, has been destroyed, but the painting of the Virgin and Christ Child [249] on the south wall is remarkably well preserved.

If the painting of Christ was composed like the extant painting, both figures, in three-quarters pose, faced eastward into the apse, breaking the pattern of near-frontality that otherwise characterizes the frieze of figures in the lower zone. By this means the paintings within the bema and the apse are set apart from the saints on the walls of the main body of the chapel and are made into a separate iconographic and compositional unit. Although there is no positive evidence that an iconostasis was ever erected on the step between them, the position and poses of the two paintings suggest that they served in lieu of the traditional templon icons; they were the counterparts of the templon mosaics of Christ and the Virgin ([186] and [187]), in similar positions on the two eastern piers flanking the sanctuary of the main church. That the painting of the Virgin was actually venerated as an icon is evident from blemishes and discoloration at two points on the footstool, at the level of her feet, which were caused by the heat and smoke of votive lamps or candles.

The full-length, standing figure of the Virgin is a splendid example of the type known as the Eleousa (the Merciful, or Compassionate). Mary holds her infant in her extended hands, as though making an offering, and her expression, though tender, is one of sadness, full of foreknowledge of the portentous mission of her divine Son. The child in an endearing gesture tilts his head sharply upward and presses his cheek against his mother's. Her head bends forward to meet that of the child, but her gaze is directed not toward him but into infinite space. The child leans forward and raises his right hand to clutch at a fold of Mary's maphorion; his left hand, in which he holds a small scroll, emerges at the waist from folds of his himation. His right leg, bare to the knee, bends over his mother's left arm, but his left leg, except for the sole of the foot, is concealed in a fall of drapery below his mother's hand.

The Virgin wears a long, tight-sleeved tunic of blue, which reaches the footstool on which she stands and all but covers her feet. Over her head and shoulders is a voluminous mantle, which falls at each side to knee level and is draped in great folds over her extended arms. As an outer garment around her shoulders she wears a maphorion, or shawl. A pointed end of this garment billows out behind; its edge, where it passes across the shoulder, is fringed with golden tassels. Both the mantle and the maphorion are dark red-violet in color. Above the forehead and again at the shoulder is a small golden star. A narrow strip of the silken headcloth that she wears beneath her outer headdress frames the upper part of her face; it is decorated with narrow vertical stripes, alternately blue-black and bluish gray. The Christ Child is clad in a short, white tunic with short, loose sleeves, a type that is often found in representations of children. Around his torso is a blue-black sash. The himation, which is represented as cloth of gold, has slid off his shoulders and is gathered about his waist in elaborate folds.

The narrow vertical faces of the Virgin's footstool are decorated at intervals with rectangular gems, between which are double rows of pearls.

Dimensions

Height of panel including painted borders, 2.29 m.; width of panel including painted borders, 1.56 m. Height of figure of Virgin from top of head to level of feet, 1.77 m.

Colors

VIRGIN *Tunic:* dark areas, left in black color of background; outlines and heavier drawing of folds, deep black; highlights, applied both as solid areas of color and as hatchings, light blue, giving effect of blue to entire garment; cuff, edged at wrist with yellow in imitation of gold. *Mantle and maphorion:* both in three values of red-violet except for highlights; darks, nearly black —full effect of red-violet obtained mainly in middle values; highlights, in two colors, yellow and very light mixture of violet and white, which appears as gray-lavender, both applied as solid areas of paint and as hatchings; edges of many of drapery folds, fringe on edge of maphorion, and stars at forehead and shoulder, picked out in narrow lines of bright yellow. *Headcloth framing upper part of face:* alternate stripes of blue-black and bluish gray highlighted with white. *Shoes:* red.

CHRIST CHILD *Tunic:* effect of white is obtained by white highlights heavily applied over base color of greenish gray, which in a darker value is used for shadows. *Girdle:* blue-black. *Himation:* basic color is rich brownish yellow, over which outlines of drapery folds are painted in brownish red and highlights, both solid and in widely spaced hatchings, in rather bright yellow ochre; effect is that of cloth of gold.

FOOTSTOOL upper face, yellow ochre outlined with red; front and side edges, two values of red, side darker than front; gems, alternately green and red; large pearls in two rows between them, white impasto.

[250]–[269]

Saints

PL. 474, 475, 488–520

SOUTH WALL, EASTERN BAY

[250] ʽΟ ἅγ(ιος) Γεώργιος   *St. George of Cappadocia   Pl. 488, 489*

[251] ʽΟ ἅγ(ιος) Φλῶρος   *St. Florus (a medallion)   Pl. 490*

[252] ʽΟ ἅγ(ιος) Λαῦρος   *St. Laurus (a medallion)   Pl. 491*

[253] ʽΟ ἅγ(ιος) [Δημήτριος]   *St. Demetrius of Thessalonike   Pl. 492, 493*

SOUTH WALL, PIER BETWEEN EASTERN AND WESTERN BAYS

[254] ʽΟ ἅγ(ιος) Θεόδωρος ὁ Τ[ί]ρω[ν]   *St. Theodore Tiro   Pl. 494, 495*

SOUTH WALL, WESTERN BAY

[255] ʽΟ ἅγ(ιος) Θεόδωρος [ὁ Στρατηλάτης]   *St. Theodore Stratelates   Pl. 496, 497*

[256] [ʽΟ ἅγ(ιος)] Μερκούριος   *St. Mercurius   Pl. 498, 499*

SOUTH WALL, WESTERN PIER

[257] ʽΟ ἅγ(ιος) Προ[κόπι]ος   *St. Procopius   Pl. 500, 501*

[258] ʽΟ ἅγ(ιος) Σάβας ὁ [Στρα]τηλ[άτης]   *St. Sabas Stratelates   Pl. 500–503*

WEST WALL, SOUTHERN PIER

[259] Ὁ ἅγ(ιος) [. . .]   *An unidentified saint*   Pl. 504, 505

WEST WALL, NORTHERN PIER

[260] Ὁ ἅγ(ιος) Δα(βί)δ ὁ ἐν Θεσσαλονίκῃ   *St. David of Thessalonike*   Pl. 506, 507

NORTH WALL, WESTERN PIER

[261] Ὁ ἅγ(ιος) Εὐστάθιος   *St. Eustathius Plakidas*   Pl. 508, 509

NORTH WALL, WESTERN BAY

[262] Ὁ ἅγ(ιος) Σαμωνᾶς   *St. Samonas of Edessa*   Pl. 510–512
[263] Ὁ ἅγ(ιος) [Γουρίας]   *St. Gurias of Edessa*   Pl. 510, 511, 513

NORTH WALL, PIER BETWEEN WESTERN AND EASTERN BAYS

[264] *Inscription lost*   *St. Artemius or St. Nicetas*   Pl. 514, 515

NORTH WALL, EASTERN BAY

[265] Ὁ ἅγ(ιος) Βάκχος   *St. Bacchus (a medallion)*   Pl. 516
[266] Ὁ ἅγ(ιος) Σέργιος   *St. Sergius (a medallion)*   Pl. 517, 518
[267] *An unidentified military saint*   Pl. 518, 519
[268] *Medallion of an unidentified saint*   Pl. 518

NORTH WALL, ARCH SOFFIT

[269] *An unidentified stylite saint*   Pl. 520

Outside the bema the frieze in the lower zone of the parecclesion consists mainly of portraits of martyr-saints, the most prominent of them full-length military figures dressed in full armor. As can be seen readily in the diagrammatic plans and sections at the back of the volume (Figs. 9–12), the north and south walls are not structural duplicates of one another; only on the south side are the walls of the two bays, between the slightly projecting piers of the arches, symmetrically constructed, with their arcosolia, or recessed niches, in the center. On the north side each bay has a door in addition to its arcosolium, so that wall space for painting is curtailed and there is no semblance of structural symmetry. Only on the south wall, therefore, could the figures be disposed in the symmetrical scheme desired by the painter, and it will be seen that only in the eastern bay is this ideal scheme still fully preserved.

The scheme, as exhibited on the south wall of the eastern bay (PL. 474), places a full-length military saint at each side of the arcosolium, guarding it, as it were, and two medallion portraits, symmetrically disposed, in the curving spandrels above it. In pose and gesture, and especially in the disposition of their military trappings, the two soldier-saints are composed to emphasize the rectangularity of the wall unit that contains them and the curvature of the arch that lies between them. The warrior at the left [250], who stands at the head of the ranks, holds his spear upright in his right hand so that it nearly parallels the left edge of the wall and provides a full stop to the rhythmic repetition of the figures along the wall; his body, in nearly frontal pose, turns slightly to the right, toward the niche and his companion at the opposite side; and his shield and sword encroach somewhat into the curving spandrel above the arch. The saint at the right [253] is well composed to fill both the vertical space and the spandrel to the right of the niche. This is accomplished by means of *contraposto;* his body is turned toward the right and his head slightly toward the left, and his steeply inclined spear and the outstretched arm that holds it are adapted to the curve of the arch. Two medallion portraits ([251] and [252]) in the narrowing wedges of wall space above the arch, the heads turned slightly toward one another, complete the composition of the south wall of the bay.

The south wall of the western bay was originally composed in like manner, but the later application of a sculptured slab as a facing for the arch of the arcosolium caused the destruction of the two medallions and parts of the two standing military saints ([255] and [256]).

The two piers of the south wall, one between the two bays and the other at the western extremity, were also decorated with full-length military saints. On the narrow pier between the bays there is room for a single figure [254]; his head is turned toward the right, but the strong curvature of his body and the arrangement of his shield and spear provide a leftward movement; in consequence he is related simultaneously to the compositions of both bays, which he unites. The considerably wider pier at the west end of the wall accommodates two standing saints, both military, one [257] dressed in full armor and the other [258] in the courtly costume of a martyr, unarmed but holding a small cross in token of his martyrdom. Because he is the terminal figure on the south wall the latter stands in nearly perfect frontality, whereas his companion to the left inaugurates, by means of a very striking pose, a strong leftward movement.

At the west end of the parecclesion the frieze is carried onto the eastern faces of the two piers, or antae, which flank the triple-arched entrance. These narrow spaces are occupied by single figures, one [259] a saint dressed in courtly costume, the other [260] a tree-dwelling saint.

In the north side, the wall of the western bay is broken by a low door and by an arcosolium, so that it was impossible to apply there the system of decoration used in the units of the south wall. Two standing figures of martyrs ([262] and [263]) were placed there, nevertheless, close beside one another in the area pierced by the door, their lower extremities in large measure cut away, as it were, by the arched opening of the door. In all probability the spandrels above the arcosolium once contained two medallions, but these, like the ones across the way, would have been destroyed when the rectangular slab was applied as a facing around the arch.

The situation in the north side of the eastern bay is much the same: an arcosolium and a rather large, arched door have a very narrow wall space between them, where only one full-length figure [267] could be accommodated; and the four spandrels of the two arches were decorated with medallions, three of which ([265], [266], [268]) still exist in whole or in part. In addition, the reveal of the arched doorway contained at least two figures, one of which, that of a stylite saint [269], is still partly preserved.

The wide pier at the west end of the north wall is pierced by an arched opening (PL. 508); the little remaining space is filled with a full-length warrior saint [261]. Another [264] occupies the narrow pier between the two bays.

Twenty-six figures, including the medallion portraits, were originally painted in the lower zone outside the bema; sixteen were full-length figures, and nine of those, as far as we can tell, were dressed in military garb. Twenty portraits, wholly or partially preserved, fifteen of them full-length, still exist.

Over the centuries a group of five or six military saints emerged as the recognized leaders among the ranks of martyrs. They constituted, as it were, the chiefs of staff, and they were often referred to as οἱ ἅγιοι μάρτυρες οἱ στρατηλάται—that is, as the commanders, or generals, of the army of the holy martyrs. Among those most frequently named in this capacity were Sts. George, Demetrius, Theodore Tiro, Theodore Stratelates, Mercurius, and Procopius. When military martyrs are introduced into the iconographic programs of churches, it is these half-dozen leaders who are usually given the most honored positions, in a hierarchical arrangement in which, more often than not, they are grouped in pairs, according to importance, and placed as pendant figures on opposite sides of the nave, chapel, or arch. In the parecclesion the structural dissimilarity between the two sides prevented the adoption of this system, and instead we find the group of leaders arrayed in hierarchical order along the south wall, beginning at the east. Thus, the two most important military saints, George and Demetrius ([250] and [253]), are paired at the east, not across the chapel from one another but at opposite sides of the arcosolium of the eastern bay. St. George is at the left, nearest the bema, because of his higher rank; he was often singled out as the τροπαιοφόρος, or bearer of the trophy of victory. The two Theodores ([254], [255]), who come next, stand side by side, as they so often do in church decoration, the Tiro at the left and the General at the right. The final pair of the great military chiefs, St. Mercurius [256] and St. Procopius [257], also stand side by side. Perhaps as a means of stressing the importance of this particular group, the terminal figure on the south wall, St. Sabas [258], although he is a general and is given that title in his inscription, is. dressed not in military uniform but in the traditional garb of a martyr.

Three soldier-saints, less illustrious than the ones on the south wall but like them dressed in military garb, are represented on the north wall at the only places where truly full-length figures could be accommodated: St. Eustathius [261], on the western pier; a saint who will be identified below as either Artemius or Nicetas [264], on the pier between the bays; and a severely damaged figure of an unidentified saint [267], between the arcosolium and door of the eastern bay.

In the spandrels of the two arcosolia where medallion portraits are still preserved, we find saints who, for various reasons, were traditionally paired. Above the arch of the tomb in the south wall of the eastern bay are Sts. Florus and Laurus ([251], [252]), twin brothers of Byzantium martyred together in Illyria, whose relics were said to have been brought to Constantinople in the reign of Constantine the Great. Above the arch of the tomb in the north wall of the eastern bay are the "twin" military saints, Bacchus and Sergius ([265], [266]), whose only military badge is the torque, or maniakion, which each wears around the neck; they are otherwise dressed as martyrs and they bear the martyr's cross. Side by side above the door in the north wall of the western bay are still another inseparable pair of martyrs, Sts. Samonas and Gurias ([262], [263]), both of Edessa. They like Laurus and Florus, and Sergius and Bacchus, are also portrayed as pairs in the mosaics of the arches of the outer narthex (see [170] and [171], [160] and [161], and [178], the last doubtless paired originally with his companion, now destroyed).

The costumes worn by the military saints are clearly derived from Hellenistic and Roman sources. In the Roman east, high military dignitaries, kings, and especially Roman emperors populated their domains with sculptured representations of themselves in military attire. Cuirassed mannequins were set up as trophies, that is, ritual monuments of victory, and cuirassed figures of "soldier gods" as commanders in chief of their religious followers were numerous.

The main elements of the late-antique military dress as it is to be seen on those cuirassed figures were a short tunic; a cuirass (the type varied, but nearly always *pteryges*, or flaps, giving the effect of a short, kilt-like skirt, were attached to it); a sash; and a chlamys. The tunic was knee-length and had sleeves that extended only slightly below the shoulders. The legs of the antique cuirassed figures were usually bare, and the feet either were bare or were shod with sandals, to which were attached various types of bindings that wrapped and tied about the ankles or lower part of the legs. The metal cuirass was sometimes of chain mail or of scale armor, but most often it was molded in form to reproduce the muscular structure of the trunk, and usually it was decorated in relief with human figures, animals, or ornamental motifs. This type of cuirass was usually supported by shoulder straps. The bottom of it, at hip level, curved downward to cover the lower abdomen, and it terminated in an ornamental motif, often in the form of large, richly decorated scales or tabs, also of metal. Attached to the undersides of the scales, and dangling from them, were the *pteryges*, the flaps of leather that protected the hips and thighs. These were suspended in one, two, or sometimes three horizontal rows, one over the other. Similar flaps were attached to the underside of the cuirass around the arm openings and hung over the upper arms to protect their flexor muscles. In most of the late-antique representations of military figures an officer's sash, the cingulum, was bound around the cuirass at the waist; it was knotted at the center, and its loose ends were tucked in at each side. The final element of dress was the chlamys, or paludamentum, a short mantle that was draped in a loop around the neck, pinned at the right shoulder by a fibula, and allowed to hang down the back. Except when warriors were represented in actual combat or a warrior god, such as Mars, was portrayed, the cuirassed figures were seldom equipped with helmets or with weapons.

It is evident from this description that the saints of the Kariye Djami were dressed in military garb of a style that, after more than a millennium, still resembled that of the Hellenistic and Roman military costume to a marked degree. Examples of this style from the earlier centuries of Christian art are rare, and it is uncertain when soldier-saints were depicted as cuirassed figures for the first time; nor can one trace with precision the modifications made by Christian artists in the pagan models. However, some of the earlier examples of uniformed saints occurring on textiles, ivory carvings, icons, etc., suggest that by the sixth century such figures were not uncommon in Byzantine art. They may well have appeared in the monumental art of Byzantine church decoration considerably later; but by the eleventh century they were a well-established feature of the iconographic program, and they appeared thereafter with ever-increasing frequency.

All the warrior saints of the parecclesion wear short military tunics, of red, blue, or violet, beneath their armor. They differ from the late-antique warrior tunics in having long, tightly fitted sleeves with cuffs of yellow, representing gold. Not usually found in the antique cuirassed figures, but of ancient origin even so, are the tightly fitting pantaloons—the anaxyrides, or *bracae*—with which the legs of all these figures are covered. The Greeks and Romans regarded this garment as a vestment of barbarians; nevertheless, their soldiery often adopted it, and in their art it was frequently represented. In our paintings the pantaloons are of striking col-

253

ors; most are purples of a bluish or reddish violet cast, but some are brown or yellow. (It is worth noting that even Roman emperors of "barbarian" dynasties of the third century, such as the Syrians Elagabalus and Alexander Severus, customarily wore *bracae* and that prior to Severus the color was uniformly purple.) Some of the pantaloons are ornamented below the knees with bands of various colors ([250], [253], [255], [256]). As can be seen in the figure of St. Theodore Stratelates [255], they were bound near the bottom with bandages, and their lower ends were slit.

Wound around the feet and lower ends of the *bracae* of most of the saints, and tied at the top, are the military fasciae—narrow, puttee-like bandages. (Fasciae are seldom found on Hellenistic and Roman cuirassed figures representing high military personages, but they were often used by soldiers who wore *bracae*.) Two other types of footwear also appear. Theodore Stratelates has red buskins ornamented with bands of yellow, similar to the Byzantine imperial buskins; St. Procopius [257] and St. Artemius or Nicetas [264] wear soft leather boots.

A peculiarity appears in the footwear of two of the saints which requires some explanation. The right foot of St. Theodore Stratelates [255] is bare and rests upon a crumpled buskin; in the case of the unidentified saint [264], the soft leather of the tip of the right boot is torn open and the bare toes are revealed. The painter was not emulating the toeless laced boots of certain Roman cuirassed figures (warriors, gods such as Mars Ultor, or Roman emperors), which are worn also by the cuirassed figure of Christ in the lunette mosaic of the archiepiscopal chapel at Ravenna. In those instances the boots are made with open toes, whereas here the right boot has been entirely removed in one instance and torn open in the other. Similar instances of warrior saints with one bare foot (*monosandalos*), or with the toes of one or both feet exposed, occur elsewhere in late-Byzantine art. In the Catholicon at the Lavra, on Mount Athos, Sts. George, Demetrius, and Theodore Stratelates are depicted with bare toes, and St. Theodore Tiro with a bare right foot. Similarly, the Archangel Michael, when represented in full armor, sometimes has one bare foot, as at the patriarchal church at Peć.

The origins of the symbolism of "one shoe off and one shoe on" are shrouded in ancient lore, and the meaning probably depended upon the category of the person who wore only one shoe or the nature of the occasion which called for this detail of costume. J. G. Frazer, in *The Golden Bough*, in dealing with the subject of "Taboo and the Perils of the Soul" indicates that it may be associated with certain magical religious ceremonies, such as rites of purification, or with the liberation from the magical effects of knots, or may be a sign of consecration on the part of one who finds himself in hazardous circumstances.[1] With specific reference to warriors, however, it appears to have become an attribute of the hero who is engaged in a perilous undertaking, although the ancients sometimes ascribed practical advantages to fighting with one bare foot. In his account of an attack by the Plataeans against the enemy's walls, Thucydides (III, 22) says that the Plataeans were not only lightly armed "but also had only the left foot sandalled" to prevent their slipping in the mud. The Scholiast on Pindar's *Pythian Odes* (IV, 133) remarks that the Aetolians were shod on only one foot "because they were so warlike," and legend has it that only one shoe was worn by the militia of ancient Latium, by Jason in his quest of the Golden Fleece, and by Perseus when he undertook to cut off the Gorgon's head.

It is especially the cuirasses and their attached *pteryges* that lend an air of antiquity to the military costumes of the saints, despite the fact that considerable liberty was taken in develop-

---

[1] Third edition, Part II (London, 1914), pp. 311 ff.

ing the Byzantine versions of the ancient types of body armor. Perhaps through misunderstanding or through a desire to obtain a wide range of types, the Byzantine painters treated the ancient forms in a highly decorative manner that at times became quite fanciful. Before the body armor of each of the military saints is described it should be pointed out that none of the cuirasses is of the "muscled" type that was prevalent in late-antique representations of military garb and that only one of them, that of St. George [250], clearly represents a solid casting; all the others, with the possible exception of the one worn by St. Theodore Tiro [254], are made of scale armor or, through a misunderstanding, adopt the scale pattern of that type of armor as a decorative surface treatment.

The cuirass of St. George [250] is the most highly decorative of any in the series. Its colors (olive greens and yellow) suggest that its material is bronze. From a boss in the form of a rosette in the center there radiates a pinwheel design of narrow, curved strips, the spaces between which are filled with what appears to be a foliate motif, repeated, from the center outward, at ever-increasing size. Below the cuirass, at the level of the hips, is a girdle with projecting tabs; like those of all the other cuirasses in the series, it is of a bluish gray color, an indication that the material is iron. Similar armlets are attached to the cuirass at the arm openings. The *pteryges*, in turn, are attached to the girdle and the armlets. These narrow flaps, which around the hips are arranged in two zones and around the upper arms, in one, are painted in red, orange-yellow, and yellow, with white highlights, in imitation of leather. The same colors are used in the wide collar that laps over the cuirass. Draped loosely over St. George's right shoulder and left arm and covering his back is his red chlamys. His left arm is thrust through the *ochanon*, or handle, on the inner face of his round, concave shield. In his left hand he holds his sheathed sword and in his right, his spear. His head is a splendid example of the type traditionally assigned to him; it is the head of a beardless youth with a rather round face, a low brow, and a rounded, bushy mop of blond hair, tightly curled and short at the back.

St. Demetrius [253] wears a cuirass of scale armor, or at any rate one with a pattern of small scales arranged in diagonal rows; it again is in colors that represent bronze. Around his body is a wide band reminiscent of the cingulum but painted in colors that indicate iron. The collar, the girdle, the armlets, and a strap over the right shoulder, which reminds one of the straps at the shoulders of antique cuirassed figures, are all of the blue-gray metallic color. The *pteryges* that hang at his hips are like those of St. George, in both form and color, but are arranged in three zones. Slung over his left shoulder is his green chlamys, and at his left side are his sword and his round shield, suspended from the opposite shoulder by a baldric. He conforms to the best traditions of his type, in which he is represented as a tall, slender youth, beardless, with a long neck and face and short, dark hair.

In representing St. Theodore Tiro [254] the artist has introduced some unusual features of costume and arms. All but concealing his cuirass is a very short, sleeveless tunic that buttons at the right shoulder. The cuirass, judging from what can be seen of it at the shoulders, is very dark brown, and it has a rather narrow yellow collar. The sleevelets and the armored skirt, which is visible only below the outer tunic, appear to be scale armor rather than the usual leather flaps. His chlamys, tied in a knot at his right side, is drawn tightly across his chest and left shoulder like a sash and floats out in a billow of drapery behind him. A triangular shield of white adorned at the edges with yellow ornament is slung from a baldric over his right shoulder and hangs behind his left. In his left hand he holds his sheathed sword and in his right, his spear. His head type seems to have been formulated in preiconoclastic times, before a distinction came to be made between the two Theodores. It is this early type that was adopted in later Byzantine art for the Tiro. He is characterized by a long face with a dark, moderately long, pointed beard and a mustache; the hair of the head is short and curly.

The form of the rather fanciful body armor of St. Theodore Stratelates [255] suggests an articulated leather jerkin rather than a metal cuirass, but the color is that of bronze. The pattern elements are aligned in slightly curved diagonal rows. Similar, but leather-colored, elements appear below the metal girdle at the hips, the upper zone of what would normally be the leather *pteryges*. The lower zone of armored skirting, on the other hand, is in the gray colors used in representing iron. Over the body of the jerkin are two diagonal bands of iron, which cross one another at the center of the chest under a lozenge-shaped boss. Around Theodore's neck is a wide leather collar surmounted by what appears to be a standing collar of metal. His upper arm, as usual, is covered by *pteryges* attached to an iron circlet below the shoulder. Hanging down his back and loosely draped over his right shoulder is a blue chlamys. In his right hand he holds a spear, but the weapons that he doubtless held at his left side were destroyed by the mounting of the slab of marble sculpture over the arcosolium beside him. He is portrayed in accordance with the commonly accepted type, which shows him with bushy hair and a beard of moderate length, rendered in the best examples with two distinct lobes at the bottom.

St. Mercurius [256] wears what appears to be a solid bronze breastplate chased with a variety of designs, including small scales and large circular motifs. As a cingulum he wears around the torso a wide metal band similar to that of St. Demetrius. His arms and thighs are protected by the usual metal armlets and girdle and leather *pteryges*, but curving over his right hip is what appears to be a piece of scale armor. Around his neck is a leather collar, formed like the *pteryges*, and over his right shoulder is a narrow strap. Drawn diagonally across his breast and tied in a knot at the center of it is his red chlamys. In his right hand he holds the hilt of a partially drawn sword and in his left, its scabbard; suspended behind him at the right by a baldric over his opposite shoulder is a round, concave shield. As usual, he is portrayed as a youth with a short, sparse beard and a mustache. The treatment of the head is a particularly good example of a device frequently found in early-Palaeologan art, in which, as it were, a profile view of the hair is combined with a three-quarters view of the face—a mode of representation that results in very pronounced bulges in the forehead and in the back of the head.

St. Procopius [257] is lightly armored. He wears no cuirass but instead a very short, sleeveless jerkin of a color that is used in representing leather; its surface, however, is treated in a scale pattern that suggests scale armor. This is true also of the very short skirt that he wears over his short tunic; the skirt is of one piece but has a slit at the right hip. The sleevelets, also, are of the color of leather, and they too bear a pattern of scales. Both skirt and sleevelets are attached to the usual metal girdle and circlets. His red chlamys is wrapped about his torso and gathered in bulky folds around his left arm, and a little of it can be seen rising slightly above the back of his shoulders. At his left side, suspended by a baldric from his opposite shoulder, is the empty scabbard of his dagger, which he holds aloft in his right hand. His sheathed sword lies across his left shoulder, the hilt above his head and the tip resting in his left hand. On the ground behind him and to the right his round, concave shield stands on its edge, apparently unsupported; it is treated in concentric zones, partly plain and partly ornamented, and at its center is a boss in the form of a human mask. His short white leather boots are held up by leather thongs tied in knots below the knees. St. Procopius is portrayed in Byzantine art, as he is here, with very distinctive features. Characteristic of him are the round and beardless face of a youth and wavy, but not curly, hair, which is pushed back behind the ears and falls almost to the shoulders.

The next saint to be represented in military garb is Eustathius Plakidas [261]. Judging from the frequency with which he is represented in art, he was, after the group of six described above, who outrank all others, one of the most popular of the military saints. Unique among our paintings is the treatment of his *bracae*, which are rendered exactly like his body armor, that is, with a pattern of diagonally arranged scales. The colors of the *bracae*, brown with yellow and white scales, are not those used in the other portraits to represent metal, and it is difficult to determine what type of mail the artist intended to depict. But it is clear, at least, that Eustathius wears not a solid cuirass but rather some kind of jerkin, which passes beneath his girdle and the single row of very short *pteryges* to form the lower zone of a short skirt. His arms are covered by the usual flaps, in browns and yellows, attached like the *pteryges* around the waist to metal circlets. His manner of wearing his red chlamys more nearly approximates the antique mode than that of his companions does; that is, it is draped over his left shoulder and fastened over his right but leaves the entire right side of his body uncovered. In the crook of his right arm he holds two spears, and he grasps his sheathed sword with both hands. The saint, as here, is usually portrayed as a somewhat older man than the saints that have preceded him. In this portrait he is shown with partly gray beard and hair, the former rather short and rounded, the latter wavy and almost reaching the shoulders.

The saint who stands on the pier between the two bays of the north wall [264] is no longer identified by an inscription. Despite the damaged condition of his face, however, his features clearly resemble those of Christ and thus identify him as St. Artemius or as St. Nicetas. The *Hermeneia* of Mount Athos, in briefly characterizing the holy martyrs, says of St. Artemius that his features were like those of Christ, and says that St. Nicetas is to be portrayed in like manner. These instructions stem from more than a literary tradition, for Byzantine monuments contain many examples of this resemblance and often pair the two "Christ-like" saints. Large areas of the figure are badly effaced, but it can be seen that he wears a cuirass of bronze ornamented with lines and motifs that radiate from a central point beneath the wide metal band around his torso. The *pteryges* at his hips and around his upper arms are attached to an iron girdle and armlets, and around his neck is a flaring collar, also of iron, as its gray paint indicates. His chlamys of red-violet is tied diagonally across his breast like a sash and wound around his left arm, which holds his circular shield. A sheathed sword dangles at his left side. He holds a spear, as do many of his companions, in his right hand.

The final saint in military garb is the severely damaged figure [267], not now identified by an inscription, who stands in the very narrow space between the two arches of the eastern bay. The falling of a wide area of plaster has destroyed all but the head, the right arm and breast, and parts of the feet, and even these areas have suffered much loss of surface paint. It can be seen, however, that the saint was clad in armor and that he was young and beardless. His body appears to have been quite frontally posed, his head turned to the left. No traces of a spear or shield are now to be seen, but he holds aloft in his right hand, in a perfectly vertical position, a naked sword, his arm extended at right angles to his body and doubled back again to bring his hand close to his shoulder; traces of the lower part of his scabbard are visible at his left side. The narrowness of the wall space and the close proximity of medallions at each side seem to have dictated this unusual pose, which emphasizes the vertical. The saint wears a cuirass and has a wide metal band across his breast and a vertical strap over his right shoulder; his upper arm is covered by the usual flaps; and a chlamys, lying over his shoulders, falls in large folds at his right side. His prominent position at the head of the military saints of the north wall ideally would have been assigned to one of the more important saints. One military saint often given considerable prominence, whose absence would be conspicuous in such a large number of warriors, is St. Nestor, whose type is not incompatible with the features exhibited by our fragmentary figure.

Of the figures who are depicted in non-military garb in the frieze outside the bema all but one are represented in the courtly costume of martyrs, and most hold the small cross that is their attribute. Most of these are also portrayed in mosaic, in the extensive series of medallion portraits of the outer narthex, which have already been discussed, and there are such great similarities between the mosaic and painted versions that the paintings need not be described. The group consists of Florus [251] (mosaic [161]) and Laurus [252] (mosaic [160]); Samonas [262] (mosaic [171]) and Gurias [263] (mosaic [170]); and Bacchus [265] and Sergius [266] (who may be compared with mosaic [178], which depicts one or the other of these saints).

Although St. Sabas Stratelates [258] was a general, as his inscription states, he is portrayed, as a full-length figure, in the traditional costume of a martyr; in this respect he can be compared with some of the full-length mosaic portraits of martyrs in the transverse arches of the outer narthex. Noteworthy in this painting is the nearly perfect state of preservation of the head, which gives us an opportunity to estimate the finesse of the painter and his high achievement in dealing with the human features. Few heads in the portraits of the parecclesion are as fully preserved (see PL. 502, 503).

The next figure [259], who must remain unidentified, is likewise attired in the costume of a martyr. The face and hair of this figure, but not the beard, are again in nearly mint condition and once more display the great capabilities of the painter at his best.

The one saint not a martyr to be included in the frieze outside the bema is St. David of Thessalonike [260]. A contemporary of the Emperor Justinian, St. David was a hermit of Thessalonike; there, according to his vita,[2] he sat in an almond tree for three years, at the end of which an angel appeared and permitted him to descend. He now resembled Abraham, it is said, for his hair had grown to the level of his loins and his beard reached his feet; his face emitted rays as of the sun. Thereafter he was endowed with miraculous powers; he was sent to Constantinople on a mission to the Emperor, held live coals in his hands on one occasion, and on his return died just before reaching Thessalonike, as he had foretold on his departure.

Extant murals of St. David are rare, and none, to my knowledge, are in quite the form that is exhibited here. Aside from some Russian representations on seals and a portrait in fresco in the Church of the Anargyroi at Kastoria, which is not conclusively identified as St. David, no existing portrayals of him are earlier than the one in the Kariye Djami. He is sometimes shown standing, without his tree or beside it, and in some very late versions the branches of the tree in which he sits entirely surround him.

In the present painting St. David is seated in a nest, composed of the tree's branches and foliage, which is perched atop a bare and gnarled tree trunk of considerable height. Only the

2 A. A. Vasiliev, "Life of David of Thessalonica," *Traditio*, IV (1946), 115–47.

upper half of his figure, dressed in a monk's tunic and scapular, rises above the nest. He holds both hands erect before him, palms turned outward. Although his beard is long, it does not have the extraordinary length attributed to it in his vita and in the descriptions contained in the *Hermeneia* and the late Russian painters' manuals. The form of the branches, their relation to the tree trunk, and the manner in which the half-figure of the saint sits within the low nest have obvious formal relationship to the representations of stylite saints (see [269]), the trunk corresponding to the column shaft and the nest to the capital and the low barrier surrounding the seated figure.

At least one stylite [269] was included among the saints on the walls of the parecclesion. The rather large arch in the north wall of the eastern bay, which gives access to the diaconicon, now contains in its western reveal and soffit a representation of a saint on his column that is complete save for the saint's head and inscription; it is likely that the now altogether missing figure in the opposite reveal of the arch represented another stylite.

There were numerous saints who chose to display their ardent asceticism by dwelling on the tops of columns, but only three or four appear at all commonly in art. The first and most famous was St. Simeon Stylites, of the first half of the fifth century. His column at Kal'at Sim'ân in Syria, on which he spent the last thirty years of his life, became the center of a great cult and was later enclosed within a magnificent cruciform church. His disciple Daniel, also a Syrian, erected his column near Constantinople; other well-known stylites, some of whom have been portrayed occasionally, were Simeon the Younger, Alypius, and Luke the Younger. When stylites are represented as pendant figures, as seems likely to have been the case in the arch of the parecclesion, it is usually either the elder Simeon and Daniel or the two Simeons who are depicted.

The stylite in the parecclesion, a half-figure, is represented in the garb and with the attribute of a martyr, that is, wearing a chlamys fastened at the breast and holding a small cross before him in his right hand; his left hand is held out in a gesture of prayer. Stylite saints are not commonly given the martyr's cross, and more often than not, even when they do hold the cross, they wear the ascetic's costume, often with a hood over the head. It is to be presumed that the endurance of extreme hardship and self-mortification entitle the stylite, in the mind of the artist, to the martyr's trophy.

For what it is worth in identification of the stylite, it is to be noted that his beard is still preserved below the level of the chin. It is moderately long, pointed, and gray. The *Hermeneia* of Mount Athos, which describes the beards of the five stylites named above, says of St. Daniel that he is to be represented as an old man with a pointed beard; the beard of the elder Simeon, on the other hand, is said to have been short and separated into two parts, while that of the younger Simeon was rounded. The description that best fits the present case is that of St. Daniel's beard.

The column, which consists of a molded base, drawn as though seen from above, a cylindrical shaft of squat proportions, and a pseudo-Corinthian capital, is surmounted by a sort of crow's-nest, also drawn as though seen from above, in which the saint is seated.

Dimensions

MEDALLIONS (diameter) [251], [252], [265], [266]: .51 m.

STANDING FIGURES [250]: height, head to foot, 1.85 m.; diameter of halo, .385 m.; height of green zone, .52 m. [253]: height, head to foot, 1.805 m.; diameter of halo, .385 m.; height of green zone, .51 m. [254]:

height, head to foot, 1.905 m.; diameter of halo, .39 m.; height of green zone, .485 m.   [255]: head to bottom of loosed boot, 1.995 m.; diameter of halo, .39 m.; height of green zone, .41 m.   [256]: height, head to foot, 1.855 m.; diameter of halo, .39 m.; height of green zone, .435 m.   [257]: height, head to foot, 1.905 m.; diameter of halo, .38 m.; height of green zone, .50 m.   [258]: height, head to foot, 1.89 m.; diameter of halo, .38 m.; height of green zone, .48 m.   [259]: average width of anta including borders, .625 m.; height of panel including borders, 2.21 m.; diameter of halo, .385 m.   [260]: average width of anta including red border at left, .50 m.; height of panel including borders, 2.20 m.; diameter of halo, .305 m.; height of green zone, .585 m.   [261]: height, head to foot, 1.865 m.; diameter of halo, .385 m.; height of green zone, .62 m.   [262] and [263]: width of wall surface from pier at left to marble slab at right, 1.635 m.; height from bottom of cornice to top of marble lintel in doorway, 1.44 m.; height of figure at left, head to foot, 1.83 m.; diameter of haloes, .39 m.   [264]: height, head to foot, 1.94 m.; diameter of halo, .385 m.; height of green zone, .535 m.   [267]: height, head to foot, 1.82 m.; diameter of halo, .375 m.; height of green zone, .625 m.   [269]: width of reveal of door including borders, .52 m.; height of fragmentary painting, from broken edge at top to bottom of red border beneath, 1.47 m. on the curved surface; width of column shaft, .185 m.; height of green zone, .535 m.

Colors

[250]: tunic, blue with golden cuffs; *bracae*, violet; fasciae, gray; chlamys, red; cuirass, olive green in middle tones, same color but very dark in background of design, and highlights of design picked out in yellow; girdle and armlets, bluish gray; *pteryges*, red, orange-yellow, yellow, and white; shield, yellows and browns on inner face and bluish gray on exterior face; sword, dark blue-violet baldric and scabbard, ornamented with yellow, and yellow and reddish brown hilt; spear, reddish brown shaft and gray head.   [251]: tunic, red with golden collar; chlamys, blue with golden tablion; cross, white; background, three zones of pink, darkest at center.   [252]: chlamys, red with indications of golden tablion at left; background, three zones of yellow, darkest at center.   [253]: tunic, red with golden cuff; *bracae*, yellow ornamented with blue bands below knees; fasciae, gray; chlamys, green; cuirass, warm greenish gray ground (applied over red underpainting) covered with bluish gray and white scales; girdles at hips and torso, armlets, collar, and strap over shoulder, all bluish gray; *pteryges*, yellow in middle tones, brown in shadows, and light blue and white in light areas; shield, bluish gray on inner face and brownish yellow on rim; baldric, black with gray buckle; sword, red baldric and scabbard, latter ornamented with yellow, and bluish gray hilt; spear, reddish brown shaft and gray head.

[254]: tunic, red with golden cuffs; *bracae*, brown; fasciae, gray; chlamys, blue-violet; cuirass, dark brown with yellow collar and armholes; sleeveless outer tunic, light yellow; sleevelets and armored skirt, yellow and brown; shield, white with yellow border design, supported by black baldric attached to black handle; sword, red scabbard, reddish brown and yellow hilt, and black baldric; spear, reddish brown shaft and gray head.   [255]: tunic, red with golden cuff; *bracae*, violet ornamented with yellow bands below knees; buskins, red ornamented with yellow; chlamys, color of blue-black background, with drawing in heavy black; armlets, girdle, and bands around torso, bluish gray; cuirass, same colors as in [250]; upper zone of skirt, brown, yellow, and white; lower zone (*pteryges*), bluish gray; *pteryges* around upper arm and collar around neck, brown and yellow; spear, reddish brown shaft and gray head.   [256]: tunic, violet with golden cuff; *bracae*, yellow ornamented with green bands above and below knees; fasciae, gray; chlamys, red; cuirass, olive green with yellow scales and ornament; armlets and girdles around hips and torso, bluish gray; *pteryges*, scale armor at right hip, collar, and strap over shoulder, brown and yellow; shield, gray inner face and yellow and brown rim; baldric, black; sword, bluish gray with scabbard and baldric of violet ornamented with yellow.   [257]: tunic, blue with golden cuff; *bracae*, blue-violet; boots, white with blue thongs; chlamys, red; short, sleeveless jerkin, skirt around hips, and sleevelets, reddish yellow with yellow scales; girdle and armlets, bluish gray; shield, bluish gray inner and outer zones, light reddish violet middle zone; scabbards of sword and dagger, light blue-violet; baldrics, dark red; dagger, gray and white.   [258]: tunic, red, decorated at hem, cuffs, collar, and shoulder with golden embroidery; chlamys, green with golden tablion (now nearly effaced); buskins, red ornamented with yellow; cross, white.

[259]: tunic, blue decorated at hem, cuff, and collar with golden embroidery; chlamys, red with golden tablia (now nearly effaced); *bracae*, green.   [260]: tunic, light red-violet; scapular, dark green with black cords; tree trunk, now dark olive green with yellow highlights; tree foliage, two values of light green, with white highlights, dark olive-green stems, black shadows and accents.

[261]: tunic, blue with golden cuff; *bracae* and cuirass, brown with yellow and white scales; fasciae, gray; chlamys, red; girdle and armlets, bluish gray; *pteryges*, brown with yellow and white highlights; scabbard, brown with blue-violet baldric; spears, yellow and brown (painted over green) with green heads.   [262]: tunic, blue with golden cuff and gold-embroidered hem, collar, and shoulder studded with green and dark red gems and with pearls; chlamys, a unique reddish brown the color of chocolate, with yellowish red border and golden tablion studded with green gems and with pearls; buskin, yellowish red; cross, white.   [263]: tunic, red ornamented at cuff, collar, and

shoulder with golden embroidery studded with green and red gems and with pearls; chlamys, green, with yellowish red border and tablion of golden embroidery studded with green and red gems and with pearls; cross, white. [264]: tunic, red with golden cuff; *bracae*, yellowish brown; boots, light reddish violet; chlamys, red-violet; cuirass, yellow over red; *pteryges*, now mostly yellow with some traces of brown or red; girdles around hips and torso, armlets, and collar, bluish gray; shield, in three zones, outer of gray, middle of light reddish violet, and center of yellow; sword scabbard and hilt, black with yellow ornaments and a black baldric; spear, yellow and reddish brown shaft and gray head.

[265]: tunic, red with yellow ornaments at collar; chlamys, blue-violet with narrow golden border and golden tablia studded with pearls and possibly gems; torque, golden; background, green in three concentric zones, darkest at center. [266]: tunic, gray (representing blue?), ornamented at collar and shoulder with golden embroidery; chlamys, green with golden tablion; traces of a golden torque; traces of a white cross; background, pink in three concentric zones, darkest at center. [267]: tunic, blue with golden cuff; *bracae*, blue-violet; fasciae, gray; chlamys, red; cuirass, traces of olive green; armlets, band around torso, collar, and strap at shoulder, bluish gray; sword, bluish gray. [268]: background of medallion, concentric zones of green; segment of halo, yellow. [269]: tunic, blue-black; chlamys, blue-violet; cross, light violet; barrier around saint, grayish green; capital, pink; shaft and base of column, gray.

The very fragmentary paintings that are described here and illustrated in Volume 3, Plates 521–529, are to be found in the two chambers that flank the main apse of the church. Collectively, these rooms are known as the pastophoria; the chamber to the north is designated as the prothesis and that to the south as the diaconicon. Closely connected with the main apse as they are, they were reserved for special priestly functions. For a description of the structure of these rooms the reader is referred to the Introduction.

By the fourteenth century a special office of Prothesis, as part of the liturgy of the Mass, had been developed; it was performed at the table of oblation in the prothesis. The rites, carried out privately by the priest and deacon, were essentially in preparation of the offerings of the bread and wine before they were taken in the procession of the Great Entry to be consecrated at the altar. Since these rites have a bearing on the iconography of the paintings that were often executed in protheses of late-Byzantine churches, it is appropriate to describe their nature briefly before the very fragmentary paintings that still exist in the prothesis of the Kariye Djami are discussed.

The altar-bread was impressed with a square seal, or stamp, the *amnos;* the stamp bore an equal-armed cross, dividing it into quarters, and the sigla $\overline{\text{IC}}$ $\overline{\text{XC}}$ NI KA in the quarters. In a symbolic emulation of Christ's sacrifice, the *amnos* was cut out of the bread with a liturgical instrument known as the holy spear (λόγχη) and placed on the paten. The particle thus cut out was likened by the priest to the Lamb, or *Amnos*, with the scriptural words: "He was led as a sheep to the slaughter. And as a spotless lamb before his shearers is dumb, so opened he not his mouth. . . . Sacrificed is the Lamb of God who taketh away the sins of the world. . . . One of the soldiers did pierce his side with a spear and straightway there came forth blood and water." Wine mingled with water was then poured into the holy chalice, and small portions of the bread, in commemoration of the Virgin, the Forerunner, and the various ranks of prophets, apostles, church Fathers, saints, and martyrs, as well as the emperor, synod, and patriarchs and finally the living and the dead, were arranged one by one on the paten in a fixed order with relation to the *amnos*. An aer, or veil, was then placed over the paten, and another over the chalice. There followed the Great Entry to the altar and the consecration there of the bread and wine and their distribution.

The dome of the prothesis (PL. 521) is so oriented that its eight flutes are centered on the longitudinal, cross, and diagonal axes of the structure beneath. Badly corroded fragments of painted plaster are still preserved in the four flutes at the north, northeast, east, and southeast (left to right in PL. 521). The figures painted on the concave surfaces of the flutes were quite evidently angels, for in each fragment at least some portion of a wing has survived. The angel in the eastern flute (PL. 522, left), the one on whom the composition of the dome would be expected to center, was evidently placed in a frontal pose: traces of his entire right wing are still preserved in the fragment to the left, as well as parts of the right side of his garments; a small

262

portion of the upper part of his left wing is preserved in the fragment to the right, and this appears to be symmetrical with the corresponding part of his right wing. Also in the fragment to the left, between his right wing and the edge of a long garment that reaches the level of his feet, is a narrow vestment hanging free of the body, its dark color contrasting with the light color of the long robe. This bit of clothing, suspended from the figure's extended right arm, might be interpreted as one end of a loros. If this interpretation is the correct one, the figure represented an archangel.

Alone among the angels, the one in the flute to the left, on the northeastern axis (PL. 523, right), though badly effaced, is still fully visible. He is turned away from the archangel on the eastern axis and stands with hands extended before him, and in near-profile, in the slightly stooped attitude of an officiating priest. That he is indeed an officiant is borne out by the fact that he wears the bishop's chasuble, apparently of white and unadorned, and the bishop's stole, which can be seen hanging down the front of his tunic, its fringed end almost reaching the level of the hem. In his hands, in an area that is much effaced, he carries an object, surely of a liturgical nature, which is now impossible to identify.

The fragmentary angel to the left (PL. 523, left), in the northern flute, appears to be in frontal pose, and he wears a light-colored garment, probably a chasuble. The dark, trilobed area of paint at the level of the hands suggests that this angel too held a liturgical object.

The fourth figure, in the southeastern flute (PL. 522, right), was apparently turned in profile to the left. The arrangement evident in the fragments that remain thus suggests that the angels of the dome were alternately in profile and frontal poses.

The evidence clearly indicates that the subject of the decoration in the dome of the prothesis was the Divine Liturgy, the celestial equivalent of the liturgical procession of the Great Entry, in which angels replace the priests and deacons in bearing the sacred elements and liturgical vessels of various kinds. In addition to the angels the complete versions of this subject represent, at the center, the figure of Christ, dressed in the vestments of an officiant and standing behind an altar. This part of the composition has been omitted from the dome of the prothesis, probably because of restrictions imposed by the fluted form of the vault. At the center of the dome there was no figural representation, and indeed no ornament of any kind, and it seems that the arrises of the flutes, unlike those of the domes in the inner narthex, were also left unadorned.

In the northeastern pendentive there is a fragment of a seraph (PL. 524); its right lateral wing, part of its right upper wing, and most of its two lower wings are still to be seen. It is quite certain, therefore, that representations of seraphim or others of the celestial powers occupied the other pendentives as well, and so became a part of the composition of the Divine Liturgy in the dome.

Turning now to the apse of the prothesis, we find that only a fragment of the painting in the conch has survived, in the lower left corner (PL. 524). Represented here is a single figure, a bishop, who bends forward toward the right in the reverent attitude of an officiating priest, with hands extended toward the missing central element of the composition. He wears the usual type of tunic with clavi and an enveloping chasuble, or *polystaurion*, covered with a pattern of crosses like that on the chasuble of St. Gregory in the apse of the parecclesion (PL. 480). His right arm, the wrist covered with the bishop's epimanikia, or sleevelets, is still preserved, and the chasuble is draped over it; his left arm, now missing, must have been above his right and held out even further, for the left side of the chasuble extends far out from his body. One end of his omophorion, which is, as usual, adorned with stripes across the ends and with widely separated crosses, hangs free between his arms. Whether he held a scroll open with his hands, as is frequently the case in representations of officiating bishops, it is now impossible to say.

At its base the painting in the conch is preserved to approximately one third of the distance around the apse along the top of the cornice. Between the figure of the bishop and the right edge of the painted fragment there is only the black paint of the background, an indication that no other figure or object existed to the left of the missing central element of the composition. It is to be supposed that in the right side of the conch there was a second bishop corresponding in attitude to the one at the left; that in the center between the two bishops stood an altar, perhaps surmounted by a ciborium; and that on the altar were placed the paten, the chalice, and a figure of the dead Christ Child as the *Amnos*, the sacrificed "Lamb of God who taketh away the sins of the world." Such a painting, placed above the table of oblation, would render in pictorial terms the meaning of the rites that were performed in the prothesis in preparing the bread and wine for the procession of the Great Entry. In late-Byzantine art such scenes involving the *Amnos* were not infrequently placed on the wall of the main apse or on the wall of the apse of the prothesis, but it is uncommon to find one, as in the Kariye Djami, in the conch of the apse.

Aside from painted ornaments in the soffits of the arches that spring from the northeastern pier, on the faces of that pier, and on the inner surfaces of the adjoining niche, the only other paintings that have survived in the prothesis are two bust figures of bishops, possibly church Fathers, at two levels on the north wall (PL. 524). Both figures are badly damaged, and neither one can now be identified. The upper one is completely visible, but much of the surface paint is lost; the lower one is largely destroyed, and what remains is even more severely effaced than the figure above it. They are portrait busts, and like the figures on the apse wall of the parecclesion they are not depicted as officiants. Each is dressed in the typical vestments of bishops, and each once held a book of the Gospels in his left arm; the figure above blesses with his right hand. It seems likely that the apse wall was decorated with a single row of bishops, who may have been portrayed in the attitudes of officiating priests, like the bishop in the conch above, that is, bent forward in profile and in all probability holding inscribed scrolls in their hands.

Of the fourteenth-century decoration in the diaconicon only a few fragmentary paintings in the dome still exist. The dome, and the drum on which it rests, as can be seen in Plate 525, are divided by ribs into eight segments; in the three eastern segments the drum is pierced by three windows. At the summit of the dome, where the ribs converge, there is a round space. A small medallion was placed there, containing a bust of Christ, the merest fragments of which remain. Above the level of the windows was an upper zone of eight standing apostles, one in each of the segments; other full-length figures, which we should presume to have been apostles as well, were placed in a lower zone in the five segments not occupied by windows. The one fragment that contains parts of both zones (PL. 528) shows no formal division between them other than that provided by the narrow zone of green ground in which the upper figures stood.

As in the dome of the prothesis, and indeed all other domes in the church, the decoration is oriented with its major axis to the east; the medallion of Christ was so placed that it was best viewed by one looking up and facing to the east, and St. Peter, the leader of the apostles, stands beneath it, in the segment above the central window of the eastern side. The medallion (PL.

526) is so small that the halo of Christ nearly fills it and at the bottom little more than the upper part of his shoulders could be included. The halo is yellow and retains, at the left, the drawing of one arm of its inscribed cross. In the lower right quadrant of the medallion is the sketchy brown underpainting of one shoulder and a lock of hair falling over it. The background of the medallion is now black.

Fragments of six apostles of the upper zone still exist (PL. 525, reading counterclockwise): at the upper left (the northwestern segment), the lower extremities of an unidentifiable apostle; at the left (the northern segment), the top of the head and halo of St. Andrew, inscribed ['O ἅγ(ιος)] 'Ανδρ[έας]; at the lower left (the northeastern segment), the upper two thirds of a figure whose features identify him as St. Paul but whose inscription is entirely effaced; at the lower center (the eastern segment), St. Peter, inscribed 'O ἅγ(ιος) Πέτρο[ς]; at the lower right (the southeastern segment), the upper two thirds of the figure of St. John, inscribed 'O ἅγ(ιος) 'Ιω(άννης) ὁ Θε(ολόγος); at the right (the southern segment), the underpainting of the head, halo, and left shoulder of an unidentified apostle. All that is left of the lower zone (PL. 525 and 528) is the underpainting of another figure presumed to be also an apostle.

The figure of St. Peter (lower right in PL. 526), as already suggested, is the pivotal one, at the east. Little more than underpainting now remains, and a large area between the left hip and knee is totally destroyed. Peter stands in frontal pose, his left arm carried in a fold of his himation, as in a sling, and his left hand holding a scroll; his right hand is extended in a gesture of blessing. Practically no color is left on his himation, but in places there is a tinge of yellow that suggests that the garment, as usual, was yellow. His tunic, visible at his right shoulder and sleeve, is a blue-black, indicative of blue, and bears a clavus that was once yellow. What can be seen of the sketch of the head reveals the usual features of St. Peter.

At Peter's right hand is the other "prince" of the apostles, St. Paul (lower left in PL. 526), turned in three-quarters view to the right to face his companion. Despite the destruction of much of his face the identification is conclusive because of the shape of the head, the high, domed brow, and the black hair, which are all characteristic of his portraits. Also supporting this identification are his position with relation to St. Peter and the red-violet color of his himation, which is well preserved where it is not totally destroyed. The tunic is blue (i.e., bluish black) and is adorned with a black clavus.

On the other side of St. Peter and reversing the pose of St. Paul is St. John the Theologian, the third-ranking apostle (lower left in PL. 527). Being also an evangelist, he is shown bearing a book of his Gospel. His head and right shoulder are destroyed, and the only garment that is still preserved is his himation, which is red-violet in color.

Of the fourth-ranking apostle, St. Andrew, who stood to the left of St. Paul (far left in PL. 526), only the top of the head and about half of the halo are now preserved. He seems to have been turned to the right to face the east.

Andrew's pendant, the figure to the right of St. John (right in PL. 527), was probably St. Matthew. Only the underpainting of the upper part of his head, a bit of his beard, and his left shoulder are preserved, but the shape of the head and the traces of features suggest an old man with a high, domed brow, a description that fits the evangelist Matthew. His himation was painted green.

Concerning the fragment in the upper zone of the northwestern segment (above in PL. 528), which contains the lower part of the figure of an apostle, all that can be said is that the figure

265

is turned to the left to face the west, that he wore a blue tunic and a yellow himation, and that he stood in a zone of green.

The figure below him, in the lower zone (below in PL. 528), is shown in three-quarters view, walking toward the right. In his left hand he holds a scroll, and a fold of fluttering drapery hangs from his left arm; his right hand is extended toward the right. The painting is so badly effaced that it is impossible to identify the original coloration of the garments.

The only other painting now to be seen in the diaconicon pertains not to the fourteenth-century decoration but to that of the earlier diaconicon of the twelfth century. The reveal of the arched doorway (PL. 529) that once led to the main apse of the church is painted with a white background above a zone of green and is framed at both sides by the usual red borders. In each jamb is a simple cross with two cross-arms, painted in dark brown, which rises from the green zone into the white area of the background. Each cross is flanked at the left by a vertical spear and at the right by a pole to the top of which a sponge is attached. Above these symbols of Christ's passion and above the larger of the two cross-arms is the painted inscription IC XC NIKA (Jesus Christ conquers). At the center of the arch is a medallion containing an eight-armed cross of dark brown set in a background of yellow.

From the period of Metochites' restorations, the only paintings that still remain to be discussed are those in the lower story of the northern annex (PL. 530), which for the sake of convenience I will designate as passageway A, and in the narrow corridor leading from the south side of the nave to the parecclesion (PL. 532 *a*), which I will designate as passageway B. These parts of the building were decorated throughout with painted ornamental motifs. The barrel vault of A, which has a span of about 3.15 m. and a length of almost 10 m., still retains parts of its overall pattern (PL. 531 *a* and *b*), which are to be seen only in the four areas left exposed when, at a later date, massive arches were built to reinforce the vault. In these areas the painting was covered with heavy coatings of whitewash, which caused rather severe damage. Below the cornice the walls of passageway A are now bare; in all probability these were originally decorated with painted imitations of marble paneling, as are the walls of passageway B. On the other hand, the painted pattern that fills the vault of B, which has a span of only 1.10 m. and a length of 3.80 m., has never been obscured by daubings of any kind and is now nearly intact; the marbleized paneling painted on its walls, however, has suffered some major losses.

In design, but not in color, the motifs of the overall pattern in the west end of the vault of passageway A (PL. 531 *b*) and of that in the vault of B (PL. 532 *b*) are akin to one another. Since the pattern in B is the more highly developed I shall describe it first. On a light gray background is a grid work of square panels alternating with outline crosses with pointed arms, formed by relatively wide, angular, interlacing strips of reddish yellow. The spaces within the crosses are filled with simple foliate motifs rather like schematized fleurs-de-lis; in each of the square panels is a floral motif consisting of a quatrefoil of pointed petals surrounded by cusped forms in a color contrasting with that of the central quatrefoil. In alternate panels the colors of the quatrefoil and surrounding forms are reversed.

In the pattern at the west end of passageway A the background is reddish yellow, the interlace is drawn in white, and each square panel as well as each cross formed by the interlace is filled with a large quatrefoil in green. The pattern at the east end (PL. 531 *a*) loses the angular character of the ones previously described; the forms are curved, so that a series of alternating quatrefoils and cusped octagonal shapes is produced, outlined by strips of white on a background of reddish yellow. Within these forms are quatrefoils of alternating red and bluish green leaves highlighted with white; in the cusped octagonal units, the quatrefoils are surrounded by other petals, which alternate between red and white in alternate units.

The oddly shaped triangular space above the cornice at the east end of passageway A, to the left of the window in the tympanum (PL. 530, 531 *c*), is filled with an especially fanciful motif, which was probably unique in the painted decorations of the church. It is an arabesque of foliate forms, painted against a white background, which grows from the bottom symmetrically, along a slightly curved axis, out of a set of three green acanthus leaves similar to those at the base of a Corinthian capital. A set of acanthus leaves appears again at midpoint in the arabesque. Between the two, the foliage is composed of leaves of various types and colors, mainly red, white, and green.

Finally, in passageway B, at the springing line of the barrel vault, there is a painted cornice, which separates the overall pattern above from the painted imitations of marble paneling on the walls below (PL. 532 c). The cornice is treated as a torus molding entwined by a spiral fillet. The rectangular panels below the cornice and their surrounding borders imitate the colors and to some extent the veining of such marbles as green serpentine and mottled red Dokimion.

IV The Sepulchral Monuments

Many of the monastic churches of Constantinople were built or restored through imperial patronage or by important personages, who were usually either members of the imperial court or of noble and aristocratic lineage. When a monastery came under such patronage, especially if its church were newly built or extensively restored, the patron was rewarded with the honored title of *ktetor*, or founder, and thereafter, especially in the Palaeologan period, the church came to be regarded as a family church. Often in the decorations of his church the *ktetor* was portrayed as donor and his monograms were carved or otherwise inscribed at various places. In his church the *ktetor* was also permitted to provide a tomb for himself and sometimes additional ones for members of his family. Thus, to cite a few well-documented examples of this practice, the monastic church of the Pantocrator, founded and erected by John II Comnenus, was provided with a special burial church for the founder, his empress, and various members of his family. The church of St. John the Baptist, built at the end of the thirteenth century by the Empress Theodora, widow of the Emperor Michael VIII Palaeologos, alongside the tenth-century church of the Panachrantos at the monastery of Constantine Lips, was constructed with wall tombs for the foundress, her mother, and her daughter, and other tombs were subsequently added for later Palaeologoi. To take still another example, the monastery of the Pammakaristos, originally a twelfth-century foundation of a certain John Comnenus and his wife Anna, of the Doukas family,[1] was taken over at the end of the thirteenth century by the Protostrator Michael Tarchaniotes Glabas, and a mortuary chapel was added to the south side, in which the *ktetor* and other members of his family were buried.

The church of the monastery of the Chora falls within the pattern of this tradition. Its last great patron, Theodore Metochites, left a portrait of himself, inscribed with the titles *ktetor* and logothete, and his monogram was carved into the cornice of the main dome and elsewhere in the church. As we have seen, he also constructed the pareclesion as a mortuary chapel and in its walls provided four arcosolia, which were to be fitted out as sepulchral monuments. Four other tombs were added at later dates in the outer and inner narthexes.[2]

These tombs have an importance that transcends their fragmentary state and the relatively poor quality of the art which most of them reveal. They are of special historical and archaeological value because they comprise the only group of sepulchral monuments of the Byzantine nobility thus far discovered in Constantinople which still retain the essential elements of their decoration and thus illustrate the type of monument, and its iconography, that formerly existed in many of the monastic churches of the city.

The eight tombs in the Kariye Djami had certain characteristics in common. Each was an arcosolium, or wall niche, wide enough and deep enough to house a sarcophagus in its lower part. Above each sarcophagus, painted on the back wall of the niche, was a portrait of the deceased accompanied in all but one case by one or more family members. It is uncertain whether everyone in the group portraits was buried in the sarcophagus or even anywhere in the church,

---

[1] See Mango and Hawkins, *D. O. Papers*, 18, 328 f.
[2] For description of the circumstances surrounding the discovery of these tombs and their condition, see the notes of the author in *D. O. Papers*, 12, 271–82, and 13, 215–28.

although some may have been placed nearby under the floor. With only one or two possible exceptions all the persons portrayed on the back walls were attired in the ceremonial garb their office or rank entitled them to wear. Some of the tombs contained additional, secondary portraits of the deceased in the jambs, at each side of the principal portrait panel, and in all cases where these exist they depict the deceased as monk or nun, in monastic garb, each inscribed with the new name that he or she adopted on taking religious vows; for in aristocratic circles it was a custom, which became most prevalent in late centuries of the empire, for a man and wife, a widow, or a widower to "retire" to a monastery late in life and thus assure burial within the walls of a church. The names that were taken on these occasions were often recorded in historical writings of the period, and they were usually, though not always, names of saints or holy men or women which had the same initial letters as their own given names. Finally, a representation of Christ or the Virgin, accompanied sometimes by busts of angels or saints, was also included in the iconographic program of a sepulchral monument. In all but one instance, the divine images were placed above the portrait groups in the upper parts of the back walls of the niches, in the soffits of the arches, or on sculptured slabs applied to the faces of the arches.

The eight tombs have been assigned letters according to their location and will be discussed in alphabetical order. The first four, the original group, are in the parecclesion: Tomb A (Figs. 10, 12 and PL. 533 *a*), possibly the tomb of Theodore Metochites, the *ktetor*, is in the north wall of the western bay; Tomb B (Figs. 10, 12; PL. 533 *b*) is in the north wall of the eastern bay; Tomb C (Figs. 10, 11; PL. 534–536) is in the south wall of the eastern bay; Tomb D (Figs. 10, 11; PL. 537–539), identified by its inscribed epitaph as the tomb of a member of the Tornikes family, is in the south wall of the western bay.

In the outer narthex three of the windows in the west wall were converted to use as tombs: Tomb E (Figs. 2, 4; PL. 540–545), in the west wall of the fifth bay, can be identified as the tomb of Irene Raoulaina Palaeologina, widow of Constantine Palaeologos (brother of the Emperor Andronicus II) and mother-in-law of Irene, the daughter of Theodore Metochites; Tomb F (Figs. 2, 4; PL. 546–547), in the west wall of the fourth bay, is now unidentifiable but belongs to a person or persons entitled to wear the monograms of the Palaeologan house; Tomb G (Figs. 2, 4; PL. 548–549), in the west wall of the second bay, is the most recent of all the monuments in the church, but its occupant cannot be identified.

The eighth tomb, here designated as Tomb H (Fig. 2; PL. 550–553), was that of a certain Demetrius, who was apparently of royal lineage; it was constructed, well after the completion of the church, against the north wall of the inner narthex.

Tomb A

FIGS. 10, 12; PL. 533 *a*

The tomb in the north wall of the western bay exceeds all others in the church in the breadth and depth of its arcosolium and in the size of its sarcophagus.[1] The sepulchral arrangements were

---

[1] Width of arcosolium at outer face of opening, 2.56 m.; depth of arcosolium, 1.06 m.; height of sarcophagus, as indicated by slots cut into masonry jambs to accommodate lid, 1.34 m. These dimensions, which governed the size of it, indicate that the sarcophagus was by far the largest in the church. Height of arch from edge of marble facing on vertical axis to floor, 3.22 m.

marked, moreover, by features, not provided in any other tombs, which gave this one a special distinction. Behind the back wall of the niche is an interior vaulted chamber, measuring 1.65 m. from east to west and 1.98 m. from north to south, which is entered through a door in the east wall of the passageway connecting the parecclesion with the nave of the church. In the north wall of the chamber was a small rectangular window which opened into the nave (see PL. 6), and in its east and west walls, flanking the back wall of the tomb, were small niches. While the function of this chamber must remain uncertain, its character and its position with relation to the nave of the church on one side and the tomb in the parecclesion on the other suggest a small chapel or oratory, in which icons with perpetually burning candles and votive lamps might have been kept and commemorative rites have been performed.

The exact place in his church where Theodore Metochites was buried is not recorded. That he had a tomb at the Chora is to be inferred from prevailing customs of the day with regard to the rights of ktetorship and from a fifteenth-century letter written by Demetrius Kabakes, who claimed descent from the Raoul and Metochites families and regarded the Chora as his family's monastery; in this interesting letter he refers to a certain tomb of another of his ancestors as being near that of the founder.[2] It must be presumed that Metochites' tomb was one of the four arcosolia that he constructed in the parecclesion and not one of those in the narthexes, which were added at later dates. If this is granted, his tomb must have been one of the two in the north wall, for the existing decorations in the two southern ones make it impossible for either one to have belonged to Metochites. Of the two in the north wall, the size and special features of Tomb A, described above, would tend to identify it as the tomb of the founder.

Sculpture was often introduced in the ornamentation of the sepulchral monuments of Constantinople. Many fragments of such sculptures, for example, were found in excavations at the church of St. John the Baptist (Fenari Isa Djami), the favored place of burial of the Palaeologoi. Among the fragments were some from an archivolt of one of the arcosolia, on which had been carved the busts of the apostles in high relief. Others were from the facing above another arch; in the center of the facing was a bust of Christ, and there were busts of angels in the spandrels and apostles in the archivolt.[3] A type of sculptural decoration for the arches and spandrels of wall tombs, this facing resembles the carved marble facing above the arcosolium of Tomb A in the Chora (PL. 533 a). The latter has an archivolt of acanthus leaves in high relief, with points turned over and undercut, which is interrupted at the center by a bust of Christ; at the top and sides is a molded border carved with a palmette motif; and in the spandrels are busts of the archangels Michael and Gabriel. The names of Christ and the archangels are inscribed in relief. The heads of the three busts have been destroyed. The facing is surmounted by a cornice that repeats at a larger scale and with minor differences the palmette motif of the frame of the spandrels.[4] The finished surfaces were coated with gesso, the background was painted blue, and the carvings were gilded. Much of the gesso, paint, and gilt have disappeared.

The sculptured slabs of the facing obviously were an addition to the arcosolium, carved and fitted into place after the paintings on the walls and vaults of the parecclesion had been finished, for the main cornice at the top of the wall and the painted plaster that had originally surrounded the arch of the tomb (which in all probability included, in the spandrels, two medallion portraits

---

2 See below, p. 286 and n. 12, 13.

3 These sculptures have been published in *D. O. Papers*, 18, in the long-delayed report of the excavations of 1929 at this church, conducted by the late Theodore Macridy.

4 Total breadth of sculptural ensemble, 3.05 m.; total height, including thin moldings at imposts and cornice above, 2.02 m.

of saints) were cut away to accommodate them. It is evident also that the masonry soffit of the arch was partially hacked away so that it sloped downward toward the back wall, to increase the height of the front face of the arch. These changes imply that the destined occupant of the tomb, or members of his family, had deferred its decoration and equipment as a place of burial for some time after the painting of the parecclesion was finished. This was true also of the two monuments in the south wall (Tombs C and D), for their decoration too was carried out later by artists whose styles of painting differed from one another and from that of the original artist who executed the paintings throughout the parecclesion. One may conjecture, therefore, that it was left to the individual owners of the tombs to provide for the decoration of their monuments at appropriate times. If Tomb A is, indeed, the tomb of Theodore Metochites, it was not necessarily the first of the tombs to be put into use. The decoration of the parecclesion was completed by the early months of 1321, and it was more than a decade later, on the 13th of March, 1332, that Metochites died.

Tomb B

FIGS. 10, 12; PL. 533 *b*

All that can be said regarding the niche in the north wall of the eastern bay is that it was constructed, and actually put into use, as a sepulchral monument.[1] When restoration work began in the parecclesion the interior of the niche was found to be covered with modern plaster, and no traces of its original decoration existed. When this plaster was removed and the masonry was laid bare, horizontal slots were found in the jambs and back wall, which had supported the lid of a sarcophagus, and cuttings in the front edges from the level of the lid to the floor indicated where the front slab of the sarcophagus had been inserted. Unlike Tombs A and D this monument was never adorned with marble facings, and in this respect it is like its pendant in the south wall of the east bay (Tomb C), which it probably resembled in having a portrait panel in the back, above the sarcophagus, and an image of Christ or the Virgin in the soffit of the arch. In the restoration of the parecclesion the interior of the niche, above the level of the sarcophagus, was covered with new plaster and painted gray; the masonry below this level was left exposed to indicate the position of the sarcophagus—the same procedure that was followed in all tombs throughout the church.

1 Width of arcosolium between masonry faces of its reveals, 2.36 m.; depth, .75 m.;
height from crown of arch to floor, 3.10 m.

Tomb C

FIGS. 10, 11; PL. 534–536 *c*

The only tomb in the church whose decoration is still relatively intact is the one designated Tomb C, in the south wall of the eastern bay of the parecclesion.[1] Its paintings, unlike those of all the other tombs where paintings still exist, have long been exposed to view; the heads and

1 Width of arcosolium, 2.54 m.; depth, .60 m.; height, 3.14 m.; height of sarcophagus, 1.32 m. For a preliminary report with an illustration of the tomb in the early stages of its repair, see Underwood, *D. O. Papers*, 12, pp. 274–76 and Fig. 10.

hands of all figures were daubed over with yellow paint, and the entire decoration was subsequently obscured with whitewash, but it seems never to have been concealed by masonry fill. The painting on the back wall was long ago described and sketched,[2] but the fact that it pertained to a funerary monument was never observed.

These paintings are clearly the work not of the master, or masters, responsible for the frescoes of the parecclesion as a whole but of an inferior painter, and they were executed at a somewhat later date. Not only is the style quite different, but at least three pigments were used that are not found in the main fresco decorations of the chapel — vermilion, indigo, and smalt.

Filling the panel in the back of the niche, above the level of the sarcophagus, are four full-length figures, standing side by side in a zone of green. The principal personages, portrayed at the center in princely costumes, a man at the left and a woman at the right, can be presumed to be the deceased man and his wife. At the far right is a woman whose dress, to judge from its form and color, might well be that of a nun. Since all inscriptions have completely disappeared, the relationship of this figure to the couple at the center must remain unknown, but for reasons that will be explained in the discussion of Tombs D and E it is possible that it may be a second portrait of the woman in princely attire at the center, but this time in her religious garb. The woman at the far left is dressed in a manner similar to that of the wife of Tornikes in Tomb D, and not in nun's habit as one might think at first glance.

In the top of the arch soffit, above the portraits, is a panel, about 1.08 m. wide, containing a bust of Christ with seraphim. This is separated by decorative borders from vertical panels in the jambs, about .75 m. high, which contain busts of angels, in three-quarters view, facing the portraits on the back wall. These panels are framed at the top by semicircular borders, and below them are square panels decorated with geometric designs.

The principal personage on the back wall is the man to left of center; he is less crowded than the others and is the only one who stands free from overlapping by others. He wears a very tall hat of a dark violet color, which flares out to its greatest width at the top. It resembles the hat worn by Michael Tornikes in Tomb D; its type is not that of an imperial crown, nor of a *skiadion* such as is worn by Metochites in the mosaic of the inner narthex (frontispiece). The undergarment, tight-sleeved and open down the front, is of a heavy material in a diaper pattern, with a large fleur-de-lis in each repeat. The pattern is painted in a grayish blue (smalt) over a ground of gray-green. The cuffs of this garment and its lining, which is visible where the garment is slightly parted in front, below knee level, are dark red. Around his waist is a yellow girdle. His outer garment is a green coat with fur lining, of the type with very long sleeves that hang empty at the sides; it is open down the front. Although the painting is badly effaced and its details are hardly visible, such a sleeve can be seen hanging down the figure's right side to a level well below his knees; the opening at the end is rendered as a very dark oval shape. In this sleeve, at about waist level, there is a slit, through which his right forearm emerges. Coats of this kind were fashionable in the fourteenth century, and examples can be seen elsewhere in the church, on figures portrayed in Tombs F and G, for instance, or on one of the full-length figures of martyrs

2 First described by Th. Mühlmann, "Die Fresko-Gemälde in der byzantinischen Klosterkirche Chora," *Archiv für kirchliche Kunst*, XI, 4 (1887), 26, 27; the figures are there said, incorrectly, to represent an imperial family consisting of two men, Michael VIII and Andronicus II, wearing crowns, and, at their sides, two women. Alexander

Rüdell pointed out that one of the "crowned" figures was in reality a woman and attempted, with only minor errors, to reconstruct the monograms on her costume (*Die Kahrie-Dschamisi in Constantinopel: Ein Kleinod Byzantinischer Kunst* [Berlin, 1908], p. 13 and Fig. 13).

([175]) in the mosaics of the outer narthex. That they were worn by women as well as men is demonstrated by the embroidered "shroud" of the Rumanian princess Maria Mangop, descendant of the Byzantine families of the Asans and Palaeologoi, on which the dead princess is depicted wearing just such a coat.[3] The strip of fur lining at one edge of the coat on the figure in the arcosolium, which the gesture of the left hand has exposed to view, is rendered in yellow and brown, in a scale pattern.

It appears that the head of this figure, like the heads of others in the group, was restored in Byzantine times, presumably because of severe damage to the original face. The face, beard, neck, and most of the hair are painted on a secondary layer of plaster, which stands out in slight relief. The eyes and nose of the restored face, in turn, are damaged. Although there is no point at which one can see whether the original plaster under the secondary layer was painted, it probably was, because in the case of other figures in this tomb whose faces and hands were covered one can see that the original painted surface continues beneath the later plaster covering.

The woman to the right of center wears a very elaborate crown, which will be described below. Her dress, visible in a wide area in front, is of green material with a pattern of widely spaced, four-petaled blossoms of yellow; one of the tightly fitting sleeves is exposed. Her outer garment is a dark red, fur-lined mantle, which hangs free at the sides. The fur lining is indicated in the same manner as that of the coat of her male companion, but in darker yellow and brown. On the right side of the garment, over the red ground, are traces of medallions containing monograms of at least two names. A careful on-the-spot inspection reveals that the medallions were arranged in vertical and horizontal rows, the two vertical rows, of seven medallions each, running the length of the garment, and it is to be presumed that such medallions also existed originally at the left. The medallions were about 11 cm. in diameter and were connected by small circles about 5 cm. in diameter. The few monograms at all legible on close inspection are recognizable as those of the Palaeologan and Asan families [4] and are very much like those on the garments of the women in Tombs E and F. Under the dark red ground, the mantle was first painted a bright red, on the order of vermilion, which shows through wherever the dark red has come away.

The face, the lower part of the crown, the neck, and the exposed parts of the shoulder of this figure were covered over with a thin layer of plaster and repainted in a Byzantine restoration. Parts of this second layer, which stood out in relief, still exist, at the shoulder and base of the neck and in the upper left part of the face, where one still sees part of the left eye and brow. When the restored face was in turn damaged, the disappearance of the plaster that had covered the lower part of the crown revealed the original paint in that area. The original crown was somewhat lower and narrower than the restored one and had a rather narrow band at the bottom, cusped along its upper edge and studded with rectangular gems of red. Centered at the top of the first crown was a fleur-de-lis. The restored crown flared out to sharp points at the sides, and its upper contour was also cusped and decorated at the center with a fleur-de-lis. At the base of the neck the restorer provided a necklace. The hands also were covered with plaster, which stands out in slight relief, and repainted.

The woman at the far right is turned toward the center, in three-quarters view; the clothing of the figure on her right partially overlaps hers. The portrait is severely damaged, in large

---

3 O. Tafrali, *Le Trésor byzantin et roumain du monastère de Poutna* (Paris, 1925), PL. 43-45.

4 See explanation of monograms in discussion of Tomb E, below.

part owing to the great fissure in the masonry, about 8 cm. in width, that passes through it, dislocating the two parts and making the figure appear much wider than it was originally. The woman is dressed in a nun's habit consisting of a tunic, or dress, of light yellowish brown with dark brown folds, over it a long mantle of dark brown, and finally a light yellowish brown headdress that fits tightly around her face and covers her shoulders. Her face, on plaster that rises in relief, seems to be a restoration, but her hands appear to be unrestored.

At the far left is another woman whose body, in three-quarters view, is turned toward the center; her face, however, like those of all the other figures, is shown frontally. As noted above, her costume resembles the one in the portrait of the wife of Michael Tornikes, on the back wall of Tomb D. Her dress, which has tight sleeves and is fitted at the waist, is of a dark violet color. Her headdress, of the type worn by the woman at the far right but white, now slightly yellowed, covers all her head but the oval of her face and drapes over her shoulders. Her face and hands seem to be unrestored, although they are now rather damaged.

It is evident that the portraits were painted after the decoration of the arch soffit had been completed, because the plaster of the back wall turns onto, and overlaps, the red border of the arch soffit. And the border surrounding the lunette of the back wall was painted red and edged with a white line before the portraits were painted, for the upper left part of the head of the woman at the far left and the upper left angle of the man's hat overlap the border. That the tomb was decorated in two stages, the soffit first and then the portraits, does not mean that the stages were of different periods or hands. Painting the soffit before the back of the niche was the normal procedure, and it avoided the damage to finished work from the accidental splashing of plaster or color that could result from a reversed order of procedure.

The panel containing the bust of Christ, in the center of the soffit, is largely preserved except at the right side, where the original plaster is destroyed (PL. 536 a). Christ's pose is frontal, and he extends both hands to the sides in blessing. He is surrounded by a complicated mandorla composed of an outer curved form and an inner rectangle from the sides of which triangles project. Long, pointed rays of glory radiate from the bust, and seraphim, partly concealed by the triangles of the mandorla, peep out from the background, one at each side. Christ wears a dark red tunic and a green himation, painted over a black ground. The rays are dark gray, bordered by a light yellow zone and by thin white outlines. The various forms of the mandorla are painted in concentric zones of gray in three values. The seraphim are yellow and brown.

The central panel of the soffit was separated from those beside it by borders of palmettes — only the left one is now preserved — drawn in white on backgrounds alternately red and blue. Below these borders are semicircular-headed panels containing half-length figures of angels with bowed heads, each holding a scepter in one hand and making a gesture of intercession with the other. The lower part of the background in each panel is green, the upper part black. The angel at the left, or east, side (PL. 536 b) wears a red tunic and a green himation; his companion at the opposite side (PL. 536 c) wears a blue tunic and a yellow himation. The outer parts of the wings are brown, the underparts gray with nearly black drawing.

Between the angel panel and the level of the sarcophagus each jamb is decorated with a square panel painted to imitate marble incrustation. In the center of each square is a disc, one in imitation of red porphyry and the other of green porphyry, surrounded by a running chevron motif in black and white, and each square is bordered in the chevron motif.

The soffit of this tomb repeats, in paint, the essential iconographic elements that in Tombs

A and D are carved in the marble slabs surmounting the arches, that is, a bust of Christ flanked by busts of angels (inscribed on the sculptures of Tomb A as the archangels Michael and Gabriel).

Tomb D, the tomb of Michael Tornikes   FIGS. 10, 11; PL. 537–539 c

The fourth tomb in the parecclesion,[1] centered in the south wall of the western bay, is the sepulchral monument of a member, or members, of the Tornikes family, according to the epitaph that forms part of the sculptural decoration around the face of the arch. This tomb utilized sculpture and mosaic in its original decoration, but when the mosaic figures on the back wall suffered partial destruction in Byzantine times they were restored in fresco.

The sculptures closely resemble those which were applied around the face of the arch of Tomb A, although they differ in dimensions and details. Each sculptural facing was made specifically for the tomb it adorns — the two are not elements taken from a single dismembered ciborium, as has been supposed.[2] Like its counterpart, the arch of Tomb D is faced with an archivolt of radiating acanthus leaves with outwardly curved, undercut points, but the bust of Christ is set above the archivolt, not within it, and is framed by a semicircular archivolt of its own, which projects above the field of the carved spandrels into the slab of the epitaph. The two angels in the spandrels hold their wings in vertical position, whereas each angel in Tomb A extends one of its wings horizontally. We can tell that the marble facing of Tomb D was already in place when the mosaics were set in the soffit of the arch, for the plaster edge of the setting bed neatly abuts the back edge of the marble and conforms exactly to its curvature; moreover, some of the red paint of the setting bed was accidentally daubed onto the back edge of the marble. The conclusion is that the mosaics and the sculpture were contemporaneous and that the marble facing was set in place as the first operation in decorating the tomb.

Between the top of the carved spandrels and the cornice that surmounts the entire slab is the incised epitaph, in two sections, flanking the central bust of Christ. In each section are six lines, each line comprising two verses of the metrical inscription of twenty-four verses. The inscription and its translation, the latter by Alexander Van Millingen,[3] except the first four lines, which have been altered, read as follows:

Ὅσους ἂν ἀθροίζοι τις ἐνθάδε κρότους	However many applauses one may collect upon this earth,
νεκροὺς ὁ ταφεὶς ἐξελέγξει Τορνίκης,	When they are all dead, Tornikes, a man of myriad
ὁ τρισαριστεὺς ἢ κονοσταῦλος μέγας,	Or Grand Constable, who lies buried here, [victories,
ὥσπερ μίμους, βέλτιστε, πιθήκους λέων.	Will put them to shame as, good friend, a lion shames
5 Ὅς, βασιλικῶν ἀποτεχθεὶς αἱμάτων,	5 He who was by birth of royal blood, [mimicking apes.
παρέσχεν αὐτοῖς προσφυῆ καὶ τὸν τρόπον.	Presented also a manner of life conformed to that [descent.

1 Width of arcosolium, between masonry jambs, 2.46 m.; depth of arcosolium, .62 m.; height of arch at center, 2.96 m.; height of sarcophagus, 1.36 m. For a preliminary report on this tomb see Underwood, *D. O. Papers*, 12, pp. 271–74 and Figs. 5–7.

2 Feodor Shmit, *Kakhrie-dzhami* (Izvestiia Russkago Arkheologicheskago Instituta v Konstantinopole, XI; text,

Sofia, album of plates, Munich, 1906), p. 95. The dimensions of the sculptured facing of Tomb A are recorded above in note 4 of the Tomb A description. Those of Tomb D are: total breadth excluding overhang of cornice, 3.02 m.; total height including cornice, 2.07 m.

3 *Byzantine Churches in Constantinople: Their History and Architecture* (London, 1912), pp. 30 f.

Ποῖον γὰρ οὐκ ἦν ἀρετῆς εἶδος φορων [sic],
ὡς ὁ πρέπων ἕκαστον ἐζήτει χρόνος;
βουληφόρος δ'οὖν, καὶ πρὸ τῆς ἡλικίας

10 καὶ δημαγωγός, καὶ κριτὴς ἦν ἀγχίνους.
Καὶ πρὸς μὲν ἐχθροὺς τακτικὴν ἔπνει φλόγα,
κεραυνὸς ὢν ἄφυκτος αὐτοῖς ἀθρόοις,
τῇ δὲ στρατιᾷ π(ατ)ρικῶς ἐπεστάτει,
φρουρῶν τὰ κοινά, μὴ κλαπῇ τὸ συμφέρον.

15 Κήδους δὲ τυχὼν εὐγενοῦς καὶ κοσμίου
καὶ βασιλικὸν προσλαβὼν αὖθις γένος
καὶ λαμπρὸν ὑπόδειγμα παρεὶς τὸν βίον,
κεῖται μοναστὴς εὐτελὴς ἐν ὀστέοις.
Ἥλιε καὶ γῆ καὶ τελευταῖοι κρότοι.

20 Πενθεῖ δὲ μικροῦ πᾶν τὸ Ῥωμαίων γένος,
ὅσον περ αὐτὸν ἀγνοοῦν οὐ τυγχάνει.
Ἀλλ' ὦ μόνε ζῶν καὶ μεθιστῶν τὰς φύσεις,
εἴ πού τι καὶ πέπραχεν αὐτῷ μὴ πρόπον [sic],
λύσιν παρασχὼν τὴν Ἐδὲμ κλῆρον δίδου.

For what form of virtue did he not possess
Such as the fitting occasion demanded each?
Therefore he was a councillor before the usual age,

10 And a popular leader and an acute judge,
And upon enemies he breathed a strategic flame,
And was an irresistible thunderbolt upon their serried
He presided over the army like a father,   [ranks.
Guarding the commonweal lest any advantage to it should be

15 Contracting a highly-born and seemly marriage   [stolen.
And securing thus again royal affinity,   [connection,
And leaving his life as a splendid example,
He lies a poor monk among bones!
O sun, O earth, O final applauses!

20 Well-nigh the whole Roman race laments him,
As much of it as is not ignorant of him.
But O only living One and transformer of natures,
If perchance he did aught that was not fitting for him,
Granting him pardon, give him Eden as his inheritance.

From this epitaph we learn that the Tornikes who was buried here held the high dignity of Grand Constable at the imperial court [4] and that both he and his wife were of royal lineage. It is implied that he possessed, in addition to the military prowess that is so extravagantly praised, such qualities of judgment that he was consulted in matters of state. At the time of his death, however, he was a poor monk. Much of this information corresponds to the statements of John Cantacuzenus, who supplies Tornikes' Christian name, Michael, and refers to him, again, as Grand Constable in the reign of Andronicus II and as a relative, on his mother's side, of the imperial family.[5] Cantacuzenus adds that Tornikes and Theodore Metochites remained loyal to Andronicus II and together served as trusted councilors of the senior emperor on the policies to be adopted with respect to Andronicus III, the rebellious younger emperor, during the period of the civil wars (1321–28).[6] It must have been the same Tornikes, described by the historian Nicephorus Gregoras as a "nobleman," who headed an important embassy to the court of the Serbian Kral Stephen Uroš III (Dečanski) at Skoplje in the spring of 1327.[7] The purpose of this mission, which Gregoras accompanied, was of such a nature as to require that it be carried out by trusted, intimate friends of the Metochites family. The mission was dispatched by the government in Constantinople (that is, by the emperor and his alter ego, Metochites) to bring back Metochites' daughter, Irene, from Skoplje, where her husband, the Caesar John Palaeologos, Despot of Salonika, had just died while on a mission of his own to Dečanski, his recently acquired son-in-law.[8] In this tragic situation Metochites' daughter, from motives of maternal

---

4 According to Ihor Ševčenko, *Études sur la polémique entre Théodore Métochite et Nicéphore Choumnos* (Corpus Bruxellense Historiae Byzantinae, Subsidia III, Brussels, 1962), p. 160, the Grand Constable ranked, at this time, twelfth in the hierarchy.

5 Joannes Cantacuzenus, *Historiarum*, Bk. I, Ch. 11; Bonn ed. (1828), I, 54.

6 This Tornikes should not be confused with Michael Palaeologos Asan, eldest son of Irene Palaeologina, sister to Andronicus II, and of the deposed Bulgarian Tsar, Ivan III

Asan (A. Papadopulos, *Versuch einer Genealogie der Palaiologen, 1259–1453* [Munich, 1938], No. 44, 45), as he was confused by R. Guilland; see "Études sur l'histoire administrative de l'empire byzantin: Le Grand Connétable," *Byzantion*, XIX (1949), p. 107. On this and other confusions see Underwood, *D. O. Papers*, 12, p. 272 and n. 5 and 7.

7 See Gregoras' description of the journey in his letter, No. 12, published by Guilland, *Correspondance de Nicéphore Grégoras* (Paris, 1927), pp. 31–51.

8 See Papadopulos, pp. 23 f.

sentiment, felt impelled to remain at the Serbian court with her very young daughter, Maria, wife of Dečanski. The fact that Gregoras was sent on the mission is understandable in view of his own close friendship with Metochites and his favorite child, and one can suppose that Tornikes was assigned to head the mission for similar reasons and because of his position as councilor. This incident, which occurred scarcely more than a year before the overthrow of the old regime in Constantinople and the cruel reprisals that were taken against those in high position who were its supporters, especially Metochites and, presumably, Tornikes, tends to explain in part the burial of Michael Tornikes in the tomb at the Chora, where in death he would remain by the side of his friend and colleague, Theodore Metochites.

As in all the other tombs where the decoration still exists, portraits of the deceased were placed within the lunette of the back wall of the niche, above the sarcophagus (PL. 538). The panel shows, even in its fragmentary state, that it was first executed in mosaic and that portraits of Michael Tornikes and his wife stood at either side of an image of the Virgin and Christ Child. The two portraits had been so severely damaged that their restoration, presumably at the instigation of members of the Tornikes family, was carried out in paint on a coating of plaster that thinly covered the gold mosaic tesserae of the background and probably some remaining mosaic fragments of the original portraits.

Early photographs and plans [9] show that the interior of the tomb was screened from view by a Turkish wall, built flush with the face of the arch and pierced by two doors; the taller, wider door at the left led to a rectangular opening in the masonry at the back of the arcosolium, the cutting of which had destroyed the lower part of the portrait of Tornikes and part of the central figure of the Virgin and Child. The smaller door at the right gave access to an improvised cupboard. About 1945 the fill of the arch was removed by the Turkish authorities and the portrait panel was exposed to view.[10]

The central mosaic of the Virgin and Child exists in two fragments: the one at the left contains parts of the Virgin's right shoulder and arm, the Child's right hand, and a bit of the rim of his halo; the second fragment contains most of the Virgin's left shoulder and arm, and the Child's left shoulder and hand. It is not possible to say whether the Virgin was depicted standing at full length, as a bust or half-figure, or seated on a throne. It is clear, however, that the Virgin and Child were frontally posed, the Child with both hands extended symmetrically to the sides in blessing, and that the type of the image was that which was used in the medallion at the summit of the dome of the parecclesion (PL. 411). The background of the mosaic was of gold glass tesserae, and the garments of the Virgin were of blue glass; the Child's garments were represented as cloth of gold. The technique exhibited in these fragments suggests a mosaic of high quality.

Tornikes, dressed in the costume of a court dignitary, was placed to the Virgin's right, in the more honored side of the lunette. Only the head and shoulders still exist, and these are badly damaged, especially in the face. The eyes and mouth have been destroyed, but to judge from present appearances Tornikes was portrayed as an elderly man with a rather long, pointed beard of gray. He wears a tall hat flaring outward at the crown, painted in a very dark purple; the upper edge has a narrow gray binding, depicted in short diagonal strokes, and at the bottom

9 Shmit, PL. 82, left, and PL. 83; Van Millingen, PL. 92; Rüdell, PL. 1.

10 The fragments of painting and mosaic were subse-quently cleaned and repaired in the restorations of the Byzantine Institute.

is a narrow band of white. His outer garment, the only one now visible, is dark green and is adorned with what appears to be a fur collar, perhaps part of a fur lining similar to that in the coat of the man in Tomb C.

The portrait of the wife of Tornikes is, by comparison, rather well preserved, and it probably reflects the posture that was her husband's. Her head is painted frontally, but her shoulders are turned toward the left; her hands and forearms are slightly raised in a gesture directed toward the Virgin. Although her eyes and nose are now destroyed, her oval face is otherwise well preserved and shows very long, arched eyebrows and a small, full-lipped mouth. She wears a tight-sleeved dress of dark purple similar to that of her husband's hat; the dress is gathered at the waist and has a very wide skirt. At the wrists are flaring white cuffs, apparently detachable, of a curious shape. Her head, all but the face, is covered by a white scarf that loops under the chin; its fringed ends are draped over her shoulders.

The frescoed background, superimposed over the gold background of the original mosaic, is painted in four horizontal zones of considerable width. The upper zone, above shoulder level, is black; the lower zones are of three values of green. The darkest zone, at the bottom, is preserved only in a small area at the lowest point of the fragment.

The soffit of the arch of the Tornikes monument still preserves much of its original mosaic decoration in unrestored condition, and, although it has suffered considerable looting of gold tesserae and in its lower slopes is totally destroyed, it nevertheless retains all the essential elements of its composition. Set in the gold background at the top of the arch is a medallion containing a jeweled, equal-armed cross against a background of three concentric zones.[11] An outside row of light gray stone tesserae borders the outer zone of the background, which is of darker gray marble. The second zone is of light blue glass, and the central disc is of dark blue glass. The arms of the cross, which increase slightly in width toward the ends, are outlined by a single row of white marble, and the field of each arm is set with gold tesserae. At the crossing of the arms and again at their ends are red gems, represented by terra cotta surrounded by dark red glass; in each arm are four "pearls," made of small discs of mat white stone, and at each corner of each arm is a teardrop of dark red glass.

The principal elements of the soffit mosaic, however, are the portraits of a monk in the slope at the left and of a nun in the slope at the right. These were originally full-length standing figures, but now the monk is completely destroyed below the level of the elbows and the nun below the level of the knees. Above their heads the figures are identified by mosaic inscriptions, which are preserved, with only minor losses, either in tesserae of black glass or in the painted setting bed, from which the tesserae of many of the letters had been scraped or picked. The inscription above the monk reads:

Ὁ αὐτὸς μοναχὸς | Μακάριος

The inscription above the nun reads:

Ἡ αὐτή μο[ναχὴ] | Εὐγενία

The use of the articles with αὐτός and αὐτή gives the inscriptions a meaning that can be expressed as "the same person, the monk Makarios" (or "the nun Eugenia"), which indicates that the monk Makarios and the nun Eugenia are the same persons who are portrayed elsewhere in the monument and therefore that the portraits in the back of the niche had indeed been executed

---

11 Diameter of medallion, .485 m.

in mosaic before their restoration in fresco. So Michael Tornikes, as the epitaph says, became a monk before his death, choosing "Makarios" as his new name in religion. It is to be noted that he followed the practice of selecting a name which has the same initial letter as the given name (Theodore Metochites adopted the name Theoleptos), and although this practice was not invariable we may assume that his wife's given name began with the letter epsilon; but of this we have no record.

In this tomb, therefore, we have an instance of the use of "double portraiture," that is, the deceased are twice represented, once in civil garb and again in monastic habit. At least one other instance of this practice, which was not uncommon in Byzantine sepulchral iconography,[12] will be found in the tombs at the Chora (see below, Tomb E).

The monk, who turns with a gesture of supplication toward the Virgin, at his left in the adjacent lunette, wears a blue scapular, which can be seen through the narrow opening of his outer garment, above his hand. His mantle and the hood that fits tightly around his face are of black glass tesserae. What remains of his face is set in light pink marble tesserae and shows little indication of modeling; his beard, almost intact, is of brown and greenish brown glasses. The nun, her pose the reverse of her husband's, wears a mantle of black glass, closed at the neck under a black collar but open down the front to reveal its black draw cords and the blue scapular beneath. To the left of the scapular is a vertical strip of dark violet glass, six rows wide, which seems to represent her tunic, exposed between the mantle and the scapular. She wears, in addition, a flat-topped hat covered by a black veil, which falls straight at the sides of her face and envelops her shoulders. Both veil and collar are outlined by single rows of gray marble.

---

12 Gabriel Millet, "Portraits byzantins," *Revue de l'art chrétien*, LXI (1911), 445–51. See also Hippolyte Delehaye, *Deux Typica byzantins de l'époque des Paléologues* (Brussels, 1921), p. 144.

Tomb E, the tomb of Irene Raoulaina Palaeologina

FIGS. 2, 4; PL. 540–545

It has always been evident that in its original form the west façade of the church was of a very open type, punctuated in each of the six bays of the outer narthex by a tall arch, its base almost at floor level; and that, except for the one in the third bay, which served as the principal entrance to the church, the arches were afterward blocked with masonry. The presumption was that these great windows had been filled when the church was converted to Moslem use. When the modern plaster was removed from the interior face of the west wall, the cut-stone and rubble fill that was revealed could indeed be recognized as late masonry, into which small, pointed windows had been set, their sills about 2.65 m. above the floor. On the exterior, however, the cut-stone fills of three of the five windows—in the second, fourth, and fifth bays counting from north to south—projected in a curious manner, rather like buttresses, from the original face of the wall, but only as far up as the sills of the pointed windows, above which they became flush with the wall surface. These projecting fills below the windows were of carefully cut stone blocks, but in courses that differed in dimensions from one window to the next, an indication that they were laid up at different periods and not contemporaneously with one another.

The removal of the stone and rubble fill from the interior of the former window of the fifth bay, with which we are concerned at this point, revealed that the cut-stone masonry projecting from the exterior face below the window was a Byzantine fill, which had originally extended to a much greater height and which had been partly destroyed in the course of later alterations. When the inner face of this truncated Byzantine wall was fully exposed it became evident that the window had been converted into an arcosolium, of the type constructed in the parecclesion, by means of the insertion of a screen wall, about .60 m. thick, half projecting on the exterior and half set within the span of the arch; a niche about .60 m. in depth remained in the inside of the arch. The arcosolium had housed a sarcophagus, and above it, both on the wall and in the reveals, were paintings pertaining to a sepulchral monument.[1]

This arcosolium [2] is unique among the three in the outer narthex in that paintings were not restricted to the back wall of the niche but were placed also in the soffit of the arch and in the jambs, between the top of the sarcophagus and the cornice. The original mosaic ornament in the soffit of the window was concealed under an archivolt of cut-stone voussoirs, which rests on the overhang of the cornice at the tops of the jambs. The face of this archivolt and its intrados were plastered and thus provided with painting surfaces. Below the cornice, the marble revetments of the jambs were removed and plaster support for paintings was applied directly to the masonry. Thus, above the sarcophagus all the surfaces within the arcosolium, with the possible exception of the semicircular lunette, were painted. While the paintings in the soffit and the jambs are still relatively complete, though in varying states of preservation, only the lower part of the painting on the back wall still survives. It exists to a height of about one meter above the presumed level of the top of the sarcophagus.

The face of the cut-stone archivolt was painted simply in geometric designs. The soffit, however, contains a bust image of the Virgin and Christ Child (Blachernitissa), the Virgin in the pose of an orant, within a cusped mandorla, which half obscures four seraphim peering out from behind. In the haunches of the soffit, flanking the Virgin, are two medallions, containing bust figures of Sts. Cosmas of Maiuma (left) and John Damascene (right), the two hymnographers depicted in the eastern pendentives of the dome of the parecclesion [225] and [224].

When the rubble fill in the upper part of the arcosolium was removed some evidence came to light, just outside the paintings in the soffit, suggesting that a semicircular window may have existed within the arch. If this was the case, the back wall of the arcosolium terminated at cornice level in the manner in which it has been reconstructed by the Byzantine Institute (PL. 540). The wall was devoted entirely to portraits of an unusually large number of persons, probably six in all, each of whom was dressed in civil garb. The panel is framed by the usual red border, but within this is a narrower one consisting of a wave motif in red on white. Within its borders the panel measures 1.57 m. in width; assuming, as the evidence indicates, that a semicircular window existed above the panel and that originally the panel rose to the same level as those in the jambs, its height would have been approximately equal to its width. The existing fragment, measuring .65 m. in height, constitutes only the lower two fifths of the original painting. Below the portraits is a horizontal panel of yellow, in imitation of marble, which formed a transition between the sarcophagus and the portraits, but the evidence indicates that

---

1 The first notices concerning the discovery of this tomb were published by the author in *D. O. Papers*, Vol. 12, pp. 278-82 and Figs. 11-13; and in Vol. 13, pp. 216-22 and Figs. 1-4.

2 Height of arcosolium from its floor (.24 m. above floor level of narthex) to soffit of its arch, 4.16 m.; height from its floor to springing line of arch (top of cornice), 3.41 m.; width between plaster surfaces of jambs, 1.77 m.; height from floor to top of fragment of painting on back wall, 2.46 m.; height from floor to top of beam holes (for support of sarcophagus lid), 1.46 m.

much of this was covered by the top of the sarcophagus. The plaster on which the portraits were painted is very thin and seems to have been applied in only one coat. Owing to the roughness and unevenness of the masonry, the plaster barely covers it in spots and the surface is unusually bumpy. There was little protection from seepage of moisture, and the painting has suffered greatly both in decomposition of the plaster and in flaking of the surface paint. In many places cleavages developed behind the plaster, and these have caused total loss in numerous, but relatively small, areas.

The figure of the Virgin in the soffit of the arch is dressed in a blue tunic exposed only at the sleeves; the cuffs are set off by two bands of red highlighted with white hatching, one at the wrist and the other halfway to the elbow. Her mantle and headdress are a dark reddish brown that gives the effect of a deep purple; over this the rather confused drapery folds are indicated in light grayish brown. Highlights, which often bear no relation to the forms, are drawn in short, very narrow strokes of white. At her shoulders and at the top of her forehead are white stars composed of alternating crosses and dots. Her flesh, and that of the Christ Child, is rendered in various values of browns, and in contrast to the paintings of the parecclesion this image shows no evidence of the use of terre-verte in the modeling or of reds for the brightening. The field of the halo is yellow ochre, and, unlike those in the parecclesion, it was never gilded. The Christ Child, posed frontally with both hands extended in blessing, wears a green tunic with yellow and white highlights and a few dark red strokes for the drawing; his himation is red with yellowish white highlights. The halo is yellow and, within the arms of the cross, gray and white. The cusped mandorla is a pale grayish blue bordered by two bands of pale bluish green. To the left of the Virgin's halo is inscribed in monogrammatic form the word Μ(ήτ)ηρ, but no trace exists of the companion word Θ(εο)ῦ. In each of the four segments between the cusps of the mandorla a half-hidden figure of a seraph is painted in yellow, with red drawing and white highlights.

The medallions of St. Cosmas of Maiuma, in the left side of the arch soffit, and St. John Damascene, in the right, measure .52 m. in diameter. The backgrounds of both medallions are red, and they are bordered by a wave pattern in red on white. Each hymnographer holds an open, inscribed scroll in his left hand; Cosmas extends his right hand to the side in blessing, and John raises his right hand, palm outward, before him.

St. Cosmas, inscribed Ὁ ἅγ(ιος) Κοσ[μ]ᾶς, has a long, dark brown beard with light blue highlights and a very high, domed brow. His tunic and hood, the latter slipped down over the back of his shoulders, are brown with grayish brown and white lights. The mantle is light green with shadows and drawing in brown and highlights in a very pale green. The inscription on his scroll, quoting the *incipit* of one of the chants for the funeral service for monks, reads as follows: Ὡς ἄνθος | μαραίνε|ται, κ(αὶ) ὡ|ς ὄναρ | π[α]ρέρχε|ται κ(αὶ) δι|[αλ]ύεται | [πᾶς] ἄνθρ|ωπο(ς),[3] that is, "Every man fades as a flower, and passes as a dream, and is dissolved."

St. John Damascene, inscribed Ὁ ἅγ(ιος) Ἰω(άννης) ὁ Δαμασκη[ν]ός, wears a turban-like headdress; his moderate-length gray beard divides below the chin into two corkscrew curls. Only the cuff of his loose-sleeved yellow and white tunic is to be seen; otherwise his body is covered by a mantle of a dark reddish brown, rather like purple, that is similar to the color of the mantle of the Virgin in the summit of the arch. A bit of light grayish blue drapery, probably representing part of a hood hanging down his back, appears over his left shoulder. His turban is

---

3 Cf. Μικρὸν εὐχολόγιον, ἢ ἁγιασματάριον τὸ μέγα, ed. E. D. Skarpas (Athens, n.d.), p. 364.

green, with wrappings and folds of yellow and white; each of the two principal bands has two cross-stripes of brown. The seven-line inscription on his scroll, quoting the *incipit* of one of the chants for the funeral service for monks, reads: Ὄντως | φοβε|ρώτατον | τὸ τοῦ θα|νάτου | μυστί|ριον,[4] "Verily, most fearful is the mystery of death."

Among the portraits below the cornice, those in the panel on the back wall depicted the deceased in their secular, ceremonial vestments. Three figures stood in the foreground, the central one, free from the others and in the most prominent position, at a slightly higher level than the two beside her. Parts of three other standing figures are to be seen at a still higher level and in the background behind and between those of the front rank: one at the upper left corner of the fragment, another between the first and second figures from the left in the front rank, and the third between the second and third figures. In so far as it is preserved and visible, the zone in which they stood is of green paint applied over a black ground, which now shows through at many points. No doubt the background above the green zone was black, perhaps overpainted with blue.

The three figures in the front rank appear to be those of an adult woman, in the center, and two children. The child at the left is dressed in a long caftan slit down the front and bound at the waist by a girdle. Owing to the flaking of the paint on this portrait, especially in a zone around the edges, one can observe several of the steps taken by the painter in its execution — and, by implication, perhaps in the execution of others of the portraits. Apparently he first put in the black of the background, but he let it overlap considerably the boundaries of the figure. He then applied green over the complete area intended for the garments, and on top of that he seems to have put a bluish gray layer, possibly smalt. Much of the green and its overpainting that were on top of the black have come away, so that there is now a largely black zone around the edges of the caftan, about 9 cm. wide at the bottom and about 5 cm. wide at the sides. Over the gray the artist painted foliate and floral motifs, representing the pattern on the material of the caftan. There are large leaf forms in yellow, on which are traces of gilding; in the centers of the leaves are vermilion dots highlighted with white; and interspersed at fairly regular intervals are small vermilion flowers composed of six roundish petals radiating from a white dot. At the top of the fragment can be seen the twisted white girdle about the waist of the figure. A white kerchief with fringed ends hangs from the girdle to the left of center. It seems likely that after the painter had completed this figure and the others he applied the green that covers the black of the background.

A second child, somewhat larger than the first, was portrayed at the far right. The figure was placed so low in the panel that the bottom border seems to cut off the lower part of the flaring skirt, leaving no space for the feet. Very small loops of drapery, fragments of the sleeves, are visible at waist level, in front and to the left; their position suggests that the forearms were extended toward the left. A light yellowish brown was applied over black underpainting, and on this a complicated series of motifs was painted. A vertical running-vine motif, repeated at regular intervals, is painted in a heavy green paint. Interspersed in the coils of the vine are heart forms drawn in white, surrounded by single rows of red dots painted over black. Between the vertical vine patterns there are vertical rows of crowns alternating with small beasts. Both crowns and beasts are yellow highlighted with white. The crowns, drawn in perspective, as though seen from underneath, have three sharp prongs on top and two streamers below. Bluish vines appear

---

4 Skarpas, p. 365.

here and there in these rows. Inscribed in white in the lower left corner of the garment are the letter omega and beneath it what seems to be a ligature of gamma and eta. On the background, immediately to the left, is the merest trace of what appears to have been another letter.

In this connection, it should be recorded that another inscription, of six lines, was painted in the lower left corner of the panel. Regrettably, this inscription is no longer legible.

Before the figure of the woman in the center is discussed, it is well to make note of the figures in the back row, the fragments of whose clothing at first glance might be regarded as the lower parts of short outer garments, such as cloaks or mantles, worn by the left and center figures in the front row. The drapery in the upper left corner of the fragment is painted mainly in browns and yellows. The small brown triangle projecting below the drapery, to the left, is the pointed toe of the right shoe of a figure whose weight rests on the left leg (invisible behind the child in the front rank). The right foot pushes the skirt out toward the left, and the hem lies in folds around it. Running through the piece of drapery to the right, between the child at the left and the central figure, is a strong black vertical line that seems to mark the right-hand edge of a piece of fur trimming; the bottom edge of the fur is oblique. To the right of this line is the wide yellow hem of a green garment decorated with a vine motif; to the left of the fur is a triangular reddish brown area on which appears part of a guilloche, or interlace, of large and small circles of yellow, rather like the pattern on the outer garment of the man in Tomb F and here too seeming to pertain to an outer garment. The larger circles may possibly have contained monograms, as they do in the other case, but this garment differs from the other in being trimmed with fur. To the right of the central figure is a bit of the clothing of yet a third background figure. There is the wide yellow hem of an inner garment at the bottom and a vertical band of yellow, possibly the edging of an outer cape or mantle, above and to the right. The cloth of the mantle, to the left of this edging, is a dark greenish gray and is decorated with a gridwork of yellow stripes. The three areas of drapery in the background do not accord with one another in color or design, and the directions of their hems are such as to make it most unlikely that they pertain in any way to the figures of the front rank.

The most important figure, and one that supplies evidence for identification of the occupant of the tomb, is that of the woman who stands, unobscured by any of the others, slightly to the right of center, between the two children and at a level midway between theirs and that of the figures in the background. The woman is dressed in a vermilion caftan, open down the front; a pattern of monogrammed medallions and small heraldic birds with outspread wings, executed in gold, covers the garment. The medallions, in horizontal and vertical rows, are linked together by small lozenges. The accompanying sketch (text Fig. E) [5] shows these details more clearly than the photographic reproduction, Plate 541 *b*.

Three distinct monograms appear in the medallions, each recurring several times. The one that appears most frequently, and in each of the four vertical rows, is the well-known monogram of the Palaeologoi. To the right-hand vertical bar of a very large pi is attached a large alpha, and above the horizontal is a small ligature formed of the letters lambda and gamma. In the first and third vertical rows this monogram alternates with one that is based on an alpha of the type with a broad horizontal bar at the top and a pendant cross-bar shaped like a Y. In one version a reversed sigma is attached to the left of the alpha and another sigma, facing correctly, to the

[5] The sketch was first published in *D. O. Papers*, 12, 281.

Fig. E. Designs on the costume of the central figure, Tomb E

right; in the one at the center of the third row, however, a reversed nu is substituted for the second sigma. This monogram, which also appears very indistinctly, together with that of the Palaeologoi, on the costume of the crowned woman in Tomb C, and again in a still different version on the costume of the woman in Tomb F, can be identified as the monogram of the powerful family who signed themselves Asanaioi-Palaeologoi. These were the descendants of the union, in the year 1278, of Irene Palaeologina, daughter of the Emperor Michael VIII Palaeologos, and the ex-Tsar of Bulgaria, Ivan III Asan ('Ασάνης), which produced four sons and two daughters.[6] The best evidence for interpreting these as versions of the Asan monogram is their close resemblance to another that appears on the embroidered "shroud," in the Rumanian monastery of Putna, of a still later descendant of the Asanaioi-Palaeologoi, Maria Mangop (d. 1476) — second wife of Stephen the Great, Voivode of Moldavia — whom Gabriel Millet identified as Maria Asanina Palaeologina.[7] That monogram differs from those in the present painting only in having a letter attached to the right side of the alpha that can be viewed as an eta or a nu, or as both. In any case, all these versions are monogrammatic forms of the name ACANHC. A third monogram shows up in the second vertical row, along with the first two. The best-preserved example of it is at the lower right corner of the costume, in the fourth row, where it seems to have alternated with the Palaeologan monogram. This is a cruciform monogram. At the top is the letter rho, at the bottom an alpha; at the right is a circular letter, prob-

6 Many of the descendants regarded themselves as members of the dynastic family and figure prominently in the genealogical study of Papadopulos — No. 18, 21, 44–46, etc.

7 For the shroud see Tafrali, loc. cit. Millet and Hélène des Ylouses, in *Broderies religieuses de style byzantin* (Paris, 1947), pp. 78–81, give the evidence for the identification of the Asan monogram, correcting Tafrali. See their PL. 43–45.

ably an omicron, and at the left a lambda. There can be little doubt that this is the monogram of the Raoul (PAOYΛ) family, who, like the Asans, were allied to the Palaeologoi.

There was also a marriage connection between the Raouls and the Cantacuzeni and, most interestingly, between them and the family of Theodore Metochites. These relationships seem to stem from the marriage, about 1261, of the Protovestiarius John Raoul to Theodora Palaeologina,[8] niece of Michael VIII and daughter of John Cantacuzenus. Their daughter Irene Raoulaina Palaeologina was married, before 1288, to Constantine Palaeologos Porphyrogennitos,[9] third son of Michael VIII, but because of his plot against his brother, Andronicus II, Constantine was imprisoned in March of 1291, and he remained so until his death on May 5, 1304;[10] having taken monastic vows, and the name Athanasius, he was buried at the monastery of Constantine Lips, the principal mortuary church of the Palaeologoi. The only issue of this marriage was John Palaeologos. Very soon after his father's death, John came to be highly favored by his uncle, the Emperor Andronicus II, and before the end of April 1305, at about the age of seventeen, he was given the title of Panhypersebastos and was married to Irene, the daughter of Theodore Metochites.[11] Thus Irene Raoulaina Palaeologina, mother of John Palaeologos, and Theodore Metochites, father of the bride, acquired relationship, and because of that fact it is not unlikely that on Irene's death she would have received burial in the Metochites family church. Evidently Tomb E became her resting place.

The hypothesis that this is the tomb of Irene Raoulaina Palaeologina seems to be confirmed by one Demetrius Raoul Kabakes, a citizen of Sparta after the Turkish conquest of Constantinople, in a letter written to his son and first published by Leo Allatius.[12] The writer, who claimed descent from the Raoul and Metochites families, recounts what he heard from his elders regarding some of his more illustrious ancestors. The pertinent passage, for our purposes, is this: "Theodore Metochites begot five sons and one daughter, and for the latter he obtained as his son-in-law the Sebastocrator John Palaeologos son of Constantine Palaeologos Porphyrogennitos, son of the Emperor Michael, who [i.e., Constantine], being born to royal rank, rightly sought the succession to the throne. . . . His wife was buried in our family's monastery of Christ in Chora, near the tomb of the *ktetor* and [that of?] her husband. Her tomb contained the following inscription: 'The wife of Constantine Palaeologos, Porphyrogennitos, son of the most high Emperor of the Romaioi, Irene Raoulaina Palaeologina.' "[13] Admittedly, the document as a whole contains numerous errors and confusions, yet what has been quoted here is, in the main, historically correct, and on such a point as Irene's place of burial there is no reason to question its accuracy, for the document and the monograms on the painting in question seem to substantiate one another.

From the point of view of the structural history of the building and the evidence concerning Irene's life this identification of the tomb is plausible. The date of Irene's death is not known. She was born not earlier than 1263 (her mother's first husband died in 1261)[14] and not much later than 1273 (her son John was born ca. 1288).[15] The tomb clearly dates some years after 1321,

8 Papadopulos, No. 34.

9 No. 37. For the date of the marriage see Ševčenko, p. 150, n. 3; he places the birth of their son in 1288–89.

10 Ševčenko, loc. cit. Papadopulos, p. 23, erroneously dates the death two years later, as does Underwood in *D. O. Papers*, 13 (Washington, 1959), 220.

11 See above, pp. 277–78, for later events in her life.

12 In *Robert Creygtoni apparatum, versionem, et notas ad*

Historiam Concilii Florentini scriptam a Silvestro Syropulo . . . exercitationes (Rome, 1674), pp. 616–21. Republished by K. N. Sathas, Μεσαιωνικὴ Βιβλιοθήκη, Τόμος Α', Βυζαντινὰ ἀνέκδοτα (Venice, 1872), pp. ρκϛ' ρλα'.

13 The Greek text of this excerpt from the letter is quoted in Underwood, loc. cit.

14 Papadopulos, No. 34.

15 Ševčenko, loc. cit.

when construction and decoration of the church were completed, and the windows in the outer narthex would not have come into demand as places for the construction of additional tombs before ca. 1325–30. These dates, setting Irene's life span at not less than fifty-two years nor more than sixty-seven, are not chronologically impossible nor at variance with the historical evidence concerning the structural phases at the church of the Chora.

In the reveals of the arcosolium, below the cornice and on a level with the portrait panel on the back wall, are two framed panels, each containing a standing figure dressed in monastic garb, a monk at the left and a nun at the right.[16] To provide the tomb with portraits at these places it was necessary to remove the marble revetments that had originally covered the reveals of the window and apply plaster directly to the masonry. The two panels were framed by a narrow wave pattern of red on white within wider red borders, like the other paintings in the tomb. The backgrounds of the panels, however, in contrast to those of the other paintings, were either left unpainted or, perhaps, covered with a thin application of lime white.

The most serious losses in the painting of the monk are in the upper parts of the figure, and the same is true of the painting of the nun; there they must have been exposed to weathering. Even though the painting is in places nearly effaced it can be seen that the monk wears a beard of moderate length and a black hood that covers his head and shoulders. The plaster in the area of his eyes is destroyed. He wears a long tunic of light yellowish brown with heavy folds, drawn in reddish brown, and a mantle of dark reddish brown, with drawing and some modeling in black. Hanging down the front of the tunic, almost to his knees, is his black scapular.

The nun wears a tightly fitting headdress of black, which covers her head completely, leaving only her oval face exposed, and falls over her shoulders. The face now retains little of its flesh color, but in the center is a patch of carefully executed Byzantine restoration, which retains more of its color and detail than the original parts do. This area includes all her right eye, most of her left eye, including the eyebrow, and all but the tip of her nose. Her mouth, which is original, still retains some drawing and some of the red of the lips. At her sides hang the long folds of her mantle, which is painted a dark reddish brown and drawn in black. Her long tunic, worn beneath the mantle, is light yellowish brown, with drawing and modeling in the reddish brown that was used for the mantle. Her shoes are black.

These two portraits were accompanied by inscriptions. Regrettably, the inscription of the monk, which seems to have consisted of four lines at each side of the head, is almost completely effaced and is no longer legible; nothing at all can be deciphered at the left, and at the right only a few letters, bits of three of the lines, are legible. Of the third line can be seen . . . καὶ κτ[ήτωρος?] . . . . The inscription accompanying the portrait of the nun has fared much better. Four lines to the left of the head read: Ἐκοιμή|θη [ἡ] δού|λη τοῦ Θ(εο)ῦ ['Α]|θανασή[α]. The inscription continues at the right, only partly legible: μοναχ[ὴ] . . .| . . . ρ[ο]ῦ τοῦ| . . . κτήτω|[ρος] . . . .[17] What now remains can be translated, "Here sleeps the servant of God, Athanasia the nun . . . of . . . founder . . . ."

It would appear, therefore, that we are again dealing with persons who were related in some way to Theodore Metochites, and in the light of the known relationship between Irene Raoulaina Palaeologina and the founder of the Chora monastery we can conclude that the painting of

---

16 Width of panels within borders, ca. .58 m.; height, ca. 1.58 m. Height of monk, 1.51 m.; height of nun, 1.47 m.

17 Photographs fail almost completely to capture these traces. For a sketch of the parts of the nun's inscription that could be seen on close inspection, see *D. O. Papers*, 13, 221.

the nun is another portrait of the mother of Metochites' son-in-law (the Caesar John Palaeologos), the principal figure in the panel on the back wall of the tomb. If this is correct, we have another instance of the "double portrait," as it occurs in the tomb of Tornikes, and, with some lacunae, the latter part of the nun's inscription might be reconstructed as follows: . . . Ἀθανασήα μοναχὴ μήτηρ τοῦ γαμπροῦ τοῦ . . . κτήτωρος . . . , that is, "Athanasia, the nun, the mother of the son-in-law of . . . the founder . . . ." There is no record that before her death Irene became a nun, but if she sought burial in the Chora, where she could be commemorated with other members of Metochites' family, she would have been obliged to do so and to take a new name. Her choice of "Athanasia" could be explained on the grounds that her husband, Constantine Porphyrogennitos, who had died in prison in 1304 and was buried at the monastery of Constantine Lips, is known to have taken the name "Athanasius" shortly before his death.[18] His burial elsewhere in 1304 need not preclude the possibility that on the death of Irene, some twenty-five years later, his remains were transferred to the Chora and placed with those of his wife. If this indeed is what happened, then the figure in monk's garb opposite that of Irene as a nun can be presumed to represent Constantine.

The question arises whether all six persons who were portrayed on the back wall were buried in or near the tomb of Irene. The sarcophagus alone could not have held them, but under the floor in front of the arcosolium, and quite obviously placed in context with it, is a vault, discovered in 1959 while the floor of the outer narthex was being relaid, which is of sufficient size to have accommodated such a large number of burials.[19]

18 Papadopulos (No. 37) cites Georgios Pachymeres, *De Michaele et Andronico Palaeologis*, II, Bonn ed. (1835), p. 424, where Constantine's death and funeral are described.

19 The vault had long since been cleared of its contents by the Turkish authorities. It is a barrel vault, made of crudely shaped stones, about 1.60 m. in height and about 2.20 m. along its main, east-west axis, which falls slightly to the north of the central axis of the wall tomb; its width at the east end is about 2 m. and at the west end, 1.80 m. A trap door to it had been constructed near its southwest corner.

Tomb F

FIGS. 2, 4; PL. 546–547

The second window of the outer narthex to have been altered for use as a sepulchral monument by the insertion of a curtain wall at the outer edge of the opening was that in the fourth bay.[1] The arch was handled differently from that in the tomb of the fifth bay (Tomb E), where the mosaic decoration in the soffit was covered by an archivolt of cut voussoirs decorated with figure paintings, in that the mosaic ornaments were left exposed and were utilized as part of the decoration of the tomb. The narrow, undecorated band of setting bed between the mosaic and the newly inserted curtain wall at the back of the niche, which is now destroyed in its upper parts, was removed by the decorators of the tomb, and a wider band of fresco ornament in a folded-ribbon pattern of green and orange-yellow was substituted to provide a transition between the mosaic and the new fresco that must have been in the lunette of the back wall. The marble revetments that originally covered the jambs of the window, below the cornice, were also left *in situ* when

1 Report on tomb first published in *D. O. Papers*, 13, pp. 223–25 and Figs. 5 and 6, but for a preliminary notice see Vol. 12, p. 282 and Fig. 15. Dimensions of tomb: height of arcosolium from its floor (.25 m. above floor level of narthex) to mosaic surface in crown of arch soffit, 4.37 m.; height from its floor to springing line of arch (top of cornice), 3.38 m.; width between masonry jambs, 1.79 m.; height from floor to bottom of fragment of painting (height of sarcophagus), 1.21 m.; height of fragment of painting, 1.17 m.

the window was made a tomb; these were subsequently removed, in all probability when the revetments on all the walls of the outer narthex were taken down. Thus, in Tomb F painting was confined to the back wall of the niche. The lower parts of three figures are all that survives of the portrait panel that occupied the wall between the top of the sarcophagus and the cornice. There must also have been, however, an image of the Virgin and Child, or one of Christ, and the only room for such an image was in a lunette above the portraits. For one to be placed there, the back wall, unlike those of the other two arcosolia of the outer narthex (Tombs E and G), would have to fill the arch completely, leaving no window in the semicircular area above the portraits. The conclusion that this was actually the case has been supported by the discovery of a small area of painted plaster (a red border framing the black paint of a background) lying at right angles to the decoration of the soffit and on the same plane as the portraits below; [2] this fragment is all that remains of the painting in the lunette of the tomb. The holy personages iconographically essential in such tombs must have been depicted here.

Approximately half of the portrait panel, below the lunette, now remains, and in remarkably good condition. Beneath the zone of standing figures is a horizontal panel, about 22 cm. high, painted a dark violet color in imitation of a slab of porphyry. This is framed by a white band about 3 cm. wide and by an outer border of red that originally extended at the sides to the marble revetments in the jambs. The red border also extended upward, with a white line inside it, to frame the panel of portraits. Within its borders the panel measures 1.595 m. in width. The height of the preserved portion is .80 m., but, assuming that the panel in its original state reached to the level of the bottom of the cornice, its original height was approximately 1.70 m.

The painting presented the portraits of three persons, probably a family: at the left a man, facing right in three-quarters pose, his feet shown in profile; at the right a woman, who may have been turned slightly to the left; and in frontal pose between them, a child. The man occupies nearly half the width of the panel and stands entirely free of the others; the child's figure, on the other hand, overlaps the woman's. No attempt is made to represent a ground plane or a setting; as far as the painting is preserved the background is uniformly green, but at a higher level it was probably black.

The man wears a long, heavy outer garment, or coat, open down the front. It has long sleeves, with narrow openings at the ends, that hang empty, an indication that he is wearing it like a mantle, over his shoulders. The ends of the sleeves nearly reach his ankles, so it is evident that the garment was never intended to be worn with the arms through the sleeves. In this respect it is of the type worn by the man in Tomb C, whose arms emerge from slits provided in the sleeves at elbow height. The same type of sleeve, exceedingly long and hanging empty, is to be found on the garment worn by the figure of the deceased in Tomb G and again on that of one of the saints portrayed in mosaic in the outer narthex [175].

In the painting in Tomb F the garment is black, with an allover pattern of alternately large and small interlacing medallions. The large medallions contain the Palaeologan monogram, the small ones a quatrefoil motif. Large, cusped spaces are left between the rows of interlacing medallions, and these are filled by the double-headed eagle, the Byzantine imperial emblem. All the ornaments are executed in gold leaf and outlined with black lines. A vertical strip of the lining of the garment is visible to the left of center, where the garment has been folded back;

2 See *D. O. Papers*, 12, p. 282 and Fig. 15.

the lining also shows at the hem and in the openings of the sleeves. It is painted in shades of violet, graduated from light at the edges to darker values within.

The inner garment is now visible only where the outer garment is parted down the front; it too seems to have opened in front, for the heavy, dark violet line running up the center apparently represents an overlapping edge. It probably had tightly fitting sleeves and a girdle at the waist, like the undergarments, which it resembles in many other respects, of various male personages in a series of portraits in a manuscript (gr. 35) of Lincoln College, Oxford, now in the Bodleian Library. The garment is vermilion and has a gold pattern similar to those appearing on some of the men's costumes in that manuscript. The principal repeat is a large, solid, leaf-like motif surrounded by a broad band that is a series of ogee curves. A similar motif is to be seen on the long-sleeved coat of the figure of Maria Mangop embroidered on Maria's "shroud," one of the treasures at the monastery of Putna;[3] this garment is also red, and the motifs are embroidered in thread of gold.

The child, at the center of the panel, wears a heavy caftan that opens down the front; about his waist is a girdle, from which a kerchief is suspended. The caftan has a field of dark red and a diaper pattern in gold leaf outlined in black. The intersecting gold bands of the pattern constrict at each crossing behind a small circle drawn in black. The girdle, knotted in front, is made of two strands of a material striped in dark red, vermilion, yellow, and white. On the white stripes are small red ornaments, and on the yellow and vermilion stripes, green ones. The kerchief is white with light gray folds, a gold border, and gold fringes. On the gold border are small scroll designs, drawn in black. The lining of the caftan, showing at the hem, is vermilion. On his feet, which were first painted fairly large but were reduced in size in an overpainting, the child wears white shoes bearing a design in red lines.

Only a small part of the clothing of the woman is obscured by the figure of the child at her right, and much can be seen of her long dress, made of a material with a foliate pattern, and of the cloak or mantle, decorated with beautifully executed monograms, which she wears over it. The dress is made of material with a black background and is decorated at the bottom by a golden hem, about 12 cm. wide, bordered at each side by two lines. In the field of the hem are three red rectangles; one is surrounded by four small triangles, drawn in black, while above and below the other two there are small circles, also drawn in black, within which flecks of the white paint that originally filled them still adhere; the rectangles represent gems and the circles, pearls. Each element of the pattern of the dress consists of a series of leaf forms arranged around an oval, and in the center of each oval is a large red dot surrounded by a white circle. The leaves are rather sketchy; some are painted in white and others in yellow. Showing below the hem of the dress are shoes of gold.

Only the right half of the vermilion and gold outer garment, which is somewhat shorter than the dress, is exposed; it is a mantle similar in form to that worn by the crowned female figure in Tomb C, in the parecclesion. Like that one, and like the garment of the central figure in Tomb E, it is covered with a pattern of large monograms contained within circles. At the bottom is a golden hem, about 10 cm. in width, which closely resembles the hem of the dress. The mantle also has a vertical golden border, about 4 cm. in width, interrupted at intervals by blue and red rectangles; between these are two rows of pearls. The monogrammed circles, of gold leaf outlined in black, are arranged in vertical and horizontal rows. Since the left side of the

3 Tafrali, p. 52.

mantle is obscured by the child, one must imagine that similar rows of medallions decorated the entire garment. In each of the cusped spaces between the medallions is a blue ornament consisting of four fleurs-de-lis assembled in the form of a cross. Only two of the vertical rows of medallions are exposed to view, and in both rows the medallions are partly cut off: in the row at the left, where the vertical border overlaps them, and in that at the right, where the garment turns away from view. In the left row are three distinct monograms; the same three are in the right row, but rearranged. If we number the monograms at the left as 1, 2, and 3, from top to bottom, their sequence at the right is 3, 1, and 2. They are thus repeated in the same order, but in the second row they are shifted downward by one monogram; presumably the same rhythm would continue, so that if the whole mantle were exposed to view, identical monograms might appear in diagonal rows, slanting downward from left to right.

The monogram that appears at the top of the first row and in the second position in the row at the right is composed of four letters in a cruciform arrangement. The complete monogram can be seen only in a combination of the two examples. The upper letter on the vertical bar of the cross is a delta, and the lower letter is a rho. The letter at the left end of the horizontal bar is a mu; the example in the first row is incomplete, but that in the second is clearly legible. Finally, at the right end of the horizontal bar is a kappa, visible only in the monogram at the left. It is probable that the letters should be read in that order. If so, they supply the name Δ(ε)ρμ(ο)κ(αΐτης).

The second monogram is a variant of the 'Ασάνης monogram that appears on the costume of Irene Raoulaina Palaeologina in Tomb E. Like its counterpart, this variant is based upon a majuscule alpha, but attached to the left side is a minuscule sigma instead of the reversed majuscule form of the letter, and at the right side is a majuscule nu, which is rather large and in this instance faces correctly. The third monogram is the now-familiar one of the Palaeologoi.

Not only is the woman entitled to wear the Palaeologan monogram because it is worn by her husband, who was evidently a member of the imperial family (vide the monograms and double-headed eagles on his outer garment), but she apparently wears all the monograms in her own right as a member of the family who styled themselves the Asanaioi-Palaeologoi and, if the above interpretation of the first monogram is correct, of the Dermokaïtes family. The genealogical study of A. Papadopulos cites only three personages of this latter name who were also Palaeologans;[4] all of these are of the fifteenth century — too late to have any direct bearing upon the identification of the portraits in this tomb. However, a Dermokaïtes who bore the title of Sebastos was the subject of a letter written to the emperor by the Patriarch Athanasius I[5] in the first decade of the fourteenth century. In it the emperor is requested to establish a commission of three, to be composed of the Sebastos Dermokaïtes and two demarchs, to inquire into the sale of bread and into the weights and measures. The title of Sebastos, in the late eleventh

4 No. 140, a Theodora Palaeologina Dermokaïtissa, who died after 1400 (see also Underwood, D. O. Papers, 12, 225); No. 141, a strategos Demetrius Palaeologos Dermokaïtes, who flourished ca. 1440 and who Papadopulos assumes was a son of No. 140; and No. 165, a Georgios Palaeologos Dromokates (Dermokaïtes), the last agent of the Byzantine state on the island of Imbros, who died shortly before the fall of Constantinople in 1453.

5 Codex Vaticanus, MS. graec. 2219, fol. 78v, an unpublished manuscript; for information regarding this document and its content I wish to thank my colleague Professor

Ihor Ševčenko. I am also indebted to Dr. Donald Nicol, who called my attention to sixteen additional members of the Dermokaïtes family, many of whom held imperial offices or titles between the eleventh and fifteenth centuries. Among them is a Michael Dermokaïtes, Pansebastos Sebastos, who is mentioned in a document in the Monastery of St. Paul on Mt. Latrus, near Miletus, which is thought to be of thirteenth-century date. The family seems to have been connected mainly with the island of Chios, and in late documents the name appears, in Italianized form, as Dromocati(s).

and the twelfth centuries, was generally conferred upon relatives of the emperor who were outside the immediate family, or now and again upon foreign princes or rulers for diplomatic purposes. Among the signatures of the dignitaries in attendance upon the council in the Palace of Blachernae under Manuel Comnenus, in 1166, the titles of the first cousins and sons-in-law of the emperor were recorded as Pansebastos Sebastos. This honorary title was the highest that was bestowed at that time upon persons related to the emperor but not of his immediate family, and in many instances it was a title without office.[6] The fact that in the first decade of the fourteenth century a Dermokaïtes bore the title of Sebastos may indicate that he, and his descendants, were related to the imperial family, albeit at some distance, and this could account for the presence of the Palaeologan monogram in conjunction with that of the Dermokaïtes family upon the vestment of a woman whose sepulchral monument must be dated within the first half of the century, although somewhat later than the period 1325–30, which was suggested above for the tomb of Irene Raoulaina Palaeologina. Examination of the foundations supporting the outer faces of the back walls of the outer-narthex tombs shows a progressive rise in level from Tomb E to Tomb G, and we should therefore regard Tomb F as the second one to have been installed in the outer narthex and date it some time after 1330.

6 See Louis Bréhier, *Les Institutions de l'empire byzantin*, Vol. II (in L'Évolution de l'humanité, Synthèse collective: Le Monde byzantin) (Paris, 1949), pp. 139, 142 ff.

Tomb G[1]

FIGS. 2, 4; PL. 548, 549

The last sepulchral monument to have been erected in the church of the Chora is Tomb G, in what was originally the window in the second bay of the outer narthex. As was the case in the construction of the other tombs of the narthex, a niche for a sarcophagus and a wall for suitable paintings were provided by the installation of a curtain wall at the outer edge of the arched opening. Originally the curtain wall rose to the level of the cornice, as it apparently did in Tomb E, leaving a semicircular window above it in the arch. In the course of later alterations, the upper part of this wall was destroyed.

Like Tomb F but in contrast with Tomb E, Tomb G was built with the original decorations of the arch left in place. The ornamental mosaic in the soffit of the window was left exposed to decorate the arch of the tomb, and this was extended at its outer edge by a band of fresco ornament in a folded-ribbon motif. The marble revetments in the jambs of the window were also left, although they were later removed along with most of the marbles on the walls of the narthex; broken fragments of marble still exist along the edges of the painting on the back wall, where it abutted the revetments.

Since the decoration of the soffit and jambs was retained, and the lunette was occupied by

1 Report on tomb first published in *D. O. Papers*, 13, pp. 225–28 and Figs. 7 and 8. See also Underwood, "Palaeologan Narrative Style and an Italianate Fresco of the Fifteenth Century in the Kariye Djami," in *Studies in the History of Art, Dedicated to William E. Suida on His Eightieth Birthday* (London, 1959), pp. 1–9; and John Beckwith, *The Art of Constantinople, An Introduction to Byzantine Art, 330–1453* (London, 1961), p. 151 f. and Fig. 203. Dimensions of tomb: height of arcosolium from its floor (.22 m. above floor level of narthex) to mosaic surface in crown of arch soffit, 4.44 m.; height from its floor to springing line of arch (top of cornice), 3.46 m.; width between masonry jambs, 1.79 m.; height from floor to bottom of fragment of painting (top of sarcophagus), 1.34 m.; maximum height of fragment of painting, 1.26 m.; approximate height of panel when complete, 2.12 m.

a window, representational painting was restricted to a rectangular panel on the back wall between the lunette window and the top of the sarcophagus, a unique situation among the tombs of the church. The limitation meant that the two indispensable elements in the iconography of a Byzantine sepulchral monument, namely, the image of a sacred person and a portrait of the deceased, would have to be juxtaposed. In this painting, which is preserved to almost three fifths of its original height, an enthroned Madonna and Child are depicted at the left, in angular perspective, facing toward a figure of the deceased, who stands at the right, in three-quarters view, facing in turn toward them. No distinction of scale is made between the figures, and they are depicted in an unusually intimate relationship. The deceased, apparently in an attitude of devotion, stands before the Virgin and Child in a direct confrontation, unaccompanied by an intermediary saint. In extant tomb paintings there are some near precedents but none to my knowledge that has all the iconographic features present in this painting. It should not be assumed that the practical space limitations dictated these unique features, for had they been considered irreverent, and therefore to be avoided, the sacred and profane persons could have been set apart from one another in the traditional manner. It will be observed below that the style of the painting is alien to Byzantine art, and when the style and the unusual relationship between the figures are considered in conjunction they betray a humanistic outlook on the part of the painter, and perhaps of the patron, that is quite new to Byzantine art and in good part attributable to influences of the Italian Renaissance.

The panel is framed at each side by the usual narrow white line and the usual red border, 3.5 cm. wide. The same border, but considerably wider (10.5 cm.), passes across the bottom of the panel. There, however, the narrow white line has been omitted, and instead the front edge of the skillfully rendered gray and white marble floor is depicted, as if it rested directly upon the lower frame of the picture. This edge is thus simultaneously a part of the floor in the scene and a part of the frame of the panel. The floor itself, surprisingly realistic, assumes a horizontal appearance, in contrast with the usual upward tilt, or slope, resulting from medieval attempts to depict horizontal surfaces. The devices used here, that is, the painting of the floor to appear horizontal and the placing of its front edge at the picture plane, are not to be found elsewhere in Byzantine art, although similar devices began to be introduced into Italian painting in the fourteenth century and were fully exploited, as here, by the mid-fifteenth century. The floor convincingly recedes to a green wall at the rear, some distance back from the front of the picture, providing a shelf-like lower plane that contributes to an equally convincing rendition of a three-dimensional space, in which the figures and the furniture take their places.

The drawing of the Virgin's footstool, which has a yellow upper face and sides the color of raw sienna, although not done entirely in two-point perspective, nevertheless does not employ the medieval divergence of orthogonals. Two of the orthogonals actually converge toward a quite low vanishing point at the left, and those that do not are at least drawn parallel. But the throne, which is painted in the same colors as the footstool, denies the existence of a single station point for the panel as a whole, and it is represented as though seen from a point higher than that from which the floor and the footstool are observed. The perspective is thus inconsistent, but the manner in which the furniture is depicted implies that the principles of Renaissance perspective had already been adopted, even though, because of insufficient understanding, they were not fully applied by the painter.

The treatment of surface and volume give the figure of the Virgin a three-dimensional, sculptural quality; and the figure is placed at such an angle that its perspective is convincingly related to the perspective of the throne and of the footstool. In these respects, again, there is a departure from Byzantine modes of representation and a kinship with Western techniques of the fifteenth century. Some of the drapery, especially that in the lower left, has sharp-edged folds, standing forward in high relief, and a series of cast shadows. The red-violet outer mantle almost completely covers the blue tunic beneath. The latter is visible in a small area on the wrist and in another at the lower left, where it touches the footstool and casts its shadow upon it. Where the mantle is draped over the extended arm it has a narrow edging of golden yellow, and very narrow yellow lines mark some of the edge of the mantle in the area of folds at the lower left. Otherwise, the highlights on the folds of the garment are in light gray or white. The Virgin's shoes and the bolster on which she sits are red. The Christ Child, who seems to have been seated on his mother's left knee with his left leg drawn up, was clad entirely in golden raiment. The effect of cloth of gold is achieved with yellow paint and a considerable amount of hatching in thin, light yellow lines. The Child wears sandals whose thongs are now only faintly visible.

At the right is the somberly but richly attired figure of the deceased, probably a woman if one may judge from the costume and the smallness of the feet. She wears a long coat of the type with almost-ankle-length sleeves that hang empty at the sides (one such sleeve, with a long slit at the elbow, can be seen at the far right).[2] This outer garment, painted in a very deep and rather glossy black pigment, seems to hang freely from the shoulders, exposing much of the front of the dress; it falls in numerous narrow folds, differing greatly in this respect from the draped clothing of the figures in the other tombs. The woman also wears a most striking, richly patterned dress, or tunic, in a material that has the appearance of a heavy damask silk. The field of this garment is a dull black, probably charcoal, of relatively light value. The pattern is drawn in the deeper, glossy black used on the coat. Each pattern repeat consists of an ogee arch framed above by two straight lines meeting at the top in a right angle and surmounted by a foliate finial; within the arch is a motif of clustered fruit and foliage. The folds of the dress too are rather narrow, and they are of a rounded, tubular form that is not to be found in the paintings of the other tombs, or in Byzantine art in general, but is paralleled in Western art of the late Middle Ages and the Renaissance. The effect of plasticity results primarily from the skill with which the painter broke up the pattern by shifting it at each individual fold to make it appear to conform to the undulation of the folds. In representations of figured garments in the other tombs, the pattern is applied over the folds in a stencil-like, continuous manner that disregards their very existence. Like the figure of the Virgin, that of the deceased woman was conceived as a three-dimensional form; convincingly she takes her place within a constructed space and in a pose that brings her, physically and psychologically, into relation with the Virgin, before whom she stands.

It has been demonstrated that in many important respects the painting in this tomb is in marked contrast with all others in the Kariye Djami. The painter appears to have combined some mannerisms that are basically Byzantine with technical devices and stylistic features that are characteristic of, or betray an acquaintance with, the achievements of Italian Renaissance painting of the mid-fifteenth century. For this reason Tomb G and its painting should be dated in the last years of the monastery's existence under Christian auspices, that is, within a period of a few years before the fall of Constantinople, in 1453.

This is the first painting found in Constantinople in which clear-cut and precise evidence of

2 For other examples of this type of sleeve, see Tombs C and F and Mosaic [175].

direct Renaissance influence can be observed. It should not, however, come as a surprise, for during the latter part of the fourteenth century and in the first half of the fifteenth the beleaguered and desperate city turned more and more to the West, and despite her isolated position there was more opportunity than before for cultural exchanges. The most important leaders of Byzantium now traveled west. One need only mention the journey to Rome of the Emperor John V Palaeologos, in 1369–71, the first journey of a Byzantine emperor into a foreign country on a peaceful mission. He was accompanied by many state dignitaries, but no clergy. And then there was the long journey of the Emperor Manuel II, in 1399; he visited Venice, London, and Paris (where he stayed almost two years). He too was accompanied by numerous members of his court, and also among the party was that intrepid warrior, Marshal Boucicault, whom Charles VI of France had sent, at the head of a small force, to the relief of Constantinople. Finally, and perhaps more important from our point of view, there was the visit to the Council of Ferrara and Florence. Late in 1437 a delegation of seven hundred of the most important personages of Constantinople set out for Ferrara. The Emperor John VIII, his brother Demetrius, and the Patriarch of Constantinople headed the delegation. They were in Florence and Ferrara for more than a year, and it is known that the Greek savants attached to the delegation came into contact with the Italian humanists, whom they astounded with their learning. That visit of the elite of Byzantium to Italy has left its record in Italian painting. Perhaps we have, here in this modest tomb at the Kariye Djami, another souvenir of that large-scale cultural exchange and an intimation of what might have been, had history taken another course.

Tomb H,[1] the tomb of Demetrius

FIG. 2; PL. 550–553

In the construction of Tomb H, in the inner narthex, the marble revetments of the entire northern wall, from floor to cornice, were removed, and an arcosolium the full width of the narthex was erected against the bare masonry (PL. 14). The marble facings on the walls at either side were left undisturbed, and the piers of the arcosolium were laid against them. The structure is built of dressed stone backed with rubble, except for the arch, which is of brick. The pier at the left is about 27 cm. wider than that at the right, with the result that the opening between the two is rather noticeably to the east of center. The lower part of the arch, up to a level 1.18 m. above the floor, was made some 10 cm. narrower than the upper part so that there would be a narrow ledge at each side on which to rest the ends of the lid of a sarcophagus. At the springs of the arch, sections taken from a marble architrave, molded and carved with a running foliate motif on the front and back sides (PL. 550), extend the full depth of the niche and serve both as imposts and as corbels, for their ends project from the masonry face of the arch, one as much as 29 cm., the other 26 cm. As imposts, these spoils from an earlier structure (perhaps the architrave of an iconostasis) were concealed; they do not protrude from the reveals of the arch, and except for their projecting ends, the corbels, they were completely covered with mortar and

---

1 Report on tomb first published, before restoration work was finished, in *D. O. Papers*, 12, pp. 276–78 and Figs. 8 and 9. Dimensions of tomb: Total breadth of monument (width of inner narthex at north end between marble revetments), 3.52 m.; total height of monument, 4.24 m.; height of arch, 3.76 m.; breadth of arch at upper level of corbels, 2.30 m.; breadth of arch at level of offset, 2.17 m.; height of sarcophagus, 1.18 m.; depth of niche, .92 m.

with the mosaics that once decorated the soffit and reveals. In the restorations of the Byzantine Institute the mortar covering the carved face of the impost at the right was removed and the carving was left exposed to view (see PL. 550); but the masonry surfaces that had become exposed on the face of the arch and within the niche, except those once concealed by the sarcophagus, were covered by the Byzantine Institute with new plaster. It should be noted that the face of the monument was originally ornamented with sculpture, marble revetments, and colonnettes, most of which had disappeared, and the interior of the niche with mosaics, fragments of which are still preserved.

The general nature of the original decoration of the outer face of the monument can be inferred from extant evidence. Attached by metal cramps to the bottom of each corbel is a square capital, the bust of a saint carved in high relief on each of the three exposed sides. All but one of the heads are destroyed. Five of the six saints are dressed in military garb, but only one of them was given an identifying inscription. The one intact bust was found on the left face of the left-hand capital, in a position where it could not be seen properly because it was very close to the western wall of the narthex. The inscribed bust, bearing the name of St. Demetrius, was also on the left-hand capital, but on its eastern face, in the position nearest to the portrait of the deceased man, whose name was Demetrius, in the panel at the back of the niche. In the restorations of the Byzantine Institute the two capitals were transposed; the perfectly preserved bust is now at the right side of the arch and can be seen easily, while the fragmentary bust of St. Demetrius now appears at the far right. It must be supposed that colonnettes, probably square in section, once flanked the opening of the arch to support the capitals. Cut into the upper face of each corbel is a shallow slot, about 15 cm. wide, which aligns with the face of the arch. This evidence and the presence of peg holes in the masonry of the face of the arch indicate that carved marble slabs, akin to those above the arches of Tombs A and D, in the parecclesion, were once attached to the face of the tomb and were supported by the corbels. Presumably, also, the outer faces of the piers were covered with revetments, abutting the colonnettes or passing behind them. In its richness of decoration, which combined sculpture with mosaic, the monument must have been comparable to Tombs A and D, and one might suppose, therefore, that its occupants were members of the more illustrious families of the city. This conclusion is substantiated, as will be seen below, by the fragmentary remains of their portraits and the accompanying inscriptions.

Above the sarcophagus the interior of the niche was covered with mosaic. Framing the panel on the back wall and extending onto the soffit was a wide, concave border of mosaic ornament, much of which survives, which separated the mosaics of the two areas. In the center of the soffit are the very fragmentary remains of a medallion which contained a bust of Christ (PL. 552 b). The medallion was framed by a border, 15 cm. wide, of three concentric bands. The inner and outer bands are in narrow wave patterns, the inner one of red glass in a white stone ground, the outer one of black glass in a white stone ground. Between the two runs a series of block-shaped motifs, perhaps intended as a dentil band. The drawing is done in black clinker-like glasses; the lighted faces of the dentils are light gray marble; the shaded faces are made up of concentric rectangles of blue and gray around small squares of terra cotta; and the small triangles between the dentils and the inner margin are of gold. The background within this border is in two concentric zones; the outer zone, which is 15 cm. wide, is of gray marble, and the inner zone is of grayish black clinker-like glass. Of the figure of Christ itself, all that now remains is parts of the two hands, extended at the sides in gestures of blessing, and a small segment of the halo. Flanking the halo is the partially preserved inscription, which doubtless read, [’Ι(ησοῦ)ς Χ(ριστὸ)ς ἡ] χώ[ρα] τῶν ζώντων (Jesus Christ, the dwelling-place of the living), repeating the epithet used in the earlier mosaics numbered [1], [3], and [186].

At each side of the medallion the soffit of the arch is ornamented with foliate elements that are so disjointed and highly conventionalized that the pattern, an interlacing of vine scrolls, is scarcely recognizable. The leaves are green, and the blossoms and calyxes are red; all are drawn in black and highlighted in white. The background is gold. The fragments of this ornamented area are broken off at each side of the arch about halfway between the medallion and the imposts. It is uncertain how far downward in the arch the ornament originally extended, but in the haunch at the right it at least covered the beardless, nimbed figure (PL. 553) that was roughly sketched on the first rendering coat of plaster, now exposed where the setting bed, with its mosaic surface, has come away. Patches of this first rendering, showing faint traces of the lower parts of the sketched figure, were found below the impost, and comparable patches appeared in the soffit at the left. In the restorations of the Byzantine Institute only the upper part of the figure in the right side of the arch was left exposed. The fact that the foliate mosaic ornament was applied over the sketch would seem to indicate that the mosaicist did not intend the sketch as a guide to the laying of tesserae but rather had at first contemplated the use of figures in the soffit, had sketched them on a trial basis, and had rejected them in favor of an overall ornamental pattern.

The wide, concave border separating the mosaics of the soffit from the panel on the back wall is composed of foliate motifs between two bands in the narrow, red-on-white wave pattern used around the medallion in the soffit. The central element of the foliate border consists of five-lobed leaves placed end to end; these are of green glasses grading from dark at the center to lighter yellow-greens at the edges, and they are surrounded by single rows of gold. The spaces alongside and between the green leaves are filled by two types of paired leaves, the larger ones of red glass bordered with gold, the smaller ones also of red, but bordered with white stones. The background of the border is of dull black glass.

Only the upper part of the mosaic on the back wall of the arcosolium has survived. In the center, at the very top of the panel, is a rather small frontal half-figure of the Virgin in the pose of an orant. Her arms, in tightly fitting blue sleeves with golden cuffs, emerge from the folds of the blue maphorion that covers all but her face and neck and the edge of the light blue kerchief framing her brow; single rows of gold tesserae mark the principal edges of the maphorion. Symmetrically disposed at the sides is the inscription Μ(ήτ)ηρ Θ(εο)ῦ ἡ ζωοδόχος πηγή (Mother of God, the life-receiving fountain, or source). Centered beneath the Virgin is a metrical inscription, which as it now exists comprises two verses in four lines (not to be confused with the fragments at either side, which are parts of two other inscriptions): Ζωῆς σὺ πηγὴ ὡς [Θεο]ῦ μή(τη)ρ λόγου. Δημή[τριος δ’] ἔγωγε σὸς [δοῦλος?] πόθω (Thou art the Fount of Life, as [thou art] the Mother of God the Word. And I am Demetrius thy slave in affection). The Demetrius who thus addresses the Virgin is the deceased personage who was portrayed in the left side of the panel. Unfortunately, all that now remains of this portrait is the right half of the headdress (in this instance it can properly be called a crown) and part of the inscribed name, between the crown and the verses addressed to the Virgin. The left edge of the preserved area of mosaic passes vertically almost exactly through the center of the crown, and the horizontal break at the bottom very nearly coincides with the crown's lower limits. Since the crown was presumably symmetrical, its form, color, and decoration can be easily reconstructed. The upper part was hemispherical; it was separated from the lower part, a wide, horizontal band, by a row of black tesserae and a row of pearls, which, at the center, curved upward in a semicircle to frame a decorative device, now largely lost. The outlines of the crown, as well as the line of demarcation between the upper and lower parts, are drawn with single rows of black glass. The hemispherical top has a red glass background and a lozenge pattern of gold; the horizontal part reverses these colors: it is ornamented by vertical bands drawn in parallel rows of red tesserae, on a field of gold. In its effect the crown is predominantly red, but there is much gold.

Of the inscription that accompanied the portrait, only one line and part of a second now exist, to the right of the head. It must have begun, however, at the opposite side of the head; the deceased's title was probably recorded, and if he were the son of an emperor the name of his father would have been as well. The part of the inscription to the right of his head seems to be devoted to his Christian name and those of the families from which he was descended. The portion of it now legible reads: Δημήτρι|[ος Δ]ούκας. . . . Anyone who used the name Doukas followed by other family names is most likely to have been a member of the Palaeologan ruling house and not merely a high functionary. In giving their full signatures to official documents, for example, Andronicus II and his eldest son Michael signed themselves Andronicus (or Michael) Δούκας Ἄγγελος Κομνηνὸς ὁ Παλαιολόγος, placing the name Doukas immediately after their Christian names, as Demetrius did in his mosaic portrait.

The nature of the crown worn by Demetrius also suggests that he was a member of the imperial family; in shape it is like those worn by the emperors Andronicus II, John VI Cantacuzenus, and Manuel II in their portraits in certain manuscript illuminations.[2] Those crowns, however, were golden, and they were studded with large gems as well as with pearls. According to Codinus,[3] the vestments of a fourteenth-century despot were similar in many respects to those of the emperor; the crown, however, was of mixed red and gold and was adorned with pearls. At this time male members of the imperial family, that is, brothers, sons, and sometimes sons-in-law, who were not coemperors were generally given the title of despot, representing the highest rank at the imperial court, and it is known that all the sons of Andronicus II bore this exalted title. The youngest son of Andronicus was the Despot Demetrius, and it is he, in my opinion, who best qualifies as the subject of the portrait under discussion. According to A. Papadopulos[4] he was born after the year 1294 and died soon after 1340, about the time of the marriage of his daughter Irene to Matthew, son of the coemperor John VI Cantacuzenus. Such a date for the mosaics of Tomb H is not impossible, although it should be reckoned as a possibility that his tomb was prepared in advance of his death, a frequent practice in the case of members of the imperial family. This Demetrius would also have used the name Doukas, followed by the other names, in the manner of his father and elder brother. A final indication that the mosaic figure could have portrayed the Despot Demetrius is that the crown, if the assumption can be drawn from the words of Codinus, is that of a despot. Other Palaeologans named Demetrius seem far less likely candidates, but they should be mentioned. One, the son of Irene and Matthew (and therefore grandson of the Despot Demetrius), is merely named in the records.[5] Demetrius, the Grand Domestic, a close relative of John V Palaeologos, died in 1375,[6] a date that seems rather too late for the tomb in question. The same objection applies to Demetrius Palaeologos Doukas Aprenos,[7] who flourished about 1400 and of whom little is known.

2 See S. P. Lampros, Λεύκωμα Βυζαντινῶν αὐτοκρατόρων (Athens, 1930), PL. 79, 81, 84.

3 De officialibus palatii Constantinopolitani, Ch. III; Bonn ed. (1839), pp. 13–17.

4 No. 63. 5 No. 64. 6 No. 135. 7 No. 134.

In the right side of the portrait panel and at nearly the same level as the crown of Demetrius is an isolated fragment of mosaic that obviously is part of the crown of the wife of Demetrius. The crown was tilted upward at the left, an indication that the wearer's head was turned somewhat in that direction. The vertical face of the crown was divided into narrow, upright units, only two of which have survived. Each came to a point at the top and was outlined in red glass; the pointed tops together formed the serrated upper contour of the crown. The field of each of these ornamental units was of gold, and each contained a gem outlined in white and pointed at the top. In addition to two gems, one green and the other red, the fragment retains a number of the pearls with which the crown was encrusted. Since this type of crown was worn only by females of the imperial family, its presence in the mosaic confirms the view expressed above that Demetrius, the husband of the wearer, was a member of the imperial family and in all probability a despot. It is regrettable that the inscription which accompanied this portrait is even less well preserved than that of Demetrius; only the upper parts of a few letters from the first line, to the left of the crown, still exist, and these are indecipherable.

The Technique of the Paintings

The mural paintings of the Kariye Djami are usually referred to as frescoes, a term that is commonly, but loosely, applied to several types of mural painting. Precisely defined, fresco is an art in which pigments in an aqueous medium are applied upon lime plaster only before it dries; strict adherence to this definition would exclude from consideration most so-called fresco paintings, including products of the Italian *stil nuovo* of the late thirteenth and the fourteenth centuries, a period during which a technique came into vogue that was thought to emulate practices most favored by the ancients. In simplest terms, this technique [1] called for the application of the pigments to small areas of freshly laid lime plaster (the *intonaco*), spread thinly in adjoining patches upon a heavier coat of dry plaster (the *arriccio*) to cover, patch by patch, the fully sketched scene or figure (the *sinopia*) that was previously drawn on the *arriccio* as a guide to the painter. In this technique the area of *buon fresco* that could be fully painted at one time was severely limited, for the durability of the painting depended upon the binding of the pigments into calcium carbonate, which would soon begin to form in a solid crystalline mass on the surface of the lime plaster through the action of atmospheric carbonic acid on the hydrate of lime. Ideally the painting of a given area of plaster should be completed before this chemical process begins. But in *buon fresco* the dryness of the *arriccio* and the thinness of the *intonaco* caused the latter to become dehydrated with relative rapidity and made it necessary to paint on quite small areas of *intonaco* applied one after another.

Recent investigations of Italian mural paintings tend to show a rather limited use of this technique in actual practice.[2] Even in the paintings of the life of St. Francis, at Assisi, which are commonly regarded as examples par excellence of true fresco, certain areas of paint were applied *a secco*.[3] To a degree, therefore, those paintings are of mixed technique. The fact that the technique used at the Kariye Djami, and in Byzantine mural painting in general, differs greatly from the Italian *buon fresco* does not mean that it cannot, to a nearly equal degree, be classified as a fresco technique, as will be seen in the following discussion.

In the course of restoration work in the parecclesion opportunities arose to observe a number of details concerning the technique of fresco painting employed by the painters. This discussion attempts to describe the materials and their preparation as well as the procedures of the painters

---

1 Described by Cennino Cennini, *Il libro dell'arte*, ed. D. V. Thompson, Jr.; Vol. I, Italian text (New Haven, 1932), pp. 40–42; Vol. II, English translation (New Haven, 1933), pp. 42–44.

2 L. Tintori and M. Meiss, *The Painting of "The Life of St. Francis" in Assisi with Notes on the Arena Chapel* (New York, 1962), pp. 15 ff.

3 Ibid., p. 64 and passim. See also their "Additional Observations on Italian Mural Technique," *The Art Bulletin*, XLVI, 3 (Sept. 1964), 377–80.

in so far as it is possible to reconstruct them.[4] Where the paintings themselves fail to yield evidence on certain points, or where observed phenomena are not in themselves explainable, I shall refer to the so-called painters' manual of Mount Athos, the *Hermeneia* of Dionysius of Fourna,[5] which seems to throw considerable light on the probable procedures of the artists; practices of late-Byzantine artists are recorded that may well have been applied, in general, in the paintings of the Kariye Djami.

In each of the three structural zones of the pareclesion (i.e., the dome over the western bay; all the lunettes, arches, and vaults between the main cornice and that of the dome; and the walls below the main cornice) there are at least two *pontate*, or horizontal bands of painted plaster, joined to one another by overlapping, which represent the various stages, or levels, at which the plasterers and painters worked as they proceeded on their scaffoldings from the highest parts of the chapel to the floor.[6] In the dome of the western bay (PL. 410), the uppermost of three *pontate* extends to a level about one and one half meters above the windows. At this level an irregular but horizontal joint, or suture, can be detected on close inspection in the ornamented ribs and above the knees of the angels (PL. 412–423), where the plaster of the work zone below overlaps that of the zone above. This does not mean, however, that the total area within the top work zone, which is very large and full of intricate painting, was plastered and painted in one continuous operation. It is evident from joints at the angles formed where the ribs return to the segments, or webbings, of the dome that within this zone the webbings were plastered and painted after the ribs had been finished; both ribs and webbings, therefore, would seem to have been done individually, one after another. Another series of horizontal joints occurs in the dome at a short distance above the cornice level, in the piers between the windows. The frescoes in the dome were thus executed in three *pontate*; in each work zone, however, the individual segments of the dome were plastered and painted one after another.

It is my conjecture that from the dome of the western bay the work moved to the domical vault to the east, where the subject is the Last Judgment (PL. 368). The total uninterrupted surface of the vault was considered to be too large to be plastered and painted in one operation, so it was divided at first into two work areas. The first to be worked on must have been the western half, in which are depicted a flying angel rolling up the scroll of heaven, at the top center, and a semicircle of clouds containing most of the Choirs of the Elect (PL. 370). The suture between the two halves, to be seen even in a photograph, runs in a straight line, north to south, across the black of the background and disappears at the edge of the scroll of heaven, where it turns to pass around the eastern edge of the spiral. Along this suture the plaster on the eastern side overlaps that on the western, an indication that the plaster in the western half was laid and painted first.

After a tone of black had been applied to the two western pendentives, it was evidently found

4 A summary report on the construction of the paintings, including analytical data and cross-section photomicrographs, was published by R. J. Gettens and George L. Stout, "A Monument of Byzantine Wall Painting—the Method of Construction," *Studies in Conservation*, III (1958), 107–18. The present discussion owes much to the statement of these experts but attempts to supplement it, somewhat speculatively, by reference to the *Hermeneia*, cited below.

5 Ἑρμηνεία τῆς ζωγραφικῆς τέχνης, ed. A. Papadopoulos-Kerameus (St. Petersburg, 1909); French translation of a corrupt manuscript of the work, by M. Didron, *Manuel d'iconographie chrétienne* (Paris, 1845); German translation by G. Schäfer from the French of Didron, *Das Handbuch der Malerei vom Berge Athos* (Trier, 1855). All references below give, first, the chapter and page numbers of the Greek edition and, second, the page of Didron's translation. My translations were made from the Greek text of Papadopoulos-Kerameus, and these I owe to the generous help of Professor Cyril Mango. The reader should be warned that Didron's translation was made from a very faulty transcription of a single manuscript and is not to be relied upon.

6 It was a very practical maxim, noted by the *Hermeneia* (Ch. 57, p. 38; Didron, p. 57), that "when you paint a church, you should begin with the highest parts and finish with the lowest."

that the area was still too large to be painted completely under favorable conditions, for a new layer of plaster was applied over the black paint and the compositions of the pendentives were then painted in. The same procedure seems to have been followed in the eastern half of the vault. Thus the vault of the Last Judgment was finally treated as six areas; each of the two semicircular ones measures nearly eleven square meters of painted surface.

The largest single area to be covered in one operation was the conch of the apse, which contains the great painting of the Anastasis (PL. 341). This work was probably executed after completion of the eastern domical vault. In the conch there are no evidences of sutures except in the red border that frames the upper limits of the painting. The total area of painted surface measures as much as fourteen square meters.

Each of the four lunettes (PL. 404, 437, 453, 458), at the north and south sides of the two bays, was plastered and painted from two levels of scaffolding, that is, in two *pontate*. Perhaps because the painters utilized the cornice as a means of support for their scaffoldings, the level from which they worked did not allow them to plaster, and subsequently to paint, all the way down to the cornice in one operation. Consequently, at the base of each lunette, above the cornice, there is a rather narrow strip of secondary plaster and paint, which includes the foreground and lower border of each painting. These strips were executed after the painting above had been finished, and the joints can easily be detected. Similar joints at about the same level occur at the bases of the soffits of the transverse arches; above these points the two sides and the summit of each soffit were painted in separate stages; the summit contains a medallion and each side, a scene. The arches, therefore, were painted in five sections: first an area containing a medallion, at the top; then the greater parts of the two scenes at the sides; and finally the narrow strips at the bottoms of the scenes.

Finally, the walls below the cornice were found to be too high for the painters' convenience, and these, too, were painted in two *pontate*. Sutures can be seen running in a more or less horizontal line beneath the feet of the saints whose full-length portraits form the frieze of figural decoration in the lowest zone (PL. 476 et al.). The very lowest work zone includes the lower part of that frieze and the dado of marbleized panels that runs the circuit of the chapel above the floor. Since pilasters separate the bays, the units into which the walls are divided are relatively narrow in both *pontate* and could be plastered and painted one by one.

It is important at this point to describe the plaster. It was applied in two coats, and the painting was done directly on the second coat. The plaster of both coats consists of lime mixed with quantities of straw chopped into lengths of up to about 3 cm. In its composition and appearance it is indistinguishable from the plaster used in the two lower coats, beneath the setting bed, in the mosaics of the Kariye Djami and other monuments of Constantinople.[7] The two coats beneath the paintings are of nearly equal thickness, and together they measure from 2 to 3 cm.; but since the masonry surface is serrated, because the joints below the brick courses are undercut, the overall thickness at the joints is appreciably greater than that.

These characteristics of the plaster would seem to correspond in all but a few particulars to the specifications of the *Hermeneia*. There only the first, or scratch, coat is described as lime with straw as a binder;[8] hemp fibers, chopped into very short lengths, are recommended for use in the second coat,[9] on which the painting is to be done. The first coat, it is said, is to be at least

---

7 See the discussion of the mosaic technique used in the Kariye Djami, p. 173.

8 Ch. 55, p. 37; Didron, p. 56.
9 Ch. 56, pp. 37 f.; Didron, pp. 56 f.

two fingers thick, if laid on brick masonry, and the second somewhat less; [10] if the plastering is to be done on stone, which the text implies is less absorbent, the first coat can be somewhat thinner than it should be on brick. At the Kariye Djami, however, the two coats of plaster were alike; both contained a straw binder, and they were slightly less thick than the text prescribed. The straw that lay very close to the surface in the final coat and was not covered by heavy paint has decayed under the humid conditions; the resulting pitting of the surface is particularly evident in the black backgrounds.

We are told by the *Hermeneia* [11] that when the work is to be done in winter, that is, under humid conditions, the first coat should be applied to the wall late in the day and the second the following morning—that is, after an interval of about twelve hours; but in summer the second coat could be applied whenever it was convenient, presumably after an appreciably shorter interval. The text stresses wetting the walls thoroughly, being liberal in the thickness of the plaster, and not delaying long in painting, all in order that the moisture of the plaster may be retained long after painting has begun. These instructions quite definitely mean that the Byzantine *Hermeneia*, which doubtless recorded the general practices that were in vogue when the Kariye Djami paintings were executed, considers that painting should be done, at least in large part, while the plaster is still moist.

The extent of the plaster area to be applied and painted in a single operation was determined by the painter on the basis of two considerations: first, an estimate of the area he could deal with before the plaster reached a condition in which it too rapidly absorbed the liquids carrying the pigments; and second, an estimate of the area he could finish painting while the hydrate of lime in the topmost layer of paint was still able to fuse with the undercoatings of paint. This fusion between one layer of paint and those beneath could occur only before the hydrate of lime in the paint and plaster, and the carbonic acid in the air, had combined in the undercoatings to form a durable and impervious calcium carbonate.

Several factors serve to explain how such relatively large areas in the parecclesion as were described above could be treated as individual working units. Since the initial coat of plaster, unlike the *arriccio* in *buon fresco*, was still moist and relatively nonabsorbent when the final coat was laid over it, the two coats, totaling some 2.5 cm. in thickness, stored up, as it were, a considerable reserve of liquid, which in itself would tend to delay the drying of the surface; and for some time after painting had begun, the painter could force liquid to the surface by the application of pressure when he found it necessary. This procedure, which is described below, is recommended in the *Hermeneia*. Moreover, the presence of considerable quantities of straw in the plaster of both coats tended to increase the absorption of water into the mix as well as its retention, although the primary function of the straw was to bind the plaster, reduce its shrinkage, and thus avoid excessive cracking and surface crazing as the plaster dried and hardened.

In only one place in the parecclesion was the first coat of plaster exposed over a large enough area to enable us to observe the manner in which its surface was treated; this occurred at an overlap, where a cleavage had developed between the coats and a substantial area of the second coat had fallen. Here it was evident that while the first coat was still soft its surface had been roughened by indentations, arranged in a herring-bone pattern, which were made with a tool having a slightly curved edge; the purpose of these indentations was to insure the cohesion of the

10 Ch. 57, p. 38; Didron, p. 57.   11 Ibid.

two coats. This surface treatment is indistinguishable from that given to the second of the three coats of plaster used in the mosaics of the Kariye Djami and a number of other monuments in Constantinople.

So little of the first coat of plaster in the parecclesion has been observed that it is impossible to determine from examining the surface whether preliminary sketches in any way comparable to the Italian *sinopie* were drawn on it before the second coat was applied. In any case, the final coat was applied over such large areas that any sketching beneath it would have served very little purpose. From a reading of the *Hermeneia* it is evident, on the contrary, that Byzantine painters laid out their compositions and sketched in their figures only on the final surface. This practice, again, corresponds to that of the mosaicists of Constantinople, for at many places in several of the churches of the city we have seen substantial areas of exposed first, second, and third coats and in only the rarest instances, and under abnormal circumstances, have sketches of any kind been found on the undercoatings beneath the setting bed.

The author of the *Hermeneia* prescribes that after the second coat of plaster has been applied it should be thoroughly worked to a fine surface, in part, at least, to extract excessive amounts of hydrate of lime, and that an unspecified interval of time should then be allowed for the surface to assume its proper consistency before the brush sketch is begun;[12] it will be seen below, however, that the plaster would be still wet when painting was begun. In the Kariye Djami paintings the detailed procedures for laying out and beginning the actual painting are not clearly evident, but in many areas where the heavier layers of overpainting have deteriorated much of the preliminary sketching can be seen. At a very early stage, probably immediately after the composition and the figures had been roughed in, the charcoal black in the background of the paintings must have been laid on. It is relatively thin in structure, and the pigment must have been applied in an almost purely aqueous medium; where it is well preserved the black has the crystalline surface characteristic of *buon fresco* after carbonation has taken place.

Instructions contained in the *Hermeneia* may again be useful as a general reflection of the methods employed by the painters of the parecclesion in laying out and sketching their figures and scenes and in executing the earlier stages of the application of color to the wet plaster, for at several points the prescribed method is corroborated by the paintings themselves. According to the text, after the second coat has been carefully prepared and has assumed its proper consistency the painter begins to lay out his sketch.[13] An extension compass with a brush attached to one arm is used to describe lightly the haloes and to establish all necessary measurements, presumably according to a canon of proportions.[14] Next the contours of the figures are very faintly sketched in ochre. The haloes should then be drawn again with a compass, presumably in greater strength.

It is important to note that at this point the painter is told to proceed with the following steps: "Polish [*stilbose*] very thoroughly the area of the background [*kampos*]; immediately apply the black [i.e., on the *kampos*]; then polish the area of the costume and apply the *proplasmos* [see below] on it. However, take care within the hour to finish as much as you have polished because if you delay the plaster sets and does not absorb the paints and later they come off. But if you are late, observe where the paint is not absorbed; strike it with your trowel (κτύπα το μὲ τὸ μιστρί) and then apply the paint and in this fashion it does not come off later."[15] This passage means that after the figures have been sketched in outline the area of the background is the first to receive

12 Ch. 57, p. 38; Didron, p. 57.
13 Ch. 58, pp. 38 f.; Didron, p. 58.

14 Ch. 51, p. 34; Didron, p. 52.
15 Ch. 58, pp. 38 f.; Didron, p. 58.

pigment; in preparation that area is well "polished," that is, freshly troweled, or closed in, in order to draw the moisture to the surface, and the black is immediately applied. From the text one also gathers that delays may make it necessary to use greater compressive force by striking the plaster with a trowel to raise moisture to the surface. After the background is applied, the painter then freshly trowels the areas within the outlines of the costumes, presumably one by one, and immediately lays in what is called the *proplasmos*. It consists of dark green, yellow, and black pigments,[16] mixed with *psimythi*, a binder of finely ground, thoroughly slaked lime (see below for a description of its preparation). The very dark, almost black *proplasmos* thus underlies the colors of the costumes, forming the opaque base on which the overpainting, which also consists of pigments carried in a lime medium, is presently to be applied. Now, at the Kariye Djami much the same procedures must have been followed, at least up to this point. In line with the description above, the black background may well have been laid on first. Furthermore, when the paintings were cleaned it was observed repeatedly, where small cleavages had occurred beneath the heavy overpainting, that a black, or nearly black, ground (the *proplasmos*) underlies the colors within the areas of the garments.

In a very interesting note Didron tells us that in 1839 he observed the painting of the narthex in the church of the monastery of Esphigmenou, on Mount Athos, and that the painter possessed a manuscript of the *Hermeneia* and still employed techniques and iconography much like those described in it.[17] One can well believe that at that time and place the practices of the monk-painters still reflected some of the traditions of late-medieval painters. According to Didron, the monk Joasaph in less than an hour sketched in on the fresh plaster an entire scene with figures of nearly life size. For his haloes and measurements he used an extension compass to which a brush was attached, and for the sketch a brush dipped in red ochre. He drew in his figures with complete spontaneity and without sketches, models, or cartoons of any kind. Starting with the central figure of his composition, Joasaph sketched in the halo and the head and worked down the body. He proceeded in this way with the other figures, first one at the right, then one at the left, back and forth symmetrically. After the entire sketch was finished an assistant applied a flat ground—in black, Didron says—within the contours of each figure, and on this ground, the *proplasmos*, still another assistant painted in the draperies and other ornaments. The heads, however, were reserved for the master, and these he executed, two at a time, after the other parts of the figures were finished; that is, each step and each color used in the process of painting a head was repeated on another head as he worked back and forth from one to the other. Presumably, the master painter also did the hands and feet. The practice of leaving the heads, hands, and feet to the last is also to be observed in the sister art of mosaic.[18]

The *Hermeneia* itself does not tell us about the painting of drapery over the *proplasmos*, and while we cannot be sure, it would seem to have preceded the painting of the heads. In late-Byzantine murals it is often the case, as it is at the Kariye Djami, that the heads have proved to be the least durable parts. This may be explained on the grounds that they were the last to be done, excepting certain minor elements that were done *a secco*, and that the delay prevented the overpainting from fusing properly with the earlier layers of paint, in which the process of carbonation had advanced too far.

The *Hermeneia* continues its instructions to the painter as follows: "In the same fashion, also

---

16 Ch. 60, pp. 39 f.; Didron, p. 59. The proportions, however, are not stated.

17 Pp. 65–69.

18 See above, pp. 179–80.

polish the face and mark it with [the point of] the trowel, or with a [sharp] stone, or with a bone which you should have with you as if it were a knife. With this [instrument] trace also the costume, then model, and draw, and apply flesh paint [to the face]. If you delay, and [the plaster] begins to set, do as we said above [i.e., strike it]." [19] The last statement suggests that at this stage it should still be possible to draw, or force, the moisture to the surface. But what is described is still in the nature of underpainting; further painting would remain to be done on it. Nevertheless, the head has now received its first applications of the more opaque paints composed of pigments in *psimythi* (lime white). What is also described here is the process of defining and sharpening the principal outlines in the figures by means of incised lines executed with a pointed instrument. This was necessary, in the case of the draperies, because any brush drawing within the contours of the sketch would have been obscured by the nearly black, and quite opaque, *proplasmos*, whereas incisions would remain visible during the overpainting. Such incisions have frequently been observed in frescoes; in those of the Kariye Djami they may be seen at many points (e.g., PL. 359), although they are not always traceable because the heavy overpainting tends to fill and obliterate them. It is evident that they were made while the plaster was still pliant, for in places, one can see that the instrument has somewhat molded the edges of the grooves and has raised them slightly from the surface of the plaster. As can be seen in Plate 359, the painter did not always adhere closely to his incised drawing in the overpainting as he developed the details of the drapery folds.

In painting the draperies, it is probable that for each color the painter had at hand a series of three or four pots, each containing a different intensity of the color, to correspond to the range of values he wished to introduce in the garment. The lighter the value the greater was the proportion of *psimythi* and the thicker and more opaque was the paint. As a general rule the painter worked first with one of his darker values, which he tended to apply over most, if not all, of the area of the garment. Over this he placed successively lighter values of the same color in those areas that were to be in half and full lights, superimposing them until he reached the pure white highlights. At the same time he must also have reinforced the darks in the outlines and in the shadows. In the process all paint layers, excepting the final highlights, were partly covered by lighter ones; conversely, only parts of each of these layers were left exposed. It can be seen that in some of the lightest areas a superposition of as many as four layers would result, and here the paint would achieve a relatively great thickness.

There are exceptions, however, to the general practice of painting a garment in values of a single color. In a few instances the darker values may be in one color and the lighter in its near-complement, so that the effect of a shot fabric, of changeable colors, is achieved. For example, the woman at the far right in Plate 363 wears a mantle in which the shaded areas are rendered in a reddish brown, the half lights in yellowish brown, and the full lights in light blue with highlights in white. Another exception occurs in the representation of many of the blue garments. It often happens that the dark areas of the "blue" garment are actually of the same black that is used in the background, to which only a little, if any, light blue is applied. The blue may be applied in relatively small areas and here and there merged with the black by means of hatching; in places the effect of very dark folds and outlines is produced by the use of a narrow bordering line of white or very light blue on each side of a narrow strip of the black underpainting, the con-

---

[19] Ch. 58, p. 39; Didron, p. 58. At this point Didron's text, or translation, is especially faulty.

trast here serving, in effect, to darken the black. So skillfully is the color handled that the effect of a blue garment is often achieved with the greatest economy of blue pigments, which were both costly and difficult to handle in fresco painting.

It might be of interest to know how, according to the author of the *Hermeneia*, the lime binder (*psimythi*) was prepared. The author recommends that the painter find a very old lime pit and, selecting the best lime from it, grind it well on a marble slab. It should be neither bitter nor styptic to the tongue but should taste like earth. If such lime is not available the text recommends using plaster from old frescoes. The paint should be scraped off and the old plaster pounded and ground; the straw and hemp should be removed, first by sifting and then by soaking in water, draining off the remaining fibers, and again grinding the residue.[20] This *psimythi* was an ingredient in most, if not all, overpainting, beginning with the *proplasmos*, as we have seen. It was also the vehicle for the mixtures that were prepared beforehand for the painting of the heads, namely, a mixture called *sarka* (flesh) and another called *glycasmos* (literally, sweetening). The *sarka* consisted of *psimythi*, Thasos ochre, and red bole;[21] the *glycasmos* was a mixture of the *sarka* with a quantity of the *proplasmos*, which contained dark green, yellow, and black pigments as well as lime white. These are formulas recommended by the *Hermeneia* for the painting of flesh and its modeling but are not necessarily those of the Kariye painters; indeed, at the Kariye there is considerable variety in the colors used for these purposes.

There are two ways to paint the faces, the text says. The preferred way, as in icon painting, is to model the features with *glycasmos* and then work in the *sarka* in the full lights.[22] A quicker way is the reverse: apply a flat field of the flesh paint and over it work in the modeling in *glycasmos*.[23] These preparations are used after the features are drawn in umber or black lines. After the flesh and modeling colors have been put in, the *Hermeneia* says, the reds are applied on the lips and cheeks or wherever necessary. For young, beardless figures red bole is recommended; for the bloom of the cheeks, bole is added to the already prepared flesh paint.[24]

In the rendering of faces at the Kariye Djami one finds that four colors and white were generally used: yellow ochre, a reddish brown (umber?), a green (which resembles terre-verte), and red. Unfortunately, a great many of the faces are partially effaced and in only a few can one now see the full use of the colors. In a number of these the modeling of the receding surfaces along the contours of the face and neck would seem to have been applied first, in a rather wide zone, possibly in terre-verte, in strokes that parallel the contours. The shading under the eyebrows and lower lids and along the sides of the nose and the shadows under the nose and chin were also sometimes painted with green. In many of the faces, however, either the green was omitted and the modeling was done in reddish brown, or the green was so extensively overpainted in brown and yellow that it is not noticeably exposed. The green around the contours, when it is exposed, is always blended into the dark brown that is applied over it at the outer edges of the contours. The areas of the foreheads and cheeks that are more or less parallel to the picture plane and were conceived to be in full and half lights are painted in yellow ochre warmed by the addition of some red and blended into the green of the shaded areas. Over this, on the curved forms that suggest the structure of the cheekbones, and again at the point of the chin in beardless faces, and sometimes in the center of the forehead, red is applied either in

20 Ch. 59, p. 39; Didron, pp. 58 f.
21 Ch. 62, p. 40; Didron, p. 60.
22 Ch. 21, p. 21; Didron, pp. 35 f.

23 Ch. 63, p. 40.
24 Ch. 64, p. 40; Didron, p. 60.

fine hatched lines or in a thin tint to enliven and brighten the face. Red hatchings are sometimes applied on one or both sides of the neck (but more prominently on the right side) in curved parallel lines that contribute to the modeling by cutting across the neck's receding curvature. Anatomical features, such as the edges of the eyelids, the wrinkles around the eyes, the shadows defining the construction of the ears, and the small curves of the nostrils, are usually drawn in reddish brown, the last sometimes in red. The upper and lower lips of the beardless figures, but only the lower lips of those who are bearded, are touched with bright red. Finally, short strokes of white are applied as highlights, most often at certain points along the left side of the ridge of the nose, below the outer end of each lower eyelid in a series of two or three parallel curved lines, and on the forehead in a series of diagonal lines above the inner ends of the eyebrows; the chin beneath the lower lip and the upper edge of the lip itself may also show such highlights.

In the hair and beards brown and yellow are predominant, but in the portrayal of old men much white is used. Strokes of color produce the straight, wavy, or curly locks required for the traditional characterization of the individual portrayed. In some instances the hair and beard are dark brown enlivened by highlights in short strokes of pale blue or white.

Although few of the pigments are definitely identified, the evidence suggests that they were natural materials, most of them minerals. Including black and white there seem to have been about eight basic colors, but a few of these occur in more than one pigment, and very limited mixing of pigments may be thought to have been the means of providing some additional colors that appear to be binary. The basic colors are blue, yellow, red, green, violet, brown, black, and white. For the blues azurite and lapis lazuli were used, the latter very sparingly. The white is calcium hydroxide (lime), and the black is charcoal. Earth colors were used for the reds and yellows, that is, red and yellow ochres; and the greens are terre-verte and possibly malachite. It was probably umber that supplied the reddish browns that appear in the features and in some of the drawing of drapery and contours. There are, finally, two violets that were widely used for garments: one is a reddish violet (probably an iron oxide), the other a deep blue-violet that may be another form of iron oxide or may have been obtained by mixing pigments.

The paintings originally possessed two striking features that the present-day beholder would hardly be aware of since their transitory nature and the effects of adverse conditions have made them all but disappear. During work with the paintings it became apparent that all the backgrounds, which are now for the most part black, had originally been covered with azurite and that a great deal of gilding had been done on the haloes, stars, and embroidered garments, and on the cloth-of-gold vestments of some of the representations of Christ. Azurite, as is well known, and as the *Hermeneia* states,[25] is one of the pigments that cannot be used in fresco painting; it can, however, be applied *a secco*. Traces of it have been found in many of the backgrounds throughout the parecclesion, and in the dome, the driest part of the structure, it still adheres rather well to the backgrounds surrounding the angels. In many places, however, and especially in the background of the southern half of the conch of the apse (the painting of the Anastasis, PL. 341), the azurite had been transformed into a brilliant green malachite. In the latter area the malachite so completely covered the black, and was so disturbing a color, that its removal seemed justified. The text of the *Hermeneia* tells us how the azurite should be applied, as one of the very last steps in executing a painting, over the black background after the plaster and its painting have become thoroughly dry. A size is prepared by soaking bran in water, boiling it,

25 Ch. 66, p. 41; Didron, p. 61.

and then draining off the liquid. Into this the azurite is mixed, and the mixture is applied over the black.[26]

These observations on their technique indicate that the paintings of the parecclesion were done largely *ad affresco* and that owing to the composition of the plaster and its relatively great thickness, which retarded its drying, it was possible for the painter to cover very large areas at one time, using a lime vehicle except in the sketches and the black of the background, the pigments for which were apparently suspended in water. While there are many areas where a failure of technique may be thought to have been responsible for some of the losses of surface paint, the technique nevertheless produced very durable results over the greater part of the painted surface. In many areas where several layers of lime paint were superimposed to a considerable thickness, the layers have successfully fused one with another, an indication that they were put on before a crust of calcium carbonate had formed which would have caused subsequent layers to lie without fusion and thus become liable to flaking so that the overpainting could be lost. The heads have suffered more consistent losses than other parts of the paintings; in part these losses may be attributed to surface carbonation beneath the layers of overpainting—the result, perhaps, of delays in their painting. There are other factors, however, that must have contributed to these losses. Rendering the parecclesion acceptable to Moslem use involved obscuring the heads, but not the draperies, with daubs of yellow paint, which adversely affected the paintings. In addition, the application of whitewash over all the paintings except those in the dome caused some damage. Humid conditions caused by condensation and even by seepage of water through fissures in the masonry, which in some places produced a very hard, calcareous deposit over the paintings, also contributed to much of the deterioration that is evident today in some parts of the parecclesion.

26 Ch. 68, pp. 41 f.; Didron, pp. 61 ff.

Selected Bibliography

Selected Bibliography

History, Architecture, and Art (Comprehensive Works)

Rüdell, Alexander. *Die Kahrie-Dschamisi in Constantinopel: Ein Kleinod Byzantinischer Kunst.* Berlin, 1908.

Shmit, Feodor Ivanovch. *Kakhrie-dzhami.* Vol. 1: *Istoriia Monastyria Khory; Arkhitektura Mecheti; Mozaiki Narfikov.* Sofia, 1906. Vol. 2: Album. Munich, 1906. (Izvestiia Russkago Arkheolo-gicheskago Instituta v Konstantinopole, XI.)

   Reviewed by Iakov Ivanovich Smirnov: *Otzyv ob Izsliedovanii F. I. Shmita Kakrie-dzhami.* Petrograd, 1915. Reprinted from *Protokoly Obshchikh Sobranii Imp. Russkago Arkheologicheskago Obshchestva za 1899–1908 g. Prilozhenie,* pp. 364–79.

Van Millingen, Alexander (assisted by Ramsay Traquair, W. S. George, and A. E. Henderson). *Byzantine Churches in Constantinople: Their History and Architecture.* London, 1912. (pp. 288–331.)

History of the Monastery

Janin, Raymond. *La Géographie ecclésiastique de l'Empire Byzantin.* Part I: *Le Siège de Constantinople et le patriarcat œcuménique.* Vol. 3: *Les Églises et les monastères.* Paris, 1953. (pp. 545–53.)

Paspates, Alexandros Georgios. Βυζαντιναὶ μελέται τοπογραφικαὶ καὶ ἱστορικαὶ μετὰ πλείστων εἰκόνων. Constantinople, 1877. (pp. 326–32.)

Shmit, F. I. Cited above.

Van Millingen, A. Cited above.

Mosaics and Frescoes

Alpatov, Michael. "Die Fresken der Kachrie Djami in Konstantinopel," *Münchener Jahrbuch der bildenden Kunst* (Munich), 6 (1929), 345–64.

Del Medico, H. E. "La Mosaïque de la Κοίμησις à Kahrie Djami," *Byzantion* (Brussels), VII (1932), 123–41.

Diehl, Charles. "Les Mosaïques de Kahrié-djami," *Gazette des beaux-arts* (Paris), 32 (1904), 352 ff.; 33 (1905), 72 ff. Reprinted in C. Diehl, *Études byzantines* (Paris, 1905), pp. 392–431.

Ebersolt, Jean. "Une Nouvelle Mosaïque de Kahrié-Djami," *La Revue de l'art* (Paris), LV (1929), 83–86; "Trois Nouveaux Fragments de mosaïques à Kahrié-Djami," ibid., LVI (1929), 163–66.

K. A. K. G. [i.e., K. A. K. Gribas]. Ὁ Χαλκίτης Χριστὸς ἐν τῇ μονῇ τῆς Χώρας, in Πυρσός, μηνιαῖο περιοδικὸ γραμμάτων καὶ τέχνης. Istanbul, 1958. (pp. 257–81.)

Kondakov, Nikodim Pavlovich. *Mozaiki Mecheti Kakhrie-dzhamisi v Konstantinopole.* (Istoriia Vizantiiskago Iskusstva i Ikonografii, II, Mozaiki.) Odessa, 1881.

————. *Vizantiiskiia Tserkvi i Pamiatniki Konstantinopolia.* Odessa, 1886. (pp. 166–97; PL. 25–45.)

Mango, Cyril. *The Brazen House, A Study of the Vestibule of the Imperial Palace of Constantinople.* (Det Kongelige Danske Videnskabernes Selskab: Arkaeologisk-kunsthistoriske Meddelelser, IV, 4.) Copenhagen, 1959. (pp. 108 ff., 138–42.)

Ogan, Aziz, and V. Mirmiroğlu. *Kaariye Camii eski Hora Manastiri.* (Türk Tarih Kurumu Yayinlarindan, VI Seri, No. 3.) Ankara, 1955. (pp. 1–37; English translation, pp. 39–61.)

Rüdell, A. Cited above.

Shmit, F. I. Cited above.

————. "Mozaiki i Freski Kakhrie-dzhamii," in Izvestiia Russkago Arkheologicheskago Instituta v Konstantinopole (Sofia), VIII (1903), pp. 119–52, PL. XVIII–XX.

Underwood, Paul A. "The Deisis Mosaic in the Kahrie Cami at Istanbul," in *Late Classical and Mediaeval Studies in Honor of Albert Mathias Friend, Jr.,* ed. Kurt Weitzmann. Princeton, 1955. (pp. 254–60.)

————. "First Preliminary Report on the Restoration of the Frescoes in the Kariye Camii at Istanbul by the Byzantine Institute: 1952–1954," *Dumbarton Oaks Papers,* 9 and 10 (Cambridge, Mass., 1956), 252–88.

————. "Second Preliminary Report . . . 1955," *D. O. Papers,* 11 (Cambridge, Mass., 1957), 173–220.

————. "Third Preliminary Report . . . 1956," *D. O. Papers,* 12 (Cambridge, Mass., 1958), 235–65.

————. "Fourth Preliminary Report . . . 1957–1958," *D. O. Papers,* 13 (Washington, 1959), 185–212.

Sepulchral Monuments

Underwood, Paul A. "Notes on the Work of the Byzantine Institute in Istanbul: 1955–1956," *Dumbarton Oaks Papers,* 12 (Cambridge, Mass., 1958), 271–82. "Notes on the Work . . . 1957," *D. O. Papers,* 13 (Washington, 1959), 215–28.

Technique and Archaeology

Gettens, Rutherford J., and George L. Stout. "A Monument of Byzantine Wall Painting—the Method of Construction," *Studies in Conservation* (London), III, 3 (1958), 107–19.

Hawkins, Ernest. "The Conservation of the Mosaics at the Kariye Camii," *Studies in Conservation,* V, 3 (1960), 102–07.

Megaw, Arthur H. S. "Notes on Recent Work of the Byzantine Institute in Istanbul," *Dumbarton Oaks Papers,* 17 (Washington, 1963), pp. 349–67, Figs. F–L, and frontispiece facing 333. Contains discussion of fragments of painted window glass discovered at Zeyrek Djami (Pantocrator) and Kariye Djami; for Kariye Djami glass see 349 and n. 49, 365–67, and frontispiece, nos. 6–9.

Oates, David. "A Summary Report on the Excavations of the Byzantine Institute in the Kariye Camii: 1957 and 1958," *D. O. Papers,* 14 (Washington, 1960), 223–31.

Underwood, Paul A. "Notes on the Work of the Byzantine Institute in Istanbul: 1954," *D. O. Papers,* 9 and 10 (Cambridge, Mass., 1956), 294–98.

Wales, Carroll. "The Treatment of Wall Paintings at Kariye Camii," *Studies in Conservation,* III, 3 (1958), 120–24.

Art History and Iconography

Ainalov, Dmitrii Vlas'evich. *Vizantiiskaia Zhivopis' XIV Stoletiia.* (Russkoe Arkheologicheskoe Obschchestvo, Klassicheskoe Otdelenie, Zapiski, 9.) Petrograd, 1917. (pp. 62–230.)

Bréhier, Louis. "La Renovation artistique sous les Paléologues et le mouvement des idées," *Mélanges Charles Diehl*. Paris, 1930. (Vol. II, 1–10.)

Demus, Otto. "Die Entstehung des Paläologenstils in der Malerei," *Berichte zum XI. Internationalen Byzantinisten-Kongress, München, 1958*, IV, 2 (Munich, 1958).

Grabar, André. "La Décoration des coupoles a Karye Camii et les peintures italiennes du Dugento," *Jahrbuch der Österreichischen Byzantinischen Gesellschaft* (Graz and Cologne), 6 (1957), 111–24.

Lafontaine-Dosogne, Jacqueline. *Iconographie de l'enfance de la Vierge dans l'Empire Byzantin et en occident*, Vol. I. Brussels, 1964. (Publication of the Royal Academy of Belgium.)

Lazarev, Victor Nikitich. *Istoriia Vizantiiskoi Zhivopisi*, Vol. 1. Moscow, 1947. (pp. 213–17.)

Millet, Gabriel. *Recherches sur l'iconographie de l'Évangile aux XIVᵉ, XVᵉ, et XVIᵉ siècles*. (Bibliothèque des Écoles Françaises d'Athènes et de Rome, no. 109.) Paris, 1916. For references to Kariye Djami, see index: Répertoire des monuments; I. Mosaiques et Fresques, s. v. "Constantinople," p. 720. Reprinted, Paris, 1960.

Muratov, Pavel Pavlovich. *La Peinture byzantine*. Paris, 1928. (pp. 145 ff.)

Radojčić, Svetozar. "Die Entstehung der Malerei der Paläologischen Renaissance," *Jahrbuch der Österreichischen Byzantinischen Gesellschaft*, 7 (1958), 105–23. A supplement to the paper of O. Demus, "Die Entstehung . . . ," cited above.

Schmidt, Théodore [Feodor Ivanovich Shmit]. "La 'Renaissance' de la peinture byzantine au XIVᵉ siècle," *Revue archéologique* (Paris), 20 (1912), 127–42.

Underwood, Paul A. "Palaeologan Narrative Style and an Italianate Fresco of the Fifteenth Century in the Kariye Djami," in *Studies in the History of Art, Dedicated to William E. Suida on his Eightieth Birthday*. London, 1959. (pp. 1–9.)

Xyngopoulos, Andreas. Ἡ κηρόχυτος γραφὴ τοῦ Χρυσοστόμου, in Ἑταιρεία Βυζαντινῶν Σπουδῶν, Ἐπετηρὶς (Athens), 21 (1951), 49 ff.

———. Ἡ ψηφιδωτὴ διακόσμησις τοῦ ναοῦ τῶν Ἁγίων Ἀποστόλων Θεσσαλονίκης, in Ἑταιρεία Μακεδονικῶν Σπουδῶν, Μακεδονικὴ Βιβλιοθήκη (Salonika), 16 (1953), 58 ff.

———. Εἰκόνες προφητῶν, in Ἑταιρεία Βυζαντινῶν Σπουδῶν, Ἐπετηρὶς, 23 (1953), 45 ff.

———. *Thessalonique et la peinture macedonienne*. Athens, 1955.

Iconographic Index

Iconographic Index

Bracketed numbers are those assigned to the mosaic and fresco subjects, in an order corresponding with the iconographic sequence of the subjects in the church; the same order is followed in the present volumes. Numbers not in brackets refer to the plates in Vols. 2 and 3. PL. 1–334 (mosaics) are in Vol. 2, PL. 335–553 (frescoes and tombs) in Vol. 3.

Plans and Sections

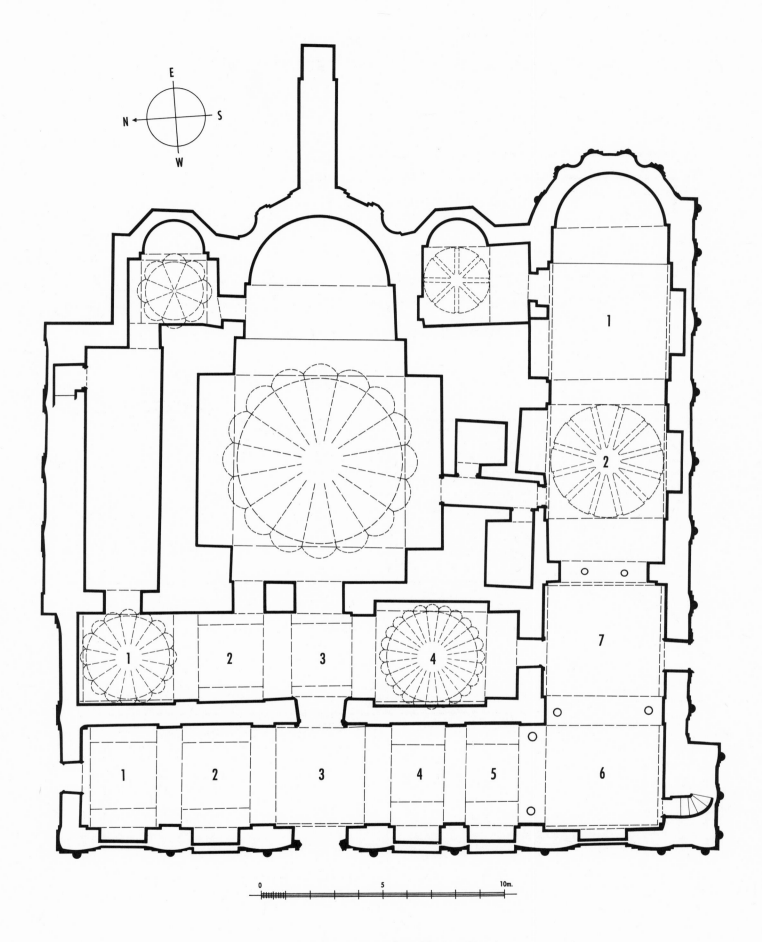

Fig. 1. General plan of the Kariye Djami

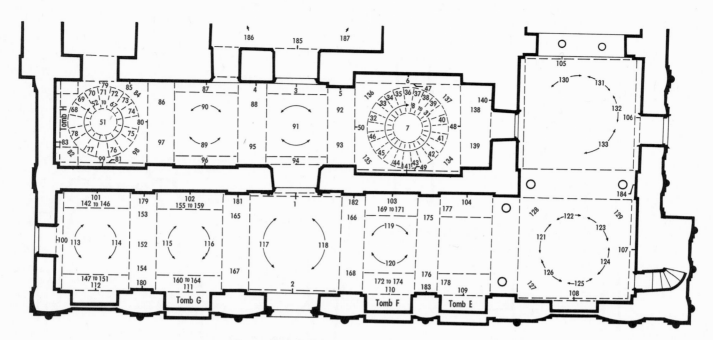

Fig. 2. Plan of the outer and inner narthexes

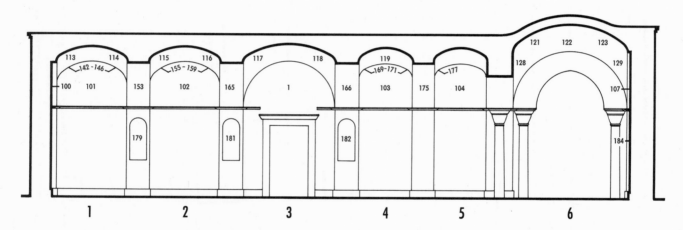

Fig. 3. Section of outer narthex, Bays 1–6, looking east

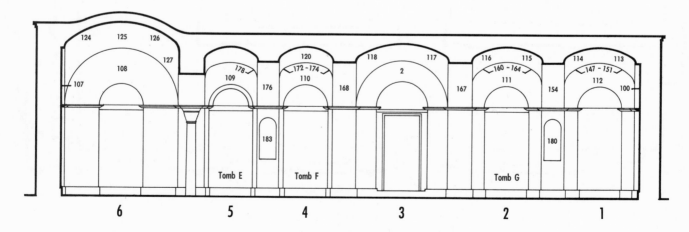

Fig. 4. Section of outer narthex, Bays 1–6, looking west

THE NARTHEXES

Key numbers in red indicate location of mosaics

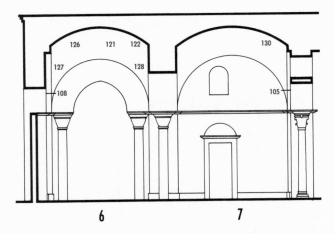

Fig. 5. Section of outer narthex, Bays 6 and 7, looking north

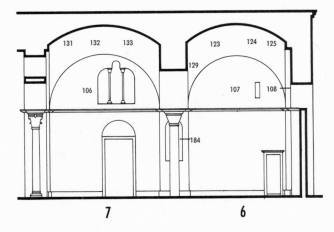

Fig. 6. Section of outer narthex, Bays 6 and 7, looking south

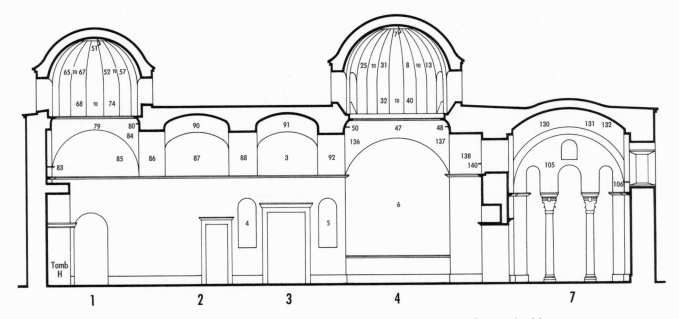

Fig. 7. Section of inner narthex, Bays 1–4, and of outer narthex, Bay 7, looking east

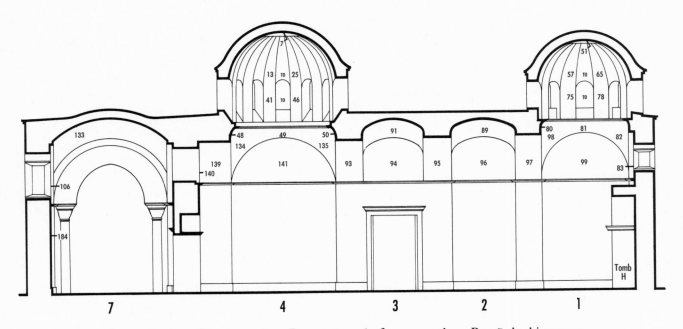

Fig. 8. Section of inner narthex, Bays 1–4, and of outer narthex, Bay 7, looking west

THE NARTHEXES

Key numbers in red indicate location of mosaics

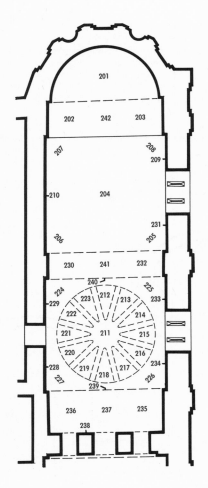

Fig. 9. Plan of the upper zone

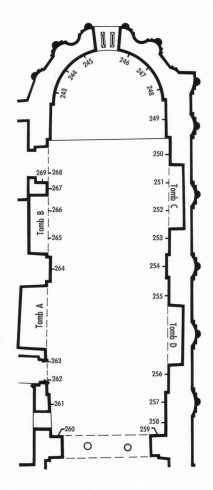

Fig. 10. Plan of the lower zone

THE PARECCLESION

Key numbers in red indicate location of frescoes

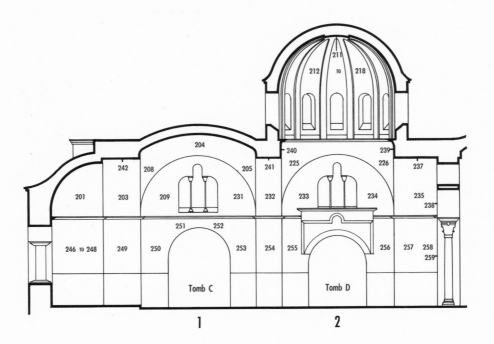

Fig. 11. Section, looking south

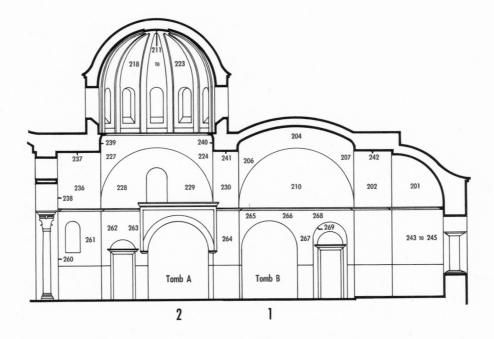

Fig. 12. Section, looking north

THE PARECCLESION

Key numbers in red indicate location of frescoes

COMPOSED, PRINTED, AND BOUND BY KINGSPORT PRESS, INC., KINGSPORT, TENNESSEE. THE FRONTISPIECE WAS ENGRAVED BY WALKER ENGRAVING CORPORATION, NEW YORK, AND PRINTED BY DAVIS, DELANEY, INC., NEW YORK.